Psychological Foundations of Organizational Behavior

SECOND EDITION

Psychological Foundations of Organizational Behavior

SECOND EDITION

EDITED BY

Barry M. Staw
University of California, Berkeley

805093

SCOTT, FORESMAN AND COMPANY   Glenview, Illinois
Dallas, Texas   Oakland, New Jersey
Tucker, Georgia   London, England   Palo Alto, California

Library of Congress Cataloging in Publication Data
Main entry under title:

Psychological foundations of organizational behavior.

Includes bibliographies.
1. Organizational behavior — Addresses, essays,
lectures. 2. Psychology, Industrial — Addresses,
essays, lectures. 3. Industrial sociology — Addresses,
essays, lectures. I. Staw, Barry M. [DNLM: 1. Behavior.
2. Organizations. 3. Psychology, Industrial.
4. Sociology. HD 58.7 P974]
HD58.7.P76 1983   302.3'5   83-3208
ISBN 0-673-16005-X

1 2 3 4 5 6 — RRC — 88 87 86 85 84 83

Preface

Organizational behavior courses often have a dual mission. They may serve both as a general introduction to the social sciences and as a study of specific problems or issues faced by organizations. I have tried, therefore, to organize a collection of readings that present some fundamental behavioral literature as well as the more typical readings that are based on organizational research. This was a distinguishing feature of the first edition and I have followed that pattern in revising the book. Nearly two-thirds of the readings are new, and their selection was guided by the idea that there is no organizational behavior if we remove the noun "behavior." Without some understanding of what makes *people* tick, there is no understanding of what makes *organizations* tick.

This edition, like the first, covers several levels of difficulty, ranging from popular pieces to scholarly articles. Although I have eliminated the more ponderous and jargon-laden works, not many of the articles will qualify as "airport reading." I have tried to balance the content-readability dilemma so that all material is accessible and at least some of the pieces qualify as exciting reading.

The topics covered in this collection range from individual motivation to organizational effectiveness. The book starts with basic models of individual motivation and then covers individual performance, attitudes, and behavior in organizational settings. The nature of perception and attribution is introduced and then its implications in organizations are treated in several applied readings. At this point, the collection turns more interpersonal in direction. Social influence and conformity are outlined and then discussion shifts to questions of organizational socialization, the exercise of power in organizational settings, and the nature of leadership. The foundations of individual decision making are then pursued, and implications for in-dividual and group decision making are explored. Finally, the nature of organizational effectiveness is discussed and specific strategies are outlined, such as learning from the Japanese, improving the management of change, and social experimentation.

Space limitations prevent coverage of all the topics in organizational behavior. The book clearly has a "micro" orientation, and does not attempt to cover the waterfront. However, the readings do *not* simply drift aimlessly amongst a lot of disconnected theories or issues. Instead, the collection helps tie theories together across chapter headings and section divisions to provide the kind of understanding that will truly be useful to practicing managers and professionals. Used on its own or with an organizational behavior text, the book should help future managers to ask some of the right questions and to search for multiple answers to the complex problems faced by organizations.

I wish to thank Jim Boyd who encouraged (and even pushed) me to revise this readings book. I also want to thank Maryann Langen, who steered the collection through the production process at Scott, Foresman, as well as my colleagues for their many suggestions for revisions. Rick Mowday and George Strauss offered the most systematic advice, which was greatly appreciated, though not always followed. Finally, I wish to note that in the preface to the first edition I was "indebted to my eighteen-month-old son, Jonah, without whose efforts the book would have been published much earlier." Because my son is now a fiercely independent seven-year-old, I must at last take full responsibility for all delays and shortcomings of the current revision.

Barry M. Staw

Contents

Part Two: Social and Self-Perception

Part Three: Social Influence

C.   Power in Organizations

D.   Leadership

Part Four: **Decision-Making**

A.   Foundations of Organizational Rationality

Part One

Individual Behavior

A.

Foundations of Work Motivation

1. Drives, Needs, and Outcomes

Edward E. Lawler III

For centuries, psychologists and philosophers have tried to explain why some objects or outcomes seem to be desired by people while others are not. The concepts of instinct, drive, intrinsic motives, functional autonomy, derived motives, and many others have been used to explain this phenomenon. This chapter will review many of these concepts and present an integrated view of present knowledge about why certain outcomes are desirable or attractive to people.

An adequate explanation of why certain outcomes are desirable must deal with three separate but interrelated questions.

1. What is it about the nature of individuals that causes outcomes to become desirable to them?
2. What general classes or groups of outcomes do people find desirable or undesirable?
3. What factors influence the desirability of outcomes, that is, how does the desirability of outcomes change over time and why do individuals differ in the importance they attach to various outcomes?

Unless the second and third questions are answered, it is impossible to predict the kind of behavior choices a person will make. Although the answer to the first question is not needed in order to predict behavior, most theorists have found that answering it is a prerequisite to answering questions two and three. That is, these theorists have found it necessary to make assumptions about what causes outcomes to be important in the first place in order to make statements about the kinds of outcomes people value and the things that are likely to influence the attractiveness of outcomes.

Our first question has typically been answered by a set of assumptions about man's internal state. For example, some theorists have assumed that man has homeostatic drives, others have talked of instincts, while still others have talked of learned drives. The second question has been answered by the development of a number of need or outcome classification systems. Some of these systems assume only two classes of needs while others assume more than 20. The third question has been answered in many different ways. Maslow (1943), for example, has theorized that needs are arrayed in a hierarchy such that the lower-level needs have to be satisfied before the higher-level needs come into play. Other psychologists have stressed that learned associations can cause change in the attractiveness of outcomes.

Not every theory that has dealt with the attractiveness of outcomes has attempted to answer all of these questions. In fact, some theories have dealt essentially with only one of the questions. For example, in his discussion of the competence motive, White (1959) is concerned with establishing the existence of that motive. He does not present a general classification of motives, nor does he make statements about what influences the importance of other motives. As we discuss the various theories dealing with the attractiveness of outcomes, it is important to note which of the three questions are answered and which are ignored.

Let us now turn to a consideration of some of the more prominent theories.

HISTORICAL APPROACHES

Prior to the 1940s three theoretical approaches to explaining why outcomes are valued dominated the thinking in psychology. The first two, instinct theory and hedonism, do not make scientifically testable predictions of what outcomes people will seek. The third, drive theory, represents an attempt to develop a theory that does make testable predictions.

Instinct Theory

Charles Darwin was the first to call the attention of the scientific world to the possibility that much of human and animal behavior may be determined by instincts. He thought that many "intelligent" actions were inherited, and he provided a number of examples from his research on animals to support this view. William James, Sigmund Freud, and William McDougall developed the instinct doctrine as an important concept in their psychological theories. Some theorists thought of instincts as mechanical and automatic rather than as conscious motivators of behavior, but McDougall, who developed the most exhaustive taxonomy of instincts, thought of them as purposive, inherited, goal-seeking tendencies.

McDougall (1908) wrote that "we may then define an instinct as an inherited or innate psycho-physical disposition that determines the possessor to perceive and pay attention to objects of a certain class, to experience an emotional excitement of a particular quality on perceiving such an object, and to act in regard to it in a particular manner, or at least to experience an impulse to such action" (p. 39). Thus, the "pugnacity instinct" was an instinct that manifested itself in fighting when the organism was exposed to appropriate stimuli. At first McDougall thought he could account for all behavior in terms of about a dozen instincts. However, as time progressed he added more and more instincts to his list so that by 1932 his list included 19 instincts. Other psychologists added more, so that by the 1920s the list of instincts totaled nearly 6,000, including the "instinct to avoid eating apples in one's own orchard" (Murray, 1964, p. 6).

In a sense, instinct theory died of its own weight. As more and more instincts were stated, psychologists began to question the explanatory usefulness of the approach. To say that an animal fights because of the instinct of pugnacity or that an individual takes a job because he has an instinct to work is merely to give a redundant description of the observed behavior that adds nothing to our understanding of why the behavior took place. The tendency of some psychologists to add a new instinct to explain each new behavior that was observed also weakened the theory. As instinct theory developed, it seemed to provide unsatisfactory answers to all of our questions. It said that heredity determined which goals or outcomes organisms would seek (which was incomplete and misleading) and that people's goals consisted of the objects they sought (a circular definition). Thus, instinct theory did not allow for the prediction of which outcomes would be sought; it allowed only for the *post hoc* explanation of why certain goals were sought. Instinct theory also failed to provide a useful classification of the type of outcomes people sought. The original list of instincts was too short and the later ones were so long that they proved useless.

Hedonism

The origins of most contemporary conceptions of motivation can be traced to the principle of hedonism (Atkinson, 1964). In turn, hedonism can be traced to the original writings of the English utilitarians. The central assumption is that behavior is directed toward outcomes that provide pleasure and away from those that produce pain. In every situation people strive to obtain those goals or outcomes that provide the most pleasure. Despite its simplicity and popularity, the principle of hedonism fails to answer any of our three questions adequately. Nothing is said about why certain things give pleasure while others don't. There is no specification of the types of outcomes that are pleasurable or painful or even how these outcomes can be determined in advance for a particular individual. Any kind of behavior can be explained after the fact by postulating that particular outcomes were sources of either pain or pleasure. Finally, nothing is said about how the attractiveness of outcomes may be modified by experience or environmental circumstances. In short, the hedonistic assumption has no real empirical content leading to predictions of behavior and, thus, it is untestable.

Despite the fact that hedonism can be described as circular and lacking in content, its influence on psychology has been extensive. As one psychologist stated, "the study of motivation by psychologists has largely been directed toward filling in the missing empirical content in hedonism" (Vroom, 1964, p. 10). It is certainly true that almost all modern theories assume that people direct their behavior toward outcomes that they find pleasurable and away from those that they find unattractive. However, most modern theories do attempt to overcome the circularity of hedonism. They specify in advance how attractive specific outcomes will be to particular individuals and they develop models that predict when the attractiveness of outcomes will change.

Drive Theory

Drive theory developed partially as a reaction to instinct theory and hedonism. It is in the tradition of hedonism, but it is more closely tied to empirical events and therefore more testable. In 1918, R. S. Woodworth published a little book entitled *Dynamic Psychology* in which he advanced the view that psychologists should study what induces people to behave in particular ways. He referred to this inducement as drive, and the concept of drive soon replaced the concept of instinct in the psychologist's glossary of important terms. Later, the term "drive" took on a very precise meaning in the writings of C. L. Hull (1943). He assumed that all behavior is motivated by either primary or secondary drives. According to Hull, the primary drives were biologically

based; they represented states of homeostatic imbalance. Hull's position was that:

The major primary needs or drives are so ubiquitous that they require little more than to be mentioned. They include the need for foods of various sorts (hunger), the need for water (thirst), the need for air, the need to avoid tissue injury (pain), the need to maintain an optimal temperature, the need to defecate, the need to micturate, the need for rest (after protracted exertion), the need for sleep (after protracted wakefulness), and the need for activity (after protracted inaction). The drives concerned with the maintenance of the species are those which lead to sexual intercourse and the need represented by nest building and care of the young [pp. 59–60].

In Hull's theory, outcomes become rewards when they are able to reduce primary drives and thereby reduce homeostatic imbalance and the tension that occurs when organisms are in a state of ecological deprivation. Thus, food is a reward to a hungry person and water is a reward to a thirsty person. Hull also stressed that drive strength can be increased by deprivation and reduced as needs become satisfied. Thus, the hungrier a person gets, the more he desires food; but as he eats food, he becomes less hungry and his desire diminishes. Although Hull assumed that all rewards and drives are ultimately based on the reduction of primary drives, he recognized that certain secondary drives and rewards could develop — or be "learned" — if in the past they were associated with food or other primary rewards. Thus, money is a secondary reward because it is often associated with food and other primary rewards. Social approval becomes a reward for children who are praised for eating well, or dressing themselves, and so on. According to Hull's view, most of the rewards used by work organizations would be considered secondary rewards.

Hull's theory represents a significant advance over the previous theories of motivation. It gives a clear-cut answer to the question of what objects or outcomes have value — that is, objects or outcomes that either reduce primary, biologically based drives or have been related to outcomes that do. It also provides a classification of drives that is still commonly used (it divides them into primary and secondary drives, and it specifies what the primary drives are). Finally, it says that deprivation increases drive strength, whereas obtaining the desired outcomes reduces drive strength. Thus,

Hull's theory has answers to all three of our questions. But the real significance of Hull's theory rests in the fact that it is empirically testable. Since it specifies in detail the relationship between such measurable things as deprivation, drive, and learning, the theory can be tested, and it has spawned a large number of research studies.

At this point it is safe to say that these studies have found Hull's theory to be inadequate in a number of important respects. The most important shortcomings have to do with the ability of the theory to explain motivation that is not based on primary drives. Hull's basic point about organisms' possessing certain primary drives that become stronger with deprivation and weaker with satisfaction still seems valid. What does not seem valid is his argument that all secondary motives are learned on the basis of primary physiological or homeostatic drives.

There is no solid evidence that drives can be learned on the basis of their association with positive drives such as hunger and thirst (Cravens and Renner, 1970). There is evidence that organisms will work for rewards that have been associated with the reduction of a primary drive if the primary drive is present. However, when the primary drive is not present, there seems to be no "acquired" drive to obtain the reward. For example, in the classic experiments of Wolfe (1936) and Cowles (1937), chimpanzees learned to associate tokens with the acquisition of food. Initially, the chimps learned to operate an apparatus that required lifting a weight to obtain grapes. They continued to operate it when the only visible reward was a token that had been associated with the grapes. However, they didn't seem to develop an acquired need for tokens, since they were willing to work to obtain the tokens only as long as they were hungry and the tokens led to something they desired—that is, food. Hence, it is difficult to see how Hull's explanation can help us understand why workers continue to work for more money even when their basic needs are satisfied.

More damaging to Hull's view than the evidence on the failure of animals to acquire learned drives is the great amount of evidence indicating that people and animals are attracted to many outcomes that do not seem to be directly related to primary needs. Rats will learn mazes in order to explore novel environments, monkeys will solve puzzles even though they receive no extrinsic rewards, and people will work simply in order to develop their skills and abilities and to increase their competence. These and many other phenomena cannot be explained easily by drive theory.

CONTEMPORARY APPROACHES

Recently, many psychologists have rejected the emphasis of drive theory on primary drives and have argued that people have many needs. This argument has come particularly from those psychologists who are interested in studying human behavior. As we shall see, they have proposed a number of needs that do not seem to be directly related to homeostatic imbalance, organism survival, or species survival. This recent work on motivation has produced two somewhat different approaches.

Researchers in one group have focused on establishing the existence of one or two human motives that they consider to be particularly important. Thus, McClelland has focused on the achievement motive and White has focused on the competence motive. They have not tried to develop complex need, or motive, classification systems. In other words, they have not tried to answer our second question. They have contented themselves with trying to understand why one set or type of outcomes is attractive to people. Other researchers have tried to develop need, or motive, classification systems in an attempt to predict which kinds of outcomes will be attractive to people. Murray's (1938) list of needs and Maslow's (1943) statement of a need hierarchy are examples of this approach. But before we consider these classification systems, we need to look at some of the needs that have been proposed as necessary additions to the primary drives observed by Hull.

The Affiliation Motive

A number of researchers have presented evidence to show that an affiliation motive exists. They have shown that social interaction is attractive to people and that it is particularly likely to occur under certain conditions. For example, Schachter (1959) has shown that people seek the companionship of others when they are anxious and confused about their motives. In Schachter's work, college students faced with the prospect of being shocked were given the opportunity to be with another person. The subjects under such anxiety were more likely to accept invitations to be with others than were subjects who were not under such anxiety. This result occurred even when the subjects were not permitted to talk to the person they were to be with. Other research suggests that people are likely to seek social interaction at times when they are doubting their self-esteem.

Harlow (1958) has presented some interesting evidence suggesting that the social motive may be innate. As part of his work with monkeys he raised some infant monkeys, providing them with two surrogate mothers in place of their natural mothers. One surrogate mother consisted of a cylinder of wire mesh with an opening in the center of the "breast" for a bottle. The other was similarly shaped but was covered with cotton terry cloth. In the experiment, baby monkeys were placed in cages containing the two "mothers." Half were fed from the cloth mother, the other half from the wire mother. According to drive theory, the monkeys who were fed by the wire mother should have become attached to the wire mother because it provided the drive reduction — that is, the milk. However, it did not work out that way. The monkeys who were fed on the wire mother spent most of their time clinging to the cloth mother. Thus, it appears that monkeys develop their attachment to their mothers based on contact comfort rather than on primary-drive reduction.

However, the important point for us about the research on the need for social contact is not whether this need is innate or acquired but that it exists in most adult human beings. It clearly is an important motivation — one that has a significant impact on behavior in organizations. Many organizations have discovered — to their sorrow — that jobs that do not provide opportunities for social contact have higher turnover and absenteeism rates because employees simply cannot stand the isolation. Frequently, unnecessary social isolation results from mechanical and architectural designs that do not consider employees' needs for social relationships.

Need for Equity

People want to be treated fairly. They observe what happens to other people and if they receive either "too much" or "too little" in comparison to other people it makes them uncomfortable. For example, one study showed that dissatisfaction with promotion was highest in Army units where promotion rates were high. Why? Because the individuals who weren't promoted in these units felt unfairly treated. Adams (1963, 1965) has developed a theory that makes a number of interesting predictions about the effects of wage inequity on work output, work quality, and attitudes toward work. Although this theory is a general theory of social inequity, it has been tested largely with respect to the effects of wage inequity, and it has some interesting things to say about how equity may affect the

attractiveness of rewards. Its predictions seem to be particularly relevant to understanding the effects of offering various sizes of pay increases and the effects of paying different wage rates.

Adams (1965) defines inequity as follows:

Inequity exists for Person when he perceives that the ratio of his outcomes to inputs and the ratio of Other's outcomes to Other's inputs are unequal. This may happen either (a) when he and Other are in a direct exchange relationship or (b) when both are in an exchange relationship with a third party, and Person compares himself to Other [p. 280].

Outcomes in the job situation include pay, fringe benefits, status, the intrinsic interest of the job, and so on. Inputs include how hard the person works, his education level, his general qualifications for the job, and so on. It must be remembered that what determines the equity of a particular input-outcome balance is the individual's perception of what he is giving and receiving; this cognition may or may not correspond to an observer's perception or to reality.

Equity theory states that the presence of inequity will motivate an individual to reduce inequity and that the strength of the motivation to reduce inequity varies directly with the perceived magnitude of the imbalance experienced between inputs and outcomes. Feelings of inequity can be produced in a variety of ways and in a variety of situations. Adams has studied inequity produced by overpayment. His research suggests that overpayment is less attractive to employees than equitable payment is. There is evidence, for example, that when a person is paid on a piece rate and feels overpaid, he will reduce his productivity in order to reduce the amount of pay he receives. The important thing for this discussion about the research on equity theory is that people tend to seek equity in their work activities, which can affect their job behavior.

Activity and Exploration

Too little stimulation is very uncomfortable for humans. In one study, college students were employed at $20 a day to stay in a low stimulation environment (Bexton, Heron, & Scott, 1954). They were asked to remain for as many days as they could, lying on a cot in a lighted, partially sound-deadened room. They wore translucent goggles, gloves, and cardboard cuffs that minimized tactile stimulation. An air conditioner provided a noise that blocked out other sounds, and the students rested their heads on a U-shaped pillow. After a certain period — usually filled with sleeping — the subjects found this situation impossible to tolerate and asked to leave the experiment. Rarely did a subject endure it for as long as 2 days despite the fact that the pay was relatively high. Other studies have reported similar results, stressing that under these conditions people seem to develop a hunger for stimulation and action leading to such responses as touching the fingers together and twitching the muscles.

Research by Scott (1969) has shown that the results are very similar when people are given repetitive tasks to perform. They develop a negative attitude toward the task, and, as time goes on, they take more breaks and try in many ways to vary their behavior. As we shall see, this finding has direct implications for the design of jobs in organizations.

Other studies have shown that both people and animals seek out opportunities to experience novel situations. Butler (1953) has shown that monkeys will learn to push open a window for no reward other than being able to see what is going on in a room, and they will keep doing it. Butler has also shown that the strength of the drive for novel stimulation can be increased by deprivation. An experiment by Smock and Holt (1962) has shown that if children are given a chance to control what they see on a television screen, they will look at objects that offer complex stimuli rather than unconflicting, simple stimuli.

Many studies of rats have shown that they will learn certain behaviors in order to experience novel stimuli. In one experiment, rats preferred a goal box that contained objects to an empty goal box. Miles (1958) found that kittens would learn things when the reward was simply the opportunity to explore a room. There is much evidence that humans and animals will try to solve puzzles simply because of the stimulation provided by working on them. Harlow (1953) has shown that monkeys will persist in solving puzzles for many days. One monkey, who was presented with a square peg and a round hole, persisted for months in trying to get the two to fit together. (The monkey finally died of perforated ulcers.)

Several theorists have suggested that the results of both the stimulus-deprivation studies and the studies of novel-stimulus environments can be explained by considering how novelty affects stimulus attractiveness (Berlyne, 1967). According to activation theory, people become used to a certain level and pattern of stimulation from the environment. For some people this adaptation level may be a relatively low level of stimulation; for others it may be a rather high level.

Regardless of where a person's level of adaptation is, however, psychologists hypothesize that deviation from it will have a strong impact on the person. Slight deviations will be experienced as pleasurable and rewarding while large deviations will be experienced as noxious and dissatisfying. Figure 1 illustrates this point graphically. According to this approach, the subjects in the stimulus-deprivation experiment were uncomfortable because the situation fell too far below the adaptation level. The animals who wanted to explore new things were attracted to them because these new things represented stimulus situations that were somewhat above their adaptation levels. Presumably if the stimulus situations had been too far above their adaptation levels, the animals would have avoided them, and indeed there is evidence that both animals and people fear situations that are very unfamiliar to them.

One of the problems with activation theory is that it can be very difficult to measure in advance what a person's adaptation level is. Still, the theory and its related research provide some interesting evidence to support the point that not all drives or needs are either primary or learned on the basis of primary drives. It is hard to see how people's reactions to different levels of stimulation can be explained by reference to a drive that has been learned on the basis of a primary drive.

Achievement

The achievement motive has been extensively studied by D. C. McClelland. It is defined by McClelland (1951, 1961) as a desire to perform in terms of a standard of excellence or as a desire to be successful in competitive situations. McClelland stresses that achievement motivation is present in most people but that the amount people have depends on a number of things, including how they were treated during childhood. One study has shown that high-need-achievement people tend to come from families where high demands were made for independence and performance at an early age. Their mothers evaluated their accomplishments favorably and rewarded them liberally.

McClelland measures the strength of people's achievement motive by scoring their responses to a series of pictures. The pictures are shown to individuals who are asked to write a five-minute story about what is going on in the picture. The stories are scored on the basis of how frequently achievement-oriented themes are mentioned (for example, "He will try his best to succeed"). The following is an example of a story

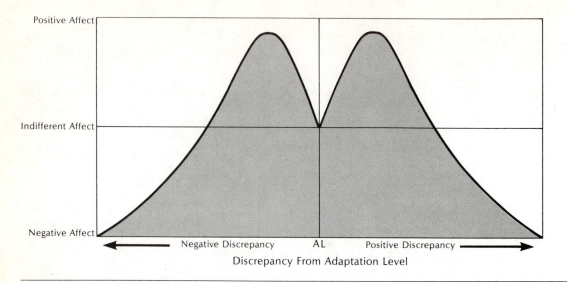

Figure 1.   The Butterfly Curve.

showing a young boy in the foreground and a hazy representation of an operation in the background.

A boy is dreaming of being a doctor. He can see himself in the future. He is hoping that he can make the grade. It is more or less a fantasy. The boy has seen many pictures of doctors in books, and it has inspired him. He will try his best and hopes to become the best doctor in the country. He can see himself as a very important doctor. He is performing a very dangerous operation. He can see himself victorious and is proud of it. He gets world renown for it. He will become the best doctor in the U.S. He will be an honest man, too. His name will go down in medical history as one of the greatest men [Atkinson, 1958, p. 193].

McClelland's research has shown that under certain conditions achievement motivation can be an important motivator of good performance in work organizations. When achievement motivation is operating, good job performance becomes very attractive to people; as a result, the motivation to perform well is higher. Achievement motivation typically does not operate when people are performing routine or boring tasks where no competition is involved. However, when challenge and competition are involved, achievement

motivation can stimulate good performance. A study by French (1955) clearly illustrates this point. In French's study, Officer Candidate School cadets performed a simple task under three different sets of instructions. Under the "relaxed" instructions the subjects were told that the experimenter was merely interested in determining what kinds of scores people make on the test. The "task-motivated" instructions said that the task was a measure of people's ability to deal rapidly with new materials. The "extrinsically motivated" instructions said that the best performers could leave while the others had to continue performing. Performance was highest under the "task-motivated" instructions and lowest under the "relaxed" instructions. Subjects with high need for achievement performed better on the "task-motivated" instructions but not under the two other kinds of instructions.

Other studies also support the view that people can be motivated simply by a drive to achieve. For example, Alper (1946) gave two groups of subjects a list of nonsense syllables to learn. Only one group was told it was an intelligence test. A test given 24 hours later showed that the "intelligence test" group remembered more of what they had learned. McClelland (1961) showed that successful people in competitive occupations tend to be universally high in achievement motivation. For example, he showed that successful managers from countries such as the United States, Italy, and India tend to be high in achievement motivation.

Overall, the research on achievement motivation suggests that such motivation is most likely to be present when moderately challenging tasks have to be performed (where about a 50–50 chance of success exists), in competitive situations, in situations where performance is perceived to depend upon some important or valued skill, and in situations where performance feedback is given. The research also suggests that people with a high need for achievement tend to seek out situations in which they can achieve, and they tend to find successful performance attractive once they are in these situations. These points have important implications for the design of jobs in organizations and for the kinds of people that are attracted to jobs in different types of work situations.

Judging from the research cited earlier on the effects of child rearing on the strength of need for achievement, it seems certain that achievement motivation is a partly learned drive. McClelland in fact argues that it is differentially present in certain cultures precisely because child-rearing practices differ. However, even though achievement motivation is a learned drive, it is hard to see how it could develop because of the primary drives. There may be some relationship here, since success often helps people to obtain primary rewards, such as food; but it is hard to see how the primary drive approach can explain the fact that early independence training leads to a strong need for achievement. Thus, even though achievement is a learned drive, it seems that it is only partially learned on the basis of primary drives.

Competence

Robert W. White (1959) has argued for the existence of a competence motive. He uses competence to refer to an organism's capacity to interact effectively with its environment. In organisms capable of little learning, competence is considered to be innate; however, competence in man—that is, his fitness to interact with the environment—is slowly attained through prolonged feats of learning. The human learning that is needed to gain competence is characterized by high persistence and a strong goal orientation. Because of this dedication to learning, White argues that it is necessary to treat competence as having a motivation aspect that is separate from motivation derived from primary drives

or instincts. He presents considerable evidence of organisms trying to cope with their environment seemingly for no other reason than that they want to master it. As White notes, there are repeated references in psychological literature.

. . . to the familiar series of learned skills which starts with sucking, grasping, and visual exploration and continues with crawling and walking, acts of focal attention and perception, memory, language and thinking, anticipation, the exploring of novel places and objects, effecting stimulus changes in the environment, manipulating and exploiting the surroundings, and achieving higher levels of motor and mental coordination. . . . Collectively they are sometimes referred to as mechanisms . . . but on the whole we are not accustomed to cast a single name over the diverse feats whereby we learn to deal with the environment. . . . I now propose that we gather the various kinds of behavior just mentioned, all of which had to do with effective interaction with the environment, under the general heading of competence . . . it is necessary to make competence a motivational concept; there is a competence motivation [1959, pp. 317–318].

White argues that competence motivation is aroused when people are faced with somewhat new situations and wanes when a situation has been explored and mastered to the point at which it no longer presents a challenge.

There is an obvious similarity between White's view of when competence motivation is aroused and the activation theorists' view of how stimulus novelty affects motivation. Both argue for high motivation when somewhat novel situations are encountered. White's theory is also very closely related to the theory of achievement motivation, since both talk of man's need to perform adequately. In fact, White says that achievement may be one outcome of competence motivation. White's theory has some interesting implications for the design of jobs in organizations. It suggests that if presented with the right task people can be motivated to perform effectively without the use of extrinsic rewards such as pay and promotion. However, once the task is mastered, competence motivation will disappear. It is also interesting to note that White, like other recent theorists, argues that the competence motive is not based on any primary drive. Although he does not say exactly where it comes from, he does imply that man's desire to be competent is innate.

Table 1.   List of Theorists Classified as Emphasizing Self-actualization, and the Term Each Uses

Kurt Goldstein (1939): Self-actualization
Erich Fromm (1941): The productive orientation
Prescott Lecky (1945): The unified personality; self-consistency
Donald Snygg and Arthur Combs (1949): The preservation and enhancement of the phenomenal self
Karen Horney (1950): The real self and its realization
David Riesman (1950): The autonomous person
Carl Rogers (1951): Actualization, maintenance, and enhancement of the experiencing organism
Rollo May (1953): Existential being
Abraham Maslow (1954): Self-actualization
Gordon W. Allport (1955): Creative becoming

Adapted from Cofer, C. N., and Appley, M. H., *Motivation: Theory and Research.* Copyright ©1964 by John Wiley & Sons, Inc. Reprinted by permission.

Self-Actualization

In the last thirty years a number of psychologists have introduced concepts into their theories that have to do with people's need to grow and develop. Table 1 lists some of these theorists and their concepts. The work of Maslow has had by far the greatest impact on the thinking concerned with motivation in organizations. Maslow uses the term ''self-actualization'' to describe the need people have to grow and develop. According to him, it is the ''desire for self-fulfillment, namely . . . the tendency [for a person] to become actualized in what he is potentially . . . the desire to become more and more of what one is, to become everything that one is capable of becoming . . .'' (1954, pp. 91–92). Maslow stresses that not all people function on the self-actualization level. He then goes on to describe the characteristics of people who are motivated by self-actualization. According to him, much of the self-actualizing person's behavior is motivated solely by the sheer enjoyment he obtains from using and developing his capacities. He does not necessarily behave in accordance with extrinsic goals or rewards. For him, the goal is simply to behave in a certain way or experience a certain feeling. Maslow makes the point like this:

. . . we must construct a profoundly different psychology of motivation for self-actualizing people, e.g., expression motivation or growth motivation, rather than deficiency motivation. Perhaps it will be useful to make a distinction between living and preparing to live. Perhaps the concept of motivation should apply only to

non-self-actualizers. Our subjects no longer strive in the ordinary sense, but rather develop. They attempt to grow to perfection and to develop more and more fully in their own style. The motivation of ordinary men is a striving for the basic need gratifications that they lack. But self-actualizing people in fact lack none of these gratifications; and yet they have impulses. They work, they try, and they are ambitious, even though in an unusual sense. For them motivation is just character growth, character expression, maturation, and development; in a word self-actualization [p. 211].

Thus, like White and others, Maslow is careful to say that all motivation is not tied to the primary drives. Maslow also stresses that people will work to obtain outcomes that are intrinsic, such as feelings of growth. He completely rejects the view that valued outcomes have to be related to such extrinsic rewards as food and water. Maslow probably goes further than any of the other theorists we have reviewed in stressing the differences between motivation based on primary drives and motivation that is independent of primary drives. He says that, unlike motivation based on primary drives, motivation based on growth needs does not decrease as the needs become satisfied. Quite to the contrary, Maslow argues that as people experience growth and self-actualization they simply want more. In his view, obtaining growth creates a desire for more growth, whereas obtaining food decreases one's desire for food.

Maslow argues that the concept of self-actualization can explain a significant amount of the motivation in organizations. He states that, particularly at the

*From *Motivation and Personality* (2nd ed.) by A. H. Maslow. Copyright© 1970 by Harper & Row, Publishers, Inc. Reprinted by permission of the publishers.

managerial level, many people are motivated by a desire to self-actualize. There is a considerable amount of evidence to support this point. In one study, managers rated the need for self-actualization as their most important need (Porter, 1964). In addition, most large organizations abound with training and development programs designed to help people develop their skills and abilities. Sometimes people do enter these programs in the hope of obtaining a raise or promotion, but on other occasions they do it only because it contributes to their self-development. There is also evidence of people seeking more challenging jobs for no other reason than to develop themselves.

An interesting contrast to Maslow's work on self-actualization is provided by the work of existential psychologists such as Allport (1955) and Rogers (1961). They too talk of people being motivated by desires that are not related to obtaining rewards such as money and status. However, they give less emphasis to the development of skills and abilities and the achievement of goals than does Maslow, and they give more emphasis to new experiences as a way of learning about one's self. Rogers, for example, talks of people being motivated ''to be that self which one truly is.'' He emphasizes self-discovery and the importance of being open to experience. Perhaps because they don't emphasize skill development and accomplishments as much as Maslow, the existential psychologists have not had much impact on the research of psychologists interested in work organizations. This is unfortunate, and it is important to remember that at times people may be motivated by nothing more than self-discovery and a desire to experience.

Need-Classification Theories

Numerous lists and classifications of needs have been presented by psychologists. One of the most important is Henry A. Murray's (1938) list of ''psychogenic'' or ''social'' needs. This list, which contains more than 20 motives, was arrived at on the basis of the study of a number of ''normal'' people. Although Murray's list has been very influential in the field of psychology, it has not been applied very much to the study of motivation in organizations, probably because its length greatly reduces its usefulness. Like the early lists of instincts, it is so long that there is almost a separate need for each behavior people demonstrate. A look at Table 2, which lists some of Murray's needs, may help the reader gain an impression of the nature of the problem. The issue is not whether Murray has identified separate kinds of behavior (he has) but whether these behaviors might not be better dealt with by a more parsimonious list of needs.

Table 2. Murray's List of Needs.

Social Motive	Brief Definition
Abasement	To surrender. To comply and accept punishment. To apologize, confess, atone. Self-depreciation. Masochism.
Achievement	To overcome obstacles, to exercise power, to strive to do something difficult as well and as quickly as possible.
Affiliation	To form friendships and associations. To greet, join, and live with others. To cooperate and converse sociably with others. To love. To join groups.
Aggression	To assault or injure an other. To murder. To belittle, harm, blame, accuse or maliciously ridicule a person. To punish severely. Sadism.
Autonomy	To resist influence or coercion. To defy an authority or seek freedom in a new place. To strive for independence.
Blamavoidance	To avoid blame, ostracism or punishment by inhibiting asocial or unconventional impulses. To be well-behaved and obey the law.
Counteraction	Proudly to refuse admission of defeat by restriving and retaliating. To select the hardest tasks. To defend one's honor in action.
Defendance	To defend oneself against blame or belittlement. To justify one's actions. To offer extenuations, explanations and excuses. To resist ''probing.''

Table 2.   Murray's List of Needs.

Social Motive	Brief Definition
Deference	To admire and willingly follow a superior allied other. To cooperate with a leader. To serve gladly.
Dominance	To influence or control others. To persuade, prohibit, dictate. To lead and direct. To restrain. To organize the behavior of a group.
Exhibition	To attract attention to one's person. To excite, amuse, stir, shock, thrill others. Self-dramatization.
Harmavoidance	To avoid pain, physical injury, illness and death. To escape from a dangerous situation. To take precautionary measures.
Infavoidance	To avoid failure, shame, humiliation, ridicule. To refrain from attempting to do something that is beyond one's powers. To conceal a disfigurement.
Nurturance	To nourish, aid or protect a helpless other. To express sympathy. To ''mother'' a child.
Order	To arrange, organize, put away objects. To be tidy and clean. To be scrupulously precise.
Play	To relax, amuse oneself, seek diversion and entertainment. To ''have fun,'' to play games. To laugh, joke and be merry. To avoid serious tension.
Rejection	To snub, ignore or exclude an other. To remain aloof and indifferent. To be discriminating.
Sentience	To seek and enjoy sensuous impressions.
Sex	To form and further an erotic relationship. To have sexual intercourse.
Succorance	To seek aid, protection or sympathy. To cry for help. To plead for mercy. To adhere to an affectionate, nurturant parent. To be dependent.
Understanding	To analyze experience, to abstract, to discriminate among concepts, to define relations, to synthesize ideas.

From H. A. Murray, *Explorations in Personality*. New York: Oxford, 1938.

Maslow's hierarchical classification of needs has been by far the most widely used classification system in the study of motivation in organizations. Maslow differs from Murray in two important ways: first, his list is shorter; second, he argues that needs are arranged in a hierarchy.

Maslow's (1943, 1954, 1970) hierarchical model is composed of a five-level classification of human needs and a set of hypotheses about how the satisfaction of these needs affects their importance.

The five need categories are as follows:

1. *Physiological needs,* including the need for food, water, air, and so on.
2. *Safety needs,* or the need for security, stability, and the absence from pain, threat, or illness.
3. *Belongingness and love needs,* which include a need for affection, belongingness, love, and so on.
4. *Esteem needs,* including both a need for personal feelings of achievement or self-esteem and also a need for recognition or respect from others.
5. *The need for self-actualization,* a feeling of self-fulfillment or the realization of one's potential.

More important than the definition of these five need groups, however, is the *process* by which each class of needs becomes important or active. According to Maslow, the five need categories exist in a hierarchy of prepotency such that the lower or more basic needs are inherently more important (prepotent) than the higher or less basic needs. This means that before any of the higher-level needs will become important, a person's physiological needs must be satisfied. Once the physiological needs have been satisfied, however, their strength or importance decreases, and the next-higher-level need becomes the strongest motivator of behavior. This process of "increased satisfaction / decreased importance / increased importance of the next higher need" repeats itself until the highest level of the hierarchy is reached. Maslow has proposed in later revisions of his theory (1968, 1970) that at the highest level of the hierarchy a reversal occurs in the satisfaction-importance relationship. He states that for self-actualization, increased satisfaction leads to *increased* need strength. "Gratification breeds increased rather than decreased motivation, heightened rather than lessened excitement" (1968, p. 30).

In short, individual behavior is motivated by an attempt to satisfy the need that is *most important* at that point in time. Further, the strength of any need is determined by its position in the hierarchy and by the degree to which it and all lower needs have been satisfied. Maslow's theory predicts a dynamic, step-by-step, causal process of human motivation in which behavior is governed by a continuously changing (though predictable) set of "important" needs. An increase (change) in the satisfaction of the needs in one category *causes* the strength of these needs to decrease, which results in an increase in the importance of the needs at the next-higher level. Maslow does say that the hierarchy of needs is not a rigidly fixed order that is the same for all individuals. Especially in the case of needs in the middle of the hierarchy, the order varies somewhat from person to person. However, this view clearly states that physiological needs are the most prepotent and that self-actualization needs are usually the least.

Two other need-hierarchy theories have been stated. One is by Langer (1937) — predating Maslow's — and another by Alderfer (1969). Alderfer's (1972) theory is the best developed of these two theories. Alderfer argues for three levels of needs: existence, relatedness, and growth. Like Maslow, he argues that the satisfaction of a need influences its importance and the importance

of higher-level needs. He agrees with Maslow's hypothesis that the satisfaction of growth needs makes them more important rather than less important to people; however, he also hypothesizes that the lack of satisfaction of higher-order needs can lead to lower-order needs becoming more important to people. He then argues that the importance of any need is influenced by the satisfaction / frustration of the needs above and below it in the hierarchy. He also assumes that all needs can be simultaneously active; thus, prepotency does not play as major a role in his theory as it does in Maslow's.

From the point of view of the three questions we asked at the beginning of the chapter, the hierarchical theories of Maslow and Alderfer provide rather complete answers to the last two questions. These theories make specific statements about what outcomes people will value (outcomes that satisfy whatever need or needs are active). They also make specific predictions about what will influence the attractiveness of various outcomes — for example, satisfaction of relevant needs including those lower on the hierarchy. They provide less complete answers to our first question, since they are not clear on why needs originate. They do, however, imply that the lower-order needs are innate and that the higher-order needs are present in most people and will appear if not blocked from appearing.

The hierarchical concept has received a great deal of attention among those interested in organizations. This interest is undoubtedly because the concept, if valid, provides a powerful tool for predicting how the importance of various outcomes will change in response to certain actions by organizations. It also can provide some important clues concerning what is likely to be important to employees. It suggests, for example, that as people get promoted in organizations and their lower-level needs become satisfied, they will become concerned with self-actualization and growth. It also suggests that if a person's job security is threatened, he will abandon all else in order to protect it. Finally, it suggests that an organization can give an employee enough of the lower-level rewards, such as security, but that it cannot give him enough growth and development. Thus, as employees receive more valued outcomes from organizations, they will *want* more; although the nature of what they want may change from things that satisfy their lower-order needs to things that satisfy their higher-order needs. As more than one manager has noted, "we have given our employees good working conditions, high pay, and a secure future.

Now they want more interesting jobs and a chance to make more decisions. Won't they ever be satisfied?" Need hierarchy suggests that they won't!

AN APPROACH TO OUTCOME ATTRACTIVENESS

The approaches of Maslow, McClelland, and others are useful in thinking about motivation in organizations. They clearly indicate a number of important points that need to be included in any approach that tries to deal with the issue of why certain outcomes are attractive to people. However, there are still many questions. The rest of this chapter will be concerned with answering these questions and with developing an approach to explaining outcome attractiveness.

Drives, Needs, Motives, or Just Outcomes?

All of the theorists discussed so far have assumed that outcomes are attractive to a person because of some drive, motive, or need the person has. On the other hand, Vroom (1964) has taken a different approach. He does not use the terms drive, need, or motive in his theory. He simply says that outcomes have value if they lead to other valued outcomes. Nothing is said about what causes people to value those other outcomes nor about what other outcomes are likely to be valued. Although it does solve the problem of trying to understand why individual outcomes are attractive, a theory that deals with the problem as Vroom's does sacrifices predictive power, in contrast to a theory of needs that states in advance what outcomes are likely to be valued and what affects their value.

A theory of needs can make some predictions — such as when outcomes will be important and what will be the effects of certain events — that Vroom's theory cannot make. For example, if it is known that pay is important to an individual because it leads to prestige, Vroom's theory can only predict that, as prestige outcomes become less important, so will pay. On the other hand, a need theory such as Maslow's can make further predictions. It can predict what conditions will affect the importance of prestige outcomes — that is, satisfaction of esteem needs or lower-level needs — and can then predict what the effect of a number of factors, such as a promotion, will be on the importance of pay.

The issue of whether needs are innate or learned is an important one; but since we are dealing with adults whose need structures are already developed, it is not crucial for us. This issue is important for us only in the sense that it might provide information about how common it is for people to have a need. Innate needs should be present in a greater proportion of the society than learned needs. Of course, at this point no one seriously argues that any needs other than the basic ones are either purely learned or purely innate. Still, it does seem that the needs that are lower on Maslow's hierarchy are more innate and, therefore, more universally present than are those that are at the top of the hierarchy.

For our purposes a theory of needs does not have to specify why people have needs, since it can say something about the needs people have and the conditions under which certain needs operate without doing this. All it has to say is that certain outcomes can be grouped together because when one is sought the others are sought and when one is obtained the others are no longer sought. People often have several groups of such outcomes. The groups can be called "needs," and, if the same ones are sought by most people, then it is reasonable to speak of a "human need" for the group of outcomes. Perhaps it should be added that before a group of outcomes is called a need the outcomes should be sought as ends in themselves rather than as instruments for obtaining other outcomes. For example, food outcomes are sought as an end in themselves, and thus we speak of a *need* for food; a big office is not an end in itself, and thus cannot be called a need. Once it is decided that people have needs, the question is "how many needs?".

How Many Needs?

Interestingly, theorists defining different categories of human needs usually don't disagree over which specific outcomes are likely to be goals for people, but they do disagree on what kinds of needs lead to outcomes taking on goal characteristics. Psychologists have argued that people have from three to several hundred needs. Part of the reason for this variance rests in the way needs are defined. Originally, the criterion was simple; needs or drives were only said to exist when it could be established that a physiological basis could be found for the attractiveness of the outcomes sought by a person.

The recent research on higher-level needs has clearly shown this approach to be too restrictive. A suggested alternative is to use the term "need" to refer to clusters of outcomes that people seek as ends in themselves.

This definition, however, does not solve the problem of how to determine what constitutes a valid cluster. Different foods provide a simple example of the problem. Various food objects can be grouped together in the sense that when a person wants one he often wants the others and when he gets enough of one he may lose interest in the others. Thus, we can say that people have a need for meat rather than saying that people have a need for roast beef or steak. By thinking in terms of outcome clusters such as the one just described, we move to a more general level and begin to group outcomes more parsimoniously. The question that arises now, however, is where to stop. That is, at what level of abstraction or generality should we stop grouping outcomes? Should we, for example, stop at the level of meat or put all food outcomes together and speak of a need for food, since food objects are somewhat similar in attractiveness as shown in Figure 2. The former is a tighter cluster in the sense that the attractiveness of different kinds of meat is probably more closely related than is the attractiveness of meat to the attractiveness of fruit. However, there are still tighter clusters (different kinds of steak), and thus there is no final answer to the question of how tight a cluster should be.

It is also possible to go to a higher level of abstraction and combine food outcomes with water and oxygen and call this combination an existence need (see Figure 3). This existence need includes all the outcomes that people need to sustain life. The criterion for grouping at this level is different from the criterion stated earlier (when one outcome is sought the other will be sought, and when one is obtained the attractiveness of the other is affected). The grouping in Figure 3 is based on the fact that all the outcomes have a common property: they are necessary for existence. Unlike the cluster shown in Figure 2, the attractiveness of one is not necessarily related to the other. Using this system, we would say that people desire food objects because of a basic need to exist; whereas, if we operated at a lower

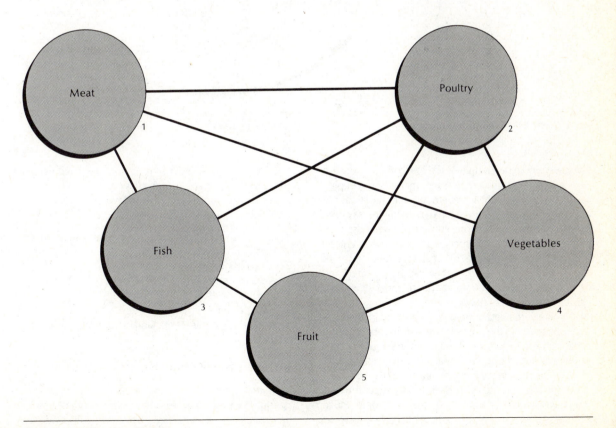

Figure 2.   An Outcome Cluster.

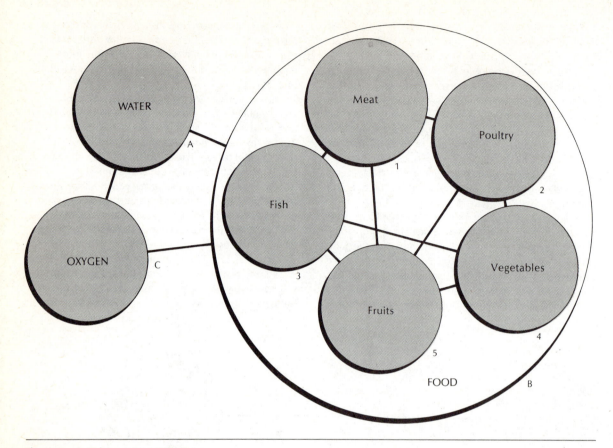

Figure 3.   An Existence-Need Cluster.

level, we would say people desire food objects because of a need for nourishment. A somewhat similar grouping problem occurs with achievement, self-actualization, and competence. Although it is possible to say that these concepts each represent separate needs, they also overlap in many respects. They all focus on the attractiveness to people of dealing effectively with challenging problems. Thus, they can be grouped and labeled as "a need for competence and growth" or they can be treated separately.

Ultimately, the best approach to categorizing needs is that which allows the greatest prediction of behavior in organizations. Unfortunately, at the moment there is not enough research evidence to allow us to state conclusively which listing of needs leads to the greatest predictability. Because of this lack of evidence, the best approach would seem to be grouping only those outcomes that have a strong empirical relationship to each other. By this condition we mean those outcomes

that can be observed to have common degrees of attractiveness to people. Using this criterion and thinking in terms of organizations, the following needs can be identified:

1. A number of existence needs — primarily sex, hunger, thirst, and oxygen.
2. A security need.
3. A social need.
4. A need for esteem and reputation.
5. An autonomy or freedom need.
6. A need for competence and self-actualization.

Is There a Need Hierarchy?

Now that we have identified a specific set of human needs, we must consider whether these needs should be arranged in a hierarchy. What does the evidence show about the existence of a need hierarchy?

There is strong evidence to support the view that unless existence needs are satisfied, none of the higher-order needs will come into play. There is also evidence that unless security needs are satisfied, people will not be concerned with higher-order needs. One report shows that subjects kept in a state of hunger think of little else than food (Keys, Brozek, Henschel, Mickelsen, & Taylor, 1950). Similar data is available in the literature on brainwashing and concentration camps (Lawler & Suttle, 1972).

There is, however, very little evidence to support the view that a hierarchy exists above the security level. Thus, it probably is not safe to assume more than a two-step hierarchy with existence and security needs at the lowest level and all the higher-order needs at the next level. This line of thinking leads to the prediction that unless these lower-order needs are satisfied, the others will not come into play. However, which higher-order needs come into play after the lower ones are satisfied and in what order they will come into play cannot be predicted. If anything, it seems that most people are simultaneously motivated by several of the same-level needs. On the other hand, people do not seem to be simultaneously motivated by needs from the two different levels. One person might, for example, be motivated by social and autonomy needs, while another might be motivated by hunger and thirst. Once a need appears, it does seem to persist until it is satisfied or the satisfaction of the lower-order needs is threatened. The one exception to this rule is the need for self-actualization and competence. Unlike the other needs, evidence shows that this need does not appear to be satiable and, thus, is not likely to cease to be important unless the satisfaction of one of the lower-level needs is threatened.

Can Outcomes Satisfy More Than One Need?

There is a considerable amount of research evidence indicating that some outcomes are relevant to the satisfaction of more than one need. That is, when these outcomes are obtained they affect the attractiveness of more than one cluster of outcomes. A classic example is pay (Lawler, 1971). Pay appears to have the ability to satisfy not only existence needs but also security and esteem needs. For example, Lawler and Porter (1963) report that the more a manager is paid, the higher is his security- and esteem-need satisfaction. This statement means that when a person is trying to satisfy either security or esteem needs, pay will be important. It is not

difficult to see why pay has the ability to satisfy a number of needs. Pay can be used to buy articles, such as food, that satisfy existence needs, and high pay also earns a certain amount of esteem and respect in our society.

How Important Are Different Needs?

Literally hundreds of studies have tried to measure the importance of different needs and outcomes to employees. Some idea of the importance of different needs can be obtained by looking at the data collected by Porter (1964), which appears in Figure 4. These data show that for over 1,900 managers sampled the higher-order needs are clearly the most important. Other data from the study show that the managers are most satisfied with the lower-order needs. Thus, it follows that these lower-order needs should be the least important. Whether this same concern with higher-order need satisfaction exists at the lower levels in organizations is not clear. The data presented in Figure 4 show that higher-order needs do seem to be somewhat less important to lower-level managers than to higher-level managers. Other data suggest that pay and certain lower-level needs are rated as more important by workers than by managers (Porter & Lawler, 1965). Dubin (1956), for example, argues that the work place is not a central part of the life of most industrial workers and that it is unwise to expect the workers to be concerned with fulfilling their higher-order needs within the context of their jobs.

Figure 5 shows the average ratings of the importance of job factors in a large number of studies (16 studies and 11,000 employees). Most of these studies were done on nonmanagerial employees. It shows job security and intrinsic job interest to be the most important factors to the employees. Lawler (1971) reviewed 43 studies in which pay was rated and found that its average rating was third. This is an interesting finding, but, like other findings that are based on employee ratings of how important various needs and job characteristics are, it must be interpreted very cautiously. These ratings are difficult for people to make and are strongly influenced by how the questions are worded. Thus, it is impossible to reach any strong conclusions about which job factors are the most important. Perhaps the most significant thing to remember from these studies is that employees rate a number of factors as very important. Some of these factors seem to be most strongly related to lower-order needs, while others are related to higher-order needs.

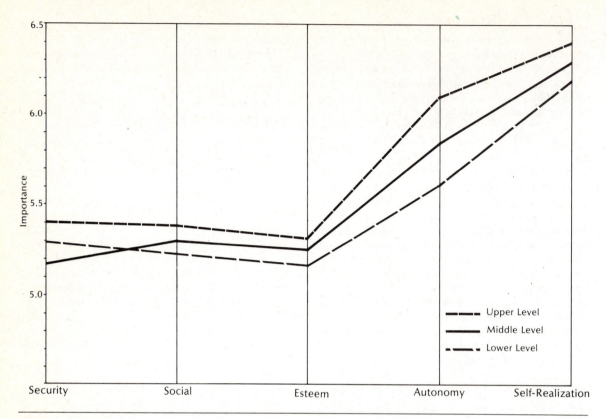

Figure 4.   Importance Attached to Five Needs by Managers from Three Organization Levels.

Individual Differences in Need Strength

Large differences clearly exist in the goals and needs people have, and these differences must be considered when viewing individual motivation in organizations. For example, Lawler reports that in about ¼ of the cases he analyzed, pay was rated as first in importance, while in many other cases it was rated sixth or lower in importance. Because of these differences a pay system that will motivate one person is often seen as irrelevant by others. Porter's (1963) data show that managers at different organization levels differ in the degree to which they are motivated by higher-order needs. Other data show that managers are motivated by different needs; some managers are motivated by self-actualization, while others are motivated by autonomy. There is also evidence that some people seem to be fixated on such lower-order needs as security.

Many individual differences in need strength are understandable if we relate them to personal character-

istics and situations. Hulin and Blood (1968), for example, point out that urban workers have different values from those of rural workers. Urban workers seem to be more alienated from work and apparently are less concerned with fulfilling higher-order needs on the job. For an interesting example of the type of individual profile that can be drawn from the research on need strength, consider the profile of a person to whom money is likely to be very important (Lawler, 1971).

The employee is a male, young (probably in his twenties); his personality is characterized by low self-assurance and high neuroticism; he comes from a small town or farm background; he belongs to few clubs and social groups, and he owns his own home and probably is a Republican and a Protestant [p. 51].

In summary then, there are significant individual differences among employees in the importance of different needs and outcomes. These differences are

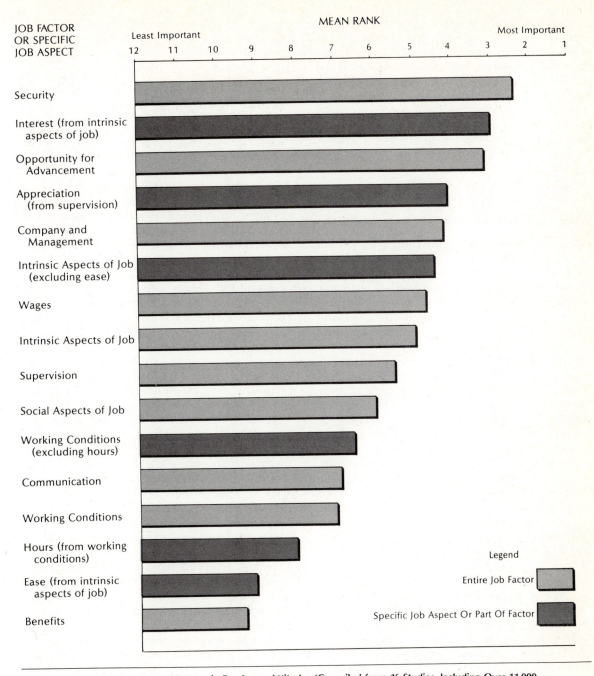

Figure 5. Average Importance of Factors in Employee Attitudes (Compiled from 16 Studies, Including Over 11,000 Employees).

From Herzberg et al., *Job Attitudes: Review of Research and Opinion*. Copyright 1957 by the Psychological Service of Pittsburgh. Reprinted by permission.

not surprising; in fact, many are predictable from what has been said about how the importance of needs is affected by the satisfaction of needs and by certain child-rearing experience. There is also evidence that these individual differences are related in meaningful ways to a number of organizational factors, such as management level, and to personal characteristics, such as age, sex, and education level. This point has some interesting implications for the management of organizations, since it means that it is possible to identify those people for whom a particular reward is likely to be important.

How Changeable Is the Importance of Needs?

There is evidence to indicate that some things can and do influence the importance of needs. Still, the evidence suggests that organizations have relatively little influence over how important various outcomes will be to their members. The importance of needs is determined partly by hereditary factors and partly by childhood experiences — things over which organizations have no control. Organizations can influence only two of the factors that determine need importance: need satisfaction and need arousal. Satisfaction influences importance, and organizational practices strongly influence satisfaction. Achievement motivation can be aroused by certain tasks and situations, as can competence motivation. Since organizations do have partial control over the situation in which their employees work, they can create conditions that will arouse certain needs. However, these needs must be present in the individual in order to be aroused, and whether the needs are present is a function of many things beyond the control of the organization.

Probably the best opportunity organizations have to influence the needs of their employees is provided by the selection process. Since need importance is relatively fixed and it is possible to identify people who are high on particular needs, organizations can select people who have the kinds of need-strength patterns they want. This would seem to be a much better approach than trying to change people's needs once they join the organization. This point also has some interesting implications for managers who have to motivate employees. It suggests that rather than trying to change the needs of their subordinates, managers should concentrate on placing people in jobs where their need structure is appropriate. The motivation system that is used must fit the needs of the person or

it will not work. If pay is not important to an employee, he or she will never be motivated by a pay-incentive system.

Has There Been an Overall Change in the Relative Importance of Needs?

Many writers (for example, Roszak, 1969) have speculated that the strength of the various needs in the population has been changing over the past 60 years. They argue that only recently has a significant proportion of the population been concerned with needs such as self-actualization and autonomy. (And it is interesting to note that only recently have psychologists been concerned with needs such as self-actualization.) The concept of man as a self-actualizing organism is essentially a development of the 1960s.

Two reasons are generally advanced for the emergence of higher-order needs. First, there is the rising level of education in our society; approximately 40 percent of the high school graduates in the United States go to college. Second, the standard of living has constantly increased so that fewer and fewer people are concerned with satisfying their existence needs and, thus, can focus on satisfying their higher-order needs.

Unfortunately, there is very little evidence to either support or disprove the view that the strength of needs is changing. To test this view adequately we would have to compare need-strength data collected 60 years ago from a random population sample with data collected recently. Unfortunately, such data do not exist. There are, however, some data that can be said to support the view that higher-order needs have become more important. We've already seen that there is evidence to support a two-step hierarchy. If we accept the fact that the standard of living is higher, then, on the basis of a two-step hierarchy, this higher standard of living supports the view that higher-order needs probably are more important. In addition, Porter's (1962) data show that younger managers place greater importance on self-actualization than older managers do. This could, of course, be simply a function of age, but it could also be due to the higher education level of these younger managers and the fact that they never experienced a depression.

There is also some direct evidence that higher-educated people are more concerned with self-actualization. Finally, there is the fact that the idea of self-actualization has gained fairly wide attention in our society. It now seems "in" to talk about self-actualization; and, as we pointed out, the concept of "self-actualization" is now prominent in psychology. Although this evidence is only indirect, it does support the view that concern with self-actualization has increased recently. In summary, although there is little direct data to support the view, it probably is true that, in general, people are somewhat more concerned with satisfying higher-order needs than they used to be.

SUMMARY AND CONCLUSIONS

The following statements summarize the major points that have been made so far about human needs.

1. Needs can be thought of as groups of outcomes that people seek.
2. Man's needs are arranged in a two-level hierarchy. At the lowest level are existence and security needs; at the other level are social, esteem, autonomy, and self-actualization needs.
3. The higher-level needs will appear only when the lower-level ones are satisfied.
4. All needs except self-actualization are satiable, and as needs become satisfied they decrease in importance.
5. A person can be motivated by more than one need at a given point in time and will continue to be motivated by a need until either it is satisfied or satisfaction of the lower-order needs is threatened.

Thus, we have answered two of the three questions asked at the beginning of the chapter. A classification system for needs has been developed, and statements have been made about what influences the importance of needs. No conclusions have been reached about why people develop needs or about whether needs are innate or learned because these questions don't seem to be answerable at this time.

REFERENCES

Adams, J. S. Toward an understanding of inequity. *Journal of Abnormal Psychology*. 1963, **67,** 422–436.

Adams, J. S. Injustice in social exchange. In L. Berkowitz (Ed.), *Advances in experimental social psychology*. Vol. 2. New York: Academic Press, 1965.

Alderfer, C. P. An empirical test of a new theory of human needs. *Organizational Behavior and Human Performance,* 1969, **4,** 142–175.

Alderfer, C. P. *Existence, relatedness, and growth: Human needs in organizational settings.* New York: The Free Press, 1972.

Allport, G. W. *Becoming: Basic considerations for a psychology of personality.* New Haven: Yale University Press, 1955.

Alper, T. G. Task-orientation vs. ego-orientation in learning and retention. *American Journal of Psychology,* 1946, **38,** 224–238.

Atkinson, J. W. Towards experimental analysis of human motivation in terms of motives, expectancies, and incentives. In J. W. Atkinson (Ed.), *Motives in fantasy, action, and society.* Princeton, N.J.: Van Nostrand Reinhold, 1958.

Atkinson, J. W. *An introduction to motivation.* Princeton, N.J.: Van Nostrand Reinhold, 1964.

Berlyne, D. E. Arousal and reinforcement. In D. Levine (Ed.), *Nebraska symposium on motivation.* Lincoln: University of Nebraska Press, 1967.

Bexton, W. H., Heron, W., & Scott, T. H. Effects of decreased variation in the sensory environment. *Canadian Journal of Psychology,* 1954, **8,** 70–76.

Butler, R. A. Discrimination learning by rhesus monkeys to visual-exploration motivation. *Journal of Comparative and Physiological Psychology.* 1953, **46,** 95–98.

Cofer, C. N., & Appley, M. H. *Motivation: Theory and research.* New York: John Wiley & Sons, 1964.

Cowles, J. T. Food tokens as incentives for learning by chimpanzees. *Comparative Psychology Monograph,* 1937, **14** (No. 71).

Cravens, R. W., & Renner, K. E. Conditioned appetitive drive states: Empirical evidence and theoretical status. *Psychological Bulletin,* 1970, **73,** 212–220.

Dubin, R. Industrial workers' worlds: A study of the "central life interests" of industrial workers. *Social Problems,* 1956, **3,** 131–142.

French, E. G. Some characteristics of achievement motivation. *Journal of Experimental Psychology,* 1955, **50,** 232–236.

Fromm, E. *Escape from freedom.* New York: Rinehart & Winston, 1941.

Goldstein, K. *The organism.* New York: American Book, 1939.

Haber, R. N. Discrepancy from adaptation level as a source of affect. *Journal of Experimental Psychology,* 1958, **56,** 370–375.

Hall, C. S., & Lindzey, G. *Theories of personality.* New York: John Wiley & Sons, 1957.

Harlow, H. F. Mice, monkeys, men, and motives. *Psychological Review,* 1953, **60,** 23–32.

Harlow, H. F. The nature of love. *American Psychologist.* 1958, **13,** 673–685.

Herzberg, F., Mausner, B., Peterson, R. O., & Capwell, D. F. *Job attitudes: Review of research and opinion.* Pittsburgh: Psychological Service of Pittsburgh, 1957.

Horney, K. *Neurosis and human growth.* New York: W. W. Norton, 1950.

Hulin, C. L., & Blood, M. R. Job enlargement, individual differences, and worker responses. *Psychological Bulletin,* 1968, **69,** 41–55.

Hull, C. L. *Principles of behavior.* New York: Appleton-Century-Crofts, 1943.

Keys, A., Brozek, J., Henschel, A., Mickelsen, O., & Taylor, H. *The biology of human starvation.* Minneapolis: University of Minnesota Press, 1950. 2 vols.

Langer, W. C. *Psychology and human living.* New York: Appleton-Century-Crofts, 1937.

Lawler, E. E. *Pay and organizational effectiveness: A psychological view.* New York: McGraw-Hill, 1971.

Lawler, E. E., & Porter, L. W. Perceptions regarding management compensation. *Industrial Relations,* 1963, **3,** 41–49.

Lawler, E. E. & Suttle, J. L. A causal correlational test of the need hierarchy concept. *Organizational Behavior and Human Performance,* 1972, **7,** 265–287.

Lecky, P. *Self-consistency: A theory of personality.* New York: Island Press, 1945.

McClelland, D. C. Measuring motivation in phantasy: The achievement motive. In H. Guetzkow (Ed.), *Groups, leadership, and men.* Pittsburgh: Carnegie Press, 1951.

McClelland, D. C. *The achieving society.* Princeton: Van Nostrand Reinhold, 1961.

McDougall, W. *An introduction to social psychology.* London: Methuen & Co., 1908.

Maslow, A. H. A theory of human motivation. *Psychological Review,* 1943, **50,** 370–396.

Maslow, A. H. *Motivation and personality.* New York: Harper & Row, 1954.

Maslow, A. H. *Toward a psychology of being.* (2nd ed.) Princeton, N.J.: Van Nostrand Reinhold, 1968.

Maslow, A. H. *Motivation and personality.* (2nd ed.) New York: Harper & Row, 1970.

May, R. *Man's search for himself.* New York: W. W. Norton, 1953.

Miles, R. C. Learning in kittens with manipulatory, exploratory, and food incentives. *Journal of Comparative and Physiological Psychology,* 1958, **51,** 39–42.

Murray, E. J. *Motivation and emotion.* Englewood Cliffs, N.J.: Prentice-Hall, 1964.

Murray, H. A. *Explorations in personality.* New York: Oxford University Press, 1938.

Porter, L. W. Job attitudes in management: I. Perceived deficiencies in need fulfillment as a function of job level. *Journal of Applied Psychology,* 1962, **46,** 375–384.

Porter, L. W. Job attitudes in management: II. Perceived importance of needs as a function of job level. *Journal of Applied Psychology,* 1963, **47,** 141–148.

Porter, L. W. *Organizational patterns of managerial job attitudes.* New York: American Foundation for Management Research, 1964.

Porter, L. W., & Lawler, E. E. Properties of organization structure in relation to job attitudes and job behavior. *Psychological Bulletin,* 1965, **64,** 23–51.

Riesman, D. *The lonely crowd.* New Haven: Yale University Press, 1950.

Rogers, C. R. *Client-centered therapy: Its current practice, implications and theory.* Boston: Houghton Mifflin, 1951.

Rogers, C. R. *On becoming a person.* Boston: Houghton Mifflin, 1961.

Roszak, Theodore. *The making of a counter culture.* Garden City, N.Y.: Doubleday, 1969.

Schachter, S. *The psychology of affiliation.* Stanford, Calif.: Stanford University Press, 1959.

Scott, W. E. The behavioral consequences of repetitive task design: Research and theory. In L. L. Cummings & W. E. Scott (Eds.), *Readings in organizational behavior and human performance.* Homewood, Ill.: Richard D. Irwin, 1969.

Smock, C. D., & Holt, B. G. Children's reactions to novelty: An experimental study of "curiosity motivation." *Child Development,* 1962, **33,** 631–642.

Snygg, D., & Combs, A. W. *Individual behavior.* New York: Harper & Row, 1949.

Vroom, V. H. *Work and motivation.* New York: John Wiley & Sons, 1964.

White, R. W. Motivation reconsidered: The concept of competence. *Psychological Review,* 1959, **66,** 297–333.

Wolfe, J. B. Effectiveness of token-rewards for chimpanzees. *Comparative Psychology Monograph,* 1936, **12,** 15.

Woodworth, R. S. *Dynamic psychology.* New York: Columbia University Press, 1918.

2.   Yankelovich on Today's Workers

Daniel Yankelovich

Our economy is not the unbeatable, dynamic, ever-growing world force it was in the first quarter-century following World War II. Our productivity is slowing for many reasons: the cost of energy, the crippling effects of government regulations, the distortions of inflation, environmental costs, a slackening of investment, a shift to services, and so on. But careful studies show that, collectively, all these factors can account for only a fraction of the present slippage.

If you look at changing American attitudes toward work, you can catch a glimpse of a major factor contributing to the decline. People who work at all levels of enterprise, and particularly younger middle-management people, are no longer motivated to work as hard and as effectively as in the past.

In the late 1960s, almost half of all employed Americans looked to their work as a source of personal fulfillment. Now that number has plunged to fewer than one in four. In the 1960s a three-fifths majority, 58 percent, believed that "hard work always pays off." Now only 43 percent hold this belief. Only 13 percent of all working Americans find their work truly meaningful and more important to them than leisure-time pursuits.

It would certainly overstate the case to attribute all the current ills of the American economy to a less involved, less committed work force. But these changes surely pose a massive challenge to people in the human resources field. Yet there is strong resistance in top-management circles, once you get beyond lip

"Yankelovich On Today's Workers" by Daniel Yankelovich from *Industry Week,* August 6, 1979. Reprinted with permission.

service, to the idea that human resources are a key to improving productivity and competitive effectiveness. The conventional wisdom holds that capital investment, technology, and management systems are more important than people's motivations.

Reasons abound for denigrating the importance of motivation in enhancing efficiency, effectiveness, and productivity. Many of the people in top management positions are trained in finance or engineering or production. They are not as comfortable with the intangibles of human behavior as with the more tangible areas of business. Also, in the past, technology and capital investment *were* the key factors in national productivity—and were, in addition, easier to deal with than they are now.

I can sum up what is happening in the American work force today in a single phrase: a growing mismatch between incentives and motivations. The incentive system does not work as well as it used to. Formerly, management had the tools to motivate people strongly enough to insure ever-increasing productivity. This is no longer true. People's values and attitudes have changed faster than the incentive system—creating a mismatch.

The idea of change in people is slippery and difficult to document. Also, this type of change is often threatening and disagreeable to contemplate. I have encountered two typical responses to my descriptions of human change in the work force and its implications for top corporate management. One is flat-out denial. The chairman looks around and says, "I don't see any change. Joe, here, our financial vice-president, he hasn't changed. My secretary hasn't changed. The directors are the same hard-working, committed people they always were." Since he does not experience the change firsthand in his own circumscribed world, it is not real to him. In the second pattern, the change is acknowledged but deplored. Typically the chairman will say, "People just aren't willing to work as hard as they used to. The old work ethic has eroded."

If you then ask, "What do you think can be done about it?" often the answer goes something like this: "Of course, I hope it doesn't happen, but a good old-fashioned depression might knock some sense into people's heads." One can be sympathetic with the frustration behind such attitudes, but this is not the kind of careful, objective analysis necessary to grasp the reality of the changing social environment of American life. Management has to adapt to this reality if we are to resume improved productivity and effectiveness in American business.

How can we grapple with a problem as elusive as this? One way is to understand the nature of the mismatch between the incentive system and people's motivations. To put it as simply as possible, I am suggesting that the tools we rely upon to give people incentives to work hard and effectively have become blunted.

There are four of these tools: (1) fear, (2) techniques that don't depend on motivation for productivity, (3) money, and (4) the assumption that people who aren't interfered with too much will just naturally want to do a good job. Every one of these four ideas upon which our incentive systems are based has lost ground in recent years.

1. Fear.   The fear factor has lost considerable clout in motivating people to be maximally effective on the job. The fear of unemployment, of being unable to make a living, of being unable to keep one's family together, is neither as much a part of people's experience nor as devastating a prospect as it once was. Further, the fear of unemployment generally tends to be confined to people who have actually lost their jobs. Don't get me wrong: job security is *very* important to people and is likely to grow even more important as an employee demand since it is part of a new psychology of entitlement. In fact, it is one of the ways in which people have changed most—feeling that job security is a *right*, to be demanded and guaranteed. Job security is not the same as an incentive to work hard, but neither withholding it nor granting it is necessarily a motivation to work.

Today there is a floor under most people's lives—unemployment compensation and other benefits. Currently 20 percent of all households have no wage earners, but live on a combination of pensions, Social Security, welfare, and similar benefits. Being fired used to be the ultimate psychological as well as practical disaster. An unemployed man suffered a devastating loss of self-esteem, a loss of his sense of being a "real man." But to today's young worker, internal feelings of inadequacy or pointlessness on the job are often more painful than being fired. Further, the growing proportion of women in the labor force and the increasing incidence of two-earner households have changed the rules of the game. As more and more women share the breadwinning role with men, there is a corresponding decline in the extent to which a man's feelings of masculinity depend upon his being the good provider. Each year in the 1950s and 1960s, we surveyed people as to how they defined a "real man." Sexual prowess ranked rather low, as did being handy around the house or being strong in a physical sense. But at the top of the list, at about the 80 percent level, was "being a good provider." All this has changed. The threat of job loss for men no longer strikes at masculinity as it once did.

The traditional head of a household was a man who worked and had a wife who stayed home and took care of young children. One or more children under 18, living at home under the care of a full-time housewife and mother, once represented the dominant pattern of American family life. About 70 percent of households were of this type in the 1950s. Today, however, only 15 percent of families fall into this category. The majority of today's Americans live in households that do not fit the old norm for one reason or another; either there are no children, or the wife works, or there is only a single person in residence, or there is only one parent, or the household differs in some other respect.

Many forces have converged to create this massive shift in the character of American family life. One consequence of the change is the way it has also altered the meaning of a job. For the majority, a job, in a sense, is no longer needed to support a *whole* family.

2. Reliance on management techniques that minimize the human factor. Automation, the organization of work into assembly-line procedures, and the use of supervision that minimizes the importance of worker motivation have long been characteristic practices of many businesses. Historically, increases in productivity have come first in agriculture and then in manufacturing. But today we are a service economy. Seventy percent of us work in service or government jobs. Even in the manufacturing sector, the very definition of productivity, the economic measure of output per man-hour, is too narrow for most businesses. Businessmen know that true productivity — in the sense of competitiveness with other nations — means the overall effectiveness and efficiency of the firm, not just output per man-hour.

If you look closely at overall effectiveness and efficiency, you will find that it depends even more than labor productivity on intangibles such as dedication, caring, and a sense of responsibility for giving real service. And you get these intangibles only when people are motivated to work hard, to give of themselves and not hold back. It isn't a question of mechanization or capital; it's a question of people and incentives and motivation.

3. Money. Perhaps the majority of incentive systems are built around money. Money is still important to

people; you'd have to be deaf and blind to think otherwise. People want and demand more money all the time. But consider three brief points about money as an incentive.

First, in a period of high inflation, it is very difficult to use money as an incentive. People find it almost impossible to keep up and get ahead. If money is to be a meaningful incentive, these things must be possible.

Second — and this is of fundamental importance for the future of our society — money just doesn't work as well as it used to as an incentive to work harder. Indeed, in many cases, more money has just the opposite effect. In New York City, where I live, the garbage men used to earn about $10,000 a year. As times changed, they became sanitation men and were paid twice that amount of money. But do they work any harder as a result of their doubled income? Their feeling is, "Well, now I can afford to live like a human being." This attitude is shared by many people. If you have more money, you can afford to live like "a human being," and part of that is being able to say to yourself, "What will I use the additional money for?" And with increasing frequency, the answer is: "For a lifestyle that permits more leisure and self-expression outside of work."

As more money allows people to look up from the grindstone, they begin to see that it costs more to live a less austere life. The desire for more money does not necessarily mean that those who get it are going to be any more highly motivated, and yet money continues to be thought of as an incentive for making people work harder.

Also, Americans no longer expect their standard of living to improve each year. This important change in expectations is reflected in an unwillingness to work hard for improvements that many feel are not likely to be forthcoming.

4. The desire to do a good job — the "work ethic." The desire to do a good job is something that people bring with them to the job; it can't be created on the job. By then it's too late. The work ethic is part of our cultural heritage, our upbringing, and our fundamental value system. The purpose of an incentive system is to encourage this feeling, sharpen it, focus it, and reward it. For an incentive system to be effective, people have to believe that hard work pays off, *whatever "payoff" means to them*. But increasingly the payoff does not mean money.

Further, the conviction that it pays to work hard is weakening today in fundamental ways. This means that management can no longer assume that people will come to the job with a built-in desire to work hard and do the best job possible. And this means, in turn, that management can no longer rely on skillful use of the carrot of money and the stick of dismissal to make people work hard and effectively. None of these four tools — fear, money, the organization of work, and the work ethic — is as effective as it once was. Their growing ineffectiveness helps account for the slippage in worker productivity and efficiency.

We need to find some positive solutions, some positive approaches, some new tools. This is a long-range problem and will require long, careful, and cogent analysis, but I'd like to suggest some lines along which such an analysis might proceed and some of the results it might have.

I have said that the old motivations no longer work as well as they used to. The way to begin our analysis is to understand precisely what this means. It does *not* mean that people don't work any more. It does *not* mean that the motivations of all American workers have changed equally. Quite the contrary. I find it useful to divide the national working population into two overall groups.

One group is composed of those for whom the old incentives still work fairly well. This group is not problem-free. It, too, is affected by new social values and lifestyles. But for all practical purposes, the mismatch between incentives and motivation is not severe for its members. This group represents approximately 56 percent of all people who work, and it consists of three subgroups.

One subgroup accounts for about 22 percent of all workers. Its members tend to be older and poorer than the median. Most of them are blue-collar. About one-third are white-collar clerical and service workers. For most people in this subgroup, work is just a habit. They go along. They're the most old-fashioned and "out-of-it" group according to the new cultural values. They are traditionalists. They're not looking for meaning in their work; they want structure, guidance, and clear-cut responsibilities. They want job security. They just want to do what they think they can do well and to have their good work acknowledged. Clearly, these workers are not a serious problem from the motivational point of view.

The members of a second subgroup, about 19 percent of workers, are more *positively work-oriented.* They come closest to the management ideal of the dedicated, hard-working employee who is strongly committed to work. Money is important to them, but not as important as work itself. These are work-

before-pleasure people who want to make a contribution to the company they work for as well as to do a good job. They, too, are older. As with the first subgroup, only one out of three is under 35.

The third subgroup represents 15 percent of all workers and consists of younger people — seven out of 10 are under 35. People in this subgroup are the real "go-getters." They are motivated primarily by money and a desire to *get ahead.* There is no mismatch here. The traditional incentive structure was made for them. A disproportionately high number are in sales. They're ambitious, and management has no problem understanding them or providing the incentives to motivate them. So, for the 56 percent majority consisting of these three subgroups, the mismatch is not a real problem — at this time.

It is a problem, however, for the remaining 44 percent, which can be divided into two subgroups. Both of these subgroups are made up of young people — that is, the majority are under 35 — but they lie at opposite ends of the socioeconomic scale and in some respects at opposite ends of the attitude scale as well.

The larger of the two subgroups, 27 percent of all working people, is a group we're calling "*turned off.*" Of all five subgroups, it is this one whose members are the least motivated to work hard. Not surprisingly, they are the least well-educated, have the lowest earnings, and represent the largest proportion of blue-collar workers. Of all workers, the people in this group have the least internal motivation to do an outstanding job for its own sake. Here we see the work ethic in its most deteriorated state. It is within this huge group of men and women, one out of every four workers, that the American dream threatens to unravel and become a mockery rather than a reality.

In this group we see signs of maladjustment and discontent. Its members are a hedonistic, live-for-today, turned-off, sensation-seeking bunch. They are hungry for diversion from boredom and fatigue. They are basically uncreative and a likely breeding ground for unrest. The conventional road to upward mobility in America — the acquisition of higher education, status, and money in exchange for substantial effort, discipline, dedication, and subordination of self to a job — is clearly not for them.

The other subgroup in the gross-mismatch category is smaller — 17 percent of all workers — but in many ways is perhaps the most pivotal of all the five subgroups regarding the *future.* This subgroup includes the most young people — three out of four of its members are under 35 — and has the largest proportion of college-educated, white-collar, and middle-management professional men and women. Of all five groups, this group's members also have the strongest need to create and to achieve. They are the most willing to sacrifice money or job security in order to fulfill this need.

It is in this group that we see the clearest evidence of changing work values, the sharpest mismatch between the incentive system and the motivation to work to the peak of effectiveness. This group, *characterizing middle management,* is the hungriest for responsibility, challenge, autonomy, informality, and less rigid authority in the organizational structure. People in this group are looking for more interesting, more vital work and a better chance to find a commitment they deem worthy of their talents and skills. But they are not finding satisfaction in their work. So they turn away, restlessly looking for other outlets in their leisure, their hobbies, and their new lifestyles. They seek self-expression by changing careers or changing mates — all in an effort to find something fulfilling that many of them could, potentially, discover in their work if only the incentive and work systems were better structured to meet their needs.

These numbers give us some rough-and-ready quantitative dimensions of national norms. In every company the distribution of these five groups will be different, of course. But even this cursory analysis demonstrates a key point. We can no longer assume that the work force is homogeneous with respect to motivation. Therefore, no single incentive system can motivate the full spectrum of today's workers.

There is a new breed among us — in fact many new breeds, white-collar and blue. The key to the incentive systems of the future is pluralism. The idea of a work force that stretches across an enormously wide spectrum — with people who are still turned toward the 19th century as well as people who are turned toward the 21st — is a difficult concept, but one that must be grasped.

Increasingly, we will need a "cafeteria" system of incentives that offers palatable choices to each individual. Throughout our history, and certainly during the last century, American *individualism* stopped at the workplace door. Now it's knocking the door down, demanding to be allowed inside. In order to satisfy the need for individualism at work, we need new kinds of human technology.

Another important point is that all programs geared to improve effectiveness on the job must distinguish sharply between job satisfaction on the one hand and motivation to work hard and effectively on the other.

People can be satisfied because their job does *not* demand that they work hard, just as they can be dissatisfied because they want to do a good job but the organization is putting obstacles in the way. Ideally, we want to create job satisfaction that comes from strong, positive motivation, but it is essential to keep in mind that measures of job satisfaction — which are the principal measures used — tell us almost nothing about motivation or effectiveness.

In the future it will be easier to provide job satisfaction than effective work incentives. Motivating people will be tougher, not only because of the need for pluralistic incentive systems, but also because of something less tangible that might be called the "holding back" phenomenon. Historically, the traditional, unwritten contract in America has been simple and fundamental: a day's work for a day's pay. Until recently, management could assume that if it lived up to its end of the bargain — providing jobs, money, and reasonable work conditions — people would respond in full measure — that is, with their utmost effort. But we are increasingly encountering among all groups — not just the 44 percent who are basically mismatched, but all groups across the board — a tendency to hold back, to bargain harder, to demand and expect more without necessarily giving anything more in return. *Holding back* is caused by many factors, among them a strong-rooted *psychology of entitlement.* People today want more out of life than they did in the past; they are demanding more. At the same time, there has been an erosion of many of the values associated with the traditional Protestant ethic — an ethic that was built on the notion of self-denial. Self-fulfillment seems in many ways almost the opposite of self-denial. But whatever workers' reasons for holding back, management must be prepared *to bargain harder in exchange for performance.* For this kind of bargaining, whether it's formal or informal, management will need a greatly expanded repertoire of incentives and a very effective set of information tools with which to gauge how well the terms of the bargain are being met on both sides.

Fortunately, the potential for an expanded grab bag of incentives already exists, and we are beginning to understand what some of them might be. Let me describe a few of the forms which the incentives of the future are going to take.

One of the most important will be innovative and ingenious ways of using time — not only flextime, which is one restructured use of time, but also vacations, sabbaticals, informal schedules, and freedom and flexibility in a whole range of different applications.

Another important source of incentives lies in leisure and health opportunities — health in the positive sense of well-being. Opportunities to build up the body as well as the mind — jogging and running and exercise of all kinds — are becoming increasingly important today.

Customized feedback mechanisms having to do with achievement and with keeping the individual's own balance sheet represent another potential area for incentives. Of course, one of the defining characteristics of the new breed, the new-values people, is the focus on the self. Focus on the self means that people frequently ask, "How well am *I* doing?" — not necessarily "How well is the job getting done?" That question creates a need and a desire for a continuing feedback system. The various ways in which you can provide feedback form a subject all of us need to be studying, and in doing so we will find thousands of methods we hadn't thought of before.

There are also opportunities for a greater distribution of amenities as work incentives than ever before, particularly among blue-collar workers. The essence of the new values — especially as expressed by some of those in the mismatched group — is the feeling that "I have a dignity that goes beyond my role." This sentiment reflects a revolt against the depersonalizing effects of role and job. For example, the blue-collar worker may not be permitted free use of the telephone, while most white-collar workers can use a phone whenever they wish. Using the telephone socially is one of the many amenities that distinguish white-collar jobs from blue-collar jobs in our society. But this creates a feeling among blue-collar workers that they are not being treated as human beings. In this context, such amenities become symbols of dignity.

The importance of the work world as a social world is something that most people do not appreciate until they retire. Then, when they find they no longer have co-workers with whom they can socialize on a daily basis, a sense of emptiness frequently sets in. On the other hand, many workers are unhappy with the social environment on the job. This is another feature of work that can be shaped, to some degree, into a work incentive.

For workers in some groups, particularly the "turned off" group, variety, stimulation, and constant change are needed if their interest is to be heightened and maintained. These needs, too, can be turned into work incentives.

Among many of the younger, new-breed people, the hunger for more responsibility earlier in life is important and can be a real incentive as well as a means to the more effective design of jobs. A lot has been written about this, and although the job-enrichment concept isn't as important to everybody as the publicity of the 1960s and 1970s suggested, neither is it something to be thrown away.

The phenomenon of a radically changing work force is not unique to the U.S. It is a problem that besets all of the industrialized democracies of the world. We have it here first, and in its most acute form, because the U.S. is the most advanced industrial nation. But it is a symptom of all societies — here, in Europe, and in Japan — that are changing in fundamental ways. It is part of a larger process of reassessment by people at all levels of what is important in life and what is not. This reassessment is taking place in the domain of the family, in the search for individual meaning in life, and in the workplace. It is all part of the same pattern, and the resulting changes are just beginning. They are the advance signs of life in the 21st century, the third milennium.

3.   Conversation with B. F. Skinner

William F. Dowling

B. F. Skinner is, in the opinion of his professional peers, the most influential psychologist in the country. He is already one of the best known among the general reading public. Certainly he is the most controversial psychologist. Whence the influence? Whence the celebrity? Whence the controversy?

Skinner is a behaviorist, which means that he seeks the explanations to human behavior not in the mind within but outside in those conditions in the environment that collectively determine behavior. His first fame came through the design of the "Skinner box," a controlled environment in which rats, pigeons, and eventually men underwent transformations in established patterns of behavior in response to changes in the environment.

Take one famous experiment with pigeons. Food was the reinforcer that moved the pigeon to behave in a particular way. Giving the food to the pigeon when it made the desired response was the reinforcement. *Operant* is the term Skinner used to define the property upon which the reinforcement depended — in this case, the height to which the bird had to raise its head before it would be fed. The change in the frequency with which the head was lifted to this height Skinner called the process of operant conditioning.

All operants grow stronger through repetition — Rome wasn't built in a day — and some operants are inherently stronger than others because they produce consequences of greater importance in the life of the pigeon — or the life of the individual man. Pigeons and man alike behave not because of the consequences that are to follow their behavior but because of the consequences that have followed similar behavior in the past. In Skinner's terms, this is the law of effect or operant conditioning. Says Skinner, "Operant conditioning shapes behavior as a sculptor shapes a lump of clay. Although at some point the sculptor seems to have produced an entirely novel object, we can always follow the process back to the original undifferentiated lump."

Skinner's early reputation came from repeated demonstrations of the law of operant conditioning with pigeons and other animals. When he moved on to man — and his writings and researches have focused on human behavior for the past 25 years — he became both famous and controversial.

He held that man's behavior was every bit as controlled as the pigeons — the difference lay in the number and complexity of the determinants. Freedom was an illusion; when J. S. Mill asserted that "Liberty consists in doing what one desires," he merely begged the question by failing to look behind the desires themselves and asking what accounted for them. The distinction that makes sense to Skinner is not between freedom and control, but between feeling free and feeling controlled, between acting to avoid something — negative reinforcement — and acting to gain something — positive reinforcement. In the former case, the individual feels coerced and controlled. In the latter, he feels free.

Skinner goes beyond description to prescription. He isn't satisfied with enumerating the various controls that together make up the technology of behavior, but he goes on to specify the ways in which the technology available can be used to create a better world.

In fact, Skinner would argue that enlightened men of good will have a responsibility to employ the controls toward benevolent ends. As Skinner points out, the technology of behavior is ethically neutral; it is available on equal terms to villain and saint. "The industrialist may design a wage system," he maintains, "that maximizes his profits, or works for the good of his employees, or most effectively produces the goods a culture needs, with a minimal consumption of resources and minimal pollution." We also suspect that Skinner still adheres to the view he expressed in *Waldon Two* over twenty years ago: that the techniques are in the wrong hands, the end product of most manipulation being private profit or personal aggrandisement.

In other words, Skinner elevates the manipulation of behavior towards benevolent ends to the level of a civic responsibility, which raises the question whether or not it is fair and accurate to label Skinner a psycho-administrative fascist, to conclude with Stephen Spender that he advocates "facism without tears."

The answer depends largely on how we define fascism. If we mean an ideology that exalts nation and race, then there is not a trace of it in Skinner. On the other hand, if we mean an ideology that asserts the positive value of economic and social regimentation, then there's a strong strain of fascism in Skinner's thinking.

The more interesting and significant question is, what goals does Skinner think the technology of behavior should be employed to reach? At two levels, the question is comparatively easy to answer. Skinner is for the maximum use of positive reinforcement and the minimal use of negative reinforcement that leaves the individual feeling controlled and coerced. And if we want Skinner's vision of the ideal society, we need only read *Walden Two*. If he's amended or altered his vision, we are unaware of it.

At the specific, pragmatic level it's much more difficult to answer the question. In general, Skinner's answer would be that benevolent ends are those that enhance the survival of the culture and of mankind. However, Skinner concedes that survival is a difficult value because it is hard to predict the conditions a culture must meet.

In reading a recent piece that Skinner wrote for *The New York Times,* the conditions that in his view enhance the survival of today's China are clear — he writes with obvious approval of the young Chinese who wear plain clothing, live in crowded quarters, eat simple diets, observe a rather puritanical sexual code, and work long hours for the greater glory of China — but it's impossible, at least based on what we have read of Skinner, to draw up an equivalent list of specific conditions for our own culture.

Given a sufficient threat to the culture we suspect that Skinner would justify the use of negative reinforcement and aversion therapy. Skinner might even approve of the drastic aversion therapy administered to Alex in the film "A Clockwork Orange" to make him good. Given the menace that the bad Alex presented, society realistically had only two choices: permanent incarceration or a drastic form of aversion therapy. This is only

conjecture. We know that in the same *Times* article Skinner took issue with the reported statement of Anthony Burgess, author of the novel on which the film is based, that "What my parable tries to state is that it is preferable to have a world of violence undertaken in full awareness — of violence chosen as an act of will — than a world conditioned to be good or harmless." Dr. Skinner dissents — as would a good many other people, ourselves included.

To what extent does Skinner beg the question of the specific conditions that enhance our culture in 1972 — the conditions that the technology of behavior should be employed to advance? The question is a difficult one to answer. As the conversation that follows makes plain, Skinner advocates some quite specific conditions in industry. The bigger social picture is not as clear nor are the mechanisms by which the destined changes will be arrived at.

Skinner consistently denies that the controlling he advocates will be done by a benevolent dictator or an equally benevolent behavioral engineer. When a bearded youth at a symposium at Yale on Skinner's ideas asked him "Who is going to program this whole thing?" Skinner replied that it was not a matter of someone pushing control buttons but of "the gradual improvement of the practices controlling the survival of the culture." At times the improvement in practices almost appears to be self-generated. Skinner asserts that "in certain respects operant reinforcement resembles the natural selection of evolutionary theory. Just as genetic characteristics which arise as mutations are selected or discarded by their consequences, so novel forms of behavior are selected and discarded through reinforcement."

These remarks on Skinner present a very partial and personal view of his ideas undertaken because our relatively brief conversation with Skinner gave us only enough time to probe the application of his ideas to business. For his general views we recommend his books, especially *Walden Two, Science and Human Behavior,* and the most recent, *Beyond Freedom and Dignity,* in which he has restated them with unexampled grace, clarity, and passion. Not the least reason for Skinner's celebrity is his command of the written word; like Freud, he is a distinguished stylist as well as a profound and original thinker.

Dowling. You draw the analogy between operant condition and its role in cultural evolution and natural selection and its role in genetic evolution.

Skinner. Yes, and I think it's important, too, because selection is a very different kind of causality. Darwin's views came very late in the history of intellectual thought, and the way in which human behavior is shaped and maintained by its consequences has taken an even longer time to surface. That's what we've been studying in the laboratory for the past 40 years now, and we've discovered that when you arrange certain kinds of consequences, certain types of behavior are selected.

Dowling. You have come under a good deal of criticism on the grounds that operant conditioning destroys autonomous man and minimizes freedom. If I understand you correctly, your answer would be that the freedom that is being defended has been an illusion all along.

Skinner. The real distinction is between whether we are really free or whether we feel free. I want people to feel freer than they feel now. When you act to avoid punishment, or to avoid any kind of unpleasantness, you *have* to act and you don't feel free. But if you act in order to produce positive results — what we call positive reinforcements — then you feel free, and I'm all for that. I want to get away from punitive control, the kind of control that is used by governments with police and military forces, or that is exercised over students by teachers who threaten them with punishment if they don't study.

Dowling. Do you feel that punitive control is widely used in industry?

Skinner. There is more of it than you might think. Many people consider a weekly wage a positive reinforcement. You work and you get paid. But you don't work on Monday morning for something that is going to happen on Friday afternoon, when you get your paycheck. You work on Monday morning because there is a supervisor who can fire you if you don't work. You're actually working to avoid the loss of the standard of living maintained by that paycheck.

On the other hand, if you're on piece-work pay, you are positively reinforced for what you do, and you build up a very high tendency to respond — so much so that labor unions and other people who have the welfare of the worker at heart usually oppose that kind of incentive system. Salesmen are usually on both a salary and a percentage basis, because you can't send a supervisor out with every salesman to make sure that he works. He works for the additional commission, but it doesn't wear him out as a straight piece-work schedule does, because he has the salary to support him. Straight commissions work well but cause trouble. The commission system in brokerage firms, for example, often leads salesmen to exaggerate opportunities and pull other tricks that cause trouble for the firm.

Dowling. Witness that student in Philadelphia who opened accounts without any money and without even showing up in person. Let's talk a little more about punishment. I wonder if you could illustrate the various controls available to the manager as forms of punishment and what you feel are the alternatives to punishment.

Skinner. When a supervisor points out that a person has done something wrong, he is mildly punishing him. His comment is a threat in the direction of his being discharged or possibly laid off without pay. And when a supervisor thinks his job is to move around a plant and discover things being done wrong and to say "Watch that" or "You got into trouble with that the last time," he establishes an atmosphere that really doesn't benefit anyone. True, the worker may be less likely to do things wrong, but you can get the same effect if the supervisor simply discovers things being done right and says something like "Good, I see you're doing it the way that works the best." Supervision by positive reinforcement changes the whole atmosphere of the workspace and produces better results. A constantly critical posture on the part of the supervisor encourages bad morale, absenteeism, and job-changing. You get the work out, but at an exorbitant price. With positive reinforcement, you get at least the same amount of work, and the worker is more likely to show up every day and less likely to change jobs. In the long run, both the company and the worker are better off.

It does not cost the company anything to use praise rather than blame, but if the company then makes a great deal more money that way, the worker may seem to be getting gypped. However, the welfare of the worker depends on the welfare of the company, and if the company is smart enough to distribute some of the fruits of positive reinforcement in the form of higher wages and better fringe benefits, everybody gains from the supervisor's use of positive reinforcement.

Dowling. What about those occasions in which punishment is inevitable? Let's take a hypothetical case: The supervisor catches three of his workers shooting craps behind the machine when they should be working the machine. Under such circumstances, in which the imposition of punishment is really inevitable, is there one best way, one best method of applying it?

Skinner.   I can't solve a problem like that sitting here in my office. I'd have to go into a given organization and see what's going on. I daresay there are times when you need some kind of punishment — docking pay, giving a verbal reprimand, threatening discharge, that kind of thing — but what you've just said is a clue to the kind of thing that would be better.

Why *are* the workers shooting craps? Look at the so-called contingencies of reinforcement. All gambling systems pay off on what is called a variable-ratio schedule of reinforcement. That's true of lotteries, roulette, poker, craps, one-armed bandits. They all pay off unpredictably, but in the long run on a certain schedule. Everyone would benefit if work could be organized so that it also pays off on that schedule. People would then work, and they would enjoy the excitement that goes with possessing a lottery ticket that may pay off at the end of the week. Management could solve some of its problems by adding a bit of a lottery to its incentive conditions. Suppose that every time a worker finished a job, he got a lottery ticket, and at the end of the week, there was a drawing. More jobs would be done, with greater pleasure.

Look at a room full of people playing bingo. They sit for hours, listening with extraordinary care to numbers being called out and placing counters on numbers with great precision. What would you give, as an industrialist, if your labor force worked that hard and that carefully! The bingo player works hard and carefully because of the schedule of payoff. It's a very poor one, because in the long run all players lose, but it commands an awesome amount of labor from people, with great precision and concentration.

Some industrial systems could be redesigned to have that same effect. And people would enjoy what they were doing as much as they enjoy playing bingo. Everybody would gain.

Dowling.   Has it ever been tried in industry?

Skinner.   I don't know, but I suspect it has. It has been tried in education very successfully, although it has not yet been widely adopted. But let's take an example of how you could use a lottery to solve the problem of absenteeism. With today's high wages, missing a day's wages doesn't much matter. But suppose you have something like a door prize every day. When you come to work, you get a ticket, and at the end of the day there's a drawing. Then a man will think twice before staying away. If absenteeism is a real problem, a reasonable prize per day might solve it.

Dowling.   What's the relationship between the ratio or frequency of the reinforcement and the size of the reinforcement? And what effect do they have on productivity?

Skinner.   The size of the reinforcement is, of course, important, but the schedule of reinforcement is more so. With a lower organism like a pigeon, we can get a fantastic amount of activity with very small amounts of reinforcement if we put it on an effective schedule. I've seen a pigeon peck a little disk on the wall ten thousand times in return for three seconds' access to pigeon feed, then go back and peck another ten thousand times. It is a long process but it's possible to build behavior up to the point at which more energy is expended than is received in the reinforcement.

Dowling.   What analogy, if any, is there between the pigeon pecking ten thousand times and the worker in industry?

Skinner.   I should hope there would be none. But there are many examples of so-called stretched schedules in everyday life. For example, people may be fond of fishing in a particular stream, but slowly they fish it out. The first time they catch the limit, the next time not quite so much, and finally they go back where they catch very little. They may seem foolish to those who have not had the same history.

Dowling.   In talking about the effectiveness or the lack of effectiveness in the incentive systems, one of the reasons that a great many people have found that incentive systems have not paid off is that the incentive system came up against the informal group organization and against the competing and conflicting reinforcement provided by the group. You have said yourself that the group is an enormously powerful reinforcer, far more effective than any individual. Would you comment on the impact of informal organization and the informal group on the operation and the relative ineffectiveness of many incentive systems?

Skinner. One question to ask is whether the group is right about it. If people are working on a piece-rate basis and the group has set a quota, presumably the schedule is having an unwarranted or even a dangerous effect. That's one thing. And if a new person comes in and starts producing beyond the quota, he will be punished by the others. They are protecting their own interests by refusing to let the schedule work them too hard, and they could be right.

But if they are holding production down to a level at which the plant is being used inefficiently, you have to improve the contingencies. The workers will come round if you make it genuinely worth their while and provide a reasonable balance between what they're being paid and what it costs them in effort and fatigue. Piece-rate schedules as such may not do the job, if the group sets a quota and punishes anyone who exceeds it.

Dowling. When you say that what needs to be done in the case of a low producing group whose output is below what an objective observer would describe as reasonable is to improve the contingencies, what specifically do you have in mind?

Skinner. It is important to remember that an incentive system isn't the only factor to take into account. How pleasant work conditions are, how easy or awkward a job is, how good or bad tools are — many things of that sort make an enormous difference in what a worker will do for what he receives.

One problem of the production-line worker is that he seldom sees any of the ultimate consequences of his work. He puts on left front wheels day in and day out, and he may never see the finished car. There are also industries in which what is being made isn't worth making, and there is no good reinforcement if the worker is not producing something people need.

I can't take a specific problem of that sort and solve it without knowing all kinds of details. Suppose I were an engineer in the bridge-building business and you came to me and said, "I want to put a bridge across a certain river — tell me what to do." I couldn't tell you. I'd have to go and see the river, see what traffic the bridge is going to handle, what the nature of the terrain is, and so on. Just because I knew all about bridge building wouldn't mean that I could tell you what to do until I looked into things. Even if I knew all about incentive systems — which I don't — I couldn't solve a particular problem without looking at the situation.

Dowling. Are you familiar with William Whyte's piece in *Psychology Today*? I think he calls it "Persons, Pigeons, and Piece Rates."

Skinner. I believe I read it. I think he makes a point that some schedules don't work as anticipated, but that isn't quite true. They work as *I* anticipate, they're just not well applied. We have clearly demonstrated that schedules that work with pigeons work perfectly well with human beings. Other things are involved, however. If I were a pigeon, I could upset an experiment, so that things wouldn't seem to be working very well, but I should do so only if the circumstances induced me to do so. It's a question of knowing all the relevant facts and not simply of trying to solve a problem with one principle as if it existed in a vacuum.

Dowling. Whyte talks about the conflicting stimuli that operate frequently in an industrial situation. You've got, for example, a worker on incentives who is also encouraged by the suggestion system to submit ideas for improving work methods. In a sense, the suggestion system is a positive reinforcer — he will get an award if management accepts his improved work method. On the other hand, he knows that there's a chance that the incentive system will be changed because of his suggestion and that he will lose out. In addition, his buddies and peers will get no award, and they will also suffer from the incentive changes. Another example of conflicting stimuli would be the case of a man who knows that the rate is relatively loose and if he puts out he is going to make a very handsome week's pay this week, next week, and maybe the week after. On the other hand, he knows that when other workers have behaved similarly the industrial engineering department has come in, restudied the job, and tightened the rates. I think we're talking about conflicting stimuli.

Skinner. I'm not sure that "conflicting stimuli" will explain it; these people are behaving exactly as you would expect under these conditions. You don't expect an elevator operator to recommend an automatic elevator, and I'm not surprised when a man does not submit a suggestion that might cut him out of a job. You can't expect a man to make suggestions that will damage him in the long run, even though you give him a prize. What are described as "conflict situations" do not mean that there is anything wrong with operant conditioning. People are behaving exactly as they ought to in the cases Whyte described.

Dowling.   In other words, it's an illustration of just how complex the variables frequently are. Speaking of variables, one phenomenon that has always fascinated me is rate busting. In a work group, under incentives, you might have maybe one or two out of thirty people who seem interested only in money; social approval or companionship mean absolutely nothing. How could you describe the rate buster in terms of operant conditioning?

Skinner.   You put it very well: The rate buster is not controlled by his peers. Their censure or punishment are not important enough to keep him within the quota. The group doesn't control him, and therefore he's controlled by the schedule. The result doesn't violate any principle; it just shows the complexity of things.

Dowling.   It would seem that there are considerable differences from individual to individual in the power of money to reinforce.

Skinner.   Not necessarily. The opposing condition may be more powerful. If you offer me a given amount of money to do something dangerous, and I accept, it may mean that danger is not very aversive to me, or that money is very reinforcing. You cannot tell which.

Dowling.   To get more to the general question of designing a compensation system, some people claim that if you want to improve performance and modify behavior, you should take whatever money is available and distribute almost all of it to the top performers — in other words, give them a really sizable reinforcer and more or less forget the rest.

Skinner.   These are practical problems that I can't solve from here. But in general it is important that a person's pay should represent some reasonable fraction of what he contributes to the company. I remember a case in which salesmen were making calls in business offices. They could do two things: they could make appointments by phone, in which case they would see people pretty well up in the company but make few calls per day, or they could make door-to-door calls, in which case they would make many more calls but see people much further down. (Actually, they weren't making sales on the spot, just describing the service involved; the sales came through later.) From the point of view of the company, it was important that they saw the top people, because they were the people who actually bought the service, but the salesmen were paid in terms

of the number of calls they made. An effective compensation system should reinforce the behavior that is worth the most to the company.

Dowling.   Job enrichment is one of the great cries now. There is a feeling that youthful workers are less interested in money than their parents were, and more interested in a job where they can control many of the conditions under which they work. How would you relate job enrichment to your own psychology?

Skinner.   I would not want to try to define "job enrichment." In interpreting what is happening with young people today, we have to take into account some very great changes that have occurred in the last generation. My father worked hard all his life because he was afraid of going to the poorhouse when he grew old. He wouldn't need to worry about that now; he would be on Social Security. People used to be afraid of losing their jobs; but now there is unemployment insurance. In other words, we have greatly reduced the significance of the money earned in a job. Diminish the significance of money, and other reinforcers obviously become important. What reinforcers do I mean? The work pace, schedules, how far you go in getting to work — these things become enormously more important. Forget about piped-in music. Look at the annoyances associated with the job and get rid of as many of them as you can. If, by moving the company into the suburbs, you can have your employees living close in, that's an important consideration.

Another question is whether what you're doing is worthwhile. People are much more alert to the ultimate value of things — for the culture and for the world — whether you're polluting the environment or using resources wastefully. Could you get any satisfaction from working in an industry that was making something that you regarded as worthless, or dangerous, or unnecessarily polluting?

Dowling.   In the list of substitutes for money as reinforcers that you have just mentioned, you haven't given much recognition to controlling the conditions under which you work — if you want to put tags on it, to democratic or participative management. I gather you don't give them much of a role.

Skinner.   The democratic principle lies in letting the worker tell you what he likes and doesn't like. He may not be the person to decide how to get rid of what he doesn't like or how to produce what he does like.

Industry is a beautiful example of the failure of a control and counter-control to produce effective contingencies. A hundred years ago, someone said this in the *Scientific American*: "Management wants as much work for as little pay as possible and the workers want as much pay for as little work as possible." So what happens? They get together and do something called bargaining. Incentive conditions emerge as a result of a bargain. And it's often a bad bargain all around. The conditions are not really very efficient as far as management goes, and not very pleasant as far as labor goes. If most people are bored with their jobs, it's because the system is the product of a battle between opposing forces. Someone should design incentive systems with the dual objectives of getting things done and making work enjoyable.

Dowling.   We recently did a survey for the first issue of *Organizational Dynamics,* in which we asked several hundred top managers what use they made of psychologists. The results were paradoxical: Top managers felt that there were many problems the psychologist could help them with, but there was very little inclination to use them. Only about 3 percent of the people surveyed had used psychologists and, even so,

they used them sporadically on minute tasks. Which raises the question, what do you think psychology has contributed to industry, and what do you think it could contribute?

Skinner.   I'm not a specialist in industrial psychology. I have only a casual acquaintance with the kinds of things done by Douglas McGregor and Abe Maslow. They do not strike me as being particularly effective. You can classify motives and still neglect contingencies of reinforcement, and the contingencies are the important things. Behavior modification is beginning to get into industry, and that may mean a change. Up to now it's been most effective in psychotherapy, in handling disturbed and retarded children, in the design of classroom management, and in programmed instruction. It is possible that we're going to see an entirely different kind of psychology in industry. Unfortunately, there are not yet many people who understand the principle. It is not something that can be taken over by the nonprofessional to use as a rule of thumb. It requires specific analysis and redesign of a situation. In the not-too-distant future, however, a new breed of industrial manager may be able to apply the principles of operant conditioning effectively.

B.

Motivating Individuals in Organizational Settings

4. Motivation: A Diagnostic Approach

David A. Nadler and Edward E. Lawler III

- What makes some people work hard while others do as little as possible?
- How can I, as a manager, influence the performance of people who work for me?
- Why do people turn over, show up late to work, and miss work entirely?

These important questions about employees' behavior can only be answered by managers who have a grasp of what motivates people. Specifically, a good understanding of motivation can serve as a valuable tool for *understanding* the causes of behavior in organizations, for *predicting* the effects of any managerial action, and for *directing* behavior so that organizational and individual goals can be achieved.

EXISTING APPROACHES

During the past twenty years, managers have been bombarded with a number of different approaches to motivation. The terms associated with these approaches are well known — "human relations," "scientific management," "job enrichment," "need hierarchy," "self-actualization," etc. Each of these approaches has something to offer. On the other hand, each of these different approaches also has its problems in both theory and practice. Running through almost all of the approaches with which managers are familiar are a series of implicit but clearly erroneous assumptions.

Assumption 1: All Employees Are Alike.   Different theories present different ways of looking at people, but each of them assumes that all employees are basically similar in their makeup: Employees all want economic gains, or all want a pleasant climate, or all aspire to be self-actualizing, etc.

Assumption 2: All Situations Are Alike.   Most theories assume that all managerial situations are alike, and that the managerial course of action for motivation (for example, participation, job enlargement, etc.) is applicable in all situations.

Assumption 3: One Best Way.   Out of the other two assumptions there emerges a basic principle that there is "one best way" to motivate employees.

When these "one best way" approaches are tried in the "correct" situation they will work. However, all of them are bound to fail in some situations. They are therefore not adequate managerial tools.

A NEW APPROACH

During the past ten years, a great deal of research has been done on a new approach to looking at motivation. This approach, frequently called "expectancy theory," still needs further testing, refining, and extending. However, enough is known that many behavioral scientists have concluded that it represents the most comprehensive, valid, and useful approach to understanding motivation. Further, it is apparent that it is a very useful tool for understanding motivation in organizations.

The theory is based on a number of specific assumptions about the causes of behavior in organizations.

Assumption 1: Behavior Is Determined by a Combination of Forces in the Individual and Forces in the Environment.   Neither the individual nor the environment alone determines behavior. Individuals come into organizations with certain "psychological baggage." They have past experiences and a developmental history which has given them unique sets of needs, ways of looking at the world, and expectations about how organizations will treat them. These all influence how individuals respond to their work environment. The work environment provides structures (such as a pay system or a supervisor) which influence the behavior of people. Different environments tend to produce different behavior in similar people just as dissimilar people tend to behave differently in similar environments.

Assumption 2: People Make Decisions About Their Own Behavior in Organizations.   While there are many constraints on the behavior of individuals in organizations, most of the behavior that is observed is the result of individuals' conscious decisions. These decisions usually fall into two categories. First, individuals make decisions about *membership behavior* — coming to work, staying at work, and in other ways being a member of the organization. Second, individuals make decisions about the amount of effort they will direct *towards performing their jobs.* This includes decisions about how hard to work, how much to produce, at what quality, etc.

Assumption 3: Different People Have Different Types of Needs, Desires and Goals.   Individuals differ on what kinds of outcomes (or rewards) they desire. These differences are not random; they can be examined systematically by an understanding of the differences in the strength of individuals' needs.

Assumption 4: People Make Decisions Among Alternative Plans of Behavior Based on Their Perceptions (Expectancies) of the Degree to Which a Given Behavior Will Lead to Desired Outcomes.   In simple terms, people tend to do those things which they see as leading to outcomes (which can also be called "rewards") they desire and avoid doing those things they see as leading to outcomes that are not desired.

In general, the approach used here views people as having their own needs and mental maps of what the world is like. They use these maps to make decisions about how they will behave, behaving in those ways which their mental maps indicate will lead to outcomes that will satisfy their needs. Therefore, they are inherently neither motivated nor unmotivated; motivation depends on the situation they are in, and how it fits their needs.

THE THEORY

Based on these general assumptions, expectancy theory states a number of propositions about the process by which people make decisions about their own behavior in organizational settings. While the theory is complex at first view, it is in fact made of a series of fairly straightforward observations about behavior. (The theory is presented in more technical terms in Appendix A.) Three concepts serve as the key building blocks of the theory:

Performance-Outcome Expectancy.   Every behavior has associated with it, in an individuals' mind, certain outcomes (rewards or punishments). In other words, the individual believes or expects that if he or she behaves in a certain way, he or she will get certain things.

Examples of expectancies can easily be described. An individual may have an expectancy that if he produces ten units he will receive his normal hourly rate while if he produces fifteen units he will receive his hourly pay rate plus a bonus. Similarly an individual may believe that certain levels of performance will lead to approval or disapproval from members of her work group or from her supervisor. Each performance can be seen as leading to a number of different kinds of outcomes and outcomes can differ in their types.

Valence. Each outcome has a "valence" (value, worth, attractiveness) to a specific individual. Outcomes have different valences for different individuals. This comes about because valences result from individual needs and perceptions, which differ because they in turn reflect other factors in the individual's life.

For example, some individuals may value an opportunity for promotion or advancement because of their needs for achievement or power, while others may not want to be promoted and leave their current work group because of needs for affiliation with others. Similarly, a fringe benefit such as a pension plan may have great valence for an older worker but little valence for a young employee on his first job.

Effort-Performance Expectancy. Each behavior also has associated with it in the individual's mind a certain expectancy or probability of success. This expectancy represents the individual's perception of how hard it will be to achieve such behavior and the probability of his or her successful achievement of that behavior.

For example, you may have a strong expectancy that if you put forth effort, you can produce ten units an hour, but that you have only a fifty-fifty chance of producing fifteen units an hour if you try.

Putting these concepts together, it is possible to make a basic statement about motivation. In general, the motivation to attempt to behave in a certain way is greatest when:

a. The individual believes that the behavior will lead to outcomes (performance-outcome expectancy)
b. The individual believes that these outcomes have positive value for him or her (valence)
c. The individual believes that he or she is able to perform at the desired level (effort-performance expectancy)

Given a number of alternative levels of behavior (ten, fifteen, and twenty units of production per hour, for example) the individual will choose that level of performance which has the greatest motivational force associated with it, as indicated by the expectancies, outcomes, and valences.

In other words, when faced with choices about behavior, the individual goes through a process of considering questions such as, "Can I perform at that level if I try?" "If I perform at that level, what will happen?" "How do I feel about those things that will happen?" The individual then decides to behave in that way which seems to have the best chance of producing positive, desired outcomes.

A General Model

On the basis of these concepts, it is possible to construct a general model of behavior in organizational settings (see Figure 1). Working from left to right in the model, motivation is seen as the force on the individual to expend effort. Motivation leads to an observed level of effort by the individual. Effort, alone, however, is not enough. Performance results from a combination of the effort that an individual puts forth *and* the level of ability which he or she has (reflecting skills, training, information, etc.). Effort thus combines with ability to produce a given level of performance. As a result of performance, the individual attains certain outcomes. The model indicates this relationship in a dotted line, reflecting the fact that sometimes people perform but do not get desired outcomes. As this process of performance-reward occurs, time after time, the actual events serve to provide information which influences the individual's perceptions (particularly expectancies) and thus influences motivation in the future.

Outcomes, or rewards, fall into two major categories. First, the individual obtains outcomes from the environment. When an individual performs at a given level he or she can receive positive or negative outcomes from supervisors, coworkers, the organization's rewards systems, or other sources. These environmental rewards are thus one source of outcomes for the individual. A second source of outcomes is the individual. These include outcomes which occur purely from the performance of the task itself (feelings of accomplishment, personal worth, achievement, etc.). In a sense, the individual gives these rewards to himself or herself. The environment cannot give them or take them away directly; it can only make them possible.

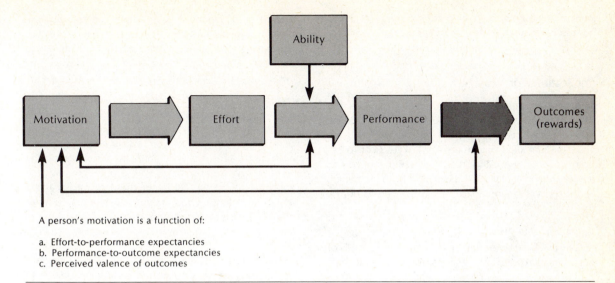

A person's motivation is a function of:

a. Effort-to-performance expectancies
b. Performance-to-outcome expectancies
c. Perceived valence of outcomes

Figure 1.   The Basic Motivation-Behavior Sequence.

Supporting Evidence

Over fifty studies have been done to test the validity of the expectancy-theory approach to predicting employee behavior.[1] Almost without exception, the studies have confirmed the predictions of the theory. As the theory predicts, the best performers in organizations tend to see a strong relationship between performing their jobs well and receiving rewards they value. In addition they have clear performance goals and feel they can perform well. Similarly, studies using the expectancy theory to predict how people choose jobs also show that individuals tend to interview for and actually take those jobs which they feel will provide the rewards they value. One study, for example, was able to correctly predict for 80 percent of the people studied which of several jobs they would take.[2] Finally, the theory correctly predicts that beliefs about the outcomes associated with performance (expectancies) will be better predictors of performance than will feelings of job satisfaction since expectancies are the critical causes of performance and satisfaction is not.

Questions About the Model

Although the results so far have been encouraging, they also indicate some problems with the model. These problems do not critically affect the managerial implications of the model, but they should be noted. The model is based on the assumption that individuals make very rational decisions after a thorough exploration of all the available alternatives and on weighing the possible outcomes of all these alternatives. When we talk to or observe individuals, however, we find that their decision processes are frequently less thorough. People often stop considering alternative behavior plans when they find one that is at least moderately satisfying, even though more rewarding plans remain to be examined.

People are also limited in the amount of information they can handle at one time, and therefore the model may indicate a process that is much more complex than the one that actually takes place. On the other hand, the model does provide enough information and is consistent enough with reality to present some clear

---

1. For reviews of the expectancy theory research see Mitchell, T. R. Expectancy models of job satisfaction, occupational preference and effort: A theoretical methodological, and empirical appraisal. *Psychological Bulletin,* 1974, 81, 1053–1077. For a more general discussion of expectancy theory and other approaches to motivation see Lawler, E. E. *Motivation in work organizations.* Belmont, Calif.: Brooks/Cole, 1973.

2. Lawler, E. E., Kuleck, W. J., Rhode, J. G. & Sorenson, J. E. Job choice and post-decision dissonance. *Organizational Behavior and Human Performance,* 1975, 13, 133–145.

implications for managers who are concerned with the question of how to motivate the people who work for them.

Implications for Managers

The first set of implications is directed toward the individual manager who has a group of people working for him or her and is concerned with how to motivate good performance. Since behavior is a result of forces both in the person and in the environment, you as manager need to look at and diagnose both the person and the environment. Specifically, you need to do the following:

Figure Out What Outcomes Each Employee Values. As a first step, it is important to determine what kinds of outcomes or rewards have valence for your employees. For each employee you need to determine "what turns him or her on." There are various ways of finding this out, including (a) finding out employees' desires through some structured method of data collection, such as a questionnaire, (b) observing the employees' reactions to different situations or rewards, or (c) the fairly simple act of asking them what kinds of rewards they want, what kind of career goals they have, or "what's in it for them." It is important to stress here that it is very difficult to change what people want, but fairly easy to find out what they want. Thus, the skillful manager emphasizes diagnosis of needs, not changing the individuals themselves.

Determine What Kinds of Behavior You Desire. Managers frequently talk about "good performance" without really defining what good performance is. An important step in motivating is for you yourself to figure out what kinds of performance are required and what are adequate measures or indicators of performance (quantity, quality, etc.). There is also a need to be able to define those performances in fairly specific terms so that observable and measurable behavior can be defined and subordinates can understand what is desired of them (e.g., produce ten products of a certain quality standard—rather than only produce at a high rate).

Make Sure Desired Levels of Performance Are Reachable. The model states that motivation is determined not only by the performance-to-outcome expectancy, but also by the effort-to-performance expectancy. The implication of this is that the levels of performance which are set as the points at which individuals receive desired outcomes must be reachable or attainable by these individuals. If the employees feel that the level of performance required to get a reward is higher than they can reasonably achieve, then their motivation to perform well will be relatively low.

Link Desired Outcomes to Desired Performances. The next step is to directly, clearly, and explicitly link those outcomes desired by employees to the specific performances desired by you. If your employee values external rewards, then the emphasis should be on the rewards systems concerned with promotion, pay, and approval. While the linking of these rewards can be initiated through your making statements to your employees, it is extremely important that employees see a clear example of the reward process working in a fairly short period of time if the motivating "expectancies" are to be created in the employees' minds. The linking must be done by some concrete public acts, in addition to statements of intent.

If your employee values internal rewards (e.g., achievement), then you should concentrate on changing the nature of the persons' job, for he or she is likely to respond well to such things as increased autonomy, feedback, and challenge, because these things will lead to a situation where good job performance is inherently rewarding. The best way to check on the adequacy of the internal and external reward system is to ask people what their perceptions of the situation are. Remember it is the perceptions of people that determine their motivation, not reality. It doesn't matter for example whether you feel a subordinate's pay is related to his or her motivation. Motivation will be present only if the subordinate sees the relationship. Many managers are misled about the behavior of their subordinates because they rely on their own perceptions of the situation and forget to find out what their subordinates feel. There is only one way to do this: ask. Questionnaires can be used here, as can personal interviews.

Analyze the Total Situation for Conflicting Expectancies. Having set up positive expectancies for employees, you then need to look at the entire situation to see if other factors (informal work groups, other managers, the organization's reward systems) have set up conflicting expectancies in the minds of the employees. Motivation will only be high when people see a number of rewards associated with good performance and few negative outcomes. Again, you can often gather this kind of information by asking your subordinates. If there are major conflicts, you need to make adjustments, either in your own performance and reward structure, or in the other sources of rewards or punishments in the environment.

Make Sure Changes in Outcomes Are Large Enough. In examining the motivational system, it is important to make sure that changes in outcomes or rewards are large enough to motivate significant behavior. Trivial rewards will result in trivial amounts of effort and thus trivial improvements in performance. Rewards must be large enough to motivate individuals to put forth the effort required to bring about significant changes in performance.

Check the System for Its Equity.   The model is based on the idea that individuals are different and therefore different rewards will need to be used to motivate different individuals. On the other hand, for a motivational system to work it must be a fair one — one that has equity (not equality). Good performers should see that they get more desired rewards than do poor performers, and others in the system should see that also. Equity should not be confused with a system of equality where all are rewarded equally, with no regard to their performance. A system of equality is guaranteed to produce low motivation.

Implications for Organizations

Expectancy theory has some clear messages for those who run large organizations. It suggests how organizational structures can be designed so that they increase rather than decrease levels of motivation of organization members. While there are many different implications, a few of the major ones are as follows:

Implication 1: The Design of Pay and Reward Systems. Organizations usually get what they reward, not what they want. This can be seen in many situations, and pay systems are a good example.[3] Frequently, organizations reward people for membership (through pay tied to seniority, for example) rather than for performance. Little wonder that what the organization gets is behavior oriented towards "safe," secure employment rather than effort directed at performing well. In addition, even where organizations do pay for performance as a motivational device, they frequently negate the motivational value of the system by keeping pay secret,

therefore preventing people from observing the pay-to-performance relationship that would serve to create positive, clear, and strong performance-to-reward expectancies. The implication is that organizations should put more effort into rewarding people (through pay, promotion, better job opportunities, etc.) for the performances which are desired, and that to keep these rewards secret is clearly self-defeating. In addition, it underscores the importance of the frequently ignored performance evaluation or appraisal process and the need to evaluate people based on how they perform clearly defined specific behaviors, rather than on how they score on ratings of general traits such as "honesty," "cleanliness," and other, similar terms which frequently appear as part of the performance appraisal form.

Implication 2: The Design of Tasks, Jobs, and Roles. One source of desired outcomes is the work itself. The expectancy-theory model supports much of the job enrichment literature, in saying that by designing jobs which enable people to get their needs fulfilled, organizations can bring about higher levels of motivation.[4] The major difference between the traditional approaches to job enlargement or enrichment and the expectancy-theory approach is the recognition by the expectancy theory that different people have different needs and, therefore, some people may not want enlarged or enriched jobs. Thus, while the design of tasks that have more autonomy, variety, feedback, meaningfulness, etc., will lead to higher motivation in some, the organization needs to build in the opportunity for individuals to make choices about the kind of work they will do so that not everyone is forced to experience job enrichment.

Implication 3: The Importance of Group Structures. Groups, both formal and informal, are powerful and potent sources of desired outcomes for individuals. Groups can provide or withhold acceptance, approval, affection, skill training, needed information, assistance, etc. They are a powerful force in the total motivational environment of individuals. Several implications emerge from the importance of groups. First, organizations should consider the structuring of at least a portion of

---

3. For a detailed discussion of the implications of expectancy theory for pay and reward systems, see Lawler, E. E. *Pay and organizational effectiveness: A psychological view.* New York: McGraw-Hill, 1971.

4. A good discussion of job design with an expectancy theory perspective is in Hackman, J. R., Oldham, G. R., Janson, R., & Purdy, K. A new strategy for job enrichment. *California Management Review,* Summer, 1975, p. 57.

rewards around group performance rather than individual performance. This is particularly important where group members have to cooperate with each other to produce a group product or service, and where the individual's contribution is often hard to determine. Second, the organization needs to train managers to be aware of how groups can influence individual behavior and to be sensitive to the kinds of expectancies which informal groups set up and their conflict or consistency with the expectancies that the organization attempts to create.

Implication 4: The Supervisor's Role. The immediate supervisor has an important role in creating, monitoring, and maintaining the expectancies and reward structures which will lead to good performance. The supervisor's role in the motivation process becomes one of defining clear goals, setting clear reward expectancies, and providing the right rewards for different people (which could include both organizational rewards and personal rewards such as recognition, approval, or support from the supervisor). Thus, organizations need to provide supervisors with an awareness of the nature of motivation as well as the tools (control over organizational rewards, skill in administering those rewards) to create positive motivation.

Implication 5: Measuring Motivation. If things like expectancies, the nature of the job, supervisor-controlled outcomes, satisfaction, etc., are important in understanding how well people are being motivated, then organizations need to monitor employee perceptions along these lines. One relatively cheap and reliable method of doing this is through standardized employee questionnaires. A number of organizations already use such techniques, surveying employees' perceptions and attitudes at regular intervals (ranging from once a month to once every year-and-a-half) using either standardized surveys or surveys developed specifically for the organization. Such information is useful both to the individual manager and to top management in assessing the state of human resources and the effectiveness of the organization's motivation systems.[5]

Implication 6: Individualizing Organizations. Expectancy theory leads to a final general implication about a possible future direction for the design of organizations. Because different people have different needs and therefore have different valences, effective motivation must come through the recognition that not all employees are alike and that organizations need to be flexible in order to accommodate individual differences. This implies the "building in" of choice for employees in many areas, such as reward systems, fringe benefits, job assignments, etc., where employees previously have had little say. A successful example of the building in of such choice can be seen in the experiments at TRW and the Educational Testing Service with "cafeteria fringe-benefits plans" which allow employees to choose the fringe benefits they want, rather than taking the expensive and often unwanted benefits which the company frequently provides to everyone.[6]

SUMMARY

Expectancy theory provides a more complex model of man for managers to work with. At the same time, it is a model which holds promise for the more effective motivation of individuals and the more effective design of organizational systems. It implies, however, the need for more exacting and thorough diagnosis by the manager to determine (a) the relevant forces in the individual, and (b) the relevant forces in the environment, both of which combine to motivate different kinds of behavior. Following diagnosis, the model implies a need to act—to develop a system of pay, promotion, job assignments, group structures, supervision, etc.—to bring about effective motivation by providing different outcomes for different individuals.

Performance of individuals is a critical issue in making organizations work effectively. If a manager is to influence work behavior and performance, he or she must have an understanding of motivation and the factors which influence an individual's motivation to come to work, to work hard, and to work well. While simple models offer easy answers, it is the more complex models which seem to offer more promise. Managers can use models (like expectancy theory) to understand the nature of behavior and build more effective organizations.

---

5. The use of questionnaires for understanding and changing organizational behavior is discussed in Nadler, D. A. *Feedback and organizational development: Using data-based methods.* Reading, Mass.: Addison-Wesley, 1977.

6. The whole issue of individualizing organizations is examined in Lawler, E. E. The individualized organization: Problems and promise. *California Management Review,* 1974, 17 (2), 31–39.

APPENDIX A: The Expectancy Theory Model in More Technical Terms

A person's motivation to exert effort towards a specific level of performance is based on his or her perceptions of associations between actions and outcomes. The critical perceptions which contribute to motivation are graphically presented in Figure 2. These perceptions can be defined as follows:

a. The effort-to-performance expectancy ($E \rightarrow P$): This refers to the person's subjective probability about the likelihood that he or she can perform at a given level, or that effort on his or her part will lead to successful performance. This term can be thought of as varying from 0 to 1. In general, the less likely a person feels that he or she can perform at a given level, the less likely he or she will be to try to perform at that level. A person's $E \rightarrow P$ probabilities are also strongly influenced by each situation and by previous experience in that and similar situations.

b. The performance-to-outcomes expectancy ($P \rightarrow O$) and valence (V): This refers to a combination of a number of beliefs about what the outcomes of successful performance will be and the value or attractiveness of these outcomes to the individual. Valence is considered to vary from $+1$ (very desirable) to -1 (very undesirable) and the performance-to-outcomes probabilities vary from $+1$ (performance sure to lead to outcome) to 0 (performance not related to outcome). In general, the more likely a person feels that performance will lead to valent outcomes, the more likely he or she will be to try to perform at the required level.

c. Instrumentality: As Figure 2 indicates, a single level of performance can be associated with a number of different outcomes, each having a certain degree of valence. Some outcomes are valent because they have direct value or attractiveness. Some outcomes, however, have valence because they are seen as leading to (or being ''instrumental'' for) the attainment of other

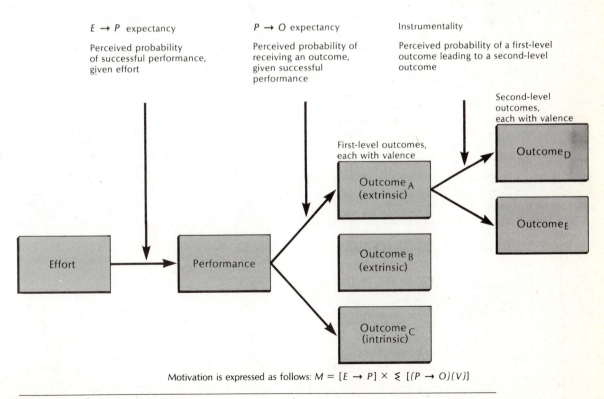

Motivation is expressed as follows: $M = [E \rightarrow P] \times \underset{\sim}{\lesseqgtr} [(P \rightarrow O)(V)]$

Figure 2. Major Terms in Expectancy Theory.

"second level" outcomes which have direct value or attractiveness.

d.   Intrinsic and extrinsic outcomes: Some outcomes are seen as occurring directly as a result of performing the task itself and are outcomes which the individual thus gives to himself (i.e., feelings of accomplishment, creativity, etc.). These are called "intrinsic" outcomes. Other outcomes that are associated with performance are provided or mediated by external factors (the organization, the supervisor, the work group, etc.). These outcomes are called "extrinsic" outcomes.

Along with the graphic representation of these terms presented in Figure 2, there is a simplified formula for combining these perceptions to arrive at a term expressing the relative level of motivation to exert effort towards performance at a given level. The formula expresses these relationships:

a.   The person's motivation to perform is determined by the $P \rightarrow O$ expectancy multiplied by the valence (*V*) of the outcome. The valence of the first order outcome subsumes the instrumentalities and valences of second order outcomes. The relationship is multiplicative since there is no motivation to perform if either of the terms is zero.

b.   Since a level of performance has multiple outcomes associated with it, the products of all probability-times-valence combinations are added together for all the outcomes that are seen as related to the specific performance.

c.   This term (the summed $P \rightarrow O$ expectancies times valences) is then multiplied by the $E \rightarrow P$ expectancy. Again the multiplicative relationship indicates that if either term is zero, motivation is zero.

d.   In summary, the strength of a person's motivation to perform effectively is influenced by (1) the person's belief that effort can be converted into performance, and (2) the net attractiveness of the events that are perceived to stem from good performance.

So far, all the terms have referred to the individual's perceptions which result in motivation and thus an intention to behave in a certain way. Figure 3 is a simplified representation of the total model, showing how these intentions get translated into actual behavior.[7] The model envisions the following sequence of events:

a.   First, the strength of a person's motivation to perform correctly is most directly reflected in his or her

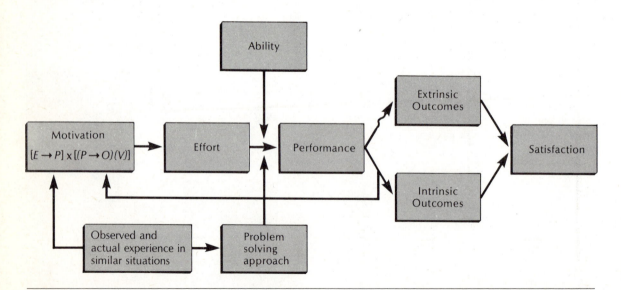

Figure 3.   Simplified Expectancy-Theory Model of Behavior.

---

7. For a more detailed statement of the model see Lawler, E. E. Job attitudes and employee motivation: Theory, research and practice. *Personnel Psychology*, 1970, 23, 223–237.

effort — how hard he or she works. This effort expenditure may or may not result in good performance, since at least two factors must be right if effort is to be converted into performance. First, the person must possess the necessary abilities in order to perform the job well. Unless both ability and effort are high, there cannot be good performance. A second factor is the person's perception of how his or her effort can best be converted into performance. It is assumed that this perception is learned by the individual on the basis of previous experience in similar situations. This "how to do it" perception can obviously vary widely in accuracy, and — where erroneous perceptions exist — performance is low even though effort or motivation may be high.

b.   Second, when performance occurs, certain amounts of outcomes are obtained by the individual.

Intrinsic outcomes, not being mediated by outside forces, tend to occur regularly as a result of performance, while extrinsic outcomes may or may not accrue to the individual (indicated by the wavy line of the model).

c.   Third, as a result of the obtaining of outcomes and the perceptions of the relative value of the outcomes obtained, the individual has a positive or negative affective response (a level of satisfaction or dissatisfaction).

d.   Fourth, the model indicates that events which occur influence future behavior by altering the $E \rightarrow P$, $P \rightarrow O$, and V perceptions. This process is represented by the feedback loops running from actual behavior back to motivation.

5.   Goal-setting—A Motivational Technique That Works

Gary P. Latham and Edwin A. Locke

The problem of how to motivate employees has puzzled and frustrated managers for generations. One reason the problem has seemed difficult, if not mysterious, is that motivation ultimately comes from within the individual and therefore cannot be observed directly. Moreover, most managers are not in a position to change an employee's basic personality structure. The best they can do is try to use incentives to direct the energies of their employees toward organizational objectives.

Money is obviously the primary incentive, since without it few if any employees would come to work. But money alone is not always enough to motivate high

performance. Other incentives, such as participation in decision making, job enrichment, behavior modification, and organizational development, have been tried with varying degrees of success. A large number of research studies have shown, however, that one very straightforward technique — goal setting — is probably not only more effective than alternative methods, but may be the major mechanism by which these other incentives affect motivation. For example, a recent experiment on job enrichment demonstrated that unless employees in enriched jobs set higher, more specific goals than do those with unenriched jobs, job enrichment has absolutely no effect on productivity. Even money has been found most effective as a motivator when the bonuses offered are made contingent on attaining specific objectives.

THE GOAL-SETTING CONCEPT

The idea of assigning employees a specific amount of work to be accomplished — a specific task, a quota, a performance standard, an objective, or a deadline — is not new. The task concept, along with time and motion study and incentive pay, was the cornerstone of scientific management, founded by Frederick W. Taylor more than 70 years ago. He used his system to increase the productivity of blue-collar workers. About 20 years ago the idea of goal setting reappeared under a new name, management by objectives, but this technique was designed for managers.

In a 14-year program of research, we have found that goal setting does not necessarily have to be part of a wider management system to motivate performance effectively. It can be used as a technique in its own right.

Laboratory and Field Research

Our research program began in the laboratory. In a series of experiments, individuals were assigned different types of goals on a variety of simple tasks — addition, brainstorming, assembling toys. Repeatedly it was found that those assigned hard goals performed better than did people assigned moderately difficult or easy goals. Furthermore, individuals who had specific, challenging goals outperformed those who were given such vague goals as to "do your best." Finally, we observed that pay and performance feedback led to improved performance only when these incentives led the individual to set higher goals.

While results were quite consistent in the laboratory, there was no proof that they could be applied to actual work settings. Fortunately, just as Locke published a summary of the laboratory studies in 1968, Latham began a separate series of experiments in the wood products industry that demonstrated the practical significance of these findings. The field studies did not start out as a validity test of a laboratory theory, but rather as a response to a practical problem.

In 1968, six sponsors of the American Pulpwood Association became concerned about increasing the productivity of independent loggers in the South. These loggers were entrepreneurs on whom the multimillion-dollar companies are largely dependent for their raw material. The problem was twofold. First, these entrepreneurs did not work for a single company; they worked for themselves. Thus they were free to (and often did) work two days one week, four days a second week, five half-days a third week, or whatever schedule they preferred. In short, these workers could be classified as marginal from the standpoint of their productivity and attendance, which were considered highly unsatisfactory by conventional company standards. Second, the major approach taken to alleviate this problem had been to develop equipment that would make the industry less dependent on this type of worker. A limitation of this approach was that many of the logging supervisors were unable to obtain the financing necessary to purchase a small tractor, let alone a rubber-tired skidder.

Consequently, we designed a survey that would help managers determine "what makes these people tick." The survey was conducted orally in the field with 292 logging supervisors. Complex statistical analyses of the data identified three basic types of supervisor. One type stayed on the job with their men, gave them instructions and explanations, provided them with training, read the trade magazines, and had little difficulty financing the equipment they needed. Still, the productivity of their units was at best mediocre.

The operation of the second group of supervisors was slightly less mechanized. These supervisors provided little training for their workforce. They simply drove their employees to the woods, gave them a specific production goal to attain for the day or week, left them alone in the woods unsupervised, and returned at night to take them home. Labor turnover was high and productivity was again average.

The operation of the third group of supervisors was relatively unmechanized. These leaders stayed on the job with their men, provided training, gave instructions and explanations, and in addition, set a specific production goal for the day or week. Not only was the crew's productivity high, but their injury rate was well below average.

Two conclusions were discussed with the managers of the companies sponsoring this study. First, mechanization alone will not increase the productivity of logging crews. Just as the average tax payer would probably commit more mathematical errors if he were to try to use a computer to complete his income tax return, the average logger misuses, and frequently abuses, the equipment he purchases (for example, drives a skidder with two flat tires, doesn't change the oil filter). This increases not only the logger's downtime, but also his costs which, in turn, can force him out of business. The second conclusion of the survey was that setting a specific production goal combined with supervisory presence to ensure goal commitment will bring about a significant increase in productivity.

These conclusions were greeted with the standard, but valid, cliché, "Statistics don't prove causation." And our comments regarding the value of machinery were especially irritating to these managers, many of whom had received degrees in engineering. So one of the companies decided to replicate the survey in order to check our findings.

The company's study placed each of 892 independent logging supervisors who sold wood to the company into one of three categories of supervisory styles our survey had identified—namely, (1) stays on the job but does not set specific production goals; (2) sets specific production goals but does not stay on the job; and (3) stays on the job and sets specific production goals. Once again, goal setting, in combination with the on-site presence of a supervisor, was shown to be the key to improved productivity.

TESTING FOR THE HAWTHORNE EFFECT

Management may have been unfamiliar with different theories of motivation, but it was fully aware of one label—the Hawthorne effect. Managers in these wood products companies remained unconvinced that anything so simple as staying on the job with the men and setting a specific production goal could have an appreciable effect on productivity. They pointed out that the results simply reflected the positive effects any supervisor would have on the work unit after giving his crew attention. And they were unimpressed by the laboratory experiments we cited—experiments showing that individuals who have a specific goal solve more arithmetic problems or assemble more tinker toys than do people who are told to "do your best." Skepticism prevailed.

But the country's economic picture made it critical to continue the study of inexpensive techniques to improve employee motivation and productivity. We were granted permission to run one more project to test the effectiveness of goal setting.

Twenty independent logging crews who were all but identical in size, mechanization level, terrain on which they worked, productivity, and attendance were located. The logging supervisors of these crews were in the habit of staying on the job with their men, but they did not set production goals. Half the crews were randomly selected to receive training in goal setting; the remaining crews served as a control group.

The logging supervisors who were to set goals were told that we had found a way to increase productivity at no financial expense to anyone. We gave the ten supervisors in the training group production tables developed through time-and-motion studies by the company's engineers. These tables made it possible to determine how much wood should be harvested in a given number of manhours. They were asked to use these tables as a guide in determining a specific production goal to assign their employees. In addition, each sawhand was given a tallymeter (counter) that he could wear on his belt. The sawhand was asked to punch the counter each time he felled a tree. Finally, permission was requested to measure the crew's performance on a weekly basis.

The ten supervisors in the control group—those who were not asked to set production goals—were told that the researchers were interested in learning the extent to which productivity is affected by absenteeism and injuries. They were urged to "do your best" to maximize the crew's productivity and attendance and to minimize injuries. It was explained that the data might be useful in finding ways to increase productivity at little or no cost to the wood harvester.

To control for the Hawthorne effect, we made an equal number of visits to the control group and the training group. Performance was measured for 12 weeks. During this time, the productivity of the goal-setting group was significantly higher than that of the control group. Moreover, absenteeism was significantly lower in the groups that set goals than in the groups who were simply urged to do their best. Injury and turnover rates were low in both groups.

Why should anything so simple and inexpensive as goal setting influence the work of these employees so significantly? Anecdotal evidence from conversations with both the loggers and the company foresters who visited them suggested several reasons.

Harvesting timber can be a monotonous, tiring job with little or no meaning for most workers. Introducing a goal that is difficult, but attainable, increases the challenge of the job. In addition, a specific goal makes it clear to the worker what it is he is expected to do. Goal feedback via the tallymeter and weekly recordkeeping provide the worker with a sense of achievement, recognition, and accomplishment. He can see how well he is doing now as against his past performance and, in some cases, how well he is doing in comparison with others. Thus the worker not only may expend greater effort, but may also devise better or more creative tactics for attaining the goal than those he previously used.

NEW APPLICATIONS

Management was finally convinced that goal setting was an effective motivational technique for increasing the productivity of the independent woods worker in the South. The issue now raised by the management of another wood products company was whether the procedure could be used in the West with company logging operations in which the employees were unionized and paid by the hour. The previous study had involved employees on a piece-rate system, which was the practice in the South.

The immediate problem confronting this company involved the loading of logging trucks. If the trucks were underloaded, the company lost money. If the trucks were overloaded, however, the driver could be fined by the Highway Department and could ultimately lose his job. The drivers opted for underloading the trucks.

For three months management tried to solve this problem by urging the drivers to try harder to fill the truck to its legal net weight, and by developing weighing scales that could be attached to the truck. But this approach did not prove cost effective, because the scales continually broke down when subjected to the rough terrain on which the trucks traveled. Consequently, the drivers reverted to their former practice of underloading. For the three months in which the problem was under study the trucks were seldom loaded in excess of 58 to 63 percent of capacity.

At the end of the three-month period, the results of the previous goal-setting experiments were explained to the union. They were told three things—that the company would like to set a specific net weight goal for the drivers, that no monetary reward or fringe benefits other than verbal praise could be expected for improved performance, and that no one would be criticized for failing to attain the goal. Once again, the idea that simply setting a specific goal would solve a production problem seemed too incredible to be taken seriously by the union. However, they reached an agreement that a difficult, but attainable, goal of 94 percent of the truck's legal net weight would be assigned to the drivers, provided that no one could be reprimanded for failing to attain the goal. This latter point was emphasized to the company foremen in particular.

Within the first month, performance increased to 80 percent of the truck's net weight. After the second month, however, performance decreased to 70 percent. Interviews with the drivers indicated that they were testing management's statement that no punitive steps would be taken against them if their performance suddenly dropped. Fortunately for all concerned, no such steps were taken by the foremen, and performance exceeded 90 percent of the truck's capacity after the third month. Their performance has remained at this level to this day, seven years later.

The results over the nine-month period during which this study was conducted saved the company $250,000. This figure, determined by the company's accountants, is based on the cost of additional trucks that would have been required to deliver the same quantity of logs to the mill if goal setting had not been implemented. The dollars-saved figure is even higher when you factor in the cost of the additional diesel fuel that would have been consumed and the expenses incurred in recruiting and hiring the additional truck drivers.

Why could this procedure work without the union's demanding an increase in hourly wages? First, the drivers did not feel that they were really doing anything differently. This, of course, was not true. As a result of goal setting, the men began to record their truck weight in a pocket notebook, and they found themselves bragging about their accomplishments to their peers. Second, they viewed goal setting as a challenging game: "It was great to beat the other guy."

Competition was a crucial factor in bringing about goal acceptance and commitment in this study. However, we can reject the hypothesis that improved performance resulted solely from competition, because no special prizes or formal recognition programs were provided for those who came closest to, or exceeded, the goal. No effort was made by the company to single out one "winner." More important, the opportunity for competition among drivers had existed before goal setting was instituted; after all, each driver knew his own truck's weight, and the truck weight of each of the 36 other drivers every time he hauled wood into the yard. In short, competition affected productivity only in the sense that it led to the acceptance of, and commitment to, the goal. It was the setting of the goal itself and the working toward it that brought about increased performance and decreased costs.

PARTICIPATIVE GOAL SETTING

The inevitable question always raised by management was raised here: "We know goal setting works. How can we make it work better?" Was there one best method for setting goals? Evidence for a "one best way" approach was cited by several managers, but it was finally concluded that different approaches would work best under different circumstances.

It was hypothesized that the woods workers in the South, who had little or no education, would work better with assigned goals, while the educated workers in the West would achieve higher productivity if they were allowed to help set the goals themselves. Why the focus on education? Many of the uneducated workers in the South could be classified as culturally disadvantaged. Such persons often lack self-confidence, have a poor sense of time, and are not very competitive. The cycle of skill mastery, which in turn guarantees skill levels high enough to prevent discouragement, doesn't apply to these employees. If, for example, these people were allowed to participate in goal setting, the goals might be too difficult or they might be too easy. On the other hand, participation for the educated worker was considered critical in effecting maximum goal acceptance. Since these conclusions appeared logical, management initially decided that no research was necessary. This decision led to hours of further discussion.

The same questions were raised again and again by the researchers. What if the logic were wrong? Can we afford to implement these decisions without evaluating them systematically? Would we implement decisions regarding a new approach to tree planting without first testing it? Do we care more about trees than we do about people? Finally, permission was granted to conduct an experiment.

Logging crews were randomly appointed to either participative goal setting, assigned (nonparticipative) goal setting, or a do-your-best condition. The results were startling. The uneducated crews, consisting primarily of black employees who participated in goal setting, set significantly higher goals and attained them more often than did those whose goals were assigned by their supervisor. Not surprisingly, their performance was higher. Crews with assigned goals performed no better than did those who were urged to do their best to improve their productivity. The performance of white, educationally advantaged workers was higher with assigned rather than participatively set goals, although the difference was not statistically significant. These results were precisely the opposite of what had been predicted.

Another study comparing participative and assigned goals was conducted with typists. The results supported findings obtained by researchers at General Electric years before. It did not matter so much *how* the goal was set. What mattered was *that* a goal was set. The study demonstrated that both assigned and participatively set goals led to substantial improvements in typing speed. The process by which these gains occurred, however, differed in the two groups.

In the participative group, employees insisted on setting very high goals regardless of whether they had attained their goal the previous week. Nevertheless, their productivity improved — an outcome consistent with the theory that high goals lead to high performance.

In the assigned-goal group, supervisors were highly supportive of employees. No criticism was given for failure to attain the goals. Instead, the supervisor lowered the goal after failure so that the employee would be certain to attain it. The goal was then raised gradually each week until the supervisor felt the employee was achieving his or her potential. The result? Feelings of accomplishment and achievement on the part of the worker and improved productivity for the company.

These basic findings were replicated in a subsequent study of engineers and scientists. Participative goal setting was superior to assigned goal setting only to the degree that it led to the setting of higher goals. Both participative and assigned-goal groups outperformed groups that were simply told to "do your best."

An additional experiment was conducted to validate the conclusion that participation in goal setting may be important only to the extent that it leads to the setting of difficult goals. It was performed in a laboratory setting in which the task was to brainstorm uses of wood. One group was asked to "do your best" to think of as many ideas as possible. A second group took part in deciding, with the experimenter, the specific number of ideas each person would generate. These goals were, in turn, assigned to individuals in a third group. In this way, goal difficulty was held constant between the assigned-goal and participative groups. Again, it was found that specific, difficult goals — whether assigned or set through participation — led to higher performance than did an abstract or generalized goal such as "do your best." And, when goal difficulty was held constant, there was no significant difference in the performance of those with assigned as compared with participatively set goals.

These results demonstrate that goal setting in industry works just as it does in the laboratory. Specific, challenging goals lead to better performance than do easy or vague goals, and feedback motivates higher performance only when it leads to the setting of higher goals.

It is important to note that participation is not only a motivational tool. When a manager has competent subordinates, participation is also a useful device for increasing the manager's knowledge and thereby improving decision quality. It can lead to better decisions through input from subordinates.

A representative sample of the results of field studies of goal setting conducted by Latham and others is shown in Figure 1. Each of these ten studies compared the performance of employees given specific challenging goals with those given "do best" or no goals. Note that goal setting has been successful across a wide variety of jobs and industries. The effects of goal setting have been recorded for as long as seven years after the

onset of the program, although the results of most studies have been followed up for only a few weeks or months. The median improvement in performance in the ten studies shown in Figure 1 was 17 percent.

A CRITICAL INCIDENTS SURVEY

To explore further the importance of goal setting in the work setting, Dr. Frank White conducted another study in two plants of a high-technology, multinational corporation on the East Coast. Seventy-one engineers, 50 managers, and 31 clerks were asked to describe a specific instance when they were especially productive and a specific instance when they were especially unproductive on their present jobs. Responses were classified according to a reliable coding scheme. Of primary interest here are the external events perceived by employees as being responsible for the high-productivity and low-productivity incidents. The results are shown in Figure 2.

The first set of events — pursuing a specific goal, having a large amount of work, working under a deadline, or having an uninterrupted routine — accounted for more than half the high-productivity events. Similarly, the converse of these — goal blockage, having a small amount of work, lacking a deadline, and suffering work interruptions — accounted for nearly 60

Figure 1. Representative Field Studies of Goal Setting

Researcher(s)	Task	Duration of Study or of Significant Effects	Percent of Change in Performance*
Blumenfeld and Leidy	Servicing soft drink coolers	Unspecified	+27
Dockstader	Keypunching	3 mos.	+27
Ivancevich	Skilled technical jobs	9 mos.	+15
Ivancevich	Sales	9 mos.	+24
Kim and Hamner	Five telephone service jobs	3 mos.	+13
Latham and Baldes	Loading trucks	9 mos.†	+26
Latham and Yukl	Logging	2 mos.	+18
Latham and Yukl	Typing	5 weeks	+11
Migliore	Mass production	2 years	+16
Umstot, Bell, and Mitchell	Coding land parcels	1–2 days‡	+16

   * Percentage changes were obtained by subtracting pre-goal-setting performance from post-goal-setting performance and dividing by pre-goal-setting performance. Different experimental groups were combined where appropriate. If a control group was available, the percentage figure represents the difference of the percentage changes between the experimental and control groups. If multiple performance measures were used, the median improvement on all measures was used. The authors would like to thank Dena Feren and Vicki McCaleb for performing these calculations.

   † Performance remained high for seven years.

   ‡ Simulated organization.

Figure 2. Events Perceived as Causing High and Low Productivity*

Event	Percent of Times Event Caused	
	High Productivity	Low Productivity
Goal pursuit/Goal blockage	17.1	23.0
Large amount of work/Small amount of work	12.5	19.0
Deadline or schedule/No deadline	15.1	3.3
Smooth work routine/Interrupted routine	5.9	14.5
Intrinsic/Extrinsic factors	50.6	59.8
Interesting task/Uninteresting task	17.1	11.2
Increased responsibility/Decreased responsibility	13.8	4.6
Anticipated promotion/Promotion denied	1.3	0.7
Verbal recognition/Criticism	4.6	2.6
People/Company conditions	36.8	19.1
Pleasant personal relationships/Unpleasant personal relationships	10.5	9.9
Anticipated pay increase/Pay increase denied	1.3	1.3
Pleasant working conditions/Unpleasant working conditions	0.7	0.7
Other (miscellaneous)	—	9.3

* *N* = 152 in this study by Frank White.

percent of the low-productivity events. Note that the first set of four categories are all relevant to goal setting and the second set to a lack of goals or goal blockage. The goal category itself — that of pursuing an attainable goal or goal blockage — was the one most frequently used to describe high- and low-productivity incidents.

The next four categories, which are more pertinent to Frederick Herzberg's motivator-hygiene theory — task interest, responsibility, promotion, and recognition — are less important, accounting for 36.8 percent of the high-productivity incidents (the opposite of these four categories accounted for 19.1 percent of the lows). The remaining categories were even less important.

Employees were also asked to identify the responsible agent behind the events that had led to high and low productivity. In both cases, the employees themselves, their immediate supervisors, and the organization were the agents most frequently mentioned.

The concept of goal setting is a very simple one. Interestingly, however, we have gotten two contradictory types of reaction when the idea was introduced to managers. Some claimed it was so simple and self-evident that everyone, including themselves, already used it. This, we have found, is not true. Time after time we have gotten the following response from subordinates after goal setting was introduced: "This is the first time I knew what my supervisor expected of me on this job." Conversely, other managers have argued that the

idea would not work, precisely *because* it is so simple (implying that something more radical and complex was needed). Again, results proved them wrong.

But these successes should not mislead managers into thinking that goal setting can be used without careful planning and forethought. Research and experience suggest that the best results are obtained when the following steps are followed:

Setting the Goal.   The goal set should have two main characteristics. First, it should be specific rather than vague: "Increase sales by 10 percent" rather than "Try to improve sales." Whenever possible, there should be a time limit for goal accomplishment: "Cut costs by 3 percent in the next six months."

Second, the goal should be challenging yet reachable. If accepted, difficult goals lead to better performance than do easy goals. In contrast, if the goals are perceived as unreachable, employees will not accept them. Nor will employees get a sense of achievement from pursuing goals that are never attained. Employees with low self-confidence or ability should be given more easily attainable goals than those with high self-confidence and ability.

There are at least five possible sources of input, aside from the individual's self-confidence and ability, that can be used to determine the particular goal to set for a given individual.

The scientific management approach pioneered by Frederick W. Taylor uses time and motion study to determine a fair day's work. This is probably the most objective technique available, but it can be used only where the task is reasonably repetitive and standardized. Another drawback is that this method often leads to employee resistance, especially in cases where the new standard is substantially higher than previous performance and where rate changes are made frequently.

More readily accepted, although less scientific than time and motion study, are standards based on the average past performance of employees. This method was used successfully in some of our field studies. Most employees consider this approach fair but, naturally, in cases where past performance is far below capacity, beating that standard will be extremely easy.

Since goal setting is sometimes simply a matter of judgment, another technique we have used is to allow the goal to be set jointly by supervisor and subordinate. The participative approach may be less scientific than time and motion study, but it does lead to ready acceptance by both employee and immediate superior in addition to promoting role clarity.

External constraints often affect goal setting, especially among managers. For example, the goal to produce an item at a certain price may be dictated by the actions of competitors, and deadlines may be imposed externally in line with contract agreements. Legal regulations, such as attaining a certain reduction in pollution levels by a certain date, may affect goal setting as well. In these cases, setting the goal is not so much the problem as is figuring out a method of reaching it.

Finally, organizational goals set by the board of directors or upper management will influence the goals set by employees at lower levels. This is the essence of the MBO process.

Another issue that needs to be considered when setting goals is whether they should be designed for individuals or for groups. Rensis Likert and a number of other human relations experts argue for group goal setting on grounds that it promotes cooperation and team spirit. But one could argue that individual goals better promote individual responsibility and make it easier to appraise individual performance. The degree of task interdependence involved would also be a factor to consider.

Obtaining Goal Commitment.   If goal setting is to work, then the manager must ensure that subordinates will accept and remain committed to the goals. Simple instruction backed by positive support and an absence of threats or intimidation were enough to ensure goal acceptance in most of our studies. Subordinates must perceive the goals as fair and reasonable and they must trust management, for if they perceive the goals as no more than a means of exploitation, they will be likely to reject the goals.

It may seem surprising that goal acceptance was achieved so readily in the field studies. Remember, however, that in all cases the employees were receiving wages or a salary (although these were not necessarily directly contingent on goal attainment). Pay in combination with the supervisor's benevolent authority and supportiveness were sufficient to bring about goal acceptance. Recent research indicates that whether goals are assigned or set participatively, supportiveness on the part of the immediate superior is critical. A supportive manager or supervisor does not use goals to threaten subordinates, but rather to clarify what is expected of them. His or her role is that of a helper and goal facilitator.

As noted earlier, the employee gets a feeling of pride and satisfaction from the experience of reaching a challenging but fair performance goal. Success in reaching a goal also tends to reinforce acceptance of future goals. Once goal setting is introduced, informal competition frequently arises among the employees. This further reinforces commitment and may lead employees to raise the goals spontaneously. A word of caution here, however: We do not recommend setting up formal competition, as this may lead employees to place individual goals ahead of company goals. The emphasis should be on accomplishing the task, getting the job done, not "beating" the other person.

When employees resist assigned goals, they generally do so for one of two reasons. First, they may think they are incapable of reaching the goal because they lack confidence, ability, knowledge, and the like. Second, they may not see any personal benefit — either in terms of personal pride or in terms of external rewards like money, promotion, recognition — in reaching assigned goals.

There are various methods of overcoming employee resistance to goals. One possibility is more training designed to raise the employee's level of skill and self-confidence. Allowing the subordinate to participate in setting the goal — deciding on the goal level — is another method. This was found most effective among uneducated and minority group employees, perhaps because it gave them a feeling of control over their fate.

Offering monetary bonuses or other rewards (recognition, time off) for reaching goals may also help.

The last two methods may be especially useful where there is a history of labor-management conflict and where employees have become accustomed to a lower level of effort than currently considered acceptable. Group incentives may also encourage goal acceptance, especially where there is a group goal, or when considerable cooperation is required.

Providing Support Elements.   A third step to take when introducing goal setting is to ensure the availability of necessary support elements. That is, the employee must be given adequate resources — money, equipment, time, help — as well as the freedom to utilize them in attaining goals, and company policies must not work to block goal attainment.

Before turning an employee loose with these resources, however, it's wise to do a quick check on whether conditions are optimum for reaching the goal set. First, the supervisor must make sure that the employee has sufficient ability and knowledge to be able to reach the goal. Motivation without knowledge is useless. This, of course, puts a premium on proper selection and training and requires that the supervisor know the capabilities of subordinates when goals are assigned. Asking an employee to formulate an action plan for reaching the goal, as in MBO, is very useful, as it will indicate any knowledge deficiencies.

Second, the supervisor must ensure that the employee is provided with precise feedback so that he will know to what degree he's reaching or falling short of his goal and can thereupon adjust his level of effort or strategy accordingly. Recent research indicates that, while feedback is not a sufficient condition for improved performance, it is a necessary condition. A useful way to present periodic feedback is through the use of charts or graphs that plot performance over time.

Elements involved in taking the three steps described are shown in Figure 3, which illustrates in outline form our model of goal setting.

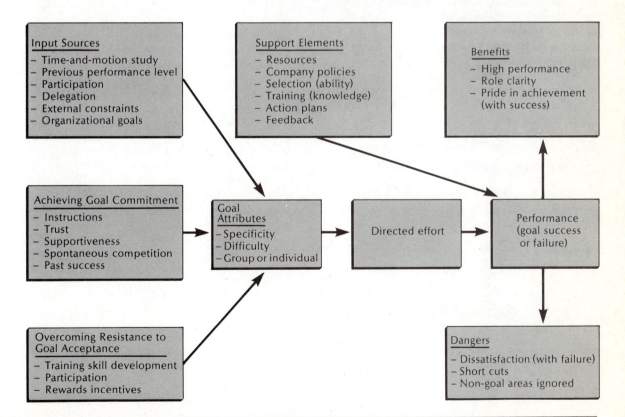

Figure 3.   Goal-Setting Model.

CONCLUSION

We believe that goal setting is a simple, straightforward, and highly effective technique for motivating employee performance. It is a basic technique, a method on which most other methods depend for their motivational effectiveness. The currently popular technique of behavior modification, for example, is mainly goal setting plus feedback, dressed up in academic terminology.

However, goal setting is no panacea. It will not compensate for underpayment of employees or for poor management. Used incorrectly, goal setting may cause rather than solve problems. If, for example, the goals set are unfair, arbitrary, or unreachable, dissatisfaction and poor performance may result. If difficult goals are set without proper quality controls, quantity may be achieved at the expense of quality. If pressure for immediate results is exerted without regard to how they are attained, short-term improvement may occur at the expense of long-run profits. That is, such pressure often triggers the use of expedient and ultimately costly methods — such as dishonesty, high-pressure tactics, postponing of maintenance expenses, and so on — to attain immediate results. Furthermore, performance goals are more easily set in some areas than in others. It's all too easy, for example, to concentrate on setting readily measured production goals and ignore employee development goals. Like any other management tool, goal setting works only when combined with good managerial judgment.

SELECTED BIBLIOGRAPHY

A summary of the early (mainly laboratory) research on goal setting may be found in E. A. Locke's "Toward a Theory of Task Motivation and Incentives" (*Organization Behavior and Human Performance,* May 1968). More recent reviews that include some of the early field studies are reported by G. P. Latham and G. A. Yukl's "Review of Research on the Application of Goal Setting in Organizations" (*Academy of Management Journal,* December 1975) and in R. M. Steers and L. W. Porter's "The Role of Task–Goal Attributes in Employee Performance" (*Psychological Bulletin,* July 1974).

An excellent historical discussion of management by objectives, including its relationship to goal-setting research, can be found in G. S. Odiorne's "MBO: A Backward Glance" (*Business Horizons,* October 1978).

A thorough review of the literature on participation, including the relationship of participation and goal setting, can be found in a chapter by E. A. Locke and D. M. Schweiger, "Participation in Decision-Making: One More Look," in B. M. Staw's edited work, *Research in Organizational Behavior* (Vol. 1, Greenwich, JAI Press, 1979). General Electric's famous research on the effect of participation in the appraisal interview is summarized in H. H. Meyer, E. Kay, and J. R. P. French, Jr.'s "Split Roles in Performance Appraisal" (*Harvard Business Review,* January–February 1965).

The relationship of goal setting to knowledge of results is discussed in E. A. Locke, N. Cartledge, and J. Koeppel's "Motivational Effects of Knowledge of Results: A Goal Setting Phenomenon?" (*Psychological Bulletin,* December 1968) and L. J. Becker's "Joint Effect of Feedback and Goal Setting on Performance: A Field Study of Residential Energy Conservation" (*Journal of Applied Psychology,* August 1978). Finally, the role of goal setting in virtually all theories of work motivation is documented in E. A. Locke's "The Ubiquity of the Technique of Goal Setting in Theories of and Approaches to Employee Motivation" (*Academy of Management Review,* July 1978).

6. On the Folly of Rewarding A, While Hoping for B

Steven Kerr

Whether dealing with monkeys, rats, or human beings, it is hardly controversial to state that most organisms seek information concerning what activities are rewarded and then seek to do (or at least pretend to do) those things, often to the virtual exclusion of activities not rewarded. The extent to which this occurs of course will depend on the perceived attractiveness of the rewards offered, but neither operant nor expectancy theorists would quarrel with the essence of this notion.

Nevertheless, numerous examples exist of reward systems that are fouled up in that behaviors which are rewarded are those which the rewarder is trying to *discourage,* while the behavior he desires is not being rewarded at all.

In an effort to understand and explain this phenomenon, this paper presents examples from society, from organizations in general, and from profit-making firms in particular. Data from a manufacturing company and information from an insurance firm are examined to demonstrate the consequences of such reward systems for the organizations involved, and possible reasons why such reward systems continue to exist are considered.

SOCIETAL EXAMPLES

Politics

Official goals are "purposely vague and general and do not indicate . . . the host of decisions that must be made among alternative ways of achieving official goals and the priority of multiple goals . . ." (8, p. 66). They usually may be relied on to offend absolutely no one, and in this sense can be considered high acceptance, low quality goals. An example might be "build better schools."

Operative goals are higher in quality but lower in acceptance, since they specify where the money will come from, what alternative goals will be ignored, etc.

The American citizenry supposedly wants its candidates for public office to set forth operative goals, making their proposed programs "perfectly clear," specifying sources and uses of funds, etc. However, since operative goals are lower in acceptance, and since aspirants to public office need acceptance (from at least 50.1 percent of the people), most politicians prefer to speak only of official goals, at least until after the election. They of course would agree to speak at the operative level if "punished" for not doing so. The electorate could do this by refusing to support candidates who do not speak at the operative level.

Instead, however, the American voter typically punishes (withholds support from) candidates who frankly discuss where the money will come from, rewards politicians who speak only of official goals, but hopes that candidates (despite the reward system) will discuss the issues operatively. It is academic whether it was moral for Nixon, for example, to refuse to discuss his 1968 "secret plan" to end the Vietnam war, his 1972 operative goals concerning the lifting of price controls, the reshuffling of his cabinet, etc. The point is that the reward system made such refusal rational.

It seems worth mentioning that no manuscript can adequately define what is "moral" and what is not. However, examination of costs and benefits, combined with knowledge of what motivates a particular individual, often will suffice to determine what for him is "rational."[1] If the reward system is so designed that it is irrational to be moral, this does not necessarily mean that immorality will result. But is this not asking for trouble?

"On the Folly of Rewarding A, While Hoping for B" by Steven Kerr from *Academy of Management Journal,* 1975, 18, no. 4:769–83. Reprinted with permission.

1. In Simon's (10, pp. 76–77) terms, a decision is "subjectively rational" if it maximizes an individual's valued outcomes so far as his knowledge permits. A decision is "personally rational" if it is oriented toward the individual's goals.

War

If some oversimplification may be permitted, let it be assumed that the primary goal of the organization (Pentagon, Luftwaffe, or whatever) is to win. Let it be assumed further that the primary goal of most individuals on the front lines is to get home alive. Then there appears to be an important conflict in goals — personally rational behavior by those at the bottom will endanger goal attainment by those at the top.

But not necessarily! It depends on how the reward system is set up. The Vietnam war was indeed a study of disobedience and rebellion, with terms such as "fragging" (killing one's own commanding officer) and "search and evade" becoming part of the military vocabulary. The difference in subordinates' acceptance of authority between World War II and Vietnam is reported to be considerable, and veterans of the Second World War often have been quoted as being outraged at the mutinous actions of many American soldiers in Vietnam.

Consider, however, some critical differences in the reward system in use during the two conflicts. What did the GI in World War II want? To go home. And when did he get to go home? When the war was won! If he disobeyed the orders to clean out the trenches and take the hills, the war would not be won and he would not go home. Furthermore, what were his chances of attaining his goal (getting home alive) if he obeyed the orders compared to his chances if he did not? What is being suggested is that the rational soldier in World War II, *whether patriotic or not,* probably found it expedient to obey.

Consider the reward system in use in Vietnam. What did the man at the bottom want? To go home. And when did he get to go home? When his tour of duty was over! This was the case *whether or not* the war was won. Furthermore, concerning the relative chance of getting home alive by obeying orders compared to the chance if they were disobeyed, it is worth noting that a mutineer in Vietnam was far more likely to be assigned rest and rehabilitation (on the assumption that fatigue was the cause) than he was to suffer any negative consequence.

In his description of the "zone of indifference," Barnard stated that "a person can and will accept a communication as authoritative only when ... at the time of his decision, he believes it to be compatible with his personal interests as a whole" (1, p. 165). In light of the reward system used in Vietnam, would it not have been personally irrational for some orders to have been obeyed? Was not the military implementing a system which *rewarded* disobedience, while *hoping* that soldiers (despite the reward system) would obey orders?

Medicine

Theoretically, a physician can make either of two types of error, and intuitively one seems as bad as the other. A doctor can pronounce a patient sick when he is actually well, thus causing him needless anxiety and expense, curtailment of enjoyable foods and activities, and even physical danger by subjecting him to needless medication and surgery. Alternately, a doctor can label a sick person well and thus avoid treating what may be a serious, even fatal ailment. It might be natural to conclude that physicians seek to minimize both types of error.

Such a conclusion would be wrong.[2] It is estimated that numerous Americans are presently afflicted with iatrogenic (physician *caused*) illnesses (9). This occurs when the doctor is approached by someone complaining of a few stray symptoms. The doctor classifies and organizes these symptoms, gives them a name, and obligingly tells the patient what further symptoms may be expected. This information often acts as a self-fulfilling prophecy, with the result that from that day on the patient for all practical purposes is sick.

Why does this happen? Why are physicians so reluctant to sustain a type 2 error (pronouncing a sick person well) that they will tolerate many type 1 errors? Again, a look at the reward system is needed. The punishments for a type 2 error are real: guilt, embarrassment, and the threat of lawsuit and scandal. On the other hand, a type 1 error (labeling a well person sick) "is sometimes seen as sound clinical practice, indicating a healthy conservative approach to medicine" (9, p. 69). Type 1 errors also are likely to generate increased income and a stream of steady customers who, being well in a limited physiological sense, will not embarrass the doctor by dying abruptly.

Fellow physicians and the general public therefore are really *rewarding* type 1 errors and at the same time *hoping* fervently that doctors will try not to make them.

---

2. In one study (4) of 14,867 films for signs of tuberculosis, 1,216 positive readings turned out to be clinically negative; only 24 negative readings proved clinically active, a ratio of 50 to 1.

GENERAL ORGANIZATIONAL EXAMPLES

Rehabilitation Centers and Orphanages

In terms of the prime beneficiary classification (2, p. 42) organizations such as these are supposed to exist for the ''public-in-contact,'' that is, clients. The orphanage therefore theoretically is interested in placing as many children as possible in good homes. However, often orphanages surround themselves with so many rules concerning adoption that it is nearly impossible to pry a child out of the place. Orphanages may deny adoption unless the applicants are a married couple, both of the same religion as the child, without history of emotional or vocational instability, with a specified minimum income and a private room for the child, etc.

If the primary goal is to place children in good homes, then the rules ought to constitute means toward that goal. Goal displacement results when these ''means become ends-in-themselves that displace the original goals'' (2, p. 229).

To some extent these rules are required by law. But the influence of the reward system on the orphanage's management should not be ignored. Consider, for example, that the:

1. Number of children enrolled often is the most important determinant of the size of the allocated budget.
2. Number of children under the director's care also will affect the size of his staff.
3. Total organizational size will determine largely the director's prestige at the annual conventions, in the community, etc.

Therefore, to the extent that staff size, total budget, and personal prestige are valued by the orphanage's executive personnel, it becomes rational for them to make it difficult for children to be adopted. After all, who wants to be the director of the smallest orphanage in the state?

If the reward system errs in the opposite direction, paying off only for placements, extensive goal displacement again is likely to result. A common example of vocational rehabilitation in many states, for example, consists of placing someone in a job for which he has little interest and few qualifications, for two months or so, and then ''rehabilitating'' him again in another

position. Such behavior is quite consistent with the prevailing reward system, which pays off for the number of individuals placed in any position for 60 days or more. Rehabilitation counselors also confess to competing with one another to place relatively skilled clients, sometimes ignoring persons with few skills who would be harder to place. Extensively disabled clients find that counselors often prefer to work with those whose disabilities are less severe.[3]

Universities

Society *hopes* that teachers will not neglect their teaching responsibilities but *rewards* them almost entirely for research and publications. This is most true at the large and prestigious universities. Clichés such as ''good research and good teaching go together'' notwithstanding, professors often find that they must choose between teaching and research oriented activities when allocating their time. Rewards for good teaching usually are limited to outstanding teacher awards, which are given to only a small percentage of good teachers and which usually bestow little money and fleeting prestige. Punishments for poor teaching also are rare.

Rewards for research and publications, on the other hand, and punishments for failure to accomplish these, are commonly administered by universities at which teachers are employed. Furthermore, publication oriented resumés usually will be well received at other universities, whereas teaching credentials, harder to document and quantify, are much less transferable. Consequently, it is rational for university teachers to concentrate on research, even if to the detriment of teaching and at the expense of their students.

By the same token, it is rational for students to act based upon the goal displacement which has occurred within universities concerning what they are rewarded for. If it is assumed that a primary goal of a university is to transfer knowledge from teacher to student, then grades become identifiable as a means toward that goal, serving as motivational, control, and feedback devices to expedite the knowledge transfer. Instead, however, the grades themselves have become much more important for entrance to graduate school, successful employment, tuition refunds, parental respect, etc., than the knowledge or lack of knowledge they are supposed to signify.

---

3. Personal interviews conducted during 1972–1973.

It therefore should come as no surprise that information has surfaced in recent years concerning fraternity files for examinations, term paper writing services, organized cheating at the service academies, and the like. Such activities constitute a personally rational response to a reward system which pays off for grades rather than knowledge.

BUSINESS RELATED EXAMPLES

Ecology

Assume that the president of XYZ Corporation is confronted with the following alternatives:

1. Spend $11 million for antipollution equipment to keep from poisoning fish in the river adjacent to the plant; or
2. Do nothing, in violation of the law, and assume a one-in-ten chance of being caught, with a resultant $1 million fine plus the necessity of buying the equipment.

Under this not unrealistic set of choices it requires no linear program to determine that XYZ Corporation can maximize its probabilities by flouting the law. Add the fact that XYZ's president is probably being rewarded (by creditors, stockholders, and other salient parts of his task environment) according to criteria totally unrelated to the number of fish poisoned, and his probable course of action becomes clear.

Evaluation of Training

It is axiomatic that those who care about a firm's well-being should insist that the organization get fair value for its expenditures. Yet it is commonly known that firms seldom bother to evaluate a new GRID, MBO, job enrichment program, or whatever, to see if the company is getting its money's worth. Why? Certainly it is not because people have not pointed out that this situation exists; numerous practitioner oriented articles are written each year to just this point.

The individuals (whether in personnel, manpower planning, or wherever) who normally would be responsible for conducting such evaluations are the same ones often charged with introducing the change effort in the first place. Having convinced top management to spend the money, they usually are quite

animated afterwards in collecting arigorous vignettes and anecdotes about how successful the program was. The last thing many desire is a formal, systematic, and revealing evaluation. Although members of top management may actually *hope* for such systematic evaluation, their reward systems continue to *reward* ignorance in this area. And if the personnel department abdicates its responsibility, who is to step into the breach? The change agent himself? Hardly! He is likely to be too busy collecting anecdotal "evidence" of his own, for use with his next client.

Miscellaneous

Many additional examples could be cited of systems which in fact are rewarding behaviors other than those supposedly desired by the rewarder. A few of these are described briefly below.

Most coaches disdain to discuss individual accomplishments, preferring to speak of teamwork, proper attitude, and a one-for-all spirit. Usually, however, rewards are distributed according to individual performance. The college basketball player who feeds his teammates instead of shooting will not compile impressive scoring statistics and is less likely to be drafted by the pros. The ballplayer who hits to right field to advance the runners will win neither the batting nor home run titles and will be offered smaller raises. It therefore is rational for players to think of themselves first and the team second.

In business organizations where rewards are dispensed for unit performance or for individual goals achieved without regard for overall effectiveness, similar attitudes often are observed. Under most Management by Objectives (MBO) systems, goals in areas where quantification is difficult often go unspecified. The organization therefore often is in a position where it *hopes* for employee effort in the areas of team building, interpersonal relations, creativity, etc., but it formally *rewards* none of these. In cases where promotions and raises are formally tied to MBO, the system itself contains a paradox in that it "asks employees to set challenging, risky goals, only to face smaller paychecks and possibly damaged careers if these goals are not accomplished" (5, p. 40).

It is *hoped* that administrators will pay attention to long-run costs and opportunities and will institute programs which will bear fruit later on. However, many organizational reward systems pay off for short-run sales and earnings only. Under such circumstances it is personally rational for officials to sacrifice long-term growth and profit (by selling off equipment and property, or by stifling research and development) for short-term advantages. This probably is most pertinent in the public sector, with the result that many public officials are unwilling to implement programs which will not show benefits by election time.

As a final, clear-cut example of a fouled-up reward system, consider the cost-plus contract or its next of kin, the allocation of next year's budget as a direct function of this year's expenditures. It probably is conceivable that those who award such budgets and contracts really hope for economy and prudence in spending. It is obvious, however, that adopting the proverb "to him who spends shall more be given," rewards not economy, but spending itself.

TWO COMPANIES' EXPERIENCES

A Manufacturing Organization

A midwest manufacturer of industrial goods had been troubled for some time by aspects of its organizational climate it believed dysfunctional. For research purposes, interviews were conducted with many employees, and a questionnaire was administered on a companywide basis, including plants and offices in several American and Canadian locations. The company strongly encouraged employee participation in the survey and made available time and space during the workday for completion of the instrument. All employees in attendance during the day of the survey completed the questionnaire. All instruments were collected directly by the researcher, who personally administered each session. Since no one employed by the firm handled the questionnaires, and since respondent names were not asked for, it seems likely that the pledge of anonymity given was believed.

A modified version of the Expect Approval scale (7) was included as part of the questionnaire. The instrument asked respondents to indicate the degree of approval or disapproval they could expect if they performed each of the described actions. A seven point Likert scale was used, with one indicating that the action would probably bring strong disapproval and seven signifying likely strong approval.

Although normative data for this scale from studies of other organizations are unavailable, it is possible to examine fruitfully the data obtained from this survey in

several ways. First, it may be worth noting that the questionnaire data corresponded closely to information gathered through interviews. Furthermore, as can be seen from the results summarized in Table 1, sizable differences between various work units, and between employees at different job levels within the same work unit, were obtained. This suggests that response bias effects (social desirability in particular loomed as a potential concern) are not likely to be severe.

Most importantly, comparisons between scores obtained on the Expect Approval scale and a statement of problems which were the reason for the survey revealed that the same behaviors which managers in each division thought dysfunctional were those which lower-level employees claimed were rewarded. As compared to job levels 1 to 8 in Division B (see Table 1), those in Division A claimed a much higher acceptance by management of "conforming" activities. Between 31 and 37 percent of Division A employees at levels 1–8 stated that going along with the majority, agreeing with the boss, and staying on everyone's good side brought approval; only once (level 5–8 responses to one of the three items) did a majority suggest that such actions would generate disapproval.

Furthermore, responses from Division A workers at levels 1–4 indicate that behaviors geared toward risk avoidance were as likely to be rewarded as to be punished. Only at job levels 9 and above was it apparent that the reward system was positively reinforcing behaviors desired by top management. Overall, the same "tendencies toward conservatism and apple-polishing at the lower levels" which divisional management had complained about during the interviews were those claimed by subordinates to be the most rational course of action in light of the existing reward system. Management apparently was not getting the behaviors it was *hoping* for, but it certainly was getting the behaviors it was perceived by subordinates to be *rewarding*.

An Insurance Firm

The Group Health Claims Division of a large eastern insurance company provides another rich illustration of a reward system which reinforces behaviors not desired by top management.

Attempting to measure and reward accuracy in paying surgical claims, the firm systematically keeps track of the number of returned checks and letters of complaint received from policyholders. However,

Table 1. Summary of Two Divisions' Data Relevant to Conforming and Risk-Avoidance Behaviors (extent to which subjects expect approval)

Dimension	Item	Division and Sample	Total Responses	Percentage of Workers Responding		
				1, 2, or 3 Disapproval	4	5, 6, or 7 Approval
Risk avoidance	Making a risky decision based on the best information available at the time, but which turns out wrong	A, levels 1–4 (lowest)	127	61	25	14
		A, levels 5–8	172	46	31	23
		A, levels 9 and above	17	41	30	30
		B, levels 1–4 (lowest)	31	58	26	16
		B, levels 5–8	19	42	42	16
		B, levels 9 and above	10	50	20	30
	Setting extremely high and challenging standards and goals and then narrowly failing to make them	A, levels 1–4	122	47	28	25
		A, levels 5–8	168	33	26	41
		A, levels 9+	17	24	6	70
		B, levels 1–4	31	48	23	29
		B, levels 5–8	18	17	33	50
		B, levels 9+	10	30	0	70
	Setting goals which are extremely easy to make and then making them	A, levels 1–4	124	35	30	35
		A, levels 5–8	171	47	27	26
		A, levels 9+	17	70	24	6
		B, levels 1–4	31	58	26	16
		B, levels 5–8	19	63	16	21
		B, levels 9+	10	80	0	20
Conformity	Being a "yes man" and always agreeing with the boss	A, levels 1–4	126	46	17	37
		A, levels 5–8	180	54	14	31
		A, levels 9+	17	88	12	0
		B, levels 1–4	32	53	28	19
		B, levels 5–8	19	68	21	11
		B, levels 9+	10	80	10	10
	Always going along with the majority	A, levels 1–4	125	40	25	35
		A, levels 5–8	173	47	21	32
		A, levels 9+	17	70	12	18
		B, levels 1–4	31	61	23	16
		B, levels 5–8	19	68	11	21
		B, levels 9+	10	80	10	10
	Being careful to stay on the good side of everyone, so that everyone agrees that you are a great guy	A, levels 1–4	124	45	18	37
		A, levels 5–8	173	45	22	33
		A, levels 9+	17	64	6	30
		B, levels 1–4	31	54	23	23
		B, levels 5–8	19	73	11	16
		B, levels 9+	10	80	10	10

underpayments are likely to provoke cries of outrage from the insured, while overpayments often are accepted in courteous silence. Since it often is impossi- ble to tell from the physician's statement which of two surgical procedures, with different allowable benefits, was performed, and since writing for clarifications will interfere with other standards used by the firm concerning "percentage of claims paid within two days of receipt," the new hire in more than one claims section is soon acquainted with the informal norm: "When in doubt, pay it out!"

The situation would be even worse were it not for the fact that other features of the firm's reward system tend to neutralize those described. For example, annual "merit" increases are given to all employees, in one of the following three amounts:

1. If the worker is "outstanding" (a select category, into which no more than two employees per section may be placed): 5 percent.
2. If the worker is "above average" (normally all workers not "outstanding" are so rated): 4 percent.
3. If the worker commits gross acts of negligence and irresponsibility for which he might be discharged in many other companies: 3 percent.

Now, since (a) the difference between the 5 percent theoretically attainable through hard work and the 4 percent attainable merely by living until the review date is small and (b) since insurance firms seldom dispense much of a salary increase in cash (rather, the worker's insurance benefits increase, causing him to be further overinsured), many employees are rather indifferent to the possibility of obtaining the extra one percent reward and therefore tend to ignore the norm concerning indiscriminant payments.

However, most employees are not indifferent to the rule which states that, should absences or latenesses total three or more in any six-month period, the entire 4 or 5 percent due at the next "merit" review must be forfeited. In this sense the firm may be described as *hoping* for performance, while *rewarding* attendance. What it gets, of course, is attendance. (If the absence-lateness rule appears to the reader to be stringent, it really is not. The company counts "times" rather than "days" absent, and a ten-day absence therefore counts the same as one lasting two days. A worker in danger of accumulating a third absence within six months merely has to remain ill (away from work) during his second absence until his first absence is more than six months old. The limiting factor is that at some point his salary ceases, and his sickness benefits take over. This usually is sufficient to get the younger workers to return, but for those with 20 or more years' service, the company provides sickness benefits of 90 percent of normal salary, tax-free! Therefore . . .)

CAUSES

Extremely diverse instances of systems which reward behavior A although the rewarder apparently hopes for behavior B have been given. These are useful to illustrate the breadth and magnitude of the phenomenon, but the diversity increases the difficulty of determining commonalities and establishing causes. However, four general factors may be pertinent to an explanation of why fouled up reward systems seem to be so prevalent.

Fascination with an "Objective" Criterion

It has been mentioned elsewhere that:

Most "objective" measures of productivity are objective only in that their subjective elements are (a) determined in advance, rather than coming into play at the time of the formal evaluation, and (b) well concealed on the rating instrument itself. Thus industrial firms seeking to devise objective rating systems first decide, in an arbitrary manner, what dimensions are to be rated, . . . usually including some items having little to do with organizational effectiveness while excluding others that do. Only then does Personnel Division churn out official-looking documents on which all dimensions chosen to be rated are assigned point values, categories, or whatever (6, p. 92).

Nonetheless, many individuals seek to establish simple, quantifiable standards against which to measure and reward performance. Such efforts may be successful in highly predictable areas within an organization but are likely to cause goal displacement when applied anywhere else. Overconcern with attendance and lateness in the insurance firm and with the number of people placed in the vocational rehabilitation division may have been largely responsible for the problems described in those organizations.

Overemphasis on Highly Visible Behaviors

Difficulties often stem from the fact that some parts of the task are highly visible while other parts are not. For example, publications are easier to demonstrate than teaching, and scoring baskets and hitting home runs are more readily observable than feeding teammates and advancing base runners. Similarly, the adverse consequences of pronouncing a sick person well are more visible than those sustained by labeling a well person sick. Team-building and creativity are other examples of behaviors which may not be rewarded simply because they are hard to observe.

Hypocrisy

In some of the instances described the rewarder may have been getting the desired behavior, notwithstanding claims that the behavior was not desired. This may be true, for example, of management's attitude toward apple-polishing in the manufacturing firm (a behavior which subordinates felt was rewarded, despite management's avowed dislike of the practice). This also may explain politicians' unwillingness to revise the penalties for disobedience of ecology laws, and the failure of top management to devise reward systems which would cause systematic evaluation of training and development programs.

Emphasis on Morality or Equity Rather than Efficiency

Sometimes consideration of other factors prevents the establishment of a system which rewards behaviors desired by the rewarder. The felt obligation of many Americans to vote for one candidate or another, for example, may impair their ability to withhold support from politicians who refuse to discuss the issues. Similarly, the concern for spreading the risks and costs of wartime military service may outweigh the advantage to be obtained by committing personnel to combat until the war is over.

It should be noted that only with respect to the first two causes are reward systems really paying off for other than desired behaviors. In the case of the third and fourth causes the system *is* rewarding behaviors desired by the rewarder, and the systems are fouled up only from the standpoints of those who believe the rewarder's public statements (cause 3), or those who seek to maximize efficiency rather than other outcomes (cause 4).

CONCLUSIONS

Modern organization theory requires a recognition that the members of organizations and society possess divergent goals and motives. It therefore is unlikely that managers and their subordinates will seek the same outcomes. Three possible remedies for this potential problem are suggested.

Selection

It is theoretically possible for organizations to employ only those individuals whose goals and motives are wholly consonant with those of management. In such cases the same behaviors judged by subordinates to be rational would be perceived by management as desirable. State-of-the-art reviews of selection techniques, however, provide scant grounds for hope that such an approach would be successful (for example, see 12).

Training

Another theoretical alternative is for the organization to admit those employees whose goals are not consonant with those of management and then, through training, socialization, or whatever, alter employee goals to make them consonant. However, research on the effectiveness of such training programs, though limited, provides further grounds for pessimism (for example, see 3).

Altering the Reward System

What would have been the result if:

1. Nixon had been assured by his advisors that he could not win reelection except by discussing the issues in detail?
2. Physicians' conduct was subjected to regular examination by review boards for type 1 errors (calling healthy people ill) and to penalties (fines, censure, etc.) for errors of either type?
3. The President of XYZ Corporation had to choose between (a) spending $11 million dollars for antipollution equipment, and (b) incurring a 50–50 chance of going to jail for five years?

Managers who complain that their workers are not motivated might do well to consider the possibility that they have installed reward systems which are paying off for behaviors other than those they are seeking. This, in part, is what happened in Vietnam, and this is what regularly frustrates societal efforts to bring about honest politicians, civic-minded managers, etc. This certainly is what happened in both the manufacturing and the insurance companies.

A first step for such managers might be to find out what behaviors currently are being rewarded. Perhaps an instrument similar to that used in the manufacturing firm could be useful for this purpose. Chances are excellent that these managers will be surprised by what they find — that their firms are not rewarding what they assume they are. In fact, such undesirable behavior by organizational members as they have observed may be explained largely by the reward systems in use.

This is not to say that all organizational behavior is determined by formal rewards and punishments. Certainly it is true that in the absence of formal reinforcement some soldiers will be patriotic, some presidents will be ecology minded, and some orphanage directors will care about children. The point, however, is that in such cases the rewarder is not *causing* the behaviors desired but is only a fortunate bystander. For an organization to *act* upon its members, the formal reward system should positively reinforce desired behaviors, not constitute an obstacle to be overcome.

It might be wise to underscore the obvious fact that there is nothing really new in what has been said. In both theory and practice these matters have been mentioned before. Thus in many states Good Samaritan laws have been installed to protect doctors who stop to assist a stricken motorist. In states without such laws it is commonplace for doctors to refuse to stop, for fear of involvement in a subsequent lawsuit. In college basketball additional penalties have been instituted against players who foul their opponents deliberately. It has long been argued by Milton Friedman and others that penalties should be altered so as to make it irrational to disobey the ecology laws, and so on.

By altering the reward system the organization escapes the necessity of selecting only desirable people or of trying to alter undesirable ones. In Skinnerian terms (as described in 11, p. 704), "As for responsibility and goodness — as commonly defined — no one . . . would want or need them. They refer to a man's behaving well despite the absence of positive reinforcement that is obviously sufficient to explain it. Where such reinforcement exists, 'no one needs goodness.' "

REFERENCE NOTES

1. Barnard, Chester I. *The functions of the executive.* Cambridge, Mass.: Harvard University Press, 1964.

2. Blau, Peter M., and Scott, W. Richard. *Formal organizations.* San Francisco: Chandler, 1962.

3. Fiedler, Fred E. Predicting the effects of leadership training and experience from the contingency model, *Journal of Applied Psychology,* 1972, 56:114-19.

4. Garland, L. H. Studies of the accuracy of diagnostic procedures, *American Journal Roentgenological, Radium Therapy Nuclear Medicine,* 1959, 82:25-38.

5. Kerr, Steven. Some modifications in MBO as an OD strategy, *Academy of Management Proceedings,* 1973:39-42.

6. Kerr, Steven. What price objectivity? *American Sociologist,* 1973, 8:92-93.

7. Litwin, G. H., and Stringer, R. A., Jr. *Motivation and organizational climate.* Boston: Harvard University Press, 1968.

8. Perrow, Charles. The analysis of goals in complex organizations, in A. Etzioni (ed.), *Readings on modern organizations.* Englewood Cliffs, N.J.: Prentice-Hall, 1969.

9. Scheff, Thomas J. Decision rules, types of error, and their consequences in medical diagnosis, in F. Massarik and P. Ratoosh (eds.), *Mathematical explorations in behavioral science.* Homewood, Ill.: Richard D. Irwin, Inc., 1965.

10. Simon, Herbert A. *Administrative behavior.* New York: Free Press, 1957.

11. Swanson, G. E. Review symposium: Beyond freedom and dignity, *American Journal of Sociology,* 1972, 78:702-705.

12. Webster, E. *Decision making in the employment interview.* Montreal: Industrial Relations Center, McGill University, 1964.

7.   A New Strategy for Job Enrichment

J. Richard Hackman, Greg Oldham, Robert Janson, and Kenneth Purdy

Practitioners of job enrichment have been living through a time of excitement, even euphoria. Their craft has moved from the psychology and management journals to the front page and the Sunday supplement. Job enrichment, which began with the pioneering work of Herzberg and his associates, originally was intended as a means to increase the motivation and satisfaction of people at work — and to improve productivity in the bargain.[1-5] Now it is being acclaimed in the popular press as a cure for problems ranging from inflation to drug abuse.

Much current writing about job enrichment is enthusiastic, sometimes even messianic, about what it can accomplish. But the hard questions of exactly what should be done to improve jobs, and how, tend to be glossed over. Lately, because the harder questions have not been dealt with adequately, critical winds have begun to blow. Job enrichment has been described as yet another "management fad," as "nothing new," even as a fraud. And reports of job-enrichment failures are beginning to appear in management and psychology journals.

This article attempts to redress the excesses that have characterized some of the recent writings about job enrichment. As the technique increases in popularity as a management tool, top managers inevitably will find themselves making decisions about its use. The intent of this paper is to help both managers and behavioral scientists become better able to make those decisions on a solid basis of fact and data.

Succinctly stated, we present here a new strategy for going about the redesign of work. The strategy is based on three years of collaborative work and cross-fertilization among the authors — two of whom are academic researchers and two of whom are active practitioners in job enrichment. Our approach is new, but it has been tested in many organizations. It draws on the contributions of both management practice and

psychological theory, but it is firmly in the middle ground between them. It builds on and complements previous work by Herzberg and others, but provides for the first time a set of tools for *diagnosing* existing jobs — and a map for translating the diagnostic results into specific action steps for change.

What we have, then, is the following:

1. A theory that specifies when people will get personally "turned on" to their work. The theory shows what kinds of jobs are most likely to generate excitement and commitment about work, and what kinds of employees it works best for.
2. A set of action steps for job enrichment based on the theory, which prescribe in concrete terms what to do to make jobs more motivating for the people who do them.
3. Evidence that the theory holds water and that it can be used to bring about measurable — and sometimes dramatic — improvements in employee work behavior, in job satisfaction and in the financial performance of the organizational unit involved.

THE THEORY BEHIND THE STRATEGY

What Makes People Get Turned on to Their Work?

For workers who are really prospering in their jobs, work is likely to be a lot like play. Consider, for example, a golfer at a driving range, practicing to get rid of a hook. His activity is *meaningful* to him; he has chosen to do it because he gets a "kick" from testing his skills by playing the game. He knows that he alone is *responsible* for what happens when he hits the ball. And he has *knowledge of the results* within a few seconds.

Behavioral scientists have found that the three "psychological states" experienced by the golfer in the above example also are critical in determining a person's motivation and satisfaction on the job.

1. *Experienced meaningfulness:* The individual must perceive his work as worthwhile or important by some system of values he accepts.
2. *Experienced responsibility:* He must believe that he personally is accountable for the outcomes of his efforts.
3. *Knowledge of results:* He must be able to determine, on some fairly regular basis, whether or not the outcomes of his work are satisfactory.

When these three conditions are present, a person tends to feel very good about himself when he performs well. And those good feelings will prompt him to try to continue to do well — so he can continue to earn the positive feelings in the future. That is what is meant by "internal motivation" — being turned on to

one's work because of the positive internal feelings that are generated by doing well, rather than being dependent on external factors (such as incentive pay or compliments from the boss) for the motivation to work effectively.

What if one of the three psychological states is missing? Motivation drops markedly. Suppose, for example, that our golfer has settled in at the driving range to practice for a couple of hours. Suddenly a fog drifts in over the range. He can no longer see if the ball starts to tail off to the left a hundred yards out. The satisfaction he got from hitting straight down the middle — and the motivation to try to correct something whenever he didn't — are both gone. If the fog stays, it's likely that he soon will be packing up his clubs.

The relationship between the three psychological states and on-the-job outcomes is illustrated in Figure 1. When all three are high, then internal work motivation, job satisfaction, and work quality are high, and absenteeism and turnover are low.

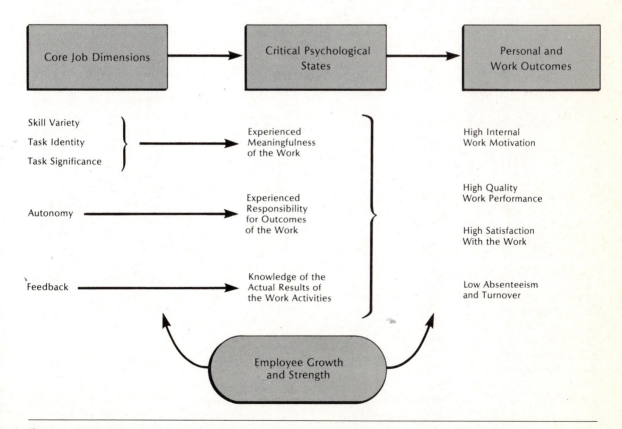

Figure 1.   Relationships Among Core Job Dimensions, Critical Psychological States, and On-the-Job Outcomes.

What Job Characteristics Make It Happen?

Recent research has identified five "core" characteristics of jobs that elicit the psychological states described above.[6-8] These five core job dimensions provide the key to objectively measuring jobs and to changing them so that they have high potential for motivating people who do them.

Toward Meaningful Work.   Three of the five core dimensions contribute to a job's meaningfulness for the worker:

1. Skill variety — the degree to which a job requires the worker to perform activities that challenge his skills and abilities. When even a single skill is involved, there is at least a seed of potential meaningfulness. When several are involved, the job has the potential of appealing to more of the whole person, and also of avoiding the monotony of performing the same task repeatedly, no matter how much skill it may require.
2. Task identity — the degree to which the job requires completion of a "whole" and identifiable piece of work — doing a job from beginning to end with a visible outcome. For example, it is clearly more meaningful to an employee to build complete toasters than to attach electrical cord after electrical cord, especially if he never sees a completed toaster. (Note that the whole job, in this example, probably would involve greater skill variety as well as task identity.)
3. Task significance — the degree to which the job has a substantial and perceivable impact on the lives of other people, whether in the immediate organization or the world at large. The worker who tightens nuts on aircraft brake assemblies is more likely to perceive his work as significant than the worker who fills small boxes with paper clips — even though the skill levels involved may be comparable.

Each of these three job dimensions represents an important route to experienced meaningfulness. If the job is high in all three, the worker is quite likely to experience his job as very meaningful. It is not necessary, however, for a job to be very high in all three dimensions. If the job is low in any one of them, there will be a drop in overall experienced meaningfulness. But even when two dimensions are low the worker may find the job meaningful if the third is high enough.

Toward Personal Responsibility.   A fourth core dimension leads a worker to experience increased responsibility in his job. This is *autonomy,* the degree to which the job gives the worker freedom, independence, and discretion in scheduling work and determining how he will carry it out. People in highly autonomous jobs know that they are personally responsible for successes and failures. To the extent that their autonomy is high, then, how the work goes will be felt to depend more on the individual's own efforts and initiatives — rather than on detailed instructions from the boss or from a manual of job procedures.

Toward Knowledge of Results.   The fifth and last core dimension is *feedback.* This is the degree to which a worker, in carrying out the work activities required by the job, gets information about the effectiveness of his efforts. Feedback is most powerful when it comes directly from the work itself — for example, when a worker has the responsibility for gauging and otherwise checking a component he has just finished, and learns in the process that he has lowered his reject rate by meeting specifications more consistently.

The Overall 'Motivating Potential' of a Job.   Figure 1 shows how the five core dimensions combine to affect the psychological states that are critical in determining whether or not an employee will be internally motivated to work effectively. Indeed, when using an instrument to be described later, it is possible to compute a "motivating potential score" (MPS) for any job. The MPS provides a single summary index of the degree to which the objective characteristics of the job will prompt high internal work motivation. Following the theory outlined above, a job high in motivating potential must be high in at least one (and hopefully more) of the three dimensions that lead to experienced meaningfulness and high in both autonomy and feedback as well. The MPS provides a quantitative index of the degree to which this is in fact the case (see Appendix for detailed formula). As will be seen later, the MPS can be very useful in diagnosing jobs and in assessing the effectiveness of job-enrichment activities.

Does the Theory Work for Everybody?

Unfortunately not. Not everyone is able to become internally motivated in his work, even when the motivating potential of a job is very high indeed.

Research has shown that the *psychological needs* of people are very important in determining who can (and who cannot) become internally motivated at work. Some people have strong needs for personal accomplishment, for learning and developing themselves beyond where they are now, for being stimulated and challenged, and so on. These people are high in "growth-need strength."

Figure 2 shows diagrammatically the proposition that individual growth needs have the power to moderate the relationship between the characteristics of jobs and work outcomes. Many workers with high growth needs will turn on eagerly when they have jobs that are high in the core dimensions. Workers whose growth needs are not so strong may respond less eagerly — or, at first, even balk at being "pushed" or "stretched" too far.

Psychologists who emphasize human potential argue that everyone has within him at least a spark of the need to grow and develop personally. Steadily accumulating evidence shows, however, that unless that spark is pretty strong, chances are it will get snuffed out by one's experiences in typical organizations. So, a person who has worked for twenty years in stultifying jobs may find it difficult or impossible to become internally motivated overnight when given the opportunity.

We should be cautious, however, about creating rigid categories of people based on their measured growth-need strength at any particular time. It is true that we can predict from these measures who is likely to become internally motivated on a job and who will be less willing

or able to do so. But what we do not know yet is whether or not the growth-need "spark" can be rekindled for those individuals who have had their growth needs dampened by years of growth-depressing experience in their organizations.

Since it is often the organization that is responsible for currently low levels of growth desires, we believe that the organization also should provide the individual with the chance to reverse that trend whenever possible, even if that means putting a person in a job where he may be "stretched" more than he wants to be. He can always move back later to the old job — and in the meantime the embers of his growth needs just might burst back into flame, to his surprise and pleasure, and for the good of the organization.

FROM THEORY TO PRACTICE: A TECHNOLOGY FOR JOB ENRICHMENT

When job enrichment fails, it often fails because of inadequate *diagnosis* of the target job and employees' reactions to it. Often, for example, job enrichment is assumed by management to be a solution to "people problems" on the job and is implemented even though there has been no diagnostic activity to indicate that the root of the problem is in fact how the work is designed. At other times, some diagnosis is made — but it provides no concrete guidance about what specific aspects of the job require change. In either case, the success of job

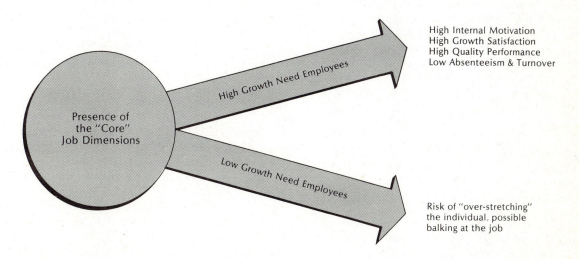

Figure 2.   The Moderating Effect of Employee Growth-Need Strength.

enrichment may wind up depending more on the quality of the intuition of the change agent — or his luck — than on a solid base of data about the people and the work.

In the paragraphs to follow, we outline a new technology for use in job enrichment which explicitly addresses the diagnostic as well as the action components of the change process. The technology has two parts: (1) a set of diagnostic tools that are useful in evaluating jobs and people's reactions to them prior to change — and in pinpointing exactly what aspects of specific jobs are most critical to a successful change attempt; and (2) a set of "implementing concepts" that provide concrete guidance for action steps in job enrichment. The implementing concepts are tied directly to the diagnostic tools; the output of the diagnostic activity specifies which action steps are likely to have the most impact in a particular situation.

The Diagnostic Tools

Central to the diagnostic procedure we propose is a package of instruments to be used by employees, supervisors, and outside observers in assessing the target job and employees' reactions to it.[9] These instruments gauge the following:

1. The objective characteristics of the jobs themselves, including both an overall indication of the "motivating potential" of the job as it exists (that is, the MPS score) and the score of the job on each of the five core dimensions described previously. Because knowing the strengths and weaknesses of the job is critical to any work-redesign effort, assessments of the job are made by supervisors and outside observers as well as the employees themselves — and the final assessment of a job uses data from all three sources.
2. The current levels of motivation, satisfaction, and work performance of employees on the job. In addition to satisfaction with the work itself, measures are taken of how people feel about other aspects of the work setting, such as pay, supervision, and relationships with coworkers.
3. The level of growth-need strength of the employees. As indicated earlier, employees who have strong growth needs are more likely to be more responsive to job enrichment than employees with weak growth needs. Therefore, it is important to know at the outset just what kinds of satisfactions the people who do the job are (and are not) motivated to obtain

from their work. This will make it possible to identify which persons are best to start changes with and which may need help in adapting to the newly enriched job.

What then, might be the actual steps one would take in carrying out a job diagnosis using these tools? Although the approach to any particular diagnosis depends upon the specifics of the particular work situation involved, the sequence of questions listed below is fairly typical.

Step 1. Are Motivation and Satisfaction Central to the Problem?   Sometimes organizations undertake job enrichment to improve the work motivation and satisfaction of employees when in fact the real problem with work performance lies elsewhere — for example, in a poorly designed production system, in an error-prone computer, and so on. The first step is to examine the scores of employees on the motivation and satisfaction portions of the diagnostic instrument. (The questionnaire taken by the employees is called the Job Diagnostic Survey and will be referred to hereafter as the JDS.) If motivation and satisfaction are problematic, the change agent would continue to Step 2; if not, he would look to other aspects of the work situation to identify the real problem.

Step 2. Is the Job Low in Motivating Potential?   To answer this question, one would examine the motivating potential score of the target job and compare it to the MPS's of other jobs to determine whether or not *the job itself* is a probable cause of the motivational problems documented in Step 1. If the job turns out to be low on the MPS, one would continue to Step 3; if it scores high, attention should be given to other possible reasons for the motivational difficulties (such as the pay system, the nature of supervision, and so on).

Step 3. What Specific Aspects of the Job Are Causing the Difficulty?   This step involves examining the job on each of the five core dimensions to pinpoint the specific strengths and weaknesses of the job as it is currently structured. It is useful at this stage to construct a "profile" of the target job, to make visually apparent where improvements need to be made. An illustrative profile for two jobs (one "good" job and one job needing improvement) is shown in Figure 3.

Job A is an engineering maintenance job and is high on all of the core dimensions; the MPS of this job is a very high 260. (MPS scores can range from 1 to about 350; an

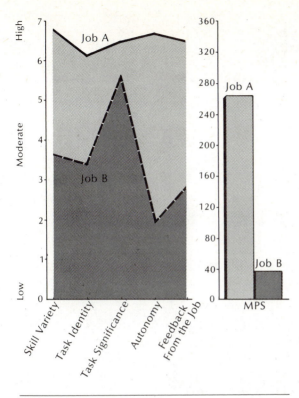

Figure 3. The JDS Diagnostic Profile for a "Good" and a "Bad" Job.

"average" score would be about 125.) Job enrichment would not be recommended for this job; if employees working on the job were unproductive and unhappy, the reasons are likely to have little to do with the nature or design of the work itself.

Job B, on the other hand, has many problems. This job involves the routine and repetitive processing of checks in the "back room" of a bank. The MPS is 30, which is quite low — and indeed, would be even lower if it were not for the moderately high task significance of the job. (Task significance is moderately high because the people are handling large amounts of other people's money, and therefore the quality of their efforts potentially has important consequences for their unseen clients.) The job provides the individuals with very little direct feedback about how effectively they are doing it; the employees have little autonomy in how they go about doing the job; and the job is moderately low in both skill variety and task identity.

For Job B, then, there is plenty of room for improvement — and many avenues to examine in planning job changes. For still other jobs, the avenues for change often turn out to be considerably more specific: for example, feedback and autonomy may be reasonably high, but one or more of the core dimensions that contribute to the experienced meaningfulness of the job (skill variety, task identity, and task significance) may be low. In such a case, attention would turn to ways to increase the standing of the job on these latter three dimensions.

Step 4. How "Ready" Are the Employees for Change? Once it has been documented that there is need for improvement in the job — and the particularly troublesome aspects of the job have been identified then it is time to begin to think about the specific action steps which will be taken to enrich the job. An important factor in such planning is the level of growth needs of the employees, since employees high on growth needs usually respond more readily to job enrichment than do employees with little need for growth. The JDS provides a direct measure of the growth-need strength of the employees. This measure can be very helpful in planning how to introduce the changes to the people (for instance, cautiously versus dramatically), and in deciding who should be among the first group of employees to have their jobs changed.

In actual use of the diagnostic package, additional information is generated which supplements and expands the basic diagnostic questions outlined above. The point of the above discussion is merely to indicate the kinds of questions which we believe to be most important in diagnosing a job prior to changing it. We now turn to how the diagnostic conclusions are translated into specific job changes.

The Implementing Concepts

Five "implementing concepts" for job enrichment are identified and discussed below.[10] Each one is a specific action step aimed at improving both the quality of the working experience for the individual and his work productivity. They are (1) forming natural work units; (2) combining tasks; (3) establishing client relationships; (4) vertical loading; (5) opening feedback channels.

The links between the implementing concepts and the core dimensions are shown in Figure 4 — which illustrates our theory of job enrichment, ranging from the concrete action steps through the core dimensions

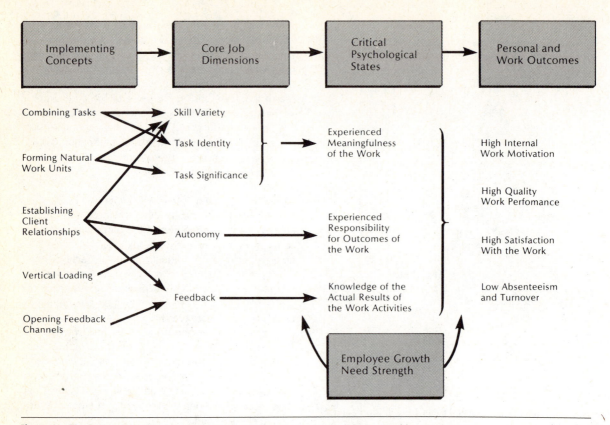

Figure 4.   The Full Model: How Use of the Implementing Concepts Can Lead to Positive Outcomes.

and the psychological states to the actual personal and work outcomes.

After completing the diagnosis of a job, a change agent would know which of the core dimensions were most in need of remedial attention. He could then turn to Figure 4 and select those implementing concepts that specifically deal with the most troublesome parts of the existing job. How this would take place in practice will be seen below.

Forming Natural Work Units.   The notion of distributing work in some logical way may seem to be an obvious part of the design of any job. In many cases, however, the logic is one imposed by just about any consideration except job-holder satisfaction and motivation. Such considerations include technological dictates, level of worker training or experience, "efficiency" as defined by industrial engineering, and current workload. In many cases the cluster of tasks a

worker faces during a typical day or week is natural to anyone *but* the worker.

For example, suppose that a typing pool (consisting of one supervisor and ten typists) handles all work for one division of a company. Jobs are delivered in rough draft or dictated form to the supervisor, who distributes them as evenly as possible among the typists. In such circumstances the individual letters, reports, and other tasks performed by a given typist in one day or week are randomly assigned. There is no basis for identifying with the work or the person or department for whom it is performed, or for placing any personal value upon it.

The principle underlying natural units of work, by contrast, is "ownership" — a worker's sense of continuing responsibility for an identifiable body of work. Two steps are involved in creating natural work units. The first is to identify the basic work items. In the typing pool, for example, the items might be "pages to be typed." The second step is to group the items in natural categories. For example, each typist might be assigned continuing responsibility for all jobs requested by one or several specific departments. The assignments should be made, of course, in such a way that workloads are about equal in the long run. (For example, one typist might end up with all the work from one busy department, while another handles jobs from several smaller units.)

At this point we can begin to see specifically how the job-design principles relate to the core dimensions (cf. Figure 4). The ownership fostered by natural units of work can make the difference between a feeling that work is meaningful and rewarding and the feeling that it is irrelevant and boring. As the diagram shows, natural units of work are directly related to two of the core dimensions: task identity and task significance.

A typist whose work is assigned naturally rather than randomly — say, by departments — has a much greater chance of performing a whole job to completion. Instead of typing one section of a large report, the individual is likely to type the whole thing, with knowledge of exactly what the product of the work is (task identity). Furthermore, over time the typist will develop a growing sense of how the work affects coworkers in the department serviced (task significance).

Combining Tasks.   The very existence of a pool made up entirely of persons whose sole function is typing reflects a fractionalization of jobs that has been a basic precept of "scientific management." Most obvious in assembly-line work, fractionalization has been applied to nonmanufacturing jobs as well. It is typically justified by efficiency, which is usually defined in terms of either low costs or some time-and-motion type of criteria.

It is hard to find fault with measuring efficiency ultimately in terms of cost-effectiveness. In doing so, however, a manager should be sure to consider *all* the costs involved. It is possible, for example, for highly fractionalized jobs to meet all the time-and-motion criteria of efficiency, but if the resulting job is so unrewarding that performing it day after day leads to high turnover, absenteeism, drugs and alcohol, and strikes, then productivity is really lower (and costs higher) than data on efficiency might indicate.

The principle of combining tasks, then, suggests that whenever possible existing and fractionalized tasks should be put together to form new and larger modules of work. At the Medfield, Massachusetts plant of

Corning Glass Works the assembly of a laboratory hot plate has been redesigned along the lines suggested here. Each hot plate now is assembled from start to finish by one operator, instead of going through several separate operations that are performed by different people.

Some tasks, if combined into a meaningfully large module of work, would be more than an individual could do by himself. In such cases, it is often useful to consider assigning the new, larger task to a small *team* of workers — who are given great autonomy for its completion. At the Racine, Wisconsin plant of Emerson Electric, the assembly process for trash disposal appliances was restructured this way. Instead of a sequence of moving the appliance from station to station, the assembly now is done from start to finish by one team. Such teams include both men and women to permit switching off the heavier and more delicate aspects of the work. The team responsible is identified on the appliance. In case of customer complaints, the team often drafts the reply.

As a job-design principle, task combination, like natural units of work, expands the task identity of the job. For example, the hot-plate assembler can see and identify with a finished product ready for shipment, rather than a nearly invisible junction of solder. Moreover, the more tasks that are combined into a single worker's job, the greater the variety of skills he must call on in performing the job. So task combination also leads directly to greater skill variety — the third core dimension that contributes to the overall experienced meaningfulness of the work.

Establishing Client Relationships.   One consequence of fractionalization is that the typical worker has little or no contact with (or even awareness of) the ultimate user of his product or service. By encouraging and enabling employees to establish direct relationships with the clients of their work, improvements often can be realized simultaneously on three of the core dimensions. Feedback increases because of additional opportunities for the individual to receive praise or criticism of his work outputs directly. Skill variety often increases because of the necessity to develop and exercise one's interpersonal skills in maintaining the client relationship. And autonomy can increase because the individual often is given personal responsibility for deciding how to manage his relationships with the clients of his work.

Creating client relationships is a three-step process. First, the client must be identified. Second, the most direct contact possible between the worker and the client must be established. Third, criteria must be set up by which the client can judge the quality of the product or service he receives. And whenever possible, the client should have a means of relaying his judgments directly back to the worker.

The contact between worker and client should be as great as possible and as frequent as necessary. Face-to-face contact is highly desirable, at least occasionally. Where that is impossible or impractical, telephone and mail can suffice. In any case, it is important that the performance criteria by which the worker will be rated by the client must be mutually understood and agreed upon.

Vertical Loading. Typically the split between the "doing" of a job and the "planning" and "controlling" of the work has evolved along with horizontal fractionalization. Its rationale, once again, has been "efficiency through specialization." And once again, the excess of specialization that has emerged has resulted in unexpected but significant costs in motivation, morale, and work quality. In vertical loading, the intent is to partially close the gap between the doing and the controlling parts of the job — and thereby reap some important motivational advantages.

Of all the job-design principles, vertical loading may be the single most crucial one. In some cases, where it has been impossible to implement any other changes, vertical loading alone has had significant motivational effects.

When a job is vertically loaded, responsibilities and controls that formerly were reserved for higher levels of management are added to the job. There are many ways to accomplish this:

1. Return to the job holder greater discretion in setting schedules, deciding on work methods, checking on quality, and advising or helping to train less experienced workers.
2. Grant additional authority. The objective should be to advance workers from a position of no authority or highly restricted authority to positions of reviewed, and eventually, near-total authority for their own work.
3. Time management. The job holder should have the greatest possible freedom to decide when to start and stop work, when to break, and how to assign priorities.
4. Troubleshooting and crisis decisions. Workers should be encouraged to seek problem solutions on their own, rather than calling immediately for the supervisor.
5. Financial controls. Some degree of knowledge and control over budgets and other financial aspects of a job can often be highly motivating. However, access to this information frequently tends to be restricted. Workers can benefit from knowing something about the costs of their jobs, the potential effect upon profit, and various financial and budgetary alternatives.

When a job is vertically loaded it will inevitably increase in *autonomy*. And as shown in Figure 4, this increase in objective personal control over the work will also lead to an increased feeling of personal responsibility for the work, and ultimately to higher internal work motivation.

Opening Feedback Channels. In virtually all jobs there are ways to open channels of feedback to individuals or teams to help them learn whether their performance is improving, deteriorating, or remaining at a constant level. While there are numerous channels through which information about performance can be provided, it generally is better for a worker to learn about his performance directly as he does his job — rather than from management on an occasional basis.

Job-provided feedback usually is more immediate and private than supervisor-supplied feedback, and it increases the worker's feelings of personal control over his work in the bargain. Moreover, it avoids many of the potentially disruptive interpersonal problems that can develop when the only way a worker has to find out how he is doing is through direct messages or subtle cues from the boss.

Exactly what should be done to open channels for job-provided feedback will vary from job to job and organization to organization. Yet in many cases the changes involve simply removing existing blocks that isolate the worker from naturally occurring data about performance — rather than generating entirely new feedback mechanisms. For example:

1. Establishing direct client relationships often removes blocks between the worker and natural external sources of data about his work.
2. Quality-control efforts in many organizations often eliminate a natural source of feedback. The quality check on a product or service is done by persons other than those responsible for the work. Feedback to the workers — if there is any — is belated and diluted. It often fosters a tendency to think of quality

as "someone else's concern." By placing quality control close to the worker (perhaps even in his own hands), the quantity and quality of data about performance available to him can dramatically increase.

3. Tradition and established procedure in many organizations dictate that records about performance be kept by a supervisor and transmitted up (not down) in the organization hierarchy. Sometimes supervisors even check the work and correct any errors themselves. The worker who made the error never knows it occurred — and is denied the very information that could enhance both his internal work motivation and the technical adequacy of his performance. In many cases it is possible to provide standard summaries of performance records directly to the worker (as well as to his superior), thereby giving him personally and regularly the data he needs to improve his performance.

4. Computers and other automated operations sometimes can be used to provide the individual with data now blocked from him. Many clerical operations, for example, are now performed on computer consoles. These consoles often can be programmed to provide the clerk with immediate feedback in the form of a CRT display or a printout indicating that an error has been made. Some systems even have been programmed to provide the operator with a positive feedback message when a period of error-free performance has been sustained.

Many organizations simply have not recognized the importance of feedback as a motivator. Data on quality and other aspects of performance are viewed as being of interest only to management. Worse still, the *standards* for acceptable performance often are kept from workers as well. As a result, workers who would be interested in following the daily or weekly ups and downs of their performance, and in trying accordingly to improve, are deprived of the very guidelines they need to do so. They are like the golfer we mentioned earlier, whose efforts to correct his hook are stopped dead by fog over the driving range.

THE STRATEGY IN ACTION: HOW WELL DOES IT WORK?

So far we have examined a basic theory of how people get turned on to their work; a set of core dimensions of jobs that create the conditions for such internal work motivation to develop on the job; and a set of five implementing concepts that are the action steps recommended to boost a job on the core dimensions and thereby increase employee motivation, satisfaction, and productivity.

The remaining question is straightforward and important: *Does it work?* In reality, that question is twofold. First, does the theory itself hold water, or are we barking up the wrong conceptual tree? And second, does the change strategy really lead to measurable differences when it is applied in an actual organizational setting?

This section summarizes the findings we have generated to date on these questions.

Is the Job-Enrichment Theory Correct?

In general, the answer seems to be yes. The JDS instrument has been taken by more than 1,000 employees working on about 100 diverse jobs in more than a dozen organizations over the last two years. These data have been analyzed to test the basic motivational theory — and especially the impact of the core job dimensions on worker motivation, satisfaction, and behavior on the job. An illustrative overview of some of the findings is given below.[11]

1. People who work on jobs high on the core dimensions are more motivated and satisfied than are people who work on jobs that score low on the dimensions. Employees with jobs high on the core dimensions (MPS scores greater than 240) were compared to those who held unmotivating jobs (MPS scores less than 40). As shown in Figure 5, employees with high MPS jobs were higher on (a) the three psychological states, (b) internal work motivation, (c) general satisfaction, and (d) "growth" satisfaction.

2. Figure 6 shows that the same is true for measures of actual behavior at work — absenteeism and performance effectiveness — although less strongly so for the performance measure.

3. Responses to jobs high in motivating potential are more positive for people with weak needs for growth. In Figure 7 the linear relationship between the motivating potential of a job and employees' level of internal work motivation is shown, separately for people with high versus low growth needs as measured by the JDS. While both groups of employees show increases in internal motivation as

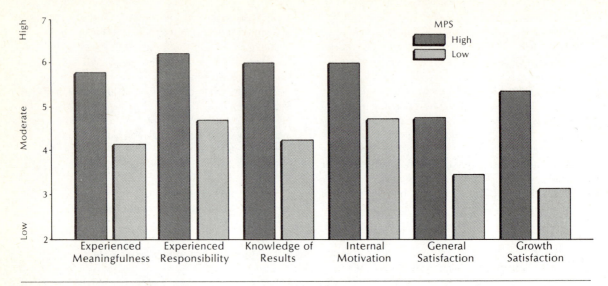

Figure 5.   Employee Reactions to Jobs High and Low in Motivating Potential for Two Banks and a Steel Firm.

MPS increases, the *rate* of increase is significantly greater for the group of employees who have strong needs for growth.

How Does the Change Strategy Work in Practice?

The results summarized above suggest that both the theory and the diagnostic instrument work when used with real people in real organizations. In this section, we summarize a job-enrichment project conducted at The Travelers Insurance Companies, which illustrates how the change procedures themselves work in practice.

The Travelers project was designed with two purposes in mind. One was to achieve improvements in morale, productivity, and other indicators of employee well-being. The other was to test the general effectiveness of the strategy for job enrichment we have summarized in this article.

The work group chosen was a keypunching operation. The group's function was to transfer information from printed or written documents onto punched cards for computer input. The work group consisted of ninety-eight keypunch operators and verifiers (both in the same job classification), plus seven assignment clerks. All reported to a supervisor who, in turn,

reported to the assistant manager and manager of the data-input division.

The size of individual punching orders varied considerably, from a few cards to as many as 2,500. Some work came to the work group with a specified delivery date, while other orders were to be given routine service on a predetermined schedule.

Assignment clerks received the jobs from the user departments. After reviewing the work for obvious errors, omissions, and legibility problems, the assignment clerk parceled out the work in batches expected to take about one hour. If the clerk found the work not suitable for punching it went to the supervisor, who either returned the work to the user department or cleared up problems by phone. When work went to operators for punching, it was with the instruction, "Punch only what you see. Don't correct errors, no matter how obvious they look."

Because of the high cost of computer time, keypunched work was 100 percent verified — a task that consumed nearly as many man-hours as the punching itself. Then the cards went to the supervisor, who screened the jobs for due dates before sending them to the computer. Errors detected in verification were assigned to various operators at random to be corrected.

The computer output from the cards was sent to the originating department, accompanied by a printout of errors. Eventually the printout went back to the supervisor for final correction.

A great many phenomena indicated that the problems being experienced in the work group might be the result of poor motivation. As the only person performing supervisory functions of any kind, the supervisor spent most of his time responding to crisis situations, which recurred continually. He also had to deal almost daily with employees' salary grievances or other complaints. Employees frequently showed apathy or outright hostility toward their jobs.

Rates of work output, by accepted work-measurement standards, were inadequate. Error rates were high. Due dates and schedules frequently were missed. Absenteeism was higher than average, especially before and after weekends and holidays.

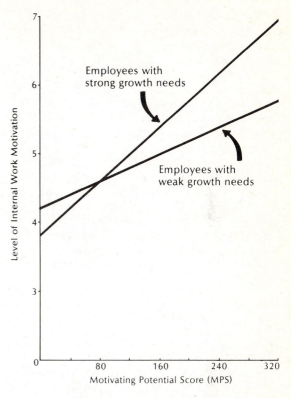

Figure 7.   Relationship Between the Motivating Potential of a Job and the Internal Work Motivation of Employees. (Shown Separately for Employees with Strong versus Weak Growth-Need Strength.)

The single, rather unusual exception was turnover. It was lower than the companywide average for similar jobs. The company has attributed this fact to poor job market in the base period just before the project began, and to an older, relatively more settled work force — made up, incidentally, entirely of women.

The Diagnosis.   Using some of the tools and techniques we have outlined, a consulting team from the Management Services Department and from Roy W. Walters & Associates concluded that the keypunch-operator's job exhibited the following serious weaknesses in terms of the core dimensions.

1. Skill variety: there was none. Only a single skill was involved — the ability to punch adequately the data on the batch of documents.

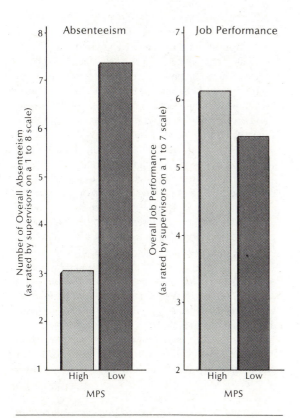

Figure 6.   Absenteeism and Job Performance for Employees with Jobs High and Low in Motivating Potential.

2. Task identity: virtually nonexistent. Batches were assembled to provide an even workload, but not whole identifiable jobs.

3. Task significance: not apparent. The keypunching operation was a necessary step in providing service to the company's customers. The individual operator was isolated by an assignment clerk and a supervisor from any knowledge of what the operation meant to the using department, let alone its meaning to the ultimate customer.

4. Autonomy: none. The operators had no freedom to arrange their daily tasks to meet schedules, to resolve problems with the using department, or even to correct, in punching, information that was obviously wrong.

5. Feedback: none. Once a batch was out of the operator's hands, she had no assured chance of seeing evidence of its quality or inadequacy.

Design of the Experimental Trial.   Since the diagnosis indicated that the motivating potential of the job was extremely low, it was decided to attempt to improve the motivation and productivity of the work group through job enrichment. Moreover, it was possible to design an experimental test of the effects of the changes to be introduced: the results of changes made in the target work group were to be compared with trends in a control work group of similar size and demographic makeup. Since the control group was located more than a mile away, there appeared to be little risk of communication between members of the two groups.

A base period was defined before the start of the experimental trial period, and appropriate data were gathered on the productivity, absenteeism, and work attitudes of members of both groups. Data also were available on turnover; but since turnover was already below average in the target group, prospective changes in this measure were deemed insignificant.

An educational session was conducted with supervisors, at which they were given the theory and implementing concepts and actually helped to design the job changes themselves. Out of this session came an active plan consisting of about twenty-five change items that would significantly affect the design of the target jobs.

The Implementing Concepts and the Changes. Because the job as it existed was rather uniformly low on the core job dimensions, all five of the implementing concepts were used in enriching it.

1. Natural units of work. The random batch assignment of work was replaced by assigning to each operator continuing responsibility for certain accounts — either particular departments or particular recurring jobs. Any work for those accounts now always goes to the same operator.

2. Task combination. Some planning and controlling functions were combined with the central task of keypunching. In this case, however, these additions can be more suitably discussed under the remaining three implementing concepts.

3. Client relationships. Each operator was given several channels of direct contact with clients. The operators, not their assignment clerks, now inspect their documents for correctness and legibility. When problems arise, the operator, not the supervisor, takes them up with the client.

4. Feedback. In addition to feedback from client contact, the operators were provided with a number of additional sources of data about their performance. The computer department now returns incorrect cards to the operators who punched them, and operators correct their own errors. Each operator also keeps her own file of copies of her errors. These can be reviewed to determine trends in error frequency and types of errors. Each operator receives weekly a computer printout of her errors and productivity, which is sent to her directly, rather than given to her by the supervisor.

5. Vertical loading. Besides consulting directly with clients about work questions, operators now have the authority to correct obvious coding errors on their own. Operators may set their own schedules and plan their daily work, as long as they meet schedules. Some competent operators have been given the option of not verifying their work and making their own program changes.

Results of the Trial.   The results were dramatic. The number of operators declined from ninety-eight to sixty. This occurred partly through attrition and partly through transfer to other departments. Some of the operators were promoted to higher-paying jobs in departments whose cards they had been handling — something that had never occurred before. Some details of the results are given below.

1. Quantity of work. The control group, with no job changes made, showed an increase in productivity of

8.1 percent during the trial period. The experimental group showed an increase of 39.6 percent.

2. Error rates. To assess work quality, error rates were recorded for about forty operators in the experimental group. All were experienced, and all had been in their jobs before the job-enrichment program began. For two months before the study, these operators had a collective error rate of 1.53 percent. For two months toward the end of the study, the collective error rate was 0.99 percent. By the end of the study the number of operators with poor performance had dropped from 11.1 percent to 5.5 percent.

3. Absenteeism. The experimental group registered a 24.1 percent decline in absences. The control group, by contrast, showed a 29 percent increase.

4. Attitudes toward the job. An attitude survey given at the start of the project showed that the two groups scored about average, and nearly identically, in nine different areas of work satisfaction. At the end of the project the survey was repeated. The control group showed an insignificant 0.5 percent improvement, while the experimental group's overall satisfaction score rose 16.5 percent.

5. Selective elimination of controls. Demonstrated improvements in operator proficiency permitted them to work with fewer controls. Travelers estimates that the reduction of controls had the same effect as adding seven operators — a saving even beyond the effects of improved productivity and lowered absenteeism.

6. Role of the supervisor. One of the most significant findings in the Travelers experiment was the effect of the changes on the supervisor's job, and thus on the rest of the organization. The operators took on many responsibilities that had been reserved at least to the unit leaders and sometimes to the supervisor. The unit leaders, in turn, assumed some of the day-to-day supervisory functions that had plagued the supervisor. Instead of spending his days supervising the behavior of subordinates and dealing with crises, he was able to devote time to developing feedback systems, setting up work modules and spearheading the enrichment effort — in other words, managing. It should be noted, however, that helping supervisors change their own work activities when their subordinates' jobs have been enriched is itself a challenging task. And if appropriate attention and help are not given to supervisors in such cases, they rapidly can become disaffected — and a job-enrichment "backlash" can result.[12]

Summary.   By applying work-measurement standards to the changes wrought by job enrichment — attitude and quality, absenteeism, and selective administration of controls — Travelers was able to estimate the total dollar impact of the project. Actual savings in salaries and machine rental charges during the first year totaled $64,305. Potential savings by further application of the changes were put at $91,937 annually. Thus, by almost any measure used — from the work attitudes of individual employees to dollar savings for the company as a whole — The Travelers test of the job-enrichment strategy proved a success.

CONCLUSIONS

In this article we have presented a new strategy for the redesign of work in general and for job enrichment in particular. The approach has four main characteristics:

1. It is grounded in a basic psychological theory of what motivates people in their work.
2. It emphasizes that planning for job changes should be done on the basis of *data* about the jobs and the people who do them — and a set of diagnostic instruments is provided to collect such data.
3. It provides a set of specific implementing concepts to guide actual job changes, as well as a set of theory-based rules for selecting *which* action steps are likely to be most beneficial in a given situation.
4. The strategy is buttressed by a set of findings showing that the theory holds water, that the diagnostic procedures are practical and informative, and that the implementing concepts can lead to changes that are beneficial both to organizations and to the people who work in them.

We believe that job enrichment is moving beyond the stage where it can be considered "yet another management fad." Instead, it represents a potentially powerful strategy for change that can help organizations achieve their goals for higher quality work — and at the same time further the equally legitimate needs of contemporary employees for a more meaningful work experience. Yet there are pressing questions about job enrichment and its use that remain to be answered.

Prominent among these is the question of employee participation in planning and implementing work redesign. The diagnostic tools and implementing concepts we have presented are neither designed nor intended for use only by management. Rather, our belief is that the effectiveness of job enrichment is likely to be enhanced when the tasks of diagnosing and changing jobs are undertaken *collaboratively* by management and by the employees whose work will be affected.

Moreover, the effects of work redesign on the broader organization remain generally uncharted. Evidence now is accumulating that when jobs are changed, turbulence can appear in the surrounding organization — for example, in supervisory-subordinate relationships, in pay and benefit plans, and so on. Such turbulence can be viewed by management either as a problem with job enrichment, or as an opportunity for further and broader organizational development by teams of managers and employees. To the degree that management takes the latter view, we believe, the oft-espoused goal of achieving basic organizational change through the redesign of work may come increasingly within reach.

The diagnostic tools and implementing concepts we have presented are useful in deciding on and designing basic changes in the jobs themselves. They do not address the broader issues of who plans the changes, how they are carried out, and how they are followed up. The way these broader questions are dealt with, we believe, may determine whether job enrichment will grow up — or whether it will die an early and unfortunate death, like so many other fledgling behavioral-science approaches to organizational change.

APPENDIX

For the algebraically inclined, the Motivating Potential Score is computed as follows

$$MPS = \frac{\left(\dfrac{\text{Skill Variety} + \text{Task Identity} + \text{Task Significance}}{3}\right) \times \text{Autonomy} \times \text{Feedback}}{}$$

It should be noted that in some cases the MPS score can be *too* high for positive job satisfaction and effective performance — in effect overstimulating the person who holds the job. This paper focuses on jobs which are toward the low end of the scale — and which potentially can be improved through job enrichment.

Acknowledgments

The authors acknowledge with great appreciation the editorial assistance of John Hickey in the preparation of this paper, and the help of Kenneth Brousseau, Daniel Feldman, and Linda Frank in collecting the data that are summarized here. The research activities reported were supported in part by the Organizational Effectiveness Research Program of the Office of Naval Research, and the Manpower Administration of the U.S. Department of Labor, both through contracts to Yale University.

NOTES

1. F. Herzberg; B. Mausner; and B. Snyderman; *The Motivation to Work* (New York: John Wiley & Sons, 1959).

2. F. Herzberg, *Work and the Nature of Man* (Cleveland: World, 1966).

3. F. Herzberg, "One More Time: How Do You Motivate Employees?" *Harvard Business Review* (1968): 53–62.

4. W. J. Paul, Jr.; K. B. Robertson; and F. Herzberg, "Job Enrichment Pays Off." *Harvard Business Review* (1969): 61–78.

5. R. N. Ford, *Motivation Through the Work Itself* (New York: American Management Association, 1969).

6. A. N. Turner and P. R. Lawrence, *Industrial Jobs and the Worker* (Cambridge, Mass.: Harvard Graduate School of Business Administration, 1965).

7. J. R. Hackman and E. E. Lawler, "Employee Reactions to Job Characteristics," *Journal of Applied Psychology Monograph* (1971): 259–86.

8. J. R. Hackman and G. R. Oldham, *Motivation Through the Design of Work: Test of a Theory,* Technical Report No. 6, Department of Administrative Sciences, Yale University, 1974.

9. J. R. Hackman and G. R. Oldham, "Development of the Job Diagnostic Survey," *Journal of Applied Psychology* (1975): 159–70.

10. R. W. Walters and Associates, *Job Enrichment for Results* (Cambridge, Mass.: Addison-Wesley, 1975).

11. Hackman and Oldham, "Development of the Job Diagnostic Survey."

12. E. E. Lawler III; J. R. Hackman; and S. Kaufman, "Effects of Job Redesign: A Field Experiment," *Journal of Applied Social Psychology* (1973): 49–62.

Job Satisfaction, Absenteeism, and Turnover

8. Satisfaction and Behavior

Edward E. Lawler III

. . . During the last 30 years, thousands of studies have been done on job satisfaction. Usually, these studies have not been theoretically oriented; instead, researchers have simply looked at the relationship between job satisfaction and factors such as age, education, job level, absenteeism rate, productivity, and so on. Originally, much of the research seemed to be stimulated by a desire to show that job satisfaction is important because it influences productivity. Underlying the earlier articles on job satisfaction was a strong conviction that ''happy workers are productive workers.'' Recently, however, this theme has been disappearing, and many organizational psychologists seem to be studying job satisfaction simply because they are interested in finding its causes. This approach to

studying job satisfaction is congruent with the increased prominence of humanistic psychology, which emphasizes human affective experience.

The recent interest in job satisfaction also ties in directly with the rising concern in many countries about the quality of life. There is an increasing acceptance of the view that material possessions and economic growth do not necessarily produce a high quality of life. Recognition is now being given to the importance of the kinds of affective reactions that people experience and to the fact that these are not always tied to economic or material accomplishments. Through the Department of Labor and the Department of Health, Education, and Welfare, the United States government has recently become active in trying to improve the affective quality of work life. Job satisfaction is one measure of the quality of life in organizations and is worth understanding and increasing even if it doesn't relate to performance. This reason for studying satisfaction is likely to be an increasingly prominent one as we begin to worry more about the effects working in organizations has on people and as our humanitarian concern for the kind of psychological experiences people have during their lives increases. What happens to people during the work day has profound effects both on the individual employee's life and on the society as a whole, and thus these events cannot be ignored if the quality of life in a society is to be high. As John Gardner has said,

Of all the ways in which society serves the individual, few are more meaningful than to provide him with a decent job. . . . It isn't going to be a decent society for any of us until it is for all of us. If our sense of responsibility fails us, our sheer self-interest should come to the rescue [1968, p. 25].

As it turns out, satisfaction is related to absenteeism and turnover, both of which are very costly to organizations. Thus, there is a very "practical" economic reason for organizations to be concerned with job satisfaction, since it can influence organizational effectiveness. However, before any practical use can be made of the finding that job dissatisfaction causes absenteeism and turnover, we must understand what factors cause and influence job satisfaction. Organizations can influence job satisfaction and prevent absenteeism and turnover only if the organizations can pinpoint the factors causing and influencing these effective responses.

THEORIES OF JOB SATISFACTION

Four approaches can be identified in the theoretical work on satisfaction. Fulfillment theory was the first approach to develop. Equity theory and discrepancy theory developed later, partially as reactions against the shortcomings of fulfillment theory. Two-factor theory, the fourth approach, represents an attempt to develop a completely new approach to thinking about satisfaction.

Fulfillment Theory

Schaffer (1953) has argued that "job satisfaction will vary directly with the extent to which those needs of an individual which can be satisfied are actually satisfied" (p. 3). Vroom (1964) also sees job satisfaction in terms of the degree to which a job provides the person with positively valued outcomes. He equates satisfaction with valence and adds "If we describe a person as satisfied with an object, we mean that the object has positive valence for him. However, satisfaction has a much more restricted usage. In common parlance, we refer to a person's satisfaction only with reference to objects which he possesses" (p. 100).* Researchers who have adopted the fulfillment approach measure people's satisfaction by simply asking how much of a given facet or outcome they are receiving. Thus, these researchers view satisfaction as depending on how much of a given outcome or group of outcomes a person receives.

Fulfillment theorists have considered how facet-satisfaction measures combine to determine overall satisfaction. The crucial issue is whether the facet-satisfaction measures should be weighted by their importance to the person when combined. We know that some job factors are more important than other job factors for each individual; therefore, the important factors need to be weighted more in determining the individual's total satisfaction. However, there is evidence that the individual's facet satisfaction scores reflect this emphasis already and thus do not need to be further weighted (Mobley & Locke, 1970).

A great deal of research shows that people's satisfaction is a function both of how much they receive and of how much they feel they should and/or want to receive (Locke, 1969). A foreman, for example, may be satisfied with a salary of $12,000, while a company president may be dissatisfied with a salary of $100,000, even though the president correctly perceives that he receives more than the foreman. The point is that people's reactions to what they receive are not simply a function of how much they receive; their reactions are strongly influenced by such individual-difference factors as what they want and what they feel they should receive. Individual-difference factors suggest that the fulfillment theory approach to job satisfaction is not valid, since this approach fails to take into account

---

*V. Vroom, *Work and Motivation.* Copyright © 1964 by John Wiley & Sons, Inc. This and all other quotes from the same source are reprinted by permission.

differences in people's feelings about what outcomes they should receive.

Morse (1953) stated this point of view as follows:

At first we thought that satisfaction would simply be a function of how much a person received from the situation or what we have called the amount of environmental return. It made sense to feel that those who were in more need-fulfilling environments would be more satisfied. But the amount of environmental return did not seem to be the only factor involved. Another factor obviously had to be included in order to predict satisfaction accurately. This variable was the strength of an individual's desires, or his level of aspiration in a particular area. If the environment provided little possibility for need satisfaction, those with the strongest desires, or highest aspirations, were the least happy [pp. 27–28].

Discrepancy theory, which will be discussed next, represents an attempt to take into account the fact that people do differ in their desires.

Discrepancy Theory

Recently many psychologists have argued for a discrepancy approach to thinking about satisfaction. They maintain that satisfaction is determined by the differences between the actual outcomes a person receives and some other outcome level. The theories differ widely in their definitions of this other outcome level. For some theories it is the outcome level the person feels should be received, and for other theories it is the outcome level the person expects to receive. All of the theoretical approaches argue that what is received should be compared with another outcome level, and when there is a difference — when received outcome is below the other outcome level — dissatisfaction results. Thus, if a person expects or thinks he should receive a salary of $10,000 and he receives one of only $8,000, the prediction is that he will be dissatisfied with his pay. Further, the prediction is that he will be more dissatisfied than the person who receives a salary of $9,000 and expects or thinks he should receive a salary of $10,000.

Katzell (1964) and Locke (1968, 1969) have probably presented the two most completely developed discrepancy-theory approaches to satisfaction. According to Katzell, satisfaction = $1 - (|X - V| / V)$, where X equals the actual amount of the outcome and V equals

the desired amount of the outcome. Like many discrepancy theorists, Katzell sees satisfaction as the difference between an actual amount and some desired amount; but, unlike most discrepancy theorists, he assumes that this difference should be divided by the desired amount of the outcome. If we use Katzell's formula, we are led to believe that the more a person wants of an outcome the less dissatisfied he will be with a given discrepancy. Katzell offers no evidence for this assumption, and it is hard to support logically. A discrepancy from what is desired would seem to be equally dissatisfying regardless of how much is desired. Katzell also speaks of "actual" discrepancies, while most discrepancy theorists talk of "perceived" discrepancies. Note also that by Katzell's formula, getting more than the desired amount should produce less satisfaction than getting the desired amount.

Locke (1969) has stated a discrepancy theory that differs from Katzell's in several ways. First, Locke emphasizes that the perceived discrepancy, not the actual discrepancy, is important. He also argues that satisfaction is determined by the simple difference between what the person wants and what he perceives he receives. The more his wants exceed what he receives, the greater his dissatisfaction. Locke says, "Job satisfaction and dissatisfaction are a function of the perceived relationship between what one wants from one's job and what one perceives it is offering" (p. 316).

Porter (1961), in measuring satisfaction, asks people how much of a given outcome there should be for their job and how much of a given outcome there actually is; he considers the discrepancy between the two answers to be a measure of satisfaction. This particular discrepancy approach has been the most widely used. It differs from Locke's approach since it sees satisfaction as influenced not by how much a person wants but by how much he feels he should receive.

A few researchers have argued that satisfaction is determined by what a person expects to receive rather than by what he wants or feels he should receive. Thus, the literature on job satisfaction contains three different discrepancy approaches; the first looks at what people want, the second at what people feel they should receive, and the third at what people expect to receive. The last of these approaches has seldom been used and can be dismissed. As Locke (1969) points out, the expectation approach is hard to defend logically. Admittedly, getting what is not expected may lead to surprise, but it hardly need lead to dissatisfaction. What if, for example, it exceeds expectations? What if it exceeds expectations but still falls below what others are getting?

It is not obvious on logical grounds that either of the first two approaches can be rejected as meaningless. Both approaches seem to be addressing important but perhaps different affective reactions to a job. There clearly is a difference between asking people how much they want and how much they think they should receive. People do respond differently to those questions (Wanous & Lawler, 1972). In a sense, the two questions help us understand different aspects of a person's feelings toward his present situation. A person's satisfaction with the fairness of what he receives for his present job would seem to be more influenced by what he feels he should receive than by what he ultimately aspires to. The difference between what the person aspires to or wants and what he receives gives us an insight into his satisfaction with his present situation relative to his long-term aspired to, or desired, situation. These two discrepancy measures can and do yield different results. For example, a person can feel that his present pay is appropriate for his present job, and in this sense he can be satisfied; however, he can feel that his present pay is much below what he wants, and in this sense he can be dissatisfied. In most cases, however, these two discrepancies probably are closely related and influence each other. Thus, the difference between the two discrepancies may not be as large or as important as some theorists have argued.

Like the fulfillment theorists, many discrepancy theorists argue that total job satisfaction is influenced by the sum of the discrepancies that are present for each job factor. Thus, a person's overall job satisfaction would be equal to his pay-satisfaction discrepancy plus his supervision-satisfaction discrepancy, and so on. It has been argued that in computing such a sum it is important to weight each of the discrepancies by the importance of that factor to the person, the argument being that important factors influence job satisfaction more strongly than unimportant ones. Locke (1969), however, argues that such a weighting is redundant, since the discrepancy score is a measure of importance in itself because large discrepancies tend to appear only for important items.

Most discrepancy theories allow for the possibility of a person saying he is receiving more outcomes than he should receive, or more outcomes than he wants to receive. However, the theories don't stress this point, which presents some problems for them. It is not clear how to equate dissatisfaction (or whatever this feeling might be called) due to over-reward with dissatisfaction due to under-reward. Are they produced in the same way? Do they have the same results? Do they both contribute to overall job dissatisfaction? These are some of the important questions that discrepancy theories have yet to answer. Equity theory, which will be discussed next, has dealt with some of these questions.

Equity Theory

Equity theory is primarily a motivation theory, but it has some important things to say about the causes of satisfaction/dissatisfaction. Adams (1963, 1965) argues in his version of equity theory that satisfaction is determined by a person's perceived input-outcome balance in the following manner: the perceived equity of a person's rewards is determined by his input-outcome balance; this perceived equity, in turn, determines satisfaction. Satisfaction results when perceived equity exists, and dissatisfaction results when perceived inequity exists. Thus, satisfaction is determined by the perceived ratio of what a person receives from his job relative to what a person puts into his job. According to equity theory, either under-reward or over-reward can lead to dissatisfaction, although the feelings are somewhat different. The theory emphasizes that over-reward leads to feelings of guilt, while under-reward leads to feelings of unfair treatment.

Equity theory emphasizes the importance of other people's input-outcome balance in determining how a person will judge the equity of his own input-outcome balance. Equity theory argues that people evaluate the fairness of their own input-outcome balance by comparing it with their perception of the input-outcome balance of their "comparison-other" (the person they compare with). This emphasis does not enter into either discrepancy theory or fulfillment theory as they are usually stated. Although there is an implied reference to "other" in the discussion of how people develop their feelings about what their outcomes should be, discrepancy theory does not explicitly state that this perception is based on perceptions of what other people contribute and receive. This difference points up a strength of equity theory relative to discrepancy theory. Equity theory rather clearly states how a person assesses his inputs and outcomes in order to develop his perception of the fairness of his input-outcome balance. Discrepancy theory, on the other hand, is vague about how people decide what their outcomes should be.

Two-Factor Theory

Modern two-factor theory was originally developed in a book by Herzberg, Mausner, Peterson, and Capwell (1957), in which the authors stated that job factors could be classified according to whether the factors contribute primarily to satisfaction or to dissatisfaction. Two years later, Herzberg, Mausner, and Snyderman (1959) published the results of a research study, which they interpreted as supportive of the theory. Since 1959, much research has been directed toward testing two-factor theory. Two aspects of the theory are unique and account for the attention it has received. First, two-factor theory says that satisfaction and dissatisfaction do not exist on a continuum running from satisfaction through neutral to dissatisfaction. Two independent continua exist, one running from satisfied to neutral and another running from dissatisfied to neutral (see Figure 1). Second, the theory stresses that different job facets influence feelings of satisfaction and dissatisfaction. Figure 2 presents the results of a study by Herzberg et al., which show that factors such as achievement, recognition, work itself, and responsibility are mentioned in connection with satisfying experiences, while working conditions, interpersonal relations, supervision, and company policy are usually mentioned in connection with dissatisfying experiences. The figure shows the frequency with which each factor is mentioned in connection with high (satisfying) and low (dissatisfying) work experiences. As can be seen, achievement was present in over 40 percent of the satisfying experiences and less than 10 percent of the dissatisfying experiences.

Perhaps the most interesting aspect of Herzberg's theory is that at the same time a person can be very satisfied and very dissatisfied. Also, the theory implies that factors such as better working conditions cannot increase or cause satisfaction, they can only affect the amount of dissatisfaction that is experienced. The only way satisfaction can be increased is by effecting changes in those factors that are shown in Figure 2 as contributing primarily to satisfaction.

The results of the studies designed to test two-factor theory have not provided clear-cut support for the theory, nor have these studies allowed for total rejection of the theory. In many cases, the studies have only fueled the controversy that surrounds the theory. It is beyond the scope of this reading to review the research that has been done on the theory. What we can do, however, is to consider some of the conclusions to which two-factor theory has led. Perhaps the most negative summary of the evidence is the account presented by Dunnette, Campbell, and Hakel (1967). According to them:

It seems that the evidence is now sufficient to lay the two-factor theory to rest, and we hope that it may be buried peaceably. We believe that it is important that this be done so that researchers will address themselves to studying the full complexities of human motivation, rather than continuing to allow the direction of motivational research or actual administrative decisions to be dictated by the seductive simplicity of two-factor theory [p. 173].

This opinion has been rejected by many researchers as too harsh and negative, and indeed research on the theory has continued since the publication of the Dunnette et al. study. Still, research on the theory has raised serious doubts about its validity. Even proponents of the theory admit that the same factors can cause both satisfaction and dissatisfaction and that a given factor can cause satisfaction in one group of people and dissatisfaction in another group of people. Other researchers have pointed out that results supporting the theory seem to be obtainable only when certain limited research methodologies are used.

The major unanswered question with respect to two-factor theory is whether satisfaction and dissatisfaction really are two separate dimensions. The evidence is not sufficient to establish that satisfaction and dissatisfaction are separate, making this the crucial unproven aspect of the theory. Neither the fact that some factors can contribute to both satisfaction and dissatisfaction nor the fact that, in some populations, factors contribute to satisfaction while, in other populations, these factors contribute to dissatisfaction is sufficient reason to reject the theory. Although these findings raise questions about the theory, they do not destroy its core concept, which is that satisfaction and dissatisfaction are, in fact, on different continua.

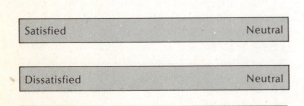

Figure 1.   Two-Factor Theory: Satisfaction Continua.

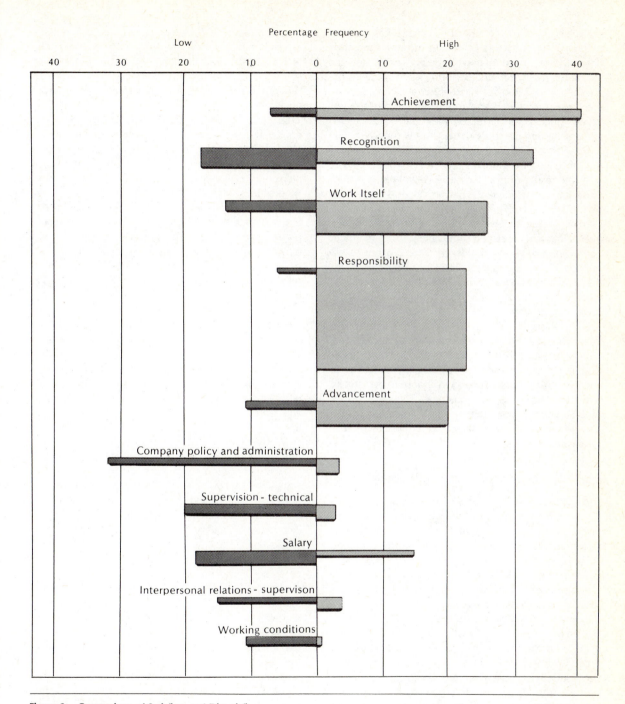

Figure 2. Comparison of Satisfiers and Dissatisfiers.

Source: Adapted from Herzberg et al., *The Motivation to Work,* 2d ed. Copyright © 1959 by John Wiley & Sons, Inc. Reprinted by permission.

Significantly, while considerable research has tried to determine which factors contribute to satisfaction and dissatisfaction, little attention has been directed toward testing the motivation and performance implications of the theory. The study of Herzberg et al. (1959) did ask the subjects (engineers and accountants) to report how various job factors affected their performance. In agreement with the theory, the subjects reported that the presence of satisfiers boosted performance, while the presence of dissatisfiers reduced performance. At best, the results of this study give weak evidence that these job factors influence performance as suggested by the theory. Only self-reports of performance were used, and in many cases the subjects were reporting on events that had happened some time prior to the date of the interviews. The evidence, although not at all conclusive, at least suggests the kinds of experiences that might lead to a strong motivation to perform effectively. Unfortunately, Herzberg et al. did not develop any theoretical concepts to explain why the job factors should affect performance. Their theory contains little explanation of why outcomes are attractive, and it fails to consider the importance of associative connections in determining which of a number of behaviors a person will choose to perform in order to obtain a desired outcome. Thus, it is not a theory of motivation; rather, it is a theory primarily concerned with explaining the determinants of job satisfaction and dissatisfaction.

Equity Theory and/or Discrepancy Theory

Equity theory and discrepancy theory are the two strongest theoretical explanations of satisfaction. Either theory could be used as a basis for thinking about the determinants of satisfaction. Fortunately it is not necessary to choose between the theories, since it is possible to build a satisfaction model that capitalizes on the strengths of each theory. In this reading, we will try to build such a model. In many ways, equity theory and discrepancy theory are quite similar. Both theories stress the importance of a person's perceived outcomes, along with the relationship of these outcomes to a second perception. In discrepancy theory, the second perception is what the outcomes should be or what the person wants the outcomes to be; in equity theory, the second perception is what a person's perceived inputs are in relation to other people's inputs and outcomes. Clearly, it could be argued that the two theories are talking about very similar concepts when they talk about perceived inputs and the subject's feeling about what

his outcomes should be. A person's perception of what his outcomes should be is partly determined by what he feels his inputs are. Thus, the "should be" phrase from discrepancy theory and the "perceived inputs relative to other people's inputs and outcomes" phrase from equity theory are very similar.

Equity theory and discrepancy theory do differ in that equity theory places explicit emphasis on the importance of social comparison, while discrepancy theory does not. This is a strength of equity theory because it helps to make explicit what influences a person's "should be" judgment. Finally, discrepancy theory talks in terms of a *difference*, while equity theory talks in terms of a *ratio*. For example, equity theory would predict that a person with 16 units of input and 4 units of outcome would feel the same as a person with 8 units of input and 2 units of outcome (same ratio, 1 to 4). Although discrepancy theory does not talk specifically in terms of inputs, if we consider input as one determinant of what outcomes should be, then discrepancy theory would not go along with equity theory. Discrepancy theory would argue that the person with 16 units of input will be more dissatisfied than the person with 8 units of input because the difference between his input and outcomes is greater. The two theories also suggest different types of relationships between dissatisfaction and feelings of what rewards should be. Discrepancy theory would predict a linear relationship such that, rewards being constant, increases in a person's perception of what his outcomes should be would be directly proportionate to increases in dissatisfaction. Equity theory, on the other hand, would predict a nonlinear relationship [satisfaction = (is getting/should be getting)] such that if a poor ratio exists, a further increase in "should be getting" will have little effect on satisfaction.

In building our "model of satisfaction," we will use the difference approach rather than the ratio approach. This choice is one of the few either/or choices that must be made between the two theories. It is not a particularly crucial choice from the point of view of measurement because methods of measurement in the field of psychology are not precise enough so that discrepancy theory and equity theory would yield very different results. Measurement scales with true zero points and equal distances between all points on the scale (for example, as in measuring weight and height) are required, and such scales are not used when attitudes are measured.

Once it has been decided to think of satisfaction in terms of a difference, the key question becomes what difference or differences should be considered. There is clear agreement that one element in the discrepancy should be what the person perceives that he actually receives. The second element could be one of two other perceptions: (1) what a person thinks he should receive, or (2) what a person wants to receive. As we've already seen, these two perceptions are closely related. However, there is a difference. Overall, it seems preferable to focus more on what a person feels he should receive than on what a person wants to receive.

If satisfaction is conceptualized as the difference between what one receives and what one wants, it is difficult to talk meaningfully about satisfaction with one's present job. Such an approach partially removes satisfaction from the context of the job and the situation. The question "How much do you want?" is an aspiration-level variable, which is not as closely related to the job situation as the question "How much should there be?" An answer to the first question is more a statement of personal goals than a statement of what is

appropriate in a particular situation. Research data show that employees consistently give higher answers to the "how much do you want" question than to the "how much should there be" question (Wanous & Lawler, 1972); answers to the "should be" question seem to vary more with such organization factors as job level. Thus, in studying people's feelings about their jobs, it seems logical to focus on what employees feel they should receive from their jobs. This perception would seem to be strongly influenced by organization practices, and it would seem to be a perception that must be studied if we are to understand employees' affective reactions to their jobs and the behavioral responses these reactions produce.

A MODEL OF FACET SATISFACTION

Figure 3 presents a model of the determinants of facet satisfaction. The model is intended to be applicable to understanding what determines a person's satisfaction

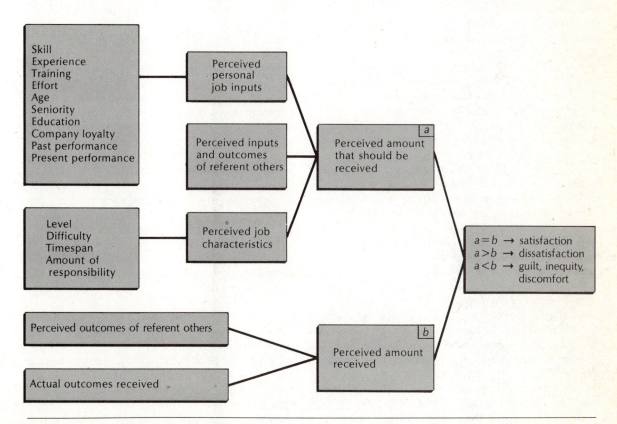

Figure 3. Model of the Determinants of Satisfaction.

with any facet of the job. The model assumes that the same psychological processes operate to determine satisfaction with job factors ranging from pay to supervision and satisfaction with the work itself. The model in Figure 3 is a discrepancy model in the sense that it shows satisfaction as the difference between a, what a person feels he should receive, and b, what he perceives that he actually receives. The model indicates that when the person's perception of what his outcome level is and his perception of what his outcome level should be are in agreement, the person will be satisfied. When a person perceives his outcome level as falling below what he feels it should be, he will be dissatisfied. However, when a person's perceived outcome level exceeds what he feels it should be, he will have feelings of guilt and inequity and perhaps some discomfort (Adams, 1965). Thus, for any job factor, the assumption is that satisfaction with the factor will be determined by the difference between how much of the factor there is and how much of the factor the person feels there should be.

Present outcome level is shown to be the key influence on a person's perception of what rewards he receives, but his perception is also shown to be influenced by his perception of what his ''referent others'' receive. The higher the outcome levels of his referent others, the lower his outcome level will appear. Thus, a person's psychological view of how much of a factor he receives is said to be influenced by more than just the objective amount of the factor. Because of this psychological influence, the same amount of reward often can be seen quite differently by two people; to one person it can be a large amount, while to another person it can be a small amount.

The model in Figure 3 also shows that a person's perception of what his reward level should be is influenced by a number of factors. Perhaps the most important influence is perceived job inputs. These inputs include all of the skills, abilities, and training a person brings to the job as well as the behavior he exhibits on the job. The greater he perceives his inputs to be, the higher will be his perception of what his outcomes should be. Because of this relationship, people with high job inputs must receive more rewards than people with low job inputs or they will be dissatisfied. The model also shows that a person's perception of what his outcomes should be is influenced by his perception of the job demands. The greater the demands made by the job, the more he will perceive he should receive. Job demands include such things as job difficulty, respon-

sibilities, and organization level. If outcomes do not rise along with these factors, the clear prediction of the model is that the people who perceive they have the more difficult, higher-level jobs will be the most dissatisfied.

The model shows that a person's perception of what his outcomes should be is influenced by what the person perceives his comparison-other's inputs and outcomes to be. This aspect of the model is taken directly from equity theory and is included to stress the fact that people look at the inputs and outcomes of others in order to determine what their own outcome level should be. If a person's comparison-other's inputs are the same as the person's inputs but the other's outcomes are much higher, the person will feel that he should be receiving more outcomes and will be dissatisfied as a result.

The model allows for the possibility that people will feel that their outcomes exceed what they should be. The feelings produced by this condition are quite different from those produced by under-reward. Because of this difference, it does not make sense to refer to a person who feels over-rewarded as being dissatisfied. There is considerable evidence that very few people feel over-rewarded, and this fact can be explained by the model. Even when people are highly rewarded, the social-comparison aspect of satisfaction means that people can avoid feeling over-rewarded by looking around and finding someone to compare with who is doing equally well. Also, a person tends to value his own inputs much higher than they are valued by others (Lawler, 1967). Because of this discrepancy, a person's perception of what his outcomes should be is often not shared by those administering his rewards, and is often above what he actually receives. Finally, the person can easily increase his perception of his inputs and thereby justify a high reward level.

As a way of summarizing some of the implications of the model, let us briefly make some statements about who should be dissatisfied if the model is correct. Other things being equal:

1. People with high perceived inputs will be more dissatisfied with a given facet than people with low perceived inputs.
2. People who perceive their job to be demanding will be more dissatisfied with a given facet than people who perceive their jobs as undemanding.
3. People who perceive similar others as having a more favorable input-outcome balance will be more

dissatisfied with a given facet than people who perceive their own balance as similar to or better than that of others.

4. People who receive a low outcome level will be more dissatisfied than those who receive a high outcome level.

5. The more outcomes a person perceives his comparsion-other receives, the more dissatisfied he will be with his own outcomes. This should be particularly true when the comparison-other is seen to hold a job that demands the same or fewer inputs.

OVERALL JOB SATISFACTION

Most theories of job satisfaction argue that overall job satisfaction is determined by some combination of all facet-satisfaction feelings. This could be expressed in terms of the facet-satisfaction model in Figure 3 as a simple sum of, or average of, all $a - b$ discrepancies. Thus, overall job satisfaction is determined by the difference between all the things a person feels he should receive from his job and all the things he actually does receive.

A strong theoretical argument can be made for weighting the facet-satisfaction scores according to their importance. Some factors do make larger contributions to overall satisfaction than others. Pay satisfaction, satisfaction with the work itself, and satisfaction with supervision seem to have particularly strong influences on overall satisfaction for most people. Also, employees tend to rate these factors as important. Thus, there is a connection between how important employees say job factors are and how much job factors influence overall job satisfaction (Vroom, 1964). Conceptually, therefore, it seems worthwhile to think of the various job-facet-satisfaction scores as influencing total satisfaction in terms of their importance. One way to express this relationship is by defining overall job satisfaction as being equal to Σ (facet satisfaction $\times$ facet importance). However, as stressed earlier, actually measuring importance and multiplying it by measured facet satisfaction often isn't necessary because the satisfaction scores themselves seem to take importance into account. (The most important items tend to be scored as either very satisfactory or very dissatisfactory; thus, these items have the most influence on any sum score.) Still, on a conceptual level, it is important to remember that facet-satisfaction scores do differentially contribute to the feeling of overall job satisfaction.

A number of studies have attempted to determine how many workers are actually satisfied with their jobs. Our model does not lead to any predictions in this area. The model simply gives the conditions that lead to people experiencing feelings of satisfaction or dissatisfaction. Not surprisingly, the studies that have been done do not agree on the percentage of dissatisfied workers. Some suggest figures as low as 13 percent, others give figures as high as 80 percent. The range generally reported is from 13 to 25 percent dissatisfied. Herzberg et al. (1957) summarized the findings of research studies conducted from 1946 through 1953. The figures in their report showed a yearly increase in the median percentage of job-satisfied persons (see Table 1). Figure 4 presents satisfaction-trend data for 1948 through 1971. These data also show an overall increase in the number of satisfied workers, which is interesting because of recent speculation that satisfaction is decreasing. However, due to many measurement problems, it is impossible to conclude that a real decline in number of dissatisfied workers has taken place.

The difficulty in obtaining meaningful conclusions from the data stems from the fact that different questions yield very different results. For example, a number of studies, instead of directly asking workers "How satisfied are you?," have asked "If you had it to do over again, would you pick the same job?" The latter question produces much higher dissatisfaction scores than does the simple "how satisfied are you" question. One literature review showed that 54 percent of the workers tended to say that they were sufficiently dissatisfied with their jobs that they would not choose

Table 1. Median Percentage of Job-Dissatisfied Persons Reported from 1946–1953

Year	Median Percentage of Job Dissatisfied
1953	13
1952	15
1951	18
1950	19
1949	19
1948	19
1946–1947	21

Source: From Herzberg et al., *Job Attitudes: Review of Research and Opinion.* Copyright 1957 by the Psychological Service of Pittsburgh. Reprinted by permission.

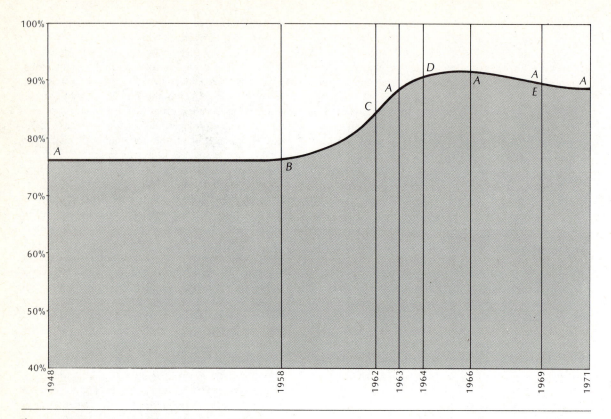

Figure 4.   Percentage of "Satisfied" Workers, 1948–1971.

Source: From Quinn, Staines, and McCullough, 1973.

Note: "Don't know" and "uncertain" have been excluded from the base of the percentages. Sources: *A* = Gallup, or Gallup as reported by Roper; *B* = Survey Research Center (Michigan); *C* = NORC; *D* = Survey Research Center (Berkeley); *E* = 1969–1970 Survey of Working Conditions.

them again. On the other hand, the straight satisfaction question shows between 13 and 25 percent dissatisfied. However, even this figure is subject to wide variation depending on how the question is asked. When the question is asked in the simple form, "Are you satisfied, yes or no?," the number of satisfied responses is large. When the question is changed so that the employees can respond yes, no, or undecided—or satisfied, dissatisfied, or neutral—the number of satisfied responses drops.

Because of these methodological complexities, it is difficult to draw conclusions about the number of workers who are or are not satisfied with their jobs or with some facet of their jobs. This drawback does not mean, however, that meaningful research on satisfac-

tion is impossible. On the contrary, interesting and important research has been and can be done on the determinants of job satisfaction. For example, the relationship between personal-input factors—such as education level, sex, and age and seniority—and job or facet satisfaction can be ascertained by simply comparing those people who report they are satisfied with those people who report they are dissatisfied and checking the results to see if the two groups differ in any systematic manner. The number of people reporting satisfaction is not crucial for this purpose. What is important is that we distinguish those people who tend to be more satisfied from those people who tend to be less satisfied. This distinction can be made with many of the better-known satisfaction-measuring instruments, such as the Job Description Index (Smith, Kendall, & Hulin, 1969) and Porter's (1961) need-satisfaction instrument.

A number of studies have tried to determine the amount of employee dissatisfaction that is associated with different job facets. Although these studies have yielded interesting results, some serious methodological problems are involved in this work. As with overall job satisfaction, factors such as type of measurement scale used and manner of wording questions seriously affect the number of people who express dissatisfaction with a given facet. For example, a question about pay satisfaction can be asked in a way that will cause few people to express dissatisfaction, while a question about security satisfaction can be asked in a way that will cause many people to express dissatisfaction. In this situation, comparing the number of people expressing security satisfaction with the number of people expressing pay dissatisfaction might produce very misleading conclusions. This problem is always present no matter how carefully the various items are worded because it is impossible to balance the items so they are comparable for all factors.

Despite methodological problems, the data on relevant satisfaction levels with different job factors are interesting. These data show that the factors mentioned earlier as being most important — that is, pay, promotion, security, leadership, and the work itself — appear in these studies as the major sources of dissatisfaction. Porter (1961) designed items using Maslow's needs as a measure of satisfaction. With these items, he collected data from various managers. The results of his study (see Table 2) show that more managers express high-order-need dissatisfaction than express lower-order-need dissatisfaction. The results also show that a large number of managers are dissatisfied with their pay and with the communications in their organizations and that middle-level managers tend to be better satisfied in all areas than lower-level managers.

Porter's data also show that managers consider the areas of dissatisfaction to be the most important areas. It is not completely clear whether the dissatisfaction causes the importance or the importance causes the dissatisfaction. The research reviewed earlier suggests that the primary causal direction is from dissatisfaction to importance, although there undoubtedly is a two-way influence process operating. The important thing to remember is that employees do report varying levels of satisfaction with different job factors, and the factors that have come out high on dissatisfaction have also been rated high on importance and have the strongest influence on overall job satisfaction.

A study by Grove and Kerr (1951) illustrates how strongly organizational conditions can affect factor satisfaction. Grove and Kerr measured employee satisfaction in two plants where normal work conditions prevailed and found that 88 percent of the workers were satisfied with their job security, which indicated that security was one of the least dissatisfying job factors for employees in these two plants. In another plant where layoffs had occurred, only 17 percent of the workers said they were satisfied with the job security, and job security was one of the most dissatisfying job factors for this plant's employees.

Table 2. Differences Between Management Levels in Percentage of Subjects Indicating Need-Fulfillment Deficiencies

Questionnaire Items	% Bottom Management (N = 64)	% Middle Management (N = 75)	% Difference
Security needs	42.2	26.7	15.5
Social needs	35.2	32.0	3.2
Esteem needs	55.2	35.6	19.6
Autonomy needs	60.2	47.7	12.5
Self-actualization needs	59.9	53.3	6.6
Pay	79.7	80.0	0.3
Communications	78.1	61.3	16.8

Source: Adapted from Porter, 1961.

DETERMINANTS OF SATISFACTION

The research on the determinants of satisfaction has looked primarily at two relationships: (1) the relationship between satisfaction and the characteristics of the job, and (2) the relationship between satisfaction and the characteristics of the person. Not surprisingly, the research shows that satisfaction is a function of both the person and the environment. These results are consistent with our approach to thinking about satisfaction, since our model (shown in Figure 3) indicates that personal factors influence what people feel they should receive and that job conditions influence both what people perceive they actually receive and what people perceive they should receive. . . .

The evidence on the effects of personal-input factors on satisfaction is voluminous and will be only briefly reviewed. The research clearly shows that personal factors do affect job satisfaction, basically because they influence perceptions of what outcomes should be. As predicted by the satisfaction model in Figure 3, the higher a person's perceived personal inputs — that is, the greater his education, skill, and performance — the more he feels he should receive. Thus, unless the high-input person receives more outcomes, he will be dissatisfied with his job and the rewards his job offers. Such straightforward relationships between inputs and satisfaction appear to exist for all personal-input factors except age and seniority. Evidence from the study of age and seniority suggests a curvilinear relationship (that is, high satisfaction among young and old workers, low satisfaction among middle-age workers) or even a relationship of increasing satisfaction with old age and tenure. The tendency of satisfaction to be high among older, long-term employees seems to be produced by the effects of selective turnover and the development of realistic expectations about what the job has to offer.

CONSEQUENCES OF DISSATISFACTION

Originally much of the interest in job satisfaction stemmed from the belief that job satisfaction influenced job performance. Specifically, psychologists thought that high job satisfaction led to high job performance. This view has now been discredited and most psychologists feel that satisfaction influences absenteeism and turnover but not job performance. However, looking at the relationship among satisfaction, absenteeism, and turnover, let's review the work on satisfaction and performance.

Job Performance

In the 1950s, two major literature reviews showed that in most studies only a slight relationship had been found between satisfaction and performance. A later review by Vroom (1964) also showed that studies had not found a strong relationship between satisfaction and performance; in fact, most studies had found a very low positive relationship between the two. In other words, better performers did seem to be slightly more satisfied than poor performers. A considerable amount of recent work suggests that the slight existing relationship is probably due to better performance indirectly causing satisfaction rather than the reverse. Lawler and Porter (1967) explained this "performance causes satisfaction" viewpoint as follows:

If we assume that rewards cause satisfaction, and that in some cases performance produces rewards, then it is possible that the relationship found between satisfaction and performance comes about through the action of a third variable — rewards. Briefly stated, good performance may lead to rewards, which in turn lead to satisfaction; this formulation then would say that satisfaction, rather than causing performance, as was previously assumed, is caused by it.

[Figure 5] shows that performance leads to rewards, and it distinguishes between two kinds of rewards and their connection to performance. A wavy line between performance and extrinsic rewards indicates that such rewards are likely to be imperfectly related to performance. By extrinsic rewards is meant such organizationally controlled rewards as pay, promotion, status, and security — rewards that are often referred to as satisfying mainly lower-level needs. The connection is relatively weak because of the difficulty of tying extrinsic rewards directly to performance. Even though an organization may have a policy of rewarding merit, performance is difficult to measure, and in dispensing rewards like pay, many other factors are frequently taken into consideration.

Quite the opposite is likely to be true for intrinsic rewards, however, since they are given to the individual by himself for good performance. Intrinsic or internally mediated rewards are subject to fewer disturbing influences and thus are likely to be more directly related

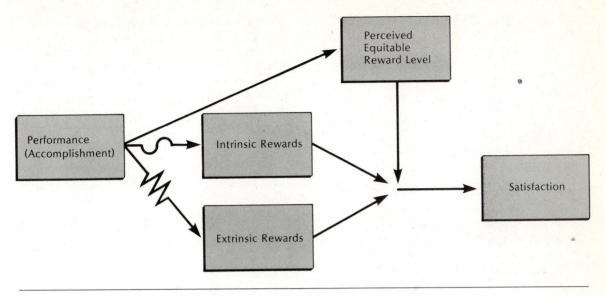

Figure 5.   Model of the Relationship of Performance to Satisfaction.

Source: From E. E. Lawler and L. W. Porter, ''The Effect of Performance on Job Satisfaction,'' *Industrial Relations* 7 (1967): 20-28. Reprinted by permission of the publisher, Industrial Relations.

to good performance. This connection is indicated in the model by a semi-wavy line. Probably the best example of an intrinsic reward is the feeling of having accomplished something worthwhile. For that matter any of the rewards that satisfy self-actualization needs or higher-order growth needs are good examples of intrinsic rewards [pp. 23-24].*

Figure 5 shows that intrinsic and extrinsic rewards are not directly related to job satisfaction, since the relationship is moderated by perceived equitable rewards (what people think they should receive). The model in Figure 5 is similar to the model in Figure 3, since both models show that satisfaction is a function of the amount of rewards a person receives and the amount of rewards he feels he should receive.

Because of the imperfect relationship between performance and rewards and the important effect of perceived equitable rewards, a low but positive relationship should exist between job satisfaction and job performance in most situations. However, in certain situations, a strong positive relationship may exist; while in other situations, a negative relationship may exist. A negative relationship would be expected where rewards are unrelated to performance or negatively related to performance.

To have the same level of satisfaction for good performers and poor performers, the good performers must receive more rewards than the poor performers. The reason for this, as stressed earlier, is that performance level influences the amount of rewards a person feels he should receive. Thus, when rewards are not based on performance — when poor performers receive equal rewards or a larger amount of rewards than good performers — the best performers will be the least satisfied, and a negative satisfaction-performance relationship will exist. If, on the other hand, the better performers are given significantly more rewards, a positive satisfaction-performance relationship should exist. If it is assumed that most organizations are partially successful in relating rewards to performance, it follows that most studies should find a low but positive

*E. E. Lawler and L. W. Porter, ''The Effect of Performance on Job Satisfaction,'' *Industrial Relations* 7 (1967): 20-28. Reprinted by permission of the publisher, Industrial Relations.

relationship between satisfaction and performance. Lawler and Porter's (1967) study was among those that found this relationship; their study also found that, as predicted, intrinsic-need satisfaction was more closely related to performance than was extrinsic-need satisfaction.

In retrospect, it is hard to understand why the belief that high satisfaction causes high performance was so widely accepted. There is nothing in the literature on motivation that suggests this causal relationship. In fact, such a relationship is opposite to the concepts developed by both drive theory and expectancy theory. If anything, these two theories would seem to predict that high satisfaction might reduce motivation because of a consequent reduction in the importance of various rewards that may have provided motivational force. Clearly, a more logical view is that performance is determined by people's efforts to obtain the goals and outcomes they desire, and satisfaction is determined by the outcomes people actually obtain. Yet for some reason, many people believed — and some people still do believe — that the "satisfaction causes performance" view is best.

Turnover

The relationship between satisfaction and turnover has been studied often. In most studies, researchers have measured the job satisfaction among a number of employees and then waited to see which of the employees studied left during an ensuing time period (typically, a year). The satisfaction scores of the employees who left have then been compared with the remaining employees' scores. Although relationships between satisfaction scores and turnover have not always been very strong, the studies in this area have consistently shown that dissatisfied workers are more likely than satisfied workers to terminate employment; thus, satisfaction scores can predict turnover.

A study by Ross and Zander (1957) is a good example of the kind of research that has been done. Ross and Zander measured the job satisfaction of 2,680 female workers in a large company. Four months later, these researchers found that 169 of these employees had resigned; those who left were significantly more dissatisfied with the amount of recognition they received on their jobs, with the amount of achievement they experienced, and with the amount of autonomy they had.

Probably the major reason that turnover and satisfaction are not more strongly related is that turnover is very much influenced by the availability of other positions. Even if a person is very dissatisfied with his job, he is not likely to leave unless more attractive alternatives are available. This observation would suggest that in times of economic prosperity, turnover should be high, and a strong relationship should exist between turnover and satisfaction; but in times of economic hardship, turnover should be low, and little relationship should exist between turnover and satisfaction. There is research evidence to support the argument that voluntary turnover is much lower in periods of economic hardship. However, no study has compared the relationship between satisfaction and turnover under different economic conditions to see if it is stronger under full employment.

Absenteeism

Like turnover, absenteeism has been found to be related to job satisfaction. If anything, the relationship between satisfaction and absenteeism seems to be stronger than the relationship between satisfaction and turnover. However, even in the case of absenteeism, the relationship is far from being isomorphic. Absenteeism is caused by a number of factors other than a person's voluntarily deciding not to come to work; illness, accidents, and so on can prevent someone who wants to come to work from actually coming to work. We would expect satisfaction to affect only voluntary absences; thus, satisfaction can never be strongly related to a measure of overall absence rate. Those studies that have separated voluntary absences from overall absences have, in fact, found that voluntary absence rates are much more closely related to satisfaction than are overall absence rates (Vroom, 1964). Of course, this outcome would be expected if satisfaction does influence people's willingness to come to work.

Organization Effectiveness

The research evidence clearly shows that employees' decisions about whether they will go to work on any given day and whether they will quit are affected by their feelings of job satisfaction. All the literature reviews on the subject have reached this conclusion. The fact that present satisfaction influences future absenteeism and turnover clearly indicates that the causal direction is from satisfaction to behavior. This conclusion is in marked contrast to our conclusion with respect to performance — that is, behavior causes satisfaction. . . .

The research evidence on the determinants of satisfaction suggests that satisfaction is very much influenced by the actual rewards a person receives; of course, the organization has a considerable amount of control over these rewards. The research also shows that, although not all people will react to the same reward level in the same manner, reactions are predictable if something is known about how people perceive their inputs. The implication is that organizations can influence employees' satisfaction levels. Since it is possible to know how employees will react to different outcome levels, organizations can allocate outcomes in ways that will either cause job satisfaction or job dissatisfaction.

Absenteeism and turnover have a very direct influence on organizational effectiveness. Absenteeism is very costly because it interrupts scheduling, creates a need for over-staffing, increases fringe-benefit costs, and so on. Turnover is expensive because of the many costs incurred in recruiting and training replacement employees. For lower-level jobs, the cost of turnover is estimated at $2,000 a person; at the managerial level, the cost is at least five to ten times the monthly salary of the job involved. Because satisfaction is manageable and influences absenteeism and turnover, organizations can control absenteeism and turnover. Generally, by keeping satisfaction high and, specifically, by seeing that the best employees are the most satisfied, organizations can retain those employees they need the most. In effect, organizations can manage turnover so that, if it occurs, it will occur among employees the organization can most afford to lose. However, keeping the better performers more satisfied is not easy, since they must be rewarded very well. . . . although identifying and rewarding the better performers is not always easy, the effort may have significant payoffs in terms of increased organizational effectiveness.

REFERENCES

Adams, J. S. "Toward an Understanding of Inequity." *Journal of Abnormal Psychology* 67 (1963): 422–36.

Adams, J. S. "Injustice in Social Exchange." In L. Berkowitz (ed.), *Advances in Experimental Social Psychology,* vol. 2, edited by L. Berkowitz. New York: Academic Press, 1965.

Dunnette, M. D.; Campbell, J. P.; and Hakel, M. D. "Factory Contributing to Job Satisfaction and Job Dissatisfaction in Six Occupational Groups." *Organizational Behavior and Human Performance* 2 (1967): 143–74.

Gardner, J. W. *No Easy Victories.* New York: Harper & Row, 1968.

Grove, E. A., and Kerr, W. A. "Specific Evidence on Origin of Halo Effect in Measurement of Employee Morale." *Journal of Social Psychology* 34 (1951): 165–70.

Herzberg, F.; Mausner, B.; Peterson, R. O.; and Capwell, D. F. *Job Attitudes: Review of Research and Opinion.* Pittsburgh: Psychological Service of Pittsburgh, 1957.

Herzberg, F.; Mausner, B.; and Snyderman, B. *The Motivation to Work,* 2nd ed. New York: John Wiley & Sons, 1959.

Katzell, R. A. "Personal Values, Job Satisfaction, and Job Behavior." In *Man in a World of Work,* edited by H. Borow. Boston: Houghton Mifflin, 1964.

Lawler, E. E. "The Multitrait-Multirater Approach to Measuring Managerial Job Performance." *Journal of Applied Psychology* 51 (1967): 369–81.

Lawler, E. E., and Porter, L. W. "The Effect of Performance on Job Satisfaction." *Industrial Relations* 7 (1967): 20–28.

Locke, E. A. "What Is Job Satisfaction?" Paper presented at the APA Convention, San Francisco, September 1968.

Locke, E. A. "What Is Job Satisfaction?" *Organizational Behavior and Human Performance* 4 (1969): 309-36.

Mobley, W. H., and Locke, E. A. "The Relationship of Value Importance to Satisfaction." *Organizational Behavior and Human Performance* 5 (1970): 463-83.

Morse, N. C. *Satisfactions in the White-Collar Job*. Ann Arbor: University of Michigan, Institute for Social Research, Survey Research Center, 1953.

Porter, L. W. "A Study of Perceived Need Satisfactions in Bottom and Middle Management Jobs." *Journal of Applied Psychology* 45 (1961): 1-10.

Ross, I. E., and Zander, A. F. "Need Satisfaction and Employee Turnover." *Personnel Psychology* 10 (1957): 327-38.

Schaffer, R. H. "Job Satisfaction as Related to Need Satisfaction in Work." *Psychological Monographs 67 (1953): 14, whole no. 364.*

Smith, P.; Kendall, L.; and Hulin, C. *The Measurement of Satisfaction in Work and Retirement*. Chicago: Rand McNally & Company, 1969.

Vroom, V. H. *Work and Motivation*. New York: John Wiley & Sons, 1964.

Wanous, J. P., and Lawler, E. E. "Measurement and Meaning of Job Satisfaction." *Journal of Applied Psychology* 56 (1972): 95-105.

9.   Major Influences on Employee Attendance: A Process Model*

Richard M. Steers and Susan R. Rhodes

Each year, it is estimated that over 400 million work days are lost in the United States due to employee absenteeism, or about 5.1 days lost per employee (Yolles, Carone, & Krinsky, 1975). In many industries, daily blue-collar absenteeism runs as high as 10% to 20% of the workforce (Lawler, 1971). A recent study by Mirvis and Lawler (1977) estimates the cost of absenteeism among non-managerial personnel to be about $66 per day per employee; this estimate includes both direct salary and fringe benefit costs, as well as costs associated with temporary replacement and estimated loss of profit. While such figures are admittedly crude, combining the estimated total days lost with the costs associated with absenteeism yields an estimated annual cost of absenteeism in the U.S. of $26.4 billion! Even taking the more conservative minimum wage rate yields an estimated annual cost of $8.5 billion. Clearly, the phenomenon of employee absenteeism is an important area for empirical research and management concern. . . .

A review of existing research indicates that investigators of employee absenteeism have typically examined bivariate correlations between a set of variables and subsequent absenteeism (Muchinsky, 1977; Nicholson, Brown & Chadwick-Jones, 1976; Porter & Steers, 1973; Vroom, 1964). Little in the way of comprehensive

*Support for this paper was provided by funds supplied under ONR Contract No. N00014-76-C-0164, NR 170-812.

theory-building can be found, with the possible exception of Gibson (1966). Moreover, two basic (and questionable) assumptions permeate the work that has been done to date. First, the current literature largely assumes that job dissatisfaction represents the primary cause of absenteeism. Unfortunately, however, existing research consistently finds only weak support for this hypothesis. Locke (1976), for example, points out that the magnitude of the correlation between dissatisfaction and absenteeism is generally quite low, seldom surpassing $r = .40$ and typically much lower. Moreover, Nicholson et al. (1976), in their review of 29 such studies, concluded that "at best it seems that job satisfaction and absence from work are tenuously related (p. 734)." Nicholson et al. also observed that the strength of this relationship deteriorates as one moves from group-based studies to individually-based studies. Similar weak findings have been reported earlier (Porter & Steers, 1973; Vroom, 1964). Implicit in these modest findings is the probable existence of additional variables (both personal and organizational) which may serve to moderate or enhance the satisfaction-attendance relationship.

The second major problem to be found in much of the current work on absenteeism is the implicit assumption that employees are generally free to choose whether or not to come to work. As noted by Herman (1973) and others, such is often not the case. In a variety of studies, important situational constraints were found which influenced the attitude-behavior relationship (Herman, 1973; Ilgen & Hollenback, 1977; Morgan & Herman, 1976; Smith, 1977). Hence, there appear to be a variety of situational constraints (e.g., poor health, family responsibilities, transportation problems) that can interfere with free choice in an attendance decision. Thus, a comprehensive model of attendance must include not only job attitudes and other influences on attendance motivation but also situational constraints that inhibit a strong motivation-behavior relationship.

In view of the multitude of narrowly-focused studies of absenteeism but the dearth of conceptual frameworks for integrating these findings, it appears useful to attempt to identify the major sets of variables that influence attendance behavior and to suggest how such variables fit together into a general model of employee attendance. Toward this end, a model of employee attendance is presented here. This model incorporates both voluntary and involuntary absenteeism and is based on a review of 104 studies of absenteeism (see Rhodes & Steers, Note 4). . . .

THE CONCEPTUAL MODEL

The model proposed here attempts to examine in a systematic and comprehensive fashion the various influences on employee attendance behavior. Briefly stated, it is suggested that an employee's attendance is largely a function of two important variables: (1) an employee's motivation to attend; and (2) an employee's ability to attend. Both of these factors are included in the schematic diagram presented in Figure 1 and each will be discussed separately as it relates to existing research. First, we shall examine the proposed antecedents of attendance motivation.

Job Situation, Satisfaction, and Attendance Motivation

A fundamental premise of the model suggested here is that an employee's motivation to come to work represents the primary influence on actual attendance, assuming one has the ability to attend (Herman, 1973; Locke, 1968). Given this, questions must be raised concerning the major influences on attendance motivation. Available evidence indicates that such motivation is determined largely by a combination of: (1) an employee's affective responses to the job situation; and (2) various internal and external pressures to attend (Vroom, 1964; Hackman & Lawler, 1971; Locke, 1976; Porter & Lawler, 1968). In this section, we will examine the relationship between an employee's satisfaction with the job situation and attendance motivation. The second major influence on attendance motivation, pressures to attend, will be dealt with subsequently.

Other things being equal, when an employee enjoys the work environment and the tasks that characterize his or her job situation, we would expect that employee to have a strong desire to come to work (Hackman & Lawler, 1971; Lundquist, 1958; Newman, 1974; Porter & Steers, 1973; Vroom, 1964). Under such circumstances, the work experience would be a pleasurable one. In view of this relationship, our first question concerns the manner in which the job situation affects one's attendance motivation. The job situation (box 1 in Figure 1), as conceived here, consists of those variables that characterize the nature of the job and the surrounding work environment. Included in the job situation are such variables as: (1) job scope; (2) job level; (3) role stress; (4) work group size; (5) leader style; (6) co-worker relations; and (7) opportunities for advancement. In essence,

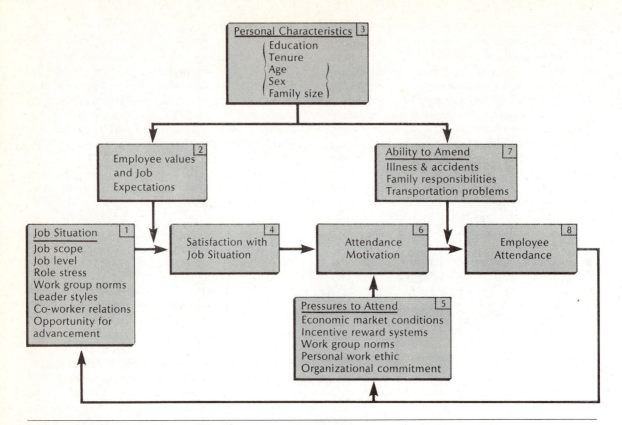

Figure 1. A Model of Employee Attendance.

available evidence suggests that variables such as these strongly influence one's level of satisfaction which, in turn, influences attendance motivation. . . .

The Role of Employee Values and Job Expectations

Considerable evidence suggests that the relationship between job situation variables and subsequent satisfaction and attendance motivation is not a direct one (Locke, 1976). Instead, a major influence on the extent to which employees experience satisfaction with the job situation is the values and expectations they have concerning the job (box 2). It has been noted previously that people come to work with differing values and job expectations; that is, they value different features in a job and expect these features to be present to a certain degree in order to maintain membership (Locke, 1976; Porter & Steers, 1973).

To a large extent these values and expectations are influenced by the personal characteristics and backgrounds of the employees (box 3). For example, employees with higher educational levels (e.g., a college degree) may value and expect greater (or at least different) rewards from an organization than those with less education (e.g., a private office, a secretary, a higher salary, greater freedom of action). Support for this contention can be found in Hedges (1973). Moreover, older and more tenured employees often value and expect certain perquisites because of their seniority (Baumgartel & Sobol, 1959; Cooper & Payne, 1965; Nicholson et al., 1976; Nicholson, Brown, & Chadwick-Jones, 1977; Hill & Trist, 1955; Martin, 1971).

Whatever the values and expectations that individuals bring to the job situation, it is important that these factors be largely met for the individual to be satisfied. In this regard, Smith (1972) found that realistic job previews created realistic job expectations among employees and led to a significant decline in absenteeism. Somewhat relatedly, Stockford (1944) found that absenteeism was higher among a sample of industrial workers whose previous training was not seen as relevant for their current positions than among a sample whose training was more closely aligned with the realities of the job situations (see also: Weaver & Holmes, 1972). Hence, based on the limited evidence that is available, it would appear that the extent to which an employee's values and expectations are met does influence the desirability of going to work.

Pressures to Attend

While satisfaction with the job situation thus apparently represents a major influence on attendance motivation, the relationship is indeed not a perfect one. Other factors can be identified which serve to enhance attendance motivation, probably in an additive fashion (Garrison & Muchinsky, 1977; Ilgen & Hollenback, 1977; Nicholson et al., 1976). These variables are collectively termed here "pressures to attend" and represent the second major influence on the desire to come to work. These pressures may be economic, social, or personal in nature and are represented in Figure 1 by box 5. Specifically, at least five major pressures can be identified: (1) economic and market conditions; (2) incentive/reward system; (3) work group norms; (4) personal work ethic; and (5) organizational commitment.

Economic and Market Conditions. The general state of the economy and the job market place constraints on one's ability to change jobs. Consequently, in times of high unemployment, there may be increased pressure to maintain a good attendance record for fear of losing one's job. Evidence suggests that there is a close inverse relationship between changes in unemployment levels within a given geographical region and subsequent absence rates (Behrend, Note 1; Crowther, 1957). Moreover, as the threat of layoff becomes even greater (e.g., when an employee's own employer begins layoffs), there is an even stronger decrease in absenteeism (Behrend, Note 1).

However, when an employee knows that *he* or *she* is to be laid off (as opposed to a knowledge that layoffs are taking place in general), the situation is somewhat different. Specifically, Owens (1966) found that railway repair employees in a depressed industry who had been

given notice of layoff because of shop closure had significantly higher absence rates prior to layoffs than a comparable group of employees who were not to be laid off. Owens suggests that, in addition to being a reflection of manifest anxiety, the increased absenteeism allowed employees time to find new positions. On the other hand, Hershey (1972) found no significant differences in absence rates between employees who were scheduled for layoffs and employees not so scheduled. Hershey argued that the subjects in his study were much in demand in the labor market and generally felt assured of finding suitable jobs. (Improved unemployment compensation in recent years may also have been a factor in minimizing absenteeism among those to be laid off.)

Hence, economic and market factors may be largely related to attendance motivation and subsequent attendance through their effects on one's ability to change jobs. When *general* economic conditions are deteriorating, employees may be less likely to be absent for fear of reprisal. However, when the *individual* employee is to be laid off, absence rates are apparently influenced by one's perceptions of his or her ability to find alternate employment. Where such alternatives are readily available, no effect of impending layoff on absenteeism is noted; when such alternatives are not readily available, absence rates can be expected to increase as employees seek other employment.

Incentive/Reward System. A primary factor capable of influencing attendance motivation is the nature of the incentive or reward system used by an organization. Several aspects of the reward system have been found to influence attendance behavior.

When perceptual measures of pay and pay satisfaction are used, mixed results are found between such measures and absenteeism. Specifically, three studies among various work samples found an inverse relationship between pay satisfaction or perceived pay equity and absenteeism (Patchen, 1960; Dittrich & Carrell, 1976; Smith, 1977), while six other studies did not find such a relationship (Hackman & Lawler, 1971; Newman, 1974; Nicholson et al., 1976; Lundquist, 1958; Garrison & Muchinsky, 1977; Nicholson et al., 1977). Three other studies found mixed results (Waters & Roach, 1971, 1973; Metzner & Mann, 1953). In short, it is difficult to draw any firm conclusions about pay and absenteeism from these perceptual measures.

In contrast, when actual wage rates or incentive systems have been studied, the results are somewhat more definitive. Lundquist (1958), Fried et al. (1972), Beatty and Beatty (1975), and Bernardin (1977) all found a direct inverse relationship between wage rate and absenteeism. The Bernardin study is particularly useful here because several potentially spurious variables (e.g., age, tenure) were partialled out of the analysis and because the results were cross-validated. Moreover, the Lundquist study employed multiple absence measures with similar results. Other studies cited in Yolles et al. (1975) point to the same conclusion. However, studies by Fried et al. (1972) and Weaver and Holmes (1972), both using the less rigorous "total days absent" measure of absenteeism, did not support this relationship. In view of the objective nature of actual wage rates as opposed to perceptual measures, it would appear that greater confidence can be placed in them than in the perceptual studies mentioned above. Hence we would expect increases in salary or wage rates to represent one source of pressure to attend, even where the employee did not like the task requirements of the job itself.

Several factors must be kept in mind when considering the role of incentives or reward systems in attendance motivation. First, the rewards offered by the organization must be seen as being both attainable and tied directly to attendance. As Lawler (1971) points out, many organizations create reward systems that at least up to a point reward nonattendance. For instance, the practice of providing 12 days "sick leave" which employees lose if they fail to use only encourages people to be "sick" 12 days a year (see also: Morgan & Herman, 1976). In this regard, Garrison and Muchinsky (1977) found a negative relationship between job satisfaction and absenteeism for employees absent without pay but no such relationship for employees absent with pay. Hence there must be an expectancy on the part of the employee that attendance (and not absenteeism) will lead to desirable rewards. Moreover, the employees must value the rewards available. If an employee would prefer a three-day weekend to having additional pay, there is little reason to expect that employee to be motivated to attend. On the other hand, an employee with a strong financial need (perhaps because of a large family) would be expected to attend if attendance was financially rewarded.

Oftentimes, a major portion of an employee's income is derived from overtime work. Consequently, the effects of such overtime on absenteeism is important to note. Two studies found that the availability of overtime work among both male and female employees was *positively* related to absenteeism (Gowler, 1969; Martin,

1971), while two other studies found no such relationship (Buck & Shimmin, 1959; Flannagan, 1974). One could argue here that the availability of overtime with premium pay can lead to an incentive system that rewards absenteeism, not attendance. That is, if an employee is absent during regular working hours (and possibly compensated for this by sick leave), he or she can then work overtime later in the week to make up for the production lost earlier due to absenteeism. Clearly, such a reward system would operate differently than it was intended to. However, in view of the fact that all four relevant studies used either weak absence measures or unduly small samples, the influence of overtime availability on absenteeism must remain in the realm of conjecture pending further study.

Several attempts have been made to examine experimentally the effects of incentive or reward systems in work organizations. In one such study, Lawler and Hackman (1969; Scheflen, Lawler, & Hackman, 1971) experimentally introduced a bonus incentive plan to reward group attendance among a sample of part-time blue-collar employees. Two important findings emerged. First, the employees working under the bonus plan were found to have better attendance records than those not working under the plan. Moreover, the group that was allowed to participate in developing the bonus plan had higher attendance rates than the other experimental group that was given the bonus plan without an opportunity to participate in its design. (See also: Glaser, 1976). Hence, both the adoption of a bonus incentive system to reward attendance and employee participation in the development of such a system appear to represent important influences on subsequent attendance.

A few studies have examined the role of punitive sanctions by management in controlling absenteeism. Results have been mixed. Two studies found that the use of stringent reporting and control procedures (e.g., keeping detailed attendance records, requiring medical verifications for reported illnesses, strict disciplinary measures) was related to lower absence rates (Baum & Youngblood, 1975; Seatter, 1961), while one found no such relationship (Rosen & Turner, 1971). Moreover, Buzzard and Liddell (Note 2) and Nicholson (1976) found that such controls did not influence average attendance rates, but did lead to fewer but longer absences. Such contradictory results concerning the use of punitive sanctions suggests that more effective results may be achieved through more positive reward systems than through punishment.

One such positive approach is the use of a lottery reward system, where daily attendance qualifies employees for an opportunity to win some prize or bonus. This approach is closely tied to the behavior modification approach to employee motivation (Hamner & Hamner, 1976). Four studies report such lotteries can represent a successful vehicle for reducing absenteeism (Nord, 1970; Tjersland, 1972; Pedalino & Gamboa, 1974; Johnson & Wallin, Note 3). However, in view of the very small magnitude of the rewards available for good attendance, it is possible here that results were caused more by the ''Hawthorne effect'' than the lottery itself. As Locke (1977) points out, in at least one of the lottery experiments (Pedalino & Gamboa, 1974), absenteeism in the experimental group declined even before anyone in the group had been, or could have been, reinforced. In addition, more conventional behavior modification techniques for reducing absenteeism, reviewed in Hamner and Hamner (1976), show only moderate results over short periods of time.

Finally, other approaches to incentives and rewards relate to modifying the traditional work week. For instance, Golembiewski et al. (1974) and Robison (Note 5) both reported a moderate decline in absenteeism following the introduction of ''flexitime,'' where hours worked can be altered somewhat to meet employee needs. Moreover, while Nord and Costigan (1973) found favorable results implementing a four-day (4–40) work week, Ivancevich (1974) did not. Since both of these studies used similar samples, it is difficult to draw meaningful conclusions about the utility of such programs for reducing absenteeism.

Work Group Norms. Pressure for or against attendance can also emerge from one's colleagues in the form of work group norms. The potency of such norms is clearly established (Cartwright & Zander, 1968; Shaw, 1976). Where the norms of the group emphasize the importance of good attendance for the benefit of the group, increased attendance would be expected (Gibson, 1966). Recent findings by Ilgen and Hollenback (1977) support such a conclusion. This relationship would be expected to be particularly strong in groups with a high degree of work group cohesiveness (Whyte, 1969). In his job attractiveness model of employee motivation, Lawler (1971) points out that members of highly cohesive groups view coming to work to help one's co-workers as highly desirable; hence, job attendance is more attractive than absenteeism. In this

regard, several uncontrolled field experiments have been carried out (summarized by Glaser, 1976) which found that the creation of ''autonomous work groups'' consistently led to increased work group cohesiveness and reduced absenteeism. It should be remembered, however, that work group norms can also have a detrimental impact on attendance where they support periodic absenteeism and punish perfect attendance.

Personal Work Ethic. A further influence on attendance motivation is the personal value system that individuals have (Rokeach, 1973). Recent research on the ''work ethic'' has shown considerable variation across employees in the extent to which they feel morally obligated to work. In particular, several investigations have noted a direct relationship between a strong work ethic and the propensity to come to work (Goodale, 1973; Ilgen & Hollenback, 1977; Feldman, 1974; Searls et al., 1974). While more study is clearly in order here, it would appear that one major pressure to attend is the belief by individuals that work activity is an important aspect of life, almost irrespective of the nature of the job itself.

Organizational Commitment. Finally, somewhat related to the notion of a personal work ethic is the concept of organizational commitment (Porter, Steers, Mowday, & Boulian, 1974). Commitment represents an agreement on the part of the employees with the goals and objectives of an organization and a willingness to work towards those goals. In short, if an employee firmly believes in what an organization is trying to achieve, he or she should be more motivated to attend and contribute toward those objectives. This motivation may exist even if the employee does not enjoy the actual tasks required by the job (e.g., a nurse's aide who may not like certain distasteful aspects of the job but who feels he or she is contributing to worthwhile public health goals). Support for this proposition can be found in Steers (1977) and Smith (1977), where commitment and attendance were found to be related for two separate samples of employees. On the other hand, where an employee's primary commitments lie elsewhere (e.g., to a hobby, family, home, or sports), less internal pressure would be exerted on the employee to attend (Morgan & Herman, 1976). This notion of competing commitments is an important one often overlooked in research on absenteeism.

Ability to Attend

A major weakness inherent in much of the current research on absenteeism is the failure to account for (and partial out) involuntary absenteeism in the study of voluntary absenteeism. This failure has led to many contradictions in the research literature that may be explained by measurement error alone. [In fact, in a comparison of five absenteeism measures, Nicholson and Goodge (1976) found an average intercorrelation of $r = .24$ between measures, certainly not an encouraging coefficient.] Thus, if we are serious about studying absenteeism, a clear distinction must be made between voluntary and involuntary attendance behavior and both must necessarily be accounted for in model-building efforts.

Even if a person wants to come to work and has a high attendance motivation, there are many instances where such attendance is not possible; that is, where the individual does not have behavioral discretion or choice (Herman, 1973). At least three such unavoidable limitations on attendance behavior can be identified: (1) illness and accidents; (2) family responsibilities; and (3) transportation problems (box 7).

Illness and Accidents. Poor health or injury clearly represents a primary cause of absenteeism (Hedges, 1973; Hill & Trist, 1955). Both illness and accidents are often associated with increased age (Baumgartel & Sobol, 1959; De La Mare & Sergean, 1961; Cooper & Payne, 1965; Martin, 1971). This influence of personal characteristics on ability to attend is shown in box 3 of Figure 1. Included in this category of health-related absences would also be problems of alcoholism and drug abuse as they inhibit attendance behavior. [See Yolles et al. (1975) for a review of the literature on health-related reasons for absenteeism.]

Family Responsibilities. The second constraint on attendance is often overlooked: namely, family responsibilities. As with health, this limitation as it relates to attendance is largely determined by the personal characteristics of the individual (sex, age, family size). In general, women as a group are absent more frequently than men (Covner, 1950; Hedges, 1973; Kerr et al., 1951; Kilbridge, 1961; Isambert-Jamati, 1962; Flanagan, 1974; Yolles et al., 1975). This finding is apparently linked, not only to the different types of jobs women typically hold compared to men, but also to the traditional family responsibilities assigned to women

(that is, it is generally the wife or mother who cares for sick children). Support for this assumption comes from Naylor and Vincent (1959), Noland (1945), and Beatty and Beatty (1975). Hence, we would expect female absenteeism to increase with family size (Ilgen & Hollenback, 1977; Nicholson & Goodge, 1976; Isambert-Jamati, 1962).

It is interesting to note, however, that the available evidence suggests that the absenteeism rate for women declines throughout their work career (possibly because the family responsibilities associated with young children declines). For males, on the other hand, unavoidable absenteeism apparently increases with age (presumably because of health reasons), while avoidable absenteeism does not (Nicholson et al., 1977; Martin, 1971; Yolles et al., 1975). In any case, gender and family responsibilities do appear to place constraints on attendance behavior for some employees.

Transportation Problems. Finally, some evidence suggests that difficulty in getting to work can at times influence actual attendance. This difficulty may take the form of travel distance from work (Isambert-Jamati, 1962; Martin, 1971; Stockford, 1944), travel time to and from work (Knox, 1961), or weather conditions that impede traffic (Smith, 1977). Exceptions to this trend have been noted by Hill (1967) and Nicholson and Goodge (1976), who found no relationship between either travel distance or availability of public transportation and absence. In general, however, increased difficulty of getting to work due to transportation problems does seem to represent one possible impediment to attendance behavior for some employees, even when the individual is motivated to attend.

Cyclical Nature of Model

Finally, as noted in Figure 1, the model as presented is a process model. That is, the act of attendance or absenteeism often influences the subsequent job situation and subsequent pressures to attend in a cyclical fashion. For example, a superior attendance record is often used in organizations as one indicator of noteworthy job performance and readiness for promotion. Conversely, a high rate of absenteeism may adversely affect an employee's relationship with his or her supervisor and co-workers and result in changes in leadership style and co-worker relations. Also, widespread absenteeism may cause changes in company incentive/reward systems, including absence control policies. Other outcomes could be mentioned. The point here is that the model, as suggested, is a dynamic one, with employee attendance or absenteeism often leading to changes in the job situation which, in turn, influence subsequent attendance motivation.

CONCLUSION AND DISCUSSION

Our review of the research literature on employee absenteeism reveals a multiplicity of influences on the decision and ability to come to work. These influences emerge both from the individuals themselves (e.g., personal work ethic, demographic factors) and from the work environment (e.g., the job situation, incentive/reward systems, work group norms). Moreover, some of these influences are largely under the control of the employees (e.g., organizational commitment), while others are clearly beyond their control (e.g., health).

We have attempted to integrate the available evidence into a systematic conceptual model of attendance behavior. In essence, it is suggested that the nature of the job situation interacts with employee values and expectations to determine satisfaction with the job situation (Locke, 1976; Porter & Steers, 1973). This satisfaction combines in an additive fashion with various pressures to attend to determine an employee's level of attendance motivation. Moreover, it is noted that the relationship between attendance motivation and actual attendance is influenced by one's ability to attend, a situational constraint (Herman, 1973; Smith, 1977). Finally, the model notes that feedback from the results of actual attendance behavior can often influence subsequent perceptions of the job situation, pressures to attend, and attendance motivation. Hence, the cyclical nature of the model should not be overlooked.

The importance of the various factors in the model would be expected to vary somewhat across employees. That is, certain factors may facilitate attendance for some employees but not for others. For instance, one employee may be intrinsically motivated to attend because of a challenging job; this individual may not feel any strong external pressures to attend because he or she likes the job itself. Another employee, however, may have a distasteful job (and not be intrinsically motivated) and yet may come to work because of other pressures (e.g., financial need). Both employees would attend, but for somewhat different reasons.

This interaction suggests a substitutability of influences up to a point for some variables. For instance, managers concerned with reducing absenteeism on monotonous jobs may change the incentive/reward system (that is, increase the attendance-reward contingencies) as a substitute for an unenriched work environment. In fact, it has been noted elsewhere that most successful applications of behavior modification (a manipulation of behavior-reward contingencies) have been carried out among employees holding unenriched jobs (Steers & Spencer, 1977). Support for this substitutability principle can be found in Ilgen and Hollenback (1977), who found some evidence that various factors influence attendance in an additive fashion, not a multiplicative one. Thus, the strength of attendance motivation would be expected to increase as more and more major influences, or pressures, emerged.

In addition, differences can be found in the manner in which the various influences on attendance affect such behavior. That is, a few of the major variables are apparently fairly *directly* related to desire to attend (if not actual attendance). For instance, highly satisfied employees would probably want strongly to attend, while highly dissatisfied employees would probably want strongly not to attend. On the other hand, certain other factors appear to serve a *gatekeeper* function and do not covary directly with attendance. The most prominent gatekeeper variable is one's health. While sick employees typically do not come to work, it does not necessarily follow that healthy employees will attend. Instead, other factors (e.g., attendance motivation) serve to influence a healthy person's attendance behavior.

In conclusion, the proposed model of employee attendance identifies several major categories of factors that have been shown to influence attendance behavior. Moreover, the model specifies, or hypothesizes, how these various factors fit together to influence the decision to come to work. Throughout, the model emphasizes the psychological processes underlying attendance behavior and in this sense is felt to be superior to the traditional bivariate correlational studies that proliferate on the topic. It remains the task of future research to extend our knowledge on this important topic and to clarify further the nature of the relationships among variables as they jointly influence an employee's desire and intent to come to work. It is hoped that the model presented here represents one useful step toward a better understanding of this process.

REFERENCE NOTES*

1. Behrend, H. Absence under full employment. Monograph A3, University of Birmingham Studies in Economics and Society, 1951.

2. Buzzard, R. B., & Liddell, F. D. K. Coal miners' attendance at work. NCB Medical Service, Medical Research Memorandum No. 3, 1958.

3. Johnson, R. D., & Wallin, J. A. Employee attendance: An operant conditioning intervention in a field setting. Paper presented at American Psychological Association annual meeting, Washington, D.C., 1976.

4. Rhodes, S. R., & Steers, R. M. Summary tables of studies of employee absenteeism. Technical Report No. 13, University of Oregon, 1977. This report is available from the second author at the Graduate School of Management. University of Oregon, Eugene, OR 97403.

5. Robison, D. Alternate work patterns: Changing approaches to work scheduling. Report of a conference sponsored by National Center for Productivity and Quality of Working Life and the Work in America Institute, Inc., June 2, 1976, Plaza Hotel, New York.

REFERENCES

Baum, J. F., & Youngblood, S. A. Impact of an organizational control policy on absenteeism, performance, and satisfaction. *Journal of Applied Psychology,* 1975, **60,** 688–694.

Baumgartel, H., & Sobol, R. Background and organizational factors in absenteeism. *Personnel Psychology,* 1959, **12,** 431–443.

Beatty, R. W., & Beatty, J. R. Longitudinal study of absenteeism of hard-core unemployed. *Psychological Reports,* 1975, **36,** 395–406.

Bernardin, H. J. The relationship of personality variables to organizational withdrawal. *Personnel Psychology,* 1977, **30,** 17–27.

Buck, L., & Shimmin, S. Overtime and financial responsibility. *Occupational Psychology,* 1959, **33,** 137–148.

Cartwright, D., & Zander, A. *Group dynamics.* New York: Harper & Row, 1968.

Cooper, R., & Payne, R. Age and absence: A longitudinal study in three firms. *Occupational Psychology,* 1965, **39,** 31 – 43.

Covner, B. J. Management factors affecting absenteeism. *Harvard Business Review,* 1950, **28,** 42–48.

Crowther, J. Absence and turnover in the divisions of one company — 1950-55. *Occupational Psychology,* 1957, **31,** 256–270.

de la Mare, G., & Sergean, R. Two methods of studying changes in absence with age. *Occupational Psychology,* 1961, **35,** 245–252.

Dittrich, J. E., & Carrel, M. R. Dimensions of organizational fairness as predictors of job satisfaction, absence and turnover. *Academy of Management Proceedings '76.* Thirty-Sixth Annual Meeting of the Academy of Management, Kansas City, Missouri, August 11-14, 1976.

Feldman, J. Race, economic class, and the intention to work: Some normative and attitudinal correlates. *Journal of Applied Psychology,* 1974, **59,** 179–186.

Flanagan, R. J., Strauss, G., & Ulman, L. Worker discontent and work place behavior. *Industrial Relations,* 1974, **13,** 101–123.

Fried, J., Wertman, M., & Davis, M. Man-machine interaction and absenteeism. *Journal of Applied Psychology,* 1972, **56,** 428–429.

---

*Reference Notes and References have been abridged.

Garrison, K. R., & Muchinsky, R. M. Attitudinal and biographical predictors of incidental absenteeism. *Journal of Vocational Behavior,* 1977, **10,** 221-230.

Gibson, J. O. Toward a conceptualization of absence behavior of personnel in organizations. *Administrative Science Quarterly,* 1966, **11,** 107-133.

Glaser, E. M. *Productivity gains through worklife improvement.* New York: The Psychological Corporation, 1976.

Golembiewski, R. T., Hilles, R., & Kagno, M. S. A longitudinal study of flex-time effects: Some consequences of an OD structural intervention. *Journal of Applied Behavioral Science,* 1974, **10,** 503-532.

Goodale, J. G. Effects of personal background and training on work values of the hard-core unemployed. *Journal of Applied Psychology,* 1973, **57,** 1-9.

Gowler, D. Determinants of the supply of labour to the firm. *Journal of Management Studies,* 1969, **6,** 73-95.

Hackman, J. R., & Lawler, E. E., III. Employee reactions to job characteristics. *Journal of Applied Psychology Monograph,* 1971, **55,** 259-286.

Hamner, W. C., & Hamner, E. P. Behavior modification on the bottom line. *Organizational Dynamics,* 1976, **4**(4), 2-21.

Hedges, J. N. Absence from work — A look at some national data. *Monthly Labor Review,* 1973, **96,** 24-31.

Herman, J. B. Are situational contingencies limiting job attitude-job performance relationships? *Organizational Behavior and Human Performance,* 1973, **10,** 208-224.

Hershey, R. Effects of anticipated job loss on employee behavior. *Journal of Applied Psychology,* 1972, **56,** 273-274.

Hill, J. M., & Trist, E. L. Changes in accidents and other absences with length of service. *Human Relations,* 1955, **8,** 121-152.

Ilgen, D. R., & Hollenback, J. H. The role of job satisfaction in absence behavior. *Organizational Behavior and Human Performance,* 1977, **19,** 148-161.

Isambert-Jamati, V. Absenteeism among women workers in industry. *International Labour Review,* 1962, **85,** 248-261.

Ivancevich, J. M. Effects of the shorter workweek on selected satisfaction and performance measures, *Journal of Applied Psychology,* 1974, **59,** 717-721.

Kerr, W., Koppelmeier, G., & Sullivan, J. Absenteeism turnover and morale in a metals fabrication factory. *Occupational Psychology,* 1951, **25,** 50-55.

Kilbridge, M. Turnover, absence, and transfer rates as indicators of employee dissatisfaction with repetitive work. *Industrial and Labor Relations Review,* 1961, **15,** 21-32.

Knox, J. B. Absenteeism and turnover in an Argentine factory. *American Sociological Review,* 1961, **26,** 424-428.

Lawler, E. E., III. *Pay and organizational effectiveness.* New York: McGraw-Hill, 1971.

Lawler, E. E., III, & Hackman, J. R. Impact of employee participation in the development of pay incentive plans: A field experiment. *Journal of Applied Psychology,* 1969, **53,** 467-471.

Locke, E. A. Toward a theory of task motivation and incentives. *Organizational Behavior and Human Performance,* 1968, **3,** 157-189.

Locke, E. A. The nature and causes of job satisfaction. In M. D. Dunnette (Ed.), *Handbook of industrial and organizational psychology.* Chicago: Rand McNally, 1976, pp. 1297-1349.

Locke, E. A. The myths of behavior mod in organizations. *Academy of Management Review,* 1977, **2,** 543-553.

Lundquist, A. Absenteeism and job turnover as a consequence of unfavorable job adjustment. *Acta Sociologica,* 1958, **3,** 119-131.

Martin, J. Some aspects of absence in a light engineering factory. *Occupational Psychology,* 1971, **45,** 77-91.

Metzner, H., & Mann, F. Employee attitudes and absences. *Personnel Psychology,* 1953, **6,** 467-485.

Mirvis, P. H., & Lawler, E. E., III. Measuring the financial impact of employee attitudes, *Journal of Applied Psychology,* 1977, **62,** 1–8.

Morgan, L. G., & Herman, J. B. Perceived consequences of absenteeism. *Journal of Applied Psychology,* 1976, **61,** 738–742.

Muchinsky, P. M. Employee absenteeism: A review of the literature. *Journal of Vocational Behavior,* 1977, **10,** 316–340.

Naylor, J. E., & Vincent, N. L. Predicting female absenteeism. *Personnel Psychology,* 1959, **12,** 81–84.

Newman, J. E. Predicting absenteeism and turnover. *Journal of Applied Psychology,* 1974, **59,** 610–615.

Nicholson, N. Management sanctions and absence control. *Human Relations,* 1976, **29,,** 139–151.

Nicholson, N., Brown, C. A., & Chadwick-Jones, J. K. Absence from work and job satisfaction. *Journal of Applied Psychology,* 1976, **61,** 728–737.

Nicholson, N., Brown, C. A., & Chadwick-Jones, J. K. Absence from work and personal characteristics. *Journal of Applied Psychology,* 1977, **62,** 319–327.

Nicholson, N., & Goodge, P. M. The influence of social, organizational and biographical factors on female absence. *Journal of Management Studies,* 1976, **13,** 234–254.

Nicholson, N., Wall, T., & Lischeron, J. The predictability of absence and propensity to leave from employees' job satisfaction and attitudes toward influence in decision-making. *Human Relations,* 1977, **30,** 499–514.

Noland, E. W. Attitudes and industrial absenteeism: A statistical appraisal. *American Sociological Review,* 1945, **10,** 503–510.

Nord, W. Improving attendance through rewards. *Personnel Administration,* November 1970, 37–41.

Nord, W. R., & Costigan, R. Worker adjustment to the four-day week: A longitudinal study. *Journal of Applied Psychology,* 1973, **58,** 660–661.

Owens, A. C. Sick leave among railwaymen threatened by redundancy: A pilot study. *Occupational Psychology,* 1966, **40,** 43–52.

Patchen, M. Absence and employee feelings about fair treatment. *Personnel Psychology,* 1960, **13,** 349–360.

Pedalino, E., & Gamboa, V. V. Behavior modification and absenteeism: Intervention in one industrial setting. *Journal of Applied Psychology,* 1974, **59,** 694–698.

Porter, L. W., & Lawler, E. E. *Managerial attitudes and performance.* Homewood, Ill.: Irwin, 1968.

Porter, L. W., & Steers, R. M. Organizational, work, and personal factors in employee turnover and absenteeism. *Psychological Bulletin,* 1973 **80,** 151–176.

Porter, L. W., Steers, R. M., Mowday, R. T., & Boulian, P. V. Organizational commitment, job satisfaction, and turnover among psychiatric technicians. *Journal of Applied Psychology,* 1974, **59,** 603–609.

Rokeach, M. *The nature of human values.* New York: The Free Press, 1973.

Rosen, H., & Turner, J. Effectiveness of two orientation approaches in hard-core unemployed turnover and absenteeism. *Journal of Applied Psychology,* 1971, **55,** 296–301.

Scheflen, K. C., Lawler, E. E., III, & Hackman, J. R. Long-term impact of employee participation in the development of pay incentive plans: A field experiment revisited. *Journal of Applied Psychology,* 1971, **55,** 182–186.

Searls, D. J., Braucht, G. N., & Miskimins, R. W. Work values and the chronically unemployed. *Journal of Applied Psychology,* 1974, **59,** 93–95.

Seatter, W. C. More effective control of absenteeism. *Personnel,* 1961, **38,** 16–29.

Shaw, M. E. *Group dynamics.* New York: McGraw-Hill, 1976.

Smith, A. L. Oldsmobile absenteeism/turnover control program. *GM Personnel Development Bulletin,* February 1972.

Smith, F. J. Work attitudes as predictors of specific day attendance. *Journal of Applied Psychology,* 1977, **62,** 16–19.

Steers, R. M. Antecedents and outcomes of organizational commitment. *Administrative Science Quarterly,* 1977, **22,** 46–56.

Steers, R. M., & Spencer, D. G. The role of achievement motivation in job design. *Journal of Applied Psychology,* 1977, **4,** 472–479.

Stockford, L. O. Chronic absenteeism and good attendance. *Personnel Journal,* 1944, **23,** 202–207.

Tjersland, T. *Changing worker behavior.* New York: Manpower Laboratory, American Telephone and Telegraph, December, 1972.

Vroom, V. *Work and motivation.* New York: Wiley, 1964.

Waters, L. K., & Roach, D. Relationship between job attitudes and two forms of withdrawal from the work situation. *Journal of Applied Psychology,* 1971, **55,** 92–94.

Waters, L. K., & Roach, D. Job attitudes as predictors of termination and absenteeism: Consistency over time and across organizations. *Journal of Applied Psychology,* 1973, **57,** 341–342.

Weaver, C. N., & Holmes, S. L. On the use of sick leave by female employees. *Personnel Administration and Public Personnel Review,* 1972, **1**(2), 46–50.

Whyte, W. F. *Organizational behavior.* Homewood, Ill.: Irwin, 1969

Yolles, S. F., Carone, P. A., & Krinsky, L. W. *Absenteeism in industry.* Springfield, Ill.: Charles C. Thomas, 1975.

10. Intermediate Linkages in the Relationship Between Job Satisfaction and Employee Turnover

William H. Mobley

Reviews of the literature on the relationship between employee turnover and job satisfaction have reported a consistent negative relationship (Brayfield & Crockett, 1955; Locke, 1975; Porter & Steers, 1973; Vroom, 1964). Locke (1976) noted that while the reported correlations have been consistent and significant, they have not been especially high (usually less than .40).

It is probable that other variables mediate the relationship between job satisfaction and the act of quitting. Based on their extensive review, Porter and Steers (1973) concluded the following:

Much more emphasis should be placed in the future on the psychology of the withdrawal process. . . . *Our understanding of the manner in which the actual decision is made is far from complete. (p. 173)*

The present paper suggests several of the possible intermediate steps in the withdrawal decision process (specifically, the decision to quit a job). Porter and Steers (1973) suggested that expressed ''intention to leave'' may represent the next logical step after experienced dissatisfaction in the withdrawal process. The withdrawal decision process presented here suggests that thinking of quitting is the next logical step after experienced dissatisfaction and that ''intention to leave,'' following several other steps, may be the last step prior to actual quitting.

A schematic representation of the withdrawal decision process is presented in Figure 1. Block A represents the process of evaluating one's existing job, while Block B represents the resultant emotional state of some degree of satisfaction-dissatisfaction. A number of models have been proposed for the process inherent in Blocks A and B — for example, the value-percept discrepancy model (Locke, 1969, 1976), an instrumentality-valence model (Vroom, 1964), a met-

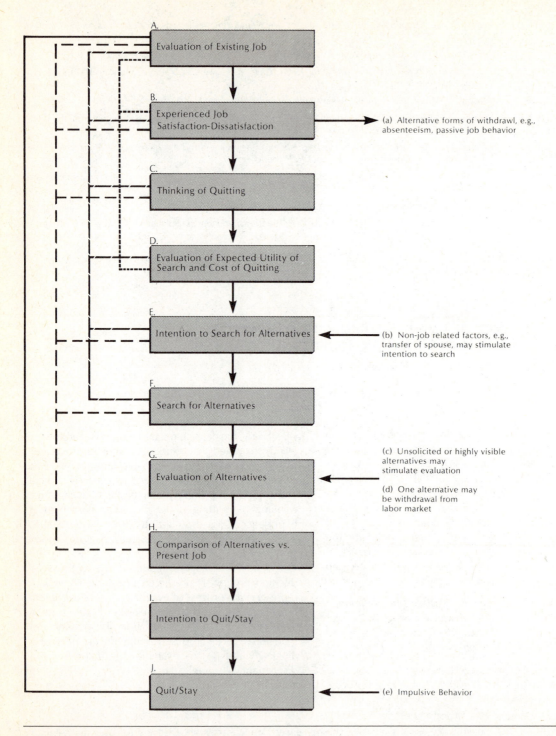

Figure 1. The Employee Turnover Decision Process.

expectations model (Porter & Steers, 1973), and a contribution/inducement ratio (March & Simon, 1958). Comparative studies that test the relative efficacy of these and other alternative models of satisfaction continue to be needed.

Most studies of turnover examine the direct relationship between job satisfaction and turnover. The model presented in Figure 1 suggests a number of possible mediating steps between dissatisfaction and actual quitting. Block C suggests that one of the consequences of dissatisfaction is to stimulate thoughts of quitting. Although not of primary interest here, it is recognized that other forms of withdrawal less extreme than quitting (e.g., absenteeism, passive job behavior) are possible consequences of dissatisfaction (see e.g., Brayfield & Crockett, 1955; Kraut, 1975).

Block D suggests that the next step in the withdrawal decision process is an evaluation of the expected utility of search and of the cost of quitting. The evaluation of the expected utility of search would include an estimate of the chances of finding an alternative to working in the present job, some evaluation of the desirability of possible alternatives, and the costs of search (e.g., travel, lost work time, etc.). The evaluation of the cost of quitting would include such considerations as loss of seniority, loss of vested benefits, and the like. This block incorporates March and Simon's (1958) perceived ease of movement concept.

If the costs of quitting are high and/or the expected utility of search is low, the individual may reevaluate the existing job (resulting in a change in job satisfaction), reduce thinking of quitting, and/or engage in other forms of withdrawal behavior. Research is still needed on the determinants of alternative forms of withdrawal behavior and on how the expression of withdrawal behavior changes as a function of time and of changes in or reevaluation of the environment.

If there is some perceived chance of finding an alternative and if the costs are not prohibitive, the next step, Block E, would be behavioral intention to search for an alternative(s). As noted by Arrow (b) in Figure 1, non-job-related factors may also elicit an intention to search (e.g., transfer of spouse, health problem, etc.). The intention to search is followed by an actual search (Block F). If no alternatives are found, the individual may continue to search, reevaluate the expected utility of search, reevaluate the existing job, simply accept the current state of affairs, decrease thoughts of quitting, and/or engage in other forms of withdrawal behavior (e.g., absenteeism, passive job behavior).

If alternatives are available, including (in some cases) withdrawal from the labor market, an evaluation of alternatives is initiated (Block G). This evaluation process would be hypothesized to be similar to the evaluation process in Block A. However, specific job factors the individual considers in evaluating the present job and alternatives may differ. (See Hellriegel & White, 1973; and Kraut, 1975, for a discussion of this point.) Independent of the preceding steps, unsolicited or highly visible alternatives may stimulate this evaluation process.

The evaluation of alternatives is followed by a comparison of the present job to alternative(s) (Block H). If the comparison favors the alternative, it will stimulate a behavioral intention to quit (Block I), followed by actual withdrawal (Block J). If the comparison favors the present job, the individual may continue to search, reevaluate the expected utility of search, reevaluate the existing job, simply accept the current state of affairs, decrease thoughts of quitting, and/or engage in other forms of withdrawal behavior.

Finally, Arrow (e) gives recognition to the fact that for some individuals, the decision to quit may be an impulsive act involving few, if any, of the preceding steps in this model. The relative incidence and the individual and situational determinants of an impulsive versus a subjectively rational decision process presents yet another area of needed research.

The model being described is heuristic rather than descriptive. There may well be individual differences in the number and sequence of steps in the withdrawal decision process, in the degree to which the process is conscious, and as noted earlier, in the degree to which the act of quitting is impulsive rather than based on a subjectively rational decision process. One value of such an heuristic model is to guide thinking and empirical research toward a valid descriptive model that can account for such individual differences.

There is a lack of research evaluating all or even most of the possible steps in the withdrawal decision process. There have been a few studies that have tested one or two of the intermediate linkages proposed in the present note. Mobley (Note 1) found high negative correlations between satisfaction and frequency of thinking of quitting (Blocks B and C). Atkinson and Lefferts (1972), who dealt with the association between Blocks C and J, found that the frequency with which people thought about quitting their job was significantly related to actual termination. Kraut (1975), looking at the associations among Blocks B, I, and J, found significant correlations between expressed intention to stay and subsequent employee participation. These correlations were much stronger than relationships between expressed satisfaction and continued participation. Finally, Armknecht and Early's (1972) review is relevant to the relationships between Blocks D and/or F and Block J. They concluded that voluntary terminations are closely related to economic conditions.

Each of these studies fails to look at a complete withdrawal decision process. Such research would appear to be sorely needed. Several researchable questions that follow from the withdrawal decision process described in the present note were mentioned earlier. Additional questions include the following. Do individuals evaluate the expected utility of search? If so, what are the determinants and consequences of this evaluation? What are the consequences and determin-

ants of behavior in the face of an unsuccessful search? In such cases, do individuals persist in search, reevaluate their existing jobs, reevaluate the cost of search, or engage in other forms of withdrawal? Is the process and/or content for evaluating alternative jobs the same as for evaluating the present job? Does satisfaction with the present job change as a function of the availability or evaluation of alternatives?

Attention to these sorts of questions rather than a continued replication of the direct relationship between job satisfaction and turnover would appear to be warranted. Particularly useful would be the longitudinal analysis of the variables and linkages suggested by the model. Such research would be responsive to Porter and Steers' (1973) conclusion that more emphasis should be placed on the psychology of the withdrawal decision process.

REFERENCE NOTE

1. Mobley, W. H. *Job satisfaction and thinking of quitting* (Tech. Rep. 75-3). Columbia: University of South Carolina, College of Business Administration, Management and Organizational Research Center, 1975.

REFERENCES

Armknecht, P. A., & Early, J. F. Quits in manufacturing: A study of their causes. *Monthly Labor Review,* 1972, **11,** 31-37.

Atkinson, T. J., & Lefferts, E. A. The prediction of turnover using Herzberg's job satisfaction technique. *Personnel Psychology,* 1972, **25,** 53-64.

Brayfield, A. H., & Crockett, W. H. Employee attitudes and employee performance. *Psychological Bulletin,* 1955, **52,** 396-424.

Hellriegel, D., & White, G. E. Turnover of professionals in public accounting: A comparative analysis. *Personnel Psychology,* 1973, **26,** 239-249.

Kraut, A. I. Predicting turnover of employees from measured job attitudes. *Organizational Behavior and Human Performance,* 1975, **13,** 233-243.

Locke, E. A. What is job satisfaction? *Organizational Behavior and Human Performance,* 1969, **4,** 309-336.

Locke, E. A. Personnel attitudes and motivation. *Annual Review of Psychology,* 1975, **26,** 457-480.

Locke, E. A. The nature and consequences of job satisfaction. In M. D. Dunnette (Ed.), *Handbook of industrial and organizational psychology.* Chicago: Rand-McNally, 1976.

March, J. G., & Simon, H. A. *Organizations.* New York: Wiley, 1958.

Porter, L. W., & Steers, R. M. Organizational, work, and personal factors in employee turnover and absenteeism. *Psychological Bulletin,* 1973, **80,** 151-176.

Vroom, V. H. *Work and motivation.* New York: Wiley, 1964.

11.   The Consequences of Turnover

Barry M. Staw

INTRODUCTION

The study of turnover has been a major interest of organizational psychologists for more than half a century. As Steers and Mowday (1980) have noted, over 1,000 separate studies on the subject can now be identified and at least 13 review articles have appeared in the literature over the last 25 years. The prime focus of all this empirical research has been to elaborate the antecedents of turnover, while theoretical efforts have largely been directed toward integrating the mass of findings into a model of turnover behavior (e.g., March and Simon, 1958; Price, 1977; Mobley *et al.,* 1979; Steers and Mowday, 1980). This paper will neither review the turnover literature nor construct a new model to explain why individuals leave organizations.

The focus of the present paper will be upon the consequences rather than the antecedents of turnover. It is this author's contention that the yield of additional studies on the determinants of turnover will be rather low given the volume of existing empirical data and the detailed theoretical models already available. The chief goal of this paper, therefore, will be to make the case for a redirection of turnover research, illustrating the reasons for this change and showing the possible shape of new research.

The Assumptions of Previous Turnover Research

Most of the existing empirical literature relates demographic, psychological, and economic data to instances of turnover, turnover being treated as a voluntary decision on the part of individuals to leave an organization. Because the goal of this research has been to predict or explain as much variance as possible in turnover rates for various jobs, occupations and organizational types, the implicit assumption underlying the effort has been that turnover is an important organizational problem – something which is costly to the organization and something which should be reduced. This assumption, as we will argue, is extremely suspect since turnover may bring positive as well as negative consequences to an organization.

The strength and endurance of the assumption that turnover is a negative consequence for organizations is understandable given three factors. First, turnover almost always involves some costs for the organization (e.g. recruitment, selection, training) and these costs may be more salient to administrators than any benefits which may result from a change in personnel. Second, because practicing organizational psychologists are generally charged with recruitment, selection, and training responsibilities within organizations, and since, as Pugh (1966) has noted, researchers in organizational psychology have tended to focus upon problems practitioners perceive as important, the negative side of turnover has been emphasized. From the perspective of a personnel department, turnover creates operating expenses for the organization and a major way for this department to contribute to the organization would seem to be a reduction in turnover expenses. Third, research in organizational psychology has tended to focus on lower-level employees in organizations such as the behavior of blue-collar workers and their immediate supervisors. Research on turnover has been no exception, relatively few studies having been conducted on the turnover of managerial or professional personnel. Although there has existed a small literature on executive succession within sociology (which has interestingly *not* assumed turnover to be detrimental to the organization), there has been almost no interface between the succession and turnover literatures. As we will outline later in this paper, negative consequences may be more likely for turnover of lower-level employees than for managerial personnel. Thus, both practitioners' and researchers' assumptions about the nature of turnover may have been reaffirmed simply by the direction of their own inquiries.

In this paper we will outline several benefits as well as costs of turnover in organizations. What makes the task of understanding turnover difficult is the possibility of multiple and conflicting outcomes. In addition, it is likely that these outcomes are each conditioned by several moderating variables adding further complexity to the picture. Therefore, rather than simply listing and discussing potential benefits as well as costs for turnover, we will attempt to specify the conditions under which the benefits are likely to be greatest, the costs lowest, and vice versa. Because there is so little research on the consequences of turnover, our current analysis will necessarily be preliminary. But, before we can redirect empirical literature and build new predictive statements there is a need for systematic hypothesis formulation and speculation.

THE COSTS OF TURNOVER

We will outline here some costs of turnover, most of which are well known and rather straightforward. We will, however, specify some moderating variables which may act to increase or decrease these costs for the organization. Thus, attention should be drawn to circumstances which can minimize or maximize the expense of turnover so that its role in organizational functioning can be more fully understood.

Selection and Recruitment Costs

The most obvious consequence of turnover is the energy and expense of finding replacement personnel. When someone leaves an organization others must be recruited, screened through some selection mechanism, and finally hired. If large numbers of people leave an organization on a regular basis, the organization will most likely have adapted to this consequence by retaining full-time specialists in recruitment and selection, thereby increasing its administrative intensity (Kasarda, 1973). In fact, for organizations who hold members for only a relatively short and specified period (e.g., the military, universities, social clubs), the search for potential members and their selection becomes a very major function of the organization. However, if turnover is low or occurs on an irregular basis, organizational staff are usually assigned to recruitment duties on a temporary basis and this function may be subcontracted to another more specialized organization (e.g., personnel consultants, executive search agencies). Because large amounts of selection and recruitment generally lead organizations to institutionalize these

functions, there may be certain economies of scale for these activities. Nonetheless, recruitment and selection can involve substantial costs to the organization, and these costs can be moderated by several additional variables.

One obvious moderator of the cost of turnover is the tightness of the labor market facing the organization for the particular position to be filled. In an extremely tight market the only place qualified candidates may be found is in competing organizations or in related occupational positions (e.g., someone with similar training but practicing an alternative specialty). Sometimes, it may even be necessary to isolate potential hires while they are still in training. The market for faculty with doctorates in accounting is so tight in American universities, for example, that doctoral students are frequently contacted by potential employers very early in their educational programs. In contrast to these efforts, recruitment in a strong labour market may require nothing more than an appropriately written advertisement in order to secure hundreds of qualified applicants (advertisements for humanities faculty in American universities would be a clear example).

A second moderator of the cost of turnover is the level of complexity of the job to be filled. At high levels, potential candidates are difficult to isolate and agree upon by organizational members. It is not uncommon, for example, that the search for an executive will stretch out over a year's time due to both the uncertainty of the criteria being attached to the choice as well as the difficulty of reaching consensus on any particular candidate. Low level positions, on the other hand, may have much clearer criteria against which to measure candidates, making both recruitment and selection a relatively routine process.

A third moderator of selection and recruitment costs is whether inside or outside succession is followed by the organization. If existing organizational personnel can be promoted or reassigned to the departed person's position, recruitment and selection costs may be drastically reduced. In fact, one person's departure from a high level position may cause a chain of welcome promotions within the organization, necessitating the hiring of only one additional person at the bottom of the hierarchy.

Training and Development Costs

Even when organizational members can be easily recruited and selected for an organization it may be months before the new employee can perform at the level of the departed member of the organization. If the role is complex the new member may need a long period of training; if the role is unprogrammed and the procedures as well as objectives undefined the individual may require time to build his or her own role in the organization (Graen, 1976). Thus, training costs can involve the direct expenses of formalized instruction programs, the costs of having other employees informally help the new organizational member, as well as the time period in which role performance is below that of the veteran employee.

The moderators of training and development costs are nearly the same variables as those considered for selection and recruitment expenses. The level and complexity of the job will clearly affect the amount of training or time necessary to reach an effective level of performance. Succession of an insider versus the hiring of an outsider also will likely moderate training and development costs. Thus, on low level jobs or inside promotions to higher level positions, training and development costs will be relatively lower than under other conditions.

Operational Disruption

Aside from the recruitment, selection, training and development costs associated with turnover, the loss of large numbers of personnel or key members of the organization will sometimes prove costly in terms of general disruption. When people leave it may affect the ability of others to produce their work because of interdependence of work roles within the organization. If a key person leaves the whole system may break down if the organization is both highly interdependent and specialized. As a result, many organizations have backup personnel for key roles, and if a large number of roles are essential for functioning, employees may be trained in a multiplicity of skills. At the extreme, when members of a team are both necessary to the functioning of a mission and at the same time vulnerable to loss, each member may be trained to carry out the most essential tasks of the entire work unit.

The chief moderator of whether turnover causes an operational disruption is the centrality of the particular role to the organization's functioning. In general, the higher the level of the position to be filled the greater is the potential for disruption. Yet, there are some exceptions to this general rule. The loss of a key production manager or even a specialized equipment repair person (Crozier, 1964) may cause greater disruption to the organization than changing executive officers. Across all positions, the predictability of turnover will also be important (Price, 1977). Some organizations expect large amounts of turnover for lower level employees and have routinized the replacement of much of the organization. For higher level positions, indication of impending departure greatly reduces risks of disruption since procedures can often be implemented to bypass the particular position in the organization or to fill it temporarily while a replacement is found.

Demoralization of Organizational Membership

Having people leave an organization may involve costs beyond replacement and operational disruption. Because people typically leave one organization for an alternative organization, turnover may undermine the attitudes of those remaining. Those remaining in the organization may see their own fates as less desirable (left behind) and they may question their own motivation for staying. In essence, turnover provides salient cues about the organization and a role model for others. Thus, turnover may by itself trigger additional turnover by prompting a deterioration in attitudes toward the organization and making salient alternative memberships.

Like the other potential costs of turnover there may be several moderators of an effect of turnover on the demoralization of membership. As Steers and Mowday (1980) have noted, the perceived reason for leaving is one key moderator. If members are perceived to leave for nonorganizational reasons such as family problems, location, or economic conditions it will produce less of a demoralization effect than if turnover is perceived to result from the nature of the work, pay, or supervision. Likewise, if those who leave are members of a cohesive work group or possess high social status among the organizational membership, turnover will likely lead to greater demoralization. Finally, if the organization considers as one of its goals the maintenance of a stable membership (e.g., a voluntary organization such as a religious or social group), turnover will be a more severe blow than if the organization trains people who frequently follow multi-organizational careers (Hall, 1977). Many professional organizations, for example, employ individuals whose careers involve a sequence of organizational memberships. In such cases, departure to another high prestige organization may actually bolster the attitudes of the membership, assuring them that commitment to the present organization is instrumental to their own long term career goals.

Summary of Potential Negative Consequences

Most people who have served on a search committee or have been employed in an organization during a turnover transition will testify that turnover presents certain costs to the organization. The cost of recruitment, selection, and training are salient to the organization and are often quantified for the replacement of lower level personnel. For the turnover of higher officials attention is generally focused upon possible disruption and demoralization effects.

We have identified several moderating variables which can serve to minimize these adverse effects of turnover. As we have noted, turnover will be least costly for persons in lower level positions, in plentiful labor markets, in noninterdependent roles, from noncohesive work groups, who leave for nonwork reasons, provide advance indication of departure, and who are replaced by persons from inside the organization. Thus, the statement that turnover is costly for organizations should really be translated to an inquiry into the extent to which turnover will prove burdensome for the organization. Only in this way will one be able to evaluate the tradeoffs between the potential costs and benefits of turnover.

Table 1. Median Years on the Job for Male Workers in Selected Industries

Industry	Median Years on Job
Railroads and railway express	19.6
Agriculture	11.5
Postal service	10.3
Federal public administration	7.6
Automobile manufacturing	7.0
Chemical and allied products manufacturing	6.8
Mining	6.4
Electrical machinery manufacturing	5.7
Communications	5.2
Instrument manufacturing	5.1
Food and kindred products manufacturing	5.1
Finance, insurance, and real estate	4.0
Rubber and plastics manufacturing	4.0
Medical and other health services	2.8
Construction	2.7
Wholesale and retail trade	2.6
Entertainment and recreation services	1.9
All durable good manufacturing	5.7
All nondurable goods manufacturing	5.3

Source: Bureau of Labor Statistics, 1975: A–13.

POSITIVE CONSEQUENCES

The potential positive consequences of turnover have received very little attention in organizational psychology. The benefits of turnover are somewhat less obvious than the costs in that they may be less quantifiable and less attainable in the near-term. Yet, the positive aspects of turnover may contribute to the long run viability of the organization.

As a rather crude way of demonstrating the potential positive consequences of turnover, one might examine some descriptive data on job tenure published by the U.S. Bureau of Labor Statistics. Table 1 compares job tenure among several major industries in the U.S. economy. One can see from this table that job tenure in the railroad industry (19.6 years) is more than three times that in durable goods manufacturing (5.7) and nondurable goods manufacturing (5.3), while over seven times that of wholesale and retail trade (2.6). Job tenure is also relatively higher in the U.S. Postal Service (10.3) than in private industrial jobs. Because the U.S. railroad industry and postal systems are reputed to be among the most inefficient units of the American economy, these data are at least suggestive of the fact that turnover may be too low rather than too high for many organizations and industries.

Increased Performance

Because turnover by its very nature leads to training and development costs, it is often implicitly assumed that there is some standard level of performance that most individuals reach after an initial time period or passage through a learning curve. This traditional perspective leads one to assume that performance of a new employee will be initially low and, only after experience, will reach the level of the preceding employee. The obvious drawback to this perspective is that insufficient attention is paid to potential gains in performance following turnover. The new arrival may be more highly motivated than the old employee and may possess greater abilities and training. As an example, consider the effective work life of employees in high-stress roles such as air traffic controllers, in roles demanding of physical endurance such as mining and construction, or in roles requiring changing technical skills such as electronics engineering. These jobs would more likely contain a performance curve that is shaped as an inverted *U* rather than the traditional *J* shape (see Figure 1). In addition, consider many public service jobs such as social work, nursing, and police work in which the psychological demands of the job are relatively high. In these jobs new employees tend to be more idealistic and motivated to serve public needs immediately upon being hired and over each subsequent year tend either to conform more to a bureaucratic role (Blau and Scott, 1962; Van Maanen, 1975) or are subject to a psychological 'burn-out' in which employees distance themselves from the client being served (Maslach, 1978).

We would argue that most jobs have an inverted *U* performance curve simply because performance is generally a joint function of skills and effort. While experience may contribute positively to job skills and knowledge, effort or motivation may be at its highest when the individual first arrives in the organization. The new employee may be characterized as optimistic, energetic, but also naive. In contrast, the long-term employee must be wise, but also cynical and sluggish. These hypothesized relationships between skills, effort and experience are outlined in Figure 2 and, as shown, can provide the basis for the inverted *U* performance

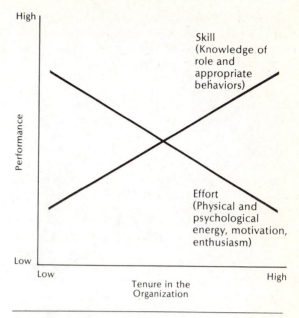

Figure 2. Hypothesized Relationship Between Motivation, Skill, and Years Experience.

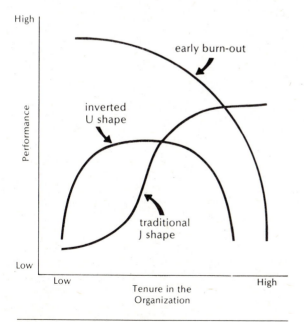

Figure 1.   Hypothetical Performance Curves.

curve. It should be noted, however, than any alteration of these underlying relationships would also change the resultant curve. There no doubt can be roles in which effort remains high over time as well as roles in which skills deteriorate with each passing year.

Greater effort should be placed into identifying jobs in which physical or psychological demand are patterned so that performance peaks early in employment and subsequently declines. In such cases, the average tenure of organizational members should be kept low in order to increase average individual performance. Thus, research should be placed into studying the relationship between individual job tenure and performance so that the *appropriate* rate of turnover could be identified. For some jobs tenure may have a positive-linear relation to performance and some a negative-linear relation, yet for most jobs tenure and performance will be nonlinearly related as either a narrowly or widely inverted *U*.

While research on the relation between job tenure and performance should be encouraged for the individual level of analysis, some research should also be directed at the effects of the *distribution* of tenure within organizations. As Pfeffer (1979) has noted, organizations and work units may differ in performance because their age and tenure distributions differ. Pfeffer argues for the study of "organizational demography" and we would support such an effort since there may not be a simple parallel between relationships at the individual and collective levels (Staw and Oldham, 1978). On the surface, one might think that a particular curve obtained for the individual tenure-performance relationship would also apply to the work group. In practice, however, tenure may not affect work groups in the same way as individuals since group functions may be dispersed among the membership (Bales, 1958; Bavelas, 1960). Within a work group some members may fulfill the knowledge function (actually serving as the unit's memory for experiences, shortcuts and traditions) while others may serve an energizing function (generating enthusiasm or providing perseverance on the most difficult tasks). Therefore, a mixture of younger and older members may lead to more effective group functioning than uniformity at any level of experience.

Wells and Pelz (1966) in a study of 83 research and development work groups found a curvilinear effect of average job tenure on scientific contribution, peaking at four to five years of "group age." Because the average of individual tenure in research groups was used to calculate "group age," it is not possible to discern from this finding whether an aggregate level of turnover or a particular distribution of tenure is related to group performance. However, organizations often display a preference for a mixture of new and experienced members. Sport teams, for example, frequently opt for a blend of veteran and rookie players. Likewise, academic departments in universities frequently employ a range of faculty at different ranks and levels of experience. It is interesting to note that, with recent budgeting cutbacks in American universities, the average age and tenure of faculty has increased dramatically. University administrators have subsequently argued that this change in tenure distribution will adversely affect scholarly output of academic departments, although no systematic research has yet examined this issue.

Implicit in our discussion of potential benefits of turnover is the assumption that organizational membership can be renewed before it reaches the downward sloping part of the performance curve. Given this reasoning, the benefits of turnover will obviously depend on the nature of the task and whether it requires physical or psychological strengths which are depletable resources. The benefits of turnover also depend on who "turns over;" if it is the older, long-tenured employees or the newcomers to the organization. Turnover rates do not as a statistic provide

such information. However, our argument for the benefits of turnover obviously assumes a normal progression of employees through the organization rather than a continual recirculation of newcomers into the system.

The issue of who "turns over" has also been addressed in some early work by Lawler (1971) in which he argued that organizational resources should be allocated on a highly contingent basis. One logical consequence of contingent pay schemes would be differential satisfaction and turnover according to performance. For example, the organization that pays its high and low performers widely differing amounts is more likely to retain its highly desired employees and lose its less desired ones. Conversely, an organization that allocates resources equally is most likely to lose its highly valued personnel, assuming they are also valued by other organizations and possess greater external opportunities. Thus, an organization with resources allocated on a highly contingent basis implicitly encourages turnover on the assumption that new employees are likely to be an improvement over departing ones. So far, there has been no research on the relationship between pay contingency and turnover nor between such turnover and subsequent unit performance. However, we do know that most employees currently perceive outcomes at their employing organizations not to be contingent on their performance (Lawler, 1973). We also know from at least three empirical studies (Allison, 1974; Bassett, 1967; Office of State Merit Systems, 1968) that leavers tend to be above average performers in the organization (Price, 1977). Therefore, one reason organizations may attempt to lower their rates of turnover is to retain their most valued employees; with contingent reward systems the exact opposite behavior would be logical on the part of organizations.

Reduction of Entrenched Conflict

Sometimes one of the precipitating causes of turnover is conflict. This conflict could be hierarchical such as that between workers and a supervisor, department heads and a higher executive, or between a vice president and the chief executive. The conflict could also be lateral such as between workers on the shop floor, members of organizational staff, or coequal executive officers. In any of these cases, turnover may result from conflicts which are not easily resolved and in which one side decides to leave the organization rather than continue to fight.

Much literature has been devoted to techniques and strategies of conflict resolution and much organizational energy is often devoted to the smoothing of conflict, arbitration of differences, or working through differences via various intervention strategies. One assumption of the conflict literature (be it based on game theory, labor relations, or organization development concepts) is that the participants in the conflict are rather permanent members of the organization. A second assumption is that conflict can and should be mediated, arbitrated, resolved, or ''worked through'' in order for the organization to function effectively. In practice, however, many conflicts, be they personal or task oriented, are not easily resolved and stem from differences in fundamental values or core beliefs. In such cases it may be functional for turnover to become the ultimate ''resolver'' of conflict. In government and business organizations, for example, it is quite frequent for one party to seek the ouster of another, to make life so difficult as to ''drive the other out.'' Turnover is thus the ultimate safety valve for organizational strife, given the fact that the conflicting parties have alternatives to which to go.

As a general statement, the more firmly held are beliefs and the more difficult they are to disconfirm, the greater will be the probability of unresolved strife. In political and religious organizations, for example, conflict among the organization's membership is likely to persist and detract from collective solidarity and purpose. Conflict in these organizations is usually resolved only by the departure of a minority, perhaps setting up its own autonomous organization or splinter group. In a study of turnover of academic department heads (Salancik, Staw, and Pondy, in press) the paradigm development of academic fields was related to the turnover of department heads. In fields with low paradigm development there is little consensus on core beliefs and it is difficult to validate one position over another. Therefore conflicts may have persisted longer in the departments with low rather than high paradigm development and resulted in more administrative turnover. Turnover, in many of these cases, may not have been a cost to the organization, but instead may have helped to resolve deep-seated conflicts among organizational membership.

Increased Mobility and Morale

Earlier we had noted that turnover might have a demoralization effect on the organization since members might impute certain motives for people leaving. In order to seek a balanced approach we should note that turnover could also have a positive effect on membership attitudes. If undesirable supervisors or coworkers leave the organization, this event might obviously cheer some members (Guest, 1962). However, even if well liked and/or productive people exit the organization, the turnover might still open positions in an otherwise impenetrable hierarchy. An organization with little turnover may have nowhere to promote highly competent employees with upward mobility strivings unless the organization is expanding rapidly by acquisition or internal growth. But, since economic growth has slackened in many industries, turnover in middle and high level positions may be the only way upwardly mobile employees can be encouraged to stay with an otherwise stable organization. Thus, turnover may be the primary determinant of promotion opportunities, contributing to a positive relation between turnover and organizational morale.

Innovation and Adaptation

An important consequence of turnover is the opportunity it provides for the organization to adapt to its environment. One means of adaptation is through strategic decision making (Chandler, 1962; Child, 1972; Miles and Snow, 1978), and along with strategic changes generally comes some reallocation of organizational resources. But resources cannot often be simply increased to accommodate new activities and purposes; they must be shifted from one department to another or from an outmoded function to a newly established endeavor. Generally a major aspect of a shift in resources is a shift of positions and personnel, and this may involve the shrinkage of one organizational unit to allow for the growth of another. Thus, turnover is a very major means by which reorientation of the organization occurs. If the shift in purpose or activity is small in comparison to the size of the organization, older units will be allowed to shrink by attrition while resources are funnelled to newer units. But, if a shift is massive, resignations may be forced or conditions of employment made difficult enough to encourage additional voluntary turnover. In either case, turnover may be integral to organizational adaptation, and the role of turnover would be especially important when resources are not easily procured from the environment.

In addition to turnover's use in conscious or strategic adaptation of the organization to its environment, turnover may also be useful from a nonpurposive, evolutionary perspective (Aldrich, 1979; Hannon and

Freeman, 1977; Weick, 1979). Although most organizations attempt to select new organizational members which match the profile of previously successful members, selection procedures (including interviews, personality inventories, and application blanks) are notoriously ineffective as screening devices (Porter, Lawler, and Hackman, 1975). This "ineffectiveness" of recruiting and selection may, however, constitute one of the most beneficial consequences of turnover. Turnover and the resulting inflow of new organizational members may be the primary source of variety (Campbell, 1965) within organizations. Almost every other process within organizations promotes homogeneity. Rules, normative sanctions, filtering of information, as well as the exposure to a common set of experiences breed similarity in point of view and knowledge. Also, participation in previous decisions fosters commitment to policies even if they may be outmoded or inappropriate (Staw, 1976; Fox and Staw, 1979). These sources of homogeneity and stability may be costly when radical changes in the environment require new values, viewpoints, and knowledge bases. An organization can therefore use turnover as a constant source of input from the environment to help keep organizational beliefs and information congruent with outside changes. Because variety increases chances for survival (Campbell, 1965; Weick, 1979), turnover can be an important source of organizational adaptation, even though this adaptation may be nonconscious and nonstrategic from the policy maker's perspective.

The effect of turnover on organizational adaptation may vary greatly with the level at which it occurs. With increased level in an organizational hierarchy typically comes increased influence over the actions of others and more central functions of the organization. Also associated with increasing levels in an organizational hierarchy is an increase in decision making and uncertainty absorption. Thus, changes in top management can be followed by major changes in organizational policy, while turnover on lower level jobs which are highly formalized or machine-paced is unlikely to provide much change to the organization.

The reason for adaptive change being associated with the hierarchical level of turnover is due to the differing discretionary component of various organizational roles and the role occupant's influence on others. However, the *potential* for innovation does exist on all organizational levels with many valuable improvements coming from middle and lower levels of the organization. For example, it is often the case that formal procedures must be bypassed, revised, and machinery altered in order for organizational members to fulfill their roles satisfactorily. Unfortunately, many of these "innovations" are not officially sanctioned by upper levels and do not diffuse freely throughout the organization. Therefore, the major impact of new employees at low or intermediate levels of the organization may be their indirect effect upon the work of longer tenured and higher level professionals (Price, 1977). More influential members of the organization may be subtly influenced by the ideas or approaches of the new employee, but ownership of any innovations may not necessarily be credited to the new arrival.

A second moderator of the effect of turnover upon organizational adaptation is whether there is a policy of inside or outside succession. While inside succession may have a beneficial effect on organizational morale it negates much of the potential adaptation value of turnover (Carlson, 1962). The new role occupant, up from the ranks, is likely to have similar background, experiences, and policy commitments to the departed member. The outside replacement, in contrast, is more likely to bring new perspectives and information to the organization, and if the new person has had reinforcing experiences elsewhere, he or she is less likely to conform to the new organization than the inside successor. Thus, turnover at high levels in the organization, accompanied by replacement with an experienced and successful outsider, may maximize the adaptive consequences of turnover.

Finally, whether turnover and any subsequent adaptation are useful for the organization depends upon the rate of change encountered by the organization. Organizations in an unchanging environment do not need diversity and could well find it more efficient to specialize by fitting its membership precisely to the current demands of its environment. However, organizations with higher rates of change and which experience unexpected developments in markets, social or political factors, may be well served by a higher level of turnover and the diversity it provides.

Summarizing the Positive Consequences

We have outlined several positive consequences of turnover and have shown how each could be moderated by other variables. Turnover can increase organizational performance, but this effect depends on the role performance curve and the contingency of the organization's reward system. In addition, turnover could increase performance simply because the labor market has improved over time, allowing the organization to recruit increasingly better members. As we have noted, turnover may also reduce conflict in the organization, but this result depends on the ideological nature of the organization and whether core beliefs or values are involved in the conflict. We also noted that turnover may benefit organizational mobility to the extent that there is little organizational growth and policies of inside succession are followed. Finally, we noted that turnover may lead to organizational innovation and adaptation, but this result may, in turn, be moderated by the hierarchical level at which turnover occurs and whether inside or outside succession is followed.

ASSESSING THE CONSEQUENCES OF TURNOVER

A large number of moderators were specified in the discussion of potential consequences of turnover and each of these is outlined in Figure 3. Once elaborated, it is evident that turnover is an extremely complex process, having an effect on multiple aspects of organizational functioning and with each of these effects themselves moderated by other contextual variables.

By examining Figure 3 is also becomes clear that some moderating variables may control the effect of turnover upon several different outcomes. For example, the higher turnover occurs in the organizational hierarchy the greater will be the costs of recruitment, selection, and training and also greater will be the potential for operational disruption. However, turnover at high levels in the organization is also associated with greater possibilities for innovation and adaptation. Likewise, inside succession following turnover eases the costs of recruitment and training and may have a positive effect on organizational morale, yet at the same time it may not produce as much innovation and adaptation as would outside succession. Thus, some moderators may affect both the costs and benefits of turnover.

Hypothetically, an administrator could use Figure 3 as a checklist for examining the consequences of turnover. By examining and categorizing the organization's current situation on each moderator variable it would be possible to assess the magnitude of various costs and benefits of turnover. Such an assessment would of course be highly speculative since there has not been

systematic research supporting each of the linkages in Figure 3. Such an assessment would also be largely qualitative since quantitative measures will likely exist only for estimating some of the more routine costs of turnover.

The outcome variables listed in Figure 3 reflect consequences that extend over several aspects of organizational functioning. Many of these outcomes (e.g., recruitment and selection costs) would normally be considered as direct costs by managers while other outcomes (e.g., reduction in conflict and increased innovation) might be considered as rather indirect means toward other more tangible goals (i.e., increased sales or profit). However, viewed from a systems perspective (Katz and Kahn, 1978), there is no substantive reason for treating routine turnover expenses differently from other outcomes. It is only because accounting systems are currently devised to account for expense items in one measure of organizational well being (profit) that selection and training costs appear most quantifiable. In terms of organizational functioning, it is not yet clear whether expenses which are directly accountable are more or less useful than other indices in measuring the effectiveness of an organization (cf. Steers, 1977). Certainly, in principle, scales could be constructed to measure each of these outcome variables on an ongoing basis.

Some sort of scale conversion is necessary for any judgment of the consequences of turnover. We must, for example, be able to tell whether an operational disruption is trivial or severe, and be able to compare the utility/disutility for this outcome with that for varying the potential for innovation. Obviously, this task entails the same problems and pitfalls as any examination of organizational effectiveness (cf. Goodman and Pennings, 1977). That is, each of the outcome variables listed in Figure 3 may be weighted differently by different constituents comprising the organization (Hall, 1977). Also, members of the same constituent group (e.g., management) may view the importance of various outcome variables differently, depending upon their own organizational roles. Immediate expenditures for recruitment or possible disruptions in production may appear important to a department manager trying to keep within budget and meet sales quotas, while interunit relations and innovations may be more heavily weighted by top levels of the organization. Thus, the perceived utility of each consequence of turnover may be conditioned by whatever administrators' lay theories of organizational effectiveness happen to be. The

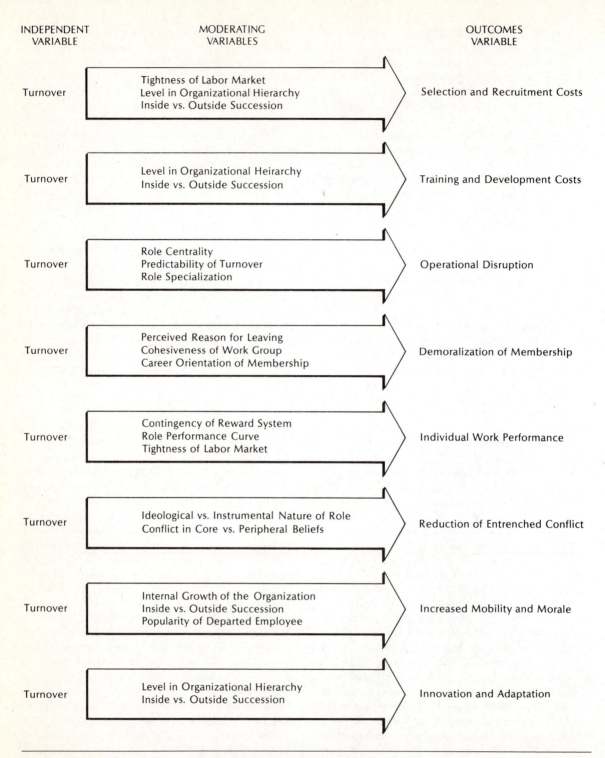

Figure 3. Positive and Negative Consequences of Turnover.

consequences of turnover will likely be moderated by administrators' conceptions of overall organizational welfare, its relevant indicators, and casual mappings (Abelson, 1976; Weick, 1979) about how each variable is believed to affect others within the system.

Given our currently primitive knowledge of organizational effectiveness, we are not yet ready to place any sort of objective weightings upon the various consequences of turnover. Some higher-order variables or "meta-moderators" of the utility of turnover do seem fairly straightforward, however, and have been implicit in our discussion throughout this paper. First, we have assumed that innovation is important for the organization because of the need to adapt to a changing environment. Thus, one moderator of the utility of innovation is the rate of change with which an organization must cope. Second, the current level of performance by the organization (e.g., sales, profitability, resource procurement) may determine how acceptable or desirable drastic change would be. When things are desperately bad, even random variations may improve the situation. Finally, turnover of the role occupant must be capable of effecting some change in organizational actions or interpersonal relations. A role which is inconsequential, routinized, or devoid of influence can rarely lead to organizational change with or without turnover.

Research on Managerial Succession

At present, the only stream of research on the consequences of turnover focuses on managerial succession. For example, early research by Grusky (1963) found that the turnover of baseball managers was related to team performance. Subsequent work, however, showed that turnover of baseball managers may primarily be a scapegoating phenomenon and may not be associated with improved performance (Gamson and Scotch, 1964). It could be that the baseball manager never does have much effect upon team performance because, as Weiss (1979) has argued, the game is not a highly interactive task which requires substantial coordination skills. It may also be that more drastic change is needed (e.g., turnover of player personnel) for outcome variables to change.

Research by Lieberson and O'Connor (1972) examined the effect of mangerial succession upon the financial performance of large corporations. They found that turnover of top executives did significantly relate to financial performance of firms but the magnitude of the effect varied greatly by industry. Likewise, Salancik and

Pfeffer (1977) found some effect of mayors upon city budget allocations, but the magnitude of the effect also differed widely by the characteristics of the city. The apparent moderator of turnover effects in both the Lieberson and O'Connor (1972) and Salancik and Pfeffer (1977) studies was the extent of external constraints facing the chief executive. When a corporate president faced many external market constraints and government regulations he/she was constrained in strategic options. Likewise, the mayor who faced highly organized political forces and interest groups within a city was greatly restrained in possible actions. In each case there are substantial forces with which leaders had to contend, and these forces accounted for more variance in organizational outcomes than the effects of leadership changes.

As evidenced in research on managerial succession, turnover of top executives does not guarantee organizational improvement or adaptation to the environment. Yet, a change in leadership sometimes accompanies and even signifies a radical change in direction for an organization. As Pfeffer and Salancik (1977) noted in the case of hospitals, newly appointed administrators are more likely to possess skills in areas which are problematic for the organization than long tenured executives. Thus, turnover among administrators can constitute a means by which the organization realigns itself with a changing environment. Turnover can also constitute a critical symbolic act that change is expected, positively sanctioned or to be initiated by the organization. Managerial shake-ups following financial adversity and cabinet realignments following political setbacks are obvious examples of the symbolic significance of turnover at high levels of an organization. It remains for future research to discover whether turnover's effect is more symbolic than substantive or whether the symbolic changes are what enable substantive changes to occur.

RESTORING THE BALANCE

Although we cannot now predict which of the consequences of turnover *should* be more important for a particular organization at a particular point in time, this does not negate the argument that turnover is probably treated inappropriately by many organizations. Our argument is based simply on the information salience of positive and negative consequences of turnover rather than any normative arguments for a reweighting of outcome criteria.

At present, negative consequences of turnover usually attract much more attention than positive outcomes. Certainly, conventional accounting systems only report realized expenses and do not account for nonmonetary gains. Also, any disruption in operations is likely to cause difficulty for line administrators charged with day to day management. Finally, possible demoralization effects will affect the immediate climate with which an administrator works, making leadership both more necessary and difficult to carry out. In sum, there are several major sources of adverse consequences for a line manager facing high turnover rates, and these consequences may directly affect the nature of the administrator's job within an immediate time horizon.

In contrast to the negative effects of turnover, most of the positive consequences affect the organization as a collectivity rather than a specific administrator's job. In addition, performance improvements resulting from turnover may depend on the abilities or efforts of a successor being superior in some respect to the departed employee. Positive consequences are thus further along in a causal chain than negative consequences, and may be weakened or confused with exogenous factors. An energetic and innovative manager may, for example, replace an outmoded administrator, yet the innovative actions of the new person may not be accepted by the organization or they may be blocked by environmental constraints (e.g., regulations, actions of competitors). In such a situation, the benefits of turnover will be masked while the expenses of turnover would still be quite evident as they are stored in the short term accounting system of the organization.

Tasks for Future Research

As we have noted, research on turnover currently concentrates on the antecedents rather than the consequences of turnover. Although turnover is a very old research topic almost nothing is therefore known about most of the questions we have addressed in this paper. The following research tasks would thus seem most relevant for future analysis:

1. We need to identify each of the consequences of turnover in longitudinal and quasi-experimental designs. Organizations experiencing increases in turnover should be identified and compared to control organizations both before and after turnover has changed. The list of variables and moderators in Figure 3 needs to be tested empirically so as to move beyond the speculation stage.

2. We need to research the relationship between the level of turnover and effectiveness indicators for various types of organizations, subunits, and organizational roles. It is important to know what the turnover rates are for organizations which are successful in particular industries or facing particular types of constraints. As noted in Table 1, there do exist differences in turnover across industries, but we do not yet know how turnover relates to performance within industries or suborganizational environments. In a sense, the outcome variables listed in Figure 3 could be viewed as intermediate variables which are in turn related to end-result variables such as sales, profit, won-loss record, resources procured, etc. Thus, any relationship found between the level of turnover and effectiveness measures would subsume the more specific and intermediate linkages.

3. We need to know more about the attributions and lay theories of administrators in regard to turnover. As Abelson (1976) has noted, people may possess scripts or scenarios of what kind of events are associated with increases in turnover. Turnover sets off a whole series of uncertainties that the administrator may find aversive. Because adverse consequences of turnover must generally be faced personally by the administrator while positive consequences are far off in time and organizational space (they may only affect one's successor!) negative scenarios may be most salient within the organization.

The three research tasks we have outlined are all designed to provide a descriptive base for understanding the consequences of turnover. The first point raises the need for research on the effects of turnover upon various aspects of organizational functioning (e.g., monetary expenses, morale, conflict, innovation). The second point stresses the need for relating turnover to more global measures of organizational effectiveness. Hypothetically, global measures of profitability, survival, won-loss record, and the like should encompass the impact of the more specific outcome variables in Figure 3. However, it may be beneficial to study the effects of turnover on intermediate outcomes at the same time as we study turnover's effect on more global measures of effectiveness. Placing intermediate outcomes into a system which relates to more global outcomes probably should await further developments in a theory of organizational effectiveness. Finally, as a third area of research, we have proposed descriptive analyses of how turnover currently is viewed by organizational administrators. If we understand more fully why administrators react to turnover the way they presently do (see Steers and Mowday, 1980) it may be easier to change these behaviors in the future.

In summary, what we have done by proposing an intensive study of turnover's consequences is to convert a rather normative field of study into one of descriptive inquiry. Because previous research has treated turnover as a simple negative consequence, turnover studies have been labeled as extremely applied research. However, when the utility of turnover is questioned, the study of turnover must stand on its own as more basic research into an important organizational phenomenon. In this way, turnover research has the potential to illuminate central aspects of organizational functioning and may accomplish this with a rather unified and delimited focus.

REFERENCES

Abelson, R. P. (1976). 'Script processing in attitude formation and decision making', In: Carroll, J. S. and Payne, J. W. (Eds), *Cognition and Social Behavior*, Lawrence Erlbaum Publishers, Hillsdale, New Jersey.

Aldrich, H. (1979). *Environments and Organizations*, Prentice-Hall, Englewood Cliffs, New Jersey.

Allison, P. D. (1974). 'Inter-organizational mobility of academic scientists', 69th annual meeting of American Sociological Association, Montreal, Canada.

Bales, R. F. (1958). 'Task roles and social roles in problem-solving groups', In: Maccoby, E. E., Newcomb, T. M. and Hartley, K. L. (Eds), *Readings in Social Psychology*, Holt, New York, pp. 437–446.

Bassett, G. (1967). *A Study of Factors Associated with Turnover of Exempt Personnel*, Personnel and Industrial Relations Services, General Electric.

Bavelas, A. (1960). 'Leadership: man and function,' *Administrative Science Quarterly*, **4**, 491–498.

Blau, P. M. and Scott, W. R. (1962). *Formal Organizations*, Chandler Publishing Co., San Francisco, California.

Campbell, D. T. (1965). 'Variation and selection retention in socio-cultural evolution,' In: Barringer, H. R., Blanksten, G. I. and Mack, R. (Eds), *Social Change in Developing Areas*, Schenkman, Cambridge Mass.

Carlson, R. O. (1962). *Executive Succession and Organizational Change*. Midwest Administration Center, University of Chicago, Chicago, Illinois.

Chandler, A. D. (1962). *Strategy and Structure*, Doubleday, Garden City, New York.

Child, J. (1972). 'Organizational structure, environment, and performance − the role of strategic choice', *Sociology*, **6**, 1–22.

Crozier, M. (1964). *The Bureaucratic Phenomenon*, University of Chicago Press, Chicago, Illinois.

Fox, F. V. and Staw, B. M. (1979). 'The trapped administrator: effects of job insecurity and policy resistance upon commitment to a course of action', *Administrative Science Quarterly*, **24**, 449–471.

Gamson, W. A. and Scotch, N. (1964). 'Scapegoating in baseball', *American Journal of Sociology*, **70**, 69–76.

Goodman, P. S. and Pennings, J. M. (1977). *New Perspectives on Organizational Effectiveness*, Jossey-Bass, San Francisco.

Graen, G. (1976). 'Role-making processes within complex organizations', In: Dunnette, M. D. (Ed.), *Handbook of Industrial and Organizational Psychology*, Rand-McNally, Chicago.

Grusky, O. (1963). 'Managerial succession and organizational effectiveness', *American Journal of Sociology*, **69**, 21–31.

Guest, R. H. (1962). 'Managerial succession in complex organization', *American Journal of Sociology*, Free Press, New York.

Hall, D. T. (1976). *Careers in Organizations*, Goodyear Publishing, Santa Monica, California.

Hall, R. H. (1977). *Organizations: Structure and Process* (2nd ed.), Prentice-Hall, Englewood Cliffs, New Jersey.

Hannon, M. and Freeman, J. (1977). 'The population ecology of organizations', *American Journal of Sociology,* **82,** 929–964.

Kasarda, J. O. (1973). 'Efforts of personnel turnover, employee qualifications, and professional staff ratios on administrative intensity and overhead', *Sociological Quarterly,* **14,** 350–358.

Katz, D. and Kahn, R. (1978). *The Social Psychology of Organizations* (2nd ed.), Wiley, New York.

Lawler, E. E. (1971). *Pay and Organizational Effectiveness: A Psychological View,* McGraw-Hill, New York.

Lawler, E. E. (1973). *Motivation in Work Organizations,* Brooks-Cole, Monterey, California.

Lieberson, S. and O'Connor, J. F. (1972). 'Leadership and organizational performance: a study of large corporations', *American Sociological Review,* **37,** 117–130.

March, J. G. and Simon, H. (1958). *Organizations,* Wiley, New York.

Maslach, C. (1978). 'Client role in staff burn-out', *Journal of Social Issues,* **34,** 111–124.

Miles, R. E. and Snow, C. C. (1978). *Organizational Strategy, Structure, and Process,* McGraw-Hill, New York.

Mobley, W. H., Griffeth, R. W., Hand, H. H. and Meglino, B. M. (1979). 'Review and conceptual analysis of the employee turnover process', *Psychological Bulletin,* **86,** 493–522.

Office of State Merit Systems (1968). 'Analysis of Appointments, Separations, Promotions', U.S. Department of Health Education, and Welfare, Washington, D.C.

Pfeffer, J. (1979). 'Some consequences of organizational demography: potential impacts of an aging work force on formal organizations'. Paper prepared for the Committee on Aging, National Research Council, National Science Foundation, Washington, D.C.

Pfeffer, J. and Salancik, G. R. (1977). 'Organizational context and the characteristics and tenure of hospital administrators', *Academy of Management Journal,* **20,** 74–88.

Porter, L. W., Lawler, E. E. and Hackman, J. R. (1975). *Behavior in Organizations,* McGraw-Hill, New York.

Price, J. L. (1977). *The Study of Turnover,* Iowa State University Press, Ames, Iowa.

Pugh, D. S. (1966). 'Modern organization theory; a psychological and sociological study', *Psychological Bulletin,* **66,** 235–251.

Salancik, G. R. and Pfeffer, J. (1977). 'Constraints on administrator discretion: the limited influence of mayors on city budgets', *Urban Affairs Quarterly,* **12,** 475–498.

Salancik, G. R., Staw, B. M. and Pondy, L. R. (1980). 'Administrative turnover as a response to unmanaged organizational interdependence', *Academy of Management Journal,* pp. 422–437.

Staw, B. M. (1976). 'Knee-deep in the big muddy: a study of escalating commitment to a chosen course of action', *Organizational Behavior and Human Performance,* **16,** 27–44.

Staw, B. M. and Oldham, G. R. (1978). 'Reconsidering our dependent variables: a critique and empirical study', *Academy of Management Journal,* **21,** 539–559.

Steers, R. M. (1977). *Organizational Effectiveness: A Behavioral View,* Goodyear Publishing Co., Santa Monica, California.

Steers, R. M. and Mowday, R. T. (1980). 'Employee Turnover and post-decision accommodation processes'. In: Cummings, L. L. and Staw, B. M. (Eds), *Research in Organizational Behavior,* JAI Press, Greenwich, Connecticut.

U.S. Department of Labor (1975). *Job Tenure of Workers: 1973,* Special Labor Report No. 172, Washington, D.C.

Van Maanen, J. (1975). 'Police socialization: a longitudinal examination of job attitudes in an urban police department', *Administrative Science Quarterly,* **20,** 207–228.

Weick, K. (1972). *The Social Psychology of Organizing,* Addison-Wesley, Reading, Massachusetts, (2nd ed.).

Weiss, R. M. (1979). 'Managerial succession and organizational effectiveness: beyond the baseball diamond'. Paper presented at 1979 meeting of Academy of Management.

Wells, W. P. and Pelz, D. C. (1966). 'Groups,' In: Pelz, D. C. and Andrews, F. M. (Eds), *Scientists in Organizations: Productive Climates for Research and Development,* Wiley, New York.

Part Two

Social and Self Perception

Foundations of Perception

12. SOCIAL PERCEPTION

Kenneth J. Gergen and Mary M. Gergen

ATTRIBUTION OF CAUSALITY

Tom, a friend of ours, was walking recently in the city when a boy of fourteen darted up behind him, plunged a knife into his back, and ran down a nearby alley. Fortunately a hospital was close by and Tom's life was saved. As Tom's friends, we were deeply upset and anxious to see the youth caught and punished. In fact, the boy was found, but our desire for punishment began to wane as his story unfolded. The stabbing proved to be an initiation rite for a neighborhood gang, and if the youth had not given in to gang pressure, his own life would have been endangered. What else could he do?

Why should this explanation be so effective in reducing our desire for revenge? How had our perception of the youth changed? As the theorist Fritz Heider (1958) suggests, our desire for revenge changed because our perception of the *causal source* of the stabbing was altered. Originally we saw the boy as the causal source, and we held him responsible. However, as we learned more about the case, we began to perceive the gang as the source of his actions. In formal terms, we first made an *internal attribution* of causality — to the actor himself; this was replaced by an *external attribution* — to the situation in which the boy lived. And as our perception of causality changed, so did our blame and corresponding desire to see the boy punished.

From Heider's standpoint the perception of personal causality plays a critical role in social life. Not only does blame depend on the perception of causality, but reward does so as well. If a person does a good deed and the action seems to have been voluntary, or self-caused, the person will receive far more rewards from others than would be the case if he or she had been paid to do the deed. If the person had been paid, the causal source would be external (Gross and Latané, 1974). Given the importance of causal attribution in social life, the first question we must ask is how do people go about deciding who has caused an action? Are there any particular rules they follow in reaching such judgments? And if there are rules, how widely are they used? Are there cases in which they are abandoned? Finally, how do we know when we have made a correct judgment of causal source? We now will consider each of these issues.

Scientists in Miniature: The Kelley Model

Harold Kelley has developed one of the most useful accounts of the common rules of causal attribution (Kelley, 1973; Kelley and Michela, 1980). Kelley suggests that people use roughly the same set of rules in their daily affairs as a scientist in the laboratory might use to sift through evidence and locate the cause of a disease. However, the scientist usually tries to follow the rules with care and precision, while the pressing and haphazard circumstances of daily life may make such procedures difficult for the average individual to follow. What are the rules? Kelley believes there are three rules, each of which is derived from the same general principle — that of *covariation*. Specifically, Kelley says, "an effect is attributed to that condition which is present when the effect is present and absent when the effect is absent" (1967, p. 194). In other words, if a condition is evident to the perceiver *when* an event occurs and is *not* evident when the event *does not* occur, people will conclude that the condition caused the event. The three rules that are derived from this tendency are described here.

The Rule of Distinctiveness.   Let us say that you have just given an important talk to your class. You aren't really sure if it was any good, but Ron comes to you after class and compliments your presentation. You want very much to know whether it was your talk (an external source) that produced the compliment or something peculiar within Ron (an internal source), such as his generally positive disposition. One of the first factors you might take into account is whether Ron's compliment is *distinctive* to you. Does Ron compliment everyone who gives an oral report? Is he generally complimentary in his daily relationships? If the compliment is distinctive to you, you may well conclude that your talk produced the compliment. In keeping with the covariation principle, the talk was present when the compliment occurred, and there was no compliment at other times. Thus, you attribute cause to the talk.

In one illustration of this principle, students were asked to judge a series of fictitious situations (McArthur, 1972). For example, some students were told that John laughs in response to a particular comedian and that he doesn't laugh at other comedians. As you can see, John's laughter in this case is distinctive to this comedian. Other students were told that John laughs in response to almost all other comedians. Clearly his laughter is not distinctive to the particular comedian. Both groups then were asked to judge whether something about the comedian (an external source) caused John to laugh or whether something about John (an internal source) caused him to laugh. In general, subjects were far more likely to view the external source as being responsible if John's reaction was distinctive — that is, if John laughed only at the particular comedian.

The Rule of Consensus.   In judging whether your talk caused Ron's compliment, you also may be concerned about whether other students agree with Ron. Thus, if many others congratulated you, you might feel more sure that your talk produced Ron's compliment. In short, the greater the consensus in people's response to a given stimulus, the greater the attribution of causality to the stimulus.

Some researchers have argued that people don't always apply the consensus rule. They often are so involved in their own actions that they don't take into account other people's responses to a stimulus (Nisbett et al., 1976). . . . However, when consensus is easily evident, people frequently take it into account (Ruble and Feldman, 1976; Wells and Harvey, 1978; Zuckerman, 1978). In fact, by overestimating the amount of consensus, people may come to feel more secure in their judgments (Goethals, Allison, and Frost, 1979). For example, at one university students who supported the women's liberation movement estimated that 57 percent of the student body shared their views. Fellow students who did not support the movement believed that 67 percent of the students shared their opinion (Ross, Greene, and House, 1977). Both groups clearly were inflating their estimates.

Consensus also influences one's judgments of others' personality. Imagine, for example, that you decide to wear blue jeans to class because you feel that any other clothing is too dressy. If all of your classmates also wear jeans, people probably will not look at your wearing jeans as being especially expressive of your own personality (internal cause). Instead, the jeans are likely to be seen as a response to the demands of an external source, the peer group (Jones and Davis, 1965). This reaction may occur even if you feel that the jeans do express something important about you. Thus, when an action is socially desirable, so that most everyone does it, the action is more likely to be seen as being externally, rather than internally, caused. In fact, if you always do what is socially desirable, you may be seen as not having any personality.

The Rule of Consistency. In judging the adequacy of your class presentation, you also would be concerned with the consistency of responses over time or across situations. For example, if you typed your talk and gave it to the teacher, would it receive a good grade? If you took the central arguments and put them into a paper to be used in another class, would the arguments still receive approval? If you see that the reaction is consistent across time and situations, you may be more confident that your work, rather than some other factor, is the causal source of the compliment. In general, the greater the consistency of a stimulus in producing a response, the greater the attribution of causality to that stimulus.

Choice of rules and the number of these rules used may depend on the circumstances (Ferguson and Wells, 1980). People may use certain of these rules to judge the cause of crime, for example, and other rules to decide what they should do to protect themselves from criminals (Kidder and Cohn, 1979). Kelley argues that sometimes people use all three rules at once. He has been especially interested in the question of how people decide between two or more competing causes. In such cases, argues Kelley (1972), positive evidence for one cause usually ends the decision-making process. Other competitors are discounted. Imagine, for example, that your younger brother took your radio and that you weren't sure whether he took it because his radio was broken or because he was angry with you. The hint that he might have been angry would probably be sufficient for you to discount wholly the possibility that his radio was broken. This tendency to discount all other causes when there is support for any given cause is called the *discounting principle.*

Achievement and Attribution: Looking Inward

Let us say that in applying Kelley's attribution rules you concluded that your talk was, indeed, responsible for Ron's compliment. Ron did not compliment anyone else (the compliment was *distinctive*), many other people

complimented you (there was high *consensus*), and you found that your teacher liked the typed draft of the talk (there was *consistency*). Would you necessarily feel pleased with yourself? Not according to Bernard Weiner and his colleagues (Meyer et al., 1980; Weiner, 1979; Weiner et al., 1979). As they argue, determining whether you yourself have caused the outcome in matters of success and failure is not enough. You also may want to identify whether the outcome was due to *effort* or *ability*. For example, if you receive a low mark on a math test, your subsequent feelings may be affected by your causal analysis. Did you fail because you are lacking in math aptitude (ability) or because you just didn't try (effort)? If you attribute failure to low ability, you might feel that you were destined to fail the course (Bar-Tal, 1979). If you think your failure was due to poor effort, you might study a lot harder the next time.

But how do you decide whether to attribute your performance to ability or to effort? It is not always so easy to know. According to Weiner, your attention would be drawn to the stability of your performance. Most people assume that ability is a stable feature of their makeup, while they expect their effort to change frequently from one situation to another. Thus, if you always fail math tests, you would most likely conclude that you lacked ability. If you always received high scores, you might perceive yourself as being highly able. However, if you sometimes fail and at other times succeed, you would be more apt to conclude that your failure was because of effort.

To demonstrate this line of reasoning, students were given information about the task performance of a hypothetical individual (Frieze and Weiner, 1971). The results showed that inconsistent performance was attributed to the individual's effort. Success on a task that the individual previously had failed was attributed to trying harder. Failure on a task previously completed successfully was due to not trying. On the other hand, an individual who was consistently successful was seen as having great ability. And an individual who always failed was judged as lacking in ability.

The Differing Perspectives of Actor and Audience

In our discussion thus far we have suggested that people often follow three common rules for deciding whether the causal source of an action lies within the person or is part of the situation. However, we also have stressed people's inconsistency. No one always follows such rules. Whether an individual chooses to do so may depend on a good many factors. One major disruptive influence is the person's perspective in the situation. Perspective varies depending on whether the individual is an actor in the situation or an observer. Return to the example of the ghetto youth who stabbed our friend. As observers we saw the youth as the cause of his own behavior and thus we wanted him to be punished. Yet, from his viewpoint he didn't have any choice. We thus looked at the same event from different perspectives.

As attribution theorists Jones and Nisbett (1971) have argued, people commonly see others as the source of their actions, while they see themselves as acting according to environmental constraints. Why should actor and observer differ in their attributions of causality? First, different quantities of information are available to each of them. Usually actors have much more information about the situation surrounding the action than do observers. Actors know about factors in their past that may propel them toward action; they can identify the specific aspects of a situation that have powerful effects on them. Observers are less knowledgeable in all these respects and thus tend to see actors as deciding for themselves. The second reason that actor and observer differ in their viewpoints is related to their focus of attention. Actors primarily focus their attention outward, toward the environment's obstacles, potentials, and so forth. Observers mainly focus on the actor. Other aspects of the situation — those which constrain the actor's choices — may go unnoticed by the observer. The observer simply sees the actor act. For these reasons, observers often tend to see people as being responsible for their own behavior, while actors see themselves as responding to the situation.

In one ethically controversial demonstration of this argument, investigators attempted to recreate the experience of the participants in the Watergate incident (West, Gunn, and Chernicky, 1975). They gave a group of students an elaborate rationale for burglarizing a local advertising firm, and they were able to secure agreement from the students that the break-in had merit. A second group (observers) simply read about the events and the subjects' agreement. When asked later about responsibility for the burglary, the subjects who had faced the facts from the actors' standpoint tended to see the burglary as being justifiably necessary. Subjects who only read about the case (observers) placed blame on the actors themselves. Thus, differences in perspective would explain both a plea by Nixon's men that their actions were demanded by the situation and the public's view that the Watergate

incident was the result of poor character. Many other studies reveal similar patterns (Miller and Ross, 1975; Sicoly and Ross, 1977; Zuckerman, 1979).

Again, we must make clear that we are speaking of tendencies, not absolute laws of behavior. For example, many people tend to attribute causality to themselves regardless of circumstance. . . . Some people generally see their actions as being under internal control, while others view their actions as being controlled by circumstances. Providing more information can also reduce the differences between actors and observers. Observers who have enough information about a situation come to resemble actors in their tendency to attribute cause to the situation (Eisen, 1979). Finally, personal goals can also change the way both actors and observers attribute causality (Jones and Thibaut, 1958).

Self-serving Bias in Causal Attribution

As we frequently have stressed, . . . interpreting human interaction can be an extremely difficult matter. People are in constant motion and one can never be too certain of the meaning of any given action. This ambiguity leaves room for many different interpretations of causality. As we have just seen, the actor and observer may come to different conclusions because they have different perspectives. We now must consider the influence of people's motives and personal goals on causal attribution. Investigators have been particularly concerned with *self-serving bias* — that is, the tendency to see oneself as the cause of one's successes but to attribute failure to external sources (Bradley, 1978).

In one early attempt to demonstrate self-serving bias, experimenters arranged for teams of students to work together for many hours in a game situation (Streufert and Streufert, 1969). Each team was given responsibility for governing a fictitious nation torn by revolution. At various intervals each team received information about the state of its nation's economy, the revolutionary force, its people's attitudes, and so forth. Many decisions were required, and their outcome was uncertain. However, the experimenters arranged matters so that during one designated period the teams consistently met with disaster. Every decision seemed to make matters worse. During a second period the experimenters caused the teams to experience consistent success. After each of these periods, members of the teams were asked to evaluate privately the causes of their success or failure. The results were clear-cut. When the team failed consistently, students placed the blame on the situation. However, when their actions met with success, they rated themselves as being highly responsible for the various outcomes. The cause of success was internal.

If such laboratory results seem remote, consider some evidence from the educational world. Who should receive credit for a student's successful performance, the teacher who uses excellent teaching methods or the student who puts in devoted effort? In one study of this issue (Johnson, Feigenbaum, and Weiby, 1964), teachers rated children in terms of whether level of performance was due primarily to the children's abilities and efforts or to their own teaching skill. The children performed in various ways — sometimes well and at other times poorly. When a child turned in a poor performance, the teachers tended to blame the child's poor ability on effort. When the child succeeded, the teachers were far more likely to take the credit themselves. We should be charitable in our judgments of the teachers, however, since students also are likely to see their successes as being their own responsibility while considering their failures to be due to circumstance (Bernstein, Stephan, and Davis, 1979). And psychotherapists have been found to demonstrate similar patterns of self-serving attribution (Weary, 1980). Although people often avoid publicly boasting that they are responsible for their successes but not their failures (Arkin, Appelman, and Burger, 1980), the private expression of self-serving biases has been demonstrated in numerous studies (Schopler and Layton, 1972; Snyder, Stephan, and Rosenfield, 1976; Wortman, Costanza, and Witt, 1973). Is taking credit for one's success always self-serving? Many studies suggest that people tend to see *every* individual's successes as being due to the individual's own efforts (Cooper and Lowe, 1977; Kelley and Michela, 1980). Most people just don't believe that anyone would try to fail.

In Search of True Cause

The preceding discussion indicates that people frequently use rules of distinctiveness, consensus, and consistency in deciding on the causal source of a given action. People's causal attributions also may shift depending on whether the persons are actors or observers and on what may benefit them in a situation. As you can see, wide disagreement is possible in tracing the responsibility for an action — that is, in deciding whether the individual should be blamed (or praised). The resolution of such disagreements sometimes can

have life-or-death consequences. Consider the situation of jury members who must decide whether a murder was voluntary (internally caused) or provoked (externally caused). How can one decide about the true cause of people's actions?

From the present standpoint, one must face the possibility that true cause is a kind of social myth — never to be located on an objective basis (Gergen and Gergen, 1979). True cause is difficult to determine because decisions about cause depend primarily on where people direct their attention (Taylor and Fiske, 1975). We have already seen how actor and observer may disagree on causal attribution. They disagree not because one of them is more objective than the other, but because one attends to the actor in motion and the other to the situational demands. The point is made with even greater clarity in research on *causal chains* — that is, series of events that may be causally linked (Brickman, Ryan, and Wortman, 1975). Consider a rape case in which the act seems to have been premeditated and thus can be attributed to internal causes. The defendant may be blamed for the action. But if the external situation preceding the rape is considered, then blame is not so certain. The defendant may have been at the mercy of an uncontrollable urge. He may have been upset because his mother and older sisters beat him during his childhood and because a month before the rape his wife left him without warning. Now it appears that the social situation should be blamed. However, looking backward once more to consider the reason for the mother's, sisters', and wife's actions, the blame may again fall on the defendant. Perhaps he provoked the women in his life. But then again, we could consider the circumstances that caused him to provoke their attack, and so on, without objective end. How much responsibility one assigns to the defendant thus depends on what point in the causal chain is being considered.

In opposition to this line of argument, some critics maintain that people know when their actions are voluntary. That is, people can distinguish between their voluntary and involuntary actions (Steiner, 1980). But can people be accurate in such assessments? If success and failure can bias causal attributions, then we may well wonder whether people can ever judge their own motives adequately. A series of studies by Richard Nisbett and his colleagues (Nisbett and Bellows, 1977; Nisbett and Wilson, 1977) demonstrate that people are generally not aware of the cognitive processes underlying their conscious decisions. If asked to give your mother's maiden name, you may quickly produce a response, but you cannot identify the particular memory processes that produced the response. Or, as the poet Howard Nemerov has revealed in conversation, "I don't know why I write what I do. My words tumble out on the page and I want to see what they say."

Yet, even though true cause may be beyond knowledge, it is nevertheless an extremely valuable concept for society. If people are not seen as the originators of their actions, no way exists to hold them accountable or responsible. And without a concept of social responsibility, trust in human relations may disappear. Further, the system of laws and courts would have no place in a world where people were not viewed as the originators of their actions. For the good of society, then, people must continue to negotiate the causes of one another's actions (Scott and Lyman, 1968; Shotter, 1980).

SELF-PERCEPTION

Social perception is not just a matter of observing others and trying to understand their behavior. People also try to understand themselves — to be aware of what they really feel, what they truly are. People question their own motives, ask why they are attracted to a given person, why they are afraid to break certain social rules, and so forth. People wonder about their values and attitudes, and they seek to define what it is they really believe about the world. They try to understand their emotions and discover their true feelings about various people and situations. Most people seem to agree with the early Greeks' belief that to "know thyself" is extremely important.

Let us examine the question of self-knowledge in light of what we have said so far in this chapter. We have argued that the perception of others is based primarily on a set of preestablished concepts or explanations that are popular within a culture. From this perspective, to understand or to perceive others properly is to apply the concept or explanation that is required to get along successfully in the culture. There is every reason to believe that people also rely on these rules of description when they try to understand their own actions. The culture furnishes labels that define action for the *actor* as well as for the *observer*. For example, if you verbally criticize your friends at a party, chances are you will be seen as having been aggressive. If you said your behavior at the party was really affectionate, your friends probably would laugh, *even if* your verbal

attacks were your own particular way of expressing affectionate respect. In this light, we will explore the problem of personal identity.

The Social Construction of Self-concept

Young people often go to great lengths to discover their true or basic selves. They talk endlessly with close friends, drop out of school for a year, join the army, see a psychotherapist, and so forth. However, the preceding discussion suggests that knowing oneself is primarily a matter of applying social labels. If feelings of personal identity are created by the choice of labels, then a person's self-concept may depend on the social situation. Thus let us examine three social processes that may influence a person's concept of self.

The Looking-glass Self.   Suppose you want to know whether you are truly warm and loving or basically alienated from others. Sometimes you seem loving enough, but you also are aware that at times being so is an effort. You wish to know what kind of person you *really* are. From the present standpoint, the answer to this question lies in the definitions supplied by the social environment. The most direct solution to the problem is simply to rely on others' opinions of you. Indeed, the early social theorist George Herbert Mead (1934) reasoned that one's concept of self is altogether a reflection of the opinions communicated by significant others. Society provides a *looking glass* in which people discover their image, or self-label.

Let us see how the social looking glass can shape a particular aspect of self-concept, namely, *self-esteem*. Self-esteem refers to an individual's perception of his or her own adequacy, competence, or goodness as a person. In one experiment, female undergraduates were interviewed by an attractive female graduate student whose field was clinical psychology (Gergen, 1965). During the interview the undergraduates were asked to evaluate themselves as honestly as possible. Each student rated her own personality, looks, social abilities, and so forth. The graduate student showed subtle signs of agreement each time the subject rated herself positively and disagreement each time the subject criticized herself. To show agreement the graduate student would smile, nod approvingly, or murmur, "Yes, I think so too." Disagreement was evidenced by silence, a frown, or an occasional disagreement with the subjects' self-doubts. The effects that this communication had on the expressions of self-esteem demonstrated by the undergraduates during the interview are shown in Figure 1. Compare the amount of positive self-evaluation evidenced by the subjects with that expressed by a control group that received no such regard from the interviewer. As you can see, the graduate student's approval produced a steady increase in the subject's self-regard. The research also revealed that the undergraduate's new definition of self continued even after the interview was completed. Approximately twenty minutes after the interview, subjects were asked to give an honest and anonymous self-appraisal. As shown in the figure, the graduate student's high opinion of the subjects carried over to this occasion. As one student later said, "I don't know why, I just felt great the whole day."

Students in this experiment allowed themselves to accept the views of the graduate student. However, people can be very selective in their choice of a looking glass. Certain people's opinions may be welcomed and others' opinions may be rejected. For example, if others' estimates disagree greatly with one's own self-estimates, they may be discredited (Bergin, 1962). In addition, people may discredit others who evaluate them unfavorably. A study of 1,500 adolescents showed that the more favorable another person's opinion was, the greater was the importance of the opinion to the individual (Rosenberg, 1979). Apparently, people bolster their self-esteem by placing greater trust in the opinions of people who evaluate them favorably.

Social Comparison Effects.   People also discover the "proper" labels for themselves through *social comparison* — that is, by estimating how they stack up in

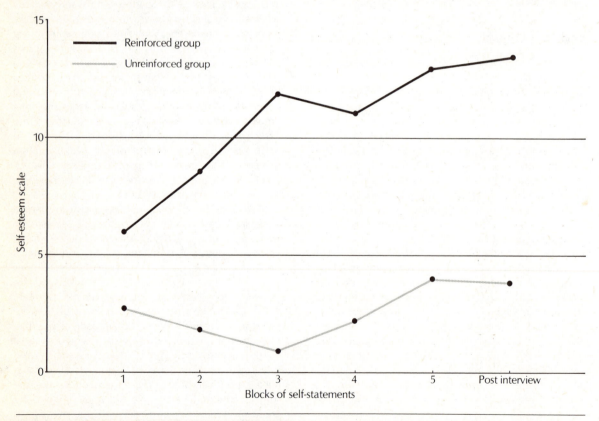

Figure 1.   The Effect of Social Reinforcement on Self-Esteem.

Note the increase in self-esteem in the group that received support from the graduate student. Increased self-esteem persisted in a different setting.

(Adapted from K. Gergen, "The Effects of Interaction Goals and Personalistic Feedback on Presentation of Self," *Journal of Personality and Social Psychology,* 1965, Vol. 1, pp. 413–425. Copyright by the American Psychological Association. Reprinted by permission of the author.)

comparison with those around them. For example, a friend may be considered by everyone to be a warm and loving person. If you find yourself behaving just like the friend, you may conclude that you too are warm and loving. The influential theorist Leon Festinger (1954) has proposed that the process of social comparison is perhaps the major vehicle through which people determine what is true and false about social life. . . . However, in one dramatic demonstration of the comparison process, a summer job was offered to a group of male college students (Morse and Gergen, 1970). When each applicant arrived for an interview, he was seated alone and given a number of forms to fill out. Among the forms was a standardized test of self-esteem. When the applicant had completed half of the self-esteem test, a secretary brought a second applicant into the room. This individual, an accomplice of the experimenters, appeared in either one of two guises. For half of the subjects, he cut an impressive figure. He wore a beautiful suit and carried an attaché case. As soon as he was seated across the table from the subject, he opened his case to reveal sharpened pencils, a philosophy book, and a slide rule. We privately labeled this applicant Mr. Clean. For the remaining subjects, the same collaborator appeared, but dressed in a smelly sweat shirt, torn pants, and several days' growth of whiskers. He looked dazed, and as he slumped into his seat he threw a dogeared copy of a cheap sex novel onto the table. He was privately knighted Mr. Dirty. No words were exchanged between the accomplice and the subject. After the accomplice was seated, the original applicant went on to complete the second half of the self-esteem test.

An examination of the self-esteem scores revealed a striking effect. In the presence of Mr. Clean, applicants showed a marked *decline* in good feelings about themselves. The ratings were far more negative than they had been before Mr. Clean arrived. Precisely the opposite effect occurred when applicants were exposed to Mr. Dirty. When they compared themselves with him, they showed a marked *increase* in self-esteem. Self-concept often may depend, then, on comparison — on who happens to be present.

Social Distinctiveness: "How do I differ?" If you were asked to talk about yourself, chances are you would not mention that you are a person with two feet, two eyes, or a nose. Yet, if you lacked a foot, an eye, or a nose, you probably would think of this as an important aspect of yourself — perhaps an essential one in understanding who you are. Apparently people also develop a sense

of self by observing the ways in which they differ from others. Observing a difference seems to increase consciousness of a particular characteristic. The characteristic then becomes a means of personal identification.

In one study of distinctiveness effects, investigators interviewed more than five hundred high-school students, asking them to talk about themselves for five minutes and to say anything that came to mind (McGuire et al., 1978). Approximately 82 percent of the students were English-speaking whites, while 9 percent were black and 8 percent were Hispanic. The black and Hispanic students were more distinctive than were the white students in this environment. As the self-descriptions revealed, very few (1 percent) of the white students spontaneously mentioned their racial identity — their being white simply was not on their minds. In contrast, 17 percent of the blacks and 14 percent of the Hispanics mentioned their race or ethnic background. Similar results were obtained in an analysis of whether students mentioned their gender (McGuire, McGuire, and Winton, 1979). Whether students identified themselves as male or female depended on how many males or females were in their household. If a male lived with a mother and three sisters, for example, his maleness became an important part of the way he saw himself.

In summary, we find that the way people define themselves at any particular time seems to depend on the responses and the presence of others. People come to know themselves by observing the way others react to their behavior, by comparing themselves with those around them, and by focusing on the aspects of the self that are different from other people's. In a sense, an individual is defined by the company he or she keeps.

Understanding Emotions

Now that we have seen how self-identity may be molded by a social situation, we can turn to a second important aspect of self-perception: the emotions. To what extent does an individual's emotional life depend on the application of labels? You may believe that your emotions are not up for social grabs: After all, you may feel that you *know* when you are angry or sad or fearful. And besides, don't emotions reflect underlying physiological differences? In discovering feelings, aren't people primarily registering the state of the nervous system at the moment? The body provides different messages for elation, hate, love, anger, and so forth.

Although these arguments sound plausible enough, let us reconsider.

First, let us examine more carefully the physiological basis of emotions. As it happens, research in this area indicates that few emotions can be clearly differentiated on a physiological basis. Thus, some physiological differences do exist between generalized positive or negative feelings (Lazarus, Kanner, and Folkman, 1980) and between extreme states of rage and fear (Ax, 1953). However, beyond very gross differences, telling one emotion from another is difficult (Holmes and Masuda, 1974; Selye, 1976). Physiology does little to discriminate, for example, among love, admiration, infatuation, sympathy, affectionate regard, or friendliness. Nor have physiological differences that distinguish among hate, envy, jealousy, spite, or anger been discovered. Instead, many different feelings seem to be accompanied by a state of *generalized physiological arousal*. But if there is little emotional discrimination on the physiological level, why are so many distinct emotions represented in language?

An intriguing answer to this puzzle is furnished by Stanley Schachter's (1964) *two-factor theory of emotions*. Schachter suggests that our emotional experience requires first *generalized arousal* and then a *cognitive label* for the arousal. Since the arousal doesn't come with a label attached, people must necessarily turn outward to their social surroundings. Social rules determine what label applies in a given situation. The rules specify, for example, that if you are aroused by a member of the opposite sex, you should call the feeling *love, infatuation,* or *sexual attraction.* If the other person is of the same sex, the arousal should be labeled *friendship.* If the person is much older, you might label the arousal *admiration.* What we think we feel thus depends importantly on the social rules governing what we are *supposed* to feel under varying circumstances (Averill, 1980).

The classic demonstration of this argument was provided by Schachter and his colleague Jerome Singer (1962). In their experiment subjects were injected with a substance they were told was a vitamin supplement. The substance was, in fact, *epinephrine,* a sympathetic nervous system stimulant. One group of participants was then told that the ''vitamin supplement'' would produce flushing, tremor, an increase in heart rate, and so forth. These subjects thus knew what effects the drug actually would produce. A second group of subjects remained uninformed. They were told nothing of the drug's effects. Once they received the shot, both groups of subjects experienced physiological arousal,

but the subjects in one group had a label that would enable them to understand their arousal, and the second group did not. As the investigators reasoned, the second group would be more open to environmental cues suggesting how to define their feelings than would the first group. A third group, injected with a nonarousing solution, was not expected to be much aroused (placebo condition).

After the injection each subject was sent to a room to wait for an experiment in vision. A confederate of the experimenters, posing as another subject, was already in the waiting room. He set the stage for emotional labeling. For half of the subjects in each of the above conditions, the confederate tried to produce *euphoria.* He happily threw paper planes, tossed wads of paper into a waste basket, and played with a hula hoop. For the other subjects the confederate tried to produce *anger.* As he filled out a questionnaire, he became angry and made increasingly critical remarks about the questionnaire and its originators. Finally, in a fit of rage he crushed the form into a ball and threw it into a waste basket.

After exposure to the confederate, subjects rated their emotional state. As you can see in Figure 2, subjects who had no label for their arousal (who were uninformed about the drug's effects) were more likely to feel euphoric or angry than were informed subjects. In other words, subjects who had no way to interpret their arousal except by using social cues were most influenced by the social circumstances. In addition, subjects who received the placebo were also less euphoric and less angry than were subjects who were aroused and uninformed. As the investigators reasoned, both arousal and a search for cues are essential for identifying emotions.

In Schachter and Singer's experiment the subjects were aroused artificially. This procedure was necessary because the investigators wanted to manipulate arousal while holding other factors constant. In daily life the sequence of events is seldom so clear. As Arlie Hochschild (1979) has argued, people often are confronted with rules about what they ought to feel *before* they are aroused. People expect to feel sad at a funeral, enthusiastic at a sports contest, or grateful when receiving a gift — and yet often these feelings are absent. At such times, observes Hochschild, people carry out *emotional work* in order to have the experience that is demanded by the occasion. That is, they try through various psychological mechanisms to align their experienced feelings with the situational requirements. These psychological mechanisms can be cognitive,

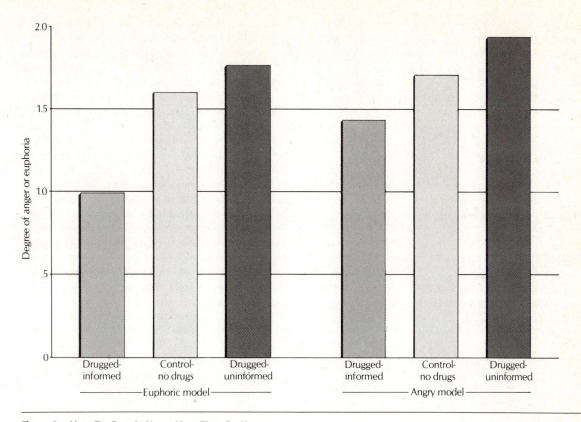

Figure 2.   How Do People Know How They Feel?

In this demonstration of Schachter's two-factor theory of emotion, note that uninformed subjects tended to give their unexplained arousal the same label as that for the behavior they were observing.

(Adapted from S. Schachter and J. L. Singer, "Cognitive, social and physiological determinants of emotional state," *Psychological Review,* 1962, Vol. 65, pp. 121–128. Copyright 1962 by the American Psychological Association. Reprinted by permission of the author.)

physiological, or expressive. For example, in order to feel grief at a funeral one might bring to mind fond memories of the deceased (cognitive), breath more deeply in order to increase heart rate and thus produce the experience of having an emotion (physiological), and adopt a posture of sadness (expressive). This emotional work helps to bring on the required state of feeling.

Although Schachter's research suggests that emotional labeling is highly dependent on social circumstances, his work has not been without criticism. Some critics have pointed out important flaws in the experimental methodology (Leventhal, 1974; Plutchik and Ax, 1962), and others have not been able to repeat the experiment successfully. For example, it has been found that most people don't like to experience unexplained arousal (Marshall, 1976; Maslach, 1979). If the dose of epinephrine is strong, for example, the subject will feel

uncomfortable regardless of the information provided by the environment. Many theorists continue to believe in a limited number of fundamental emotions (Ekman, Friesen, and Ellsworth, 1972; Izard, 1977). Yet, even though Schachter's work has its critics, it has stimulated much fascinating research.

Research on the *reattribution of emotional states* deserves special attention. If emotional feelings are as ambiguous as Schachter maintains them to be, then label selection can be rather arbitrary—people need only agree that a label is appropriate. Therefore, giving people different kinds of information should produce a reattribution of their emotional state—a shift from one label to another. This set of assumptions offers exciting possibilities for workers in the fields of mental health and medicine. Think about using reattribution to reduce pain. Can it be done? The fact that people can walk on hot coals or lie on a bed of nails suggests that cognitive factors can be important in determining how much pain a person feels. To explore this possibility more directly, the Schachter group gave subjects a ''drug'' — a harmless substance that had no effect (Nisbett and Schachter, 1966). Half of the subjects were told that the drug would cause an arousal reaction similar to that produced by electric shock, while the others were informed that it would have few or no side effects. Later the subjects were given a test of pain tolerance. They received increasingly high dosages of electric shock and were told they could terminate the experiment whenever the shocks became too painful. The two groups differed markedly in the amount of shock they could tolerate. Individuals in the group that had been told that the drug had shocklike effects were able to withstand more shock than were those who had not received this information. Seemingly, those who thought that the drug had side effects attributed the effects of the shock to the ''drug'' and did not label the shock as pain. Thus, through reattribution the experience of pain was reduced greatly.

What are the limits of reattribution techniques? Are psychological anesthetics feasible? Are there more effective means for reducing anxiety or depression in therapy patients? Some steps have been taken toward developing such techniques. Research has shown, for example, that altering people's attributions can reduce insomnia (Storms et al., 1979), rid people of snake phobias (Dienstbier, 1972), increase sexual satisfaction (Morris and O'Neal, 1974), reduce fear (Ross, Rodin, and Zimbardo, 1969), and reduce the pain of giving up cigarettes (Barefoot and Girodo, 1972). Other researchers are exploring the possibility that menstrual pain is dependent on conceptual labeling (Koeske and Koeske, 1975). At this point it is too early to know how effective relabeling of emotional states can be. Some investigators feel that long-established habits of labeling can be altered and that new habits can be established (Loftis and Ross, 1974). However, other investigators have discovered defects in the early studies (Calvert-Bozanowsky, and Leventhal, 1975; Kellog and Baron, 1975). Clearly, reattribution has interesting and important potential.

REFERENCES

Arkin, R. M., Appelman, A. J., & Burger, J. M. Social anxiety, self-presentation and the self-serving bias in causal attribution. *Journal of Personality and Social Psychology,* 1980, *38,* 23–35.

Averill, J. R. A constructivist view of emotion. In R. Plutchik & H. Kellerman (Eds.), *Emotion: Theory, research and experience.* New York: Academic Press, 1980.

Ax, A. F. The physiological differentiation between fear and anger in humans. *Psychosomatic Medicine,* 1953, *15,* 433–442.

Barefoot, J. C., & Girodo, M. The misattribution of smoking cessation symptoms. *Canadian Journal of Behavior Science,* 1972, *4,* 358–363.

Bar-Tal, D. Interactions of teachers and pupils. In I. H. Frieze, D. Bar-Tal, & J. Carroll (Eds.), *New approaches to social problems.* San Francisco: Jossey-Bass, 1979.

Bergin, A. E. The effects of dissonant persuasive communications upon changes in self-referring attitudes. *Journal of Personality,* 1962, *30,* 423–438.

Bernstein, A. M., Stephan, W. G., & Davis, M. H. Explaining attribution for achievement: A path analytic approach. *Journal of Personality and Social Psychology,* 1979, *37,* 1810–1821.

Bradley, G. W. Self-serving biases in the attribution process: A re-examination of the fact or fiction question. *Journal of Personality and Social Psychology,* 1978, *36,* 56–71.

Brickman, P., Ryan, K., & Wortman, C. Causal chains: Attribution of responsibility as a function of immediate and prior causes. *Journal of Personality and Social Psychology,* 1975, *32,* 1060–1067.

Calvert-Boyanowsky, J., & Leventhal, H. The role of information in attenuating behavioral responses to stress: A reinterpretation of the misattribution phenomenon. *Journal of Prsonality and Social Psychology,* 1975, *32,* 214–221.

Cooper, H. M., & Lowe, C. A. Task, information and attributions for academic performance by professional teachers and roleplayers. *Journal of Personality,* 1977, *45,* 469–483.

Dienstbier, R. A. The role of anxiety and arousal attribution in cheating. *Journal of Experimental Social Psychology,* 1972, *8,* 168–179.

Eisen, S. V. Actor-observer differences in information inference and causal attribution. *Journal of Personality and Social Psychology,* 1979, *37,* 261–272.

Ekman, P., Friesen, W. V., & Ellsworth, P. *Emotion in the human face.* Elmsford, N.Y.: Pergamon Press, 1972.

Ferguson, T. J., & Wells, G. L. Priming of mediators in causal attribution. *Journal of Personality and Social Psychology,* 1980, *38,* 461–470.

Frieze, I. H., & Weiner, B. Cue utilization and attributional judgments for success and failure. *Journal of Personality,* 1971, *39,* 559–605.

Gergen, K. J. The effects of interaction goals and personalistic feedback on presentation of self. *Journal of Personality and Social Psychology,* 1965, *1,* 413–425.

Goethals, G. R., Allison, S. J., & Frost, M. Perceptions of the magnitude and diversity of social support. *Journal of Experimental Social Psychology,* 1979, *15,* 570–581.

Gross, A. E., & Latané, J. G. Receiving help, reciprocation and interpersonal attraction. *Journal of Applied Social Psychology,* 1974, *4,* 210–223.

Hochschild, A. R. Emotion work, feeling rules and social structure. *American Journal of Sociology,* 1979, *85,* 551–575.

Holmes, T. H., & Masuda, M. Life change and illness susceptibility. In B. S. Dohrenwend & B. P. Dohrenwend (Eds.), *Stressful life events: Their nature and effects.* New York: John Wiley & Sons, 1974.

Izard, C. E. *Human emotions.* New York: Plenum, 1977.

Johnson, T. J., Feigenbaum, R., & Weiby, M. Some determinants and consequences of the teacher's perception of causality. *Journal of Educational Psychology,* 1964, *55,* 237–246.

Jones, E. E., & Davis, K. E. From acts to dispositions. In L. Berkowitz (Ed.), *Advances in experimental social psychology* (Vol. 2). New York: Academic Press, 1965.

Jones, E. E. & Nisbett, R. E. *The actor and the observer: Divergent perceptions of the cause of behavior.* Morristown, N.J.: Silver Burdett/General Learning Press, 1971.

Jones, E. E., & Thibaut, J. W. Interaction goals as bases of inference in interpersonal perception. In R. Tagiuri & L. Petrullo (Eds.), *Person perception and interpersonal behavior.* Stanford, Calif.: Stanford University Press, 1958.

Kelley, H. H. Attribution theory in social psychology. In D. Levine (Ed.), *Nebraska Symposium on Motivation* (Vol. 15). Lincoln: University of Nebraska Press, 1967.

Kelley, H. H. *Causal schemata and the attribution process.* Morristown, N.J.: Silver Burdett/General Learning Press, 1972.

Kelley, H. H. The processes of causal attribution. *American Psychologist,* 1973, *28,* 107–128.

Kelley, H. H., & Michela, S. L. Attribution theory and research. *Annual Review of Psychology,* 1980, *31,* 457–502.

Kellogg, R., & Baron, R. S. Attribution theory, insomnia and the reverse placebo effect: A reversal of Storm's and Nisbett's findings. *Journal of Personality and Social Psychology,* 1975, *32,* 231–236.

Kidder, L. H., & Cohn, E. S. Public views of crime and crime prevention. In I. Frieze, D. Bar-Tal, & J. Carroll (Eds.), *New approaches to social problems.* San Francisco: Jossey-Bass, 1979.

Koeske, G. F., & Koeske, R. K. Deviance and a generalized disposition toward internality: An attributional approach. *Journal of Personality,* 1975, *43,* 634–646.

Lazarus, R. S., Kanner, A. D., & Folkman, S. Emotions: A cognitive-phenomenological analysis. In R. Plutchik & H. Kellerman (Eds.), *Emotion: Theory, research, and experience.* New York: Academic Press, 1980.

Leventhal, H. Emotions: A basic problem for social psychology. In C. Nemeth (Ed.), *Social psychology: Classic and contemporary integrations.* Chicago: Rand McNally, 1974.

Loftis, J., & Ross, L. Retrospective misattribution of a conditioned emotional response. *Journal of Personality and Social Psychology,* 1974, *30,* 683–687.

McArthur, L. Z. The how and what of why: Some determinants and consequences of causal attribution. *Journal of Personality and Social Psychology,* 1972, *22,* 171–193.

McGuire, W. J., McGuire, C. V., Child, P., & Fujioka, T. Salience of ethnicity in the spontaneous self-concept as a function of one's ethnic distinctiveness in the social environment. *Journal of Personality and Social Psychology,* 1978, *36,* 511–520.

McGuire, W. J., McGuire, C. V., & Winton, W. Effects of household sex composition on the salience of one's gender in the spontaneous self-concept. *Journal of Experimental Social Psychology,* 1979, *15,* 77–90.

Marshall, G. *The affective consequences of ''inadequately explained'' physiological arousal.* Unpublished doctoral dissertation, Stanford University, Stanford, Calif., 1976.

Maslach, C. Negative emotional biasing of unexplained arousal. *Journal of Personality and Social Psychology,* 1979, *37,* 953–969.

Mead, G. H. *Mind, self, and society.* Chicago: University of Chicago Press, 1934.

Meyer, J. P. Causal attribution for success and failure: A multivariate investigation of dimensionality, formation and consequences. *Journal of Personality and Social Psychology,* 1980, *38,* 704–718.

Miller, D., & Ross, M. Self-serving biases in the attribution of causality: Fact or fiction? *Psychological Bulletin,* 1975, *82,* 213–225.

Morris, L. A., & O'Neal E. C. Drug name familiarity and the placebo effect. *Journal of Clinical Psychology,* 1974, *7,* 280–282.

Morse, S. J., & Gergen, K. J. Social comparison, self-consistency and the concept of self. *Journal of Personality and Social Psychology,* 1970, *16,* 149–156.

Nisbett, R. E., & Bellows, N. Verbal reports about causal influences as social judgments: Private access versus public theories. *Journal of Personality and Social Psychology,* 1977, *35,* 613–624.

Nisbett, R. E., Borgida, E., Crandall, R., & Reed, H. Popular induction: Information is not necessarily informative. In J. S. Carroll & J. W. Payne (Eds.), *Cognition and social behavior.* Hillsdale, N.J.: Lawrence Erlbaum, 1976.

Nisbett, R. E., & Schachter, S. Cognitive manipulation of pain. *Journal of Experimental Social Psychology,* 1966, *2,* 227–236.

Nisbett, R. E., & Wilson, T. D. Telling more than we can know: Verbal reports on mental processes. *Psychological Review,* 1977, *84,* 231–259.

Plutchik, R., & Ax, A. F. A critique of ''Determinants of emotional state'' by Schachter and Singer. *Psychophysiology,* 1967, *4,* 79–82.

Rosenberg, M. *Conceiving the self.* New York: Basic Books, 1979.

Ross, L. The intuitive psychologist and his shortcomings: Distortions in the attribution process. In L. Berkowitz (Ed.), *Advances in experimental social psychology* (Vol. 10). New York: Academic Press, 1977.

Ross, L., Greene, S., & House, P. The ''false consensus effect'': An egocentric bias in social perception and attribution processes. *Journal of Experimental Social Psychology,* 1977, *13,* 279–301.

Ross, L., Rodin, J., & Zimbardo, P. G. Toward an attribution therapy: The reduction of fear through induced cognitive-emotional misattribution. *Journal of Personality and Social Psychology,* 1969, *12,* 279–288.

Ruble, D., & Feldman, N. Order of concensus, distinctiveness and consistency information and causal attribution. *Journal of Personality and Social Psychology,* 1976, *34,* 930–937.

Schachter, S. The interaction of cognitive and physiological determinants of emotional state. In L. Berkowitz (Ed.), *Advances in experimental social psychology* (Vol. 1). New York: Academic Press, 1964.

Schachter, S., & Singer, J. L. Cognitive, social and physiological determinants of emotional state. *Psychological Review,* 1962, *65,* 121–128.

Schiltz, M. E. *Public attitudes toward social security,* 1935–1956. Washington, D.C.: U.S. Government Printing Office, 1970.

Schopler, J., & Layton, B. D. Determinants of the self-attribution of having influenced another person. *Journal of Personality and Social Psychology,* 1972, *22,* 326–332.

Scott, M., & Lyman, S. Accounts. *American Sociological Review,* 1968, *33,* 46–62.

Selye, H. *The stress of life.* New York: McGraw-Hill, 1976.

Shotter, J. Action, joint action and intentionality. In M. Brenner (Ed.), *The structure of action.* Oxford: Blackwell, 1980.

Sicoly, F., & Ross, M. The facilitation of ego-biased attributions by means of self-serving observer feedback. *Journal of Personality and Social Psychology,* 1977, *35,* 734-741.

Snyder, M. L., Stephan, W. G., & Rosenfield, D. Egotism and attribution. *Journal of Personality and Social Psychology,* 1976, *33,* 435-441.

Steiner, I. D. Attribution of choice. In M. Fishbein (Ed.), *Progress in social psychology* (Vol. 1). Hillsdale, N.J.: Lawrence Erlbaum, 1980.

Storms, M. D., Denney, D. R., McCaul, K. D., & Lowery, C. R. Treating insomnia. In I. Frieze, D. Bar-Tal, & T. Carrol (Eds.), *New approaches to social psychology.* San Francisco: Jossey-Bass, 1979.

Streufert, S., & Streufert, S. C. Effects of conceptual structure, failure and success on attribution of causality and interpersonal attitudes. *Journal of Personality and Social Psychology,* 1969, *11,* 138-147.

Taylor, S. E., & Fiske, S. T. Point of view and perception of causality. *Journal of Personality and Social Psychology,* 1975, *32,* 439-445.

Weary, G. Examination of affect and egotism as mediators of bias in causal attributions. *Journal of Personality and Social Psychology,* 1980, *38,* 348-357.

Weiner, B., Russell, D., & Lerman, D. The cognition-emotion process in achievement-related contexts. *Journal of Personality and Social Psychology,* 1979, *37,* 1211-1220.

Wells, G. L., & Harvey, J. Do people use concensus information in making causal attributions? *Journal of Personality and Social Psychology,* 1978, *35,* 279-293.

West, S. G., Gunn, S. P., & Chernicky, P. Ubiquitous Watergate: An attributional analysis. *Journal of Personality and Social Psychology,* 1975, *32,* 55-65.

Wortman, C. B., Costanza, P. R., & Witt, T. R. Effect of anticipated performance on the attributions of causality to self and others. *Journal of Personality and Social Psychology,* 1973, *27,* 372-381.

Zuckerman, M. Actions and occurrences in Kelley's cube. *Journal of Personality and Social Psychology,* 1978, *36,* 647-656.

Zuckerman, M. Attribution of success and failure revisited, or: The motivational bias is alive and well in attribution theory. *Journal of Personality,* 1979, *47,* 245-287.

Effects of Perception on Organizational Behavior

13. The Self-Perception of Motivation

Barry M. Staw

Within the area of interpersonal perception, it has been noted (Heider, 1958) that an individual may infer the causes of another's actions to be a function of personal and environmental force:

Action = f (personal force + environmental force)

This is quite close to saying that individuals attempt to determine whether another person is intrinsically motivated to perform an activity (action due to personal force), or extrinsically motivated (action due to environmental force), or both. The extent to which an individual will infer intrinsic motivation on the part of another is predicted to be affected by the clarity and strength of external forces within the situation (Jones & Davis, 1965; Jones & Nisbett, 1971; Kelley 1967). When there are strong forces bearing on the individual to perform an activity, there is little reason to assume that

a behavior is self-determined, whereas a high level of intrinsic motivation might be inferred if environmental force is minimal. Several studies dealing with interpersonal perception have supported this general conclusion (Jones, Davis, & Gergen, 1961; Jones & Harris, 1967; Strickland, 1958; Thibaut & Riecken, 1955).

Bem (1967a, b) extrapolated this interpersonal theory of causal attribution to the study of self-perception or how one views his *own* behavior within a social context. Bem hypothesized that the extent to which external pressures are sufficiently strong to account for one's behavior will determine the likelihood that a person will attribute his own actions to internal causes. Thus if a person acts under strong external rewards or punishments, he is likely to assume that his behavior is under external control. However, if extrinsic contingencies are not strong or salient, the individual is likely to assume that his behavior is due to his own interest in the activity or that his behavior is intrinsically motivated. De Charms has made a similar point in his discussion of individual's perception of personal causation (1968, p. 328):

As a first approximation, we propose that whenever a person experiences himself to be the locus of causality for his own behavior (to be an Origin), he will consider himself to be intrinsically motivated. Conversely, when a person perceives the locus of causality for his behavior to be external to himself (that he is a Pawn), he will consider himself to be extrinsically motivated.

De Charms emphasized that the individual may attempt psychologically to label his actions on the basis of whether or not he has been instrumental in affecting his own behavior; that is, whether his behavior has been intrinsically or extrinsically motivated.

THE CASE FOR A NEGATIVE RELATIONSHIP BETWEEN INTRINSIC AND EXTRINSIC MOTIVATION

The self-perception approach to intrinsic and extrinsic motivation leads to the conclusion that there may be a negative interrelationship between these two motivational factors. The basis for this prediction stems from the assumption that individuals may work backward from their own actions in inferring sources of causation (Bem, 1967a, b; 1972). For example, if external pressures on an individual are so high that they would ordinarily cause him to perform a given task regardless of the internal characteristics of the activity, then the individual might logically infer that he is extrinsically motivated. In contrast, if external reward contingencies are extremely low or nonsalient, the individual might then infer that his behavior is intrinsically motivated. What is important is the fact that a person, in performing an activity, may *seek out* the probable cause of his own actions. Since behavior has no doubt been caused by something, it makes pragmatic, if not scientific, sense for the person to conclude that the cause is personal (intrinsic) rather than extrinsic if he can find no external reasons for his actions.

Two particular situations provide robust tests of the self-perception prediction. One is a situation in which there is insufficient justification for a person's actions, a situation in which the intrinsic rewards for an activity are very low (e.g., a dull task) and there are no compensat-

ing extrinsic rewards (e.g., monetary payment, verbal praise). Although rationally, one ordinarily tries to avoid these situations; there are occasions when one is faced with the difficult question of "why did I do that?" The self-perception theory predicts that in situations of insufficient justification, the individual may cognitively reevaluate the intrinsic characteristics of an activity in order to justify or explain his own behavior. For example, if the individual performed a dull task for no external reward, he may "explain" his behavior by thinking that the task was not really so bad after all.

Sometimes a person may also be fortunate enough to be in a situation in which his behavior is oversufficiently justified. For example, a person may be asked to perform an interesting task and at the same time be lavishly paid for his efforts. In such situations, the self-perception theory predicts that the individual may actually reevaluate the activity in a downward direction. Since the external reward would be sufficient to motivate behavior by itself, the individual may mistakenly infer that he was extrinsically motivated to perform the activity. He may conclude that since he was forced to perform the task by an external reward, the task probably was not terribly satisfying in and of itself.

Figure 1 graphically depicts the situations of insufficient and overly sufficient justification. From the figure,

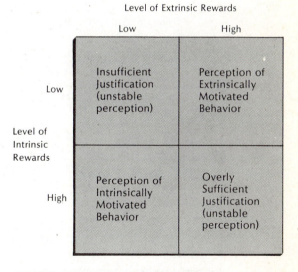

Figure 1. A Conceptual Framework of Self-Perception Theory.

we can see that the conceptual framework supporting self-perception theory raises several interesting issues. First, it appears from this analysis that there are only two fully stable attributions of behavior: (1) the perception of extrinsically motivated behavior in which the internal rewards associated with performing an activity are low while external rewards are high; and (2) the perception of intrinsically motivated behavior in which the task is inherently rewarding but external rewards are low. Furthermore, it appears that situations of insufficient justification (where intrinsic and extrinsic rewards are both low) and oversufficient justification (where intrinsic and extrinsic rewards are both high) involve unstable attribution states. As shown in Figure 2, individuals apparently resolve this attributional instability by altering their perceptions of intrinsic rewards associated with the task.

An interesting question posed by the self-perception analysis is why individuals are predicted to resolve an unstable attribution state by cognitively reevaluating a task in terms of its intrinsic rewards rather than changing their perceptions of extrinsic factors. The answer to this question may lie in the relative clarity of extrinsic as compared with intrinsic rewards, and the individual's relative ability to distort the two aspects of the situation. Within many settings (and especially within laboratory

experiments) extrinsic rewards are generally quite salient and specific, whereas an individual must judge the intrinsic nature of a task for himself. Any shifts in the perception of intrinsic and extrinsic rewards may therefore be more likely to occur in the intrinsic factor. As shown in Figure 2 it is these predicted shifts in perceived intrinsic rewards that may theoretically underlie a negative relationship between intrinsic and extrinsic motivation.

Empirical Evidence: Insufficient Justification

Several studies have shown that when an individual is induced to commit an unpleasant act for little or no external justification, he may subsequently conclude that the act was not so unpleasant after all. Actually, the first scientific attempt to account for this phenomenon was the theory of cognitive dissonance (Festinger, 1957). It was predicted by dissonance theorists (Aronson, 1966; Festinger, 1957) that, since performing an unpleasant act for little or no reward would be an inconsistent (and seemingly irrational) thing to do, an individual might subsequently change his attitude toward the action in order to reduce the inconsistency or to appear rational. Bem's self-perception theory yields the same predictions but does not require one to posit that there is a motivating state such as dissonance reduction or self-rationalization. To Bem, since the individual examines his own behavior in light of the forces around him, he is simply more likely to come to the conclusion that his actions were intrinsically satisfying if they were performed under minimal external force.

In general, two types of experiments have been designed to assess the consequences of insufficient justification. One type of design has involved the performance of a dull task with varied levels of reward (Brehm & Cohen, 1962; Freedman, 1963; Weick, 1964; Weick & Penner, 1965). A second and more popular design has involved some form of counterattitudinal advocacy, either in terms of lying to a fellow subject about the nature of an experiment or writing an essay against one's position on an important issue (Carlsmith, Collins, & Helmreich, 1966; Festinger & Carlsmith, 1959; Linder, Cooper, & Jones, 1967). Fundamentally, the two types of designs are not vastly different. Both require subjects to perform an intrinsically dissatisfying act under varied levels of external inducement, and both predict that, in the low payment condition, the subject will change his attitude toward the activity (i.e., think

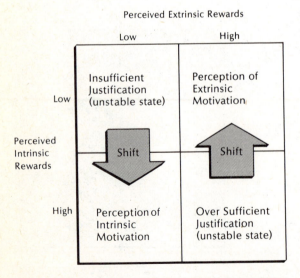

Figure 2. A Schematic Analysis of the Self-Perception of Intrinsic and Extrinsic Motivation.

more favorably of the task or begin to believe the position advocated).

The most well-known experiment designed to test the insufficient justification paradigm was conducted by Festinger and Carlsmith (1959). Subjects participated in a repetitive and dull task (putting spools on trays and turning pegs) and were asked to tell other waiting subjects that the experiment was enjoyable, interesting, and exciting. Half the experimental subjects were paid $1, and half were paid $20 for the counterattitudinal advocacy (and to be "on call" in the future), while control subjects were not paid and did not perform the counterattitudinal act. As predicted, the smaller the reward used to induce subjects to perform the counterattitudinal act, the greater the positive change in their attitudes toward the task. Although the interpretation of the results of this study have been actively debated (e.g., between dissonance and self-perception theorists) the basic findings have been replicated by a number of different researchers. It should be noted, however, that several mediating variables have also been isolated as being necessary for the attainment of this dissonance or self-perception effect: free choice (Linder, Cooper, & Jones, 1967), commitment or irrevocability of behavior (Brehm & Cohen, 1962), and substantial adverse consequences (Calder, Ross, & Insko, 1973; Collins & Hoyt, 1972).

Recently, a strong test of the insufficient justification paradigm was also conducted outside the laboratory (Staw, 1974a). A natural field experiment was made possible by the fact that many young men had joined an organization (Army ROTC) in order to avoid being drafted, *and* these same young men subsequently received information (a draft lottery number) that changed the value of this organizational reward. Of particular relevance was the fact that those who joined ROTC did so not because of their intrinsic interest in the activities involved (e.g., drills, classes, and summer camp), but because they anticipated a substantial extrinsic reward (draft avoidance). As a result, those who received draft numbers that exempted them from military service subsequently faced a situation of low extrinsic as well as intrinsic rewards, a situation of insufficient justification. In contrast, persons who received draft numbers that made them vulnerable to military call-up found their participation in ROTC perfectly justified — they were still successfully avoiding the draft by remaining in the organization. To test the insufficient justification effect, both the attitudes and the performance of ROTC cadets were analyzed by draft number before and after the national draft lottery. The results showed that those in the insufficient justification situation enhanced their perception of ROTC and even performed somewhat better in ROTC courses after the lottery. It should be recognized, however, that this task enhancement occurred only under circumstances very similar to those previously found necessary for the dissonance or self-perception effect (i.e., high commitment, free choice, and adverse consequences).

Empirical Evidence: Overly Sufficient Justification

There have been several empirical studies designed to test the self-perception prediction within the context of overly sufficient justification. Generally, a situation in which an extrinsic reward is added to an intrinsically rewarding task has been experimentally contrived for this purpose. Following self-perception theory, it is predicted that an increase in external justification will cause individuals to lose confidence in their intrinsic interest in the experimental task. Since dissonance theory cannot make this prediction (it is neither irrational nor inconsistent to perform an activity for too many rewards), the literature on overly sufficient justification provides the most important data on the self-perception prediction. For this reason, we will examine the experimental evidence in some detail.

In an experiment specifically designed to test the effect of overly sufficient justification on intrinsic motivation, Deci (1971) enlisted a number of college students to participate in a problem-solving study. All the students were asked to work on a series of intrinsically interesting puzzles for three experimental sessions. After the first session, however, half of the students (the experimental group) were told that they would also be given an extrinsic reward (money) for correctly solving the second set of puzzles, while the other students (the control group) were not told anything about the reward. In the third session, neither the experimental nor the control subjects were rewarded. This design is schematically outlined below:

Basic Design of Deci (1971) Study

	Time 1	Time 2	Time 3
Experimental group	No payment	Payment	No payment
Control group	No payment	No payment	No payment

Deci had hypothesized that the payment of money in the second experimental session might decrease subjects' intrinsic motivation to perform the task. That is, the introduction of an external force (money) might cause participants to alter their self-perception about why they are working on the puzzles. Instead of being intrinsically motivated to solve the interesting puzzles, they might find themselves working primarily to get the money provided by the experimenter. Thus Deci's goal in conducting the study was to compare the changes in subjects' intrinsic motivation from the first to third sessions for both the experimental and control groups. If the self-perception hypothesis was correct, the intrinsic motivation of the previously paid experimental subjects would decrease in the third session, whereas the intrinsic motivation of the unpaid controls should remain unchanged.

As a measure of intrinsic motivation, Deci used the amount of free time participants spent on the puzzle task. To obtain this measure, the experimenter left the room during each session, supposedly to feed some data into the computer. As the experimenter left the room, he told the subjects they could do anything they wanted with their free time. In addition to the puzzles, current issues of *Time, The New Yorker,* and *Playboy* were placed near the subjects. However, while the first experimenter was out of the laboratory, a second experimenter, unknown to the subjects, observed their behavior through a one-way mirror. It was reasoned that if the subject worked on the puzzles during this free time period, he must be intrinsically motivated to perform the task. As shown in Table 1, the amount of free time spent on the task decreased for those who were previously paid to perform the activity, while there was a slight increase for the unpaid controls. Although the difference between the experimental and control

groups was only marginally significant, the results are suggestive of the fact that an overly sufficient extrinsic reward may decrease one's intrinsic motivation to perform a task.

Lepper, Greene, and Nisbett (1973) also conducted a study that tested the self-perception prediction in a situation of overly sufficient justification. Their study involved having nursery school children perform an interesting activity (playing with Magic Markers) with and without the expectation of an additional extrinsic reward. Some children were induced to draw pictures with the markers by promising them a Good Player Award consisting of a big gold star, a bright red ribbon, and a place to print their name. Our children either performed the activity without any reward or were told about the reward only after completing the activity. Children who participated in these three experimental conditions (expected reward, no reward, unexpected reward) were then covertly observed during the following week in a free-play period. As in the Deci (1971) study, the amount of time children spent on the activity when they could do other interesting things (i.e., playing with other toys) was taken to be an indicator of intrinsic motivation.

The findings of the Lepper, Greene, and Nisbett study showed that the introduction of an extrinsic reward for performing an already interesting activity caused a significant decrease in intrinsic motivation. Children who played with Magic Markers with the expectation of receiving the external reward did not spend as much subsequent free time on the activity as did children who were not given a reward or those who were unexpectedly offered the reward. Moreover, the rated quality of drawings made by children with the markers was significantly poorer in the expected-reward group than either the no-reward or unexpected-reward groups.

The results of the Lepper et al. study help to increase our confidence in the findings of the earlier Deci experiment. Not only are the earlier findings replicated with a different task and subject population, but an important methodological problem is minimized. By reexamining Table 1, we can see that the second time period in the Deci experiment was the period in which payment was expected by subjects for solving the puzzles. However, we can also see that in time 2 there was a whopping increase in the free time subjects spent on the puzzles. Deci explained this increase as an attempt by subjects to practice puzzle solving to increase their chances of earning money. However, what Deci did not discuss is the possibility that the subsequent decrease in time 3 was due not to the prior

Table 1. Mean Number of Seconds Spent Working on the Puzzles during the Free Time Periods

Group	Time 1	Time 2	Time 3	Time 3 – Time 1
Experimental (n = 12)	248.2	313.9	198.5	-49.7
Control (n = 12)	213.9	202.7	241.8	27.9

Source: E. L. Deci, "The Effects of Externally Mediated Rewards on Intrinsic Motivation," *Journal of Personality and Social Psychology* 18 (1971): 105–15. Copyright 1971 by the American Psychological Association. Reprinted by permission.

administration of rewards but to the effect of satiation or fatigue. One contribution of the Lepper et al. study is that its results are not easily explained by this alternative. In the Lepper et al. experiment, there was over one week's time between the session in which an extrinsic reward was administered and the final observation period.

Although both the Deci and Lepper et al. studies support the notion that the expectation of an extrinsic reward may decrease intrinsic interest in an activity, there is still one important source of ambiguity in both these studies. You may have noticed that the decrease in intrinsic motivation follows not only the prior administration of an extrinsic reward, but also the withdrawal of this reward. For example, in the Deci study, subjects were not paid in the third experimental session in which the decrease in intrinsic motivation was reported. Likewise, subjects were not rewarded when the final observation of intrinsic motivation was taken by Lepper, Greene, and Nisbett. It is therefore difficult to determine whether the decrease in intrinsic interest is due to a change in the self-perception of motivation following the application of an extrinsic reward or merely to frustration following the removal of the reward. An experiment by Kruglanski, Freedman, and Zeevi (1971) helps to resolve this ambiguity.

Kruglanski et al. induced a number of teenagers to volunteer for some creativity and memory tasks. To manipulate extrinsic rewards, the experimenters told half the participants that because they had volunteered for the study, they would be taken on an interesting tour of the psychology laboratory; the other participants were not offered this extrinsic reward. The results showed that teenagers offered the reward were less satisfied with the experimental tasks and were less likely to volunteer for future experiments of a similar nature than were teenagers who were not offered the extrinsic reward. In addition, the extrinsically rewarded group did not perform as well on the experimental task (in terms of recall, creativity, and the Zeigarnik effect) as the nonrewarded group. These findings are similar to those of Deci (1971) and Lepper et al. (1973), but they cannot be as easily explained by a frustration effect. Since in the Kruglanski et al. study the reward was never withdrawn for the experimental group, the differences between the experimental (reward) and control (no reward) conditions are better explained by a change in self-perception than by a frustration effect.

The designs of the three overly sufficient justification studies described above have varying strengths and weaknesses (Calder & Staw, 1975a), but taken together,

their results can be interpreted as supporting the notion that extrinsic rewards added to an already interesting task can decrease intrinsic motivation. This effect, if true, has important ramifications for educational, industrial, and other work settings. There are many situations in which people are offered extrinsic rewards (grades, money, special privileges) for accomplishing a task which may already be intrinsically interesting. The self-perception effect means that, by offering external rewards, we may sometimes be sacrificing an important source of task motivation and not necessarily increasing either the satisfaction or the performance of the participant. Obviously, because the practical implications of the self-perception effect are large, we should proceed with caution. Thus, in addition to scrutinizing the validity of the findings themselves (as we have done above), we should also attempt to determine the exact conditions under which they might be expected to hold.

Earlier, Deci (1971, 1972) had hypothesized that only rewards contingent on a high level of task performance are likely to have an adverse effect on intrinsic motivation. He had reasoned that a reward contingent upon specific behavioral demands is most likely to cause an individual to infer that his behavior is extrinsically rather than intrinsically motivated and that a decrease in intrinsic motivation may result from this change in self-perception. Although this assumption seems reasonable, there is not a great deal of empirical support for it. Certainly in the Kruglanski et al. and Lepper et al. studies all that was necessary to cause a decrease in intrinsic motivation was for rewards to be contingent upon the completion of an activity. In each of these studies what seemed to be important was the cognition that one was performing an activity in order to get an extrinsic reward rather than a prescribed goal for a particular level of output. Thus as long as it is salient, a reward contingency based upon the completion of an activity may decrease intrinsic motivation just like a reward contingency based on the quality or quantity of performance.

Ross (1975) recently conducted two experiments that dealt specifically with the effect of the salience of rewards on changes in intrinsic motivation. In one study, children were asked to play a musical instrument (drums) for either no reward, a nonsalient reward, or a salient reward. The results showed that intrinsic motivation, as measured by the amount of time spent on the drums versus other activities in a free play situation, was lowest for the salient reward condition. Similar results were found in a second study in which some children were asked to think either of the reward (marshmallows) while playing a musical instrument, think of an extraneous object (snow), or not think of anything in particular. The data for this second study showed that intrinsic motivation was lowest when children consciously thought about the reward while performing the task.

In addition to the salience of an external reward, there has been empirical research on one other factor mediating the self-perception effect, the existing norms of the task situation. In examining the prior research using situations of overly sufficient justification. Staw, Calder, and Hess (1976) reasoned that there is one common element which stands out. Always, the extrinsic reward appears to be administered in a situation in which persons are not normally paid or otherwise reimbursed for their actions. For example, students are not normally paid for laboratory participation, but the Deci (1971) and Kruglanski et al. (1971) subjects were. Likewise, nursery school children are not normally enticed by special recognition or rewards to play with an interesting new toy, but both the Lepper et al. (1973) and Ross (1975) subjects were. Thus Staw, Calder, and Hess (1976) manipulated norms for payment as well as the actual payment of money for performing an interesting task. They found an interaction of norms and payment such that the introduction of an extrinsic reward decreased intrinsic interest in a task only when there existed a situational norm for no payment. From these data and the findings of the Ross study, it thus appears that an extrinsic reward must be both salient and situationally inappropriate for there to be a reduction in intrinsic interest.

Reassessing the Self-perception Effect

At present there is growing empirical support for the notion that intrinsic and extrinsic motivation *can* be negatively interrelated. The effect of extrinsic rewards on intrinsic motivation has been replicated by several researchers using different classes of subjects (males, females, children, college students) and different activities (puzzles, toys), and the basic results appear to be internally valid. As we have seen, however, the effect of extrinsic rewards is predicated on certain necessary conditions (e.g., situational norms and reward salience), as is often the case with psychological findings subjected to close examination.

To date, the primary data supporting the self-perception prediction have come from situations of insufficient and overly sufficient justification. Empirical findings have shown that individuals may cognitively reevaluate intrinsic rewards in an upward direction when their behavior is insufficiently justified and in a downward direction when there is overly sufficient justification. In general, it can be said that the data of these two situations are consistent with the self-perception hypothesis. Still, theoretically, it is not immediately clear why previous research has been restricted to these two particular contexts. No doubt it is easier to show an increase in intrinsic motivation when intrinsic interest is initially low (as under insufficient justification) or a decrease when intrinsic interest is initially high (as under overly sufficient justification). Nevertheless, the theory should support a negative interrelationship of intrinsic and extrinsic factors at *all levels*, since it makes the rather general prediction that the greater the extrinsic rewards, the less likely is the individual to infer that he is intrinsically motivated.

One recent empirical study has tested the self-perception hypothesis by manipulating *both* intrinsic and extrinsic motivation. Calder and Staw (1975b) experimentally manipulated both the intrinsic characteristics of a task as well as extrinsic rewards in an attempt to examine the interrelationship of these two factors at more than one level. In the study male college students were asked to solve one of two sets of puzzles identical in all respects except the potential for intrinsic interest. One set of puzzles contained an assortment of pictures highly rated by students (chiefly from *Life* magazine but including several *Playboy* centerfolds); another set of puzzles was blank and rated more neutrally. To manipulate extrinsic rewards, half the subjects were promised $1 for their 20 minutes of labor (and the dollar was placed prominently in view), while for half of the subjects, money was neither mentioned nor displayed. After completing the task, subjects were asked to fill out a questionnaire on their reactions to the puzzle-solving activity. The two primary dependent variables included in the questionnaire were a measure of task satisfaction and a measure of subjects' willingness to volunteer for additional puzzle-solving exercises. The latter consisted of a sign-up sheet on which subjects could indicate the amount of time they would be willing to spend (without pay or additional course credit) in future experiments of a similar nature.

The results of the Calder and Staw experiment showed a significant interaction between task and payment on subjects' satisfaction with the activity and a marginally significant interaction on subjects' willingness to volunteer for additional work without extrinsic reward. These data provided empirical support for the self-perception effect in a situation of overly sufficient justification, but not under other conditions. Specifically, when the task was initially interesting (i.e., using the picture puzzle activity), the introduction of money caused a reduction of task satisfaction and volunteering. However, when the task was initially more neutral (i.e., using the blank puzzle activity), the introduction of money increased satisfaction and subjects' intentions to volunteer for additional work. Thus if we consider Calder and Staw's dependent measures as indicators of intrinsic interest, the first finding is in accord with the self-perception hypothesis, while the latter result is similar to what one might predict from a reinforcement theory. The implications of these data, together with previous findings, are graphically depicted in Figure 3.

As shown in the figure, self-perception effects have been found *only* at the extremes of insufficient and overly sufficient justification. Thus it may be prudent to withhold judgment on the general hypothesis that there is a uniformly negative relationship between intrinsic and extrinsic motivation. Perhaps we should no longer broadly posit that the greater external rewards and pressures, the weaker the perception of intrinsic interest in an activity; and the lower external pressures, the stronger intrinsic interest. Certainly, under conditions

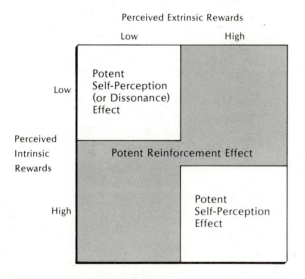

Figure 3. The Relative Potency of Self-Perception and Reinforcement Mechanisms.

other than insufficient and overly sufficient justification, reinforcement effects of extrinsic rewards on intrinsic task satisfaction have readily been found (Cherrington, 1973; Cherrington, Reitz, & Scott, 1971; Greene, 1974).

At present it appears that only in situations of insufficient or overly sufficient reward will there be attributional instability of such magnitude that shifts will occur in the perception of intrinsic rewards. We might therefore speculate that either no attributional instability is evoked in other situations or it is just not strong enough to overcome a countervailing force. This writer would place his confidence in the latter theoretical position. It seems likely that both self-perception *and* reinforcement mechanisms hold true, but that their relative influence over an individual's task attitudes and behavior varies according to the situational context. For example, only in situations with insufficient or overly sufficient justification will the need to resolve attributional instability probably be strong enough for external rewards to produce a decrease in intrinsic motivation. In other situations we might reasonably expect a more positive relationship between intrinsic and extrinsic factors, as predicted by reinforcement theory.

Although this new view of the interrelationship between intrinsic and extrinsic motivation remains speculative, it does seem reasonable in light of recent theoretical and empirical work. Figure 4 graphically elaborates this model and shows how the level of intrinsic and extrinsic motivation may depend on the characteristics of the situation. In the figure, secondary reinforcement is depicted to be a general force for producing a positive relationship between intrinsic and extrinsic motivation. However, under situations of insufficient and oversufficient justification, self-perception (and dissonance) effects are shown to provide a second but still potentially effective determinant of a negative interrelationship between intrinsic and extrinsic motivation. Figure 4 shows the joint operation of these two theoretical mechanisms and illustrates their ultimate effect on individuals' satisfaction, persistence, and performance on a task.

IMPLICATIONS OF INTRINSIC AND EXTRINSIC MOTIVATION

In this discussion we have noted that the administration of both intrinsic and extrinsic rewards can have important effects on a person's task attitudes and

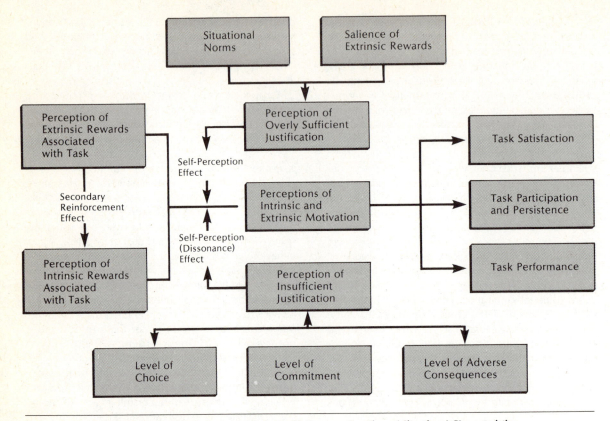

Figure 4. **The Interrelationship of Intrinsic and Extrinsic Motivation as a Function of Situational Characteristics.**

behavior. Individually, extrinsic rewards may direct and control a person's activity on a task and provide an important source of satisfaction. By themselves, intrinsic rewards can also motivate task-related behavior and bring gratification to the individual. As we have seen, however, the joint effect of intrinsic and extrinsic rewards may be quite complex. Not only may intrinsic and extrinsic factors not be additive in their overall effect on motivation and satisfaction, but the interaction of intrinsic and extrinsic factors may under some conditions be positive and under other conditions negative. As illustrated in Figures 3 and 4, a potent reinforcement effect will often cause intrinsic and extrinsic motivation to be positively interrelated, although on occasion a self-perception mechanism may be so powerful as to create a negative relationship between these two factors.

The reinforcement predictions of Figures 3 and 4 are consistent with our common sense. In practice, extrinsic rewards are relied upon heavily to induce desired behaviors, and most allocators of rewards (administrators, teachers, parents) operate on the theory that extrinsic rewards will positively affect an individual's intrinsic interest in a task. We should therefore concentrate on those situations in which our common sense may be in error—those situations in which there may in fact be a negative relationship between intrinsic and extrinsic motivation.

Motivation in Educational Organizations

One of the situations in which intrinsic and extrinsic motivation may be negatively interrelated is our schools. As Lepper and Green (1975) have noted, many educational tasks are inherently interesting to students and would probably be performed without any external force. However, when grades and other extrinsic inducements are added to the activity, we may, via overly sufficient justification, be converting an interesting activity into work. That is, by inducing students to perform educational tasks with strong extrinsic rewards or by applying external force, we may be converting learning activities into behaviors that will not be performed in the future without some additional outside pressure or extrinsic force.

Within the educational context, a negative relationship between intrinsic and extrinsic motivation poses a serious dilemma for teachers who allocate external rewards. For example, there is no doubt that grades, gold stars, and other such incentives can alter the direction and vigor of specific ''in school'' behaviors (e.g., getting students to complete assigned exercises by a particular date). But because of their effect on intrinsic motivation, extrinsic rewards may also weaken a student's general interest in learning tasks and decrease voluntary learning behavior that extends beyond the school setting. In essence, then, the extrinsic forces that work so well at motivating and controlling specific task behaviors may actually cause the extinction of these same behaviors within situations devoid of external reinforcers. This is an important consideration for educational organizations, since most of an individual's learning activity will no doubt occur outside the highly regulated and reinforced setting of the classroom.[1]

In order to maintain students' intrinsic motivation in learning activities it is recommended that the use of extrinsic rewards be carefully controlled. As a practical measure, it is recommended that when a learning task is inherently interesting (and would probably be performed without any external force) all external pressures on the individual be minimized. Only when a task is so uninteresting that individuals would not ordinarily perform it should extrinsic rewards be applied. In addition, it is suggested that the student role be both enlarged and enriched to increase rather directly the level of intrinsic motivation. The significance of learning tasks, responsibility for results, feedback, and variety in student activities are all areas of possible improvement.

Motivation in Work Organizations

Voluntary work organizations are very much like educational organizations; their members are often intrinsically motivated to perform certain tasks and extrinsic rewards are generally not necessary to induce the performance of many desired behaviors. Moreover, if for some reason extrinsic rewards were to be offered

to voluntary workers for performing their services we would expect to find, as in the educational setting, a decrease in intrinsic motivation. As in the educational context, we would expect an external reward to decrease self-motivated (or voluntary) behavior in settings free from external reinforcement, although the specific behaviors which are reinforced might be increased. As a concrete example, let us imagine a political candidate who decides to ''motivate'' his volunteer campaign workers by paying them for distributing flyers to prospective voters. In this situation, we might expect that the administration of an extrinsic reward will increase the number of flyers distributed. However, the political workers' subsequent interest in performing other campaign activities *without pay* may subsequently be diminished. Similarly, the volunteer hospital worker who becomes salaried may no longer have the same intrinsic interest in his work. Although the newly professionalized worker may exert a good deal of effort on the job and be relatively satisfied with it, his satisfaction may stem from extrinsic rather than intrinsic sources of reward.

Let us now turn to the implications of intrinsic and extrinsic motivation for nonvoluntary work organizations. Deci (1972), in reviewing his research on intrinsic motivation, cautioned strongly against the use of contingent monetary rewards within industrial organizations. He maintained that paying people contingently upon the performance of specific tasks may reduce intrinsic motivation for these activities, and he recommended noncontingent reinforcers in their stead. As we have seen, however, a decrease in intrinsic motivation does not always occur following the administration of extrinsic rewards; certain necessary conditions must be present before there is a negative relationship between intrinsic and extrinsic motivation. Generally, industrial work settings do not meet these necessary conditions.

First, within industrial organizations, a large number of jobs are not inherently interesting enough to foster high intrinsic motivation. Persons would not ordinarily perform many of the tasks of the industrial world (e.g., assembly line work) without extrinsic inducements, and this initial lack of intrinsic interest will probably preclude the effect of overly sufficient justification. Second, even when an industrial job is inherently interesting, there exists a powerful norm for extrinsic payment. Not only do workers specifically join and contribute their labor in exchange for particular inducements, but the instrumental relationship between task behavior and extrinsic rewards is supported by both social and legal standards. Thus the industrial work situation is quite unlike that of either a voluntary organization or an educational system. In the latter cases, participants may be initially interested in performing certain tasks without external force, and the addition of overly sufficient rewards may convey information that the task is not intrinsically interesting. Within industrial organizations, on the other hand, extrinsic reinforcement is the norm, and tasks may often be perceived to be even more interesting when they lead to greater extrinsic rewards.

The very basic distinction between nonvoluntary work situations and other task settings (e.g., schools and voluntary organizations) is that, without extrinsic rewards, nonvoluntary organizations would be largely without participants. The important question for industrial work settings is therefore not one of payment versus nonpayment, but of the recommended degree of contingency between reward and performance. On the basis of current evidence, it would seem prudent to suggest that, within industrial organizations, rewards continue to be made contingent upon behavior. This could be accomplished through performance evaluation, profit sharing, or piece-rate incentive schemes. In addition, intrinsic motivation should be increased directly via the planned alteration of specific job characteristics (e.g., by increasing task variety, complexity, social interaction, task identity, significance, responsibility for results, and knowledge of results).

A FINAL COMMENT

Although the study of the interaction of intrinsic and extrinsic motivation is a relatively young area within psychology, it has been the intent of this paper to outline a theoretical model and provide some practical suggestions based upon the research evidence available to date. As we have seen, the effects of intrinsic and extrinsic motivation are not always simple, and several moderating variables must often be taken into account before specific predictions can be made. Thus in addition to providing "answers" to theoretical and practical problems, this paper may illustrate the complexities involved in drawing conclusions from a limited body of research data. The main caution for the reader is to regard these theoretical propositions and practical recommendations as working statements subject to the influence of future empirical evidence.

NOTES

1. It is interesting to note that Kazdin and Bootzin (1972) have made a quite similar point in their recent review of research on token economies. They noted that while operant conditioning procedures have been quite effective in altering focal behaviors within a controlled setting, seldom have changes been found to generalize to natural, nonreinforcing environments.

2. The author wishes to express his gratitude to Bobby J. Calder and Greg R. Oldham for their critical reading of the manuscript, and to the Center for Advanced Study at the University of Illinois for the resources and facilities necessary to complete this work.

REFERENCES

Aronson, E. "The Psychology of Insufficient Justification: An Analysis of Some Conflicting Data." In *Cognitive Consistency: Motivational Antecedents and Behavior Consequences,* edited by S. Feldman. Academic Press, 1966.

Bem, D. J. "Self-perception: An Alternative Interpretation of Cognitive Dissonance Phenomena." *Psychological Review* 74 (1967): 183–200. (a)

———."Self-perception: The Dependent Variable of Human Performance." *Organizational Behavior and Human Performance* 2 (1967): 105–21. (b)

_____."Self-perception Theory." In *Advances in Experimental Social Psychology*, vol. 6, edited by L. Berkowitz. New York: Academic Press, 1972.

Brehm, J. W., and Cohen, A. R. *Explorations in Cognitive Dissonance*. New York: Wiley, 1962.

Calder, B. J.; Ross, M.; and Insko, C. A. "Attitude Change and Attitude Attribution: Effects of Incentive, Choice, and Consequences." *Journal of Personality and Social Psychology* 25 (1973): 84-100.

_____, and Staw, B. M. "The Interaction of Intrinsic and Extrinsic Motivation: Some Methodological Notes." *Journal of Personality and Social Psychology* 31 (1975): 76-80. (a)

_____, and Staw, B. M. "Self-perception of Intrinsic and Extrinsic Motivation." *Journal of Personality and Social Psychology* 31 (1975): 599-605. (b)

Carlsmith, J. M.; Collins, B. E.; and Helmreich, R. L. "Studies in Forced Compliance: The Effect of Pressure for Compliance on Attitude Change Produced by Face-to-Face Role Playing and Anonymous Essay Writing." *Journal of Personality and Social Psychology* 4 (1966): 1-13.

Cherrington, D. J. "The Effects of a Central Incentive—Motivational State on Measures of Job Satisfaction." *Organizational Behavior and Human Performance* 10 (1973): 271-89.

_____, Reitz, H. J.; and Scott, W. E. "Effects of Reward and Contingent Reinforcement on Satisfaction and Task Performance." *Journal of Applied Psychology* 55 (1971): 531-36.

Collins, B. E., and Hoyt, M. F. "Personal Responsibility-for-Consequences: An Integration and Extension of the Forced Compliance Literature." *Journal of Experimental Social Psychology* 8 (1972): 558-94.

de Charms, R. *Personal Causation: The Internal Affective Determinants of Behavior*. New York: Academic Press, 1968.

Deci, E. L. "The Effects of Externally Mediated Rewards on Intrinsic Motivation." *Journal of Personality and Social Psychology* 18 (1971): 105-15.

_____."The Effects of Contingent and Noncontingent Rewards and Controls on Intrinsic Motivation." *Organizational Behavior and Human Performance* 8 (1972): 217-29.

Festinger, L. *A Theory of Cognitive Dissonance*. Palo Alto: Stanford University Press, 1957.

_____, and Carlsmith, J. M. "Cognitive Consequences of Forced Compliance." *Journal of Abnormal and Social Psychology* 58 (1959): 203-10.

Freedman, J. L. "Attitudinal Effects of Inadequate Justification," *Journal of Personality* 31 (1963): 371-85.

Greene, C. N. "Causal Connections Among Managers' Merit Pay, Job Satisfaction, and Performance." *Journal of Applied Psychology* 58 (1974): 95-100.

Heider, F. *The Psychology of Interpersonal Relations*. New York: Wiley, 1958.

Jones, E. E., and Davis, K. E. "From Acts to Dispositions: The Attribution Process in Person Perception." In *Advances in Experimental Psychology*, vol. 2, edited by L. Berkowitz. New York: Academic Press, 1965.

_____; Davis, K. E.; and Gergen, K. E. "Role Playing Variations and Their Informational Value for Person Perception." *Journal of Abnormal and Social Psychology* 63 (1961): 302-10.

_____, and Harris, V. A. "The Attribution of Attitudes." *Journal of Experimental Social Psychology* 3 (1967): 1-24.

_____, and Nisbett, R. E. *The Actor and the Observer: Divergent Perceptions of the Causes of Behavior*. New York: General Learning Press, 1971.

Kazdin, A. E., and Bootzen, R. R. "The Token Economy: An Evaluative Review." *Journal of Applied Behavior Analysis* 5 (1972): 343-72.

Kelley, H. H. "Attribution Theory in Social Psychology." In *Nebraska Symposium on Motivation*, vol. 15, edited by D. Levine. University of Nebraska Press, 1967.

Kruglanski, A. W.; Freedman, I.; and Zeevi, G. "The Effects of Extrinsic Incentives on Some Qualitative Aspects of Task Performance." *Journal of Personality* 39 (1971): 606-17.

Lepper, M. R., and Greene, D. "Turning Play into Work: Effects of Adult Surveillance and Extrinsic Rewards on Children's Intrinsic Motivation." *Journal of Personality and Social Psychology*, in press.

_____; Greene, D.; and Nisbett, R. E. "Undermining Children's Intrinsic Interest with Extrinsic Rewards: A Test of the 'Overjustification' Hypothesis." *Journal of Personality and Social Psychology* 28 (1973): 129-37.

Linder, D. E.; Cooper, J.; and Jones, E. E. "Decision Freedom as a Determinant of the Role of Incentive Magnitude in Attitude Change." *Journal of Personality and Social Psychology* 6 (1967): 245-54.

Ross, M. "Salience of Reward and Intrinsic Motivation." *Journal of Personality and Social Psychology* 32 (1975): 245–254.

Staw, B. M. "Attitudinal and Behavioral Consequences of Changing a Major Organizational Reward: A Natural Field Experiment." *Journal of Personality and Social Psychology* 6 (1974): 742–51. (a)

_____. "Notes Toward a Theory of Intrinsic and Extrinsic Motivation." Paper presented at Eastern Psychological Association, 1974. (b)

_____; Calder, B. J.; and Hess, R. "Intrinsic Motivation and Norms About Payment." Working paper, Northwestern University, 1975.

Strickland, L. H. "Surveillance and Trust." *Journal of Personality* 26 (1958): 200–215.

Thibaut, J. W., and Riecken, H. W. "Some Determinants and Consequences of the Perception of Social Causality." *Journal of Personality* 24 (1955): 113–33.

Weick, K. E. "Reduction of Cognitive Dissonance Through Task Enhancement and Effort Expenditure." *Journal of Abnormal and Social Psychology* 68 (1964): 533–39.

_____, and Penner, D. D. "Justification and Productivity." Unpublished manuscript, University of Minnesota, 1965.

14.   Job Enrichment Versus Social Cues: A Comparison and Competitive Test

Sam E. White and Terence R. Mitchell

Forty-one part-time student employees were randomly assigned in a 2 × 2 factorial research design including 2 types of social cues and 2 levels of job enrichment to investigate the effects of the independent variables on perceptions of job enrichment, job ambiguity, job satisfaction, and productivity. All employees worked in a simulated organizational setting involving a routine clerical task. The results showed that both the cues given off by co-workers as well as the physical properties of the task have an effect on employee perceptions of job enrichment and job ambiguity. In addition, people receiving positive social cues from co-workers were more satisfied and more productive than people receiving negative social cues from co-workers. These results are discussed in terms of their relevance for current theories of job motivation.

Job enrichment has become an increasingly important issue in both the empirical and practical literature about the quality of work life in America. It is argued that job enrichment will increase commitment and satisfaction as well as the productivity of employees (e.g., Hackman & Oldham, 1975; Herzberg, 1966). These benefits supposedly result from increased levels of certain job characteristics such as task variety, task identity, significance of the job, job autonomy, and feedback

This research was partially supported by the Office of Naval Research Contract N00014-76-C-0193 (Terence R. Mitchell and Lee Roy Beech, principal investigators).

We would like to thank Michael Ferri for his assistance in developing the experimental task, and our research assistants, Carole Sherwood and Allen Mandelbaum, for their efforts.

(Hackman & Lawler, 1971; Hackman & Oldham, 1976; Turner & Lawrence, 1965). It is also argued that these effects are strongest for those individuals who have high needs for achievement and growth (Oldham, Hackman, & Pearce, 1976; Steers & Spencer, 1977; Stone, Mowday, & Porter, 1977). Thus, job enrichment, when properly applied, may be a means to increase both the satisfaction and productivity of employees.

A number of criticisms have recently been raised about the job enrichment approach. First, reviews of the empirical literature on enrichment suggest that the effects are often weak (O'Reilly, 1977; Pierce & Dunham, 1976; Salancik & Pfeffer, 1977). In general, the findings would suggest that attitudes such as job satisfaction are more readily affected by enrichment than is productivity (Pierce & Dunham, 1976; Umstot, Mitchell, & Bell, in press). For example, a study by Umstot, Bell, and Mitchell (1976), investigating the joint effects of job enrichment and goal setting, found that goal setting resulted in higher productivity, whereas enrichment resulted in greater satisfaction. The support for the enrichment–productivity relationship is weak.

A second and perhaps more damaging criticism has been raised by Salancik and Pfeffer (1977). These authors take issue with the basic need satisfaction model that forms the foundation of job enrichment approaches. They suggest that social and informational cues may be better predictors of employees' reactions to a task than the objective characteristics of the task. That is, job satisfaction and motivation may be more a result of how one's co-workers react to a task than the task characteristics themselves.

To date, only one empirical study has tested this last assumption (O'Reilly & Caldwell, in press). These investigators manipulated both the task characteristics (high enrichment vs. low enrichment) and informational cues (positive vs. negative) in a simulated selection task. They found that the informational cues (what other workers wrote about the task) had a greater impact on perceptions of enrichment than the objective characteristics of the task itself.

The purpose of the present research was to pursue these two areas of criticism one step further. More specifically, we wanted to test two questions. First, we were interested in replicating and extending the work presented by O'Reilly and Caldwell (in press). In their study, the informational cues about co-workers' views of the task were presented on a typed sheet in the absence of the co-worker. We wished to have co-workers actually commenting on the task as the work activity was carried out. This difference is potentially significant in that the present procedure removes any possibility that experimental demand characteristics may account for differences in satisfaction or productivity. We also wanted to manipulate job enrichment in such a way that the task itself was the same but the surrounding job characteristics resulted in different perceptions of enrichment. In the O'Reilly and Caldwell study, enrichment was manipulated by having people do slightly different tasks.

The second question we wished to answer had to do with whether enrichment or social cues had a more substantive effect on job satisfaction and productivity. From previous research (White, Mitchell, & Bell, 1977) we knew that social cues could have a substantial effect on job performance — one that controlled approximately the same amount of variance as goal setting. The issue investigated in the current study was whether social cues were more important than job enrichment in producing satisfied and productive employees.

METHOD

Overview of Study

The study was composed of two independent variables (enrichment vs. no enrichment and positive vs. negative social cues) resulting in a 2 × 2 design. Checks on the manipulations were made and the dependent variables were (a) perceptions of enrichment, (b) job satisfaction, (c) other job attitudes, and (d) productivity. Three employees worked together at one time (two naive subjects and one confederate).

Subjects

Forty-three undergraduate business students served as employees in the research. Data from 2 employees were omitted from the analysis because one employee failed to follow prescribed work procedures and the other expressed feelings of suspicion about the experimental cover story and the work sessions. The remaining 41 subjects were randomly assigned to the four experimental conditions. The ratio of males to females in all treatments was 2:1, and the average age was 21.5 years (range: 20–24 years). The average age between treatment conditions varied from 21.2 to 21.7 years.

Establishing the Task Setting

Students were contacted in their classes and asked to volunteer for part-time work. Subjects were told that they were being hired to work for a group of university professors interested in compiling information about the stock market. This statement was highly credible because the New York Stock Exchange had just reported 2 record volume days that were heavily publicized in the newspaper and other news broadcasts. Also, the students were told that we were interested in their reaction to the work environment and that we would ask them some questions about it.

Several tangible features of the experimental setting contributed to establishing a realistic work environment. A large graphic sign bearing the title "Stock Pricing Project" hung on the entrance door, and other experimental material also carried this heading. In addition, the work area was located in a campus building that housed similar projects. The questionnaire was explained and presented as a part of the normal work routine. Each employee was paid $2.50 per hour and worked for a total of 2 hours.

The experimental area consisted of two separate rooms, a reception area containing a large desk and other secretarial equipment and a work area containing a large table and three chairs. When the employees were at work, they were out of sight of the "receptionist," although their comments could be overheard.

The Task

Employees were asked to complete three separate sets of job activities. The first activity was looking up stock prices from weekly American Stock Exchange quotations listed in a local newspaper. These reports were photocopied on 8½ × 14 inch (21.59 × 35.56 cm) paper and organized by date in a single stock price booklet. Each employee worked from a separate but identical booklet. After looking up a closing price, subjects recorded them on an IBM Fortran coding form that had been specially marked into columns for date and price. The second part of the task was calculating and recording the percentage price change from week to week with the information compiled in Stage 1. Each employee, working with a calculator, computed percentage change by dividing the current price by the price at Week 1. These percentages were recorded in a column next to the current weekly prices. The third component of the task was graphing the weekly price changes on specially prepared 8½ × 14 inch graph paper. Each graph was marked by date and quarter, and an average percentage index was superimposed on it. The task also required the employees to staple the coding and graphing sheets together and to identify the stock by name on each sheet before turning them in to the research assistant.

Procedure

When the employees arrived, they entered the reception area where they filled out a ½-page employment sheet asking for biographical information. This activity took 3–5 minutes. After completing this form, the employee was taken into the work area. Once all three employees were settled, the experimenter–supervisor demonstrated the task for 15 minutes and answered questions about the task procedures. During this demonstration the enrichment manipulation was carried out. The supervisor's comments were made according to a prescribed script so that the task instructions and explanations were exactly the same for every condition except for the enrichment manipulation.

Following the task demonstration, the supervisor asked each employee to look up 15 different prices from a randomly selected stock. Interviews with pilot study subjects ($n = 10$) indicated that they became proficient after working with 10–15 items in the booklet. Since other activities involved in the task were straightforward, once the employees learned how to use the stock price booklet, other practice times were not given. These work procedures were followed for approximately 90 minutes. The last 5–10 minutes of the 2-hour session were spent filling out the postsession questionnaire.

Manipulating the Independent Variables

Job enrichment was manipulated by verbal instructions and task procedures focusing on the five critical job characteristics suggested by Hackman and Oldham (1976): significance, autonomy, variety, identity, and feedback. In the enriched condition, the employees were told, "Your task is the initial one in a larger process that will include computer analysis and evaluation. The outcome of this later work will be directly influenced by how well you do your job" (significance). In the unenriched condition, employees were simply told

"You have been hired to prepare information about stocks from the American Stock Exchange." An explanation of the task procedures immediately followed this introduction. Task procedures for the enriched condition included choosing stocks to work on from a listing of over 150 stocks that were grouped by industry in alphabetical order (*autonomy*), identifying the chosen stocks on a poster behind the employee and in view of the other workers (*identity*), choosing one's own process or sequencing for completing the compiling, computing, and graphing activities for each stock, and scheduling one's own work breaks during the 2-hour session (*autonomy, variety*). Completed work was stacked beside the employees' work areas so that employees could visualize their progress and contribution toward finishing the project (*feedback*). At the end of the work session, the total output of each employee was clipped together and collected by the work supervisor. For the unenriched condition, task procedures included the supervisor randomly assigning stocks one-at-a-time, and an explanation of single activities throughout the work session (e.g., the computing activities were not explained until the compiling activities and the supervisor-scheduled rest periods were completed). In addition, employees worked on different stocks during each phase of the task. For example, they did not compute price changes or graph a stock for which they had compiled the original prices. Completed work was collected by the work supervisor as soon as it was finished.

One additional note about the task procedures in the two job enrichment conditions is in order. Since the total task was divided into three sets of activities, each requiring different amounts of time to complete a single unit (e.g., it takes longer to look up a stock price in the Stock Price booklet and to write it down than it takes to calculate the percentage change between two prices on a calculator), it was important to assure that the amount of time spent doing each set of activities was approximately equal in the enriched and unenriched conditions. Based on results from pilot study subjects in the enriched condition ($n = 5$), the amount of time spent doing each of the three sets of task activities in the unenriched condition of the present study was 38 minutes of compiling, 25 minutes of calculating, and 35 minutes of graphing. A random check of subjects ($n = 10$) working in the enriched condition in the current study showed that they were dividing their time in substantially the same manner. Thus, differences in productivity between enriched and unenriched groups cannot be attributed to different amounts of working time on the three subtasks.

Two types of social cues were used: positive and negative. These cue conditions were established behaviorally and verbally by a confederate during the work session. A script consisting of 12 verbal cues was prepared and memorized to assure that these cues were consistent across experimental conditions. There were three response themes in the 12 social cues: (a) the task itself, (b) the importance of the output, and (c) one's performance on the task. A positive role consisted of issuing positive comments about the three response themes (e.g., "This is interesting. It is nice to finally use the skills I've developed in school," and "This job becomes more meaningful as you do it") and completing the total task activities for three stocks. A negative role consisted of issuing negative comments about the three response themes (e.g., "This isn't very interesting. It doesn't require any of the skills I've developed in school," and "The more you do this job the less meaningful it is") and completing the total task activities for two stocks. As one can see, these social cues were not extreme (e.g., "This is the worst job I've ever seen. It's the pits!!") but are moderately positive or negative in content. Also, confederates delivered the social cues with moderate intensity so that both content and emphasis were similar to the comments that would normally be expected in a temporary work setting. Confederates presented the social cues when it seemed most natural and in conjunction with the appropriate behavioral cues of smiling, frowning, body posture, and so on.

More information about the use of confederates in this study is necessary. First, the confederates were treated the same as every other employee. They filled out the biographical forms and questionnaires and were subject to the same work procedures as the other participants. In addition, they arrived at the work setting in the same manner as others; that is, they were not waiting in the work area for the naive subjects to enter. Third, the confederates practiced the two roles until they were comfortable in both roles before the experiment began. Each of the two confederates who participated in the study played the two roles an approximately equal number of times. Finally, although the confederates were obviously aware of differences in the instructions for doing the task, they were not briefed about the experimental hypotheses, nor did they know which role to play until they entered the work area along with the other workers. The supervisor placed an unobtrusive P (for positive) or N (for negative) on a cardboard file box that was sitting among several other similar boxes, and the confederates acted accordingly.

Measures

Data were collected for four major classes of variables: (a) manipulation checks, (b) attitudes toward the job, (c) job satisfaction, and (d) productivity. The job enrichment characteristics were examined by having a separate control group of 18 employees ($n = 9$ in the enriched and unenriched task conditions) experience the task without the social cues manipulation. These employees were required to follow the same work procedures as in the actual experimental session, and they rated the task using the Job Diagnostic Survey.

The social cues manipulation check consisted of questionnaire items administered during the last 5–10 minutes of the experimental session. To assess the effectiveness of the social cues manipulation, each employee was asked to respond to eight questionnaire items concerning their co-workers (e.g., "My co-workers think this job is important," and "My co-workers were able to figure out how well they were performing on this job") on a 7-point scale ranging from agree strongly (7) to disagree strongly (1). Social cues items were intermixed with other questionnaire items described below, and the individual responses were summed to form a social cues index.

The employees' attitudes toward the job were measured by having them respond to the questionnaire items (e.g., "This job is quite simple and repetitive," and "This job is arranged so that I do not have the chance to do an entire piece of work from beginning to end") that define the five core job-dimension scales of the Job Diagnostic Survey (Hackman & Oldham, 1975). The subjects answered questions concerning their perception of skill variety, task identity, task significance, job autonomy, and feedback from the job itself. Composite scores were computed for each job characteristic according to the procedures outlined by Hackman and Oldham (1974). In addition, perceptions of job ambiguity were assessed by a six-item role-ambiguity scale (Rizzo, House, & Lirtzman, 1970). Subjects responded to statements (e.g., "I know exactly what is expected of me," and "I know what my responsibilities are on this job") on a 7-point scale ranging from very true (7) to very false (1). Individual responses to these 6 items were averaged to form a job-ambiguity score.

Motivational value of the job was established with three different measures. Two scales from the Job Diagnostic Survey—the Internal Work Motivation scale (IWM) and the Motivational Potential score (MPS)—were used. Both of these scales were computed according to the procedures presented in Hackman and Oldham (1974). The MPS score is a combination of the five job factors and represents an overall estimate of the motivating properties of the task. It was computed using the following formula:

$$MPS = \left[\frac{\text{Skill Variety} + \text{Task Identity} + \text{Task Significance}}{3} \times (\text{Autonomy}) \times (\text{Feedback}). \right]$$

The degree to which employees were self-motivated to perform effectively on the job (IWM) was computed by averaging employee responses to four questionnaire items (e.g., "My opinion of myself went up when I did well on this job," and "I will feel bad and unhappy if I discover that I have performed poorly on this job"). Employees responded to the IWM questions on a 7-point scale ranging from strongly agree (7) to strongly disagree (1), and the IWM items were intermixed with questions from other scales on the questionnaire.

One other motivational measure, a modification of the MPS, was used: the Social Cues Motivational Index (SCMI). This index consisted of the three job-dimension scales for which the confederate issued specific comments—skill variety, job autonomy, and feedback from the job itself. Computations of the index value were identical to the Hackman and Oldham motivation potential score procedures (e.g., Skill Variety $\times$ Autonomy $\times$ Feedback). This modification provided a means of more clearly assessing the effects of social cues on the motivational value of the job.

Job satisfaction was assessed by postsession questionnaires using the three general satisfaction items (e.g., "I am generally satisfied with the kind of work I did on this job," "I frequently thought about quitting this job," and "Generally speaking, I am very satisfied with this job") from the Job Diagnostic Survey (Hackman & Oldham, 1974). Employees responded to these questions on 7-point scales ranging from strongly agree (7) to strongly disagree (1). Employee job satisfaction was computed by averaging the person's three responses.

Productivity was assessed by measuring the employee's total output during the work sessions.

Whenever output was collected during the experiment, a research assistant would secretly record the subjects' code numbers and the starting and ending times on the back of the output form. At the end of the work session, the research assistant recorded the number of items compiled, computed, and graphed as well as the total time worked for each employee. Productivity was established by dividing the total number of items produced by the total time worked. This procedure produced an items per minute output measure for each employee.

In summary, 41 subjects were randomly assigned to one of four experimental conditions in a 2 X 2 factorial design consisting of 2 levels of job enrichment and 2 types of social cues. Job enrichment was manipulated by experimenter inductions and actual work procedures and social cues were manipulated by confederate comments and actions during a 1½-hour work session. The primary dependent measures were perceptions of specific job characteristics, job satisfaction, and productivity.

RESULTS

Manipulation Checks

A 2 X 2 analysis of variance was computed on the SCMI. The mean score was 4.35 for subjects in the positive cues condition and 2.89 for the subjects in the negative cues condition. The main effect was significant, $F(1,37) = 28.76, p < .001$. The task condition main effect (enrichment) and the interaction effect were not significant. The co-worker was clearly seen as having a more favorable reaction to the task in the positive social cue condition than in the negative social cue condition.

The Job Diagnostic Survey ratings of the 18 control group employees were used to compute t-test comparisons for all five job characteristics. The means for skill variety, task identity, task significance, job autonomy, and feedback, respectively, were 3.78, 5.67, 5.56, 5.00, and 4.22 in the enriched condition. The means (in the same order) were 1.39, 2.50, 3.72, 1.89, and 2.22 in the unenriched condition. The difference between means was significant for each job dimension: (a) skill variety, $t(16) = 5.75, p < .01$; (b) task identity, $t(16) = 4.30, p < .01$; (c) task significance, $t(16) = 4.63, p < .01$; (d) job autonomy, $t(16) = 6.07, p < .01$; and (e) feedback, $t(16) = 3.57, p < .01$. These data provide convincing

evidence that the two manipulations were effective. Because there was no interaction effect or task condition effect on the SCMI and because a separate control group perceived significant differences in the task on the five job characteristics, we may feel confident that the two independent variables were separately manipulated and are conceptually distinct variables.

Attitudes Toward the Job

Two-way analyses of variance were calculated using the five job-dimension scales and job-ambiguity measure from the postsession questionnaire as the dependent variables. Table 1 presents a summary of the results. Only main effects are presented except for the feedback and ambiguity indices because of the absence of interaction effects on the other attitude measures.

Results are mixed on the six scales. Task condition had a significant effect on employee perceptions of task identity, task significance, and job autonomy. The means were 5.31, 4.26, and 3.74 for the enriched group

Table 1. A Summary of Results of Analyses of Variance on Job Attitude Measures

Dependent Variable	F	p
Skill variety		
Task condition	.07	.79
Type of social cues	8.26	.01
Task identity		
Task condition	10.02	.01
Type of social cues	.03	.87
Task significance		
Task condition	4.46	.04
Type of social cues	.03	.86
Job autonomy		
Task condition	4.57	.04
Type of social cues	.06	.81
Feedback from the job		
Task condition	.28	.60
Type of social cues	.28	.60
Task X Cues	3.90	.05
Job ambiguity		
Task condition	.28	.60
Type of social cues	3.36	.08
Task X Cues	34.32	.01

Note. df =1, 37.

on these three measures. The means were 3.30, 3.28, and 2.78 for the unenriched group on the three measures, respectively. Type of social cues had a significant effect on employee perceptions of skill variety. The mean for the positive cues group was 3.38, and the mean for the negative cues group as 1.88. This pattern of results suggests that the use of social information varies in perceiving the different task characteristics. Objective information (e.g., the task itself) was the primary source of perceptions of task identity, job autonomy, and task significance, but social information (e.g., the comments of co-workers) was the primary source of perception of skill variety. One explanation for this result is that skill variety was the least objective task characteristic evaluated. In the absence of objective information, employees relied more heavily on social cues in evaluating this aspect of the work environment.

There were no significant main effects on the feedback or job ambiguity indices, but there were significant interaction effects on both of these measures. For the feedback index, the means were 3.50, 4.30, 4.30, and 2.85 for the unenriched-positive group, the enriched-negative group, the unenriched-positive group, and the unenriched-negative group, respectively. The employees perceived more feedback from the job itself when the task characteristics were incongruent with the comments of their co-workers. The amount of job ambiguity experienced by the employees follows the opposite pattern. The means were 6.05, 3.05, 3.57, and 5.22 for the enriched-positive group, the enriched-negative group, the unenriched-positive group, and unenriched-negative group, respectively (high score = low ambiguity). Subjects were more certain about their jobs and what was expected of them when the task characteristics were congruent with the comments of co-workers. The results of multiple comparisons of the means (Winer, 1971) in the congruent and incongruent treatment conditions were significant on the ambiguity variable, $F(3, 38) = 55.44$, $p < .01$, and approached significance on the feedback variable, $F(3, 38) = 3.91$, $p < .06$. It appears that employees used both the task and the social cues of co-workers as sources of information in forming perceptions of their progress on the task and in their task role. When the two sources provided incongruent information, the employees' certainty about progress on the task and in their job role was reduced. But when both sources provided congruent information, one source confirmed the other and increased the employees' certainty about the job role and about progress on the task. Thus, it was the incongruity of information in the work setting that was the source of the significant interaction.

Motivational Value of the Job

Analyses of variance using two enrichment conditions and two types of social cues as the independent variables were calculated on the IWM, the MPS, and the SCMI. A summary of the results are presented in Table 2. Since there were no significant interaction effects, only the main effects are presented.

The IWM data show no significant task condition or type of social cues effect. However, the task condition effect was marginally significant, $F(1, 37) = 3.43$, $p < .07$. The means were 4.23 and 3.48 for the enriched and unenriched groups, respectively, suggesting that the enrichment condition resulted in greater internal work motivation than the unenriched condition.

A two-way analysis of variance computed with the MPS as the dependent variable showed a significant main effect for task condition, $F(1, 37) = 12.77$, $p < .01$, and a social cue effect that was marginally significant, $F(1, 37) = 3.37$, $p < .07$. The mean MPS score for the enriched group was 58.68, and the mean MPS score for the unenriched group was 28.56. For the positive cues group, the mean MPS score was 50.80, and for the negative cues group the mean MPS score was 36.83. These data suggest that both the physical properties of the task as well as the cues given off by co-workers have an effect on perceptions of the task environment.

Because the comments of co-workers (confederates) were not directed at all five of the job dimensions

Table 2. A Summary of Results of Analyses of Variance on Motivational Value, Job Satisfaction, and Productivity

Dependent Variable	F	p
Internal work motivation		
Task condition	3.43	.07
Type of social cues	1.21	.28
Motivation potential score		
Task condition	12.77	.01
Type of social cues	3.37	.07
Social cues motivation index		
Task condition	.24	.63
Type of social cues	5.97	.02

Note. $df = 1, 37$.

measured, a modified MPS (the SCMI) was developed that included only the job-dimension scales for which co-workers made direct comments. We could expect scores on this index to more accurately reflect the effects of co-worker cues on perceptions of the job. An analysis of variance was computed on the SCMI, and only the type of social cues had a significant main effect, $F(1, 37) = 5.97, p < .02$. The mean SCMI for the positive cues group was 44.52, and the mean SCMI for the negative cues group was 20.95. These results provided additional evidence that social cues did have a significant effect on the employees' perceptions of job characteristics when co-workers provided direct comments about specific job dimensions.

Job Satisfaction

The results of a 2 × 2 analysis of variance on job satisfaction produced no main effect for task condition or for the interaction of task condition and social cues. The main effect for type of social cues was significant, $F(1, 37) = 4.51, p < .04$. The mean general satisfaction score for the group receiving positive social cues was 5.19, and the mean general satisfaction score for the group receiving negative social cues was 4.08. These results are quite interesting. Apparently, in this situation, differences in task characteristics did not affect the employees' affective response to the job. It appears that the critical factor in determining job satisfaction was the expressed affective responses of one's co-worker. These results are incongruent with the theoretical model described by Hackman and Oldham (1974) and the empirical evidence reported by others (e.g., Pierce & Durnham, 1976; Umstot, Bell, & Mitchell, 1976).

Productivity

A two-way analysis of variance was carried out on the productivity measure, with task condition and type of social cues serving as the independent variables. Similar to the job satisfaction results, the main effect for type of social cues was the only significant effect observed, $F(1, 37) = 14.28, p < .01$. The mean productivity level for the positive cues group was 4.78 items per minute, and the mean productivity level for the negative cues group was 3.94 items per minute. Interestingly, the productivity means for the two task conditions were almost identical. For the enriched group, the mean was 4.37 items per minute, and for the unenriched group the mean was 4.36 items per minute. These data seem to suggest that objective differences in task characteristics

had no effect on job performance but that social cues were highly significant in influencing the level of employee output. These results are consistent with those reported earlier by Umstot et al. (1976; Umstot et al., in press) and by White, Mitchell, and Bell (1977).

DISCUSSION

The results of this study are interesting in a number of respects. First, the data provide support for the contention that the social cues of co-workers may be an important determinant of whether a job is perceived as enriched or unenriched. Admittedly, the actual job factors had a somewhat more substantial effect on enrichment perceptions (as measured by the MPS) than did the social cues, but one would hope that this would be the case. The demonstration that social cues can in some cases be as powerful a determinant of these perceptions (as measured by the SCMI and the interaction effect on the feedback scale) provides additional support for the arguments brought forward by Salancik and Pfeffer (1977) and O'Reilly and Caldwell (in press). Employee perceptions of the task environment are a joint function of objective task characteristics and social cues.

To some extent we have known for a long time that social cues are important. The early work of Asch (1951) and Sherif (1935) are good examples of the importance of social cues. However, to date, most researchers concerned with job enrichment have neglected to include social cues in their conceptualizations of enrichment. Although we are not arguing that social cues are the only or even the most important determinant of enrichment perceptions, our results do suggest that they are important.

A second and equally important finding was that both job satisfaction and productivity were significantly affected by social cues but were unaffected by job enrichment. The job enrichment manipulation clearly worked. Both the manipulation check and the perceptions of the actual employees (e.g., the MPS) showed significant enrichment effects. Yet the job outcomes, productivity, and satisfaction were unaffected by these task differences. Apparently, at least in this instance, the comments of co-workers were a more powerful motivating force than the actual properties of the task.

When compared to an actual ongoing job situation, we believe that the present co-worker effects are in some sense conservative. That is, the effect of the comments of an unknown co-worker in a short work session would intuitively seem to be less important than the comments of a co-worker with whom one works 8 hours a day, 5 days a week, because the ad hoc nature of the present groups probably produced far less social pressure to conform than could be expected by members of a long-term integrated work team. However, one cannot simply draw the inference that all we need is a stooge to talk up the task in order to increase job satisfaction and productivity. Our results clearly indicate that incongruous job settings (enriched/negative cues or unenriched/positive cues) result in greater role ambiguity, and many studies discuss the detrimental effects of role ambiguity on the job (e.g., Brief & Aldag, 1976; Miles & Perreault, 1976). What the present results do suggest (along with the White et al., 1977, study) is that social cues and co-worker support may be as important as job enrichment, goal setting, and performance evaluation in creating high motivation and productivity. It is perhaps true that greater attention should be directed toward the motivational properties of social interaction if we are to more fully explain the performance and satisfaction of organizational employees. One final point should be mentioned. The social cues presented in this research were clearly positive or negative (although not extremely so) and were clearly task related. In many settings one would expect that the incongruous situations (co-workers who dislike an enriched task or like an unenriched one) would dissipate over time. Poor person–job fits frequently get resolved through turnover, absenteeism, or transfers. It is also true that much of the social interaction that takes place on the job is not task related. Thus, the objects of future research should probably be those enduring aspects of the social interaction that are task related. These are the kinds of cues that must be incorporated into our theories of employees' relations to their work environment.

REFERENCES

Asch, E. Effects of group pressure on the modification and distortion of judgments. In H. Guetzkow (Ed.), *Groups, leadership, and men.* Pittsburgh, Pa.: Carnegie Press, 1951.

Brief, A. P., & Aldag, R. J. Correlates of role indices. *Journal of Applied Psychology,* 1976, 61, 467–472.

Hackman, J. R., & Lawler, E. Employee reactions to job characteristics. *Journal of Applied Psychology,* 1971, 55, 259–286.

Hackman, J. R., & Oldham, G. R. *The job diagnostic survey: An instrument for the diagnosis of jobs and the evaluation of job redesign projects* (Tech. Rep. No. 4). New Haven, Conn.: Yale University Press, 1974.

Hackman, J. R., & Oldham, G. R. Development of the job diagnostic survey. *Journal of Applied Psychology,* 1975, 60, 159–170.

Hackman, J. R., & Oldham, G. R. Motivation through the design of work: Test of a theory. *Organizational Behavior and Human Performance,* 1976, 16, 250–279.

Herzberg, F. *Work and the nature of man.* New York: World Publishing, 1966.

Miles, R. H., & Perreault, W. D. Organizational role conflict: Its antecedents and consequences. *Organizational Behavior and Human Performance,* 1976, 17, 19–44.

Oldham, G. R., Hackman, J. R., & Pearce, J. L. Conditions under which employees respond positively to enriched work. *Journal of Applied Psychology,* 1976, 61, 395–403.

O'Reilly, C. A. Personality-job fit: Implications for individual attitudes and performance. *Organizational Behavior and Human Performance,* 1977, 18, 36–46.

O'Reilly, C. A., & Caldwell, D. F. Informational influence as a determinant of task characteristics and job satisfaction. *Journal of Applied Psychology,* in press.

Pierce, J., & Dunham, R. Task design: A literature review. *Academy of Management Review,* 1976, 1, 83–97.

Rizzo, J. R., House, R. J., & Lirtzman, S. I. Role conflicts and ambiguity in complex organizations. *Administrative Science Quarterly,* 1970, 15, 150–163.

Salancik, G., & Pfeffer, J. An examination of need–satisfaction models of job attitudes. *Administrative Science Quarterly,* 1977, 22, 427–456.

Sherif, M. A study of some social factors in perception. *Archives of Psychology,* 1935, No. 187.

Steers, R. M., & Spencer, D. G. The role of achievement motivation in job design. *Journal of Applied Psychology,* 1977, 62, 472–479.

Stone, E., Mowday, R., & Porter, L. Higher order needs strengths as moderators of the job scope–job satisfaction relationship. *Journal of Applied Psychology,* 1977, 62, 466–471.

Turner, A., & Lawrence, P. *Industrial jobs and the worker.* Cambridge, Mass.: Harvard University Press, 1965.

Umstot, D. D., Bell, C. H., Jr., & Mitchell, T. R. Effects of job enrichment and task goals on satisfaction and productivity: Implications for job design. *Journal of Applied Psychology,* 1976, 61, 379–394.

Umstot, D. D., Mitchell, T. R., & Bell, C. H., Jr. Goal setting and job enrichment: An integrated approach to job design. *Academy of Management Review,* in press.

White, S. E., Mitchell, T. R., & Bell, C. H., Jr. Goal setting, evaluation apprehension, and social cues as determinants of job performance and job satisfaction in a simulated organization. *Journal of Applied Psychology,* 1977, 62, 665–673.

Winer, B. J. *Statistical principles in experimental design* (2nd ed.). New York: McGraw-Hill, 1971.

15. Organizational Stories: More Vivid and Persuasive than Quantitative Data

Joanne Martin and Melanie E. Powers

Many organizations have become adept at symbolic means of communicating information about their philosophy of management, the culture of their organization, and the humanistic rationale for their policies. Symbolic forms of management include the creation of rituals of initiation and transition, the evolution of shared jargon and special metaphors, and — the focus of this chapter — the telling of organizational sagas, myths, legends, and stories.

COLLECTING HEADS, TAMING WILD DUCKS, AND J.F.K.

One organization that has become known for its attention to symbolic forms of management is I.B.M. Under the guidance of its founder, T. J. Watson, Sr., I.B.M. developed a distinctive culture, a well-articulated philosophy of management, and a strong demand for conformity (cf. Belden & Belden, 1962; Foy, 1975; Malik,

1975). For example the famous I.B.M. dress code required male employees to wear dark suits, crisp white shirts, and narrow black ties. The organizational culture included rules concerning sexual relations between employees (not advisable), the use of coarse language or alcohol during working hours (don't), and the way to make a speech (list key points using simple words on a flip chart). T. J. Watson, Sr., reinforced these forms of organizational control with numerous rituals and ceremonies. For example, until the company became too large, employees lived temporarily in tents on company grounds during the annual picnic. There they sang company songs and listened to speeches given with evangelical fervor.

When T. J. Watson, Jr., took over the leadership of I.B.M. from his father, he wanted to improve the functioning of the corporation and leave his personal mark on its distinctive philosophy of management and culture. One means to these ends was to change the rhetoric, and perhaps the reality, of the corporation's demands for conformity. T. J. Watson, Jr. stated this objective directly in his speeches at company functions: "I just wish somebody would stick his head in my office and say (to me) 'you're wrong.' I would really like to hear that. I don't want yes-men around me" (Malik, 1975:210).

Watson, Jr., justified his encouragement of dissent by citing *The Organization Man:* "When an organization tries to get too close to its people and makes a lot of the team idea, the individual gets swallowed up, loses his identity, and becomes a carbon copy of his fellow employees" (Watson, Jr., 1963:24-25). He claimed that the company already had in its ranks a number of employees who would dare express dissent:

[Our company] has more than 125,000 employees. A substantial number of them, many of whom I could pick out by name, are highly individualistic men and women. They value their intellectual freedom and I question whether they would surrender it at any price. Admittedly, they may like their jobs and the security and salaries that go along with them. But I know of few who would not put on their hats and slam the door if they felt the organization had intruded so heavily on them they no longer owned themselves. (Watson, Jr., 1963:25-26)

Such abstract, direct statements of this change in the demand for the conformity were dismissed as corporate propaganda by many employees: "[Watson, Jr.] says to us to stick our heads into his office and say 'you are wrong'; you should see the collection of heads that he has" (Malik, 1975:210).

Watson, Jr., seemed to recognize the difficulty of convincing I.B.M. employees that this change in policy was truthful, and not corporate propaganda. He repeatedly supplemented abstract, direct statements, such as that quoted above, with stories illustrating his point. His favorite story concerned wild ducks:

The moral is drawn from a story by the Danish philosopher, Soren Kierkegaard. He told of a man on the coast of Zealand who liked to watch the wild ducks fly south in great flocks each fall. Out of charity, he took to putting feed for them in a nearby pond. After a while some of the ducks no longer bothered to fly south; they wintered in Denmark on what he fed them.

In time they flew less and less. When the wild ducks returned, the others would circle up to greet them but then head back to their feeding grounds on the pond. After three or four years they grew so lazy and fat that they found difficulty in flying at all.

Kierkegaard drew his point—you can make wild ducks tame, but you can never make tame ducks wild

again. One might also add that the duck who is tamed will never go anywhere anymore.

We are convinced that any business needs its wild ducks. And in I.B.M. we try not to tame them. (Watson, Jr., 1963:27-28)

This metaphorical story also failed to convince many employees. Indeed, some researchers (cf. Ott, 1979) expressed skepticism about it. One employee put his reaction succinctly: "Even wild ducks fly in formation" (Malik, 1975:210). Watson, Jr., had another story he told which made a similar point. The main characters in this story were I.B.M. employees.

Early in 1961, in talking to our sales force, I attempted to size up the then new Kennedy Administration as I saw it. It was not a political talk. I urged no views on them. It was an optimistic assessment, nothing more. But at the close of the meeting, a number of salesmen came up front. They would listen to what I had to say about business, they said, but they didn't want to hear about the new Administration in a company meeting.

On my return to New York, I found a few letters in the same vein. Lay off, they seemed to say, you're stepping on our toes in something that's none of your business.

At first I was a bit annoyed at having been misunderstood. But when I thought about it, I was pleased, for they had made it quite clear they wore no man's collar and they weren't at all hesitant to tell me so. From what I have read of organization men, that is not the way they are supposed to act. (Watson, Jr., 1963:26)

This last story was more credible than his other statements which encouraged dissent. Even self-appointed critics of I.B.M. do not usually doubt the truthfulness of this particular story (cf. Malik, 1975), although they may continue to be skeptical of the company's actual tolerance of dissent.

This skepticism is not misplaced. Even in public statements, Watson, Jr., betrayed his unchanged desire for conformity:

It's going to be a prodigious job for every one of us to make all of them look and act and have the same basic philosophies in their business lives and their community lives that all of us have . . . I wish I could put it in a page or two and hand it out and say "Give this to every new employee," who will then automatically start to look and act and think as we do. (Belden & Belden, 1962:249)

In this I.B.M. example, Watson, Jr.'s policy change was more rhetoric than reality. Of all the various forms of communicating this purported policy change, the story about organizational employees seemed to arouse the least skepticism. Thus, it was most likely to generate commitment to the policy. Direct statements of the policy in abstract language were apparently less effective.

If organizational stories are a particularly effective means of generating commitment, they are a potentially powerful management tool. From a management point of view, it would be useful to know whether in fact an organizational story is a more effective way to generate commitment than other forms of communicating information. It would also be useful to know the conditions under which an organizational story would lose its impact.

From an employee's point of view, different issues are salient. An employee needs to know whether to believe a given statement is true or whether to dismiss it as corporate propaganda. It is also useful for an employee to know if a particular form of communication, such as a story, is likely to be particularly persuasive. If so, the employee can be wary when information is communicated in this form. These concerns of top management and lower-level employees suggest that symbolic forms of management, such as organizational stories, are an important topic for researchers to investigate.

ORGANIZATIONAL STORIES, MYTHS, LEGENDS, AND SAGAS

Some organizational research indicates that the persuasive power of the story in the I.B.M. example is representative of other organizational settings. This research focuses on organizational stories, myths, sagas, and legends (e.g., Clark, 1970; Meyer & Rowan, 1978; Selznick, 1957). Wilkins and Martin (1979) define an organizational story as an anecdote about an event sequence, apparently drawn from an accurate version of an organization's history. The main characters are organizational participants, usually employees rather than clients.

This research on organizational stories has relied predominantly on qualitative methods (e.g., Clark, 1970; Selznick, 1957). Researchers have found examples of organizational stories in the transcripts of open-ended interviews and in archival material, such as memoranda, brochures, letters, and records of speeches given by company executives.

This organizational research speculates that organizational stories may serve many of the same functions that anthropologists have found myths to serve in tribal societies (e.g., Cohen, 1969; Malinowski, 1948): organizational stories legitimate the power relations within the organization; they rationalize existing practices, traditions, and rituals; and they articulate through examplars the philosophy of management and the policies which make the organization distinctive. In short, this research suggests the proposition that there is an association between stories and organizational commitment. The next section of this chapter examines this proposition in detail.

STORIES AND COMMITMENT

Alan Wilkins (1978) tested this proposition using a mixture of qualitative and quantitative methods. He obtained transcripts of organizational stories through interviews with employees of two companies, and measured levels of employee commitment with a survey instrument. In the organization in which commitment was stronger, a larger number of stories were told, and their content was more favorable to the organization. Thus Wilkins' research found an association between organizational stories and commitment.

The organizational research discussed above, including Wilkins' work, raises two interesting questions. The first concerns causality. Does the telling of organizational stories increase employee commitment to the organization? Or, is the direction of causality reversed, so that committed employees are more likely to tell favorable stories? Another possibility is that there may not be a causal relationship at all between stories and commitment. The second question concerns the relative impact of stories on commitment, compared to other methods of communicating information about management philosophy or policy. Such other means of communicating information might include abstract policy statements, such as corporate objectives, or a table of statistical data. Are stories a more effective means of generating commitment than these other forms of information? The types of research designs and methodologies used in the organizational research discussed above raised these questions, but did not attempt to provide answers to them (Clark, 1970; Meyer & Rowan, 1978; Selznick, 1957; Wilkins, 1978).

We decided to seek answers to these two questions by using experimental laboratory methods. This methodology is well suited to address these questions. In an experiment it is possible to manipulate the form of information presented to subjects. Potentially confounding variables such as tenure can be controlled by the design of the experimental context and by random assignment of subjects to conditions. Hence a well-designed experiment can provide a context for testing questions of causality and for measuring the comparative strength of various means of communicating information.

We designed experiments to test two propositions based on the organizational research discussed above. We proposed, first, that supporting a management philosophy statement with an organizational story would increase the subjects' commitment to that philosophy. Second, we proposed that stories would produce more commitment than other forms of information.

As considered in more detail elsewhere (Martin, in press), a body of experimental social cognition research is relevant to these propositions. This cognitive research begins with a premise concerning sample size which is familiar to all students of statistical inference: a judgment based on multiple observations should be more reliable than a judgment based on a single observation. Furthermore, if data based on multiple observations is supplemented by an additional observation, then that additional data point should be treated merely as one of the set of observations.

This premise concerning sample size raises some issues about the impact of an organizational story. A story — indeed, any case example — is based on a single observation. Therefore, if the sample size premise is followed, a story should have much less impact than would data based on multiple observations.

Considerable cognitive research suggests that people do not behave in a manner consistent with the sample size premise (Borgida & Nisbett, 1977; McArthur, 1972, 1976; Nisbett & Borgida, 1975; Nisbett & Ross, 1980; Tversky & Kahneman, 1973). Typically in this research, some subjects were randomly selected to receive distributional data about the behavior of a number of other people (consensus information) or the characteristics of a sample (base-rate information). The remaining subjects received the distributional information, plus additional information about a single case example. The dependent variables usually required subjects to make rational cognitive judgments about relatively academic tasks.

The engineers and lawyers problem is representative of these experimental tasks (Kahneman & Tversky, 1973). Subjects were given base-rate data about the percentages of engineers and lawyers in a given sample. Some of the subjects were also given personally descriptive information about a single individual. Subjects were then asked to estimate the probability that this individual was an engineer.

In accord with the sample size premise, subjects exposed only to the distributional data based their cognitive judgments on that data. Subjects exposed both to the distributional data and to the case example, however, weighted the case example much more heavily in their judgments than they should have, had they behaved in accord with sample size considerations.

More recently, researchers have attempted to find the limits of this phenomenon. Some recent research has found that for tasks such as this, the impact of distributional data was equal to or greater than the impact of a single case example (Azjen, 1977; Feldman, Higgins, Karlovac, & Ruble, 1976; Hansen & Donoghue, 1977; Manis, Dovalina, Avis, & Cardoze, 1980; Wells & Harvey, 1977). Even in these studies, though, case examples are usually given weight beyond that dictated by the sample size premise. To summarize, social cognition research provides an experimental paradigm for examining the two hypotheses discussed above. It also provides additional support for the second of the two propositions to be tested: a case example, such as an organizational story, may have strong impact on judgments, stronger than that predicted by sample size considerations alone.

These conclusions, however, assume that the cognitive research results are generalizable to organizational contexts. This assumption may not be warranted, for two reasons. First, the experimental tasks used in the cognitive research require subjects to make rational, usually statistical, judgments. Subjects' knowledge of statistical principles may be sufficient to produce a correct solution to the problem. In organizational contexts, judgments are usually more complex and subjective. Second, the source of the distributional and case example information appears to be objective in the cognitive research. Subjects would have little reason to doubt the truthfulness of this information. In organizational contexts, though, the credibility of the source of information is often questionable. Organizational representatives have been known to distort information about their organizations.

Both of these limitations of the cognitive research suggest the importance of exploring ideas drawn from the cognitive research in contexts which are organizationally relevant. In such contexts, experimental tasks would require complex and subjective solutions, not derivable from statistical principles. The source of the information, whether it is based on single or multiple observations, would be of potentially questionable credibility.

We conducted two experiments with these organizationally relevant characteristics. In each experiment we gave all subjects a statement of an organizational policy, phrased in abstract language. Some subjects also received additional information presented in the form of data (based on multiple observations); others received additional information in the form of an organizational story (based on a single observation). Still others received both the data and the story. Because of the complexity of the information, we were able to incorporate into our questionnaire a broader range of dependent variables than were used in the cognitive research. We included the usual cognitive dependent variables plus accuracy of recall and attitudinal dependent variables such as belief in and commitment to the policy statement. Our two experiments are described below.

SELLING CALIFORNIA WINE WITH A STORY

In the first experiment (Martin & Powers, 1979) M.B.A. students were recruited as subjects for a study of the effectiveness of an advertisement for a winery. An abstract policy statement (an advertisement) was read by all subjects. According to this statement, the new Joseph Beaumont Winery used many of the same excellent winemaking techniques as used in the famed Chablis region of France, thus producing California wine as fine as French chablis.

The text of the advertisement contained this policy statement plus some supplemental information. The supplemental information detailed the winemaking procedures used by the Joseph Beaumont winery. Subjects were randomly assigned to receive this information in one of three forms: a story, a table of statistics, or a combination of story plus statistics. Like many organizational stories, the story concerned the founder of a business:

Joseph Beaumont's father spent most of his life growing grapes in Chablis, the famous winemaking area of France. After World War II, Joe's father came to the United States, to live in the Napa area of California. The gravelly soil and cool climate there reminded him of the stony fields and cool nights in Chablis. All the time Joe was growing up, his father would tell him how the wonderful, flinty, dry wines of Chablis were made. Before his father died, Joe promised him that someday

he would make a California wine using the traditional winemaking techniques of Chablis.

For ten years, Joe worked at some of the most famous vineyards in the Napa Valley, putting all his savings into a winery and vineyard, which he named Beaumont. Although money was sometimes scarce, Joe has struggled for the last two years to duplicate the old, but unfortunately expensive, methods of winemaking of Chablis. His Pinot Chardonnay vines were too new; they didn't supply all the grapes he needed and he was forced to buy some inferior grape varieties. He wanted to use glass-lined tanks, like those in Chablis, but could only afford 7 of the 10 he needed, so he had to use a few of the steel tanks usually used in California. In spite of these difficulties, Joe made no other compromises. He ordered special Limosin oak barrels, from the same suppliers used by Chablis winemakers. He filtered his wine using natural methods – egg whites rather than the chemical filters favored by other California wineries. As Joe tasted his first vintage wine he thought, ''My father would have been proud of this wine.''

In the statistics condition, subjects were given a table summarizing information comparing the winemaking procedures (such as the types of grapes and oak barrels) used at the Joseph Beaumont Winery, at other California wineries, and in Chablis, France. In the story condition, subjects received the story, but no statistical data. In the combination condition, subjects received both the story and the table of statistics. After reading this material, subjects answered a questionnaire about the advertisement which contained the dependent measures of willingness to predict that the organization would behave in accord with the abstract policy statement; willingness to believe the policy statement; ability to recognize its content accurately; and willingness to consider the advertisement a persuasive marketing technique.

Our hypothesis, labeled *the story hypothesis,* predicted the same pattern of results for each of these classes of dependent variables: the story should have the greatest impact, followed by the combination condition, and then the statistics condition. An alternate hypothesis, labeled *the data hypothesis,* predicted the opposite pattern of results: statistics > combination > story.

In contrast to subjects in the other two conditions, subjects who read only the story were slightly more likely to predict that the winery would continue to use the winemaking procedures from France. These subjects were significantly more likely to believe that the advertisement was truthful, to believe that the Beaumont winery actually had used the French wine-making procedures, and to distort their memory of the policy statement, in a direction favorable to the winery. In summary, in accord with the story hypothesis, the story generally had stronger impact than the combination of story plus statistics; and the combination had more impact than did the statistics by themselves.

Interestingly, the subjects were apparently unaware of the strong impact of the story. In accord with the data hypothesis, subjects in the statistics condition rated the advertisement they had read as somewhat more persuasive than did subjects who had read both the story and the statistics. Furthermore, subjects in the statistics condition rated the advertisement as considerably more persuasive than did subjects in the other conditions. Thus the subjects did not realize how powerfully the story had affected their responses. It created a "true believer" reaction even in these quantitatively well-trained M.B.A. students.

GENERATING COMMITMENT TO A POLICY STATEMENT WITH A STORY

In the first experiment the supplemental information supported the policy statement. In this second study (Martin & Powers, 1980), the supplemental information either supported or disconfirmed the policy statement. As in the first study, three forms of that information were used: a story, a table of statistics, or a combination of story plus statistics. Thus in this second study two independent variables were manipulated, creating a two-by-three factorial design.

The M.B.A. subjects all read a policy statement. This policy, based on an actual company policy studied by Wilkins (1978), stated that the company would avoid mass layoffs in times of economic difficulty by asking employees to take a temporary 10% cut in pay. In the story condition, the subjects read about a single employee, Phil Locke. The product which was produced by Phil's division was going to have to be discontinued. According to the story, Phil was worried:

Phil had a wife and two kids. Add to that the usual mortgage payments, car payments, insurance premiums, taxes — you know, he was overextended financially. Well, all that was pretty unsettling for Phil. He's one of those Yankee conservatives who thinks borrowing money is immoral.

Phil knew he was really banking on Electrotec's layoff policy. In fact, that policy was one reason why he had come to Electrotec in the first place. Still, he knew he

shouldn't depend totally on the company to protect his career and his family's welfare. He began to look at sales jobs at other firms in the area — just in case. The problem was that none of these jobs fit his training and interests as well as the job he already had, and the market was getting worse.

Phil was in the cafeteria when his secretary came after him with the news that his boss wanted to see him right away.

Phil broke out in a cold sweat as he walked into his boss's office. His boss didn't say much, just something like, "I'm sorry, Phil. I just got the news we've all been dreading; the inertial navigation products are going to be dropped from our line. You and I have been together for a long time, and I will miss you, but . . ."

Two endings for this story were prepared. Subjects in the policy supporting conditions read that:

". . . you'll still have a job with Electrotec. I even think we'll be able to set one up for you in one of the other military hardware divisions. Of course, this means a temporary 10% cut in pay." Not fired! Phil said later he felt as if he had been given a reprieve from a death sentence.

Subjects in the disconfirming conditions read a different ending to the story: " '. . . I have to let you go' Fired! Phil said later he felt as if he had been given the death sentence."

In the statistics conditions subjects were given numerical data concerning the frequencies of turnover (voluntary and involuntary) and paycuts, both before and after the products were discontinued. In the supporting conditions, the turnover data indicated that no mass layoffs had occurred and that most employees had taken a 10% cut in pay after the product was discontinued. In the disconfirming conditions, the frequency of turnover implied that a mass layoff had occurred and that pay cuts were rare. In the combination conditions subjects received either the supporting story plus the supporting statistics or the disconfirming story plus the disconfirming statistics.

When the information supported the policy statement, subjects in the story condition, in contrast to subjects in the combination and statistics conditions, were more likely to predict that mass layoffs would be avoided, to believe the policy statement was truthful, and to require a larger salary increase before they would quit for a comparable job at another company. The opposite pattern of effects was found when the information disconfirmed the policy condition. The disconfirming story had an impact equal to or less than the impact of the disconfirming statistics or the combination of disconfirming story plus disconfirming statistics.

In summary, when subjects were given information which supported a policy statement and were then asked to make predictions, to assess their belief in the truthfulness of the policy, or to indicate their commitment to the organization, the supporting story had a stronger impact than the other forms of communication. The power of a story however, is not limitless. When the information disconfirmed the policy statement, the story never had a stronger impact, and frequently had a significantly weaker impact, than the disconfirming statistics and the disconfirming combination of story plus statistics.

CONCLUSIONS

In this final section of the chapter, the theoretical contributions of these experimental results are discussed. The practical implications for organizational employees are outlined and several ethical concerns are raised.

The results of these two studies can be summarized in terms of the two questions raised by the organizational research. First, stories caused commitment. Second, stories caused more commitment than other means of communicating information, such as statistics.

In addition to addressing questions raised by the organizational research, these two experiments extend the results of the cognitive research. A wider range of dependent variables was considered. Whereas previous cognitive research had used dependent measures concerning cognitive judgments, these two experiments also measured belief in the truthfulness of information and commitment to the values underlying the information. The two experiments demonstrated that case examples, such as organizational stories, have strong impact on these attitudes as well as on cognitions.

The second experiment also produced a finding which was not anticipated by previous organizational or cognitive research. It demonstrated a boundary condition or limit to the powerful impact of case examples such as stories. When the content of the information disconfirmed, rather than supported, the policy statement, the story lost its power. Disconfirming statistics had an impact on attitudes and cognitions that was equal to, sometimes even greater than, a disconfirming story. Subjects apparently dismissed the disconfirming story as the single exception to the general rule. The results of the second experiment suggest that if a story is to have strong impact, it must be congruent with prior knowledge.

The results of these two experiments have some clear practical implications. Frequently managers wish to communicate information about a policy change or their philosophy of management. Obviously, they want their messages to be memorable and believable, so that employees will be committed to these ideas. The studies discussed above indicate that the most effective tactic would be to support their points with an organizational story, rather than with statistical information.

Watson, Jr., of I.B.M. was using this tactic when he told the stories about the wild ducks or about the negative reaction to his speech supporting John F. Kennedy. Unfortunately, Watson ran afoul of the boundary condition discovered in the second experiment. He told stories which disconfirmed the employees' prior knowledge about the I.B.M. emphasis on conformity. Consequently, these disconfirming stories were dismissed, by many employees, as corporate propaganda.

The I.B.M. example raises some ethical issues. Employees need to be wary of the potentially powerful impact that a seemingly innocuous story can have. Management, indeed anyone, could use the power of a story to manipulate beliefs about a policy and to generate commitment to an organization when the information is, in fact, corporate propaganda. As this caveat indicates, symbolic forms of management, such as the telling of organizational stories, are powerful and potentially dangerous tools.

REFERENCES

Azjen, I. Intuitive theories of events and the effects of base-rate information on prediction. *Journal of Personality and Social Psychology,* 1977, *35,* 303–314.

Belden, T. G., & Belden, M. R. *The lengthening shadow: The life of Thomas J. Watson.* Boston: Little, Brown, 1962.

Borgida, E., & Nisbett, R. E. The differential impact of abstract vs. concrete information on decisions. *Journal of Applied Social Psychology*, 1977, *7*, 258–271.

Clark, B. *The distinctive college: Antioch, Reed and Swarthmore*. Chicago: Aldine, 1970.

Cohen, P. S. Theories of myth. *Man*, 1969, *4*, 337–353.

Feldman, N. S., Higgins, E. T., Karlovac, M., & Ruble, D. N. Use of consensus information in causal attributions as a function of temporal presentation and availability of direct information. *Journal of Personality and Social Psychology*, 1976, *34*, 694–698.

Foy, N. *The sun never sets on IBM*. New York: William Morrow & Company, Inc., 1975.

Hansen, R. D., & Donoghue, J. The power of consensus: Information derived from one's and others' behavior. *Journal of Personality and Social Psychology*, 1977, *35*, 294–302.

Kahneman, D., & Tversky, A. On the psychology of prediction. *Psychological Review*, 1973, *80*, 237–251.

Malik, R. *And tomorrow . . . the world? Inside IBM*. London: Millington HD, 1975.

Malinowski, B. Myth in primitive psychology. In *Magic, science, and religion, and other essays*. Boston: Beach Press, 1948.

Manis, M., Dovalina, I., Avis, N., & Cardoze, S. Base rates can affect individual predictions. *Journal of Personality and Social Psychology*, 1980, *38*, 231–248.

Martin, J. Stories and scripts in organizational settings. In A. Hastorf and A. Isen (Eds.), *Cognitive Social Psychology*. New York: Elsevier-North Holland, Inc., In Press.

Martin, J., & Powers, M. E. *If case examples provide no proof, why under-utilize statistical information?* Paper presented at the meetings of the American Psychological Association, New York, September 1979.

Martin, J., & Powers, M. E. *Skepticism and the true believer: The effects of case and/or base rate information on belief and commitment*. Paper presented at the meeting of the Western Psychological Association, Honolulu, May 1980.

McArthur, L. Z. The how and what of why: Some determinants and consequences of causal attribution. *Journal of Personality and Social Psychology*, 1972, *22*, 171–193.

McArthur, L. Z. The lesser influence of consensus than distinctiveness information on causal attributions: A test of the person-thing hypothesis. *Journal of Personality and Social Psychology*, 1976, *33*, 733–742.

Meyer, J. W., & Rowan, B. Institutionalized organizations: Formal structure as myth and ceremony. In M. M. Meyer & Associates, *Environment and organizations: Theoretical and empirical perspectives*. San Francisco: Jossey-Bass, Inc., 1978, 78–109.

Nisbett, R. E., & Borgida, E. Attribution and the psychology of prediction. *Journal of Personality and Social Psychology*, 1975, *32*, 932–943.

Nisbett, R. E., & Ross, L. *Human inference: Strategies and shortcomings of social judgment*. Englewood Cliffs, N.J.: Prentice-Hall, Inc., 1980.

Ott, R. *Are wild ducks really wild: Symbolism and behavior in the corporate environment*. Paper presented at the meeting of the Northeastern Anthropological Association, March 1979.

Selznick, P. *Leadership and administration*. Evanston, Ill.: Row, Peterson, 1957.

Tversky, A., & Kahneman, D. Availability: A heuristic for judging frequency and probability. *Cognitive Psychology*, 1973, *5*, 207–232.

Watson, Jr., T. J. *A business and its beliefs: The ideas that helped build IBM*. New York: McGraw-Hill Book Company, Inc., 1963.

Wells, G. L., & Harvey, J. H. Do people use consensus information in making causal attributions? *Journal of Personality and Social Psychology*, 1977, *35*, 279–293.

Wilkins, A. *Organizational stories as an expression of management philosophy: Implications for social control in organizations*. Unpublished doctoral dissertation, Stanford University, 1978.

Wilkins, A., & Martin, J. *Organizational legends* (Research Paper No. 521). Graduate School of Business, Stanford University, 1979.

Part Three

Social Influence

Foundations of Social Influence

16. Imitation, Conformity, and Compliance

Leonard Berkowitz

IMITATION AND MODELING

In some instances an individual follows another's actions in the absence of any social pressures. The other person sets an example which is copied in one way or another. Psychologists usually speak of *imitation* when the observer duplicates what he or she sees fairly closely, but they talk about *modeling* when the examplar's influence is somewhat broader and the observer's action isn't an exact replica of the model's behavior (Bandura, 1969, 1970). Since it is a more extensive concept than imitation, modeling refers to a wider range of processes. The conditions that produce imitation don't necessarily operate in every case of modeling.

Albert Bandura (1969, 1970) at Stanford University is perhaps the leading theorist in this area; he has discussed three kinds of modeling effects: response stimulation

(which he terms "response facilitation"), observational learning, and the lowering of inhibitions. We'll follow his analysis with some modifications.

Response Stimulation

Reflexive Imitation. Researchers tell us that several species of animals have a "monkey see, monkey do" tendency, in which one animal sometimes copies the behavior of another almost reflexively (Tolman, 1968). Human infants imitate the facial expressions of nearby adults in this involuntary manner, and even grown-ups may show this simple copying, as when one person's yawn causes a contagion of yawning throughout a group. Most important, this relatively primitive imitation doesn't involve the transmission of information from the model to the observer. The model's action doesn't explicitly tell the observer, "Do what I do if you want to get a reward." The imitation is largely involuntary and can thus be viewed as an instance of our Theme I, involuntary responses to external events.

I occasionally exhibit this kind of reaction on fall Sunday afternoons when I look at football on TV. Watching a particular player closely, not having any distracting thoughts, and not being engaged in any competing activities, I sometimes dart and lunge along with him as he moves. This reflexive copying of another may not have been learned, although learning can add to and complicate the reaction.

A team of investigators at the University of Texas may have observed such a blend of learned reactions and stimulus-elicited copying as they recorded the behavior of pedestrians at a traffic light (Lefkowitz, Blake, and Mouton, 1955).

At the appropriate time, right after the traffic signal at a busy street corner commanded the pedestrians to "wait," a 31-year-old man (the experimenters' accomplice) disregarded the red light and walked across the street. On some occasions his clothing (business suit, shirt and tie, and highly polished shoes) indicated he had a relatively high social status, whereas at other times he wore soiled and patched work clothes, suggesting that he had a lower status. The violator's apparent social level affected the extent to which the other pedestrians crossed the street with him. As is typical in this kind of situation, the traffic light violator's action probably stimulated some onlookers to move. He started crossing and some other pedestrians automatically did the same thing. But the stimulation effect was greater when the violator seemed to have a high social status. (While only 1 percent of the pedestrians crossed against the traffic when the accomplice hadn't violated the signal, 4 percent of the onlookers disregarded the light when the illegally acting model had low status, and 14 percent crossed when he was well-dressed.) The onlookers may have paid greater attention to the high-status than to the low-status model. Whatever the explanation, in this study one person's movement prompted others to start forward also . . .

The Contagion of Violence. News stories reporting violent crimes can [also] have [an] imitative effect. The widespread publicity produces a contagion of violence as other persons are stimulated to carry out similar actions. In the late nineteenth century the French sociologist Gabriel Tarde described what he called "suggesto-imitative-assaults." Coining what used to be a well-known phrase, he wrote that epidemics of crime "follow the line of the telegraph." That is, news of a spectacular crime in one community suggests the idea to other people, leading to imitative crimes. According to Tarde (1912), the brutal Jack the Ripper murders in London inspired a series of female mutilation cases in other sections of England. Police officials in the United States have offered similar observations. The Chicago Police Department reported, for example, that Richard Speck's murder of 8 nurses in Chicago in July 1966 and Charles Whitman's shooting of 45 people from the University of Texas Tower the next month were followed by an unusually sharp increase in homicides in Chicago (*Look Magazine*, September 19, 1967). Also, that fall an 18-year-old high school senior shot 4 women and a child in an Arizona beauty parlor. He told police afterwards that he had gotten the idea for a mass killing from the news stories of the Speck and Whitman crimes.

Other illustrations of the contagion of violence can also be cited if we classify suicides as violence. Evidence (Phillips, 1974) indicates that suicides increase immediately after a suicide story has been publicized in the newspapers. And the greater the publicity devoted to a suicide story, the greater is the subsequent rise in the suicide rate. When movie actress Marilyn Monroe committed suicide, there was a 12-percent increase in the suicides in the United States and a 10-percent rise in England and Wales in the next month. The ideas and feelings evoked in susceptible people when they see these news stories need not produce only a close imitation; they may end their own lives by any available means. In a careful statistical analysis, Phillips (1978) has demonstrated that widely publicized murder-suicides tend to be followed by a significant increase in private and business airplane crashes. The greater the publicity given to any murder-suicide, the more crashes occurred. Some people with suicidal tendencies are apparently stirred to action by news stories of suicides, so that they may use the opportunity of an airplane flight to kill themselves, even if they take other persons' lives as well. . . . You may recall the television movie *The Doomsday Flight*. . . . The film portrays an attempt to extort money from an airline by threatening to blow up a passenger plane in flight. The showing of this movie in the United States and abroad provoked a rash of hoax telephone calls warning about bombs aboard airlines, and some flights had to be recalled or canceled. Indeed, this happened so regularly each time the film was telecast that the Federal Aviation Administration asked television stations not to air it. Similarly, airplane hijackings have shown a contagion effect (see Figure 1). Besides giving some people ideas they may otherwise not have had (an involuntary reaction), the story provides information: It tells them how they can get money (or some other goal) and just what they have to do to reach this goal.

A good deal of what we know and much of what we do has been acquired through observational learning. We have learned how to get to some locations in our community, play certain games, put on some items of clothing, and carry out at least part of our jobs by watching other persons engage in similar activities. Adults serve as models for children and deliberately or inadvertently teach them how to behave in various situations. Parental actions often speak louder than words. Parents frequently exhort their sons and daughters to work hard, although they themselves seem bent on having an easy time; to be honest, although they themselves try to cheat whenever possible; and to be helpful and considerate toward others, although they themselves are often selfish and inconsiderate. Needless to say, youngsters who see adult hypocrisy frequently copy what their parents do and not what they say (Bryan, 1970).

The influence any model will have depends on several considerations. Observers don't automatically learn every detail of the lesson before them. If the learning is to last, the watchers have to *attend* to the model's action and then *rehearse* what they see. Onlookers won't watch the model carefully, however, if they aren't interested in the activity or if the model isn't attractive or prestigious enough to command their attention. Moreover, observers will probably remember the witnessed action better if they describe or repeat the lesson to themselves as they watch (Bandura, Grusec, & Menlove, 1966; Jeffery, 1976).

Qualities of Influential Models. The models' characteristics often affect the extent to which their actions are copied, partly by influencing what the observers learn (Bandura, 1969). Especially important is the models' control over the observers' goals (Bandura, Ross, & Ross, 1963; Grusec, 1971; Mischel & Grusec, 1966). If the observers realize that the model can determine whether they will get what they want or whether they'll be punished, they are more likely to look closely at what the model does and to think about his activity, implicitly practicing it, as he performs.

Investigations of the effects of the model's power illustrate how laboratory experiments can throw light on child development. Social scientists have long been interested in *identification,* the process by which a child adopts someone else's qualities and ways of acting.

Bandura et al. (1963) studied identification experimentally by establishing three-person groups composed of two adults and a child to represent the nuclear family — a "father," "mother," and "child." Researchers' accomplices filled the parental roles, whereas the subject — a nursery-school-aged boy or girl — played the part of the offspring. It was quickly apparent that one of the adults — sometimes the man and sometimes the woman — was the powerful member of the "family" and determined who could play with the attractive toys in

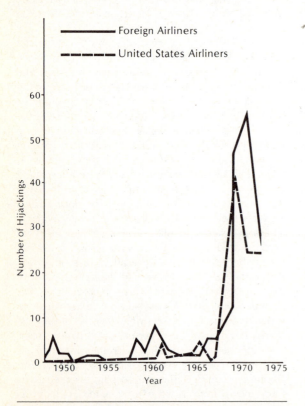

Figure 1.   The Number of Airplane Hijackings in the United States and Abroad Between 1947 and 1972.

Courtesy of Albert Bandura.

the room. As the power in the family, this adult dispensed the rewards. The powerful adult rewarded the subject allowing the rewarded individual to have the attractive toys, in some cases and the other adult in other cases. After these conditions had been established, the two adults exhibited distinctively different behaviors while working on another task, and the child was given an opportunity to copy them. Defining "identification" for their purposes as imitation, the psychologists recorded the number of times each child imitated either adult's actions. As Table 1 shows, the children were most likely to copy the powerful adult rather than the less powerful one (the sex of the model didn't have any significant effect). Furthermore, the subjects tended to imitate even a powerful model who had been somewhat frustrating to them.

In Bandura et al.'s study (1963) the subjects carried out the novel behaviors they learned, but this is not always the case. People usually don't display the lesson taught to them unless they are also motivated to act. By seeing a violent model we can learn how to be aggressive and even that violence is appropriate behavior in some situations, but we can still restrain ourselves if we think aggression will be punished in the particular setting (Bandura, 1965). Aggressive models can teach others that aggression is sometimes desirable and can even evoke aggressive inclinations (as indicated earlier), but this readiness to carry out the witnessed behavior may not be translated into open action if the observers are strongly inhibited or have good reason to believe that they won't benefit by acting this way or (in the absence of an incentive) if they aren't sufficiently excited as they watch the model's behavior.

Table 1.   Mean Number of Imitative Responses Shown by Children in Reaction to Model's Power and Extent to Which the Model Had Rewarded the Subject

	Object of Imitation	
Reward Conditions	Powerful Model	Less Powerful Model
When other adult is rewarded	26.88	13.60
When the subject is rewarded	27.46	22.38

Adapted from Ross A. Bandura and S. A. Ross, "A comparative test of the status envy, social power, and secondary reinforcement theories of identificatory learning." *Journal of Abnormal Social Psychology, 67,* 1963, pp. 527–34. Copyright 1963 by the American Psychological Association. Reprinted by permission of the author.

The observer's similarity to the model is another important factor affecting the likelihood of imitation. Both children and adults have a greater tendency to copy the actions of someone who is similar to them than of someone who is greatly different (Bandura, 1969). It's easy to see why this should occur. As we watch someone similar to us behave, we're apt to infer that what happens to this individual will also happen to us. We're less likely to make this assumption if we're very different from the person we're observing. If the similar model is rewarded, or at least isn't punished, we're inclined to think our behavior will have the same outcome, and we accordingly imitate the model's behavior.

Bandura (1969) suggested that the most important kind of similarity is *similarity in previous reinforcements.* Let me explain what this concept means. As children grow up, they find that they get the same kind of benefits that certain other persons obtain when they exhibit a given kind of behavior. Susan learns that she and other young girls receive approval when they act like grown-up women in some ways; all of these persons (Susan, other young girls, grown-up women) are thus similarly reinforced for displaying certain actions. This similarity in reinforcement contingencies heightens the chances of imitation, so that Susan will be particularly likely to copy other females. Bussey and Perry (1976) verified this reasoning in an experiment with Australian schoolchildren. When the young boys and girls watched an adult make a series of choices, they were more imitative of the adult in their later choices if they had previously experienced the same reinforcement contingencies as the adult model. That is, when the children saw that both they and the adult had been given the same rewards for doing the same things, they tended to copy the adult's behavior afterwards.

Seeing Others Be Brave.   ◯Observational learning of the kind described here can have very powerful effects. As a consequence of the experiences (and reinforcements) we share with others in the course of growing up, we can be profoundly influenced by the things we see happen to other persons. We may react emotionally to the painful treatment someone else receives (Berger, 1962) or get over some of our fears by watching other persons act fearlessly. In one experiment (Bandura, Blanchard, & Ritter, 1969) adults who were very afraid of snakes watched a series of models handle snakes. Where many of the adults hadn't been able to even look at the reptiles, after only two hours of exposure to the fearless models, over 90 percent of the subjects could allow a snake to crawl freely over their hands, neck and arms. Seeing someone else be brave can lessen our own fear.

This effect isn't necessarily a matter of putting up a brave front. Let's say that Daphne Wardle is so frightened of electric shocks that she is upset by even the possibility of a mild electrical tingle on her hands. Now imagine that Daphne sees another woman receive a series of electric shocks of increasing intensity and not show any signs of discomfort. Soon afterwards, when it's Daphne's turn to be shocked, she may be able to take a fairly high level of electric shocks herself, higher than otherwise would have been the case. It's not that Daphne is only trying to look just as good as the other woman and is gritting her teeth in order to withstand the pain. If she is typical of the subjects in two experiments reported by Kenneth Craig (Craig & Neidermeyer, 1974; Craig & Prkachin, 1978), the model's fearless response to the shocks could actually make Daphne experience less pain. The information transmitted by the model's behavior can influence the way that observers interpret their own sensations. To a great extent, our feeling of pain is the result of our interpretations of physical sensations; and these interpretations can be shaped by external events, including the actions of others.

Raising and Lowering Restraints

In addition to stimulating certain reponses within us and teaching us something, a model's behavior or its outcome may also affect our attitude toward the kind of conduct we see. As we look at the model and note what happens to her, we get some idea of the likely consequences should we behave the same way. We're not particularly inclined to copy the model's aggressiveness, at least for a while, if we see her punished for being violent; we may be more willing to emulate her if we see that her conduct pays off (Bandura, 1965).

Our moral judgments can also be temporarily influenced by the events we watch. This has been demonstrated repeatedly in research on movie violence, in my own laboratory (Berkowitz & Geen, 1967; Berkowitz & Rawlings, 1963), elsewhere (Hoyt, 1970; Meyer, 1972), and in experiments with juvenile delinquents as well as with college men (Berkowitz, Parke, Leyens, & West, 1974). All of these studies found that angry subjects became more willing to attack the person who had provoked them earlier if they had just seen a movie "bad guy" get the beating he supposedly deserved, than if they had watched "less justified" aggression in which a sympathetic movie character

received unwarranted punishment. The events on the screen apparently colored the subjects' judgment of the propriety of their own aggression. "Good" aggression in the film—a scoundrel supposedly getting what was coming to him—meant that they could hurt the scoundrel in their own lives.

Hollywood movies often portray such "good" aggression. As the hero triumphs over the villains, he frequently beats them up, giving them their just desserts. All this is often emotionally satisfying for the audience—justice has been served, an eye has been given for an eye, equity has been attained, bad people have gotten their deserved punishment. But the "warranted" violence on the screen may also induce angry people in the audience to think (for a short while) that their own aggression is also warranted.

CONFORMITY: YIELDING TO OTHERS

In most of the above instances an individual imitated the actions of others with relatively little thought or, in other cases, with little questioning. The person wasn't under any social pressure and copied others' behavior quite freely. This type of modeling influence should be differentiated from *conformity*, which social psychologists usually define as yielding to group pressure of some sort. When people conform, they change their behavior or beliefs, moving from an earlier way of acting or thinking toward the position advocated by those around them "as a result of real or imagined group pressure" (Kiesler & Kiesler, 1969). Patricia Hearst's conduct right after she joined the Symbionese Liberation Army may be viewed as conformity. Because of the psychological power the terrorists had over her, she may have felt some pressure to conform to her captors' views.

This definition refers to a *change* in behavior or belief, which means that people aren't necessarily conforming when they go along with or act in the same way as others. They could be following a social rule or convention which they accept just because they have grown up in a particular society. When Americans answer the telephone, they usually say "Hello" or give their name, because this is what one does in this type of situation. People can also be conventional in their tastes in home furnishings or clothing. Their choices reflect what they are accustomed to or what they are used to wearing. They haven't given up other tastes or other modes of conduct in response to real or implied pressures.

The Benefits of Conformity

We are especially likely to accede to social pressures when we think it is to our benefit to do so. On these occasions we follow the old political dictum, "If you want to get along, go along." We realize there's something to be gained by conforming to other persons' views and something to be lost if we are different. This is a very commonplace observation, but it's still impressive how widespread is the tendency to conform in order to avoid social costs.

The Asch Experiments.   One of the classic demonstrations of people yielding to others can be found in Solomon Asch's research (1958) on conformity, which started in the early 1950s.

Seven male undergraduates listened to the experimenter explain that they were participating in a study of the judgment of perceptual relations. On each trial in the series, the men were told, they would be shown four lines — a standard line and three others of varying lengths. Their task was simply to say which of the latter three lines was the same length as the standard. The experiment began with each subject expressing his judgments aloud. Then, on the third trial, something unexpected happened. To his surprise, subject 6 heard one person after another report that the standard's best match was with line A — which actually appeared somewhat longer than the standard — even though he clearly saw that line C was the closest in length. What should he say when his turn came? The other men were unanimously contradicting the evidence provided by his own senses.

   Not realizing that the other undergraduates were the experimenter's confederates and had been instructed to express wrong judgments on certain trials, subject 6 was faced perhaps for the first time in his life with a situation in which he had to decide whether to go along with the group's unanimous judgment or report what his eyes told him was correct. Even though he knew the judgment was incorrect, the typical subject 6 in this study went along with the group on about 4 of the 12 trials in which the majority gave a wrong answer.

This is a graphic case of conformity. The subjects in these experiments seemed to be well aware of the correct answer, yet about one-third of them surrendered to the erroneous majority by voicing the wrong answer. Was it possible that a good portion of those who went along with the majority actually believed that the majority was right? When Asch interviewed his subjects afterwards, many of the conformists claimed that they had thought the majority opinion was probably correct. Since all of the others were in agreement, these subjects said, they suspected something was wrong with their own eyesight. Now, is this the case? Did many of the conformists actually believe the majority judgment was probably right?

   An interesting answer to this question is given in a later variation of the Asch experiments. A few years after Asch published the first report of his research, Deutsch and Gerard (1955) repeated the study with some modifications. Most important for our purposes, they established one condition in which subjects could express their estimates anonymously, so that no one else in the group supposedly knew who gave what judgment. This anonymity greatly reduced conformity to the incorrect majority to well below the incidence observed by Asch. Many of the conformists in Asch's initial studies apparently tried to justify their yielding by claiming that they thought the majority was right. They had evidently known the majority was wrong, but went along anyway. Even though the others in the room were strangers whom they might not see again, the yielders publicly conformed to the erroneous majority judgment in order to avoid seeming different.

Types of Conformity.   In the words of some social psychologists (Kiesler & Kiesler, 1969), Asch's subjects exhibited *compliance* in going along with the others without a true (or private) acceptance of the group's opinions. If the stimulus had been much more ambiguous, so that these subjects hadn't been so certain of what was right, many more of them would have acceded to the group's judgments and would have believed that the majority was probably correct. Deutsch and Gerard used two now well-known concepts to refer to these different kinds of social influence. Adapting their terminology, we would say that the compliance shown by Asch's conformists arose through *normative social influence;* these persons conformed to the others' view because they thought that it would be to their benefit. Other people's opinions are truly accepted, however, when there is *informational social influence,* and other's views are taken "as evidence about reality."

Independence Versus Rebelliousness.   So far we've been talking about distinctions in cases of going along with others. Are there any differentiations we should make when an individual doesn't follow the others around her? In a variation of the Asch procedure (Milgram, 1961), Norwegian and French university students were led to think that other students occasionally differed with them in judging the duration of sounds. The Norwegians were more inclined than the French to yield to the wrong opinions of their peers. But what were the French students doing when they didn't conform? Were they truly independent in the sense of being indifferent to the majority judgment, or did they notice the majority view and decide to rebel against it? We can't tell which reaction occurred in this situation. Truly *independent* people know what others expect of them, but don't use these expectations as a guide for their own behavior; they are indifferent to them. *Rebelliousness*—or what some social psychologists call *anticonformity*—exists when the individual reacts against the group's expectations and moves away from the actions or beliefs it advocates (Hollander & Willis, 1967).

Perhaps we can apply this distinction between independence and rebelliousness to the social scene of the mid-1960s to early 1970s. Although some young men and women prided themselves on their independence, they weren't indifferent to society's rules and conventions, but only rebelled against them. They were self-conscious rebels rather than being quietly and self-confidently independent.

Factors Influencing Compliance

Deviation May Be Dangerous. Compliance basically arises because we realize that we are likely to be punished in some way if we don't conform. The other people around us are apt to hurt us, psychologically or at times even physically, if we depart from their norms, their standards defining what is proper behavior. For example, throughout much of the 1960s long-haired youths were often subjected to scorn and even harassment because many people assumed that the youths rejected other social norms and values besides those concerned with appearance and dress. Workers in industry frequently apply sanctions against others in their group who deviate from the work norms they've informally agreed on (Homans, 1961). I recently heard that a young and still eager janitor at my university had been punched, harried, and generally mistreated by other janitors in his section who thought he worked too hard and did too much.

Even if the majority is in no real danger as a result of the nonconformist's failure to adhere to its standards,

such resistance to the group norm can be disturbing. The deviation may cast doubt on the majority's cherished attitudes and values; seeing the "odd man out" cling to his discrepant views, the majority may begin to wonder if their own beliefs are right (Moscovici & Faucheux, 1972). Young married couples with babies who hear their friends insist that they won't have any children may question the wisdom of their own decision to raise a family. Then too, as some writers have pointed out (Kiesler, 1973), people holding the predominant position often regard the norm violator as disturbingly unpredictable. The deviant may be doing something unexpected when she insists on her unusual views, and this unpredictability can be bothersome.

Most of us are aware of these possibilities. We know that we may be punished by being rejected or by not being liked or worse, and we're inclined to comply with others' expectations, especially if these people can give us something we desire.

The Person's Goals. An individual will follow the views of the people around her, even when she doesn't agree with them, if she thinks that compliance will bring her something she wants. On the other hand, if she's basically interested in determining what is the right belief or in defending her own opinion, she may not yield to others' pressure on her to change. She's much more apt to submit if she is concerned with gaining their approval or keeping their goodwill.

Thibaut and Strickland (1956) have demonstrated how a person's goals can affect his reaction to group pressures. Male students at the University of North Carolina were assembled in small groups and required to make complex judgments of physical stimuli. Each subject was induced to become somewhat committed to his initial opinion (by telling him he would have to justify his answers later). Then the experimenter led him to think that the other group members unanimously disagreed with him. At this point the student received written messages, ostensibly from his partners, which put either high, moderate, or low pressure on him to alter his judgment. Cross-cutting this variation, half of the subjects were made to be concerned about the task and about getting the best answer to the problem, while the others were led to be more interested in their social relationships.

The proportion of subjects in each condition who conformed to group pressure is shown in Figure 2. Look first at the responses of those who were primarily interested in getting the best answer to the problem.

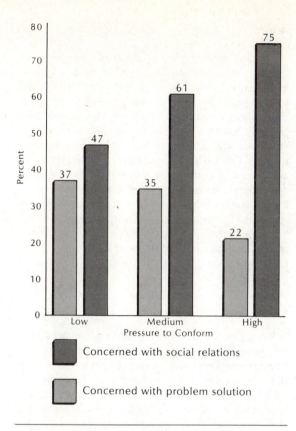

Figure 2. Percentage of Subjects Yielding to a Fictitious Majority Under Different Degrees of Group Pressure.

Adapted from Thibaut and Strickland (1956).

Being somewhat committed to their own ideas, the more pressure the other persons placed on them, the more likely these subjects were to hold on to their initial beliefs. The subjects who were problem oriented evidently experienced reactance . . . and resented the pressure on them to change; they were apt to cling doggedly to their own views. However, the students who were concerned with their social relationships showed a very different pattern. The greater the pressure the other group members imposed on them, the more likely they were to yield and go along with them.

Many Americans appear to be equally concerned with their social relationships. When we meet someone new, we usually want to get along with her or even be liked by her. If we aren't strongly committed to a particular attitudinal position, we may be inclined to accede to her opinions, at least overtly, in order to win her acceptance, especially if we know we'll meet again in the future (Lears, et al., 1972).

Many of us especially desire to be accepted after we find that we've expressed deviant views on some issue. Knowing that people are usually suspicious of those who are "different," we may become anxious at learning we've just voiced a minority opinion. If we have another opportunity to state our beliefs (on another issue) right afterwards, we may take care to go along with someone else in order to avoid being frowned on as an oddball (Darley, Moriarty, Darley, & Berscheid, 1974).

The Others' Attractiveness. While many of us seek the approval of strangers, we are even more intent on keeping the goodwill of those who are attractive to us. We like being with them and would be hurt if they rejected us. The more we care for people, the more apt we are to go along with their views if we know how they want us to act and if they can see what we do (Berkowitz, 1954). Unless we're very sure of these people, we don't want to risk offending them by conspicuously departing from their standards.

There may be personality differences in this regard, however. In connection with the Thibaut and Strickland study, we saw that conformity is heightened when a person is interested in social relationships with others rather than in getting the best answer. Some individuals are preoccupied with having others like them, while other persons mainly want to find out what's right. The former are more inclined to yield to the majority's opinions (McDavid, 1959) and are probably also particularly responsive to the views of people they find attractive. By contrast, people who usually focus on learning the correct solution tend to go along with unattractive people as readily as with those they find attractive (Wilson, 1960).

Social Status and Compliance

Much of what we have been discussing can be translated into power terms. When we learn that other people are important to us because they can either provide us with the rewards we greatly desire or punish us in ways we especially fear (for example, by rejecting us), we come under their control to a considerable extent. They have some power over us. Attractive people have power over us because they control something we want — their approval. An individual's status in a group often determines how much power the other group members have over him and how much influence he can exert over them.

Low Status.   We are in a very precarious position if we have low status in our group, aren't well accepted by the others, or are afraid that we may be completely excluded. Clinging to our precious foothold in the group — maybe even hoping that we can better our position — we walk the straight and narrow, not daring to deviate openly from the group's standards. We may not even like the other group members because they don't seem to care for us, so that we don't truly adopt their point of view (Dittes & Kelley, 1956). However, such surface compliance comes about when the low-status individual is interested in maintaining or even improving her standing in the group. If we've given up on the others, we won't bother to hide our real opinions and will show our noncompliance (Harvey & Consalvi, 1960).

High Status.   The high-status group member is in a much more fortunate position, especially if his rank is unlikely to change. His status gives him the security to express disagreement if he differs from the majority at any time. Norma Feshbach (1967) assembled four-man groups of fraternity members, seeing that two of the members were among the most popular people in the fraternity (high status) and the other two were relatively unpopular (low status). Moreover, the high- and low-status members had the task of deciding which card of the two presented to them on each trial contained the greater number of dots. Even though incorrect estimates would hurt their group and possibly cost their fraternity a $25 prize, the low-status members were generally reluctant to disagree with the high-status members' incorrect judgments. When each person was misled into thinking that his partners were unanimously wrong, the high-status fraternity members were much more willing to deviate from this view than were their less popular counterparts.

There are most likely two interrelated reasons for the high-status fraternity members' feeling that they could safely stand apart from their group. One has to do with differences in power. The highly popular people were undoubtedly aware that their partners needed their approval more than they required these others' goodwill. Then too, groups may actually permit high-status members greater freedom to deviate from the majority position. These persons are often given

"idiosyncrasy credit," as Hollander (1958) put it, and allowed to be oddballs.

I suspect that high-status members who occupy a formally designated position symbolizing the group's ideals, such as the President of the United States or the king of England, don't have an idiosyncrasy credit in matters that are important to the group. Indeed, they probably have less freedom to deviate from approved standards in these areas than the average group member. Edward VIII couldn't marry a divorced woman and remain king; and Princess Margaret was discouraged from marrying a divorced man, even though a British commoner could do so, without suffering ostracism. The group may hold fairly stringent expectations for certain high-status members on important matters at least, and would be quite annoyed if the high-status people violated these expectations (Wahrman, 1970).

Compliance with Authority

In January 1942 a group of top-level civil servants in the Nazi government met in a suburb of Berlin to coordinate efforts to the Final Solution, Hitler's plan to exterminate the Jews of Europe. Adolf Eichmann, head of the Jewish Office in the German Secret Police, or Gestapo, was impressed by the meeting. Here he was chatting and drinking with high governmental officials, despite his humble background.

There was another reason that made the day . . . unforgettable for Eichmann. Although he had been doing his best right along to help with the Final Solution, he had still harbored some doubts about "such a bloody solution through violence," and these doubts had now been dispelled. "Here now . . . the most prominent people had spoken. . . ." Not only Hitler . . . not just the S.S. or the Party, but the elite of the good old Civil Service were vying and fighting with each other for the honor of taking the lead in these bloody matters. "At that moment, I sensed a kind of Pontius Pilate feeling, for I felt free of all guilt." Who was he to judge? (Arendt, 1963, p. 101)

Eichmann was reassured and led to believe that the plan must be all right, since all these important people agreed on it. As he told the court during his trial in Jerusalem in 1961, his conscience was soothed because "he could see no one, no one at all, who actually was against the Final Solution" (quoted in Arendt, 1963, p. 103). Moreover, even if he had any misgivings in the coming months and years, as millions of Jewish men, women, and children were slaughtered, he could always tell himself that "This was the way things were, this was the new law of the land, based on the Fuhrer's order; whatever he did he did, as far as he could see, as a law-abiding citizen. He did his duty, as he told the [Jerusalem] court over and over again; he not only obeyed orders, he also obeyed the law" (Arendt, 1963, p. 120).

"Following orders" is a defense that the German generals were to repeat again and again after World War II: "I wasn't really responsible for the deaths of those thousands of civilians ruthlessly shot by my soldiers; I was a soldier myself, obeying a superior's orders" (see, for example, Shirer, 1960, p. 380). The Germans aren't the only ones who have tried to excuse or explain their actions in such terms. In every country "good soldiers" have said that if they hurt someone in the performance of their duties, they were absolved of blame because they were only following orders or obeying the law. Hannah Arendt, the author of the book on Eichmann just cited, has maintained that this pattern of behavior is now all too prevalent in our society. Western history, she believes, has produced a type of official who, "for the sake of his pension, his life insurance, the security of his wife and children [is] prepared to do literally anything" (Arendt, 1978). He follows his superiors' orders, partly because he believes they have the right to tell him what to do, but also because he believes compliance is to his benefit.

In some ways, such compliance is part of an age-old problem: the relation of the individual to the authority systems of society, or the conflict between personal freedom and the requirements of the social order. Long before the rise of Nazi Germany, the Greek philosopher Plato asked whether a person is obliged to obey an unjust law. Plato's teacher Socrates had thought there were only a few limited alternatives to obedience to the state and had accepted his society's right to condemn him to death.

The Right to Give Orders.   We have now observed that people have sometimes given other persons the right to tell them what to do in some domains of life. In my view, this permission may be an automatic, relatively unthinking, response (Theme I) to persons who carry the symbols of legitimate authority.

The social order is a network of interlocking roles and statuses in which some positions have authority over other roles. Thus, judges can impose fines, parents can legitimately tell children what to do in some situations, teachers can influence their students' activities in the

classroom, and employers can properly direct their workers. These expectations hold for subordinates as well as for those exerting power, so that on at least some occasions, most of us think we ought to obey those having recognized authority over us.

Research on Reactions to Legitimate Authority.   A well-known research program conducted by Stanley Milgram (1963), now of the City University of New York, demonstrates how many United States citizens have learned to follow the dictates of those in authority.

Milgram's male subjects, recruited by newspaper ads, had a much more diverse background than is customary in psychological experiments. They were blue-collar workers, salesmen, businessmen, and professionals between 20 and 50 years of age. Each man thought he was a "teacher" in a learning experiment who had the job of punishing another subject (actually the investigator's accomplice) each time that person made a mistake on the learning task. The teacher was to administer electric shocks as the punishment, increasing the shock intensity regularly as the mistakes continued. The "mistakes" were prearranged so that each subject was required to raise the shock intensity 30 times, supposedly in 15-volt steps, going from 15 to 450 volts, with the last electric switch bearing the sign, "Danger, Severe Shock." If the subject seemed reluctant to proceed with this assignment and was slow to go on to the next shock switch, the watching experimenter instructed him to continue, even though the confederate learner in the next room occasionally pounded the wall and cried out in pain. No one was really shocked, but almost every subject thought he was hurting the person next door (although he had been reassured that there would be "no permanent tissue damage").

All of the subjects complied with the experimenter's orders until they reached the 300-volt level (switch 20), the point at which the learner next door began pounding the wall. Either then or at the next switch, 22 percent refused to continue despite the experimenter's insistence. A few more went a little bit further and then refused to go on. But only a minority resisted the authority of the experimenter; 65 percent obeyed the instructions and steadily increased the punishment they inflicted up to the maximum, and supposedly dangerous, level. They believed they were hurting someone badly, yet they did what they were told.

Other experiments have since determined how our willingness to inflict pain in response to the dictates of authority is affected by various situational conditions.

For example, Milgram (1965) found that the investigator's commands became less effective as the victim's suffering was made clearer. While only 35 percent of the subjects refused to follow the experimenter's orders at some point in the procedure when the victim was next door, about 60 percent defied the authority's instructions before they reached the maximum intensity if the victim was in the same room, and 70 percent refused to go all the way if they had to forcibly hold the victim's hand on the shockplate as the shocks were administered. Evidently, it became more difficult for the subjects to hurt someone in compliance with orders when they could readily see the consequences of their acquiescence (also see Tilker, 1970). They couldn't keep punishing the victim severely unless they had a strong respect for the authority or, possibly, a low regard for the victim.

Another factor is also at work here. Notice that subjects showed the greatest resistance to authority when they had to hold the victim down. These men couldn't pass the buck; they couldn't tell themselves that they were passively following orders because they actively contributed to the injury done to the other person. So they had to take some of the blame if they continued. Not wanting to feel personal responsibility for the pain they inflicted, they defied their instructions. Two other experiments — one in West Germany (Mantell, 1971) and the other in the United States (Tilker, 1970) — have shown that many people are reluctant to hurt others if they have to take personal responsibility for their actions. Thus, in the West German study (Mantell, 1971), only 7 percent of the "teachers" gave the maximum shocks when they were told it was up to them to decide whether and how much the "learner" was to be punished. By contrast, in the baseline condition (exactly the same as Milgram's original condition) 85 percent of the subjects administered the maximum punishment.

We can easily translate the research on obedience to authority into terms applicable to our own country. Suppose you were an American soldier in Vietnam in the late 1960s. On patrol in possibly dangerous territory, your platoon enters a small village. Everyone is on edge, even scared. Then your commanding officer orders the platoon to shoot any Vietnamese on sight. What would you do? Would you obey orders?

Unthinking Reactions to Legitimate Authority. Authorities are obeyed to a very substantial extent because we have learned to give them the right to tell us what to do in certain situations. Much of the time we don't have to be forced to comply. Indeed, coercion is unlikely to hold an organization together for long. If the group is to be stable, its members must submit voluntarily to those in command (Weber, 1947). As the eminent sociologist Robert Nisbet (1970) observed, "For most persons, most of the time, in most places, the authorities they obey are perceived as legitimate authorities. Obedience is willed, or at least not checked, in light of this legitimacy" (p. 140). As one testimonial to the power of legitimacy, the West German version of Milgram's study (Mantell, 1971) demonstrated a drop in subjects' compliance with the experimenter's instructions when his legitimacy was undermined. The subjects accorded him less right to control their actions when they didn't think his job was to tell them what to do.

Since the authority's legitimacy is so important any comprehensive analysis of compliance requires a greater understanding of the sources of legitimacy than we now possess. Why are some people empowered with the right to influence others, and — an especially intriguing question nowadays — why do previously accepted authorities sometimes come under attack so that their areas of influence shrink?

Probably more than any other factor, *collective approval* — the agreement of the group members — legitimates the patterns of dominance and subordination in the group (Blau, 1964). In our society collective approval usually becomes explicit when someone is elected to the authority role. What we often see, then, is that election justifies the adoption of power. We may strongly oppose a politician's candidacy in an election campaign, but if she is elected we usually accept her right to exert the authority of the office. By the same token, when a person in a small work group starts telling the other group members what to do, these people are more apt to feel that he has a right to prescribe behavior for them if he has been elected to the supervisory position than if he has simply usurped this job. And in the former case, group members are also more inclined to adopt the leader's prescriptions as their own beliefs (French & Raven, 1959; Raven & French, 1958); the election has legitimated his influence attempts.

The great sociological theorist Max Weber (1947) has also pointed out that legitimacy is frequently derived from rational considerations. Modern societies tend to regard authorities as legitimate if they operate in a reasonable manner. Thus, the authorities exercise their control on the basis of their knowledge rather than because they have been born into the right family or group. Evan and Zelditch (1961) used this conception in a laboratory analog of a bureaucratic organization. In this experiment college students worked under the guidance of an appointed supervisor, who they were led to believe knew either more, the same, or less about the job than they did. Supervisors should be more expert than their subordinates, and their appointment isn't reasonable (or legitimate) if they know less. In keeping with Weber's view, the students were more disobedient to the supervisor's commands, particularly in hard-to-see ways, if his knowledge was supposedly inferior to theirs. His position was apparently not totally legitimate if it had an illogical basis.

Some Concluding Thoughts.   Authority is not a simple matter, and there is no easy way to eliminate the wrongs committed in authority's name. As long as society continues, some people will violate the trust we place in them or abuse the power given them or hurt other persons if they think their job requires this. But we can't do away with all authority. Even the leading theorists of the anarchist movement thought that some authority was necessary and indispensable (Nisbet, 1970, p. 141). Every social order must have a regulatory system (hopefully one that is humane and just), an agreed-upon conception of what is legitimate authority, and a widespread willingness to comply with the rules laid down in the appropriate, "proper" manner — or else brute force will control how people interact. Maybe, as some writers have suggested and as the founders of the American Republic recognized, it is best to have institutionalized checks and balances in which countervailing authorities press against each other. "Whether authority is in fact limited or total depends upon norms of freedom and authority . . . and also . . . upon the degree to which that authority is checked, limited, challenged, and countervailed by other authorities in the social order" (Nisbet, 1970, p. 135).

TRUE ACCEPTANCE OF OTHERS' STANDARDS

Social Consensus and Informational Influence

Authoritative Opinions.   Most of us not only comply with the dictates of authority, but frequently think that the attitudes or practices advocated by government officials are correct. Throughout the Johnson and Nixon administrations, millions of Americans approved of the Vietnam war because this was the President's policy. Since the government had undertaken to fight this war, many citizens believed that it must be the right thing to

do. Similarly, when English university students were told that laws defined certain behaviors as legal (or illegal), their judgments of the moral propriety of these actions were correspondingly affected to a slight but significant degree (Berkowitz & Walker, 1967). Actions certified by legal authority gained in moral rightness, whereas conduct condemned by the laws was regarded more morally improper than it had been before.

Consensus and the Social Definition of Reality.   There are a number of reasons why legitimate authority can validate particular opinions or actions. One possibility has to do with the social consensus implicitly supporting the authority. We're generally aware that duly constituted government ultimately rests upon the approval of the governed. Thus, a law is implicitly right or correct to the extent that it is backed by a widespread social consensus. The obvious defiance of the no-liquor laws of the Prohibition era probably further weakened their effectiveness; people who once thought Prohibition was a good idea no longer backed this policy when they saw that many of their peers disapproved of it.

Adolf Eichmann's belief that the Final Solution was a proper course of action is also a testimony to the power of social consensus. His doubts about "such a bloody solution through violence" were largely obliterated by the agreement of the top-level officials meeting to implement the plan. Not one person disagreed with the proposal, he said, so he thought it must be all right.

In all of these instances the group consensus defined the validity, the correctness, perhaps even the "truth," of the issue. We can look at this in terms of Theme III and say that the agreement among the people in the situation affected any one person's interpretation of the ambiguous stimulation (that is, the nature of the information received). As some social psychologists have stated, the consensus provided a social definition of reality. Social agreement creates reality in many different walks of life and even, to some extent, in the Asch experiment and its later variations. Earlier in this chapter I mentioned the variation of Asch's experiment in which the subjects were permitted to express their views anonymously (Deutsch & Gerard, 1955). Although this procedure reduced the amount of compliance to the erroneous majority opinion, as I reported, a small number of subjects still yielded to the majority view. These few were apparently so lacking in self-confidence that they doubted their own senses in the face of others' unanimity. Questioning themselves, they thought the others might be right since everyone else had the same judgment.

The Sherif Experiment.   A classic experiment carried out by Muzafer Sherif (1936) in the mid-1930s illustrates how agreement among the members of a group can define reality. In contrast to the Asch study, where the subject could easily see what was right, the situation was much more ambiguous in Sherif's experiment.

In this investigation, the subject sat in a completely darkened room, along with two other college students, looking at a point of light waving back and forth in the distance. The walls were not visible, nor were there any other physical frames of reference for subjects to use in their task of judging how far the light moved as it followed its erratic course in the darkness. Because the stimulus was so ambiguous, the three people didn't "see" it in exactly the same way at first. After a while, however, their estimates converged. They developed a common perception, a shared way of viewing the light. In the next phase of the experiment the subject was alone in the darkened room, and he again had to say how far the light moved. As he stared at the faint glow, he wondered if the light was acting in the same way as before. Yes it was, he decided. It appeared to be moving just as much as it had in the group session.

Unknown to the subject, however, the light actually was physically stationary at all times and only *seemed* to be moving, an illusion called the "autokinetic effect." The ambiguous stimulus was defined in a certain way by the group, and the subjects then carried the group's definition with them when they were alone. This earlier experience in the group taught them how to view the stimulus.

Social Support May Break Consensus.   We can also see the effects of consensus when we look at what happens when the group's unanimity is broken. In Asch's original research the subjects were less likely to yield to the erroneous majority when there was another dissident in the room than when they were alone against the group. Destroying the group's unanimity increased the student's resistance to the pressures of the majority. There are several reasons for this finding. For example, the naive subject may have been less afraid of being ostracized or laughed at if someone else also refused to go along with the group. In addition, the other deviant (who gave his judgments before subject 6 did) might have weakened the group's credibility—the majority opinion seemed less right—and also heightened the individual's confidence in his own belief.

An experiment by Allen and Levine (1969) at the University of Wisconsin shows how the group's credibility is lessened when the members are no longer unanimous.

Using a modification of the Asch procedure devised by Crutchfield, the psychologists placed five people in separate booths. Each subject was told he would be the fifth person in the group to express his answer to the presented problem and that signal lights in his cubicle would let him know how each of the others had responded. . . . Unknown to the subjects, these lights were actually controlled by the experimenter, who gave each student prearranged information about his partners' views.

The first three persons answering were always in agreement, and on the 18 critical trials they expressed highly unusual judgments (as determined by prior testing with college students) that were different from the subjects' own opinions. The fourth member's answers varied with the experimental condition. In the social support condition his responses were in complete accord with the subjects' judgments (which had been ascertained previously), while in the extreme dissent condition his answers were even more incorrect than those stated by the erroneous majority. Finally, in the no-support condition the fourth person always went along with the majority. Thus, there were two conditions in which the group consensus was lowered; but only in the first of these treatments, the social support group, did the deviant agree with the subject's own views.

The subjects were given three types of problems — visual (as in the original Asch experiment), information, and opinion. Allen and Levine found that the weakened group consensus in both the social support and extreme dissent conditions significantly reduced the level of conformity to the incorrect majority on the visual and information items, and substantially decreased the yielding to the majority on the opinion items (see Figure 3). However, on the opinion items there was less conformity in the social support than in the extreme dissent treatment.

As Allen and Levine (1969) suggest, most people probably expect complete agreement on factual matters such as the visual and information problems. Should the consensus be less complete, the group is regarded as a defective judge of reality and can be disregarded. In other words, on objective problems it doesn't matter whether others agree with us or if they have another judgment; as long as the group is not

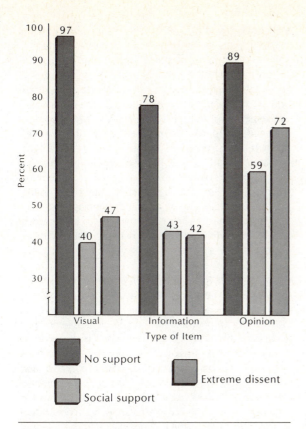

Figure 3.   Mean Conformity to Majority as a Function of Type of Item and Type of Support.

Adapted from V. L. Allen and J. M. Levine, "Consensus and conformity," *Journal of Experimental Psychology,* 1969, Vol. 5, pp. 389–399. Copyright 1969 by the American Psychological Association. Reprinted by permission.

unanimous, its credibility is suspect. On more subjective issues, such as opinions, we're not surprised if there's less than perfect agreement. In this case we usually think that the greater the consensus, the greater the probability that the others may be right. But if someone sides with us on such ambiguous issues, we're more confident of our own judgments (Allen & Levine, 1971). Social agreement defines reality primarily in subjective matters for which we know there is no single, unquestioned truth.

Another study indicates that the time at which its consensus is broken can be very important in determining the amount of power the majority will have over the individual. According to Morris and Miller (1975), we are less likely to go along with a majority holding a very

different view if someone else expresses a judgment close to our own ideas before we hear the people in the majority. Then, when it's our turn to offer an opinion, we're more likely to hold on to our own judgment. The other person's initial statement corroborates our own first thoughts, strengthening our confidence in our own views, so that we can withstand the majority's divergent judgment. More strongly convinced of the rightness of our initial opinion because of the support provided by the other person, we don't believe the majority has correctly defined what is real and true. . . .

Influence of the Minority on the Majority

Until now we've focused on the effects of the group on the individual. Two French social psychologists, Moscovici and Faucheux (1972), have pointed out, however, that such a one-sided emphasis neglects the considerable impact that a few determined persons sometimes have on the larger group. Every now and then a small band has triumphed over the many, convincing a once scornful majority to accept ideas it had previously rejected. History has been made by such innovators as Copernicus in astronomy, Luther in religion, and Freud in psychology. If social psychology is to say anything about social innovations, it must consider the minority's influence as well as the majority's power.

Moscovici and his associates (Moscovici & Faucheux, 1972; Moscovici & Nemeth, 1974) have argued that a persistent few can change the prevailing group norms by maintaining their own deviant views consistently, coherently, and forcefully. The minority's continuous and determined pressure raises doubts where certainty existed before. The others begin to wonder if the majority consensus does indeed define what is true or correct, and they open their minds to the ideas they repudiated earlier. Thus, in keeping with our present information-processing theme (Theme III), a determined minority can influence the majority by shaping the majority's understanding. Other investigators have obtained some evidence consistent with this reasoning (see Nemeth & Wachtler, 1974).

Reasonably Self-confident.   According to this later research, dedicated dissidents are particularly likely to be convincing when they express their minority views with confidence and with reason. Let's suppose that Daphne Wardle is involved in an argument with the other women in her dormitory and finds herself holding a minority position. Where most of the residents favor one policy, Daphne and one or two others prefer a very different proposal. How can Daphne convince the majority? Well, an experiment by a Swiss psychologist (Mugny, 1975) tells us she should appear firm, but not dogmatic. In this study a group member's minority opinion was less likely to be accepted by the others if he seemed to be rigidly dogmatic rather than reasonably firm. The people in the majority were more inclined to go along with the deviant when he acknowledged that their views were reasonable while arguing for his position. . . . If we want to convince other persons, we're often better off if we don't flatly repudiate their beliefs in a head-on confrontation. But the minority has to seem self-confident; individuals who appear very sure of themselves are especially likely to be influential (Spitzer & Davis, 1978). Charlan Nemeth and her colleagues (Nemeth, Swedlund, & Kanki, 1974; Nemeth & Wachtler, 1974) have demonstrated that dissidents can waver occasionally and still be convincing, as long as their variations don't create an impression of uncertainty. Thus, Daphne Wardle doesn't have to be rigidly consistent if she states her views with confidence.

As I said before, this self-assurance makes the people in the majority question the correctness of their own beliefs and causes them to wonder if the minority isn't right after all. But the minority's persuasiveness is also helped by anything else that adds credence to its position, such as someone's past history of success and even the size of the minority.

Minority Size and the Perceived Correctness of the Minority. Consider the matter of the minority's size. Would Daphne Wardle be better off in her efforts to convince the majority in her dormitory if she had only a few people on her side or if she had lots of adherents?

Nemeth pointed out that we can expect two different things to happen as the minority gets larger (Nemeth, Wachtler, & Endicott, 1977). For one thing, the majority may assume that the dissidents are less self-confident as their numbers grow. Think of this in attribution theory terms. If a single person holds out as the lone dissenter against the pressure of the majority, we tend to assume this individual must be quite self-confident. The majority thus attributes the deviation to an internal factor, the person's self-assurance. However, the discounting principle may come into play as the minority gets larger. . . . We tend to rule out internal factors as a possible cause of someone's behavior if we can reasonably attribute the action to external circum-

stances (Kelley, 1972, 1973). This means observers will be less likely to believe that any one deviant is self-confident, the more dissidents there are. The majority assigns the minority's stance to an external factor (the support the dissidents provide each other) and not to internal self-confidence. On the other hand, as Nemeth also noted, increased numbers may also enhance the perceived correctness of the minority position, as when social consensus defines reality in ambiguous matters. The more people there are who share a given opinion, up to some maximum number, the more likely it is that we will think they are probably right (Asch, 1958). Putting all of these findings together, we would expect an increasing minority to be regarded as (1) somewhat less self-confident, but (2) more correct.

Nemeth et al. (1977) examined the effect of the minority's size upon its persuasiveness as a function of the two components of perceived self-confidence and correctness. Undergraduate women were assembled in groups of six naive subjects together with a certain number of the investigators' confederates. Some groups had only one confederate, other groups had two, and some other groups had either three or four confederates. All of the people in the group had to express judgments about the colors of stimuli that were shown to them, but where the naive subjects in the majority were quite sure these stimuli were blue, the confederates adopted the minority position and persisted in labeling the stimuli "blue-green."

The subjects' ratings of the minority at the end of the session are summarized in Table 2. As you can see, the larger the size of the minority, the more correct (competent), but less self-confident, they were thought to be. In this study at least, the minority's perceived correctness was generally more important than their self-assurance in determining their persuasiveness. In general, even though the majority rejected the dissident viewpoint most of the time (the stimulus was much too clear-cut), the naive subjects were somewhat more accepting of the minority judgment, the more people there were in the minority. Despite this finding, other evidence indicates that both the perceived self-confidence and the perceived correctness of the minority contributed to the minority's influence. When the researchers formed a composite index based on the subjects' ratings of both of these qualities, this combination was a better predictor of the minority's influence than either characteristic alone.

Table 2. Reactions of Majority Members to Those in Minority

	Minority Size			
	1	2	3	4
Number of times minority judgment was adopted*	1.35	1.31	2.25†	1.88
Perceived confidence of minority‡	5.67	5.22	5.29	5.13
Perceived competence of minority‡	3.78	4.28	4.42	4.52

*In the control condition containing no confederates, no subject ever gave the response persistently voiced by the confederates.
    †This mean is significantly greater than the mean in the 1-confederate condition.
    ‡There were significant linear trends for these two measures so that we can say there was a regular decrease in the minority's assumed confidence and a regular increase in their perceived competence.
    Data from Nemeth et al. (1977).

If we can generalize from this particular experiment, Daphne would be well advised to seek additional adherents to her cause. The other women might think Daphne and her supporters weren't especially self-confident, but the dissident arguments might appear more valid as the minority grew.

Breaking the Majority's Consensus. Just as the dissidents' consensus can affect the onlookers' estimate of how correct their own opinions are, so can agreement among the majority influence its members' confidence in their own viewpoint. This point has implications for how the minority may go about convincing the majority. What happens, we may ask, if some people desert the majority cause and take up the minority opinion? Kiesler and Pallak's study (1975) indicates that those in the minority should "chip away" at a susceptible member of the majority in order to get her over to their side. The people who remain in the majority aren't going to like the "switcher," according to Kiesler and Pallak, and may even regard her as a renegade, but the switch tends to make the majority lose confidence. "Maybe there's a good reason why that person joined the other side," they think. As their doubts mount, they can be more easily persuaded by the persistent minority.

My impression is that this type of process was at work in the United States during the Vietnam war. As the war continued, quite a few people who initially supported the United States government's policy in Asia began to side with the antiwar protestors. The former supporters' desertion of the majority cause undoubtedly contributed to the majority's growing doubts about the wisdom of continuing the struggle.

SELF-PERCEPTION IN COMPLIANCE

Low Balling the Customer

Joe Arbuthnot received a substantial amount of money as a birthday present and decided to buy a new car. Determined to be a smart customer, he told a salesperson at one of the largest automobile dealerships in the city that he would only buy a new car from that firm if he received a good deal on his present vehicle as a trade-in. The salesperson assured Joe he would get the best trade-in value in town, and Joe chose the new model he wanted. But when Joe sat down to sign the necessary papers for the purchase, the salesperson told Joe that the manager would have to approve the amount offered for Joe's old car. In a little while the salesperson returned and said the manager had rejected the trade-in price. The manager was supposed to have said that the firm wouldn't make enough money on the sale if he paid that much for Joe's old car. If Joe wanted the new automobile he had selected, he would have to spend several hundred dollars more than he had thought just a few minutes earlier.

Joe's experience wasn't unique. He was the victim of "low balling," a reprehensible but widespread practice used by many salespeople, especially in the automobile industry (*Consumer Reports,* May 1974, p. 368). The idea is to get the customer committed to the purchase on the basis of a very favorable deal and then eliminate some of the favorable features after the customer is "hooked." Joe had made his decision after being told he would have to pay only a certain amount of money for the new car. However, once Joe "bit" and was psychologically committed to the purchase, the salesperson informed him that he would have to spend more. This manipulative technique is frequently effective.

I think we can see why low balling works if we look at it in connection . . . with the self in social behavior. A customer who agrees to make the purchase does two things: (1) He *activates his intentions.* . . . It's not enough just to expect or intend to do something. We also have to think *actively* of carrying out that behavior if the intention is to be translated into action (Leventhal, Singer, & Jones, 1965). Thus, the customer's decision to buy the product could start him moving psychologically toward that goal. (2) As Cialdini, Cacioppo, Bassett, and Miller (1978) have suggested, the decision makes the customer feel *personally committed* to the purchase. From our present point of view, we can say his failure to carry through might then reflect negatively on his self-image. ``I agreed to do this and I should be consistent,'' he may tell himself.

Cialdini et al. (1978) have reported three experiments which testify to the effectiveness of the low-balling technique. These investigations were carried out in naturalistic and artificial settings. We'll discuss their last study, which provides a good example of low balling. Male and female undergraduates serving in the study to gain extra class credit were told that the research required them to take one of two different personality tests, and they were provided with a brief description of the tests. In two conditions (both analogs of the low-balling procedure) the students were informed that they would receive twice as much credit if they worked on one test (call it test A) rather than on the other. And one of these groups was also told the choice was up to the subjects. Needless to say, when the people in this group made their selection right after this, they overwhelmingly preferred test A. The subjects in the second condition had no choice and were instructed to work on test A. After the students in these two conditions had rated their impressions of the personality tests, the experimenter supposedly noticed that he had made a mistake and said he wouldn't be able to award the extra credit for test A. Then, whether or not they had been told the choice was up to them, all of the people in these conditions were instructed that they were free to work on either of the two tests. In a third, control condition the experimenter didn't say anything about extra credit for test A. Here too, the subjects were asked which test they wanted to take after they read the description of the tests.

The findings indicated the students typically wanted to carry through with the commitment they had voluntarily undertaken, even when the extra inducement used to win this commitment was withdrawn. Sixty-one percent of the subjects in the choice condition still agreed to do test A, as compared to only 42 percent of those in the no-choice group and 31 percent in the control condition.

Most of the students in the choice group evidently wanted to be consistent. They had freely agreed to carry out the given activity (they thought), and they went through with it. Their self-image would suffer if they changed their mind. Of course, many more subjects would have refused to honor this commitment if they believed they had been tricked into making their decision. In real life, people can stop such manipulation if they realize the salesperson's initial offer may simply be a trick to get them hooked on the line before the attractive inducement is withdrawn.

The Foot in the Door

Low balling is quite similar to another procedure used by salespeople and others. In this second technique the would-be influencer makes a small and fairly reasonable request in order to get a foot in the door. When the unknowing individual complies, the influencer then brings the real major request forward.

Two well-known field experiments by Jonathan Freedman and Scott Fraser (1966) illustrate how effective this procedure can be. In one of these investigations the experimenters started out with a small request. They asked housewives to install a small sign on their lawns urging motorists to drive carefully. Several weeks later, when other interviewers contacted the women and asked them to put up a monstrous sign with the same message, three-quarters of them complied. By contrast, fewer than one-fifth of another group of women who hadn't received the first request agreed to install the large, ugly sign. The researchers had increased their persuasiveness by getting subjects to do them a small favor (the foot in the door) and then asking for a much more substantial favor. This phenomenon isn't limited to cases in which the first and second requests are very similar, such as in putting up signs. Other findings indicate that the tendency to comply can generalize to quite different situations. Freedman and Fraser first asked another group of housewives to sign a petition in favor of keeping their state beautiful. Even though this initial request was different in both form (petition) and topic (state beauty), almost half of the women later agreed to put up the big, ugly safe-driving sign — as against less than one-fifth of the control group.

The foot-in-the-door technique can also be understood in terms of . . . the role of self-concept in social behavior. Freedman and Fraser suggest that when the women complied with the first request they thought of themselves as people who acted responsibly. They were people who did good things such as supporting highway safety or state beautification. When the interviewers came along with the second request, they essentially reminded the women of this self-conception and thus motivated them to live up to this image of themselves.

The issues need not be as socially desirable as those used by Freedman and Fraser for this technique to work. As long as we can induce people to think of themselves in a certain way, we theoretically should be able to have them try to live up to this self-conception. After Snyder and Cunningham (1975) led some of their subjects to view themselves as people who agreed to reasonable requests, these subjects were inclined to go along with even larger requests of the same nature. The researchers telephoned a sample of Minneapolis residents, soliciting their participation in a telephone survey for a public service organization. Some were asked if they would answer 8 questions in this survey (small request), whereas others were requested to answer a long series of 50 questions. Two days later all of these persons were called back and a moderate favor was solicited for a different organization: Would they answer 30 questions? In comparison with control subjects, for whom no request was made, those who had complied to the previous small request were much more likely to agree (52 percent saying yes). The persons who had been asked to do the much more substantial favor, on the other hand, were much less inclined to comply (22 percent acquiescing). As you can see, as a result of going along with the first small request, the former subjects apparently thought of themselves as

the kind of people who would do a reasonable favor for others; and they later acted in keeping with this self-concept, even though the second requester was supposedly someone else.

The findings also tell us something else. The initial request has to be small enough so that the first favor is granted, but not so small that the right kind of self-concept isn't established. If we ask people to do something trivial, they may well agree without viewing themselves as good persons; the action is just too easy. Seligman, Bush, and Kirsch (1976) showed this in a study similar to that of Snyder and Cunningham. Bush and Kirsch's telephone callers first asked for favors of various magnitudes, ranging from very easy to more difficult. Those who complied with the easiest requests weren't inclined to grant the second, more substantial favor two days later. When people grant the first favor, the compliance has to be significant enough that they think of themselves as having done something special.

This research reveals how people can be manipulated through their self-concepts. We often urge those we know to be true to themselves, as if they will become more independent if they live up to their image of themselves. The paradox is that a would-be influencer can alter people's self-concepts (at least temporarily and to some degree), so that people are exploited as they try to adhere to their self-concepts. The persuasion operates through people's desire to be true to themselves.

REFERENCES

Allen, V. L., and Levine, J. M. Consensus and conformity. *Journal of Experimental Psychology,* 1969, *5,* 389–399.

Allen, V. L., and Levine, J. M. Social support and conformity. The role of independent assessment of reality. *Journal of Experimental Social Psychology,* 1971, *7,* 48–58.

Arendt, H. *Eichmann in Jerusalem.* New York: Viking, 1963.

Asch, S. E. Effects of group pressures upon modification and distortion of judgments. In E. E. Maccoby, T. M. Newcomb, and E. L. Hartley (Eds.), *Readings in social psychology.* New York: Holt, Rinehart and Winston, 1958, 174–183.

Bandura, A. Vicarious processes: A case of no-trial learning. In L. Berkowitz (Ed.), *Advances in experimental social psychology, Vol. 2.* New York: Academic Press, 1965.

Bandura, A. *Principles of behavior modification.* New York: Holt, Rinehart and Winston, 1969.

Bandura, A. *Theories of modeling.* New York: Atherton Press, 1970.

Bandura, A., Blanchard, B., and Ritter, B. Relative efficacy of desensitization and modeling approaches for inducing behavioral, affective, and attitudinal changes. *Journal of Personality and Social Psychology,* 1969, *13,* 173–199.

Bandura, A., Grusec, J. E., and Menlove, F. L. Observational learning as a function of symbolization and incentive set. *Child Development,* 1966, *37,* 499-506.

Bandura, A., Ross, D., and Ross, S. A. A comparative test of the status envy, social power, and secondary reinforcement theories of identificatory learning. *Journal of Abnormal Social Psychology,* 1963, *67,* 527-534.

Berger, S. M. Conditioning through vicarious instigation. *Psychological Review,* 1962, *69,* 450-466.

Berkowitz, L. Group standards, cohesiveness and productivity. *Human Relations,* 1954, *7,* 509-519.

Berkowitz, L. Some determinants of impulsive aggression: The role of mediated associations with reinforcements for aggression. *Psychological Review,* 1974, *81,* 165-176.

Berkowitz, L., and Geen, R. G. Stimulus qualities of the target of aggression: A further study. *Journal of Personality and Social Psychology,* 1967, *5,* 364-368.

Berkowitz, L., Parke, R. D., Leyens, J-P., and West, S. G. Reactions of juvenile delinquents to "justified" and "less justified" movie violence. *Journal of Research in Crime and Delinquency,* 1974, *11,* 16-24.

Berkowitz, L., and Rawlings, E. Effects of film violence on inhibitions against subsequent aggression. *Journal of Abnormal and Social Psychology,* 1963, *66,* 405-412.

Berkowitz, L., and Walker, N. Laws and moral judgments. *Sociometry,* 1967, *30,* 410-422.

Blau, P. M. *Exchange and power in social life.* New York: Wiley, 1964.

Bryan, J. H. Children's reactions to helpers: Their money isn't where their mouths are. In J. Macaulay and L. Berkowitz (Eds.), *Altruism and helping behavior.* New York: Academic Press, 1970, 61-73.

Bussey, K., and Perry, D. G. Sharing reinforcement contingencies with a model: A social-learning analysis of similarity effects in imitation research. *Journal of Personality and Social Psychology,* 1976, *34,* 1168-1176.

Cialdini, R. B., Cacioppo, J. T., Bassett, R., and Miller, J. A. Low-ball procedure for producing compliance: Commitment then cost. *Journal of Personality and Social Psychology,* 1978, *36,* 463-476.

Craig, K. D., and Neidermeyer, H. Autonomic correlates of pain thresholds influenced by social modeling. *Journal of Personality and Social Psychology,* 1974, *29,* 246-252.

Craig, K. D., and Prkachin, K. M. Social modeling influences on sensory decision theory and psychophysiological indexes of pain. *Journal of Personality and Social Psychology,* 1978, *36,* 805-815.

Darley, J. M., Moriarty, T., Darley, S., and Berscheid, E. Increased conformity to a fellow deviant as a function of prior deviation. *Journal of Experimental Social Psychology,* 1974, *10,* 211-223.

Deutsch, M., and Gerard, H. B. A study of normative and informational social influences upon individual judgment. *Journal of Abnormal and Social Psychology,* 1955, *51,* 629-636.

Dittes, J. E., and Kelley, H. H. Effects of different conditions of acceptance upon conformity to group norms. *Journal of Abnormal and Social Psychology,* 1956, *53,* 100-107.

Evan, W., and Zelditch, M., Jr. A laboratory experiment on bureaucratic authority. *American Sociological Review,* 1961, *26,* 883-893.

Feshbach, N. D. Nonconformity to experimentally induced group norms of high-status versus low-status members. *Journal of Personality and Social Psychology,* 1967, *6,* 55-63.

Freedman, J. L., and Fraser, S. C. Compliance without pressure: The foot-in-the-door technique. *Journal of Personality and Social Psychology,* 1966, *4,* 195-202.

French, J. R. P., Jr., and Raven, B. The bases of social power. In D. Cartwright (Ed.), *Studies in social power.* Ann Arbor, Mich.: Institute for Social Research, 1959.

Grusec, J. E. Power and the internalization of self-denial. *Child Development,* 1971, *42,* 93-105.

Harvey, O. J., and Consalvi, C. Status and conformity to pressures in informal groups. *Journal of Abnormal and Social Psychology,* 1960, *60,* 182-187.

Hollander, E. P. Conformity, status and idiosyncracy credit. *Psychological Review,* 1958, *65,* 117-127.

Hollander, E. P., and Willis, R. H. Some current issues in the psychology of conformity and nonconformity. *Psychological Bulletin,* 1967, *68,* 62-76.

Homans, G. C. *Social behavior: Its elementary forms.* New York: Harcourt, Brace Jovanovich, 1961.

Hoyt, J. L. Effect of media violence "justification" on aggression. *Journal of Broadcasting,* 1970, *16,* 455-464.

Jeffery, R. W. The influence of symbolic and motor rehearsal on observational learning. *Journal of Research in Personality,* 1976, *10,* 116-127.

Kelley, H. H. *Causal schemata and the attribution process.* Morristown, N.J.: General Learning Press, 1972.

Kelley, H. H. The process of causal attribution. *American Psychologist,* 1973, *28,* 107-128.

Kiesler, C. A., and Kiesler, S. B. *Conformity.* Reading, Mass.: Addison-Wesley, 1969.

Kiesler, C. A., and Pallak, M. S. Minority influence: The effect of majority reactionaries and defectors, and minority and majority compromisers, upon majority opinion and attraction. *European Journal of Social Psychology,* 1975, *5,* 237-256.

Kiesler, S. B. Preference for predictability or unpredictability as a mediator of reactions to norm violations. *Journal of Personality and Social Psychology,* 1973, *27,* 354-359.

Lefkowitz, M., Blake, R. R., and Mouton, J. S. Status factors in pedestrian violation of traffic signals. *Journal of Abnormal and Social Psychology,* 1955, *51,* 704-706.

Leventhal, H., Singer, R., and Jones, S. Effects of fear and specificity of recommendations upon attitudes and behavior. *Journal of Personality and Social Psychology,* 1965, *2,* 20-29.

Mann, J., Berkowitz, L., Sidman, J., Starr, S., and West, S. Satiation of the transient stimulating effects of erotic films. *Journal of Personality and Social Psychology,* 1974, *30,* 729-735.

Mann, J., Sidman, J., and Starr, S. Effects of erotic films on the sexual behavior of married couples. In *Technical report of the Commission on Obscenity and Pornography, Vol. 8.* Washington, D.C.: U.S. Government Printing Office, 1971, 170-254.

Mantell, D. M. The potential for violence in Germany. *Journal of Social Issues,* 1971, *27,* 101-112.

McDavid, J. W. Personality and situational determinants of conformity. *Journal of Abnormal and Social Psychology,* 1959, *58,* 241-246.

Meyer, T. P. Effects of viewing justified and unjustified real film violence on aggressive behavior. *Journal of Personality and Social Psychology,* 1972, *23,* 21-29.

Milgram, S. Nationality and conformity. *Scientific American,* 1961, *205,* 45-51.

Milgram, S. Behavioral study of obedience. *Journal of Abnormal and Social Psychology,* 1963, *67,* 371-378.

Milgram, S. Some conditions of obedience and disobedience to authority. *Human Relations,* 1965, *18,* 57-75.

Mischel, W., and Grusec, J. Determinants of the rehearsal and transmission of natural and aversive behaviors. *Journal of Personality and Social Psychology,* 1966, *3,* 197-203.

Morris, W. N., and Miller, R. S. The effects of consensus-breaking and consensus-preempting partners on reduction of conformity. *Journal of Experimental Social Psychology,* 1975, *11,* 215-223.

Moscovici, S., and Faucheux, C. Social influence, conformity bias, and the study of active minorities. In L. Berkowitz (Ed.), *Advances in experimental social psychology, Vol. 6.* New York: Academic Press, 1972, 149-202.

Moscovici, S., and Nemeth, C. Social influence. II. Minority influence. In C. Nemeth (Ed.), *Social psychology: Classic and contemporary integrations.* Chicago: Rand McNally, 1974.

Mugny, G. Negotiations, image of the other and the process of minority influence. *European Journal of Social Psychology,* 1975, *5,* 209-228.

Nemeth, C., Swedlund, M., and Kanki, B. Patterning of the minority's responses and their influence on the majority. *European Journal of Social Psychology,* 1974, *4,* 53-64.

Nemeth, C., and Wachtler, J. Creating the perceptions of consistency and confidence: A necessary condition for minority influence. *Sociometry,* 1974, *37,* 529-540.

Nemeth, C., Wachtler, J., and Endicott, J. Increasing the size of the minority: Some gains and some losses. *European Journal of Social Psychology,* 1977, *7*(1), 15-27.

Nisbet, R. A. *The social bond.* New York: Knopf, 1970.

Phillips, D. P. The influence of suggestion on suicide: Substantive and theoretical implications of the Werther effect. *American Sociological Review,* 1974, *39,* 340-354.

Phillips, D. P. Airplane accident fatalities increase after newspaper stories about murder and suicide. *Science,* 1978, *201,* 748–750.

Raven, B. H., and French, J. R. P., Jr. Legitimate power, coercive power, and observability in social influence. *Sociometry,* 1958, *21,* 83–97.

Seligman, C., Bush, M., and Kirsch, K. Relationship between compliance in the foot-in-the-door paradigm and size of the first request. *Journal of Personality and Social Psychology,* 1976, *33,* 517–520.

Sherif, M. *The psychology of social norms.* New York: Harper & Row, 1936.

Shirer, W. L. *The rise and fall of the third reich.* New York: Simon and Schuster, 1960.

Snyder, M., and Cunningham, M. R. To comply or not comply: Testing the self-perception explanation of the ''foot-in-the-door'' phenomenon. *Journal of Personality and Social Psychology,* 1975, *31,* 64–67.

Spitzer, C. E., and Davis, J. H. Mutual social influence in dynamic groups. *Social Psychology,* 1978, *41,* 24–33.

Tarde, G. *Penal philosophy.* Boston: Little, Brown, 1912.

Thibaut, J. W., and Strickland, L. H. Psychological set and social conformity. *Journal of Personality,* 1956, *25,* 115–129.

Tilker, H. A. Socially responsible behavior as a function of observer responsibility and victim feedback. *Journal of Personality and Social Psychology,* 1970, *14,* 95–100.

Tolman, C. W. The role of the companion in social facilitation of animal behavior. In E. C. Simmel, R. A. Hoppe, and G. A. Milton (Eds.), *Social facilitation and imitative behavior.* Boston: Allyn and Bacon, 1968, 33–54.

Wahrman, R. High status, deviance and sanctions. *Sociometry,* 1970, *33,* 485–504.

Weber, M. *The theory of social and economic organization.* New York: Oxford University Press, 1947.

Wilson, R. S. Personality patterns, source attractiveness, and conformity. *Journal of Personality,* 1960, *28,* 186–199.

B.

Socializing Individuals into Organizational Roles

17. Organizational Socialization and the Profession of Management

Edgar H. Schein

INTRODUCTION

Ladies and gentlemen, colleagues and friends. There are few times in one's professional life when one has an opportunity, indeed something of a mandate, to pull together one's thoughts about an area of study and to communicate these to others.

I can define my topic of concern best by reviewing very briefly the kinds of issues upon which I have focused my research over the last several years. In one way or another I have been trying to understand what happens to an individual when he enters and accepts membership in an organization. My interest was originally kindled by studies of the civilian and military prisoners of the Communists during the Korean War. I thought I could discern parallels between the kind of indoctrination to which these prisoners were subjected, and some of the indoctrination which goes on in American corporations when college and business school graduates first go to work for them. My research efforts came to be devoted to learning what sorts of attitudes and values students had when they left school, and what happened to these attitudes and values in the first few years of work. To this end I followed several panels of graduates of the Sloan School into their early career.

When these studies were well under way, it suddenly became quite apparent to me that if I wanted to study the impact of an organization on the attitudes and values of its members, I might as well start closer to home. We have a school through which we put some 200 men per year—undergraduates, regular Master's students, Sloan Fellows, and Senior Executives. Studies of our own students and faculty revealed that not only

Edgar H. Schein, "Organizational Socialization and the Profession of Management." *Industrial Management Review,* Winter 1968, © 1968 by the Industrial Management Review Association; all rights reserved.

did the student groups differ from each other in various attitude areas, but that they also differed from the faculty.

For example, if one takes a scale built up of items which deal with the relations of government and business, one finds that the Senior Executives in our program are consistently against any form of government intervention, the Sloans are not as extreme, the Master's students are roughly in the middle, and the faculty are in favor of such intervention. A similar lineup of attitudes can be found with respect to labor-management relations, and with respect to cynicism about how one gets ahead in industry. In case you did not guess, the Senior Executives are least cynical and the faculty are most cynical.

We also found that student attitudes change in many areas during school, and that they change away from business attitudes toward the faculty position. However, a recent study of Sloan Fellows, conducted after their graduation, indicated that most of the changes toward the faculty had reversed themselves to a considerable degree within one year, a finding which is not unfamiliar to us in studies of training programs of all sorts.

The different positions of different groups at different stages of their managerial career and the observed changes during school clearly indicate that attitudes and values change several times during the managerial career. It is the process which brings about these changes which I would like to focus on today — a process which the sociologists would call ''occupational socialization,'' but which I would prefer to call ''organizational socialization'' in order to keep our focus clearly on the setting in which the process occurs.

Organizational socialization is the process of ''learning the ropes,'' the process of being indoctrinated and trained, the process of being taught what is important in an organization or some subunit thereof. This process occurs in school. It occurs again, and perhaps most dramatically, when the graduate enters an organization on his first job. It occurs again when he switches within the organization from one department to another, or from one rank level to another. It occurs all over again if he leaves one organization and enters another. And it occurs again when he goes back to school, and again when he returns to the organization after school.

Indeed, the process is so ubiquitous and we go through it so often during our total career, that it is all too easy to overlook it. Yet it is a process which can make or break a career, and which can make or break organizational systems of manpower planning. The speed and effectiveness of socialization determine

employee loyalty, commitment, productivity, and turnover. The basic stability and effectiveness of organizations therefore depends upon their ability to socialize new members.

Let us see whether we can bring the process of socialization to life by describing how it occurs. I hope to show you the power of this process, particularly as it occurs within industrial organizations. Having done this, I would like to explore a major dilemma which I see at the interface between organizations and graduate management schools. Schools socialize their students toward a concept of a profession, organizations socialize their new members to be effective members. Do the two processes of socialization supplement each other or conflict? If they conflict, what can we do about it in organizations and in the schools?

SOME BASIC ELEMENTS OF ORGANIZATIONAL SOCIALIZATION

The term socialization has a fairly clear meaning in sociology, but it has been a difficult one to assimilate in the behavioral sciences and in management. To many of my colleagues it implies unnecessary jargon, and to many of my business acquaintances it implies the teaching of socialism — a kiss of death for the concept right there. Yet the concept is most useful because it focuses clearly on the interaction between a stable social system and the new members who enter it. The concept refers to the process by which a new member learns the value system, the norms, and the required behavior patterns of the society, organization, or group which he is entering. It does not include all learning. It included only the learning of those values, norms, and behavior patterns which, from the organization's point of view or group's point of view, it is necessary for any new member to learn. This is defined as the price of membership.

What are such values, norms, and behavior patterns all about? Usually they involve:

1. The basic *goals* of the organization.
2. The preferred *means* by which these goals should be attained.
3. The basic *responsibilities* of the member in the role which is being granted to him by the organization.
4. The *behavior patterns* which are required for effective performance in the role.
5. A set of rules or principles which pertain to the *maintenance of the identity and integrity* of the organization.

The new member must learn not to drive Chevrolets if he is working for Ford, not to criticize the organization in public, not to wear the wrong kind of clothes or be seen in the wrong kinds of places. If the organization is a school, beyond learning the content of what is taught, the student must accept the value of education, he must try to learn without cheating, he must accept the authority of the faculty and behave appropriately to the student role. He must not be rude in the classroom or openly disrespectful to the professor.

By what processes does the novice learn the required values and norms? The answer to this question depends in part upon the degree of prior socialization. If the novice has correctly anticipated the norms of the organization he is joining, the socialization process merely involves a reaffirmation of these norms through various communication channels, the personal example of key people in the organization, and direct instructions from supervisors, trainers, and informal coaches.

If, however, the novice comes to the organization with values and behavior patterns which are in varying degrees out of line with those expected by the organization, then the socialization process first involves a destructive or unfreezing phase. This phase serves the function of detaching the person from his former values, of proving to him that his present self is worthless from the point of view of the organization and that he must redefine himself in terms of the new roles which he is to be granted.

The extremes of this process can be seen in initiation rites or novitiates for religious orders. When the novice enters his training period, his old self is symbolically destroyed by loss of clothing, name, often his hair, titles, and other self-defining equipment. These are replaced with uniforms, new names and titles, and other self-defining equipment consonant with the new role he is being trained for.

It may be comforting to think of activities like this as being characteristic only of primitive tribes of total institutions like military basic training camps, academies, and religious orders. But even a little examination of areas closer to home will reveal the same processes both in our graduate schools and in the business organizations to which our graduates go.

Perhaps the commonest version of the process in school is the imposition of a tight schedule, of an impossibly heavy reading program, and of the assignment of problems which are likely to be too difficult for the student to solve. Whether these techniques are deliberate or not, they serve effectively to remind the student that he is not as smart or capable as he may

have thought he was, and therefore, that there are still things to be learned. As our Sloan Fellows tell us every year, the first summer in the program pretty well destroys many aspects of their self-image. Homework in statistics appears to enjoy a unique status comparable to having one's head shaved and clothes burned.

Studies of medical schools and our own observations of the Sloan program suggest that the work overload on the students leads to the development of a peer culture, a kind of banding together of the students as a defense against the threatening faculty and as a problem-solving device to develop norms of what and how to study. If the group solutions which are developed support the organizational norms, the peer group becomes an effective instrument of socialization. However, from the school's point of view, there is the risk that peer group norms will set up counter-socializing forces and sow the seeds of sabotage, rebellion, or revolution. The positive gains of a supportive peer group generally make it worthwhile to run the risks of rebellion, however, which usually motivates the organization to encourage or actually facilitate peer group formation.

Many of our Sloan Fellow alumni tell us that one of the most powerful features of the Sloan program is the fact that a group of some 40 men share the same fate of being put through a very tough educational regimen. The peer group ties formed during the year have proven to be one of the most durable end-results of the educational program and , of course, are one of the key supports to the retention of some of the values and attitudes learned in school. The power of this kind of socializing force can be appreciated best by pondering a further statement which many alumni have made. They stated that prior to the program they identified themselves primarily with their company. Following the program they identified themselves primarily with the other Sloan Fellows, and such identification has lasted, as far as we can tell, for the rest of their career.

Let me next illustrate the industrial counterpart of these processes. Many of my panel members, when interviewed about the first six months in their new jobs, told stories of what we finally labeled as ''upending experiences.'' Upending experiences are deliberately planned or accidentally created circumstances which dramatically and unequivocally upset or disconfirm some of the major assumptions which the new man holds about himself, his company, or his job.

One class of such experiences is to receive assignments which are so easy or so trivial that they carry the clear message that the new man is not worthy of being given anything important to do. Another class of such experiences is at the other extreme — assignments which are so difficult that failure is a certainty, thus proving unequivocally to the new man that he may not be as smart as he thought he was. Giving work which is clearly for practice only, asking for reports which are then unread or not acted upon, protracted periods of training during which the person observes others work, all have the same upending effect.

The most vivid example came from an engineering company where a supervisor had a conscious and deliberate strategy for dealing with what he considered to be unwarranted arrogance on the part of engineers whom they hired. He asked each new man to examine and diagnose a particular complex circuit, which happened to violate a number of textbook principles but actually worked very well. The new man would usually announce with confidence, even after an invitation to doublecheck, that the circuit could not possibly work. At this point the manager would demonstrate the circuit, tell the new man that they had been selling it for several years without customer complaint, and demand that the new man figure out why it did work. None of the men so far tested were able to do it, but all of them were thoroughly chastened and came to the manager anxious to learn where their knowledge was inadequate and needed supplementing. According to this manager, it was much easier from this point on to establish a good give-and-take relationship with his new man.

It should be noted that the success of such socializing techniques depends upon two factors which are not always under the control of the organization. The first factor is the initial motivation of the entrant to join the organization. If his motivation is high, as in the case of a fraternity pledge, he will tolerate all kinds of uncomfortable socialization experiences, even to extremes of hell week. If his motivation for membership is low, he may well decide to leave the organization rather than tolerate uncomfortable initiation rites. If he leaves, the socialization process has obviously failed.

The second factor is the degree to which the organization can hold the new member captive during the period of socialization. His motivation is obviously one element here, but one finds organizations using other forces as well. In the case of basic training there are legal forces to remain. In the case of many schools, one must pay one's tuition in advance, in other words, invest one's self materially so that leaving the system becomes expensive. In the case of religious orders, one must make strong initial psychological commitments in the form of vows and the severing of relationships

outside the religious order. The situation is defined as one in which one will lose face or be humiliated if one leaves the organization.

In the case of business organizations the pressures are more subtle but nevertheless identifiable. New members are encouraged to get financially committed by joining pension plans, stock option plans, and/or house purchasing plans which would mean material loss if the person decided to leave. Even more subtle is the reminder by the boss that it takes a year or so to learn any new business; therefore, if you leave, you will have to start all over again. Why not suffer it out with the hope that things will look more rosy once the initiation period is over.

Several of my panel members told me at the end of one year at work that they were quite dissatisfied, but were not sure they should leave because they had invested a year of learning in that company. Usually their boss encouraged them to think about staying. Whether or not such pressures will work depends, of course, on the labor market and other factors not under the control of the organization.

Let me summarize thus far. Organizations socialize their new members by creating a series of events which serve the function of undoing old values so that the person will be prepared to learn the new values. This process of undoing or unfreezing is often unpleasant and therefore requires either strong motivation to endure it or strong organizational forces to make the person endure it. The formation of a peer group of novices is often a solution to the problem of defense against the powerful organization, and, at the same time, can strongly enhance the socialization process if peer group norms support organizational norms.

Let us look next at the positive side of the socialization process. Given some readiness to learn, how does the novice acquire his new learning? The answer is that he acquires it from multiple sources — the official literature of the organization; the example set by key models in the organization; the instructions given to him directly by his trainer, coach, or boss; the example of peers who have been in the organization longer and thus serve as big brothers; the rewards and punishments which result from his own efforts at problem solving and experimenting with new values and new behavior.

The instructions and guidelines given by senior members of the organization are probably one of the most potent sources. I can illustrate this point best by recalling several incidents from my own socialization into the Sloan School back in 1956. I came here at the invitation of Doug McGregor from a research job. I had no prior teaching experience or knowledge of organizational or managerial matters. Contrary to my expectations, I was told by Doug that knowledge of organizational psychology and management was not important, but that some interest in learning about these matters was.

The first socializing incident occurred in an initial interview with Elting Morison, who was then on our faculty. He said in a completely blunt manner that if I knew what I wanted to do and could go ahead on my own, the Sloan School would be a great place to be. If I wasn't sure and would look to others for guidance, not to bother to come.

The second incident occurred in a conversation with our then Dean, Penn Brooks, a few weeks before the opening of the semester. We were discussing what and how I might teach. Penn said to me that he basically wanted each of his faculty members to find his own approach to management education. I could do whatever I wanted—so long as I did not imitate our sister school up the river. Case discussion leaders need not apply, was the clear message.

The third incident (you see I was a slow learner) occurred a few days later when I was planning my subject in social psychology for our Master's students. I was quite nervous about it and unsure of how to decide what to include in the subject. I went to Doug and innocently asked him to lend me outlines of previous versions of the subject, which had been taught by Alex Bavelas, or at least to give me some advice on what to include and exclude. Doug was very nice and very patient, but also quite firm in his refusal to give me either outlines or advice. He thought there was really no need to rely on history, and expressed confidence that I could probably make up my own mind. I suffered that term but learned a good deal about the value system of the Sloan School, as well as how to organize a subject. I was, in fact, so well socialized by these early experiences that nowadays no one can get me to coordinate anything with anybody else.

Similar kinds of lessons can be learned during the course of training programs, in orientation sessions, and through company literature. But the more subtle kinds of values which the organization holds, which indeed may not even be well understood by the senior people, are often communicated through peers operating as helpful big brothers. They can communicate the subtleties of how the boss wants things done, how higher management feels about things, the kinds of things which are considered heroic in the organization, the kinds of things which are taboo.

Of course, sometimes the values of the immediate group into which a new person is hired are partially out of line with the value system of the organization as a whole. If this is the case, the new person will learn the immediate group's values much more quickly than those of the total organization, often to the chagrin of the higher levels of management. This is best exemplified at the level of hourly workers where fellow employees will have much more socializing power than the boss.

An interesting managerial example of this conflict was provided by one recent graduate who was hired into a group whose purpose was to develop cost reduction systems for a large manufacturing operation. His colleagues on the job, however, showed him how to pad his expense account whenever they traveled together. The end result of this kind of conflict was to accept neither the cost reduction values of the company nor the cost inflation values of the peer group. The man left the company in disgust to start up some business of his own.

One of the important functions of organizational socialization is to build commitment and loyalty to the organization. How is this accomplished? One mechanism is to invest much effort and time in the new member and thereby build up expectations of being repaid by loyalty, hard work, and rapid learning. Another mechanism is to get the new member to make a series of small behavioral commitments which can only be justified by him through the acceptance and incorporation of company values. He then becomes his own agent of socialization. Both mechanisms involve the subtle manipulation of guilt.

To illustrate the first mechanism, one of our graduates went to a public relations firm which made it clear to him that he had sufficient knowledge and skill to advance, but that his values and attitudes would have to be evaluated for a couple of years before he would be fully accepted. During the first several months he was frequently invited to join high ranking members of the organization at their luncheon meetings in order to learn more about how they thought about things. He was so flattered by the amount of time they spent on him, that he worked extra hard to learn their values and became highly committed to the organization. He said that he would have felt guilty at the thought of not learning or of leaving the company. Sending people to expensive training programs, giving them extra perquisites, indeed the whole philosophy of paternalism, is built on the assumption that if you invest in the employee he will repay the company with loyalty and hard work. He would feel guilty if he did not.

The second mechanism, that of getting behavioral commitments, was most beautifully illustrated in Communist techniques of coercive persuasion. The Communists made tremendous efforts to elicit a public confession from a prisoner. One of the key functions of such a public confession, even if the prisoner knew he was making a false confession, was that it committed him publicly. Once he made this commitment, he found himself under strong internal and external pressure to justify why he had confessed. For many people it proved easier to justify the confession by coming to believe in their own crimes than to have to face the fact that they were too weak to withstand the captor's pressure.

In organizations, a similar effect can be achieved by promoting a rebellious person into a position of responsibility. The same values which the new member may have criticized and jeered at from his position at the bottom of the hierarchy suddenly look different when he has subordinates of his own whose commitment he must obtain.

Many of my panel members had very strong moral and ethical standards when they first went to work, and these stood up quite well during their first year at work even in the face of less ethical practices by their peers and superiors. But they reported with considerable shock that some of the practices they had condemned in their bosses were quickly adopted by them once they had themselves been promoted and faced the pressures of the new position. As one man put it very poignantly — "my ethical standards changed so gradually over the first five years of work that I hardly noticed it, but it was a great shock to suddenly realize what my feelings had been five years ago and how much they had changed."

Another version of obtaining commitment is to gain the new member's acceptance of very general ideals like "one must work for the good of the company," or "one must meet the competition." Whenever any counter-organizational behavior occurs one can then point out that the ideal is being violated. The engineer who does not come to work on time is reminded that his behavior indicates lack of concern for the good of the company. The employee who wears the wrong kind of clothes, lives in the wrong neighborhood, or associates with the wrong people can be reminded that he is hurting the company image.

One of my panel members on a product research assignment discovered that an additive which was approved by the Food and Drug Administration might in fact be harmful to consumers. He was strongly encouraged to forget about it. His boss told him that it was the F.D.A.'s problem. If the company worried about things like that it might force prices up and thus make it tough to meet the competition.

Many of the upending experiences which new members of organizations endure are justified to them by the unarguable ideal that they should learn how the company really works before expecting a position of real responsibility. Once the new man accepts this ideal, it serves to justify all kinds of training and quantities of menial work which others who have been around longer are unwilling to do themselves. This practice is known as "learning the business from the ground up," or "I had to do it when I first joined the company, now it's someone else's turn." There are clear elements of hazing involved not too different from those associated with fraternity initiations and other rites of passage.

The final mechanism to be noted in a socialization process is the transition to full-fledged member. The purpose of such transitional events is to help the new member incorporate his new values, attitudes, and norms into his identity so that they become part of him, not merely something to which he pays lip-service. Initiation rites which involve severe tests of the novice serve to prove to him that he is capable of fulfilling the new role — that he now is a man, no longer merely a boy.

Organizations usually signal this transition by giving the new man some important responsibility or a position of power which, if mishandled or misused, could genuinely hurt the organization. With this transition often come titles, symbols of status, extra rights or prerogatives, sharing of confidential information, or other things which in one way or another indicate that the new member has earned the trust of the organization. Although such events may not always be visible to the outside observer, they are felt strongly by the new member. He knows when he has finally "been accepted," and feels it when he becomes "identified with the company."

So much for examples of the process of socialization. Let us now look at some of the dilemmas and conflicts which arise within it.

FAILURES OF SOCIALIZATION— NONCONFORMITY AND OVERCONFORMITY

Most organizations attach differing amounts of importance to different norms and values. Some are pivotal. Any member of a business organization who does not believe in the value of getting a job done will not survive long. Other pivotal values in most business organizations might be belief in a reasonable profit, belief in the free enterprise system and competition, belief in a hierarchy of authority as a good way to get things done, and so on.

Other values or norms are what may be called relevant. These are norms which it is not absolutely necessary to accept as the price of membership, but which are considered desirable and good to accept. Many of these norms pertain to standards of dress and decorum, not being publicly disloyal to the company, living in the right neighborhood and belonging to the right political party and clubs. In some organizations some of these norms may be pivotal. Organizations vary in this regard. You all know the stereotype of IBM as a company that requires the wearing of white shirts and hats. In some parts of IBM such values are indeed pivotal; in other parts they are only relevant, and in some parts they are quite peripheral. The point is that not all norms to which the new member is exposed are equally important for the organization.

The socialization process operates across the whole range of norms, but the amount of reward and punishment for compliance or noncompliance will vary with the importance of the norm. This variation allows the new member some degrees of freedom in terms of how far to conform and allows the organization some degrees of freedom in how much conformity to demand. The new man can accept none of the values, he can accept only the pivotal values, but carefully remain independent on all those areas not seen as pivotal, or he can accept the whole range of values and norms. He can tune in so completely on what he sees to be the way others are handling themselves that he becomes a carbon-copy and sometimes a caricature of them.

These basic responses to socialization can be labeled as follows:

Type 1. Rebellion: Rejection of all values and norms.
Type 2. Creative individualism: Acceptance only of pivotal values and norms; rejection of all others.
Type 3. Conformity: Acceptance of all values and norms.

Most analyses of conformity deal only with the type 1 and 3 cases, failing to note that both can be viewed as socialization failures. The rebellious individual either is expelled from the organization or turns his energies toward defeating its goals. The conforming individual curbs his creativity and thereby moves the organization toward a sterile form of bureaucracy. The trick for most organizations is to create the type 2 response — acceptance of pivotal values and norms, but rejection of all others, a response which I would like to call "creative individualism."

To remain creatively individualistic in an organization is particularly difficult because of the constant re-socialization pressures which come with promotion or lateral transfer. Every time the employee learns part of the value system of the particular group to which he is assigned, he may be laying the groundwork for conflict when he is transferred. The engineer has difficulty accepting the values of the sales department, the staff man has difficulty accepting the high pressure ways of the production department, and the line manager has difficulties accepting the service and helping ethic of a staff group. With each transfer, the forces are great toward either conforming or rebelling. It is difficult to keep focused on what is pivotal and retain one's basic individualism.

PROFESSIONAL SOCIALIZATION AND ORGANIZATIONAL SOCIALIZATION

The issue of how to maintain individualism in the face of organizational socialization pressures brings us to the final and most problematical area of concern. In the traditional professions like medicine, law, and teaching, individualism is supported by a set of professional attitudes which serve to immunize the person against some of the forces of the organization. The questions now to be considered are (1) Is management a profession? (2) If so, do professional attitudes develop in managers? and (3) If so, do these support or conflict with organizational norms and values?

Professionalism can be defined by a number of characteristics:

1. Professional decisions are made by means of general principles, theories, or propositions which are independent of the particular case under consideration. For management this would mean that there are certain principles of how to handle people, money, information, etc., independent of any particular company. The fact that we can and do teach general subjects in these areas would support management's claim as a profession.

2. Professional decisions imply knowledge in a specific area in which the person is expert, not a generalized

body of wisdom. The professional is an expert only in his profession, not an expert at everything. He has to license to be a ''wise man.'' Does management fit by this criterion? I will let you decide.

3. The professional's relations with his clients are objective and independent of particular sentiments about them. The doctor or lawyer makes his decisions independent of his liking or disliking of his patients or clients. On this criterion we have a real difficulty since, in the first place, it is very difficult to specify an appropriate single client for a manager, and, in the second place, it is not at all clear that decisions can or should be made independent of sentiments. What is objectively best for the stockholder may conflict with what is best for the enterprise, which, in turn may conflict with what is best for the customer.

4. A professional achieves his status by accomplishment, not by inherent qualities such as birth order, his relationship to people in power, his race, religion, or color. Industry is increasingly moving toward an acceptance of this principle for managerial selection, but in practice the process of organizational socialization may undermine it by rewarding the conformist and rejecting the individualist whose professional orientation may make him look disloyal to the organization.

5. A professional's decisions are assumed to be on behalf of the client and to be independent of self-interest. Clearly this principle is at best equivocal in manager-customer relations, though again one senses that industry is moving closer to accepting the idea.

6. The professional typically relates to a voluntary association of fellow professionals, and accepts only the authority of these colleagues as a sanction on his own behavior. The manager is least like the professional in this regard, in that he is expected to accept a principle of hierarchical authority. The dilemma is best illustrated by the previous example which I gave of our Sloan Fellow alumni who, after the program, related themselves more to other Sloans than to their company hierarchy. By this criterion they had become truly professionalized.

7. A professional has sometimes been called someone who knows better what is good for his client than the client. The professional's expertness puts the client into a very vulnerable position. This vulnerability has necessitated the development of strong professional codes and ethics which serve to protect the client.

Such codes are enforced through the colleague peer group. One sees relatively few attempts to develop codes of ethics for managers or systems of enforcement.

On several bases, then, management is a profession, but on several others it is clearly not yet a profession.

This long description of what is a profession was motivated by the need to make a very crucial point. I believe that management education, particularly in a graduate school like the Sloan School, is increasingly attempting to train professionals, and in this process is socializing the students to a set of professional values which are, in fact, in severe and direct conflict with typical organizational values.

For example, I see us teaching general principles in the behavioral sciences, economics, and quantitative methods. Our applied subjects like marketing, operations management, and finance are also taught as bodies of knowledge governed by general principles which are applicable to a wide variety of situations. Our students are given very broad concepts which apply to the corporation as a whole, and are taught to see the relationship between the corporation, the community, and the society. They are taught to value the long-range health and survival of economic institutions, not the short-range profit of a particular company. They come to appreciate the necessary interrelationships between government, labor, and management rather than to define these as mutually warring camps. They are taught to look at organizations from the perspective of high ranking management, to solve the basic problems of the enterprise rather than the day-to-day practical problems of staff or line management. Finally, they are taught an ethic of pure rationality and emotional neutrality — analyze the problem and make the decisions independent of feelings about people, the product, the company, or the community. All of these are essentially professional values.

Organizations value many of the same things, in principle. But what is valued in principle by the higher ranking and senior people in the organization often is neither supported by their own behavior, nor even valued lower down in the organization. In fact, the value system which the graduates encounter on their first job is in many respects diametrically opposed to the professional values taught in school. The graduate is immediately expected to develop loyalty and concern for a particular company with all of its particular idiosyncrasies. He is expected to recognize the limitation of his general knowledge and to develop the sort of *ad hoc* wisdom which the school has taught him to avoid. He is expected to look to his boss for evaluation rather than to some group of colleagues outside the company.

Whereas the professional training tells him that knowledge is power, the graduate now must learn that knowledge by itself is nothing. It is the ability to sell knowledge to other people which is power. Only by being able to sell an application of knowledge to a highly specific, local situation, can the graduate obtain respect for what he knows. Where his education has taught the graduate principles of how to manage others and to take the corporate point of view, his organizational socialization tries to teach him how to be a good subordinate, how to be influenced, and how to sell ideas from a position of low power.

On the one hand, the organization via its recruiters and senior people tells the graduate that it is counting on him to bring fresh points of view and new techniques to bear on its problems. On the other hand, the man's first boss and peers try to socialize him into their traditional mold.

A man is hired to introduce linear programming into a production department, but once he is there he is told to lay off because if he succeeds he will make the old supervisors and engineers look bad. Another man is hired for his financial analysis skills but is not permitted access to data worth analyzing because the company does not trust him to keep them confidential. A third man is hired into a large group responsible for developing cost reduction programs in a large defense industry, and is told to ignore the fact that the group is overstaffed, inefficient, and willing to pad expense accounts. A fourth man, hired for his energy and capability, put it this way as an explanation of why he quit to go into private consulting: "They were quite pleased with work that required only two hours per day; I wasn't."

In my panel of 1962 graduates, 73 percent have already left their first job and many are on their third or fourth. In the class of 1963, the percentage is 67, and in the class of 1964, the percentage is 50. Apparently, most of our graduates are unwilling to be socialized into organizations whose values are incompatible with the ones we teach. Yet these organizations are precisely the ones who may need creative individualists most.

What seems to happen in the early stages of the managerial career is either a kind of postponement of professional socialization while organizational socializa-

tion takes precedence, or a rebelling by the graduate against organizational socialization. The young man who submits must first learn to be a good apprentice, a good staff man, a good junior analyst, and perhaps a good low level administrator. He must prove his loyalty to the company by accepting this career path with good graces, before he is trusted enough to be given a position of power. If he has not lost his education by then, he can begin to apply some general principles when he achieves such a position of power.

The businessman wants the school to provide both the professional education and the humility which would make organizational socialization smoother. He is not aware that teaching management concepts of the future precludes justifying the practices of today. Some professional schools clearly do set out to train for the needs of the profession as it is designed today. The Sloan School appears to me to reject this concept. Instead we have a faculty which is looking at the professional manager of five, ten, or twenty years from now, and is training its graduates in management techniques which we believe are coming in the future.

Symptomatic of this approach is the fact that in many of our subjects we are highly critical of the management practices of today, and highly committed to reeducating those managers like Sloan Fellows and Senior Executives who come back to study at M.I.T. We get across in a dozen different ways the belief that most organizations of today are obsolete, conservative, constipated, and ignorant of their own problems. Furthermore, I believe that this point of view is what society and the business community demands of a good professional school.

It would be no solution to abandon our own vision of the manager of the future, and I doubt that those of you in the audience from business and industry would really want us to do this. What you probably want is to have your cake and eat it too — you want us to teach our students the management concepts of tomorrow, and you want us to teach them how to put these concepts into deep freeze while they learn the business of today. Then when they have proven themselves worthy of advancement and have achieved a position of some influence, they should magically resurrect their education and put it to work.

Unfortunately, socialization processes are usually too powerful to permit that solution. If you succeed in socializing your young graduates to your organizations, you will probably also succeed in proving to them that their education was pretty worthless and might as well be put on a permanent rather than temporary shelf. We have resarch evidence that many well-educated graduates do learn to be complacent and to play the organizational game. It is not all clear whether they later ever resurrect their educational arsenal.

WHAT IS TO BE DONE ABOUT THIS SITUATION?

I think we need to accept, at the outset, the reality of organizational socialization phenomena. As my colleague, Leo Moore, so aptly put it, organizations like to put their fingerprints on people, and they have every right to do so. By the same token, graduate schools of business have a right and an obligation to pursue professional socialization to the best of their ability. We must find a way to ameliorate the conflicts at the interface, without, however, concluding that either schools or organizations are to blame and should stop what they are doing.

What the Schools Can Do

The schools, our school in particular, can do several concrete things which would help the situation. First, we can insert into our total curriculum more apprenticeship experience which would bring the realities of organizational life home to the student earlier. But such apprenticeship experiences will not become educational unless we combine them with a second idea, that of providing a practicum on how to change organizations. Such a practicum should draw on each of the course specialties and should be specifically designed to teach a student how to translate his professional knowledge into viable action programs at whatever level of the organization he is working.

Ten years ago we would not have known how to do this. Today there is no excuse for not doing it. Whether the field is operations research, sophisticated quantitative marketing, industrial dynamics, organizational psychology or whatever, we must give our students experience in trying to implement their new ideas, and we must teach them how to make the implementation effective. In effect, we must teach our students to become change-agents, whatever their disciplinary specialty turns out to be. We must teach them how to influence their organizations from low positions of power without sacrificing their professional values in the process. We must teach them how to remain creative

individualists in the face of strong organizational socialization pressures.

Combined with these two things, we need to do a third thing. We need to become more involved in the student's efforts at career planning, and we need to coordinate our activities more closely with the company recruiters and the university placement officers. At the present I suspect that most of our faculty is quite indifferent to the student's struggles to find the right kind of a job. I suspect that this indifference leaves the door wide open to faulty selection on the part of the student, which can only lead, in the end, to an undermining of the education into which we pour so much effort. We need to work harder to insure that our graduates get jobs in which they can further the values and methods we inculcate.

What the Companies Can Do

Companies can do at least two things. First, they can make a genuine effort to become aware of and understand their own organizational socialization practices. I fear very few higher level executives know what is going on at the bottom of their organization where all the high priced talent they call for is actually employed. At the same time, I suspect that it is their own value system which ultimately determines the socialization activities which occur throughout all segments of the organization. Greater awareness and understanding of these practices should make possible more rational choices as to which practices to encourage and which to deemphasize. The focus should be on pivotal values only, not on peripheral or irrelevant ones.

Second, companies must come to appreciate the delicate problems which exist both for the graduate and for his first boss in the early years of the career when socialization pressures are at the maximum. If more companies appreciated the nature of this dilemma they would recognize the necessity of giving some training to the men who will be the first bosses of the graduates.

I have argued for such training for many years, but still find that most company effort goes into training the graduate rather than his boss. Yet it is the boss who really has the power to create the climate which will lead to rebellion, conformity, or creative individualism. If the companies care whether their new hires use one or the other of these adaptation strategies, they had better start looking at the behavior of the first boss and training him for what the company wants and hopes for. Too many bosses concentrate on teaching too many peripheral values and thus undermine the possibilities for creative individualism and organizational improvement.

CONCLUSION

The essence of management is to understand the forces acting in a situation and to gain control over them. It is high time that some of our managerial knowledge and skill be focused on those forces in the organizational environment which derive from the fact that organizations are social systems who do socialize their new members. If we do not learn to analyze and control the forces of organizational socialization, we are abdicating one of our primary managerial responsibilities. Let us not shrink away from a little bit of social engineering and management in this most important area of the human side of the enterprise.

REFERENCES

Blau, P. M., and Scott, R. W. *Formal Organizations.* San Francisco: Chandler, 1962.

Goffman, E. *Asylums.* Garden City, N.Y.: Doubleday Anchor, 1961.

Schein, E. H. "Management Development as a Process of Influence," *Industrial Management Review* II (1961): 59-77.

_____. "Forces Which Undermine Management Development," *California Management Review* V, Summer 1963.

_____. "How to Break in the College Graduate," *Harvard Business Review* XLII, 1964.

_____. "Training in Industry: Education or Indoctrination," *Industrial Medicine and Surgery* XXXIII, 1964.

_____. *Organizational Psychology.* Englewood Cliffs, N.J.: Prentice-Hall, 1965.

_____. "The Problem of Moral Education for the Business Manager." *Industrial Management Review* VIII (1966): 3-14.

_____. "Attitude Change During Management Education," *Administrative Science Quarterly* XI (1967): 601-28.

_____. "The Wall of Misunderstanding on the First Job," *Journal of College Placement,* February/March 1967.

_____; Schneier, Inge; and Barker, C. H. *Coercive Persuasion.* New York: W. W. Norton, 1961.

18.   Commitment and the Control of Organizational Behavior and Belief

Gerald R. Salancik

Most articles on organizational commitment extol the virtues of commitment. In them, you will find that the committed employee is the happy employee, the success of the organization is a matter of its members sacrificing their time and effort, and commitment to the values of the organization gives meaning to a person's life. In them commitment enhances productivity, assures quality in the final product, and guarantees the flow of adaptive innovation. In them, you will find, in short, a lot of nonsense mixed with a lot of common sense. But from them your understanding of commitment may not be enhanced. . . .

The view of commitment we present in this paper is one which is grounded in behavior and the implications of behavior in one situation for behavior in another. The view derives primarily from the model of commitment developed by Kiesler (1971), with intellectual roots going back to Festinger (1957; 1964) and Lewin (1947). We borrow considerably from Kiesler's work, and deviate in significant ways. As a working definition, "commitment is the binding of the individual to behavioral acts" (Kiesler and Sakumura, 1966). The important words are "binding" and "acts."

To act is to commit oneself. A person may talk about how important it is to keep the population growth rate down, but to be sterilized is to give eloquent, unshakeable force to the statement. An adulterer may proclaim unrelenting devotion to a lover, but to give up children, home, and joint bank accounts is to put meaning into the proclamation. Thus, at a minimum, a concept of commitment implies that behavior, or action, be a central focus.

DETERMINANTS OF COMMITMENT

While action is a necessary ingredient in commitment, all behaviors are not equally committing. There are degrees of commitment. A statement of a belief or attitude is a less committing action than the signing of a petition in favor of the belief, which in turn is less committing than actively advocating the belief to a hostile or skeptical audience.

The degree of commitment derives from the extent to which a person's behaviors are binding. Four characteristics of behavioral acts make them binding, and hence determine the extent of commitment: explicitness; revocability; volition; and publicity. The first is the *explicitness* or deniability of the act, and concerns the extent to which an action can be said to have taken place. Two contributors to explicitness are the observability of the act and the unequivocality of the act. Some acts are not observable and we may know them only by inference from assumed consequences. You leave a dollar bill on a checkout counter, turn away for a moment, then find it missing. The consequence is obvious, but do you know if the customer next to you took it or if it was carried away by a draft from the open door? Acts themselves can be equivocal, forgotten, or otherwise intractable. A person who says, "I sometimes think . . ." is behaving more equivocally than one who says, "I think. . . ."

A second characteristic of behavior affecting commitment is the *revocability* or reversibility of the action. Some actions are like trials. We try them out, see how they fit with us, and if they don't suit us we change our minds and do something else. Few actions are really irreversible. Even a vasectomy can be undone. Promises can be made and broken. Jobs can be quit. Marriages can be dissolved; engagements, broken. Contracts can be torn up. On the other hand, some actions are permanent and having occurred, they cannot be undone. They are committing. Slapping someone in the face can be excused, forgiven, forgotten or reciprocated, but it cannot be taken back. Consumption of food or drink may be regretted but not reversed. Pulling the trigger of a loaded gun pointed at a friend commits all to its gross reality.

The explicitness and irrevocability of an act link action to an indelible reality. *Volition,* a third characteristic of committing behaviors, links action to the individual. This is one of the more difficult characteristics of human action to define precisely, and is frequently associated with such concepts as freedom and personal responsibility. What makes definition difficult is that all human action is both free and constrained, being done under one's own volition and in response to contingencies. Even the most seemingly free and personal action can be perceived as constrained. Artists and writers, such as Dostoevski and George Bernard Shaw, describe their acts of creation as the result of compulsions and external forces. And even the most seemingly constrained acts can be considered free. A person with a gun to his head ultimately is free to choose, whether to comply or accept the consequences of noncompliance. The perception of volition, moreover, can vary with the consequences that follow acts. A manager who takes a decision which turns out to be a disaster for his firm may make every effort to divest himself of responsibility. And one can observe in the annual reports of most corporations the following simple relationship. When sales increase from the previous year, the annual report points out how management's ingenious investments and development programs are paying off; when, the next year, sales decrease, an astounding downturn in the economy is lugubriously noted.

Despite difficulties in developing a precise concept of volition, volition wields powerful influences on the attitudes and behaviors of people, at least in Western culture. Some major characteristics found to relate to the degree of perceived volition of action are: (1) choice; (2) the presence of external demands for action; (3) the presence of extrinsic bases for action; and (4) the presence of other contributors to action. Thus a person who works hard in order to make a lot of money is not perceived as having as much volition as a person who works hard for nothing. A person who works hard because his superior stands over him constantly is not perceived as having as much volition as one who does as much on his own. With regard to choice, a person who buys a Ford because that is the only car available for sale is not perceived as having as much volition as one who passes over a hundred other models to make the same purchase. . . .

A fourth characteristic of action affecting commitment is the *publicity* or publicness of the act. This characteristic links the action into a social context. While all action and behavior is by definition observable, publicity refers to the extent to which others know of the action and the kinds of persons who know of it. Some audiences are unimportant to us, as are their observations of our behavior. One of the simplest ways to commit yourself to a course of action is to go around telling all your friends that you are definitely going to do something. You will find yourself bound by your own statements. The same commitment will not develop from proclamations to strangers you meet on trains. The publicity of one's action places the action in a social context which is more or less binding and, as we shall describe, contributes to directing the effect of those behaviors on subsequent behaviors. . . .

COMMITMENT TO ORGANIZATIONS

A careless interpretation of the consistency assumption might lead one to infer that having chosen to join an organization or to do a job, individuals will be willing to stay with it and be quite satisfied. After all, one implication of taking a job is that the person likes it. Choice, however, is not enough. The choice itself must be committing. The person must be bound to this choice. . . .

Sacrifice and Initiation Rites

Some organizations prefer not to leave a member's commitment to the happenstance of his own decision process. Corporations frequently publicize the decisions of their new managers. The *Wall Street Journal* is crammed with advertisements by companies announcing that a particular individual has joined their firm, an act giving instant status to the manager's new role. Friends and past associates call in their congratulations and set into motion a climate of expectation that he is part of that firm. In recent years, insurance companies have been taking full spreads in such magazines as *Time* and *Newsweek* to publish the pictures of their sales personnel. Western Electric has done the same with television scans of their employees working on the job. For a few hundred dollars, an individual is identified with the organization. Next-door neighbors rush to ask, "Say, is this you?" One implication of the advertisement to both the employee and his friends is that the company really cares about its employees, and as a consequence it becomes more and more difficult to complain about it to friends. Harvard Business School uses a particularly effective method of maintaining long-term commitment from its graduates. Entering MBAs are immediately assigned to a group of classmates. This class does everything together from then on. They live in the same dormitories, hear the same lectures, and take the same exams. Virtually everything is scheduled for the class as a whole. Within each class, individuals are identified by namecards so that everyone knows the name of everyone else and is referred to by name in classroom discussions. Twenty years later, when the individuals have long departed the ivy-draped halls, the social network created there continues to operate. One of the things it is used for is to drum donations to the "B School," as it is fondly called.

In addition to advertising a person's commitment, some organizations take pains to make sure the individual is aware he has made a decision. Like the experiments with a well-constructed social psychological choice manipulation, the new employer commits the beginner: "Now, we want to be sure you're taking this job because you want to. We know you've given up a lot to come here and we're grateful. You left your home, your old friends. It must have been very difficult for you. And the salary we're offering, while more than you were making, is never enough to compensate for that."

The idea of giving up something to join the organization is one exploited in many ways. A common form is the initiation rites which still persist in college fraternities and sororities, fraternal clubs like the Masons or Elks, prisons, military organizations, revolutionary cadres, communal living experiments, police academies and religious organizations, orders and cults. An important part of the initiation process is the forcing of a sacrifice, in which members are asked to give up something as a price of membership (Karter, 1968). College fraternities require pledges to do hours of push-ups, to take verbal abuse, to have their privileges restricted, to accept subservient roles; in the end, those who endure love it. The effect is obvious. The individual in order to give meaning to his sacrifices is left to conclude they were made because of his devotion to the organization, a conclusion made more likely by his public pledge to enter the organization out of his own choosing. Other organizations have less colorful forms of sacrifice. Exclusive country clubs require their new members to make large initial donations in addition to yearly fees. The donations themselves provide for no services, and members pay for almost all services. But having given up an initial thousand, or a few thousand dollars, members feel a certain compulsion to spend $3.00 for a martini at the club's bar rather than half that at a public lounge.

Investments and Tenure

Many organizations do not exploit the idea of sacrifice as a price of membership. Instead they emphasize the instrumental or exchange bases for participation. Members are hired rather than invited into the organization. Commitment under such circumstances will obviously be more difficult.

Studies on commitment to organizations that emphasize the instrumental bases for membership — work organizations — have consistently found two factors as most reliably related to commitment. The two factors are position in the organization and tenure with the organization. Study after study on the issue comes down to: People with good jobs are willing to stay in them, and, the longer a person has been with an organization, the more he wants to stay. Unfortunately, most of the studies were done in such ways that it is difficult, and in many cases impossible, to interpret the meaning of the findings.

The relationship of tenure to organizational commitment is predictable from the model of commitment presented in this chapter and has been discussed in a related manner. Howard Becker (1960) suggested that individuals build up commitment over time through certain "side-bets" they make in the organization. One obvious form of accumulation investments in an organization is the build-up of pension benefits and credits over the course of a lifetime. Until recently, such employee benefits, often called the "golden padlock," were not transferable from one organization to another. If an individual terminated in one organization, he lost some of his future wealth or security and had to begin accumulating it again in another organization. The costs of leaving the organization thus increase the longer one's involvement and one becomes more and more likely to continue where one is.

Regardless of financial investments, mobility also declines with tenure in an organization. As time goes by, one becomes less employable. And one's expertise becomes increasingly specific to one's current organization. Some organizations purposely manipulate the costs of leaving for some individuals. Universities will promote some of their assistant professors at rapid rates, making it more costly for other organizations to entice them away. Some business organizations will give young managers attractive positions unusual for their age, knowing it would be difficult for them to obtain equivalent offers elsewhere and also knowing it is cheaper to buy their commitment at an early age than it would be when they become industry hot-shots. . . .

WORK ENVIRONMENTS AND ORGANIZATIONAL COMMITMENT

Thus far we have discussed commitment to the organization as the result of the constraints on an individual's ability to leave the organization, and the extent to which the individual himself has made a definite and committing choice. In reading this over, one gets the feeling that commitment to an organization is an entrapment: an individual is either cut off from other alternatives because no one else wants him or because his own situation doesn't allow him to change it. Thus, individuals rarely make job changes involving moves when their children are entrenched in a school. In all, it is a rather negative view of commitment. You are committed because the facts of your life have bound you.

What about more positive features? Do people become committed to their jobs because they are attracted to them and find them enjoyable? The research on this issue is unimpressive. Much is based on termination interviews which find that workers who quit say they quit because they didn't like the job or the pay. Having taken so decisive a step, it would be rather amusing to find them saying that they loved the job. Studies attempting to predict employee turnover or absenteeism from prior reports of job satisfaction have been notoriously unsuccessful from a practical point of view; that is, the studies report statistically reliable relationships of so low a magnitude that they predict little about behavior. Even superior measurement techniques do poorly (Newman, 1974).

The typical relationship found between job attitudes and turnover or absenteeism is clouded by other factors. We have already discussed that one of these factors is the tenure of the employee. Job satisfaction increases with age and tenure, as does commitment to the organization (see Grupp and Richards, 1975; Organ and Greene, 1974; Gow, Clark, and Dossett, 1974 for illustrative studies). Where investigators have bothered to make the necessary causal analyses, they have found that the change is a "real" one and not simply a function of changes in position, jobs, or salary (Stagner, 1975). As a person becomes more experienced in what he does he becomes more able to cope with the negative and positive features of his job. . . .

Commitment and Job Features

Despite the rather unpredictable relationship between job attitudes, absenteeism, turmoil, and turnover, the model of commitment presented here does suggest that certain features of a person's job situation will affect his commitment. In general, any characteristic of a person's job situation which reduces his felt responsibility will reduce his commitment. As for the relationship between commitment and satisfaction, our own view is that enjoyment is more likely to follow commitment than the reverse.

Many characteristics of job situations can affect a person's perception of responsibility. Some positions simply carry more responsibility, and persons in higher positions tend to be more committed. Similarly, some jobs offer more discretion and self-determination to their occupants, and it has been found that employees in autonomous positions generally have more favorable attitudes than those with little freedom to decide how to do their jobs (Hackman and Lawler, 1971; Hackman and Oldham, 1974).

In addition to the job and the freedom it permits, the manner by which the job is supervised or monitored can affect perceptions of responsibility. The supervisor who stands over a subordinate provides an excuse for the subordinate's behavior. When unpleasant aspects of the job become apparent, rather than coping with them, and finding some joy in the job, the subordinate can attribute his endurance to the supervisor's tenacious pressure. Lepper and Greene (1975) found that surveillance deteriorates interest in a task. Zanna (1970) found that when students are led to believe they worked very hard for a nasty supervisor, they enjoyed the task more than when they worked very hard for a nice supervisor. When they work for a nice person they attribute their effort to their liking for him, not the job. This would be an unrealistic attribution to a nasty boss, so they like the job more.

If a supervisor merely stands by without taking an active part in determining the subordinate's behavior, his presence may serve to reinforce the subordinate's felt responsibility. Maguire and Ouchi (1975) found that close output supervision improves employee satisfaction but that close behavioral supervision does not. Monitoring and providing an individual with feedback about his work performance can increase a person's felt responsibility. The person, knowing his outcomes and knowing his outcomes are known by others, may become more aware that the outcomes are his responsibility. Hackman and Oldham (1974) found worker's perception of responsibility was in part a function of feedback about their performance. While the precise effects of various supervisory conditions on commitment have not been well studied, we would expect that high output monitoring coupled with low behavioral control would lead to the greatest felt responsibility on the part of the worker. Whether or not these conditions will lead to greater satisfaction, would depend on whether or not the worker can handle the task. Maguire and Ouchi (1975) found more satisfaction among monitored workers who could do their jobs without depending on others (i.e., low interdependence), than those who could not.

Commitment also derives from the relation of an employee's job to those of others in the organization. Some jobs are rather isolated and can be done independently of other jobs in the organization. It has been found that jobs which are not integrated with the work activities of others tend to be associated with less favorable attitudes (Sheperd, 1973). Gow, Clark and Dossett (1974), for instance, find that telephone operators who quit tend to be those who are not integrated into the work group. Work integration can affect commitment by the fact that integrated jobs are likely to be associated with salient demands from others in the organization. If a person has a job which affects the work of others in the organization, it is likely that those others will communicate their expectations for performance of that job. Such expectations can be committing in that the other people implicitly or explicitly hold the person accountable for what he does. Earlier we mentioned that when individuals did not know what was expected of them they tended to be less committed to the organization. One reason an

individual will not know what is expected is because no one is telling him. In general, we would expect that anything which contributes to creating definite expectations for a person's behavior would enhance his felt responsibility, and hence commitment. Integration may be one such contributor.

Perhaps the most pervasive condition of a job which affects commitment is its instrumentality, the fact that work is a means to some other end. While all jobs in industrial and commercial organizations are done in exchange for salary, there are perhaps great variations in the extent to which the instrumental basis for the work is salient or not. In general, we would expect that when the instrumental basis for work is salient it will reduce a person's felt responsibility. The attribution, "I am doing this job only for the money," should inhibit commitment. A similar point was raised by Ingham (1970), who analyzed absenteeism and turnover in light engineering firms in Bradford, England. Observing that larger organizations had more absenteeism (but lower turnover), he argued that workers were attracted to large firms because of the higher pay offered, but that this instrumental orientation led to little personal involvement with the organization. . . .

There is far too little empirical work on the nature of commitment to jobs, and how features of the work situation lead to or detract from feelings of personal responsibility for work. Much more detailed accountings of the particulars of job situations need to be made.

REFERENCES

Becker, H. S. Notes on the concept of commitment. *American Journal of Sociology,* 1960, 66, 32–40.

Festinger, L. *A theory of cognitive dissonance.* Stanford, Calif.: Stanford University Press, 1957.

Festinger, L. *Conflict, decision, and dissonance.* Stanford, Calif.: Stanford University Press, 1964.

Gow, J. S., Clark, A. W., & Dossett, G. S. A path analysis of variables influencing labour turnover. *Human Relations,* 1974, 27, 703–19.

Hackman, J. R., & Lawler, E. E. Employee reactions to job characteristics. *Journal of Applied Psychology,* 1971, 55, 259–86.

Hackman, J. R., & Oldham, G. R. Motivation through the design of work: Test of a theory. Technical Report no. 6, Administrative Sciences, Yale University, 1974.

Ingham, G. K. *Size of industrial organizations and worker behavior.* Cambridge: Cambridge University Press, 1970.

Kanter, R. M. Commitment and social organizations. *American Sociological Review,* 1968.

Kiesler, C. A. *The psychology of commitment: Experiments linking behavior to belief.* New York: Academic Press, 1971.

Kiesler, C. A., & Sakumura, J. A test of a model for commitment. *Journal of Personality and Social Psychology,* 1966, **3,** 349–53.

Lepper, M. R., Greene, D., & Nisbett, R. E. Undermining children's intrinsic interest with extrinsic rewards: A test of the "overjustification" hypothesis. *Journal of Personality and Social Psychology,* 1973, 28, 129–37.

Lewin, K. Group decision and social change. In T. M. Newcomb and E. L. Hartley (Eds.), *Readings in social psychology.* New York: Holt, Rinehart & Winston, 1947, pp. 330–44.

Maguire, M. A., & Ouchi, W. Organizational control and work satisfaction. Research Paper no. 278, Graduate School of Business, Stanford University, 1975.

Newman, J. E. Predicting absenteeism and turnover: A field comparison of Fishbein's model and traditional job attitude measures. *Journal of Applied Psychology,* 1974, 59, 610–15.

Organ, D. W., & Greene, N. The perceived purposefulness of job behavior: Antecedents and consequences. *Academy of Management Journal,* 1974, 17, 69–78.

Stagner, R. Boredom on the assembly line: Age and personality variables. *Industrial Gerontology,* 1975, 21, 23–44.

Zanna, M. P. Attitude inference in a low choice setting. Ph.D. dissertation, Yale University, 1970.

19. How the Top Is Different

Rosabeth Moss Kanter

Corporate headquarters of the company I have called Indsco occupied many floors in a glass and steel office building in a large city. The surroundings were luxurious. At ground level was a changing art exhibit in glass cases with displays of awards to Indsco executives for meritorious public service or newspaper clippings about the corporation. There might be piles of company newspapers on a nearby table or special publications like the report by foreign students who spent the summer with Indsco families. Such public displays almost always stressed Indsco's contributions to the welfare of the larger community. Across from gleaming chrome elevators and a watchman's post were doors leading into the employees' dining room. In the morning a long table with coffee, sweet rolls, and bagels for sale was set up outside the dining room; during the day coffee carts were available on each floor. Inside, the dining room was divided into two parts; a large cafeteria for

everyone and a small area with already set tables, hostess seating, menus, and waitress service. Those tables were usually occupied by groups of men; the largely female clerical work force tended to eat in the cafeteria. Special luncheon meetings arranged by managers were held in the individual executive dining rooms and conference areas on the top floor; to use these rooms, reservations had to be made well in advance by someone with executive status.

Indsco executives were also likely to go out for lunch, especially if they were entertaining an outside visitor, to any of the numerous posh restaurants in the neighborhood. At these lunches a drink was a must; at one time it was two extra-dry martinis, but more recently it became a few glasses of wine. However, despite the fact that moderate social drinking was common, heavy drinking was frowned upon. A person's career could be ruined by the casual comment that he or she had alcoholic tendencies. Stories told about men who cavorted and caroused in bars, staying up all night, were told with the attitude that "that was really crazy."

The office floors were quietly elegant, dominated by modern design, white walls, and beige tones. At one end, just off the elevators, sat a receptionist who [called] on a company telephone line to announce visitors. A secretary would then appear to escort a visitor to his or her appointment. Offices with windows were for higher status managers, and their secretaries were often proud of having drapes. Corner offices were reserved for the top. They were likely to be larger in size, with room for coffee tables and couches, and reached through a reception area where a private secretary sat. Inside offices went to assistants and other lower-status salaried personnel; conference rooms were also found along the inside rim. Secretaries and other hourly workers occupied rows of desks with banks of cabinets and files in the public spaces between. There were few signs of personal occupancy of space, except around the secretaries' desks. Managers might put up a painting or poster on a wall, and they usually had a small set of photographs of their families somewhere on or near their desk. Rarely would more than a few books or reports be visible, and the overall impression was one of tidiness, order, and uniformity from office to office. In fact, it was often true that the higher the status of an executive, the less cluttered was his desk. Office furnishings themselves reflected status rather than personality. There was a clear system of stratification. As status increased, desks went from a wood top with steel frame through solid wood to the culmination in a marble-top desk. Type of ashtray was also determined by the status system; and a former executive secrtary, promoted into a management position herself, reported that her former peers were upset that she took her stainless steel file trays with her because a secretary working for her would not be entitled to such luxurious equipment. The rational distribution of furniture and supplies was thought to make the system more equitable and to avoid competition for symbols of status. . . .

The secretary also contributed in minor ways to the boss's status. Some people have argued that secretaries function as "status symbols" for executives, holding that the traditional secretarial role is developed and preserved because of its impact on managerial egos, not its contribution to organizational efficiency. Robert Townsend, iconoclastic former president of Avis, claimed in *Up the Organization* that the existence of private secretaries was organizationally inefficient, as

proven by his experience in gaining half a day's time by giving up what he called "standard executive equipment." One writer was quite explicit about the meaning of secretary: "In many companies a secretary outside your door is the most visible sign that you have become an executive; a secretary is automatically assigned to each executive, whether or not his work load requires one. . . . When you reach the vice-presidential level, your secretary may have an office of her own, with her name on the door. At the top, the president may have two secretaries. . . ." A woman professional at Indsco agreed with the idea that secretaries were doled out as rewards rather than in response to job needs, as she talked about her own problems in getting enough secretarial help.

At Indsco, the secretary's function as a status symbol increased up the ranks as she became more and more bound to a specific boss. "It's his image, his status, sitting out in front," a personnel administrator said. "She's the sign of how important he is." . . .

Physical height corresponded to social height at Indsco, like other major corporations. Corporate officers resided at the very top on the forty-fifth floor, which was characterized by many people in Indsco as a "hospital ward." The silence was deafening. The offices were huge. According to one young executive who had served as an assistant to an officer, "One or two guys are sitting there; there's not much going on. It's the brain center, but there is no activity. It's like an old folks' home. You can see the cobwebs growing. A secretary every quarter mile. It's very sterile." An executive secretary told the story of her officer boss's first reaction to moving onto the forty-fifth floor. "He was the one human being," she said, who was uncomfortable with the trappings of status. When he moved up, he had to pick an office." She wouldn't let him take anything but a corner—it was the secretary who had to tell him that. Finally he agreed for the sake of the corporate image, but he was rarely there, and he set up the office so that everything was in one corner and the rest was useless space.

Some people felt that the physical insulation of top executives also had its counterpart in social insulation. Said a former officer's assistant, "There are courtiers around the top guys, telling them what they want to hear, flattering them. For example, there was a luncheon with some board members. The vice-chairman mentioned that he was looking for a car for his daughter. A courtier thought, 'We'll take care of it.' He went down the line, and someone in purchasing had to spend half a day doing this. The guy who had to do it resented it, so he became antagonistic to the top. The vice-chairman had no idea this was going on, and if he had known, he would probably have stopped it; but you can't say anything at the top without having it be seen as an order. Even ambiguous remarks may get translated into action. At the top you have to figure out the impact of all of your words in advance because an innocent expression can have a major effect. A division president says, 'It might be a good idea to _____.' He's just reminating, but that gets sent down to the organization as an ultimatum, and everyone scrambles around to make sure it gets done. He looks down and says, 'What the hell is happening?' ''

At the same time, officers could also be frustrated by their distance from any real action. One remarked, "You get into a position like mine, and you think you can get anything done, but I shout down an order, and I have to wait years for any action. The guy in the plant turns a valve and sees the reaction, or the salesman offers a price, but I may never live to see the impact of my decisions." For this reason, it was known that once in a while officers could be expected to leave their protected environment and try to get involved in routine company activities. Some would go down and try to do something on the shop floor. Once in a while one would make a sales call at a very high level or make an appearance at a customer golf outing. It was also a legend that an early president had his own private laboratory outside of his office — his own tinkering room. As a manager put it, "He would close the door and go play. It was almost as though he was babied. He was given a playroom." . . .

CONFORMITY PRESSURES AT THE TOP: UNCERTAINTY AND THE GROWTH OF INNER CIRCLES

Leaders who already have power seek as new recruits those they can rely upon and trust. They demand that the newcomers to top positions be loyal, that they accept authority, and that they conform to a prescribed pattern of behavior.

Unlike a more communal environment, where eccentrics can be lovingly tolerated because trust is based on mutual commitments and deep personal knowledge, those who run the bureaucratic corporation often rely on outward manifestations to determine who is the "right sort of person." Managers tend to carefully guard power and privilege for those who fit in, for those they see as "their kind." Wilbert Moore was

commenting on this phenomenon when he used the metaphor of a "bureaucratic kinship system" to describe the corporation — but a kinship system based on homosocial reproduction in which men reproduce themselves in their own image. The metaphor is apt. Because of the *situation* in which managers function, because of the position of managers in the corporate structure, social similarity tends to become extremely important to them. The structure sets in motion forces leading to the replication of managers as the same kind of social individuals. And people at the top reproduce themselves in kind.

Conformity pressures and the development of exclusive management circles closed to "outsiders" stem from the degree of uncertainty surrounding managerial positions. Bureaucracies are social inventions that supposedly reduce the uncertain to the predictable and routine. Yet much uncertainty remains — many situations in which individual people rather than impersonal procedures must be trusted. "Uncertainty," James Thompson wrote in a recent major statement on organizations, "appears as the fundamental problem for complex organizations, and coping with uncertainty as the essence of the administrative process." Thompson identified three sources of uncertainty in even the most perfect of machinelike bureaucracies; a lack of cause-effect understanding in the culture at large (limiting the possibility for advance planning); contingencies caused by the fact that the bureaucracy is not alone, so that outcomes of organizational action are in part determined by action of other elements in the environment; and the interdependence of parts, the human interconnections inside the organization itself, which can never fully be reduced to predictable action. The requirements for a perfectly technically "rational" bureaucracy that never has to rely on the personal discretion of a single individual can never be met; complete knowledge of all cause-effect relationships plus control over all of the relevant variables. Thus, sources of uncertainty that are inherent in human institutions mean that some degree of reliance on individual persons must always be present.

It is ironic that in those most impersonal of institutions the essential communal problem of trust remains. For wherever there is uncertainty, *someone* (or some group) must decide, and thus, there must be personal discretion. And discretion raises not technical but human, social, and even communal questions: trust, and its origins in loyalty, commitment, and mutual understanding based on the sharing of values. It is the uncertainty quotient in managerial work, as it has come to be defined in the large modern corporation, that causes management to become so socially restricting; to develop tight inner circles excluding social strangers; to keep control in the hands of socially homogeneous peers; to stress conformity and insist upon a diffuse, unbounded loyalty; and to prefer ease of communication and thus social certainty over the strains of dealing with people who are "different."

If conditions of uncertainty mean that people have to be relied on, then people fall back on social bases for trust. The greater the uncertainty, the greater the pressures for those who have to trust each other to form a homogeneous group. At different times in an organization's history, and at different places in its structure, a higher degree of uncertainty brings with it more drive for social similarity. . . .

Uncertainty can stem from either the time-span of decisions and the amount of information that must be collected, or from the frequency with which nonroutine events occur and must be handled. The impossibility of specifying contingencies in advance, operating procedures for all possible events, leaves an organization to rely on personal discretion. (It is also this pressure that partly accounts for the desire to centralize responsibility in a few people who can be held accountable for discretionary decisions.) Commented a sales manager at Indsco, "The need for flexibility is primary in my job. The situation changes from minute to minute. One minute it's a tank truck that collapsed. Another it's a guy whose wife just had a hysterectomy and is going to die. . . . I'm dealing with such different problems all the time."

The importance of discretion increases with closeness to the top of a hierarchical organization. Despite the institutionalization and routinization of much of the work of large organizations and despite the proliferation of management experts, uncertainty remains a generic condition, increasing with rank. Jobs are relatively unstructured, tasks are nonroutine, and decisions must be made about a variety of unknown elements. Issues such as "direction" and "purpose" cannot be reduced to rational formulae. Organizational improvement, or even maintenance, is not a simple matter that can be summarized in statements about "the ten functions of managers" or techniques of operation. If the "big picture" can be viewed from the top, it also looks bigger and fuzzier. Computers have not necessarily reduced the uncertainty of decisions at the top; in some cases, they have merely increased the amount of information that decision-makers must take into account. A major executive of Indsco confessed in a meeting that "we don't know how to manage these giant structures; and

I suspect no one does. They are like dinosaurs, lumbering on of their own accord, even if they are no longer functional."

Criteria for "good decisions" or good management performance also get less certain closer to the top. The connection between an upper management decision and a factor such as production efficiency several layers below or gross sales is indirect, if it is even apparent. (An Indsco division president said, "In the 1960s we thought we were really terrific. We patted ourselves on the back a lot because every decision was so successful. Business kept on expanding. Then came the recession, and we couldn't do anything to stop it. We had been lucky before. Everything turned to gold in the 1960s. But it became clear that we don't know the first thing about how to make this enterprise work.")

Financial measures of performance are sometimes even artifactual because of the juggling of figures; for example, when and how a loss is recorded. There are also a variety of dilemmas in trying to evaluate the success of managers: qualitative versus quantitative measures, short-run versus long-run outcomes. Decisions that look good in the short-term might be long-term disasters, but by that time the failure can be blamed on other factors, and those responsible for the decisions might be so entrenched in power that they now call the shots anyway. A former public relations manager at DuPont formulated what he called the Law of Inverse Certainty: "The more important the management decision, the less precise the tools to deal with it . . . and the longer it will take before anyone knows it was right." One example was a rigid cost cutter who helped increase profits by eliminating certain functions; by the time the company began to feel the loss of those functions, he had been promoted and was part of the inner power group. Someone else picked up the pieces.

The uncertainty up the ranks, like the uncertainty of beginnings, also puts trust and homogeneity at a premium. The personal loyalty normally demanded of subordinates by officials is most intense at the highest levels of organizations, as others have also noted. The lack of structure in top jobs makes it very important for decision-makers to work together closely in at least the harmony of shared understanding and a degree of mutual trust. Since for an organization to function at all requires that, to some extent, people will pull together around decisions, the solidarity that can be mustered through common membership in social networks, and the social control this provides, is a helpful supplement for decision-makers. Indeed, homogeneity of class and ethnic background and prior social experiences is one important "commitment mechanism" found to build a feeling of communion among members of viable utopian communities. Situational pressures, then, place a great emphasis on personal relations and social homogeneity as functional elements in the carrying out of managerial tasks. And privilege is also kept within a small circle.

The social homogeneity of big business leaders from the early-to-middle twentieth century has been noted frequently by critics such as C. Wright Mills as well as business historians. Their class background and social characteristics tended to be similar: largely white, Protestant men from elite schools. Much attention has also been paid to the homogeneity of type within any particular company. In one industrial organization, managers who moved ahead needed to be members of the Masonic Order and the local yacht club; not Roman Catholic; Anglo-Saxon or Germanic in origin; and Republican.

At Indsco, until ten years ago, top executives in the corporation were traceable to the founders of the company or its subsidiaries — people who held stock or were married to people who did. There was a difference between who did well in the divisions, where performance tended to account for more, and who got into top positions in the corporation itself. To get ahead in the corporation, social connections were known to be very important. Indeed, corporate staff positions became a place to put people who were nonmovers, whose performance was not outstanding, but were part of the "family." The social homogeneity of corporate executives was duly noted by other managers. One asked a consultant, "Do all companies have an ethnic flavor? Our top men all seem to be Scotch-Irish." (But as management has become more rationalized, and the corporation has involved itself more heavily in divisional operations, there has also been a trend, over the past five years, toward more "objective" criteria for high-level corporate positions.)

We expect a direct correlation, then, between the degree of uncertainty in a position — the extent to which organizations must rely on personal discretion — and a reliance on "trust" through "homosocial reproduction" — selection of incumbents on the basis of social similarity. . . .

Management becomes a closed circle in the absence of better, less exclusionary responses to uncertainty and communication pressures. Forces stemming from organizational situations help foster social homogeneity as a selection criterion for managers and promote social conformity as a standard for conduct. Concerned about giving up control and broadening discretion in the organization, managers choose others that can be "trusted." And thus they reproduce themselves in kind. Women are occasionally included in the inner circle when they are part of an organization's ruling family, but more usually this system leaves women out, along with a range of other people with discrepant social characteristics. Forces insisting that trust means total dedication and nondiffuse loyalty also serve to exclude those, like women, who are seen as incapable of such a single-minded attachment.

There is a self-fulfilling prophecy buried in all of this. The more closed the circle, the more difficult it is for "outsiders" to break in. Their very difficulty in entering may be taken as a sign of incompetence, a sign that the insiders were right to close their ranks. The more closed the circle, the more difficult it is to share power when the time comes, as it inevitably must, that others challenge the control by just one kind. And the greater the tendency for a group of people to try to reproduce themselves, the more constraining becomes the emphasis on conformity. It would seem a shame, indeed, if the only way out of such binds lay in increasing bureaucratization — that is, in a growth in routinization and rationalization of areas of uncertainty and a concomitant decline in personal discretion. But somehow corporations must grapple with the problem of how to reduce pressures for social conformity in their top jobs. . . .

CONFORMITY REACHES HOME

It is one of the prevailing ironies of modern corporate life that the closer to the top of the organization, the more traditional and non-"modern" does the system look. As Max Weber noted, at this point more charismatic, symbolic, and "non-rational" elements come into play. At the top — and especially in interaction with its environment — the organization is most likely to show strong elements of a personal, familistic system imbued with ritual, drawing on traditional behavior modes, and overlaid with symbolism. The irony stems from the fact that it is the top level that prescribes routine and impersonality — the absence of particularism and familism — for the rest of the organization. The modern organization formally excludes the family from participation in organizational life and excludes family ties as a basis for organizational position, even to the extent of antinepotism rules. Yet, at the top the wife may come into the picture as a visible member of the husband's ''team''; she may be given a position and functions (and, in some cases, may even jump over qualified employees in taking on an official, paid, executive position). The wife who is excluded below may be included at the top, as part of the diplomatic apparatus of the corporation. And she has little freedom to refuse participation.

The dilemma that can confront people at this level is the issue of publicness/privateness. Both husband and wife can be made into public figures, with no area of life remaining untinged with responsibilities for the company. Here, as Wilbert Moore said, ''The man, and his wife, simply cannot divest themselves of corporate identification. Their every activity with persons outside the immediate family is likely to be tinged with a recognition of the man's position. He represents the company willy-nilly. His area of privacy, and that of his wife, is very narrowly restricted.'' One rising young Indsco executive felt that the following had to be considered the ''modern risks'' of corporate vice-presidential and presidential jobs: traveling 80 percent of the time, getting shot at or kidnapped by radicals, prostituting yourself to customers, and opening your private life to scrutiny.

The higher executive's work spills over far beyond the limits of a working day. There may be no distinction between work and leisure. Activities well out of the purview of the organization's goals and defined as pleasure for other people (golf club memberships, symphony attendance, party-giving) are allowable as business expenses on income tax returns because the definition of what is ''business'' becomes so broad and nonspecific. People entertain one another on yachts or over long, lavish lunches — all in an attempt to mutually obligate, to create personal relations that will give someone an inside track when it comes to more formal negotiations. Whenever ''selling'' is a part of the organization's relations with its environment and sufficient sums of money rest on each deal, those who sell tend to offer gifts (tickets to a sports event, dinners at fancy restaurants, expensive pen and pencil sets) to those who buy, trying to bind the others beyond the limits of a rational contractual relationship. Entertaining in the home with the wife as hostess is especially binding, since it appears to be a more personal offering not given to all, sets up a social obligation, implicates others, and also calls on ancient and traditional feelings about the need to reward hospitality.

Fusion of business and private life also occurs around longer-term relationships. At the top, all friendships may have business meaning. Business relations can be made because of social connections. (One unlikely merger between two companies in very different fields was officially said to result from one company's need for a stock exchange listing held by the other, but off the record it was known to have been brought about by the friendship of the two presidents and their wives.) Charitable and community service activities, where the life's role is especially pivotal, may generate useful business and political connections. Wives may meet each other through volunteer work and bring their husbands into contact, with useful business results. Stratification of the volunteer world paralleling class and ethnic differentiation in the society ensures that husbands and wives can pinpoint the population with which they desire connections by an appropriate choice of activity. As one chief executive wife wrote, ''Any public relations man worth his salt will recognize the corporate wife as an instrument of communication with the community far more sincere and believable than all the booze poured down the press to gain their favor.''

The importance of the wife stems not only from her own skills and activities (which could be, and are, performed by paid employees) but also from the testimony her behavior provides, its clue to the character and personal side of her husband. The usefulness of this testimony, in turn, is derived from unique aspects of top leadership. Image, appearance, background, and likability are all commodities traded at the top of the system, where actors are visible and where they put pressure on one another to demonstrate trustworthiness. . . . Farther down a hierarchy, jobs can be broken down into component skills and decisions about people and jobs made on the basis of ability to demonstrate those skills. At the top, decisions about people are not so easy or mechanical; they rest on personal factors to a degree perhaps much greater than systems themselves officially admit. The situations that a corporation president or a president of a country face are not routine and predictable; indeed, constituents are less interested in their handling of routine matters than in their capacities for the unexpected. So there is no test except a vague one: Is this person trustworthy? Even questions about philosophy and intelligence are proxies for trust.

Furthermore, the capacities of an organization itself are unknown and cannot be reduced precisely either to history or to a set of facts and figures. Thus, the character of its leaders can become a critical guide to making a decision about a future relationship with it: whether to invest, to donate funds, to allow it into the community, to provide some leeway in the regulation of its activities. Indsco was always concerned about character in its managers. Company newspapers from field locations routinely stressed church leadership in articles about individual managers, and "integrity" and "acceptance of accountability" appeared on the list of eleven traits that must be possessed by candidates for officer-level jobs. Disclosures of corrupt practices by other companies in the mid-1970s enhanced Indsco's concerns about public respectability. Whereas, at lower levels of the organization, there was a tendency to formalize demands, to create routinized job descriptions, to ensure continuity of functioning by seeing to it that the occupant did not make over the job in his own image, and to exclude as much as possible of the personal and emotional life of the worker, close to the top, opposite pressure prevailed. Those with whom leaders entered into relationships looked for the private person behind the role and for the qualities and capacities that could not be encompassed by a job description but on which they must bet when deciding to trust the leader or the organization. Here's where the wives are important.

One way leaders can offer glimpses of their private beings is by bringing along their wives, by inviting others into their homes, and by making sure that their wives confirm the impression of themselves they are trying to give. By meeting in social circumstances, by throwing open pieces of private life for inspection, leaders try to convey their taste and their humanity. Wives, especially, are the carriers of this humanity and the shapers of the image of the private person. Of course, to the extent that social events and "informal" occasions are known to communicate an image for the purposes of making appropriate relationships, they may come to be as carefully managed and rationally calculated as any production task within the organization. The public relations department might even stage-manage the performance of the leader and his wife; when Dollie Ann Cole, wife of a General Motors president, wrote that PR departments no longer tell the wife what to wear and what to say, she made it explicit that they once did: ". . . a new day has dawned. Corporate wives no longer ask the public relations office what charity they should work with or whether they can debate for a cause on a local or national radio or television show — or even who is coming to dinner."

The wife is thus faced with an added task at the boundary of the public and the private: to make an event seem personal that is instead highly ritualized and contrived. She must recognize also the meanings conveyed by small acts (who sits next to whom, how much time she and her husband spend with each person, the taste implied by objects in the home, how much she drinks, who seem to be the family friends) and manage even small gestures with extreme self-consciousness, as one high-level wife at Indsco recalled she did at managers' meetings: "I had to be very careful to be invariably cordial, friendly, to remember everyone's names — and then to stay away. If I was too involved with someone, it would look like I was playing favorites; that would set up waves in highly inappropriate ways. Some of the young wives were terrified, but there was only so much I could do because I had other things to worry about."

Private life thus becomes penetrable and not very private at the top. Wives face the demand to suppress private beliefs and self-knowledge in the interest of public appearance. As an instrument of diplomacy and a critical part of her husband's image, the corporate wife must often hide her own opinions in order to preserve a united front, play down her own abilities to keep him looking like the winner and the star. The women's intelligence and superior education — assets when the men looked for wives — give way to other, more social traits, such as gregariousness, adaptability, attractiveness, discretion, listening ability, and social graces.

Thus, unless serving as a surrogate for the husband, voicing opinions was not easily allowed of corporate wives as Indsco, like those political wives who must beware of outshining their husbands. An aide to Eleanor McGovern spoke of the contradictory pressures on a candidate's wife: to be able to give the speech when he can't make it but to shut her mouth and listen adoringly when he is there. Indeed, Eleanor was told to stop looking so good when she started getting better press notices than George. Abigail McCarthy recalled the anxiety she felt about how words would affect her husband's prospects: "After every interview, I lay awake in a black nightmare of anxiety, fearful that I had said something which would do Gene irreparable harm." Betty Ford became an object of controversy (and of admiration) precisely because she violated these rules of the game and refused to distort her private life. Yet, wives of upper management at Indsco felt they did not have that luxury, even though they characterized the pressure to suppress independent opinions as "nonsense" and frustrating. Not everyone complained. One wife reported that she was proud of never having unburdened herself, even to a confidante, and never having forgotten her public role throughout her husband's career.

Stresses, choices, and dilemmas in the top leadership phase, then, center around the tension between the public and the private. If men and their wives at the top gained public recognition, they also lost private freedoms. The emotional pressure this entailed was too much for some wives, as literature in the corporate-wives-as-victims tradition made clear; but it should be pointed out, too, that emotional breakdowns and secret deviances could also reflect defiant independence, unobtainable in any other way under constraining role definitions. The wishes expressed by wives in this position were of two kinds. Some women said that if they were going to be used by the company anyway, they would like the opportunity to do a real job, exercise real skills — by which they meant take on official areas of responsibility. Others wanted merely to be able to carve out more areas of privacy and independence in an otherwise public existence.

POWER AND ITS PRICES

The top leadership of an organization has all of the privileges of office: the signs of status, the benefits and perquisites, the material advantages their position is seen to warrant. They play ball in a large field, and the scope of their decisions is vast and far-reaching. They have, on occasion, gigantic power which does not even

have to be used; a mere wish on their part is translated into action, with full cooperation and without the show of force.

But such power exists in a vise of checks and constraints; it comes out of a system, and the system, in turn, exacts its price. What if a top leader tries to exercise power that violates the expectations of other top leaders and organization members — if he or she steps out of line, out of character, or out of role? Would obedience be so easily forthcoming? Power at the top is contingent on conformity. Pressures to "fit in" also mean restraints on the unbridled exercise of power.

Furthermore, power which in some respects is contingent on trust for its effective exercise also, ironically, breeds suspicion: Can people at the top trust what they hear? Can they trust each other? What, beyond social appearance, can they use as keys to trust? Sometimes cut off from the "real action," they are seen by the organization's rank and file as remote from the daily events which truly constitute the organization — as once potent actors who now make whimsical decisions with little real understanding of organizational operations. And, as the final price of power, top leaders have to acknowledge the organization's ownership of that ultimate piece of property, their own private lives and beings. Life at the top is life in a goldfish bowl, an existence in which all the boundaries can be rendered transparent at the twitch of the public's curiosity.

The room at the top is all windows.

---

20. Type Z Organization: Stability in the Midst of Mobility

William G. Ouchi and Alfred M. Jaeger

Now all the evidence of psychiatry ... shows that membership in a group sustains a man, enables him to maintain his equilibrium under the ordinary shocks of life, and helps him to bring up children who will in turn be happy and resilient. If his group is shattered around him, if he leaves a group in which he was a valued member, and if, above all, he finds no new group to which he can relate himself, he will, under stress, develop disorders of thought, feeling and behavior. . . . The cycle is vicious; loss of group membership in one generation may make men less capable of group membership in the next. The

---

"Type Z Organization: Stability in the Midst of Mobility" by William G. Ouchi and Alfred M. Jaeger. Reprinted with permission from *Academy of Management Review,* April 1978.

civilization that, by its very process of growth, shatters small group life will leave men and women lonely and unhappy (1, p. 457).

Society traditionally has relied upon kinship, neighborhood, church, and family networks to provide the social support and normative anchors which made collective life possible. As Mayo (2) pointed out, the advent of the factory system of production and the rapid rate of technological change produced high rates of urbanization, mobility, and division of labor. These forces weakened the community, family, church, and friendship ties of many Americans. Social observers point to this weakening of associational ties as the basic cause of increasing rates of alcoholism, divorce, crime, and other symptoms of mental illness at a societal level (3–5).

While worrying over the disappearance of family, church, neighborhood, and the friendship network, predispositions can blind us to the most likely alternative source of associational ties or cohesion: the work organization. The large work organization which brought about urbanization and its consequent social ills can also provide relief from them. Donham notes:

Mayo shows us for the first time in the form of specific instances that it is within the power of industrial administrators to create within industry itself a partially effective substitute for the old stabilizing effect of the neighborhood. Given stable employment, it might make of industry (as of the small town during most of our national life) a social satisfying way of life as well as a way of making a living (2).

Employment already defines many aspects of people's lives: socio-economic status, their children's education, kinds and length of vacations, frequency and severity with which they can afford to become ill, and even the way in which pension benefits allow them to live their retirement years. From childhood to the grave, the work organization plays a central role in identifying people and molding their lives. Japan (6), Poland (7), and China (8) provide models of work systems which organize life and society, but we have been unwilling to borrow these models, because they do not permit the individual freedom that is valued in American life.

With memories of the totalitarian paternalism of the mines and plantations still not healed by time, Americans have been reluctant to even consider the work organization as the social umbrella under which people can live free, happy, and productive lives. The ideology of independence that is part of the basic fabric of the American persona recoils at the thought of individual freedom subordinated to collective commitment. American idols are the rough, tough individualists, the John Waynes, the Evel Knievals, the Gloria Steinems. Our most pitiable figures are those who lose their individuality in some larger, corporate entity and become "organization men," faceless persons "in gray flannel suits."

We must discover that ideologically unique American solution which allows individual freedom while using the work organization to support and encourage the stability of associational ties.

The beginnings of this solution were found in a study by one of the authors (9). Interviews were conducted with employees of all levels of Japanese and American firms which had operations in both the United States and Japan. In Japanese companies in Japan were found the now-familiar characteristics first reported by Abegglen (6): almost total inclusion of the employee into the work organization so that the superior concerns himself or herself with the personal and family life of each subordinate; a collective, nonindividual approach to work and responsibility; and extremely high identification of the individual with the company. These characteristics are largely the result of the lifetime employment system which characterizes large companies in Japan (5, 6, 10–12).

The surprising finding was that Japanese companies with operations in the United States are applying a modified form of the pure Japanese type with some success. While they do not provide company housing or large bonuses as in Japan, they attempt to create the same sort of complete inclusion of the employee into the company. Supervisors are taught to be aware of all aspects of an employee's life; extrawork social life is often connected to other employees; corporate values are adjusted to reflect employee needs as well as profit needs, and high job security is protected above all else. The American employees expressed liking for this "atmosphere" or "climate," with the managerial staff in particular noting the difference from their previous employers.

The study gave evidence that, while Americans probably do not want a return to old-style paternalism, they favor a work organization which provides associational ties, stability, and job security. The Japanese-American mixed form suggested the model which may simultaneously permit individual freedom and group cohesion.

Some American companies, by reputation, have many of the characteristics of this mixed model. Best known are Kodak, Cummins Engine Company, IBM, Levi

Strauss, National Cash Register, Procter and Gamble, and Utah International. Their historical rates of turnover are low; loyalty and morale are reputed to be very high, and identification with the company is reputed to be strong. In addition, each company has been among the most successful of American companies for many decades, a record which strongly suggests that something about the form of organization, rather than solely a particular product or market position, has kept the organization vital and strong. It is widely believed that these companies have been co-opted by their employees; they do not express goals of short-term profitability but rather pay some cost in order to maintain employment stability through difficult times. These work organizations may have created the alternative to village life to which Mayo referred.

Compare persons associated with this mixed model to the "ideal type" of bureaucrat described by Toennies (13), Weber (14), and Merton (15) – a person involved in the limited, contractual, only partially inclusive relationships that characterize traditional American organizations. In a sense, the scheme being proposed here is an organizational analogue of Toennies' *Gemeinschaft* and *Gesellschaft* (13). Just as societies suffer from poor mental health as a result of size, density, and heterogeneity, which lead to contractualism and segmentalism in life, work organizations also can become segmented and contractual as they grow. This is what Weber (14) expected. He advocated development of a contractual *Gesellschaft* in work organizations to shield the meritocracy from outside ascriptive values and ties (16, 17). In a stable society, individuals can develop ties outside work to complement the impersonal nature of participation in a contractual organization. But in a mobile and changing society, societal values and outside ties are weaker, posing less threat to the efficiency of the organization. More individuals are less likely to have developed personal ties outside of work which satisfactorily complement the impersonal interactions

engaged in at work. Thus, organizations whose goals and philosophy are in tune with today's general societal values can survive and even thrive by being more "personal."

THE IDEAL TYPES: TYPE A, TYPE J, AND TYPE Z

This section describes three ideal types of work organization. It is argued that each type is an integrated system and will yield either positive or negative outcomes for the society depending on certain environmental conditions. Type A represents the Western organization, especially the North American and Western European forms. Type J represents the Japanese and mainland Chinese forms, and Type Z is an emergent form which is particularly suited to the United States of America today.

Each ideal type contains seven dimensions (Table 1). Length of employment refers to the average number of years served within the corporation, considering all employees. This is important in two respects. First, if mean number of years of tenure is high, employees will be more familiar with the workings of the organization and more likely to have developed friendships among their co-workers; second, if the new employee anticipates a long career within one organization, he or she will be willing to incur greater personal costs in order to become integrated into the culture of the organization.

The mode of decision-making refers to typical ways of dealing with nonroutine problems. Individual decision-making is a mode by which the manager may or may not solicit information or opinion from others, but he or she expects and is expected by others to arrive at a decision without obligation to consider the views of others. Under consensual decision-making, the manager will not decide until others who will be affected have had sufficient time to offer their views, feel they have

Table 1. Characteristics of Two Familiar Organizational Ideal Types: A and J

Type A (American)	Type J (Japanese)
Short-term employment	Lifetime employment
Individual decision-making	Consensual decision-making
Individual responsibility	Collective responsibility
Rapid evaluation and promotion	Slow evaluation and promotion
Explicit, formalized control	Implicit, informal control
Specialized career path	Nonspecialized career path
Segmented concern	Holistic concern

been fairly heard, and are willing to support the decision even though they may not feel that it is the best one (18).

Although responsibility is not easily distinguished from decision-making style in all cases, it represents an important, independent dimension. Individual responsibility as a value is a necessary precondition to conferring rewards upon individuals in a meritocracy. A manager possibly could engage in consensual decision-making while clearly retaining individual responsibility for the decision. Indeed, the Type Z organization exhibits just this combination. In the J organization, responsibility for overseeing projects and for accepting rewards or punishments is borne collectively by all members of a subunit. American companies in Japan which have attempted to introduce the notion of individual responsibility among managers and blue-collar workers have found strong resistance from their employees. But in the United States individual responsibility is such a central part of the national culture that no organization can replace it with the collective value of the J type.

The speed of evaluation and promotion category is self-explanatory, but its effects are subtle. If promotion is slow, managers have time to become acquainted with the people and the customs which surround their jobs. Workers will be shaped by and ultimately assimilated into the corporate culture. For better or worse, the maverick will not be promoted until he or she has learned to abide by local customs. An organization with a history of rapid promotion will not have as unified a culture as an organization with slower rates of upward mobility.

Speed of evaluation also has significant effects upon the character of interpersonal relationships. In an achievement-oriented organization, evaluations of performance must be free of dimensions such as friendship or kinship. The only solution open to an evaluator is an impersonal relationship. If evaluations occur rapidly, for example once each six months, the subject of the evaluation will typically be known only to the direct supervisor, who will be charged with the responsibility of rendering the evaluation. The supervisor is thus blocked from forming personal, friendship ties with the subordinate. But if major evaluations occur only once every five or ten years (as is common in Japanese firms), the evaluation is no longer explicitly rendered by one superior but emerges through a nonexplicit process of agreement between the many superiors who know the subordinate. Being one among many judges, the direct superior is freed from the need to preserve an "objective" attitude toward the subordinate and thus can take a personal interest in him or her.

The dimension of control is represented in an oversimplified manner. In a sense, the whole ideal type represents a form of social control, and each ideal type achieves this social control in a different manner. But we can identify in Type A organizations the use of explicit standards, rules and regulations, and performance measures as the primary technique of ensuring that actual performance meets desired performance. In Type Z, expectations of behavior or output are not explicitly stated but are to be deduced from a more general understanding of the corporate philosophy.

For example, during one of the author's visits to a Japanese bank in California, the Japanese president and the American vice-presidents of the bank accused each other of being unable to formulate objectives. The Americans meant that the Japanese president could not or would not give them explicit, quantified targets to attain over the next three or six months, while the Japanese meant that the Americans could not see that once they understood the company's philosophy, they would be able to deduce for themselves the proper objective for any conceivable situation.

The degree to which a career path is typically specialized according to function differs greatly between organizational types. In the A organization, an upwardly mobile manager typically remains within a functional specialty, for example going from book-keeper to clerical supervisor to assistant department head of accounting to head of the accounting department. In the J organization, the typical career path is not specialized by function, but may go from bookkeeper to supervisor of the planning department.

A specialized career path yields professionalization, decreases organizational loyalty, and facilitates movement of the individual from one firm to another. A nonspecialized career path yields localism, increases organizational loyalty, and impedes interfirm mobility. Career specialization also increases problems of coordination between individuals and subunits, while nonspecialization eases the coordination problem. Career specialization also yields the scale economies of task specialization and expertise, whereas nonspecialized career paths often sacrifice these benefits. A and J organizations may be the same in formal structure — having equal divisional separation, for example — but individuals will move through those subunits in quite different patterns.

Concern refers to the holism with which employees view each other and especially to the concern with which the supervisor views the subordinate. In the A organization, the supervisor regards the subordinate in a purely task-oriented manner and may consider it improper to inquire into her or his personal life. In comparison to this segmented view of people, the J organization manager considers it part of the managerial role to be fully informed of the personal circumstances of each subordinate.

Each ideal type represents a set of interconnected parts, each dependent on at least one other part. The systematic nature of each type is best understood by putting it in an environmental context.

The Type A has developed in a society characterized by high rates of individual mobility, in a culture which supports norms of independence, self-reliance, and individual responsibility. A work organization in such a setting must contend with high rates of interfirm mobility and a short average tenure of employment. It reduces interdependence between individuals, avoiding the start-up costs of replacing one part of a team. Individual decision-making and individual responsibility provide an adaptive response to rapid change of personnel. If interfirm mobility is high, it becomes impossible to integrate new members into the organization on a large number of dimensions. It is simpler to attend to only the one or two necessary task dimensions of the new member and integrate those. Thus a segmented concern evolves, because a concern for the whole person presents an impossible problem to an organization with high turnover. But as a result, the employee has only limited, contractual ties to the organization, has not internalized its values, and must be dealt with in a compliant relationship, in which control is explicit and formalized.

The A type organization has a relatively short time in which to realize productive benefits from the necessary investment in an individual employee (cost of search and training). It can best realize these benefits by having the person follow a highly specialized career path in which necessary learning can occur rapidly and scale economies are soon achieved. Finally, rapid turnover requires replacement of managers and thus rapid promotion of those at lower levels. Because promotion must be preceded by evaluation, to preserve the impression if not the fact of a meritocracy, evaluation also will occur rapidly.

Ideal Type J organizations evolved in a society in which individual mobility has been low in a culture which supported norms of collectivism. Through historical accidents which preserved a feudal society in Japan into the 19th century and then, after the Meiji restoration, rushed Japan into full-blown industrialism (19), fuedal loyalties were transferred to major industrial institutions, with owners and employees taking the appropriate historical roles of lord and vassal. Because employees are expected to be in the same firm for a lifetime, control can be implicit and internalized rather than explicit and compliant (as in the A type). This form of control evolves because it is more reliable and can account for a wide variety of task and personally oriented actions, whereas no explicit system of rules and regulations could be sufficiently comprehensive to encompass that range of behavior.

Type J employees need not follow specialized career paths, because the organization can invest in them for a long period of time and be assured of repayment in later years. By following nonspecialized career paths, they become experts in the organization rather than experts in some function. They are no longer interchangeable with other organizations, since their particular set of skills and values is unique to one firm, but that is not a cost to them or to the firm. Rather, their loyalty to the firm has increased and the firm need not monitor them closely, thus saving managerial overhead.

Furthermore, coordination problems are reduced, since employees have the information and inclination to accommodate each other in jointly taking action. Since they are to spend a lifetime together, they have an interest in maintaining harmonious relationships and engaging in consensual decision-making. The larger culture supports norms of collectivism which are mirrored in the organization. No individual can properly take credit or blame for actions, since organizational action by its very nature is a joint product of many individuals. Given joint responsibility, rapid evaluation would be difficult, since the task would be like that of performing a multivariate analysis with a sample of one observation. But since turnover and promotion occur slowly, evaluation need not proceed quickly. Many observations of the individual are accumulated over a period of years before the first major evaluation is made. This slow evaluation takes the pressure off a single superior and frees him or her to take a holistic concern for the employee.

The complex relationships between elements of the ideal types are not yet completely specified; that is one task of the present research, which will be aided through empirical analysis. But clearly, the major driving force behind development of the ideal types is the rate of interfirm mobility, which is closely related to the cultural values which aid or inhibit mobility. It can be argued that the A type is an adaptive response to high rates of social mobility while the J type is a response to low rates of social mobility, both forms fitting naturally with their environments. The work organization in this view represents just one way in which members of a society are integrated; it is both influenced by and influences the structure of its surrounding society.

Having concluded that each ideal type represents a natural adaptation to a particular environment, how is it that the J type apparently has succeeded in the United States (9)? The United States provided the social environment in which the A type evolved. Americans are highly urbanized, move about, lead segmented lives, and thus have created a situation in which a work organization must be able to rely on people who are strangers to each other and still get coordinated effort out of them. The answer was the A type, which is contractual, formalized, and impersonal. How can a very different type, the J, flourish in this same social environment?

Interviews with managers from a large number of companies over the past two years were focused on companies which, by reputation, have many characteristics of Type J. Out of these interviews came a conception of a third ideal type, which initially appeared to be the J but differs from it in some essential characteristics.

The ideal Type Z (Table 2) combines a basic cultural commitment to individualistic values with a highly collective, nonindividual pattern of interaction. It simultaneously satisfies old norms of independence and present needs for affiliation. Employment is effectively (although not officially) for a lifetime, and turnover is low. Decision-making is consensual, and there is often a highly self-conscious attempt to preserve the consensual mode.

But the individual still is ultimately the decision-maker, and responsibility remains individual. This procedure puts strains on the individual, who is held responsible for decisions singly but must arrive at them collectively.

Table 2.   Characteristics of Organizational Type Z

Type Z (Modified American)

Long-term employment
Consensual decision-making
Individual responsibility
Slow evaluation and promotion
Implicit, informal control with explicit, formalized measures
Moderately specialized career path
Holistic concern, including family

These strains are mitigated by the fact that evaluation and promotion take place slowly and that the basic control is implicit and subtle. Thus the complexities of collective decision-making are taken into account in rendering personal evaluations, but there are explicit measures of performance as in Type A. In the Z organization, although there are lots of formal accounting measures of performance, the real evaluation is subjective and highly personal. No one gets rapidly promoted or punished solely because their performance scores are good or bad. In an A organization, by contrast, people's careers often succeed or fail solely on explicit performance measures, as must be the case in any purely formalized system.

Career paths in the Z organization tend to be moderately specialized, but quite nonspecialized by comparison with the Type A organization. The slowness of evaluation and the stability of membership promote a holistic concern for people, particularly from superior to subordinate. This holism includes the employee and his or her family in an active manner. Family members regularly interact with other organization members and their families and feel an identification with the organization.

IMPLICATIONS FOR SOCIETY AT LARGE

Why is the Z type useful in thinking about American organizations if the A type is the natural adaptation to a society and culture? If a second ideal type can be accommodated, social conditions must have changed.

The critical aspect of the environment is its ability to provide stable affiliations for individuals. Traditional sources of affiliation in American society (family, church, neighborhood, voluntary association, and long-term friendship) have been weakened by urbanization and geographical mobility. Figure 1 represents the combination of societal and organizational sources of affiliation. It includes only ideal Types A and Z; ideal Type J, the pure adaptation to a Japanese society, is not useful as a representation of American organizations.

Throughout most of its history, this nation has been high in sources of affiliation outside of the workplace. Under this condition, Type A organizations evolved, creating a stable, integrated state in which most people devoted most of their energies to affiliative networks away from the workplace and were only partially included in the work organization. Had the work organization been Type Z, each employee would have been torn between two mistresses and in an overload-

Affiliation in the Organization	Affiliation in Society	
	High	Low
High (Type Z)	I Overloaded	II Integrated
Low (Type Z)	III Integrated	IV Underloaded

Figure 1. Societal and Organizational Sources of Affiliation.

ed state (Cell I). In the past few decades, much of American society has moved from the "High" to the "Low" affiliation state (20–23). High mobility has broken the traditional patterns of interaction, but the values which supported those patterns will change more slowly. Those values support the notion of partial inclusion, of individuality, of the Type A organization. Thus many find themselves largely in the Underloaded cell (Cell IV), with society unable to provide affiliation and work organizations not organized to do so. To return to a balanced state, affiliation will have to come mostly from the organization and not from society at large.

Because not all people need the same level of affiliation (or achievement or power), each person will respond differently to being in each of the cells I through IV. According to Maslow (24), all people have a need for affiliation, belongingness, or love, which can be satisfied through feeling that they are part of a group or company. On the average, people in Cell IV ("Underloaded") will have unfulfilled needs for affiliation. They will experience "anomie," the sensation that there are no anchors or standards, and thus a feeling of being lost.

All these elements can be combined in one model which describes how the organization interacts with its social environment and with the needs of its individual members to produce high or low loyalty for the organization and high or low mental health for the employees (see Figure 2).

If American society is moving from high to low affiliation, people who are employed in a Type Z organization should be better able to deal with stress and should be happier than the population at large. Certainly the Type Z organization will be more appropriate for that segment of society which lacks stable and strong affiliative ties. That is not to suggest that the work organization will in any way replace or compete with other national institutions. Quite the opposite: if the company provides a strong basic stability in people's lives, then the family, church, and neighborhood can all flourish.

Some may object that they will never support a Type Z approach in their company or that it would never work in their industry. They may be right. Society contains a range of people and environments; some prefer an employer who leaves them alone, evaluates them purely on objective measures, and recognizes achievement through rapid promotion even over the heads of others. There will always be organizations for such people and such tastes. Stability of employment is not possible in some industries. Aerospace is one example of an industry where a Type Z organization would be harmful; if people built rich ties with each other and a control system based on personal knowledge, both would be wrenched and destroyed when the contract came to an end and massive layoffs became necessary. The Type Z form will not be for everyone.

Due to chance, some models of the Type Z organization are available to study and learn from. Until recently, the Type A organization was the most successful form in American society. When people had relatives, neighbors, and churches, they did not need Dr. Spock to tell them why the baby was purple, and they did not need a company that provided them with a rich network of social contacts. But in a few cases, companies grew up in small towns, or in places like California that were populated by emigrants, or in industries which required frequent relocation of employees. In all three cases, one side effect was that people had no immediate form of social contact available except through their employer. The extreme case is the military base, which looks, feels, and smells the same whether it is in Hawaii, Illinois, or New York. To make life possible under conditions of high geographical mobility, the military has developed a culture which is immediately familiar and secure no matter where its employees go. These organizations, public and private, created a social vacuum for their

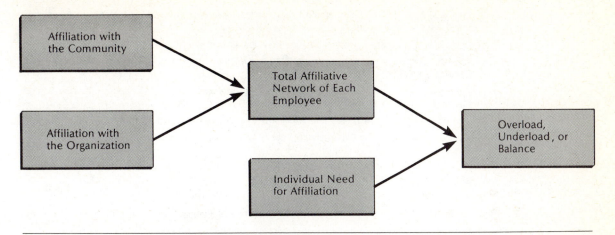

Figure 2.   A Model of Organizational and Individual Affiliation Needs.

employees and then had to develop internal sources of support to replace what had been taken away. Now the rest of the country is "catching up" with them as stable sources of support disappear elsewhere. One can look to such models for ideas about how to cope with the new society.

The future problem confronting the work organization seems relatively clear. American society, which has been in a constant process of change during its turbulent 200 years, has reached a critical point. Church membership is declining; violent crimes increasingly involve a victim who is completely unknown to the assailant; workers feel less commitment to employers; all of us long for stability and structure in our lives. These changes signify a decline in belongingness and suggest the fate assigned by Homans (1) to societies which lose the feeling of membership; we will become, "a dust heap of individuals without links to one another."

REFERENCES

1. Homans, G. C. *The Human Group* (New York: Harcourt, Brace and World, 1950).

2. Mayo, E. *The Social Problems of an Industrial Civilization* (Boston: Harvard Business School, 1945).

3. Angell, R. C. *The Moral Integration of American Cities* (Chicago: University of Chicago Press, 1951).

4. Angell, R. C. "The Moral Integration of American Cities, Part II," *American Journal of Sociology*, Vol. 80 (1974), 607–29.

5. Form, W. H. "The Social Construction of Anomie: A Four Nation Study of Industrial Workers," *American Journal of Sociology*, Vol. 80 (1975), 1165–91.

6. Abegglen, J. C. *The Japanese Factory: Aspects of its Social Organization* (Glencoe, Ill.: Free Press, 1958).

7. Kolarska, L. "Interorganizational Networks and Politics: The Case of Polish Industry." Unpublished MS (1975).

8. Whyte, M. K. "Bureaucracy and Modernization in China: The Maoist Critique," *American Sociological Review*, Vol. 38 (1973), 149–63.

9. Johnson, R. T., and W. G. Ouchi. "Made in America (under Japanese Management)," *Harvard Business Review*, Vol. 52, No. 5 (1974), 61–69.

10. Cole, R. Japanese Blue Collar: The Changing Tradition (Berkeley: University of California Press, 1971).

11. Cole, R. "Functional Alternatives and Economic Development: An Empirical Example of Permanent Employment in Japan," *American Sociological Review,* Vol. 38 (1973), 424–38.

12. Dore, R. British Factory — Japanese Factory (Berkeley: University of California Press, 1973).

13. Toennies, Ferdinand. *Gemeinschaft und Gesellschaft,* trans. by Loomis (New York: American Book Company, 1940).

14. Weber, Max. *The Theory of Social and Economic Organization,* trans. by A. M. Henderson and T. Parsons (Glencoe, Ill.: Free Press and Falcon's Wing Press, 1947).

15. Merton, Robert K. *Social Theory and Social Structure,* 2d ed. Glencoe, Ill.: Free Press, 1957).

16. Udy, S. "Bureaucracy and Rationality in Weber's Organization Theory: An Empirical Study," *American Sociological Review,* Vol. 24 (1959).

17. Udy, S. "Administrative Rationality, Social Setting, and Organizational Development," *American Journal of Sociology,* Vol. 68 (1962), 299–308.

18. Schein, E. *Process Consultation* (Reading, Mass.: Addison-Wesley, 1969).

19. Nakane, C. *Japanese Society,* rev. ed. (Middlesex, England: Penguin Books, 1973).

20. Kasarda, J. D., and M. Janowitz. "Community Attachment in a Mass Society," *American Sociological Review,* Vol. 39 (1974), 328–39.

21. Reissman, L. *The Urban Process* (Glencoe, Ill.: Free Press, 1964).

22. Short, J. F. *The Social Fabric of the Metropolis* (Chicago: University of Chicago Press, 1971).

23. Warren, R. L. *The Community in America* (Chicago: Rand McNally, 1972).

24. Maslow, A. H. *Motivation and Personality* (New York: Harper, 1954).

Power in Organizations

21. Power Tactics

Norman H. Martin and John Howard Sims

Executives — whether in business, government, education, or the church — have power and use it. They maneuver and manipulate in order to get a job done and, in many cases, to strengthen and enhance their own position. Although they would hate the thought and deny the allegation, the fact is that they are politicians. "Politics," according to one of the leading authorities in this complex and fascinating field, "is . . . concerned with relationships of control or of influence. To phrase the idea differently, politics deal with human relationships of superordination and subordination, or dominance and submission, of the governors and the governed."[1] In this sense, everyone who exercises power must be a politician.

It is true, as many others have pointed out in different connections, that we in this country have an instinctive revulsion against the term *power*. It carries immoral connotations for us, despite the definitions of men like R. H. Tawney, the economic historian, who divorces it

from any ethical attributes by calling it simply "the capacity of an individual or group of individuals to modify the conduct of other individuals or groups in the manner which he desires, and to prevent his own conduct from being modified in the manner which he does not."[2]

Furthermore, though we glorify ambition in the abstract, we frown on its practices and are distressed at the steps which must be taken if ambition is to be translated into actual advancement. Thus when power is coupled with ambition, we shy away and try to pretend that neither really exists.

But the fact is that we use power and exercise our ambitions just the same — troubled though we may be by the proverbial New England conscience which "doesn't prevent you from doing anything — it just keeps you from enjoying it!"

The complexity of the problem is increased when we recall that the real source of power is not the superior

Reprinted from the *Harvard Business Review,* November-December 1956, pp. 25-29, by permission of the authors and the publisher. © 1956 by the President and Fellows of Harvard College; all rights reserved.

but the subordinate. Men can only exercise that power which they are allowed by other men — albeit their positions are buttressed by economic, legal, and other props. The ultimate source of power is the group; and a group, in turn, is made up of people with consciousness and will, with emotion and irrationality, with intense personal interests and tenaciously held values.

The human being resists being treated as a constant. Knowledge, reason, and technical know-how will not suffice as means of control but give way to the arts of persuasion and inducement, of tactics and maneuver, of all that is involved in interpersonal relationships. Power cannot be given; it must be won. And the techniques and skills of winning it are at the same time the methods of employing it as a medium of control. This represents the political function of the power holder.

In such a light, we see why the successful functioning and advancement of the executive is dependent not only on those aspects of an enterprise which are physical and logical, but on morale, teamwork, authority, and obedience — in a word, on the vast intricacy of human relationships which make up the political universe of the executive.

The real question then becomes: How can power be used most effectively? What are some of the political stratagems which the administrator must employ if he is to carry out his responsibilities and further his career? This is an area that has carefully been avoided by both students and practitioners of business — as if there were something shady about it. But facts are facts, and closing our eyes to them will not change them. Besides, if they are important facts, they should be brought into the open for examination.

Accordingly, we present here some of the first stage of a fairly extensive investigation of just how the executive functions in his political-power environment. We have searched the biographies of well-known leaders of history, from Alexander to Roosevelt; we have explored the lives of successful industrialists like Rockefeller and Ford; and we have interviewed a number of contemporary executives.

There follows an account of certain tactics which we have found to be practiced by most men whose success rests on ability to control and direct the actions of others — no doubt, raw and oversimplified when reduced to a few black-and-white words, but for this very reason more likely to be provocative. With further refinement, these generalizations will serve as hypotheses in the succeeding stages of our research, but in the meantime we present them to businessmen to look at

openly and objectively — to ask, ``Do we not use just such techniques frequently?'' and, if so, to ponder, ``How can we best operate in this particular area, for our own interest as managers and for the good of people under us?''

TAKING COUNSEL

The able executive is cautious about how he seeks and receives advice. He takes counsel only when he himself desires it. His decisions must be made in terms of his own grasp of the situation, taking into account the views of others when he thinks it necessary. To act otherwise is to be subject, not to advice, but to pressure; to act otherwise too often produces vacillation and inconsistency.

Throwing a question to a group of subordinates is all too often interpreted as a delegation of power, and the executive may find himself answered with a decision instead of counsel. He must remember that he, not the group under him, is the responsible party. If an executive allows his subordinates to provide advice when he does not specifically call for it, he may find himself subject, not only to pressure, but to conflicting alignments of forces within his own ranks. A vague sort of policy which states, ``I am always ready to hear your advice and ideas on anything,'' will waste time, confuse issues, dilute leadership, and erode power.

ALLIANCES

In many respects, the executive system in a firm is composed of complexes of sponsor-protégé relationships.[3] For the protégé, these relationships provide channels for advancement; for the sponsor, they build a loyal group of followers. A wise administrator will make it a point to establish such associations with those above and below him. In the struggles for power and influence that go on in many organizations, every executive needs a devoted following and close alliances with other executives, both on his own level and above him, if he is to protect and to enhance his status and sphere of influence.

Alliances should not be looked upon, however, merely as a protective device. In addition, they provide ready-made systems of communications, through which the executive can learn firsthand how his decisions are being carried out, what unforeseen obstacles are being encountered, and what the level of morale in the organization is at any moment.

MANEUVERABILITY

The wise executive maintains his flexibility, and he never completely commits himself to any one position or program. If forces beyond his control compel a major change in company policy, he can gracefully bend with the wind and cooperate with the inevitable, thus maintaining his status.

An executive should preserve maneuverability in career planning as well. He ought never to get in a situation that does not have plenty of escape hatches. He must be careful, for instance, that his career is not directly dependent on the superior position of a sponsor. He should provide himself with transferable talents, and interfirm alliances, so that he will be able to move elsewhere if the conditions in his current organization become untenable.

COMMUNICATION

During recent years emphasis has been placed on the necessity for well-dredged channels of communication which run upward, downward, and sideways. Top management should supply its subordinates with maximum information, according to this theory; subordinates, in turn, must report fully to their chiefs.

It is possible, however, that executives have been oversold on maximizing the flow of information. It simply is not good strategy to communicate everything one knows. Instead, it may often be advantageous to withhold information or to time its release. This is especially true with reference to future plans—plans which may or may not materialize; it is also valid in the case of information that may create schism or conflict within the organization; and it is prudent when another executive is a threat to one's own position. Furthermore, information is an important tactical weapon, and should be considered as such.

It would appear, then, that executives should be concerned with determining "who gets to know what and when" rather than with simply increasing the flow. Completely open communication deprives the executive of the exclusive power of directing information which should be his.

COMPROMISING

The executive should accept compromise as a means of settling differences with his tongue in his cheek. While appearing to alter his view, he should continue to press forward toward a clear-cut set of goals. It is frequently necessary to give ground on small matters, to delay, to move off tangents, even to suffer reverses in order to retain power for future forward movement. Concessions, then, should be more apparent than real.

NEGATIVE TIMING

The executive is often urged to take action with which he is not in agreement. Sometimes pressure for such action arises from the expectations of subordinates, the influence of his associates with his superiors, the demands of custom and tradition, or other sources he would be unwise to ignore.

To give in to such demands would be to deny the executive's prerogative; to refuse might precipitate a dangerous crisis, and threaten his power. In such situations the executive may find it wise to use what might be called the technique of "negative timing." He initiates action, but the process of expedition is retarded. He is considering, studying, and planning for the problem; there are difficulties to be overcome and possible ramifications which must be considered. He is always *in the process* of doing something but never quite does it, or finally he takes action when it is actually too late. In this way the executive escapes the charge of dereliction, and at the same time the inadvisable program "dies on the vine."

SELF-DRAMATIZATION

Most vocal communication in which an executive engages—whether with his superiors, his colleagues, or his subordinates—is unpremeditated, sincere, spontaneous. His nonvocal communication—the impression projected by his posture, gestures, dress, or facial expressions—is commonly just as natural.

But executives would do well to reexamine this instinctive behavior, for many of them are overlooking an important political stratagem. The skill of the actor—whose communication is "artistic" as opposed to "natural"—represents a potential asset to an administrator. Dramatic art is a process by which selections from reality are chosen and arranged by the artists for the particular purpose of arousing the emotions, of convincing, of persuading, of altering the behavior of the audience in a *planned direction*.

The actor's purpose is no different from that of the manager who wants to activate his subordinates in certain specific directions—to secure a certain response from those with whom he communicates. The actor's peculiar gift is in deliberately shaping his own speech and behavior to accomplish his purpose. The element of chance, the variable of the unknown, is diminished, if not removed; and rehearsal with some foreknowledge of what is to occur takes place. The *how* of communicating is considered as well as the *what*.

Of course, this is no easy task. The effectiveness of the actor's performance depends on his ability to estimate what will stimulate the audience to respond. And once he makes his choices, he must be able to use them skillfully. His voice and body must be so well disciplined, so well trained, that the images he chooses may be given life. The question is, How can an executive acquire the skill of artistic communication? How can he learn to dramatize himself?

The development of sharper powers of observation is the first step. Having witnessed effective communication — whether a TV drama or an actual meeting of the board of directors — the executive should try to determine what made it effective. He should pay attention to *how* a successful man handled himself, not what he said or did. Formal classes can provide the executive with control over his voice — its pitch, tone, color, speed, diction; training can do the same for his body — gesture, posture, and mime. Most important, the executive should seize any opportunity to gain actual experience in putting such skills to work, in amateur theatricals or "role-playing" sessions.

It would be foolish to deny that such skills cannot be entirely learned; to some extent they depend on the unknowns of flair, talent, and genius. But such an acknowledgment does not excuse the executive from making an effort, for the range of possible improvement is very great.

CONFIDENCE

Related to, but not identical with, self-dramatization is the outward appearance of confidence. Once an executive has made a decision, he must look and act decided. In some instances genuine inner conviction may be lacking, or the manager may find it difficult to generate the needed dynamics. The skillful executive who finds himself in such a situation will either produce the effect of certainty or postpone any contact with his associates in order to avoid appearing in an unfavorable light.

Thus, the man who constantly gives the impression of knowing what he is doing — even if he does not — is using his power and increasing it at the same time.

ALWAYS THE BOSS

Warm personal relations with subordinates have sometimes been considered the mark of a good executive. But in practice an atmosphere of social friendship interferes with the efficiency of an operation and acts to limit the power of the manager. Personal feelings should not be a basis for action — either negative or positive. The executive should never permit himself to be so committed to a subordinate as a friend that he is unable to withdraw from this personal involvement and regard the man objectively as an element in a given situation.

Thus, a thin line of separation between executive and subordinate must always be maintained. The situation should be one of isolation and contact — of the near and far — of marginality. No matter how cordial he may be, the executive must sustain a line of privacy which cannot be transgressed; in the final analysis, he must always be the boss. If we assume, then, that the traditional "open-door" policy of the modern executive is good strategy, we must always ask the question: "How far open?"

The foregoing discussion will undoubtedly raise questions, and even indignation, in the minds of some readers. In the last two decades, the finger of censure has often been pointed at the interpersonal relations in the management of industrial organizations, questioning whether they are harmonious with a democratic society and ideology.[4] Executives have been urged to adopt practices and programs aimed at "democratizing" their businesses. Perhaps they have even developed a sense of guilt from the realization of their own position of authority and that they cannot be completely frank, sincere, honest, and aboveboard in their interpersonal relations. We live in an era of "groupiness"; we are bombarded with admonitions which insist that everyone who is participating in an enterprise should have a part in the management of it.

In the light of such a trend even the terminology used in this article — "power," "maneuver," "tactics," "techniques" — appears disturbing when set down in black and white. But in fact it is neither immoral nor cynical to recognize and describe the actual daily practices of power. After all, sweeping them under the rug — making believe that they are not actually part of the executive's activity — does not cause them to vanish. Open and honest discussion of the political aspects in the administrator's job exposes these stratagems to the constructive spotlight of knowledge. They exist; therefore, we had better take a look at them and see what they are really like.

As we delve deeper into the study of political tactics in business management, the contrast with modern human relations theory and practice will stand out in ever-sharper relief. Mutual confidence, open communication, continuing consultation and participation by subordinates, friendship, and an atmosphere of democracy seem hard to reconcile with much of the maneuvering and power plays that go on in the nation's offices and factories every day.

Yet businessmen must develop some rationale of executive behavior which can encompass the idealism of democracy and the practicality of politics — and, at the same time, be justified in terms of ultimate values. If they do not, they will feel like hypocrites as the day-to-day operation of their offices clashes with their speeches before women's clubs. The old cliché that *business is business* is no longer satisfying to the general public nor to the executive himself.

One way to try to fit human relations theory and political tactics together is to state that the means of exercising power are neutral. In and of themselves, they have no moral value. They take on moral qualities only in connection with the ends for which they are used. Power can be used for good or ill according to this theory, and we should have the courage and knowledge to use it wisely. Conscious, deliberate, and skilled use of executive power means responsible use of power. If men in the past have employed power for evil ends, that is unfortunate; it is just as true that other men, if they had made use of business politics in an effective fashion, might have been a greater force for good.

The difficulty with this line of thought lies in the well-known pitfalls inherent in the timeless means-ends controversy. In real life, what are means and what are ends? Can you achieve good ends by bad means? If the way one man conducts his relationship with another has no moral implications, what human activity does have moral significance?

Others may take the position that "so long as my general philosophy is sound and moral, the specific actions I have to take in the course of my job don't matter." But one may question the validity of a philosophy of life that breaks down every time it comes into contact with reality.

Still another formula could be found in the statement, "The good of the company comes before that of an individual. If I have to violate moral codes and democratic principles in dealing with one man, that is too bad for him. But I cannot allow any single person to overshadow the interests of all our other employees, stockholders, and customers." The skeptical listener might then raise the issue of collectivism versus individualism, and ask whether the general welfare really overrides the worth and dignity of the individual. Can we build a society on the idea of the individual's importance if we violate the principle whenever it interferes with what we consider to be the good of the group?

There are, of course, other approaches, but they too are fraught with internal contradictions. The riddle, then, remains unsolved; the conflict between the use of power and the principles of democracy and enlightened management is unrelieved. Businessmen, who face this paradox every day in countless situations, cannot avoid the responsibility of explaining or resolving it. If a viable philosophy of management is to be developed, they must contribute their ideas — for the sake of their own peace of mind, if nothing else.

If this article succeeds in getting more businessmen to do some thinking along this line, then it will have served its purpose.

NOTES

1. V. O. Key Jr., *Politics, Parties and Pressure Groups,* 2d ed. (New York: Thomas Y. Crowell Co., 1948), p. 3.

2. R. H. Tawney, *Equality,* 4th ed. (London: George Allen & Unwin, Ltd., 1952), p. 175.

3. See Norman H. Martin and Anselm S. Strauss, "Patterns of Mobility within Industrial Organizations," *Journal of Business,* April 1956, p. 101.

4. See Thomas C. Cochran, "Business and the Democratic Tradition," *Harvard Business Review,* March-April 1956, p. 39.

22.   Sources of Power of Lower Participants in Complex Organizations

David Mechanic

It is not unusual for lower participants[1] in complex organizations to assume and wield considerable power and influence not associated with their formally defined positions within these organizations. In sociological terms they have considerable personal power but no authority. Such personal power is often attained, for example, by executive secretaries and accountants in business firms, by attendants in mental hospitals, and even by inmates in prisons. The personal power achieved by these lower participants does not necessarily result from unique personal characteristics, although these may be relevant, but results rather from particular aspects of their location within their organizations.

INFORMAL VERSUS FORMAL POWER

Within organizations the distribution of authority (institutionalized power) is closely if not perfectly correlated with the prestige of positions. Those who have argued for the independence of these variables[2] have taken their examples from diverse organizations and do not deal with situations where power is clearly comparable.[3] Thus when Bierstedt argues that Einstein had prestige but not power, and the policeman power but not prestige, it is apparent that he is comparing categories that are not comparable. Generally persons occupying high-ranking positions within organizations have more authority than those holding low-ranking positions.

One might ask what characterizes high-ranking positions within organizations. What is most evident, perhaps, is that lower participants recognize the right of higher-ranking participants to exercise power, and yield without difficulty to demands they regard as legitimate. Moreover, persons in high-ranking positions tend to have considerable access to and control over information and persons both within and outside the organization, and to instrumentalities or resources. Although higher supervisory personnel may be isolated from the task activities of lower participants, they maintain access to them through formally established intermediary positions and exercise control through intermediary participants. There appears, therefore, to be a clear correlation between the prestige of positions within organizations and the extent to which they offer access to information, persons, and instrumentalities.

Since formal organizations tend to structure lines of access and communication, access should be a clue to institutional prestige. Yet access depends on variables other than those controlled by the formal structure of an organization, and this often makes the informal power structure that develops within organizations somewhat incongruent with the formally intended plan. It is these variables that allow work groups to limit production through norms that contravene the goals of the larger organization, that allow hospital attendants to thwart changes in the structure of a hospital, and that allow prison inmates to exercise some control over prison guards. Organizations, in a sense, are continuously at the mercy of their lower participants, and it is this fact that makes organizational power structure especially interesting to the sociologist and social psychologist.

CLARIFICATION OF DEFINITIONS

The purpose of this paper is to present some hypotheses explaining why lower participants in organizations can often assume and wield considerable power which is not associated with their positions as formally defined within these organizations. For the purposes of this analysis the concepts "influence," "power," and "control" will be used synonymously. Moreover, we shall not be concerned with type of power, that is, whether the power is based on reward, punishment, identification, power to veto, or whatever.[4] Power will be defined as *any force that results in behavior that*

Administrative Science Quarterly 7 (1962): 349-64.

would not have occurred if the force had not been present. We have defined power as a force rather than a relationship because it appears that much of what we mean by power is encompassed by the normative framework of an organization, and thus any analysis of power must take into consideration the power of norms as well as persons.

I shall also argue, following Thibaut and Kelley,[5] that power is closely related to dependence. To the extent that a person is dependent on another, he is potentially subject to the other person's power. Within organizations one makes others dependent upon him by controlling access to information, persons, and instrumentalities which I shall define as follows:

Information includes knowledge of the organization, knowledge about persons, knowledge of the norms, procedures, techniques, and so forth.

Persons include anyone within the organization or anyone outside the organization upon whom the organization is in some way dependent.

Instrumentalities include any aspect of the physical plant of the organization or its resources (equipment, machines, money, and so on). Power is a function not only of the extent to which a person controls information, persons, and instrumentalities, but also of the importance of the various attributes he controls.[6]

Finally, following Dahl,[7] we shall agree that comparisons of power among persons should, as far as possible, utilize comparable units. Thus we shall strive for clarification by attempting to oversimplify organizational processes; the goal is to set up a number of hypothetical statements of the relationship between variables taken two at a time, "all other factors being assumed to remain constant."

To state the hypotheses suggested somewhat more formally:

H1 Other factors remaining constant, organizational power is related to access to persons, information, and instrumentalities.

H2 Other factors remaining constant, as a participant's length of time in an organization increases, he has increased access to persons, information, and instrumentalities.

While these hypotheses are obvious, they do suggest that a careful scrutiny of the organizational literature, especially that dealing with the power or counterpower of lower participants, might lead to further formalized statements, some considerably less obvious than the ones stated.

SOURCES OF POWER OF LOWER PARTICIPANTS

The most effective way for lower participants to achieve power is to obtain, maintain, and control access to persons, information, and instrumentalities. To the extent that this can be accomplished, lower participants make higher-ranking participants dependent upon them. Thus dependence together with the manipulation of the dependency relationship is the key to the power of lower participants.

A number of examples can be cited which illustrate the preceding point. Scheff, for example, reports on the failure of a state mental hospital to bring about intended reform because of the opposition of hospital attendants.[8] He noted that the power of hospital attendants was largely a result of the dependence of ward physicians on attendants. This dependence resulted from the physician's short tenure, his lack of interest in administration, and the large amount of administrative responsibility he had to assume. An implicit trading agreement developed between physicians and attendants, whereby attendants would take on some of the responsibilities and obligations of the ward physician in return for increased power in decision-making processes concerning patients. Failure of the ward physician to honor his part of the agreement resulted in information being withheld, disobedience, lack of cooperation, and unwillingness of the attendants to serve as a barrier between the physician and a ward full of patients demanding attention and recognition. When the attendant withheld cooperation, the physician had difficulty in making a graceful entrance and departure from the ward, in handling necessary paper work (officially his responsibility), and in obtaining information needed to deal adequately with daily treatment and behavior problems. When attendants opposed change, they could wield influence by refusing to assume responsibilities officially assigned to the physician.

Similarly, Sykes describes the dependence of prison guards on inmates and the power obtained by inmates over guards.[9] He suggests that although guards could report inmates for disobedience, frequent reports would give prison officials the impression that the guard was unable to command obedience. The guard, therefore, had some stake in ensuring the good behavior of prisoners without use of formal sanctions against them. The result was a trading agreement whereby the guard allowed violations of certain rules in return for cooperative behavior. A similar situation is found in respect to officers in the Armed Services or foremen in industry. To the extent that they require formal sanctions to bring about cooperation, they are usually perceived by their superiors as less valuable to the organization. For a good leader is expected to command obedience, at least, if not commitment.

FACTORS AFFECTING POWER

Expertise

Increasing specialization and organizational growth have made the expert or staff person important. The expert maintains power because high-ranking persons in the organization are dependent upon him for his special skills and access to certain kinds of information. One possible reason for lawyers obtaining many high governmental offices is that they are likely to have access to rather specialized but highly important means to organizational goals.[10]

We can state these ideas in hypotheses, as follows:

H3 Other factors remaining constant, to the extent that a low-ranking participant has important expert knowledge not available to high-ranking participants, he is likely to have power over them.

Power stemming from expertise, however, is likely to be limited unless it is difficult to replace the expert. This leads to two further hypotheses:

H4 Other factors remaining constant, a person difficult to replace will have greater power than a person easily replaceable.
H5 Other factors remaining constant, experts will be more difficult to replace than nonexperts.

While persons having expertise are likely to be fairly high-ranking participants in an organization, the same hypotheses that explain the power of lower participants are relevant in explaining the comparative power positions of intermediate and high-ranking persons.

As a result of growing specialization, expertise is increasingly important in organizations. As the complexity of organizational tasks increases, and as organizations grow in size, there is a limit to responsibility that can be efficiently exercised by one person. Delegation of responsibility occurs, experts and specialists are brought in to provide information and research, and the higher participants become dependent upon them. Experts have tremendous potentialities for power by withhold-

ing information, providing incorrect information, and so on, and to the extent that experts are dissatisfied, the probability of organizational sabotage increases.

Effort and Interest

The extent to which lower participants may exercise power depends in part on their willingness to exert effort in areas where higher-ranking participants are often reluctant to participate. Effort exerted is directly related to the degree of interest one has in an area.

H6 Other factors remaining constant, there is a direct relationship between the amount of effort a person is willing to exert in an area and the power he can command.

For example, secretarial staffs in universities often have power to make decisions about the purchase and allocation of supplies, the allocation of their services, the scheduling of classes, and, at times, the disposition of student complaints. Such control may in some instances lead to sanctions against a professor by polite reluctance to furnish supplies, ignoring his preferences for the scheduling of classes, and giving others preference in the allocation of services. While the power to make such decisions may easily be removed from the jurisdiction of the lower participant, it can only be accomplished at a cost — the willingness to allocate time and effort to the decisions dealing with these matters. To the extent that responsibilities are delegated to lower participants, a certain degree of power is likely to accompany the responsibility. Also, should the lower participant see his perceived rights in jeopardy, he may sabotage the system in various ways.

Let us visualize a hypothetical situation where a department concludes that secretarial services are being allocated on a prejudicial basis as a result of complaints to the chairman of the department by several of the younger faculty. Let us also assume that, when the complaint is investigated, it is found to be substantially correct; that is, some of the younger faculty have difficulty obtaining secretarial services because of preferences among the secretarial staff. If in attempting to eliminate discretion by the secretarial staff, the chairman establishes a rule ordering the allocation of services on the basis of the order in which work appears, the rule can easily be made ineffective by complete conformity to it. Deadlines for papers, examinations, and the like will occur, and flexibility in the allocation of services is required if these deadlines are to be met. Thus the need for flexibility can be made to conflict with the rule by a staff usually not untalented in such operations.

When an organization gives discretion to lower participants, it is usually trading the power of discretion for needed flexibility. The cost of constant surveillance is too high, and the effort required too great; it is very often much easier for all concerned to allow the secretary discretion in return for cooperation and not too great an abuse of power.

H7 Other factors remaining constant, the less effort and interest higher-ranking participants are willing to devote to a task, the more likely are lower participants to obtain power relevant to this task.

Attractiveness

Another personal attribute associated with the power of low-ranking persons in an organization is attractiveness or what some call ''personality.'' People who are viewed as attractive are more likely to obtain access to persons, and, once such access is gained, they may be more likely to succeed in promoting a cause. But once again dependence is the key to the power of attractiveness, for whether a person is dependent upon another for a service he provides, or for approval or affection, what is most relevant is the relational bond, which is highly valued.

H8 Other factors remaining constant, the more attractive a person, the more likely he is to obtain access to persons and control over these persons.

Location and Position

In any organization the person's location in physical space and position in social space are important factors influencing access to persons, information, and instrumentalities.[11] Propinquity affects the opportunities for interaction, as well as one's position within a communication network. Although these are somewhat separate factors, we shall refer to their combined effect as centrality[12] within the organization.

H9 Other factors remaining constant, the more central a person is in an organization, the greater is his access to persons, information, and instrumentalities.

Some low participants may have great centrality within an organization. An executive's or university president's secretary not only has access, but often controls access in making appointments and scheduling events. Although she may have no great formal authority, she may have considerable power.

CONDITIONS

It should be clear that the variables we are considering are at different levels of analysis; some of them define attributes of persons, while others define attributes of communication and organization. Power processes within organizations are particularly interesting in that there are many channels of power and ways of achieving it.

In complex organizations different occupational groups attend to different functions, each group often maintaining its own power structure within the organization. Thus hospitals have administrators, medical personnel, nursing personnel, attendants, maintenance personnel, laboratory personnel, and so on. Universities, similarly, have teaching personnel, research personnel, administrative personnel, maintenance personnel, and so on. Each of these functional tasks within organizations often becomes the sphere of a particular group that controls activities relating to the task. While these tasks usually are coordinated at the highest levels of the organization, they often are not coordinated at intermediate and lower levels. It is not unusual, however, for coalitions to form among lower participants in these multiple structures. A secretary may know the man who manages the supply of stores, or the person assigning parking stickers. Such acquaintances may give her the ability to handle informally certain needs that would be more time-consuming and difficult to handle formally. Her ability to provide services informally makes higher-ranking participants in some degree dependent upon her, thereby giving her power, which increases her ability to bargain on issues important to her.

RULES

In organizations with complex power structures lower participants can use their knowledge of the norms of the organization to thwart attempted change. In discussing the various functions of bureaucratic rules, Gouldner maintains that such rules serve as excellent substitutes for surveillance, since surveillance in addition to being expensive in time and effort arouses considerable hostility and antagonism.[13] Moreover, he argues, rules are a functional equivalent for direct, personally given orders, since they specify the obligations of workers to do things in specific ways. Standardized rules, in addition, allow simple screening of violations, facilitate remote control, and to some extent legitimize punishment when the rule is violated. The worker who violates a bureaucratic rule has little recourse to the excuse that he did not know what was expected, as he might claim for a direct order. Finally, Gouldner argues that rules are "the 'chips' to which the company staked the supervisors and which they could use to play the game";[14] that is, rules established a punishment which could be withheld, and this facilitated the supervisors' bargaining power with lower participants.

While Gouldner emphasizes the functional characteristics of rules within an organization, it should be clear that full compliance to all the rules at all times will probably be dysfunctional for the organization. Complete and apathetic compliance may do everything but facilitate achievement of organizational goals. Lower participants who are familiar with an organization and its rules can often find rules to support their contention that they do not do what they have been asked to do, and rules are also often a rationalization for inaction on their part. The following of rules becomes especially complex when associations and unions become involved, for there are then two sets of rules to which the participant can appeal.

What is suggested is that rules may be chips for everyone concerned in the game. Rules become the "chips" through which the bargaining process is maintained. Scheff, as noted earlier, observed that attendants in mental hospitals often took on responsibilities assigned legally to the ward physician, and when attendants refused to share these responsibilities the physician's position became extremely difficult.[15]

The ward physician is legally responsible for the care and treatment of each ward patient. This responsibility requires attention to a host of details. Medicine, seclusion, sedation, and transfer orders, for example, require the doctor's signature. Tranquilizers are particularly troublesome in this regard since they require frequent adjustment of dosage in order to get the desired effects. The physician's order is required to each change in dosage. With 150 patients under his care on tranquilizers, and several changes of dosages a week desirable, the physician could spend a major portion of his ward time in dealing with this single detail.

Given the time-consuming formal chores of the physician, and his many other duties, he usually worked out an arrangement with the ward personnel, particularly the charge (supervisory attendant), to handle these duties. On serveral wards, the charge called specific problems to the doctor's attention, and the two of them, in effect, would have a consultation. The charge actually made most of the decisions concerning dosage change in the back wards. Since the doctor delegated portions of his formal responsibilities to the charge, he was dependent on her goodwill toward him. If she withheld her cooperation, the physician had absolutely no recourse but to do all the work himself.[16]

In a sense such delegation of responsibility involves a consideration of reward and cost, whereby the decision to be made involves a question of what is more valuable — to retain control over an area, or to delegate one's work to lower participants.

There are occasions, of course, when rules are regarded as illegitimate by lower participants, and they may disregard them. Gouldner observed that, in the mine, men felt they could resist authority in a situation involving danger to themselves.[17] They did not feel that they could legitimately be ordered to do anything that would endanger their lives. It is probably significant that in extremely dangerous situations organizations are more likely to rely on commitment to work than on authority. Even within nonvoluntary groups dangerous tasks are regarded usually as requiring task commitment, and it is likely that commitment is a much more powerful organizational force than coercive authority.

SUMMARY

The preceding remarks are general ones, and they are assumed to be in part true of all types of organizations. But power relationships in organizations are likely to be molded by the type of organization being considered, the nature of organizational goals, the ideology of organizational decision making, the kind of commitment participants have to the organization, the formal structure of the organization, and so on. In short, we have attempted to discuss power processes within organizations in a manner somewhat divorced from other major organizational processes. We have emphasized variables affecting control of access to persons, information, and facilities within organizations. Normative definitions, perception of legitimacy, exchange, and coalitions have all been viewed in relation to power processes. Moreover, we have dealt with some attributes of persons related to power; commitment, effort, interest, willingness to use power, skills, attractiveness, and so on. And we have discussed some other variables; time, centrality, complexity of power structure, and replaceability of persons. It appears that these variables help to account in part for power exercised by lower participants in organizations.

NOTES

1. The term *lower participants* comes from Amitai Etzioni, *A Comparative Analysis of Complex Organizations* (New York, 1961) and is used by him to designate persons in positions of lower rank; employees, rank-and-file, members, clients, customers, and inmates. We shall use the term in this paper in a relative sense denoting position vis-à-vis a higher-ranking participant.

2. Robert Bierstedt, "An Analysis of Social Power," *American Sociological Review* 15 (1950): 730-38.

3. Robert A. Dahl, "The Concept of Power," *Behavioral Science* 2 (1957): 201-13.

4. One might observe, for example, that the power of lower participants is based primarily on the ability to "veto" or punish. For a discussion of bases of power, see John R. P. French, Jr., and Bertram Raven, "The Bases of Social Power," in D. Cartwright and A. Zander, eds., *Group Dynamics* (Evanston, Ill., 1960), pp. 607-23.

5. John Thibaut and Harold H. Kelley, *The Social Psychology of Groups* (New York: 1959). For a similar emphasis on dependence, see Richard M. Emerson, "Inter-Dependence Relationships." *American Sociological Review* 27 (1962): 31-41.

6. Although this paper will not attempt to explain how access may be measured, the author feels confident that the hypotheses concerned with access are clearly testable.

7. Op. cit.

8. Thomas J. Scheff, "Control over Policy by Attendants in a Mental Hospital," *Journal of Health and Human Behavior* 2 (1961): 93-105.

9. Gresham M. Sykes, "The Corruption of Authority and Rehabilitation," in A. Etzioni, ed., *Complex Organizations* (New York, 1961), pp. 191-97.

10. As an example, it appears that 6 members of the cabinet, 30 important subcabinet officials, 63 senators, and 230 congressmen are lawyers (*New Yorker,* April 14, 1962, p. 62). Although one can cite many reasons for lawyers holding political posts, an important one appears to be their legal expertise.

11. There are considerable data showing the powerful effect of propinquity on communication. For summary see Thibaut and Kelley, op. cit., pp. 39-42.

12. The concept of centrality is generally used in a more technical sense in the work of Bavelas, Shaw, Gilchrist, and others. For example, Bavelas defines the central region of a structure as the class of all cells with the smallest distance between one cell and any other cell in the structure, with distance measured in link units. Thus the most central position in a pattern is the position closest to all others. Cf. Harold Leavitt, "Some Effects of Certain Communication Patterns on Group Performance," in F. Maccoby, I. N. Newcomb, and F. I. Hartley, eds., *Readings in Social Psychology* (New York, 1958), p. 559.

13. Alvin W. Gouldner, *Patterns of Industrial Bureaucracy* (Glencoe, Ill., 1954).

14. Ibid., p. 173.

15. Scheff, op. cit.

16. Ibid., p. 87.

17. Gouldner, op. cit.

23. Who Gets Power—and How They Hold on to It: A Strategic-Contingency Model of Power

Gerald R. Salancik and Jeffrey Pfeffer

Power is held by many people to be a dirty word or, as Warren Bennis has said, "It is the organizations's last dirty secret."

This article will argue that traditional "political" power, far from being a dirty business, is, in its most naked form, one of the few mechanisms available for aligning an organization with its own reality. However, institutionalized forms of power — what we prefer to call the cleaner forms of power: authority, legitimization, centralized control, regulations, and the more modern "management information systems" — tend to buffer the organization from reality and obscure the demands of its environment. Most great states and institutions declined, not because they played politics, but because they failed to accommodate to the political realities they faced. Political processes, rather than being mechanisms for unfair and unjust allocations and appointments, tend toward the realistic resolution of conflicts among interests. And power, while it eludes definition, is easy enough to recognize by its consequences — the ability of those who possess power to bring about the outcomes they desire.

The model of power we advance is an elaboration of what has been called strategic-contingency theory, a view that sees power as something that accrues to organizational subunits (individuals, departments) that cope with critical organizational problems. Power is used by subunits, indeed, used by all who have it, to enhance their own survival through control of scarce critical resources, through the placement of allies in key positions, and through the definition of organizational problems and policies. Because of the processes by which power develops and is used, organizations become both more aligned and more misaligned with their environments. This contradiction is the most interesting aspect of organizational power and one that makes administration one of the most precarious of occupations.

WHAT IS ORGANIZATIONAL POWER?

You can walk into most organizations and ask without fear of being misunderstood, "Which are the powerful groups or people in this organization?" Although many organizational informants may be *unwilling* to tell you, it is unlikely they will be *unable* to tell you. Most people do not require explicit definitions to know what power is.

Power is simply the ability to get things done the way one wants them to be done. For a manager who wants an increased budget to launch a project that he thinks is important, his power is measured by his ability to get that budget. For an executive vice president who wants to be chairman, his power is evidenced by his advancement toward his goal.

People in organizations not only know what you are talking about when you ask who is influential but they are likely to agree with one another to an amazing extent. Recently, we had a chance to observe this in a regional office of an insurance company. The office had 21 department managers; we asked 10 of these managers to rank all 21 according to the influence each one had in the organization. Despite the fact that ranking 21 things is a difficult task, the managers sat down and began arranging the names of their colleagues and themselves in a column. Only one person bothered to ask, "What do you mean by influence?" When told "power," he responded, "Oh," and went on. We compared the rankings of all ten managers and found virtually no disagreement among them in the managers ranked among the top five or the bottom five. Differences in the rankings came from department heads claiming more influence for themselves than their colleagues attributed to them.

Such agreement on those who have influence, and those who do not, was not unique to this insurance company. So far we have studied over 20 very different organizations — universities, research firms, factories, banks, retailers, to name a few. In each one we found individuals able to rate themselves and their peers on a scale of influence or power. We have done this both for specific decisions and for general impact on organizational policies. Their agreement was unusually high, which suggests that distributions of influence exist well enough in everyone's mind to be referred to with ease — and we assume with accuracy.

WHERE DOES ORGANIZATIONAL POWER COME FROM?

Earlier we stated that power helps organizations become aligned with their realities. This hopeful prospect follows from what we have dubbed the strategic-contingencies theory of organizational power. Briefly, those subunits most able to cope with the organization's critical problems and uncertainties acquire power. In its simplest form, the strategic-contingencies theory implies that when an organization faces a number of lawsuits that threaten its existence the legal department will gain power and influence over organizational decisions. Somehow other organizational interest groups will recognize its critical importance and confer upon it a status and power never before enjoyed. This influence may extend beyond handling legal matters and into decisions about product design, advertising production, and so on. Such extensions undoubtedly would be accompanied by appropriate, or acceptable, verbal justifications. In time, the head of the legal department may become the head of the corporation, just as in times past the vice president for marketing had become the president when market shares were a worrisome problem and, before him, the chief engineer, who had made the production line run as smooth as silk.

Stated in this way, the strategic-contingencies theory of power paints an appealing picture of power. To the extent that power is determined by the critical uncertainties and problems facing the organization and, in turn, influences decisions in the organization, the organization is aligned with the realities it faces. In short, power facilitates the organization's adaptation to its environment — or its problems.

We can cite many illustrations of how influence derives from a subunit's ability to deal with critical contingencies. Michael Crozier described a French cigarette factory in which the maintenance engineers had a considerable say in the plant-wide operation.

After some probing he discovered that the group possessed the solution to one of the major problems faced by the company, that of trouble-shooting the elaborate, expensive, and irascible automated machines that kept breaking down and dumbfounding everyone else. It was the one problem that the plant manager could in no way control.

The production workers, while troublesome from time to time, created no insurmountable problems; the manager could reasonably predict their absenteeism or replace them when necessary. Production scheduling was something he could deal with since, by watching inventories and sales, the demand for cigarettes was known long in advance. Changes in demand could be accommodated by slowing down or speeding up the line. Supplies of tobacco and paper were also easily dealt with through stockpiles and advance orders.

The one thing that management could neither control nor accommodate to, however, was the seemingly happenstance breakdowns. And the foremen couldn't instruct the workers what to do when emergencies developed since the maintenance department kept its records of problems and solutions locked up in a cabinet or in its members' heads. The breakdowns were, in truth, a critical source of uncertainty for the organization, and the maintenance engineers were the only ones who could cope with the problem.

The engineers' strategic role in coping with breakdowns afforded them a considerable say on plant decisions. Schedules and production quotas were set in consultation with them. And the plant manager, while formally their boss, accepted their decisions about personnel in their operation. His submission was to his credit, for without their cooperation he would have had an even more difficult time in running the plant.

Ignoring Critical Consequences

In this cigarette factory, sharing influence with the maintenance workers reflected the plant manager's awareness of the critical contingencies. However, when organizational members are not aware of the critical contingencies they face and do not share influence accordingly, the failure to do so can create havoc. In one case, an insurance company's regional office was having problems with the performance of one of its departments, the coding department. From the outside, the department looked like a disaster area. The clerks who worked in it were somewhat dissatisfied; their supervisor paid little attention to them, and they resented the hard work. Several other departments were critical of this manager, claiming that she was inconsistent in meeting deadlines. The person most critical was the claims manager. He resented having to wait for work that was handled by her department, claiming that it held up his claims adjusters. Having heard the rumors about dissatisfaction among her subordinates, he attributed the situation to poor supervision. He was second in command in the office and therefore took up the issue with her immediate boss, the head of administrative services. They consulted with the personnel manager, and the three of them concluded that the manager needed leadership training to improve her relations with her subordinates. The coding manager objected, saying it was a waste of time, but agreed to go along with the training and also agreed to give more priority to the claims department's work. Within a week after the training, the results showed that her workers were happier but that the performance of her department had decreased, save for the people serving the claims department.

About this time, we began, quite independently, a study of influence in this organization. We asked the administrative services director to draw up flow charts of how the work of one department moved onto the next department. In the course of the interview, we noticed that the coding department began or interceded in the work flow of most of the other departments and casually mentioned to him, "The coding manager must be very influential." He said "No, not really. Why would you think so?" Before we could reply, he recounted the story of her leadership training and the fact that things were worse. We then told him that it seemed obvious that the coding department would be influential from the fact that all the other departments depended on it. It was also clear why productivity had fallen. The coding manager took the training seriously and began spending more time raising her workers' spirits than she did worrying about the problems of all the departments that depended on her. Giving priority to the claims area only exaggerated the problem, for their work was getting done at the expense of the work of the other departments. Eventually the company hired a few more clerks to relieve the pressure in the coding department and performance returned to a more satisfactory level.

Originally we got involved with this insurance company to examine how the influence of each manager evolved from his or her department's handling of critical organizational contingencies. We reasoned that one of the most important contingencies faced by

all profit-making organizations was that of generating income. Thus we expected managers would be influential to the extent to which they contributed to this function. Such was the case. The underwriting managers, who wrote the policies that committed the premiums, were the most influential; the claims managers, who kept a lid on the funds flowing out, were a close second. Least influential were the managers of functions unrelated to revenue, such as mailroom and payroll managers. And contrary to what the administrative services manager believed, the third most powerful department head (out of 21) was the woman in charge of the coding function, which consisted of rating, recording, and keeping track of the codes of all policy applications and contracts. Her peers attributed more influence to her than could have been inferred from her place on the organization chart. And it was not surprising, since they all depended on her department. The coding department's records, their accuracy, and the speed with which they could be retrieved, affected virtually every other operating department in the insurance office. The underwriters depended on them in getting the contracts straight; the typing department depended on them in preparing the formal contract document; the claims department depended on them in adjusting claims; and accounting depended on them for billing. Unfortunately, the "bosses" were not aware of these dependences, for unlike the cigarette factory, there were no massive breakdowns that made them obvious, while the coding manager, who was a hard-working but quiet person, did little to announce her importance.

The cases of this plant and office illustrate nicely a basic point about the source of power in organizations. The basis for power in an organization derives from the ability of a person or subunit to take or not take actions that are desired by others. The coding manager was seen as influential by those who depended on her department, but not by the people at the top. The engineers were influential because of their role in keeping the plant operating. The two cases differ in these respects: The coding supervisor's source of power was not as widely recognized as that of the maintenance engineers, and she did not use her source of power to influence decisions; the maintenance engineers did. Whether power is used to influence anything is a separate issue. We should not confuse this issue with the fact that power derives from a social situation in which one person has a capacity to do something and another person does not but wants it done.

POWER SHARING IN ORGANIZATIONS

Power is shared in organizations; and it is shared out of necessity more than out of concern for principles of organizational development or participatory democracy. Power is shared because no one person controls all the desired activities in the organization. While the factory owner may hire people to operate his noisy machines, once hired they have some control over the use of the machinery. And thus they have power over him in the same way he has power over them. Who has more power over whom is a mooter point than that of recognizing the inherent nature of organizing as a sharing of power.

Let's expand on the concept that power derives from the activities desired in an organization. A major way of managing influence in organizations is through the designation of activities. In a bank we studied, we saw this principle in action. This bank was planning to install a computer system for routine credit evaluation. The bank, rather progressive-minded, was concerned that the change would have adverse effects on employees and therefore surveyed their attitudes.

The principal opposition to the new system came, interestingly, not from the employees who performed the routine credit checks, some of whom would be relocated because of the change, but from the manager of the credit department. His reason was quite simple. The manager's primary function was to give official approval to the applications, catch any employee mistakes before giving approval, and arbitrate any difficulties the clerks had in deciding what to do. As a consequence of his role, others in the organization, including his superiors, subordinates, and colleagues, attributed considerable importance to him. He, in turn, for example, could point to the low proportion of credit approvals, compared with other financial institutions, that resulted in bad debts. Now, to his mind, a wretched machine threatened to transfer his role to a computer programmer, a man who knew nothing of finance and who, in addition, had ten years less seniority. The credit manager eventually quit for a position at a smaller firm with lower pay, but one in which he would have more influence than his redefined job would have left him with.

Because power derives from activities rather than individuals, an individual's or subgroup's power is never absolute and derives ultimately from the context of the situation. The amount of power an individual has at any one time depends, not only on the activities he or she controls, but also on the existence of other persons or means by which the activities can be achieved and on those who determine what ends are desired and, hence, on what activities are desired and critical for the organization. One's own power always depends on other people for these two reasons. Other people, or groups or organizations, can determine the definition of what is a critical contingency for the organization and can also undercut the uniqueness of the individual's personal contribution to the critical contingencies of the organization.

Perhaps one can best appreciate how situationally dependent power is by examining how it is distributed. In most societies, power organizes around scarce and critical resources. Rarely does power organize around abundant resources. In the United States, a person doesn't become powerful because he or she can drive a car. There are simply too many others who can drive with equal facility. In certain villages in Mexico, on the other hand, a person with a car is accredited with enormous social status and plays a key role in the community. In addition to scarcity, power is also limited by the need for one's capacities in a social system. While a racer's ability to drive a car around a 90° turn at 80 mph may be sparsely distributed in a society, it is not likely to lend the driver much power in the society. The ability simply does not play a central role in the activities of the society.

The fact that power revolves around scarce and critical activities, of course, makes the control and organization of those activities a major battleground in struggles for power. Even relatively abundant or trivial resources can become the bases for power if one can organize and control their allocation and the definition of what is critical. Many occupational and professional groups attempt to do just this in modern economies. Lawyers organize themselves into associations, regulate the entrance requirements for novitiates, and then get laws passed specifying situations that require the services of an attorney. Workers had little power in the conduct of industrial affairs until they organized themselves into closed and controlled systems. In recent years, women and blacks have tried to define themselves as important and critical to the social system, using law to reify their status.

In organizations there are obviously opportunities for defining certain activities as more critical than others. Indeed, the growth of managerial thinking to include defining organizational objectives and goals has done much to foster these opportunities. One sure way to liquidate the power of groups in the organization is to define the need for their services out of existence.

David Halberstam presents a description of how just such a thing happened to the group of correspondents that evolved around Edward R. Murrow, the brilliant journalist, interviewer, and war correspondent of CBS News. A close friend of CBS chairman and controlling stockholder William S. Paley, Murrow, and the news department he directed, were endowed with freedom to do what they felt was right. He used it to create some of the best documentaries and commentaries ever seen on television. Unfortunately, television became too large, too powerful, and too suspect in the eyes of the federal government that licensed it. It thus became, or at least the top executives believed it had become, too dangerous to have in-depth, probing commentary on the news. Crisp, dry, uneditorializing headliners were considered safer. Murrow was out and Walter Cronkite was in.

The power to define what is critical in an organization is no small power. Moreover, it is the key to understanding why organizations are either aligned with their environments or misaligned. If an organization defines certain activities as critical when in fact they are not critical, given the flow of resources coming into the organization, it is not likely to survive, at least in its present form.

Most organizations manage to evolve a distribution of power and influence that is aligned with the critical realities they face in the environment. The environment, in turn, includes both the internal environment, the shifting situational contexts in which particular decisions are made, and the external environment that it can hope to influence but is unlikely to control.

THE CRITICAL CONTINGENCIES

The critical contingencies facing most organizations derive from the environmental context within which they operate. This determines the available needed resources and thus determines the problems to be dealt with. That power organizes around handling these problems suggests an important mechanism by which organizations keep in tune with their external environments. The strategic-contingencies model implies that subunits that contribute to the critical resources of the organization will gain influence in the organization. Their influence presumably is then used to bend the organization's activities to the contingencies that determine its resources. This idea may strike one as obvious. But its obviousness in no way diminishes its importance.

Indeed, despite its obviousness, it escapes the notice of many organizational analysts and managers, who all too frequently think of the organization in terms of a descending pyramid, in which all the departments in one tier hold equal power and status. This presumption denies the reality that departments differ in the contributions they are believed to make to the overall organization's resources, as well as to the fact that some are more equal than others.

Because of the importance of this idea to organizational effectiveness, we decided to examine it carefully in a large midwestern university. A university offers an excellent site for studying power. It is composed of departments with nominally equal power and is administered by a central executive structure much like other bureaucracies. However, at the same time it is a situation in which the departments have clearly defined identities and face diverse external environments. Each department has its own bodies of knowledge, its own institutions, its own sources of prestige and resources. Because the departments operate in different external environments, they are likely to contribute differentially to the resources of the overall organization. Thus a physics department with close ties to NASA may contribute substantially to the funds of the university; and a history department with a renowned historian in residence may contribute to the intellectual credibility or prestige of the whole university. Such variations permit one to examine how these various contributions lead to obtaining power within the university.

We analyzed the influence of 29 university departments throughout an 18-month period in their history. Our chief interest was to determine whether departments that brought more critical resources to the university would be more powerful than departments that contributed fewer or less critical resources.

To identify the critical resources each department contributed, the heads of all departments were interviewed about the importance of seven different resources to the university's success. The seven included undergraduate students (the factor determining size of the state allocations by the university), national prestige, administrative expertise, and so on. The most critical resource was found to be contract and grant monies received by a department's faculty for research or consulting services. At this university, contract and grants contributed somewhat less than 50 percent of the overall budget, with the remainder primarily coming from state appropriations. The importance attributed to contract and grant monies, and the rather minor importance of undergraduate students, was not surprising for this particular university. The university was a major center for graduate education; many of its departments ranked in the top ten of their respective fields. Grant and contract monies were the primary source of discretionary funding available for maintaining these programs of graduate education, and hence for maintaining the university's prestige. The prestige of the university itself was critical both in recruiting able students and attracting top-notch faculty.

From university records it was determined what relative contributions each of the 29 departments made to the various needs of the university (national prestige, outside grants, teaching). Thus, for instance, one department may have contributed to the university by teaching 7 percent of the instructional units, bringing in 2 percent of the outside contracts and grants, and having a national ranking of 20. Another department, on the other hand, may have taught one percent of the instructional units, contributed 12 percent to the grants, and be ranked the third best department in its field within the country.

The question was: Do these different contributions determine the relative power of the departments within the university? Power was measured in several ways; but regardless of how measured, the answer was "Yes." Those three resources together accounted for about 70 percent of the variance in subunit power in the university.

But the most important predictor of departmental power was the department's contribution to the contracts and grants of the university. Sixty percent of the variance in power was due to this one factor, suggesting that the power of departments derived primarily from the dollars they provided for graduate education, the activity believed to be the most important for the organization.

THE IMPACT OF ORGANIZATIONAL POWER ON DECISION MAKING

The measure of power we used in studying this university was an analysis of the responses of the department heads we interviewed. While such perceptions of power might be of interest in their own right, they contribute little to our understanding of how the distribution of power might serve to align an organization with its critical realities. For this we must look to how

power actually influences the decisions and policies of organizations.

While it is perhaps not absolutely valid, we can generally gauge the relative importance of a department of an organization by the size of the budget allocated to it relative to other departments. Clearly it is of importance to the administrators of those departments whether they are squeezed in a budget crunch or are given more funds to strike out after new opportunities. And it should also be clear that when those decisions are made and one department can go ahead and try new approaches while another must cut back on the old, then the deployment of the resources of the organization in meeting its problems is most directly affected.

Thus our study of the university led us to ask the following question: Does power lead to influence in the organization? To answer this question, we found it useful first to ask another one, namely: Why should department heads try to influence organizational decisions to favor their own departments to the exclusion of other departments? While this second question may seem a bit naive to anyone who has witnessed the political realities of organizations, we posed it in a context of research on organizations that sees power as an illegitimate threat to the neater rational authority of modern bureaucracies. In this context, decisions are not believed to be made because of the dirty business of politics but because of the overall goals and purposes of the organization. In a university, one reasonable basis for decision making is the teaching workload of departments and the demands that follow from that workload. We would expect, therefore, that departments with heavy student demands for courses would be able to obtain funds for teaching. Another reasonable basis for decision making is quality. We would expect, for that reason, that departments with esteemed reputations would be able to obtain funds both because their quality suggests they might use such funds effectively and because such funds would allow them to maintain their quality. A rational model of bureaucracy intimates, then, that the organizational decisions taken would favor those who perform the stated purposes of the organization — teaching undergraduates and training professional and scientific talent — well.

The problem with rational models of decision making, however, is that what is rational to one person may strike another as irrational. For most departments, resources are a question of survival. While teaching undergraduates may seem to be a major goal for some members of the university, developing knowledge may seem so to others; and to still others, advising governments and other institutions about policies may seem to be the crucial business. Everyone has his own idea of the proper priorities in a just world. Thus goals rather than being clearly defined and universally agreed upon are blurred and contested throughout the organization. If such is the case, then the decisions taken on behalf of the organization as a whole are likely to reflect the goals of those who prevail in political contests, namely, those with power in the organization.

Will organizational decisions always reflect the distribution of power in the organization? Probably not. Using power for influence requires a certain expenditure of effort, time, and resources. Prudent and judicious persons are not likely to use their power needlessly or wastefully. And it is likely that power will be used to influence organizational decisions primarily under circumstances that both require and favor its use. We have examined three conditions that are likely to affect the use of power in organizations: scarcity, criticality, and uncertainty. The first suggests that subunits will try to exert influence when the resources of the organization are scarce. If there is an abundance of resources, then a particular department or a particular individual has little need to attempt influence. With little effort, he can get all he wants anyway.

The second condition, criticality, suggests that a subunit will attempt to influence decisions to obtain resources that are critical to its own survival and activities. Criticality implies that one would not waste effort, or risk being labeled obstinate, by fighting over trivial decisions affecting one's operations.

An office manager would probably balk less about a threatened cutback in copying machine usage than about a reduction in typing staff. An advertising department head would probably worry less about losing his lettering artist than his illustrator. Criticality is difficult to define because what is critical depends on people's beliefs about what is critical. Such beliefs may or may not be based on experience and knowledge and may or may not be agreed upon by all. Scarcity, for instance, may itself affect conceptions of criticality. When slack resources drop off, cutbacks have to be made—those ''hard decisions,'' as congressmen and resplendent administrators like to call them. Managers then find themselves scrapping projects they once held dear.

The third condition that we believe affects the use of power is uncertainty: When individuals do not agree about what the organization should do or how to do it, power and other social processes will affect decisions. The reason for this is simply that, if there are no clear-cut criteria available for resolving conflicts of interest, then the only means for resolution is some form of social process, including power, status, social ties, or some arbitrary process like flipping a coin or drawing straws. Under conditions of uncertainty, the powerful manager can argue his case on any grounds and usually win it. Since there is no real consensus, other contestants are not likely to develop counterarguments or amass sufficient opposition. Moreover, because of his power and their need for access to the resources he controls, they are more likely to defer to his arguments.

Although the evidence is slight, we have found that power will influence the allocations of scarce and critical resources. In the analysis of power in the university, for instance, one of the most critical resources needed by departments is the general budget. First granted by the state legislature, the general budget is later allocated to individual departments by the university administration in response to requests from the department heads. Our analysis of the factors that contribute to a department getting more or less of this budget indicated that subunit power was the major predictor, overriding such factors as student demand for courses, national reputations of departments, or even the size of a department's faculty. Moreover, other research has shown that when the general budget has been cut back or held below previous uninflated levels, leading to monies becoming more scarce, budget allocations mirror departmental powers even more closely.

Student enrollment and faculty size, of course, do themselves relate to budget allocations, as we would expect since they determine a department's need for resources, or at least offer visible testimony of needs. But departments are not always able to get what they need by the mere fact of needing them. In one analysis it was found that high-power departments were able to obtain budget without regard to their teaching loads and, in some cases, actually in inverse relation to their teaching loads. In contrast, low-power departments could get increases in budget only when they could justify the increases by a recent growth in teaching load, and then only when it was far in excess of norms for other departments.

General budget is only one form of resource that is allocated to departments. There are others such as special grants for student fellowships or faculty research. These are critical to departments because they affect the ability to attract other resources, such as outstanding faculty or students. We examined how power influenced the allocations of four resources department heads had described as critical and scarce.

When the four resources were arrayed from the most to the least critical and scarce, we found that departmental power best predicted the allocations of the most critical and scarce resources. In other words, the analysis of how power influences organizational allocations leads to this conclusion: Those subunits most likely to survive in times of strife are those that are more critical to the organization. Their importance to the organization gives them power to influence resource allocations that enhance their own survival.

HOW EXTERNAL ENVIRONMENT IMPACTS EXECUTIVE SELECTION

Power not only influences the survival of key groups in an organization, it also influences the selection of individuals to key leadership positions, and by such a process further aligns the organization with its environmental context.

We can illustrate this with a recent study of the selection and tenure of chief administrators in 57 hospitals in Illinois. We assumed that since the critical problems facing the organization would enhance the power of certain groups at the expense of others, then the leaders to emerge should be those most relevant to the context of the hospitals. To assess this we asked each chief administrator about his professional background and how long he had been in office. The replies were then related to the hospitals' funding, ownership, and competitive conditions for patients and staff.

One aspect of a hospital's context is the source of its budget. Some hospitals, for instance, are run much like other businesses. They sell bed space, patient care, and treatment services. They charge fees sufficient both to cover their costs and to provide capital for expansion. The main source of both their operating and capital funds is patient billings. Increasingly, patient billings are paid for, not by patients, but by private insurance companies. Insurers like Blue Cross dominate and represent a potent interest group outside a hospital's control but critical to its income. The insurance companies, in order to limit their own costs, attempt to hold down the fees allowable to hospitals, which they do effectively from their positions on state rate boards. The squeeze on hospitals that results from fees increasing slowly while costs climb rapidly more and more demands the talents of cost accountants or people trained in the technical expertise of hospital administration.

By contrast, other hospitals operate more like social service institutions, either as government healthcare units (Bellevue Hospital in New York City and Cook County Hospital in Chicago, for example) or as charitable institutions. These hospitals obtain a large proportion of their operating and capital funds, not from privately insured patients, but from government subsidies or private donations. Such institutions rather than requiring the talents of a technically efficient administrator are likely to require the savvy of someone who is well integrated into the social and political power structure of the community.

Not surprisingly, the characteristics of administrators predictably reflect the funding context of the hospitals with which they are associated. Those hospitals with larger proportions of their budget obtained from private insurance companies were most likely to have administrators with backgrounds in accounting and least likely to have administrators whose professions were business or medicine. In contrast, those hospitals with larger proportions of their budget derived from private donations and local governments were most likely to have administrators with business or professional backgrounds and least likely to have accountants. The same held for formal training in hospital management. Professional hospital administrators could easily be found in hospitals drawing their incomes from private insurance and rarely in hospitals dependent on donations or legislative appropriations.

As with the selection of administrators, the context of organizations has also been found to affect the removal of executives. The environment, as a source of organizational problems, can make it more or less difficult for executives to demonstrate their value to the organization. In the hospitals we studied, long-term administrators came from hospitals with few problems. They enjoyed amicable and stable relations with their local business and social communities and suffered little competition for funding and staff. The small city hospital director who attended civic and Elks meetings while running the only hospital within a 100-mile radius, for example, had little difficulty holding on to his job. Turnover was highest in hospitals with the most problems, a phenomenon similar to that observed in a study of industrial organizations in which turnover was highest among executives in industries with competitive environments and unstable market conditions. The interesting thing is that instability characterized the industries rather than the individual firms in them. The troublesome conditions in the individual firms were attributed, or rather misattributed, to the executives themselves.

It takes more than problems, however, to terminate a manager's leadership. The problems themselves must be relevant and critical. This is clear from the way in which an administrator's tenure is affected by the status of the hospital's operating budget. Naively we might assume that all administrators would need to show a surplus. Not necessarily so. Again, we must distinguish between those hospitals that depend on private donations for funds and those that do not. Whether an endowed budget shows a surplus or deficit is less important than the hospital's relations with benefactors. On the other hand, with a budget dependent on patient billing, a surplus is almost essential; monies for new equipment or expansion must be drawn from it, and without them quality care becomes more difficult and patients scarcer. An administrator's tenure reflected just these considerations. For those hospitals dependent upon private donations, the length of an administrator's term depended not at all on the status of the operating budget but was fairly predictable from the hospital's relations with the business community. On the other hand, in hospitals dependent on the operating budget for capital financing, the greater the deficit the shorter was the tenure of the hospital's principal administrators.

CHANGING CONTINGENCIES AND ERODING POWER BASES

The critical contingencies facing the organization may change. When they do, it is reasonable to expect that the power of individuals and subgroups will change in turn. At times the shift can be swift and shattering, as it was recently for powerholders in New York City. A few years ago it was believed that David Rockefeller was one of the ten most powerful people in the city, as tallied by New York magazine, which annually sniffs out power for the delectation of its readers. But that was before it was revealed that the city was in financial trouble, before Rockefeller's Chase Manhattan Bank lost some of its own financial luster, and before brother Nelson lost some of his political influence in Washington. Obviously David Rockefeller was no longer as well positioned to help bail the city out. Another loser was an attorney with considerable personal connections to the political and religious leaders of the city. His talents were

no longer in much demand. The persons with more influence were the bankers and union pension fund executors who fed money to the city; community leaders who represent blacks and Spanish-Americans, in contrast, witnessed the erosion of their power bases.

One implication of the idea that power shifts with changes in organizational environments is that the dominant coalition will tend to be that group that is most appropriate for the organization's environment, as also will the leaders of an organization. One can observe this historically in the top executives of industrial firms in the United States. Up until the early 1950's, many top corporations were headed by former production line managers or engineers who gained prominence because of their abilities to cope with the problems of production. Their success, however, only spelled their demise. As production became routinized and mechanized, the problem of most firms became one of selling all those goods they so efficiently produced. Marketing executives were more frequently found in corporate boardrooms. Success outdid itself again, for keeping markets and production steady and stable requires the kind of control that can only come from acquiring competitors and suppliers or the invention of more and more appealing products — ventures that typically require enormous amounts of capital. During the 1960's, financial executives assumed the seats of power. And they, too, will give way to others. Edging over the horizon are legal experts, as regulation and antitrust suits are becoming more and more frequent in the 1970s, suits that had their beginnings in the success of the expansion generated by prior executives. The more distant future, which is likely to be dominated by multinational corporations, may see former secretaries of state and their minions increasingly serving as corporate figureheads.

THE NONADAPTIVE CONSEQUENCES OF ADAPTATION

From what we have said thus far about power aligning the organization with its own realities, an intelligent person might react with a resounding ho-hum, for it all seems too obvious: Those with the ability to get the job done are given the job to do.

However, there are two aspects of power that make it more useful for understanding organizations and their effectiveness. First, the "job" to be done has a way of expanding itself until it becomes less and less clear what the job is. Napoleon began by doing a job for France in the war with Austria and ended up Emperor, convincing many that only he could keep the peace. Hitler began by promising an end to Germany's troubling postwar depression and ended up convincing more people than is comfortable to remember that he was destined to be the savior of the world. In short, power is a capacity for influence that extends far beyond the original bases that created it. Second, power tends to take on institution-alized forms that enable it to endure well beyond its usefulness to an organization.

There is an important contradiction in what we have observed about organizational power. On the one hand we have said that power derives from the contingencies facing an organization and that when those contingen-cies change so do the bases for power. On the other hand we have asserted that subunits will tend to use their power to influence organizational decisions in their own favor, particularly when their own survival is threatened by the scarcity of critical resources. The first statement implies that an organization will tend to be aligned with its environment since power will tend to bring to key positions those with capabilities relevant to the context. The second implies that those in power will not give up their positions so easily; they will pursue policies that guarantee their continued domination. In short, change and stability operate through the same mechanism, and as a result, the organization will never be completely in phase with its environment or its needs.

The study of hospital administrators illustrates how leadership can be out of phase with reality. We argued that privately funded hospitals needed trained technical administrators more so than did hospitals funded by donations. The need as we perceived it was matched in most hospitals, but by no means in all. Some organiza-tions did not conform with our predictions. These deviations imply that some administrators were able to maintain their positions independent of their suitability for those positions. By dividing administrators into those with long and short terms of office, one finds that the characteristics of longer-termed administrators were virtually unrelated to the hospital's context. The shorter-termed chiefs on the other hand had character-istics more appropriate for the hospital's problems. For a hospital to have a recently appointed head implies that the previous administrator had been unable to endure by institutionalizing himself.

One obvious feature of hospitals that allowed some administrators to enjoy a long tenure was a hospital's ownership. Administrators were less entrenched when their hospitals were affiliated with and dependent upon

larger organizations, such as governments or churches. Private hospitals offered more secure positions for administrators. Like private corporations, they tend to have more diffused ownership, leaving the administra-tor unopposed as he institutionalizes his reign. Thus he endures, sometimes at the expense of the performance of the organization. Other research has demonstrated that corporations with diffuse ownership have poorer earnings than those in which the control of the manager is checked by a dominant shareholder. Firms that overload their boardrooms with more insiders than are appropriate for their context have also been found to be less profitable.

A word of caution is required about our judgment of "appropriateness." When we argue some capabilities are more appropriate for one context than another, we do so from the perspective of an outsider and on the basis of reasonable assumptions as to the problems the organization will face and the capabilities they will need. The fact that we have been able to predict the distribution of influence and the characteristics of leaders suggests that our reasoning is not incorrect. However, we do not think that all organizations follow the same pattern. The fact that we have not been able to predict outcomes with 100 percent accuracy indicates they do not.

MISTAKING CRITICAL CONTINGENCIES

One thing that allows subunits to retain their power is their ability to name their functions as critical to the organization when they may not be. Consider again our discussion of power in the university. One might wonder why the most critical tasks were defined as graduate education and scholarly research, the effect of which was to lend power to those who brought in grants and contracts. Why not something else? The reason is that the more powerful departments argued for those criteria and won their case, partly because they were more powerful.

In another analysis of this university, we found that all departments advocate self-serving criteria for budget allocation. Thus a department with large undergraduate enrollments argued that enrollments should determine budget allocations, a department with a strong national reputation saw prestige as the most reasonable basis for distributing funds, and so on. We further found that advocating such self-serving criteria actually benefited a department's budget allotments but, also, it paid off more for departments that were already powerful.

Organizational needs are consistent with a current distribution of power also because of a human tendency to categorize problems in familiar ways. An accountant sees problems with organizational performance as cost accountancy problems or inventory flow problems. A sales manager sees them as problems with markets, promotional strategies, or just unaggressive sales-people. But what is the truth? Since it does not automatically announce itself, it is likely that those with prior credibility, or those with power, will be favored as the enlightened. This bias, while not intentionally self-serving, further concentrates power among those who already possess it, independent of changes in the organizations's context.

INSTITUTIONALIZING POWER

A third reason for expecting organizational contingencies to be defined in familiar ways is that the current holders of power can structure the organization in ways that institutionalize themselves. By institutionalization we mean the establishment of relatively permanent structures and policies that favor the influence of a particular subunit. While in power, a dominant coalition has the ability to institute constitutions, rules, procedures, and information systems that limit the potential power of others while continuing their own.

The key to institutionalizing power always is to create a device that legitimates one's own authority and diminishes the legitimacy of others. When the "Divine Right of Kings" was envisioned centuries ago it was to provide an unquestionable foundation for the supremacy of royal authority. There is generally a need to root the exercise of authority in some higher power. Modern leaders are no less affected by this need. Richard Nixon, with the aid of John Dean, reified the concept of executive privilege, which meant in effect that what the President wished not to be discussed need not be discussed.

In its simpler form, institutionalization is achieved by designating positions or roles for organizational activities. The creation of a new post legitimizes a function and forces organization members to orient to it. By designating how this new post relates to older, more established posts, moreover, one can structure an organization to enhance the importance of the function in the organization. Equally, one can diminish the importance of traditional functions. This is what happened in the end with the insurance company we

mentioned that was having trouble with its coding department. As the situation unfolded, the claims director continued to feel dissatisfied about the dependency of his functions on the coding manager. Thus he instituted a reorganization that resulted in two coding departments. In so doing, of course, he placed activities that affected his department under his direct control, presumably to make the operation more effective. Similarly, consumer-product firms enhance the power of marketing by setting up a coordinating role to interface production and marketing functions and then appoint a marketing manager to fill the role.

The structures created by dominant powers sooner or later become fixed and unquestioned features of the organization. Eventually, this can be devastating. It is said that the battle of Jena in 1806 was lost by Frederick the Great, who died in 1786. Though the great Prussian leader had no direct hand in the disaster, his imprint on the army was so thorough, so embedded in its skeletal underpinnings, that the organization was inappropriate for others to lead in different times.

Another important source of institutionalized power lies in the ability to structure information systems. Setting up committees to investigate particular organizational issues and having them report only to particular individuals or groups facilitates their awareness of problems by members of those groups while limiting the awareness of problems by the members of other groups. Obviously, those who have information are in a better position to interpret the problems of an organization, regardless of how realistically they may, in fact, do so.

Still another way to institutionalize power is to distribute rewards and resources. The dominant group may quiet competing interest groups with small favors and rewards. The credit for this artful form of co-optation belongs to Louis XIV. To avoid usurpation of his power by the nobles of France and the Fronde that had so troubled his father's reign, he built the palace at Versailles to occupy them with hunting and gossip. Awed, the courtiers basked in the reflected glories of the "Sun King" and the overwhelming setting he had created for his court.

At this point, we have not systematically studied the institutionalization of power. But we suspect it is an important condition that mediates between the environment of the organization and the capabilities of the organization for dealing with that environment. The more institutionalized power is within an organization, the more likely an organization will be out of phase with the realities it faces. President Richard Nixon's structuring of his White House is one of the better documented illustrations. If we go back to newspaper and magazine descriptions of how he organized his office from the beginning in 1968, most of what occurred subsequently follows almost as an afterthought. Decisions flowed through virtually only the small White House staff; rewards, small presidential favors of recognition, and perquisites were distributed by this staff to the loyal; and information from the outside world — the press, Congress, the people on the streets — was filtered by the staff and passed along only if initialed "bh." Thus it was not surprising that when Nixon met war protestors in the early dawn, the only thing he could think to talk about was the latest football game, so insulated had he become from their grief and anger.

One of the more interesting implications of institutionalized power is that executive turnover among the executives who have structured the organization is likely to be a rare event that occurs only under the most pressing crisis. If a dominant coalition is able to structure the organization and interpret the meaning of ambiguous events like declining sales and profits or lawsuits, then the "real" problems to emerge will easily be incorporated into traditional molds of thinking and acting. If opposition is designed out of the organization, the interpretations will go unquestioned. Conditions will remain stable until a crisis develops, so overwhelming and visible that even the most adroit rhetorician would be silenced.

IMPLICATIONS FOR THE MANAGEMENT OF POWER IN ORGANIZATIONS

While we could derive numerous implications from this discussion of power, our selection would have to depend largely on whether one wanted to increase one's power, decrease the power of others, or merely maintain one's position. More important, the real implications depend on the particulars of an organizational situation. To understand power in an organization, one must begin by looking outside it — into the environment — for those groups that mediate the organization's outcomes but are not themselves within its control.

Instead of ending with homilies, we will end with a reversal of where we began. Power, rather than being the dirty business it is often made out to be, is probably one of the few mechanisms for reality testing in organizations. And the cleaner forms of power, the institutional forms, rather than having the virtues they

are often credited with, can lead the organization to become out of touch. The real trick to managing power in organizations is to ensure somehow that leaders cannot be unaware of the realities of their environments and cannot avoid changing to deal with those realities. That, however, would be like designing the "self-liquidating organization," an unlikely event since anyone capable of designing such an instrument would be obviously in control of the liquidations.

Management would do well to devote more attention to determining the critical contingencies of their environments. For if you conclude, as we do, that the environment sets most of the structure influencing organizational outcomes and problems, and that power derives from the organization's activities that deal with those contingencies, then it is the environment that needs managing, not power. The first step is to construct an accurate model of the environment, a process that is quite difficult for most organizations. We have recently started a project to aid administrators in systematically understanding their environments. From this experience, we have learned that the most critical blockage to perceiving an organization's reality accurately is a failure to incorporate those with the relevant expertise into the process. Most organizations have the requisite experts on hand but they are positioned so that they can be comfortably ignored.

One conclusion you can, and probably should, derive from our discussion is that power — because of the way it develops and the way it is used — will always result in the organization suboptimizing its performance. However, to this grim absolute, we add a comforting caveat: If any criteria other than power were the basis for determining an organization's decisions, the results would be even worse.

SELECTED BIBLIOGRAPHY

The literature on power is at once both voluminous and frequently empty of content. Some is philosophical musing about the concept of power, while other writing contains popularized palliatives for acquiring and exercising influence. Machiavelli's *The Prince,* if read carefully, remains the single best prescriptive treatment of power and its use. Most social scientists have approached power descriptively, attempting to understand how it is acquired, how it is used, and what its effects are. Mayer Zald's edited collection *Power in Organizations* (Vanderbilt University Press, 1970) is one of the more useful sets of thoughts about power from a sociological perspective, while James Tedeschi's edited book, *The Social Influence Processes* (Aldine-Atherton, 1972) represents the social psychological approach to understanding power and influence. The strategic contingencies's approach, with its emphasis on the importance of uncertainty for understanding power in organizations, is described by David Hickson and his colleagues in ''A Strategic Contingencies Theory of Intraorganizational Power'' (*Administrative Science Quarterly*, December 1971, pp. 216–29).

Unfortunately, while many have written about power theoretically, there have been few empirical examinations of power and its use. Most of the work has taken the form of case studies. Michel Crozier's *The Bureaucratic Phenomenon* (University of Chicago Press, 1964) is important because it describes a group's source of power as control over critical activities and illustrates how power is not strictly derived from hierarchical position. J. Victor Baldridge's *Power and Conflict in the University* (John Wiley & Sons, 1971) and Andrew Pettigrew's study of computer purchase decisions in one English firm (*Politics of Organizational Decision Making*, Tavistock, 1973) both present insights into the acquisition and use of power in specific instances. Our work has been more empirical and comparative, testing more explicitly the ideas presented in this article. The study of university decision making is reported in articles in the June 1974, pp. 135–51, and December 1974, pp. 453–73, issues of the *Administrative Science Quarterly*, the insurance firm study in J. G. Hunt and L. L. Larson's collection, *Leadership Frontiers* (Kent State University Press, 1975), and the study of hospital administrator succession appeared in 1977 in the *Academy of Management Journal*.

24. Organizational Governance

William G. Scott, Terence R. Mitchell, and Philip H. Birnbaum

Organizational governance is the vehicle management uses to promulgate acceptable value structures. Organizational governance establishes the legitimacy of these structures by obtaining consensus on essential resource allocation decisions. Thus, consensus and legitimacy are very closely related, and they are governance objectives which have remained virtually unchanged in management over the years. For example, mutuality of interests has been highly regarded in management thought since the time of Frederick W. Taylor. This concept suggests that equitable rewards induce employees to see their interests as inextricably connected to the interests of ownership and management.

Consensus can be considered as a problem of technical or organizational rationality, but it is also a problem of political rationality. The ways in which management allocates resources, defines equity, and administers justice are apparent in various organizational policies. Such policies are determined by two governance processes: substantive and procedural due process.

SUBSTANTIVE DUE PROCESS

Decisions have to be made allocating organizational resources to various individuals, interest groups, and economic sectors within an organization. These types of decisions are legislative, because they set the terms and establish the distribution rules for who gets what and how much of an organization's wealth. The important questions for organization governance are how such decisions are made and what are the consequences that result. Allocation decisions can be made democratically, autocratically, constitutionally, or a number of other ways with various degrees of shading and overlapping.

At most state universities, for example, when the legislature decides to give money for raises (e.g., 5 percent of current salary costs), there is always the question of how it should be distributed. Should it be distributed on the basis of merit alone, or should everyone get an across-the-board increase? The decision on this issue may be made by the dean with the consultation and advice of the faculty; or the dean might decide alone; or the faculty might make a decision which was binding on the dean. The point is that there are numerous ways in which this decision could be made, and different procedures will probably result in different amounts of consensus.

One of the most obvious modes of increasing consensus via the legislative process is through participation in organizational decision making. To date, participation appears in two general forms. The first, which is representative of the American experience, is an attempt to have participation at the task level. In this frame of reference, participation is a method for increasing productivity and effectiveness. The goal is efficiency, and the motive is technical rationality. The second form is participation at an organizational or occupational level. The power base is broader, the conflicts more general, and the underlying rationality is political rather than technical. This distinction is made by Hall and Clark, when they discuss work participation as an ideology "which can be political in the sense that there is a belief that workers ought to have more control over their lives and their work" or as a practical ideology concerned with the work environment.[1] Participation, therefore, can be seen as both a technically rational decision or a political decision concerned with the redistribution of power.

Participation at the Task Level

Participation at the task level is based on the concept of technical rationality. Management should and probably will use any technique that is likely to increase productivity. In their review of this literature, Heller and Rose argue that "in modern, large and progressive companies participation and power are seen to be anchored in the situation, particularly in the nature of the task." They label this a form of "sociotechnical analysis." It is the technical demands of the situation that prompt the need for participation.[2]

The research on this technique has typically come from psychologists doing work in the field or laboratory. This approach is essentially experimental in nature. Researchers are interested in where participation works best, and why it works when it does. The underlying rationale for the research is not political. Researchers generally are more interested in the psychological processes operating in a participative environment than in political implications. A number of areas where participation has been tried are mentioned below.

In some cases, employees have participated in the performance-appraisal system. The argument is that performance goals and appraisal should be carried out jointly so that the employees participate in setting the goal and evaluating their own progress. Supposedly, by participating, the individual will be less defensive in evaluating his or her work and will have higher motivation to reach the explicit, agreed-upon targets. Also, this system provides better data for training and development systems. These are all technically rational reasons for participation.

A second area where people advocate participation is in the organizational-change process. Many authors argue that participation is a fundamental necessity for effective organizational change. Employees will be more committed to the change and illustrate greater acceptance of new rules or norms if they have contributed to their formulation. There should be better coordination and less conflict about implementing change.

The third area concerns participation in decisions about ongoing, day-to-day work practices. Participation at this level means increases in the accuracy and amount of information workers have available. Thus, participation creates more certainty in the organizational environment, and group norms are likely to develop to support these practices. As group members have more control over work policies, it is more likely that they will

1. R. H. Hall and J. P. Clark, "Participation and Interorganizational Relationships: Some Suggestions and Tentative Findings," *Proceeedings of the First International Sociological Conference on Participation and Self-Management,* Dubrovnik, Yugoslavia, 4 (1972), 47-55, 97.

2. R. A. Heller and J. S. Rose, "Participation and Decision Making Re-examined," *Proceedings of the First International Sociological Conference on Participation and Self-Management,* Dubrovnik, Yugoslavia, 4 (1972), 123-33.

support these policies through their informal group norms.

Most current reviews of participation present a qualified perspective. They suggest that participation is only effective some of the time, in some places, and with some people. People have to (1) have some expertise about the issue, (2) have a desire to participate, and (3) feel as if they are actually making a contribution before participation seems to be effective. These reservations have led to contingency approaches for participation where a manager's decision style (i.e., degree of participation) is matched to the decision problems.

The most thorough analysis of this type has been developed by Vroom and Yetton.[3] They outline the major decision guidelines that management should use in determining the degree of participation that will generate effective decision making. These guidelines refer to what sort of information is held by subordinates, whether the subordinates' acceptance is critical for implementation, the likelihood of conflict, and whether subordinates can be trusted to consider the organization's goals before their own. These factors determine the level of participation necessary for making the right decision.

The emphasis on the strategy of participation provides interesting insights. In most American organizations, participation is introduced because management believes it will increase the effort, motivation, and productivity of its employees, and *not* because of concerns about equity, equality, or rights. A vastly different emphasis is apparent in the European experience.

Participation as Power Redistribution

The other major perspective on participation comes from those who view participation in terms of the political redistribution of power. Socialists such as Trotsky spoke of the justification of any process which abolished the power of man over man. Political scientists have also discussed the issue of ''social equity,'' as contrasted with the more traditional technical or utilitarian points of view. Harmon, for example, states that ''For the sake of convenience, the two contempo-

rary conceptions of organizational man will be labeled 'professional-technocratic' man, and 'politico-administrative' man, the former being an outgrowth of public administration's historical ties with management science, and the latter the result of the recognition that the public administrator's role was inherently political in nature.''[4]

The power redistribution position is couched in ethical and political terms, not in technically rational ones. Advocates of this approach do not usually talk about participation; they speak of workers' control as the means of avoiding arbitrary power in public or private organizations. Employee self-management is the goal of a socialist society.

Experimentation with these ideas has been extensive and varied throughout Europe. In some cases, there is as much variability within a country as there is among different countries. In Sweden, for example, there are bodies such as the Development Council (trade-union members) and the Committee for Industrial Democracy. The latter is more concerned with power redistribution and has cited successful examples, such as the Swedish Tobacco Company. Other groups, such as the Development Council, are sometimes viewed as supporting a more paternalistic consultation strategy. England has tended to follow the more consultative view. Joint councils are established containing management and worker representatives, and a review of many British enterprises shows that acceptance seems to vary according to the ability of a given group to manipulate the committee according to its interests. England has also developed the idea of the shop steward who is a union member paid by management but who promotes worker demands and interests.

In Germany, there are workers' councils with elected representatives from management and workers. They decide jointly on issues, such as the work schedule, social services, vocational training, and some personnel matters. A Works Council in the Netherlands also has representatives from management and labor. Their purpose is to deal with general consultation and descriptions of tasks, jobs, and required competencies. The success of this strategy seems to vary according to a number of variables, such as the size of the company, the age and length of service of the workers, and other factors.

3. V. H. Vroom and P. W. Yetton, *Leadership and Decision Making* (Pittsburgh: University of Pittsburgh Press, 1973).

4. M. Harmon, ''Social Equity and Organization Man: Motivation and Organizational Democracy,'' *Public Administration Review* 34 (1974), 12.

The Eastern European countries have systems that provide the worker with more actual control. Yugoslavia emphasizes assemblies of working people and the idea of ''self-management.'' However, when one reviews the writings about the approach, it is obvious that many workers are dissatisfied and that the present experiment has not changed traditional work patterns. Experiences in Poland have been somewhat similar. Here, there is the Conference of Workers' Self-Government, and research has shown that in many cases there is minimal worker support for such systems. ''Self-government'' is seen more as a concern for discipline and production schedules than a concern for the quality of working life.

Limitations of Power Redistribution

There are a number of reasons why these attempts at self-management have failed to yield the type of support and redistribution of power originally sought. In some cases, representatives became hard to control. And, in a situation similar to one that occurs occasionally in the United States with union representatives, the European representatives have developed a separate professional role. That is, they are neither workers nor managers. Another problem has to do with the areas in which participation seems to be most effective. Major proponents have noted the better communication and more explicit exchanges between workers and management. Most reports, however, suggest that little action is really taken on issues that are of vital concern to the worker.

Perhaps the most interesting paradox has been raised by Tannenbaum.[5] He argues that participation in many cases will increase the power of managers over workers, and he suggests some reasons why this should be the case. First, worker representatives frequently become more sympathetic to management's point of view. By jointly working on the problem, they see the other side of the issue. Second, managers by and large have more technical expertise than workers and can, therefore, have a greater impact in decisions because of their ''expert'' power. Finally, workers feel more committed to the decisions made by councils simply because their representatives participated in the meetings. Research in Yugoslavia, England, Israel, Italy, Austria, and the United States by Tannenbaum and his colleagues has shown support for these ideas. They explain their findings by suggesting that workers generally trust management and when they feel a sense of responsibility in the plant, they are likely to be responsive to management's influence attempts. Managers are, therefore, more likely to be influential under these conditions. The idea of increased worker power through participation may, in fact, lead to less power.

Thus, there are severe qualifications one must make when evaluating the success of participation. From a psychological perspective (or technically rational view), it seems as if participation can increase commitment and consensus for certain types of activities. It may also increase motivation. From a political perspective, it may increase commitment to the normative order which is, of course, the aim of a politically rational decision-making process. It may not, however, increase the actual power of the participants. This is a controversial topic that will undoubtedly be researched further.

Participation, therefore, can be seen as a negotiated agreement (e.g., unions), as an experiment (e.g., participative managerial leadership styles), or as a right (e.g., workers' councils). Whatever the rationale, the outcome seems to be that participation does increase consensus and commitment when applied at the appropriate time and place. Since we suspect that a concern for political support will increase in the near future, we also suspect that participation will play an increasing role in the legislative process of organizations.

PROCEDURAL DUE PROCESS

An argument often advanced in the participation literature is that when allocation decisions are unilaterally made by management, it is easy for a real or an imagined perception of injustice to creep into people's assessment of their rewards relative to others. Differential rewards are distributed to employees depending on a number of factors, such as the type of work performed, level in the hierarchy, amount of bargaining power, and pure managerial whim. The way employees perceive fairness in reward distribution results in a perception of equity or inequity, and this feeling of equity is related to motivation, cooperation, and political support. In an

---

5. A. S. Tannenbaum et al., *Hierarchy in Organizations: An International Comparison* (San Francisco: Jossey-Bass, 1974).

equitable situation, people are more likely to work hard, cooperate with others, and agree upon the norms established. Thus, equity can affect technical, organizational, and political rationality.

Equity

Equity is perceptual, and it is relative. A person feels justly or unjustly treated only in relation to how other people are being treated in the same situation. If a woman is paid less for doing the same work as a man, then it is appropriate that she feels she has been done an injustice. However, most cases of inequitable treatment are not as clear-cut. People may feel unjustly treated, even if no objective discrimination exists. A sense of equity or inequity exists in individual minds, and it occurs through perceptual apparatus, regardless of how imperfectly or accurately their apparatus works.

No matter how the norms of an organization originate, be it through participation or through unilateral acts of management, it follows that if people think they are being dealt with unfairly, they should have the right to appeal in order to obtain equity. The purpose of procedural due process is to provide a judicial function in organizations that limits and corrects arbitrariness and unfairness in the administration of allocation policies.

Examples of Judicial Procedures

There are many examples of such procedures, some formal, some informal. Formal appeal systems occasionally arise from the benevolence of management. That is, they may be granted to employees as a unilateral act of management. Others may be traced to a popular movement on the part of employees, such as unionization, to force management to give them channels for securing justice. Virtually every contract that management and unions sign contains a clause having a written grievance procedure. Still other appeal programs begin with public law. Most federal civil service employees have numerous avenues guaranteed to them by civil service law and agency regulations for appealing complaints of injustice. Thus, there are widespread judicial procedures for obtaining corrective justice in organizations.

Two principles underlie these procedures.[6] The first is that appeal mechanisms must be available to all employees without prejudice. This is to say, people must be able to appeal for justice within the organization without fear of reprisal. The second principle is the separation of governance power, which simply means that those who make and execute the laws of the organization should not be the ones to interpret the laws by judging disputes that arise from them. While these two principles are the minimum requirements necessary to assure that the adjudication of disputes is done fairly and dispassionately, they are frequently honored in the breach rather than in the observance of organizational governance.

The chief exception to this is found in collective-bargaining agreements between labor and management. Union contracts generally have a clause that provides union members the opportunity to appeal alleged violations of their contract rights. Most negotiated grievance procedures have arbitration as a final step. At this stage, unresolved issues are submitted for impartial arbitration and for final and binding decisions.

For the most part, however, separation of power is virtually unheard of in organizations. More often than not, the level of corrective justice in organizations has not progressed beyond the feudal practice that allowed aggrieved people to approach the lord or the king to seek redress of an injustice. Likewise, in modern organizations, people may be directed informally to key executives who act in the role of a judge in resolving conflicts and correcting injustices. Thus, even where formal redress systems are absent, some sort of informal channel may be available.

As an example, what would you do if you did not like the grade you received on a paper you wrote for one of your courses? You could argue with the professor, you could agree to do additional work, or in some cases, you might be able to convince the professor to seek another evaluation. Beyond that, what could you do? Unless there was some final court of appeal, you would be stuck.

As it turns out, many universities have recently introduced appeal procedures. In these cases, a board of students and faculty listens to both sides of the issue and makes a final binding decision. But this sort of procedure is relatively new and infrequently used. The prevailing norm is that professors have the right to

---

6.   William G. Scott, *The Management of Conflict* (Homewood, Ill.: Irwin-Dorsey Press, 1965).

determine the grade, and there are few limitations on this power. Probably because of this lack of redress, students sometimes see the grading procedure as arbitrary.

Informal versus Formal Procedures

The important point is that the procedural due-process function, whether formal or informal, must be performed in organizational governance. As with substantive due process, *how* it is performed determines the nature of the governance activity. The informal approach to corrective justice has the advantage of flexibility, but it does little to protect the employees' *right* to appeal and to prevent arbitrariness in the administration of justice. The formal approach, which depends upon written guarantees and specified legalistic procedures, offers the assurance that appeal privileges are available but has the danger that employee appeals will get bogged down in elaborate judicial machinery.

Another difficulty with informal due process is that the laws of organization are seldom codified. It is frequently difficult for an employee to know what is appealable and what is not. The lack of codification results in clogging the judicial system with gripes and complaints. While such minor expressions of discontent are often important barometers of morale, they tend to create a lot of noise in the system and prevent major incidents of individual injustice from being heard and resolved.

In conclusion, substantive and procedural due-process guarantees are established as part of an evolution in organization design. Both processes provide the individual employee with a feeling of equity and fairness. By participating in the decision process, people feel more committed to the actions taken and are more likely to support such positions. They are likely to say something such as, "Well, we all agreed this is what we would do, and even though it is not my first preference, I can support it." It is the process of contributing that causes these feelings of fairness.

However, in many cases, participation is not available. In these settings, the basic minimum requirement for establishing equity and fairness is some system of procedural due process. The employee has to feel that there is at least some control on the whims and capriciousness of management. Formal or informal appeal systems provide some assurance against arbitrary action. The employee is likely to say, "I may not have much say around here, but I do know one thing, if they treat me wrong, the union will stand up for me."

D.

Leadership

25. Path-Goal Theory of Leadership

Robert J. House and Terence R. Mitchell

An integrated body of conjecture by students of leadership, referred to as the "Path-Goal Theory of Leadership," is currently emerging. According to this theory, leaders are effective because of their impact on subordinates' motivation, ability to perform effectively, and satisfactions. The theory is called Path-Goal because its major concern is how the leader influences the subordinates' perceptions of their work goals, personal goals, and paths to goal attainment. The theory suggests that a leader's behavior is motivating or satisfying to the degree that the behavior increases subordinate goal attainment and clarifies the paths to these goals.

HISTORICAL FOUNDATIONS

The path-goal approach has its roots in a more general motivational theory called expectancy theory.[1] Briefly, expectancy theory states that an individual's attitudes (e.g., satisfaction with supervision or job satisfaction) or behavior (e.g., leader behavior or job effort) can be predicted from: (1) the degree to which the job, or behavior, is seen as leading to various outcomes (expectancy) and (2) the evaluation of these outcomes (valences). Thus, people are satisfied with their job if they think it leads to things that are highly valued, and they work hard if they believe that effort leads to things that are highly valued. This type of theoretical rationale can be used to predict a variety of phenomena related to leadership, such as why leaders behave the way they do, or how leader behavior influences subordinate motivation.[2]

This latter approach is the primary concern of this article. The implication for leadership is that subordinates are motivated by leader behavior to the extent

---

"Path-Goal Theory of Leadership" by Robert J. House and Terence R. Mitchell. Reprinted with permission from *Journal of Contemporary Business,* University of Washington, Autumn 1974, 3, no. 4, pp. 81–97.

1. T. R. Mitchell, "Expectancy Model of Job Satisfaction, Occupational Preference and Effort: A Theoretical, Methodological and Empirical Appraisal," *Psychological Bulletin* (1974).

2. D. M. Nebeker and T. R. Mitchell, "Leader Behavior: An Expectancy Theory Approach," *Organization Behavior and Human Performance,* 11(1974): 355–67.

that this behavior influences expectancies, e.g., goal paths and valences, e.g., goal attractiveness.

Several writers have advanced specific hypotheses concerning how the leader affects the paths and the goals of subordinates.[3] These writers focused on two issues: (1) how the leader affects subordinates' expectations that effort will lead to effective performance and valued rewards, and (2) how this expectation affects motivation to work hard and perform well.

While the state of theorizing about leadership in terms of subordinates' paths and goals is in its infancy, we believe it is promising for two reasons. First, it suggests effects of leader behavior that have not yet been investigated but which appear to be fruitful areas of inquiry. And, second, it suggests with some precision the situational factors on which the effects of leader behavior are contingent.

The initial theoretical work by Evans asserts that leaders will be effective by making rewards available to subordinates and by making these rewards contingent on the subordinate's accomplishment of specific goals.[4] Evans argued that one of the strategic functions of the leader is to clarify for subordinates the kind of behavior that leads to goal accomplishment and valued rewards. This function might be referred to as path clarification. Evans also argued that the leader increases the rewards available to subordinates by being supportive toward subordinates, i.e., by being concerned about their status, welfare, and comfort. Leader supportiveness is in itself a reward that the leader has at his or her disposal,

and the judicious use of this reward increases the motivation of subordinates.

Evans studied the relationship between the behavior of leaders and the subordinates' expectations that effort leads to rewards and also studied the resulting impact on ratings of the subordinates' performance. He found that when subordinates viewed leaders as being supportive (considerate of their needs) and when these superiors provided directions and guidance to the subordinates there was a positive relationship between leader behavior and subordinates' performance ratings.

However, leader behavior was only related to subordinates' performance when the leader's behavior also was related to the subordinates' expectations that their effort would result in desired rewards. Thus, Evans's findings suggest that the major impact of a leader on the performance of subordinates is clarifying the path to desired rewards and making such rewards contingent on effective performance.

Stimulated by this line of reasoning, House, and House and Dessler advanced a more complex theory of the effects of leader behavior on the motivation of subordinates.[5] The theory intends to explain the effects of four specific kinds of leader behavior on the following three subordinate attitudes or expectations: (1) the satisfaction of subordinates, (2) the subordinates' acceptance of the leader and (3) the expectations of subordinates that effort will result in effective performance and that effective performance is the path to rewards. The four kinds of leader behavior included in the theory are: (1) directive leadership, (2) supportive

3. M. G. Evans, "The Effects of Supervisory Behavior on the Path-Goal Relationship," *Organization Behavior and Human Performance,* 55(1970): 277–98; T. H. Hammer and H. T. Dachler, "The Process of Supervision in the Context of Motivation Theory," Research Report no. 3 (University of Maryland, 1973); F. Dansereau, Jr., J. Cashman, and G. Graen, "Instrumentality Theory and Equity Theory as Complementary Approaches in Predicting the Relationship of Leadership and Turnover among Managers," *Organization Behavior and Human Performance,* 10(1973): 184–200; R. J. House, "A Path-Goal Theory of Leader Effectiveness, *Administrative Science Quarterly,* 16, 3(September 1971): 321–38; T. R. Mitchell, "Motivation and Participation: An Integration," *Academy of Management Journal,* 16 4(1973): 160–79; G. Graen, F. Dansereau, Jr., and T. Minami, "Dysfunctional Leadership Styles," *Organization Behavior and Human Performance,* 7(1972): 216–36; G. Graen, F. Dansereau, Jr. and T. Minami, "An Empirical Test of the Man-in-the-Middle Hypothesis among Executives in a Hierarchical Organization Employing a Unit Analysis," *Organization Behavior and Human Performance,* 8(1972): 262–85; R. J. House and G. Dessler, "The Path-Goal Theory of Leadership: Some Post Hoc and A Priori Tests," to appear in J. G. Hunt, ed., *Contingency Approaches to Leadership* (Carbondale, Ill.: Southern Illinois University Press, 1974).

4. M. G. Evans, "Effects of Supervisory Behavior"; M. G. Evans, "Extensions of a Path-Goal Theory of Motivation," *Journal of Applied Psychology,* 59 (1974): 172-78.

5. R. J. House, "A Path-Goal Theory"; R. J. House and G. Dessler, "Path-Goal Theory of Leadership."

leadership, (3) participative leadership and (4) achievement-oriented leadership. Directive leadership is characterized by a leader who lets subordinates know what is expected of them, gives specific guidance as to what should be done and how it should be done, makes his or her part in the group understood, schedules work to be done, maintains definite standards of performance and asks that group members follow standard rules and regulations. Supportive leadership is characterized by a friendly and approachable leader who shows concern for the status, well-being and needs of subordinates. Such a leader does little things to make the work more pleasant, treats members as equals, and is friendly and approachable. Participative leadership is characterized by a leader who consults with subordinates, solicits their suggestions, and takes these suggestions seriously into consideration before making a decision. An achievement-oriented leader sets challenging goals, expects subordinates to perform at their highest level, continuously seeks improvement in performance *and* shows a high degree of confidence that the subordinates will assume responsibility, put forth effort, and accomplish challenging goals. This kind of leader constantly emphasizes excellence in performance and simultaneously displays confidence that subordinates will meet high standards of excellence.

A number of studies suggest that these different leadership styles can be shown by the same leader in various situations.[6] For example, a leader may show directiveness toward subordinates in some instances and be participative or supportive in other instances.[7] Thus, the traditional method of characterizing a leader as either highly participative and supportive *or* highly directive is invalid; rather, it can be concluded that leaders vary in the particular fashion employed for supervising their subordinates. Also, the theory, in its present stage, is a tentative explanation of the effects of leader behavior — it is incomplete because it does not explain other kinds of leader behavior and does not explain the effects of the leader on factors other than subordinate acceptance, satisfaction, and expectations. However, the theory is stated so that additional

variables may be included in it as new knowledge is made available.

PATH-GOAL THEORY

General Propositions

The first proposition of path-goal theory is that leader behavior is acceptable and satisfying to subordinates to the extent that the subordinates see such behavior as either an immediate source of satisfaction or as instrumental to future satisfaction.

The second proposition of this theory is that the leader's behavior will be motivational, i.e., increase effort, to the extent that (1) such behavior makes satisfaction of subordinate's needs contingent on effective performance and (2) such behavior complements the environment of subordinates by providing the coaching, guidance, support, and rewards necessary for effective performance.

These two propositions suggest that the leader's strategic functions are to enhance subordinates' motivation to perform, satisfaction with the job, and acceptance of the leader. From previous research on expectancy theory of motivation, it can be inferred that the strategic functions of the leader consist of: (1) recognizing and/or arousing subordinates' needs for outcomes over which the leader has some control, (2) increasing personal payoffs to subordinates for work-goal attainment, (3) making the path to those payoffs easier to travel by coaching and direction, (4) helping subordinates clarify expectancies, (5) reducing frustrating barriers and (6) increasing the opportunities for personal satisfaction contingent on effective performance.

Stated less formally, the motivational functions of the leader consist of increasing the number and kinds of personal payoffs to subordinates for work-goal attainment and making paths to these payoffs easier to travel by clarifying the paths, reducing road blocks and pitfalls, and increasing the opportunities for personal satisfaction en route.

---

6. R. J. House and G. Dessler, "Path-Goal Theory of Leadership"; R. M. Stogdill, *Managers, Employees, Organization* (Ohio State University, Bureau of Business Research, 1965); R. J. House, A. Valency, and R. Van der Krabben, "Some Tests and Extensions of the Path-Goal Theory of Leadership" (in preparation).

7. W. A. Hill and D. Hughes, "Variations in Leader Behavior as a Function of Task Type," *Organization Behavior and Human Performance,* 11, 1(1974): 83–96.

Contingency Factors

Two classes of situational variables are asserted to be contingency factors. A contingency factor is a variable which moderates the relationship between two other variables such as leader behavior and subordinate satisfaction. For example, we might suggest that the degree of structure in the task moderates the relationship between leaders' directive behavior and subordinates' job satisfaction. Figure 1 shows how such a relationship might look. Thus, subordinates are satisfied with directive behavior in an unstructured task and are satisfied with nondirective behavior in a structured task. Therefore, we say that the relationship between leader directiveness and subordinate satisfaction is contingent upon the structure of the task.

The two contingency variables are *(a)* personal characteristics of the subordinates and *(b)* the environmental pressures and demands with which subordinates must cope in order to accomplish the work goals and to satisfy their needs. While other situational factors also may operate to determine the effects of leader behavior, they are not presently known.

With respect to the first class of contingency factors, the characteristics of subordinates, path-goal theory asserts that leader behavior will be acceptable to subordinates to the extent that the subordinates see such behavior as either an immediate source of satisfaction or as instrumental to future satisfaction. Subordinates' characteristics are hypothesized to determine this perception partially. For example, Runyon[8] and Mitchell[9] show that the subordinate's score on a measure called Locus of Control moderates the relationship between participative leadership style and subordinate satisfaction. The Locus-of-Control measure reflects the degree to which an individual sees the environment as systematically responding to his or her behavior. People who believe that what happens to them occurs because of their behavior are called internals; people who believe that what happens to them occurs because of luck or chance are called externals. Mitchell's findings suggest that internals are more satisfied with a participative leadership style and externals are more satisfied with a directive style.

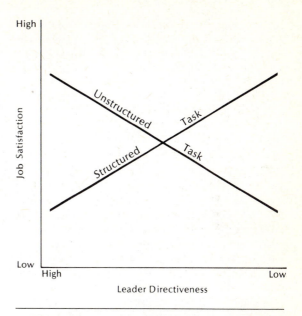

Figure 1. Hypothetical Relationship Between Directive Leadership and Subordinate Satisfaction with Task Structure as a Contingency Factor.

A second characteristic of subordinates on which the effects of leader behavior are contingent is subordinates' perception of their own ability with respect to their assigned tasks. The higher the degree of perceived ability relative to task demands, the less the subordinate will view leader directiveness and coaching behavior as acceptable. Where the subordinate's perceived ability is high, such behavior is likely to have little positive effect on the motivation of the subordinate and to be perceived as excessively close control. Thus, the acceptability of the leader's behavior is determined in part by the characteristics of the subordinates.

The second aspect of the situation, the environment of the subordinate, consists of those factors that are not within the control of the subordinate but which are important to need satisfaction or to ability to perform effectively. The theory asserts that effects of the leader's behavior on the psychological states of

8. K. E. Runyon, "Some Interactions between Personality Variables and Management Styles," *Journal of Applied Psychology*, 57, 3(1973): 288–94; T. R. Mitchell, C. R. Smyser, and S. E. Weed, "Locus of Control: Supervision and Work Satisfaction," *Academy of Management Journal*, 18, 3(1975): 623–31.

9. T. R. Mitchell, "Locus of Control."

subordinates are contingent on other parts of the subordinates' environment that are relevant to subordinate motivation. Three broad classifications of contingency factors in the environment are:

The subordinates' tasks.
The formal authority system of the organization.
The primary work group.

Assessment of the environmental conditions makes it possible to predict the kind and amount of influence that specific leader behaviors will have on the motivation of subordinates. Any of the three environmental factors could act upon the subordinate in any of three ways: first, to serve as stimuli that motivate and direct the subordinate to perform necessary task operations; second, to constrain variability in behavior. Constraints may help the subordinate by clarifying expectancies that effort leads to rewards or by preventing the subordinate from experiencing conflict and confusion. Constraints also may be counterproductive to the extent that they restrict initiative or prevent increases in effort from being associated positively with rewards. Third, environmental factors may serve as rewards for achieving desired performance, e.g., it is possible for the subordinate to receive the necessary cues to do the job and the needed rewards for satisfaction from sources other than the leader, e.g., co-workers in the primary work group. Thus, the effect of the leader on subordinates' motivation will be a function of how deficient the environment is with respect to motivational stimuli, constraints, or rewards.

With respect to the environment, path-goal theory asserts that when goals and paths to desired goals are apparent because of the routine nature of the task, clear group norms or objective controls of the formal authority systems, attempts by the leader to clarify paths and goals will be both redundant and seen by subordinates as imposing unnecessary, close control. Although such control may increase performance by preventing soldiering or malingering, it also will result in decreased satisfaction (see Figure 1). Also with respect to the work environment, the theory asserts that the more dissatisfying the task, the more the subordinates will resent leader behavior directed at increasing productivity or enforcing compliance to organizational rules and procedures.

Finally, with respect to environmental variables the theory states that leader behavior will be motivational to the extent that it helps subordinates cope with environmental uncertainties, threats from others or sources of frustration. Such leader behavior is predicted to increase subordinates' satisfaction with the job context and to be motivational to the extent that it increases the subordinates' expectations that their effort will lead to valued rewards.

These propositions and specification of situational contingencies provide a heuristic framework on which to base future research. Hopefully, this will lead to a more fully developed, explicitly formal theory of leadership.

Figure 2 presents a summary of the theory. It is hoped that these propositions, while admittedly tentative, will provide managers with some insights concerning the effects of their own leader behavior and that of others.

EMPIRICAL SUPPORT

The theory has been tested in a limited number of studies which have generated considerable empirical support for our ideas and also suggest areas in which the theory requires revision. A brief review of these studies follows.

Leader Directiveness

Leader directiveness has a positive correlation with satisfaction and expectancies of subordinates who are engaged in ambiguous tasks and has a negative correlation with satisfaction and expectancies of subordinates engaged in clear tasks. These findings were predicted by the theory and have been replicated in seven organizations. They suggest that when task demands are ambiguous or when the organization procedures, rules, and policies are not clear a leader behaving in a directive manner complements the tasks and the organization by providing the necessary guidance and psychological structure for subordinates.[10]

10. R. J. House, "A Path-Goal Theory"; R. J. House and G. Dessler, "Path-Goal Theory of Leadership"; A. D. Szalagyi and H. P. Sims, "An Exploration of the Path-Goal Theory of Leadership in a Health Care Environment," *Academy of Management Journal* (in press); J. D. Dermer, "Supervisory Behavior and Budget Motivation" (Cambridge, Mass.: unpublished, MIT, Sloan School of Management, 1974); R. W. Smetana, "The Relationship between Managerial Behavior and Subordinate Attitudes and Motivation: A Contribution to a Behavioral Theory of Leadership" (Ph.D. dissertation, Wayne State University, 1974).

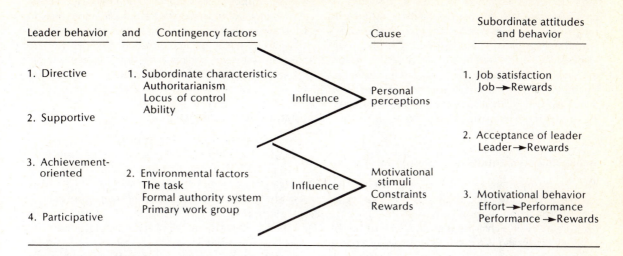

Figure 2.   Summary of Path-Goal Relationships.

However, when task demands are clear to subordinates, leader directiveness is seen more as a hindrance.

However, other studies have failed to confirm these findings.[11] A study by Dessler[12] suggests a resolution to these conflicting findings — he found that for subordinates at the lower organizational levels of a manufacturing firm who were doing routine, repetitive, unambiguous tasks, directive leadership was preferred by closed-minded, dogmatic, authoritarian subordinates and nondirective leadership was preferred by nonauthoritarian, open-minded subordinates. However, for subordinates at higher organizational levels doing nonroutine, ambiguous tasks, directive leadership was preferred for both authoritarian and nonauthoritarian subordinates. Thus, Dessler found that two contingency factors appear to operate simultaneously: subordinate task ambiguity and degree of subordinate authoritarianism. When measured in combination, the findings are as predicted by the theory; however, when the subordinate's personality is not taken into account, task ambiguity does not always operate as a contingency variable as predicted by the theory. House, Burill, and Dessler recently found a similar interaction between subordinate authoritarianism and task ambiguity in a second manufacturing firm, thus adding confidence in Dessler's original findings.[13]

Supportive Leadership

The theory hypothesizes that supportive leadership will have its most positive effect on subordinate satisfaction

11. S. E. Weed, T. R. Mitchell, and C. R. Smyser, "A Test of House's Path-Goal Theory of Leadership in an Organizational Setting" (paper presented at Western Psychological Assn., 1974); J. D. Dermer and J. P. Siegel, "A Test of Path-Goal Theory: Disconfirming Evidence and a Critique" (unpublished, University of Toronto, Faculty of Management Studies, 1973); R. S. Schuler, "A Path-Goal Theory of Leadership: An Empirical Investigation" (Ph.D. dissertation, Michigan State University, 1973); H. K. Downey, J. E. Sheridan, and J. W. Slocum, Jr., "Analysis of Relationships among Leader Behavior, Subordinate Job Performance and Satisfaction: A Path-Goal Approach" (unpublished mimeograph, 1974); J. E. Stinson and T. W. Johnson, "The Path-Goal Theory of Leadership: A Partial Test and Suggested Refinement," *Proceedings* (Kent, Ohio: 7th Annual Conference of the Midwest Academy of Management, April 1974): 18–36.

12. G. Dessler, "An Investigation of the Path-Goal Theory of Leadership" (Ph.D. dissertation, City University of New York, Bernard M. Baruch College, 1973).

13. R. J. House, D. Burrill, and G. Dessler, "Tests and Extensions of Path-Goal Theory of Leadership, I" (unpublished, in process).

for subordinates who work on stressful, frustrating, or dissatisfying tasks. This hypothesis has been tested in 10 samples of employees,[14] and in only one of these studies was the hypothesis disconfirmed.[15] Despite some inconsistency in research on supportive leadership, the evidence is sufficiently positive to suggest that managers should be alert to the critical need for supportive leadership under conditions where tasks are dissatisfying, frustrating, or stressful to subordinates.

Achievement-oriented Leadership

The theory hypothesizes that achievement-oriented leadership will cause subordinates to strive for higher standards of performance and to have more confidence in the ability to meet challenging goals. A recent study by House, Valency, and Van der Krabben provides a partial test of this hypothesis among white-collar employees in service organizations.[16] For subordinates performing ambiguous, nonrepetitive tasks, they found a positive relationship between the amount of achievement orientation of the leader and subordinates' expectancy that their effort would result in effective performance. Stated less technically, for subordinates performing ambiguous, nonrepetitive tasks, the higher the achievement orientation of the leader, the more the subordinates were confident that their efforts would pay off in effective performance. For subordinates performing moderately unambiguous, repetitive tasks, there was no significant relationship between achievement-oriented leadership and subordinate expectancies that their effort would lead to effective performance. This finding held in four separate organizations:

Two plausible interpretations may be used to explain these data. First, people who select ambiguous, nonrepetitive tasks may be different in personality from those who select a repetitive job and may, therefore, be more responsive to an achievement-oriented leader. A second explanation is that achievement orientation only affects expectancies in ambiguous situations because

there is more flexibility and autonomy in such tasks. Therefore, subordinates in such tasks are more likely to be able to change in response to such leadership style. Neither of the above interpretations have been tested to date; however; additional research is currently under way to investigate these relationships.

Participative Leadership

In theorizing about the effects of participative leadership, it is necessary to ask about the specific characteristics of both the subordinates and their situation that would cause participative leadership to be viewed as satisfying and instrumental to effective performance.

Mitchell recently described at least four ways in which a participative leadership style would impact on subordinate attitudes and behavior as predicted by expectancy theory.[17] First, a participative climate should increase the clarity of organizational contingencies. Through participation in decision making, subordinates should learn what leads to what. From a path-goal viewpoint participation would lead to greater clarity of the paths to various goals. A second impact of participation would be that subordinates, hopefully, should select goals they highly value. If one participates in decisions about various goals, it makes sense that this individual would select goals he or she wants. Thus, participation would increase the correspondence between organization and subordinate goals. Third, we can see how participation would increase the control the individual has over what happens on the job. If our motivation is higher (based on the preceding two points), then having greater autonomy and ability to carry out our intentions should lead to increased effort and performance. Finally, under a participative system, pressure towards high performance should come from sources other than the leader or the organization. More specifically, when people participate in the decision process, they become more ego-involved; the decisions made are in some part their own. Also, their peers know what is expected and the social pressure has a greater

---

14. R. J. House, "A Path-Goal Theory"; R. J. House and G. Dessler, "Path-Goal Theory of Leadership"; A. D. Szalagyi and H. P. Sims, "Exploration of Path-Goal"; J. E. Stinson and T. W. Johnson, *Proceedings;* R. S. Schuler, "Path-Goal: Investigation"; H. K. Downey, J. E. Sheridan, and J. W. Slocum, Jr., "Analysis of Relationships"; S. E. Weed, T. R. Mitchell, and C. R. Smyser, "Test of House's Path-Goal."

15. A. D. Szalagyi and H. P. Sims, "Exploration of Path-Goal."

16. R. J. House, A. Valency, and R. Van der Krabben, "Tests and Extensions of Path-Goal Theory of Leadership, II" (unpublished, in process).

17. T. R. Mitchell, "Motivation and Participation."

impact. Thus, motivation to perform well stems from internal and social factors as well as formal external ones.

A number of investigations prior to the above formulation supported the idea that participation appears to be helpful,[18] and Mitchell presents a number of recent studies that support the above four points.[19] However, it is also true that we would expect the relationship between a participative style and subordinate behavior to be moderated by both the personality characteristics of the subordinate and the situational demands. Studies by Tannenbaum and Alport and Vroom have shown that subordinates who prefer autonomy and self-control respond more positively to participative leadership in terms of both satisfaction and performance than subordinates who do not have such preferences.[20] Also, the studies mentioned by Runyon[21] and Mitchell[22] showed that subordinates who were external in orientation were less satisfied with a participative style of leadership than were internal subordinates.

House also has reviewed these studies in an attempt to explain the ways in which the situation or environment moderates the relationship between participation and subordinate attitudes and behavior.[23] His analysis suggests that where participative leadership is positively related to satisfaction, regardless of the predispositions of subordinates, the tasks of the subjects appear to be ambiguous and ego-involving. In the studies in which the subjects' personalities or predispositions moderate the effect of participative leadership, the tasks of the subjects are inferred to be highly routine and/or nonego-involving.

House reasoned from this analysis that the task may have an overriding effect on the relationship between leader participation and subordinate responses and that individual predispositions or personality characteristics of subordinates may have an effect only under some tasks. It was assumed that when task demands are ambiguous subordinates will have a need to reduce the ambiguity. Further, it was assumed that when task demands are ambiguous participative problem solving between the leader and the subordinate will result in more effective decisions than when the task demands are unambiguous. Finally, it was assumed that when the subordinates are ego-involved in their tasks they are more likely to want to have a say in the decisions that affect them. Given these assumptions, the following hypotheses were formulated to account for the conflicting findings reviewed above:

When subjects are highly ego-involved in a decision or a task and the decision or task demands are ambiguous, participative leadership will have a positive effect on the satisfaction and motivation of the subordinate, *regardless* of the subordinate's predisposition toward self-control, authoritarianism, or need for independence.

When subordinates are not ego-involved in their tasks and when task demands are clear, subordinates who are not authoritarian and who have high needs for independence and self-control will respond favorably to leader participation and their opposite personality types will respond less favorably.

These hypotheses were derived on the basis of path-goal theorizing, i.e., the rationale guiding the analysis of prior studies was that both task characteristics and characteristics of subordinates interact to determine the effect of a specific kind of leader behavior on the satisfaction, expectancies, and performance of subordinates. To date, one major investigation has

---

18. H. Tosi, "A Reexamination of Personality as a Determinant of the Effects of Participation," *Personnel Psychology,* 23(1970): 91–99; J. Sadler "Leadership Style, Confidence in Management and Job Satisfaction," *Journal of Applied Behavioral Sciences,* 6(1970): 3–19; K. N. Wexley, J. P. Singh, and J. A. Yukl, "Subordinate Personality as a Moderator of the Effects of Participation in Three Types of Appraisal Interviews," *Journal of Applied Psychology,* 83 1(1973): 54–59.

19. T. R. Mitchell, "Motivation and Participation."

20. A. S. Tannenbaum and F. H. Allport, "Personality Structure and Group Structure: An Interpretive Study of Their Relationship through an Event-Structure Hypothesis," *Journal of Abnormal and Social Psychology,* 53(1956): 272–80; V. H. Vroom, "Some Personality Determinants of the Effects of Participation," *Journal of Abnormal and Social Psychology,* 59(1959): 322–27.

21. K. E. Runyon, "Some Interactions between Personality Variables and Management Styles," *Journal of Applied Psychology,* 57, 3(1973): 288–94.

22. T. R. Mitchell, C. R. Smyser, and S. E. Weed, "Locus of Control."

23. R. J. House, "Notes on the Path-Goal Theory of Leadership" (University of Toronto, Faculty of Management Studies, May 1974).

supported some of these predictions[24] in which personality variables, amount of participative leadership, task ambiguity, and job satisfaction were assessed for 324 employees of an industrial manufacturing organization. As expected, in nonrepetitive, ego-involving tasks, employees (regardless of their personality) were more satisfied under a participative style than a nonparticipative style. However, in repetitive tasks which were less ego-involving, the amount of authoritarianism of subordinates moderated the relationship between leadership style and satisfaction. Specifically, low authoritarian subordinates were *more satisfied* under a participative style. These findings are exactly as the theory would predict; thus, it has promise in reconciling a set of confusing and contradictory findings with respect to participative leadership.

SUMMARY AND CONCLUSIONS

We have attempted to describe what we believe is a useful theoretical framework for understanding the effect of leadership behavior on subordinate satisfaction and motivation. Most theorists today have moved away from the simplistic notions that all effective leaders have a certain set of personality traits or that the situation completely determines performance. Some researchers have presented rather complex attempts at matching certain types of leaders with certain types of situations. . . . But, we believe that a path-goal approach goes one step further. It not only suggests what type of style may be most effective in a given situation — it also attempts to explain *why* it is most effective.

We are optimistic about the future outlook of leadership research. With the guidance of path-goal theorizing, future research is expected to unravel many confusing puzzles about the reasons for and effects of leader behavior that have, heretofore, not been solved. However, we add a word of caution: the theory, and the research on it, are relatively new to the literature of organizational behavior. Consequently, path-goal theory is offered more as a tool for directing research and stimulating insight than as a proven guide for managerial action.

---

24. R. S. Schuler, "Leader Participation, Task Structure, and Subordinate Authoritarianism" (unpublished mimeograph, Cleveland State University, 1974).

26. Leadership Revisited

Victor H. Vroom

RESEARCH ON LEADERSHIP TRAITS

Early research on the question of leadership had roots in the psychology of individual differences and in the personality theory of that time. The prevailing theory held that differences among people could be understood in terms of their traits — consistencies in behavior exhibited over situations. Each person could be usefully described on such dimensions as honesty-dishonesty, introversion-extroversion or masculine-feminine. In extrapolating this kind of theory to the study of leadership, it seemed natural to assume that there was such a thing as a trait of leadership, i.e., it was something that people possessed in different amounts. If such differences existed, they must be measurable in some way. As a consequence, psychologists set out, armed with a wide variety of psychological tests, to measure differences between leaders and followers. A large number of studies were conducted including comparisons of bishops with clergymen, sales managers with salesmen and railway presidents with station agents. Since occupancy of a leadership position may not be a valid reflection of the degree of leadership, other investigators pursued a different tack by looking at the relationship between personal traits of leaders and criteria for their effectiveness in carrying out their positions.

If this search for the measurable components of this universal trait of leadership had been effective, the implications for society would have been considerable. The resulting technology would have been of countless value in selecting leaders for all of our social institutions and would have eliminated errors inevitably found in the subjective assessments which typically guide this process. But the search was largely unsuccessful and the dream of its byproduct — a general technology of leader selection — was unrealized. The results, which have been summarized elsewhere (Bass, 1960; Gibb, 1969; Stogdill, 1948) cast considerable doubt on the usefulness of the concept of leadership as a personality trait. They do not imply that individual differences have nothing to do with leadership, but rather that their significance must be evaluated in relation to the situation.

Written more than 25 years ago, Stogdill's conclusions seem equally applicable today:

The pattern of personal characteristics of the leader must bear some relevant relationship to the characteristics, activities and goals of the followers . . . It becomes clear that an adequate analysis of leadership involves not only a study of leaders, but also of situations. (1948, pp. 64–65)

The study of leadership based on personality traits had been launched on an oversimplified premise. But as Stogdill's conclusions were being written, social scientists at Ohio State University and at the University of Michigan were preparing to launch another and quite different attack on the problem of leadership. In these ventures, the focus was not on personal traits but on leader behavior and leadership style. Effective and ineffective leaders may not be distinguishable by a battery of psychological tests but may be distinguished by their characteristic behavior patterns in their work roles.

RESEARCH ON EFFECTIVE LEADERSHIP METHODS

The focus on behavior of the leader rather than his personal traits was consistent with Lewin's classic dictum that behavior is a function of both person and environment (Lewin, 1951) and of growing recognition that the concept of trait provided little room for environmental or situational influences on behavior. Such a focus also envisioned a greater degree of consistency in behavior across situations than has been empirically demonstrated (Hartshorne and May, 1928; Mischel, 1968; Vroom and Yetton, 1973).

If particular patterns of behavior or leadership styles were found which consistently distinguished leaders of effective and ineffective work groups, the payoff to organizations and to society would have been considerable, but of a different nature than work based on the trait approach. Such results would have less obvious implications for leader selection but would have significant import for leader development and training. Knowledge of the behavior patterns which characterize effective leaders would provide a rational basis for the design of educational programs in an attempt to instill these patterns in actual or potential leaders.

Space does not permit a detailed account of the Ohio State and Michigan research or of its offshoots in other institutions. It is fair to say, however, that the success of this line of inquiry in developing empirically based generalizations about effective leadership styles is a matter of some controversy. There are some who see in the results a consistent pattern sufficient to constitute the basis of technologies of organization design or leader development. Likert (1967), reviewing the program of research at Michigan, finds support for what he calls System 4, a participative group-based conception of management. Similarly, Blake and Moulton (1964), with their conceptual roots in the Ohio State research program, argue that the effective leader exhibits concern for both production and employees (their 9-9 style) and have constructed a viable technology of management and organization development based on that premise.

On the other hand, other social scientists including the present writer (Korman, 1966; Sales, 1966; Vroom, 1964) have reviewed the evidence resulting from these studies and commented lamentably on the variability in results and the difficulty in making from them any definitive statements about effective leader behavior without knowledge of the situation in which the behavior has been exhibited.

At first glance, these would appear to be two directly opposing interpretations of the same results, but that would probably be too strong a conclusion. The advocates of general leadership principles have stated these principles in such a way that they are difficult to refute by empirical evidence and at the same time provide considerable latitude for individual interpretation. To say that a leader should manage in such a way that personnel at all levels feel real responsibility for the attainment of the organization's goals (Likert, 1967) or alternatively that he should exhibit concern for both production and his employees (Blake and Mouton, 1964) are at best general blueprints for action rather

than specific blueprints indicating how these objectives should be achieved. The need for adapting these principles to the demands of the situation is recognized by most social scientists. For example, Likert writes:

Supervision is . . . always a relative process. To be effective and to communicate as intended, a leader must always adapt his behavior to take into account the expectations, values, and interpersonal skills of those with whom he is interacting. . . . There can be no specific rules of supervision which will work well in all situations. Broad principles can be applied in the process of supervision and furnish valuable guides to behavior. These principles, however, must be applied always in a manner that takes fully into account the characteristics of the specific situation and of the people involved. (1961, p. 95)

To this writer, the search for effective methods of supervision management and leadership has come close to foundering on the same rocks as the trait approach. It too has failed to deal explicitly with differences in situational requirements for leadership. If the behavioral sciences are to make a truly viable contribution to the management of the contemporary organization, they must progress beyond an advocacy of power equalization with appropriate caveats about the need for consideration of situational differences and attempt to come to grips with the complexities of the leadership process.

INVESTIGATION ON LEADERSHIP STYLES

These convictions, whether right or wrong, provided the basis for a new approach to the investigation of leadership style — its determinants and consequences — launched about six years ago by the author and Phillip Yetton, then a graduate student at Carnegie Mellon University. We set ourselves two goals: (1) to formulate a normative or prescriptive model of leader behavior which incorporated situational characteristics in an explicit manner and which was consistent with existing empirical evidence concerning the consequences of alternative approaches; and (2) to launch an empirical attack on the determinants of leader behavior which would reveal the factors both within the person and in the situation which influence leaders to behave in various ways.

In retrospect, these goals were ambitious ones and the reader will have to judge for himself the extent to which either has been achieved. We attempted to make the task more manageable by focusing on one dimension of leader behavior — the degree to which the leader encourages the participation of his subordinates in decision-making. This dimension was chosen both because it was at the core of most prescriptive approaches to leadership and because a substantial amount of research had been conducted on it.

The first step was to review that evidence in detail. No attempt will be made here to repeat that review. (The reader interested in this question may consult Lowin, 1968; Vroom, 1964; or Wood, 1974.) Instead, we will restrict our attention to a summary of the major conclusions which appeared justifiable by the evidence.

1. Involvement of subordinates in "group decision-making" is costly in terms of time. Autocratic decision-making processes are typically faster (and thus of potential value in emergency or crisis situations) and invariably require less investment in man-hours of the group in the process of decision-making than methods which provide greater opportunities for participation by subordinates, particularly those decision processes which require consensus by the group.

2. Participation by subordinates in decision-making creates greater acceptance of decisions which in turn is reflected in better implementation. There is a wide range of circumstances under which "people support what they helped to build." Increasing the opportunity for subordinates to have a significant voice in decisions which affect them results in greater acceptance and commitment to the decisions, which will in turn be reflected in more effective and reliable implementation of the decision.

3. The effects of increased participation by subordinates in decision making on the quality or rationality of decisions tend to be positive, although the effects are likely to depend on several identifiable factors. Extensive research has been conducted on group and individual problem solving. Group decisions tend to be higher in quality when the relevant information is widely distributed among group members, when the problem is unstructured, and when there exists a mutual interest or common goal among group members.

4. Involvement of subordinates in decision making leads to growth and development of subordinates. This consequence of participation has been least researched and its assertion here is based primarily on theoretical rather than empirical grounds. It is different from the three previous factors (time, acceptance, and quality of decision) in its long-term nature.

From this general research foundation a normative model was constructed. The model utilized five decision processes which vary in the amount of opportunity afforded subordinates to participate in decision making. These processes are shown in Table 1.

The model to be described is a contingency model. It rests on the assumption that no one decision-making

Table 1. Types of Management Decision Styles

AI	You solve the problem or make the decision yourself using information available to you at that time.
AII	You obtain necessary information from subordinate(s) and then decide on a solution to the problem yourself. You may or may not tell subordinates what the problem is in getting the information from them. The role played by your subordinates in making the decision is clearly one of providing the necessary information to you, rather than generating or evaluating alternative solutions.
CI	You share the problem with relevant subordinates individually, getting their ideas and suggestions without bringing them together as a group. Then you make the decision which may or may not reflect your subordinates' influence.
CII	You share the problem with your subordinates as a group, collectively obtaining their ideas and suggestions. Then, *you* make the decision which may or may not reflect your subordinates' influence.
GII	You share the problem with your subordinates as a group. Together you generate and evaluate alternatives and attempt to reach agreement (consensus) on a solution. Your role is much like that of chairman. You do not try to influence the group to adopt "your" solution and are willing to accept and implement any solution which has the support of the entire group.

process is best under all circumstances, and that its effectiveness is dependent upon identifiable properties of the situation. However, it is different from other contingency models in the fact that the situational characteristics are attributes of the particular problem or decision rather than more general role characteristics. To distinguish this type of situational variable from others we have designated them as problem attributes. These attributes are the building blocks of the model and represent the means of diagnosing the nature of the problem or decision at hand so as to determine the optimal decision process.

The most recent form of the model is shown in Figure 1. It is expressed here in the form of a decision tree. The problem attributes are arranged along the top and are shown here in the form of yes-no questions. To use the model to determine the decision process, one starts at the left-hand side of the diagram and asks the question pertaining to attribute *A*. The answer (yes or no) will determine the path taken. When a second box is encountered, the question pertaining to that attribute is asked and the process continued until a terminal node is reached. At that node one will find a number (indicating problem type) and a feasible set of decision processes.

For some problem types only one decision process is shown; for others there are two, three, four or even all five processes. The particular decision processes shown are those that remain after a set of seven rules has been applied. The rules function to protect both the quality and the acceptance by eliminating methods that have a substantial likelihood of jeopardizing either of these two components of an effective decision. The interested reader should consult Vroom and Yetton (1973) for a detailed statement, in both verbal and mathematical form, of these rules.

If more than one alternative remains in the feasible set, there are a number of bases for choosing among them. One of them is time. The methods are arranged in ascending order of the time in man-hours which they require. Accordingly, a time minimizing model (which we have termed Model A) would select that alternative that is farthest to the left within the feasible set. An alternative to minimizing time is maximizing development of subordinates. This model (which we have termed Model B) would select that decision process which is farthest to the right within the feasible set.

While we have attempted to phrase the questions pertaining to the problem attributes in as meaningful a fashion as possible, the reader should keep in mind that

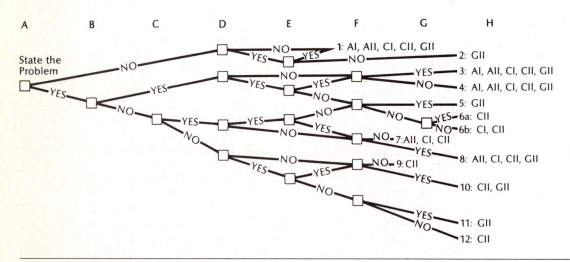

Figure 1.   Decision-Process Flow Chart for Group Problems.

A. Is there a quality requirement such that one solution is likely to be more rational than another?
B. Do I have sufficient info to make a high quality decision?
C. Is the problem structured?
D. Is acceptance of decision by subordinates critical to effective implementation?
E. If I were to make the decision by myself, is it reasonably certain that it would be accepted by my subordinates?
F. Do subordinates share the organizational goals to be attained in solving this problem?
G. Is conflict among subordinates likely in preferred solutions? (This question is irrelevant to individual problems.)
J. Do subordinates have sufficient info to make a high quality decision?

they are really surrogates for more detailed specifications of the underlying variables. The reader interested in more information on the meaning of the attributes, the threshold for yes-no judgments or their rationale for inclusion in the model should consult Vroom and Yetton (1973). Illustrations of the models' application to concrete cases can be found in Vroom (1973); Vroom and Yetton (1973); and Vroom and Jago (1974).

The model shown in Figure 1 is intended to apply to a domain of managerial decision-making which Maier, Solem, and Maier (1957) refer to as group problems, i.e., problems which have potential effects on all or a substantial subset of the manager's subordinates. Recently, we have become interested in extending the model to "individual problems," i.e., those affecting only one subordinate. For these decisions, the first three decision processes shown in Table 1 represent potentially reasonable alternatives, but there are at least two other viable alternatives not yet represented. One of these we have called GI, which is a form of group decision involving only a single subordinate. (A GI manager shares the problem with the subordinate and together they analyze the problem and arrive at a mutually satisfactory solution.) The other, which we have designated as DI, consists of delegating the problem or decision to the subordinate.

Many of the considerations used in building the model for group problems — such as problem attributes and rules — could easily be adapted to the domain of individual problems. There remained, however, one major structural difference. For group problems, there was a tradeoff between the short-run consideration of time efficiency (which favored autocratic methods) and longer-range considerations involving subordinate development (which favored participative methods). The reader will recall that Model A and Model B represented two extreme modes of resolution of that tradeoff. For individual problems, the differences in time requirements of the five processes (AI, AII, CI, GI, DI) are not nearly as large and the alternative which provides the greatest amount of subordinate influence or participation, DI, can hardly be argued to be least time efficient. This difference in the correlation between time efficiency and participation for individual and group problems required an adjustment in the location of DI in the ordering of alternatives in terms of time. Model A and Model B retain their original meaning from the earlier model, but they are no longer polar opposites.

Figure 2 contains a model also expressed as a decision tree which purports to guide choices among decision processes for both individual and group problems. The only difference lies in the specifications of two feasible sets (one for group and one for individual problems) for each problem type.

Is the model in its present form an adequate guide to practice? Would managers make fewer errors in their choices of decision processes if they were to base them on the model? We would be less than honest if we said we knew the answers to such questions. Most managers who have had sufficient training in the use of the model to be able to use it reliably report that it is a highly useful guide, although there are occasionally considerations not presently contained in the model — such as geographical dispersion of subordinates — which prevent implementation of its recommendations. Some research has been conducted in an attempt to establish the validity of the model (see Vroom and Yetton, 1973: 182–84), but the results, while promising, are not conclusive. Perhaps the most convincing argument for the development of models of this kind is that they can serve as a guide for research that can identify their weaknesses and that superior models can later be developed.

The reader will note that flexibility in leader behavior is one of the requirements of use of the model. To use it effectively, the leader must adapt his approach to the situation. But how flexible are leaders in the approaches they use? Do they naturally try and vary their approach with the situation? Is it possible to develop such flexibility through training? These questions were but a few of those which guided the next phase of our inquiry into how leaders do in fact behave and into the factors both within the leader himself and in the situations with which he deals which cause him to share decision-making power with his subordinates.

Two different research methods have been used in an attempt to answer questions such as these. The first investigation utilized a method that can be referred to as "recalled problems." Over 500 managers from 11 different countries representing a variety of firms were asked to provide a written description of a problem that they had recently had to solve. These varied in length from one paragraph to several pages and covered virtually every facet of managerial decision making. For each case, the manager was asked to indicate which of the decision processes shown in Table 1 he used to solve the problem. Finally, each manager was asked to answer the questions corresponding to the problem attributes used in the normative model with his own case in mind.

These data made it possible to determine the frequency with which the managers' decision process

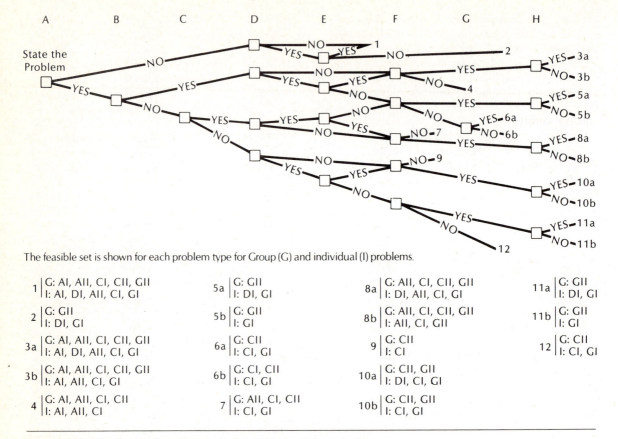

The feasible set is shown for each problem type for Group (G) and individual (I) problems.

1 | G: AI, AII, CI, CII, GII
   | I: AI, DI, AII, CI, GI

2 | G: GII
   | I: DI, GI

3a | G: AI, AII, CI, CII, GII
    | I: AI, DI, AII, CI, GI

3b | G: AI, AII, CI, CII, GII
    | I: AI, AII, CI, GI

4 | G: AI, AII, CI, CII
   | I: AI, AII, CI

5a | G: GII
    | I: DI, GI

5b | G: GII
    | I: GI

6a | G: CII
    | I: CI, GI

6b | G: CI, CII
    | I: CI, GI

7 | G: AII, CI, CII
   | I: CI, GI

8a | G: AII, CI, CII, GII
    | I: DI, AII, CI, GI

8b | G: AII, CI, CII, GII
    | I: AII, CI, GII

9 | G: CII
   | I: CI

10a | G: CII, GII
     | I: DI, CI, GI

10b | G: CII, GII
     | I: CI, GI

11a | G: GII
     | I: DI, GI

11b | G: GII
     | I: GI

12 | G: CII
    | I: CI, GI

Figure 2. Decision-Process Flow Chart for Both Individual and Group Problems.

A. Is there a quality requirement such that one solution is likely to be more rational than another?
B. Do I have sufficient info to make a high quality decision?
C. Is the problem structured?
D. Is acceptance of decision by subordinates critical to effective implementation?
E. If I were to make the decision by myself, is it reasonably certain that it would be accepted by my subordinates?
F. Do subordinates share the organizational goals to be attained in solving this problem?
G. Is conflict among subordinates likely in preferred solutions? (This question is irrelevant to individual problems.)
H. Do subordinates have sufficient info to make a high quality decision?

was similar to that of the normative model and the factors in their description of the situation which were associated with the use of each decision process. This investigation provided results which were interesting but also led to the development of a second more powerful method for investigating the same questions. This method, which will be termed "standardized problems," used some of the actual cases written by the managers in the construction of a standardized set of cases, each of which depicts a manager faced with a problem to solve or decision to make. In each case, a

leader would be asked to assume the role of the manager faced with the situation described and to indicate which decision process he would use if faced with that situation.

Several such sets of cases have been developed. In early research, each set consisted of thirty cases, but more recently longer sets of forty-eight and fifty-four cases have been used. Composition of each set of standardized cases was in accordance with multifactorial experimental design. Cases varied in terms of each of the eight problem attributes used in the normative model, and variation in each attribute was independent of each other attribute. This feature permits the assessment of the effects of each of the problem attributes on the decision processes used by a given manager.

The cases themselves spanned a wide range of managerial problems including production scheduling, quality control, portfolio management, personnel allocation, and research and development project selection. To date, several thousand managers in the United States and abroad have been studied using this approach.

RESULTS AND CONCLUSIONS

To summarize everything learned in the course of this research is well beyond the scope of this reading, but it is possible to discuss some of the highlights. Since the results obtained from the two research methods—recalled and standardized problems—are consistent, the major results can be presented independent of the method used.

Perhaps the most striking finding is the weakening of the widespread view that participativeness is a general trait that individual managers exhibit in different amounts. To be sure, there were differences among managers in their general tendencies to utilize participative methods as opposed to autocratic ones. On the standardized problems, these differences accounted for about 10 percent of the total variance in the decision processes observed. Furthermore, those managers who tended to use more participative methods such as CH and GH with group problems also tended to use more participative methods like delegation for dealing with individual problems.

However, these differences in behavior between managers were small in comparison with differences within managers. On the standardized problems, no manager has indicated that he would use the same decision process on all problems or decisions, and most use all methods under some circumstances. Taking managers' reports of their behavior in concrete situations, it is clear that they are striving to be flexible in their approaches to different situations.

Some of this variance in behavior within managers can be attributed to widely shared tendencies to respond to some situations by sharing power and others by retaining it. It makes more sense to talk about participative and autocratic situations than it does to talk about participative and autocratic managers. In fact, on

the standardized problems, the variance in behavior across problems or cases is from three to five times as large as the variance across managers.

What are the characteristics of an autocratic as opposed to a participative situation? An answer to this question would constitute a partial descriptive model of this aspect of the decision-making process and has been the goal of much of the research conducted. From observations of behavior on both recalled problems and on standardized problems, it is clear that the decision-making process employed by a typical manager is influenced by a large number of factors, many of which also show up in the normative model. Following are several conclusions substantiated by the results on both recalled and standardized problems.

Managers use decision processes providing less opportunity for participation (1) when they possess all the necessary information rather when they lack some of the needed information; (2) when the problem they face is well-structured rather than unstructured; (3) when their subordinates' acceptance of the decision is not critical for the effective implementation of the decision or when the prior probability of acceptance of an autocratic decision is high; and (4) when the personal goals of their subordinates are not congruent with the goals of the organization as manifested in the problem.

These findings concern relatively common or widely shared ways of dealing with organizational problems. The results also strongly suggest that managers have ways of "tailoring" their decision process to the situation that distinguish one manager from another. Theoretically, these can be thought of as differences among managers in decision rules that they employ about when to encourage participation.

Consider, for example, two managers who have identical distributions of the use of the five decision processes shown in Table 1 on a set of thirty cases. In a sense, they are equally participative (or autocratic). However, the situations in which they permit or encourage participation in decision making on the part of their subordinates may be very different. One may restrict the participation of his subordinates to decisions without a quality requirement, whereas the other may restrict their participation to problems with a quality requirement. The former would be more inclined to use participative decision processes (like GII) on such decisions as what color the walls should be painted or when the company picnic should be held. The latter would be more likely to encourage participation in decision making on decisions that have a clear and demonstrable impact on the organization's success in achieving its external goals.

Use of the standardized problem set permits the assessment of such differences in decision rules that govern choices among decision-making processes. Since the cases are selected in accordance with an experimental design, they can indicate differences in the behavior of managers attributable not only to the existence of a quality requirement in the problem but also in the effects of acceptance requirements, conflict, information requirements, and the like.

The research using both recalled and standardized problems has also permitted the examination of similarities and differences between the behavior of the normative model and the behavior of a typical manager. Such an analysis reveals, at the very least, what behavioral changes could be expected if managers began using the normative model as the basis for choosing their decision-making processes.

A typical manager says he would (or did) use exactly the same decision process as that shown in Figure 1 in about 40 percent of the group problems. In two-thirds of the situations, his behavior is consistent with the feasible set of methods proposed in the model. However, in the remaining one-third of the situations, his behavior violates at least one of the seven rules underlying the model. Results show significantly higher agreement with the normative model for individual problems than for group problems.

The rules designed to protect the acceptance or commitment of the decision have substantially higher probabilities of being violated than do the rules designed to protect the quality or rationality of the decision. Assuming for the moment that these two sets of rules have equal validity, these findings strongly suggest that the decisions made by typical managers are more likely to prove ineffective due to deficiencies of acceptance by subordinates than due to deficiencies in decision quality.

Another striking difference between the behavior of the model and of the typical manager lies in the fact that the former shows far greater variance with the situation. If a typical manager voluntarily used the model as the basis for choosing his methods of making decisions, he would become both more autocratic and more participative. He would employ autocratic methods more frequently in situations in which his subordinates were unaffected by the decision and participative methods more frequently when his subordinates' cooperation and support were critical and/or their information and expertise were required.

It should be noted that the typical manager to whom we have been referring is merely a statistical average of the several thousand who have been studied over the last three or four years. There is a great deal of variation around that average. As evidenced by their behavior on standardized problems, some managers are already behaving in a manner that is highly consistent with the model, while others' behavior is clearly at variance with it.

The research program that has been summarized was conducted in order to shed new light on the causes and consequences of decision-making processes used by leaders in formal organizations. In the course of research, it was realized that the data collection procedures, with appropriate additions and modifications, might also serve a useful function in leadership development. From this realization evolved an important byproduct of the research activities — a new approach to leadership training based on the concepts in the normative model and the empirical methods of the descriptive research.

A detailed description of this training program and of initial attempts to evaluate its effectiveness may be found in Vroom and Yetton (1973, chap. 8). It is based on the premise that one of the critical skills required of all leaders is the ability to adapt their behavior to the demands of the situation and that a component of this skill involves selecting the appropriate decision-making process for each problem or decision they confront. The purpose of the program is not to "train" managers to use the model in their everyday decision-making activities. Instead the model serves as a device for encouraging managers to examine their leadership styles and for coming to a conscious realization of their own, often implicit, choices among decision processes, including their similarity and dissimilarity with the model. By helping managers to become aware of their present behavior and of alternatives to it, the training provides a basis for rethinking their leadership style to be more consistent with goals and objectives. Succinctly, the training is intended to transform habits into choices rather than to program a leader with a particular method of making choices.

A fundamental part of the program in its present form is the use of a set of standardized cases previously described in connection with the descriptive phase of the research. Each participant specifies the decision process he would employ if he were the leader described in the case. His responses to the entire set of cases are processed by computer, which generates a highly detailed analysis of his leadership style. The responses for all participants in a single course are typically processed simultaneously, permitting the calculation of differences between the person and others in the same program.

In its latest form, a single computer printout for a person consists of seven 15" by 11" pages, each filled with graphs and tables highlighting different features of his behavior. Understanding the results requires a detailed knowledge of the concepts underlying the model, something already developed in one of the previous phases of the training program. The printout is accompanied by a manual that aids in explaining the results and provides suggested steps to be followed in extracting the full meaning from the printout.

Following are a few of the questions that the printout answers:

1. How autocratic or participative am I in my dealings with subordinates in the program?
2. What decision processes do I use more or less frequently than the average?
3. How close does my behavior come to that of the model? How frequently does my behavior agree with the feasible set? What evidence is there that my leadership style reflects the pressure of time as opposed to a concern with the development of my subordinates? How do I compare in these respects with other participants in the program?
4. What rules do I violate most frequently and least frequently? On what cases did I violate these rules? Does my leadership style reflect more concern with getting decisions that are high in quality or with getting decisions that are accepted?

When a typical manager receives his printout, he immediately goes to work trying to understand what it tells him about himself. After most of the major results have been understood, he goes back to the set of cases to reread those on which he has violated rules. Typically, managers show an interest in discussing and comparing their results with others in the program. Gatherings of four to six people comparing their results and their interpretations of them, often for several hours at a

stretch, were such a common feature that they have recently been institutionalized as part of the procedure.

It should be emphasized that this method of providing feedback on their leadership style is just one part of the total training experience which encompasses over thirty hours over a period of three successive days. To date, no long-term evaluations of its effectiveness have been undertaken, but initial results appear quite promising.

SUMMARY

How far has the understanding of leadership progressed in the 50 years since the Hawthorne Studies? The picture that has been painted in this reading is one of false starts stemming from oversimplified conceptions of the process. An encouraging sign, however, is the increased interest in contingency theories or models incorporating both leader and situational variables. In this reading I have spent much time describing one kind of contingency model; Professor Fiedler, who accompanies me on this panel, has developed another form of contingency model.

These two models share a number of qualities, but are different in several important aspects. I believe that Professor Fiedler sees much greater consistency and less flexibility in leader behavior than is required by the normative model or exhibited in managers' statements of how they would behave on the problem set. I suspect that we also have substantially different views on the potential for modification of leadership style through training and development.

Both of these are fascinating and important questions, and I for one would enjoy exploring them during our later discussion. But there is one prediction about which I feel quite confident. Fifty years from now, both contingency models will be found wanting in detail if not in substance. If either Professor Fiedler or I am remembered at that time, it will be for the same reason that we meet to commemorate the Hawthorne Studies this week — the kinds of questions we posed rather than the specific answers we provided.

REFERENCES

Bass, B. M. *Leadership, Psychology and Organizational Behavior.* New York: Harper, 1960.

Blake, R., and Mouton, J. *The Managerial Grid.* Houston: Gulf, 1964.

Gibb, C. A. "Leadership," in *Handbook of Social Psychology,* edited by G. Lindzey and E. Aronson, vol. 4. Reading, Mass.: Addison-Wesley, 1969.

Hartshorne, H., and May, M. A. *Studies in Deceit*. New York: Macmillan, 1928.

Korman, A. K. " 'Consideration,' 'Initiating Structure,' and Organizational Criteria-A Review," *Personnel Psychology* 19 (1966).

Lewin, K. *Field Theory in Social Science,* edited by D. Cartwright. New York: Harper, 1941.

Likert, R. *New Patterns of Management*. New York: McGraw-Hill, 1961.

_____. *The Human Organization*. New York: McGraw-Hill, 1967.

Lowin, A. "Participative Decision-Making: A Model, Literature Critique, and Prescriptions for Research." *Organizational Behavior and Human Performance* 3 (1968).

Mischel, W. *Personality and Assessment*. New York: Wiley, 1968.

Maier, N. R. F.; Solem, A. R., and Maier, A. A. *Supervisory and Executive Development: A Manual for Role Playing*. New York: Wiley, 1954.

Sales, S. M. "Supervisory Style and Productivity: Review and Theory." *Personnel Psychology* 19 (1966).

Stogdill, R. M. "Personal Factors Associated with Leadership: A Survey of the Literature. *Journal of Psychology* 25 (1948).

Vroom, V. H. *Work and Motivation*. New York: Wiley, 1964.

_____. "A New Look at Managerial Decision-Making." *Organizational Dynamics* 1 (1973).

_____, and Jago, A. G. "Decision-Making as a Social Process: Normative and Descriptive Models of Leader Behavior." *Decision Science,* 1974.

_____, and Yetton, P. W. "A Normative Model of Leadership Styles. In *Readings in Managerial Psychology,* edited by H. J. Leavitt and L. Pondy, 2d ed. Chicago: University of Chicago Press, 1973.

Wood, M. J. "Power Relationships and Group Decision Making in Organizations." *Psychological Bulletin,* 1974.

27.   The Manager's Job: Folklore and Fact

Henry Mintzberg

If you ask a manager what he does, he will most likely tell you that he plans, organizes, coordinates, and controls. Then watch what he does. Don't be surprised if you can't relate what you see to these four words.

When he is called and told that one of his factories has just burned down, and he advises the caller to see whether temporary arrangements can be made to supply customers through a foreign subsidiary, is he planning, organizing, coordinating, or controlling? How about when he presents a gold watch to a retiring employee? Or when he attends a conference to meet people in the trade? Or on returning from that conference, when he tells one of his employees about an interesting product idea he picked up there?

The fact is that these four words, which have dominated management vocabulary since the French industrialist Henri Fayol first introduced them in 1916, tell us little about what managers actually do. At best, they indicate some vague objectives managers have when they work.

The field of management, so devoted to progress and change, has for more than half a century not seriously addressed *the* basic question: What do managers do? Without a proper answer, how can we teach management? How can we design planning or information systems for managers? How can we improve the practice of management at all?

Our ignorance of the nature of managerial work shows up in various ways in the modern organization — in the boast by the successful manager that he never spent a single day in a management training program; in the turnover of corporate planners who never quite understood what it was the manager wanted; in the computer consoles gathering dust in the back room because the managers never used the fancy on-line MIS some analyst thought they needed. Perhaps most important, our ignorance shows up in the inability of our large public organizations to come to grips with some of their most serious policy problems.

Somehow, in the rush to automate production, to use management science in the functional areas of marketing and finance, and to apply the skills of the behavioral scientist to the problem of worker motivation, the manager — that person in charge of the organization or one of its subunits — has been forgotten.

My intention in this article is simple: to break the reader away from Fayol's words and introduce him to a more supportable, and what I believe to be a more useful, description of managerial work. This description derives from my review and synthesis of the available research on how various managers have spent their time.

In some studies, managers were observed intensively ("shadowed" is the term some of them used); in a number of others, they kept detailed diaries of their activities; in a few studies, their records were analyzed. All kinds of managers were studied — foremen, factory supervisors, staff managers, field sales managers, hospital administrators, presidents of companies and nations, and even street gang leaders. These "managers" worked in the United States, Canada, Sweden, and Great Britain. [A brief review of the major studies that I found most useful in developing this description, including my own study of five American chief executive officers, is informative.]

A synthesis of these findings paints an interesting picture, one as different from Fayol's classical view as a cubist abstract is from a Renaissance painting. In a sense, this picture will be obvious to anyone who has ever spent a day in a manager's office, either in front of the desk or behind it. Yet, at the same time, this picture may turn out to be revolutionary, in that it throws into doubt so much of the folklore that we have accepted about the manager's work.

I first discuss some of this folklore and contrast it with some of the discoveries of systematic research — the hard facts about how managers spend their time. Then I synthesize these research findings in a description of ten roles that seem to describe the essential content of all managers' jobs. In a concluding section, I discuss a number of implications of this synthesis for those trying to achieve more effective management, both in classrooms and in the business world.

SOME FOLKLORE AND FACTS ABOUT MANAGERIAL WORK

There are four myths about the manager's job that do not bear up under careful scrutiny of the facts.

1

Folklore.   The manager is a reflective, systematic planner. The evidence on this issue is overwhelming, but not a shred of it supports this statement.

Fact.   Study after study has shown that managers work at an unrelenting pace, that their activities are characterized by brevity, variety, and discontinuity, and that they are strongly oriented to action and dislike reflective activities. Consider this evidence:

- Half the activities engaged in by the five chief executives of my study lasted less than nine minutes, and only 10% exceeded one hour.[1] A study of 56 U.S. foremen found that they average 583 activities per eight-hour shift, an average of 1 every 48 seconds.[2] The work pace for both chief executives and foremen was unrelenting. The chief executives met a steady stream of callers and mail from the moment they arrived in the morning until they left in the evening. Coffee breaks and lunches were inevitably work related, and ever-present subordinates seemed to usurp any free moment.

- A diary study of 160 British middle and top managers found that they worked for a half hour or more

1. All the data from my study can be found in Henry Mintzberg, *The Nature of Managerial Work* (New York: Harper & Row, 1973).

2. Robert H. Guest, "Of Time and the Foreman," *Personnel,* May 1956, p. 478.

without interruption only about once every two days.[3]

- Of the verbal contacts of the chief executives in my study, 93% were arranged on an ad hoc basis. Only 1% of the executives' time was spent in open-ended observational tours. Only 1 out of 368 verbal contacts was unrelated to a specific issue and could be called general planning. Another researcher finds that "in *not one single case* did a manager report the obtaining of important external information from a general conversation or other undirected personal communication."[4]

- No study has found important patterns in the way managers schedule their time. They seem to jump from issue to issue, continually responding to the needs of the moment.

Is this the planner that the classical view describes? Hardly. How, then, can we explain this behavior? The manager is simply responding to the pressures of his job. I found that my chief executives terminated many of their own activities, often leaving meetings before the end, and interrupted their desk work to call in subordinates. One president not only placed his desk so that he could look down a long hallway but also left his door open when he was alone — an invitation for subordinates to come in and interrupt him.

Clearly, these managers wanted to encourage the flow of current information. But more significantly, they seemed to be conditioned by their own work loads. They appreciated the opportunity cost of their own time, and they were continually aware of their ever-present obligations — mail to be answered, callers to attend to, and so on. It seems that no matter what he is doing, the manager is plagued by the possibilities of what he might do and what he must do.

When the manager must plan, he seems to do so implicitly in the context of daily actions, not in some abstract process reserved for two weeks in the organization's mountain retreat. The plans of the chief executives I studied seemed to exist only in their heads — as flexible, but often specific, intentions. The

traditional literature notwithstanding, the job of managing does not breed reflective planners; the manager is a real-time responder to stimuli, an individual who is conditioned by his job to prefer live to delayed action.

2

Folklore. The effective manager has no regular duties to perform. Managers are constantly being told to spend more time planning and delegating, and less time seeing customers and engaging in negotiations. These are not, after all, the true tasks of the manager. To use the popular analogy, the good manager, like the good conductor, carefully orchestrates everything in advance, then sits back to enjoy the fruits of his labor, responding occasionally to an unforeseeable exception.

But here again the pleasant abstraction just does not seem to hold up. We had better take a closer look at those activities managers feel compelled to engage in before we arbitrarily define them away.

Fact. In addition to handling exceptions, managerial work involves performing a number of regular duties, including ritual and ceremony, negotiations, and processing of soft information that links the organization with its environment. Consider some evidence from the research studies:

- A study of the work of the presidents of small companies found that they engaged in routine activities because their companies could not afford staff specialists and were so thin on operating personnel that a single absence often required the president to substitute.[5]

- One study of field sales managers and another of chief executives suggest that it is a natural part of both jobs to see important customers, assuming the managers wish to keep those customers.[6]

- Someone, only half in jest, once described the manager as that person who sees visitors so that

3. Rosemary Stewart, *Managers and Their Jobs* (London: Macmillan, 1967); see also Sune Carlson, *Executive Behaviour* (Stockholm: Strombergs, 1951), the first of the diary studies.

4. Francis J. Aguilar, *Scanning the Business Environment* (New York: Macmillan, 1967), p. 102.

5. Unpublished study by Irving Choran, reported in Mintzberg, *The Nature of Managerial Work.*

6. Robert T. Davis, *Performance and Development of Field Sales Managers* (Boston: Division of Research, Harvard Business School, 1957); George H. Copeman, *The Role of the Managing Director* (London: Business Publications, 1963).

The Manager's Job: Folklore and Fact**273**

everyone else can get his work done. In my study, I found that certain ceremonial duties — meeting visiting dignitaries, giving out gold watches, presiding at Christmas dinners — were an intrinsic part of the chief executive's job.

- Studies of managers' information flow suggest that managers play a key role in securing "soft" external information (much of it available only to them because of their status) and in passing it along to their subordinates.

3

Folklore. The senior manager needs aggregated information, which a formal management information system best provides. Not too long ago, the words *total information system* were everywhere in the management literature. In keeping with the classical view of the manager as that individual perched on the apex of a regulated, hierarchical system, the literature's manager was to receive all his important information from a giant, comprehensive MIS.

But lately, as it has become increasingly evident that these giant MIS systems are not working — that managers are simply not using them — the enthusiasm has waned. A look at how managers actually process information makes the reason quite clear. Managers have five media at their command — documents, telephone calls, scheduled and unscheduled meetings, and observational tours.

Fact. Managers strongly favor the verbal media — namely, telephone calls and meetings. The evidence comes from every single study of managerial work. Consider the following:

- In two British studies, managers spent an average of 66% and 80% of their time in verbal (oral) communication.[7] In my study of five American chief executives, the figure was 78%.

- These five chief executives treated mail processing as a burden to be dispensed with. One came in Saturday morning to process 142 pieces of mail in just over three hours, to "get rid of all the stuff." This same manager looked at the first piece of "hard"

mail he had received all week, a standard cost report, and put it aside with the comment, "I never look at this."

- These same five chief executives responded immediately to 2 of the 40 routine reports they received during the five weeks of my study and to four items in the 104 periodicals. They skimmed most of these periodicals in seconds, almost ritualistically. In all, these chief executives of good-sized organizations initiated on their own — that is, not in response to something else — a grand total of 25 pieces of mail during the 25 days I observed them.

An analysis of the mail the executives received reveals an interesting picture — only 13% was of specific and immediate use. So now we have another piece in the puzzle: not much of the mail provides live, current information — the action of a competitor, mood of a government legislator, or the rating of last night's television show. Yet this is the information that drove the managers, interrupting their meetings and rescheduling their workdays.

Consider another interesting finding. Managers seem to cherish "soft" information, especially gossip, hearsay, and speculation. Why? The reason is its timeliness; today's gossip may be tomorrow's fact. The manager who is not accessible for the telephone call informing him that his biggest customer was seen golfing with his main competitor may read about a dramatic drop in sales in the next quarterly report. But then it's too late.

To assess the value of historical, aggregated, "hard" MIS information, consider two of the manager's prime uses for his information — to identify problems and opportunities[8] and to build his own mental models of the things around him (e.g., how his organization's budget system works, how his customers buy his product, how changes in the economy affect his organization, and so on). Every bit of evidence suggests that the manager identifies decision situations and builds models not with the aggregated abstractions an MIS provides, but with specific tidbits of data.

Consider the words of Richard Neustadt, who studied the information-collecting habits of Presidents Roosevelt, Truman, and Eisenhower:

---

7. Stewart, *Managers and Their Jobs;* Tom Burns, "The Directions of Activity and Communication in a Departmental Executive Group," *Human Relations 7,* no. 1 (1954): 73.

8. H. Edward Wrapp, "Good Managers Don't Make Policy Decisions," HBR September-October 1967, p. 91; Wrapp refers to this as spotting opportunities and relationships in the stream of operating problems and decisions; in his article Wrapp raises a number of excellent points related to this analysis.

"*It is not information of a general sort that helps a President see personal stakes; not summaries, not surveys, not the* bland amalgams. *Rather . . . it is the odds and ends of* tangible detail *that pieced together in his mind illuminate the underside of issues put before him. To help himself he must reach out as widely as he can for every scrap of fact, opinion, gossip, bearing on his interests and relationships as President. He must become his own director of his own central intelligence.*"[9]

The manager's emphasis on the verbal media raises two important points:

First, verbal information is stored in the brains of people. Only when people write this information down can it be stored in files of the organization — whether in metal cabinets or on magnetic tape — and managers apparently do not write down much of what they hear. Thus the strategic data bank of the organization is not in the memory of its computers but in the minds of its managers.

Second, the manager's extensive use of verbal media helps to explain why he is reluctant to delegate tasks. When we note that most of the manager's important information comes in verbal form and is stored in his head, we can well appreciate his reluctance. It is not as if he can hand a dossier over to someone; he must take the time to "dump memory" — to tell that someone all he knows about the subject. But this could take so long that the manager may find it easier to do the task himself. Thus the manager is damned by his own information system to a "dilemma of delegation" — to do too much himself or to delegate to his subordinates with inadequate briefing.

4

Folklore.   Management is, or at least is quickly becoming, a science and a profession. By almost any definitions of *science* and *profession*, this statement is false. Brief observation of any manager will quickly lay to rest the notion that managers practice a science. A science

involves the enaction of systematic, analytically determined procedures or programs. If we do not even know what procedures managers use, how can we prescribe them by scientific analysis? And how can we call management a profession if we cannot specify what managers are to learn? For after all, a profession involves "knowledge of some department of learning or science" (*Random House Dictionary*).[10]

Fact.   The managers' programs — to schedule time, process information, make decisions, and so on — remain locked deep inside their brains. Thus, to describe these programs, we rely on words like *judgment* and *intuition,* seldom stopping to realize that they are merely labels for our ignorance.

I was struck during my study by the fact that the executives I was observing — all very competent by any standard — are fundamentally indistinguishable from their counterparts of a hundred years ago (or a thousand years ago, for that matter). The information they need differs, but they seek it in the same way — by word of mouth. Their decisions concern modern technology, but the procedures they use to make them are the same as the procedures of the nineteenth-century manager. Even the computer, so important for the specialized work of the organization, has apparently had no influence on the work procedures of general managers. In fact, the manager is a kind of loop, with increasingly heavy work pressures but no aid forthcoming from management science.

Considering the facts about managerial work, we can see that the manager's job is enormously complicated and difficult. The manager is overburdened with obligations; yet he cannot easily delegate his tasks. As a result, he is driven to overwork and is forced to do many tasks superficially. Brevity, fragmentation, and verbal communication characterize his work. Yet these are the very characteristics of managerial work that have impeded scientific attempts to improve it. As a result, the management scientist has concentrated his efforts on the specialized functions of the organizations, where he could more easily analyze the procedures and quantify the relevant information.[11]

---

9. Richard E. Neustadt, *Presidential Power* (New York: John Wiley, 1960), pp. 153–154; italics added.

10. For a more thorough, though rather different, discussion of this issue, see Kenneth R. Andrews, "Toward Professionalism in Business Management," HBR March-April 1969, p. 49.

11. C. Jackson Grayson, Jr., in "Management Science and Business Practice." HBR July-August 1973, p. 41, explains in similar terms why, as chairman of the Price Commission, he did not use those very techniques that he himself promoted in his earlier career as a management scientist.

But the pressures of the manager's job are becoming worse. Where before he needed only to respond to owners and directors, now he finds that subordinates with democratic norms continually reduce his freedom to issue unexplained orders, and a growing number of outside influences (consumer groups, government agencies, and so on) expect his attention. And the manager has had nowhere to turn for help. The first step in providing the manager with some help is to find out what his job really is.

BACK TO A BASIC DESCRIPTION OF MANAGERIAL WORK

Now let us try to put some of the pieces of this puzzle together. Earlier, I defined the manager as that person in charge of an organization or one of its subunits. Besides chief executive officers, this definition would include vice presidents, bishops, foremen, hockey coaches, and prime ministers. Can all of these people have anything in common? Indeed they can. For an important starting point, all are vested with formal authority over an organizational unit. From formal authority comes status, which leads to various interpersonal relations, and from these comes access to information. Information, in turn, enables the manager to make decisions and strategies for his unit.

The manager's job can be described in terms of various "roles," or organized sets of behaviors identified with a position. My description, shown in Figure 1, comprises ten roles. As we shall see, formal authority gives rise to the three interpersonal roles, which in turn give rise to the three informational roles; these two sets of roles enable the manager to play the four decisional roles.

Interpersonal Roles

Three of the manager's roles arise directly from his formal authority and involve basic interpersonal relationships.

1. First is the *figurehead* role. By virtue of his position as head of an organizational unit, every manager must perform some duties of a ceremonial nature. The president greets the touring dignitaries, the foreman attends the wedding of a lathe operator, and the sales manager takes an important customer to lunch.

The chief executives of my study spent 12% of their contact time on ceremonial duties; 17% of their

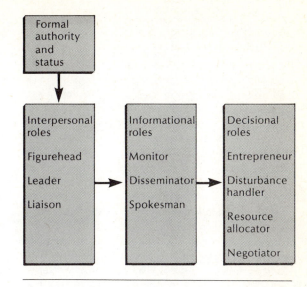

Figure 1.   The Manager's Roles.

incoming mail dealt with acknowledgments and requests related to their status. For example, a letter to a company president requested free merchandise for a crippled schoolchild; diplomas were put on the desk of the school superintendent for his signature.

Duties that involve interpersonal roles may sometimes be routine, involving little serious communication and no important decision making. Nevertheless, they are important to the smooth functioning of an organization and cannot be ignored by the manager.

2. Because he is in charge of an organizational unit, the manager is responsible for the work of the people of that unit. His actions in this regard constitute the *leader* role. Some of these actions involve leadership directly — for example, in most organizations the manager is normally responsible for hiring and training his own staff.

In addition, there is the indirect exercise of the leader role. Every manager must motivate and encourage his employees, somehow reconciling their individual needs with the goals of the organization. In virtually every contact the manager has with his employees, subordinates seeking leadership clues probe his actions: "Does he approve?" "How would he like the report to turn out?" "Is he more interested in market share than high profits?"

The influence of the manager is most clearly seen in the leader role. Formal authority vests him with great potential power; leadership determines in large part how much of it he will realize.

3. The literature of management has always recognized the leader role, particularly those aspects of it related to motivation. In comparison, until recently it has hardly mentioned the *liaison* role, in which the manager makes contacts outside his vertical chain of command. This is remarkable in light of the finding of virtually every study of managerial work that managers spend as much time with peers and other people outside their units as they do with their own subordinates — and, surprisingly, very little time with their own superiors.

In Rosemary Stewart's diary study, the 160 British middle and top managers spent 47% of their time with peers, 41% of their time with people outside their unit, and only 12% of their time with their superiors. For Robert H. Guest's study of U.S. foremen, the figures were 44%, 46%, and 10%. The chief executives of my study averaged 44% of their contact time with people outside their organizations, 48% with subordinates, and 7% with directors and trustees.

The contacts the five CEOs made were with an incredibly wide range of people: subordinates; clients, business associates, and suppliers; and peers — managers of similar organizations, government and trade organization officials, fellow directors on outside boards, and independents with no relevant organizational affiliations. The chief executives' time with and mail from these groups is shown in Figure 2. Guest's study of foremen shows, likewise, that their contacts were numerous and wide ranging, seldom involving fewer than 25 individuals, and often more than 50.

As we shall see shortly, the manager cultivates such contacts largely to find information. In effect, the liaison role is devoted to building up the manager's own external information system — informal, private, verbal, but, nevertheless, effective.

Informational Roles

By virtue of his interpersonal contacts, both with his subordinates and with his network of contacts, the manager emerges as the nerve center of his organizational unit. He may not know everything, but he typically knows more than any member of his staff.

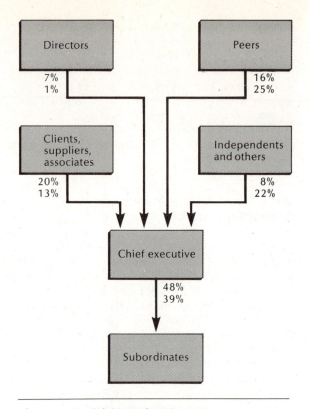

Figure 2. The Chief Executives' Contacts.

Note: The top figure indicates the proportion of total contact time spent with each group and the bottom figure, the proportion of mail from each group.

Studies have shown this relationship to hold for all managers, from street gang leaders to U.S. presidents. In *The Human Group*, George C. Homans explains how, because they were at the center of the information flow in their own gangs and were also in close touch with other gang leaders, street gang leaders were better informed than any of their followers.[12] And Richard Neustadt describes the following account from his study of Franklin D. Roosevelt:

"The essence of Roosevelt's technique for information-gathering was competition. 'He would call you in,' one of his aides once told me, 'and he'd ask you to get the story on some complicated business, and you'd come back after a couple of days of hard labor and present

---

12. George C. Homans, *The Human Group* (New York: Harcourt, Brace & World, 1950), based on the study by William F. Whyte entitled *Street Corner Society,* rev. ed. (Chicago: University of Chicago Press, 1955).

the juicy morsel you'd uncovered under a stone somewhere, and then *you'd find out he knew all about it, along with something else you* didn't *know. Where he got this information from he wouldn't mention, usually, but after he had done this to you once or twice you got damn careful about* your *information.' "* [13]

We can see where Roosevelt "got this information" when we consider the relationship between the interpersonal and informational roles. As leader, the manager has formal and easy access to every member of his staff. Hence, as noted earlier, he tends to know more about his own unit than anyone else does. In addition, his liaison contacts expose the manager to external information to which his subordinates often lack access. Many of these contacts are with other managers of equal status, who are themselves nerve centers in their own organization. In this way, the manager develops a powerful data base of information.

The processing of information is a key part of the manager's job. In my study, the chief executives spent 40% of their contact time on activities devoted exclusively to the transmission of information; 70% of their incoming mail was purely informational (as opposed to requests for action). The manager does not leave meetings or hang up the telephone in order to get back to work. In large part, communication *is* his work. Three roles describe these informational aspects of managerial work.

1. As *monitor,* the manager perpetually scans his environment for information, interrogates his liaison contacts and his subordinates, and receives unsolicited information, much of it as a result of the network of personal contacts he has developed. Remember that a good part of the information the manager collects in his monitor role arrives in verbal form, often as gossip, hearsay, and speculation. By virtue of his contacts, the manager has a natural advantage in collecting this soft information for his organization.

2. He must share and distribute much of this information. Information he gleans from outside personal contacts may be needed with his organization. In his *disseminator* role, the manager passes some of his privileged information directly to his subordinates, who would otherwise have no access to it. When his

subordinates lack easy contact with one another, the manager will sometimes pass information from one to another.

3. In his *spokesman* role, the manager sends some of his information to people outside his unit — a president makes a speech to lobby for an organization cause, or a foreman suggests a product modification to a supplier. In addition, as part of his role as spokesman, every manager must inform and satisfy the influential people who control his organizational unit. For the foreman, this may simply involve keeping the plant manager informed about the flow of work through the shop.

The president of a large corporation, however, may spend a great amount of his time dealing with a host of influences. Directors and shareholders must be advised about financial performance; consumer groups must be assured that the organization is fulfilling its social responsibilities; and government officials must be satisfied that the organization is abiding by the law.

Decisional Roles

Information is not, of course, an end in itself; it is the basic input to decision making. One thing is clear in the study of managerial work: the manager plays the major role in his unit's decision-making system. As its formal authority, only he can commit the unit to important new courses of action; and as its nerve center, only he has full and current information to make the set of decisions that determines the unit's strategy. Four roles describe the manager as decision-maker.

1. As *entrepreneur,* the manager seeks to improve his unit, to adapt it to changing conditions in the environment. In his monitor role, the president is constantly on the lookout for new ideas. When a good one appears, he initiates a development project that he may supervise himself or delegate to an employee (perhaps with the stipulation that he must approve the final proposal).

There are two interesting features about these development projects at the chief executive level.

First, these projects do not involve single decisions or even unified clusters of decisions. Rather, they emerge as a series of small decisions and actions sequenced over time. Apparently, the chief executive prolongs each project so that he can fit it bit by bit into his busy,

---

13. Neustadt, *Presidential Power,* p. 157.

disjointed schedule and so that he can gradually come to comprehend the issue, if it is a complex one.

Second, the chief executives I studied supervised as many as 50 of these projects at the same time. Some projects entailed new products or processes; others involved public relations campaigns, improvement of the cash position, reorganization of a weak department, resolution of a morale problem in a foreign division, integration of computer operations, various acquisitions at different stages of development, and so on.

The chief executive appears to maintain a kind of inventory of the development projects that he himself supervises — projects that are at various stages of development, some active and some in limbo. Like a juggler, he keeps a number of projects in the air; periodically, one comes down, is given a new burst of energy, and is sent back into orbit. At various intervals, he puts new projects on-stream and discards old ones.

2.   While the entrepreneur role describes the manager as the voluntary initiator of change, the *disturbance handler* role depicts the manager involuntarily responding to pressures. Here change is beyond the manager's control. He must act because the pressures of the situation are too severe to be ignored: strike looms, a major customer has gone bankrupt, or a supplier reneges on his contract.

It has been fashionable, I noted earlier, to compare the manager to an orchestra conductor, just as Peter F. Drucker wrote in *The Practice of Management:*

"The manager has the task of creating a true whole that is larger than the sum of its parts, a productive entity that turns out more than the sum of the resources put into it. One analogy is the conductor of a symphony orchestra, through whose effort, vision and leadership individual instrumental parts that are so much noise by themselves become the living whole of music. But the conductor has the composer's score; he is only interpreter. The manager is both composer and conductor." [14]

Now consider the words of Leonard R. Sayles, who has carried out systematic research on the manager's job:

"[The manager] is like a symphony orchestra conductor, endeavouring to maintain a melodious performance in which the contributions of the various instruments are coordinated and sequenced, patterned and paced, while the orchestra members are having various personal difficulties, stage hands are moving music stands, alternating excessive heat and cold are creating audience and instrument problems, and the sponsor of the concert is insisting on irrational changes in the program." [15]

In effect, every manager must spend a good part of his time responding to high-pressure disturbances. No organization can be so well run, so standardized, that it has considered every contingency in the uncertain environment in advance. Disturbances arise not only because poor managers ignore situations until they reach crisis proportions, but also because good managers cannot possibly anticipate all the consequences of the actions they take.

3.   The third decisional role is that of *resource allocator.* To the manager falls the responsibility of deciding who will get what in his organizational unit. Perhaps the most important resource the manager allocates is his own time. Access to the manager constitutes exposure to the unit's nerve center and decision-maker. The manager is also charged with designing his unit's structure, that pattern of formal relationships that determines how work is to be divided and coordinated.

Also, in his role as resource allocator, the manager authorizes the important decisions of his unit before they are implemented. By retaining this power, the manager can ensure that decisions are interrelated; all must pass through a single brain. To fragment this power is to encourage discontinuous decision making and a disjointed strategy.

There are a number of interesting features about the manager's authorizing others' decisions. First, despite the widespread use of capital budgeting procedures — a means of authorizing various capital expenditures at one time — executives in my study made a great many authorization decisions on an ad hoc basis. Apparently, many projects cannot wait or simply do not have the quantifiable costs and benefits that capital budgeting requires.

Second, I found that the chief executives faced incredibly complex choices. They had to consider the impact of each decision on other decisions and on the

---

14. Peter F. Drucker, *The Practice of Management* (New York: Harper & Row, 1954), pp. 431–442.

15. Leonard R. Sayles, *Managerial Behavior* (New York: McGraw-Hill, 1964), p. 162.

organization's strategy. They had to ensure that the decision would be acceptable to those who influence the organization, as well as ensure that resources would not be overextended. They had to understand the various costs and benefits as well as the feasibility of the proposal. They also had to consider questions of timing. All this was necessary for the simple approval of someone else's proposal. They also had to consider questions of timing. At the same time, however, delay could lose time, while quick approval could be ill considered and quick rejection might discourage the subordinate who had spent months developing a pet project.

One common solution to approving projects is to pick the man instead of the proposal. That is, the manager authorizes those projects presented to him by people whose judgment he trusts. But he cannot always use this simple dodge.

4. The final decisional role is that of *negotiator*. Studies of managerial work at all levels indicate that managers spend considerable time in negotiations: the president of the football team is called in to work out a contract with the holdout superstar; the corporation president leads his company's contingent to negotiate a new strike issue; the foreman argues a grievance problem to its conclusion with the shop steward. As Leonard Sayles puts it, negotiations are a "way of life" for the sophisticated manager.

These negotiations are duties of the manager's job; perhaps routine, they are not to be shirked. They are an integral part of his job, for only he has the authority to commit organizational resources in "real time," and only he has the nerve center information that important negotiations require.

The Integrated Job

It should be clear by now that the ten roles I have been describing are not easily separable. In the terminology of the psychologist, they form a gestalt, an integrated whole. No role can be pulled out of the framework and the job be left intact. For example, a manager without liaison contacts lacks external information. As a result, he can neither disseminate the information his employees need nor make decisions that adequately reflect external conditions. (In fact, this is a problem for the new person in a managerial position, since he cannot make effective decisions until he has built up his network of contacts.)

Here lies a clue to the problems of team management.[16] Two or three people cannot share a single managerial position unless they can act as one entity. This means that they cannot divide up the ten roles unless they can very carefully reintegrate them. The real difficulty lies with the informational roles. Unless there can be full sharing of managerial information — and, as I pointed out earlier, it is primarily verbal — team management breaks down. A single managerial job cannot be arbitrarily split, for example, into internal and external roles, for information from both sources must be brought to bear on the same decisions.

To say that the ten roles form a gestalt is not to say that all managers give equal attention to each role. In fact, I found in my review of the various research studies that

. . . sales managers seem to spend relatively more of their time in the interpersonal roles, presumably a reflection of the extrovert nature of the marketing activity;

. . . production managers give relatively more attention to the decisional roles, presumably a reflection of their concern with efficient work flow;

. . . staff managers spend the most time in the informational roles, since they are experts who manage departments that advise other parts of the organization.

Nevertheless, in all cases the interpersonal, informational, and decisional roles remain inseparable.

TOWARD MORE EFFECTIVE MANAGEMENT

What are the messages for management in this description? I believe, first and foremost, that this description of managerial work should prove more important to managers than any prescription they might derive from it. That is to say, *the manager's effectiveness is significantly influenced by his insight into his own work.* His performance depends on how well he understands and responds to the pressures and dilemmas of the job. Thus managers who can be

16. See Richard C. Hodgson, Daniel J. Levinson, and Abraham Zaleznik, *The Executive Role Constellation* (Boston: Division of Research, Harvard Business School, 1965), for a discussion of the sharing of roles.

introspective about their work are likely to be effective at their jobs. . . .

Let us take a look at three specific areas of concern. For the most part, the managerial logjams — the dilemma of delegation, the data base centralized in one brain, the problems of working with the management scientist — evolve around the verbal nature of the manager's information. There are great dangers in centralizing the organization's data bank in the minds of its managers. When they leave, they take their memory with them. And when subordinates are out of convenient verbal reach of the manager, they are at an informational disadvantage.

1

The manager is challenged to find systematic ways to share his privileged information. A regular debriefing session with key subordinates, a weekly memory dump on the dictating machine, the maintaining of a diary of important information for limited circulation, or other similar methods may ease the logjam of work considerably. Time spent disseminating this information will be more than regained when decisions must be made. Of course, some will raise the question of confidentiality. But managers would do well to weigh the risks of exposing privileged information against having subordinates who can make effective decisions.

If there is a single theme that runs through this article, it is that the pressures of his job drive the manager to be superficial in his actions — to overload himself with work, encourage interruption, respond quickly to every stimulus, seek the tangible and avoid the abstract, make decisions in small increments, and do everything abruptly.

2

Here again, the manager is challenged to deal consciously with the pressures of superficiality by giving serious attention to the issues that require it, by stepping back from his tangible bits of information in order to see a broad picture, and by making use of analytical inputs. Although effective managers have to be adept at responding quickly to numerous and varying problems, the danger in managerial work is that they will respond to every issue equally (and that means abruptly) and that

they will never work the tangible bits and pieces of informational input into a comprehensive picture of their world.

As I noted earlier, the manager uses these bits of information to build models of his world. But the manager can also avail himself of the models of the specialists. Economists describe the functioning of markets, operations researchers simulate financial flow processes, and behavioral scientists explain the needs and goals of people. The best of these models can be searched out and learned.

In dealing with complex issues, the senior manager has much to gain from a close relationship with the management scientists of his own organization. They have something important that he lacks — time to probe complex issues. An effective working relationship hinges on the resolution of what a colleague and I have called "the planning dilemma."[17] Managers have the information and the authority; analysts have the time and the technology. A successful working relationship between the two will be effected when the manager learns to share his information and the analyst learns to adapt to the manager's need. For the analyst, adaptation means worrying less about the elegance of the method and more about its speed and flexibility.

It seems to me that analysts can help the top manager especially to schedule his time, feed in analytical information, monitor projects under his supervision, develop models to aid in making choices, design contingency plans for disturbances that can be anticipated, and conduct "quick-and-dirty" analysis for those that cannot. But there can be no cooperation if the analysts are out of the mainstream of the manager's information flow.

3

The manager is challenged to gain control of his own time by turning obligations to his advantage and by turning those things he wishes to do into obligations. The chief executives of my study initiated only 32% of their own contacts (and another 5% by mutual agreement). And yet to a considerable extent they seemed to control their time. There were two key factors that enabled them to do so.

First, the manager has to spend so much time discharging obligations that if he were to view them as

---

17. James S. Hekimian and Henry Mintzberg, "The Planning Dilemma," *The Management Review,* May 1968, p. 4.

just that, he would leave no mark on his organization. The unsuccessful manager blames failure on the obligations; the effective manager turns his obligations to his own advantage. A speech is a chance to lobby for a cause; a meeting is a chance to reorganize a weak department; a visit to an important customer is a chance to extract trade information.

Second, the manager frees some of his time to do those things that he—perhaps no one else—thinks important by turning them into obligations. Free time is made, not found, in the manager's job; it is forced into the schedule. Hoping to leave some time open for contemplation or general planning is tantamount to hoping that the pressures of the job will go away. The manager who wants to innovate initiates a project and obligates others to report back to him; the manager who needs certain environmental information establishes channels that will automatically keep him informed; the manager who has to tour facilities commits himself publicly.

The Educator's Job

Finally, a word about the training of managers. Our management schools have done an admirable job of training the organization's specialists—management scientists, marketing researchers, accountants, and organizational development specialists. But for the most part they have not trained managers.[18]

Management schools will begin the serious training of managers when skill training takes a serious place next to cognitive learning. Cognitive learning is detached and informational, like reading a book or listening to a lecture. No doubt much important cognitive material must be assimilated by the manager-to-be. But cognitive learning no more makes a manager than it does a swimmer. The latter will drown the first time he jumps into the water if his coach never takes him out of the lecture hall, gets him wet, and gives him feedback on his performance.

In other words, we are taught a skill through practice plus feedback, whether in a real or a simulated situation. Our management schools need to identify the skills managers use, select students who show potential in these skills, put the students into situations where these skills can be practiced, and then give them systematic feedback on their performance.

My description of managerial work suggests a number of important managerial skills—developing peer relationships, carrying out negotiations, motivating subordinates, resolving conflicts, establishing information networks and subsequently disseminating information, making decisions in conditions of extreme ambiguity, and allocating resources. Above all, the manager needs to be introspective about his work so that he may continue to learn on the job.

Many of the manager's skills can, in fact, be practiced, using techniques that range from role playing to videotaping real meetings. And our management schools can enhance the entrepreneurial skills by designing programs that encourage sensible risk taking and innovation.

No job is more vital to our society than that of the manager. It is the manager who determines whether our social institutions serve us well or whether they squander our talents and resources. It is time to strip away the folklore about managerial work, and time to study it realistically so that we can begin the difficult task of making significant improvements in its performance.

---

18. See J. Sterling Livingston, "Myth of the Well-Educated Manager," HBR January-February 1971, p. 79.

28.   The Ambiguity of Leadership

Jeffrey Pfeffer

Leadership has for some time been a major topic in social and organizational psychology. Underlying much of this research has been the assumption that leadership is casually related to organizational performance. Through an analysis of leadership styles, behaviors, or characteristics (depending on the theoretical perspective chosen), the argument has been made that more effective leaders can be selected or trained or, alternatively, the situation can be configured to provide for enhanced leader and organizational effectiveness.

Three problems with emphasis on leadership as a concept can be posed: *(a)* ambiguity in definition and measurement of the concept itself; *(b)* the question of whether leadership has discernible effects on organizational outcomes; and *(c)* the selection process in succession to leadership positions, which frequently uses organizationally irrelevant criteria and which has implications for normative theories of leadership. The argument here is that leadership is of interest primarily as a phenomenological construct. Leaders serve as symbols for representing personal causation of social events. How and why are such attributions of personal effects made? Instead of focusing on leadership and its effects, how do people make inferences about and react to phenomena labeled as leadership (5)?

THE AMBIGUITY OF THE CONCEPT

While there have been many studies of leadership, the dimensions and definition of the concept remain unclear. To treat leadership as a separate concept, it must be distinguished from other social influence phenomena. Hollander and Julian (24) and Bavelas (2) did not draw distinctions between leadership and other processes of social influence. A major point of the Hollander and Julian review was that leadership research might develop more rapidly if more general theories of

social influence were incorporated. Calder (5) also argued that there is no unique content to the construct of leadership that is not subsumed under other, more general models of behavior.

Kochan, Schmidt, and DeCotiis (33) attempted to distinguish leadership from related concepts of authority and social power. In leadership, influence rights are voluntarily conferred. Power does not require goal compatibility — merely dependence — but leadership implies some congruence between the objectives of the leader and the led. These distinctions depend on the ability to distinguish voluntary from involuntary compliance and to assess goal compatibility. Goal statements may be retrospective inferences from action (46, 53) and problems of distinguishing voluntary from involuntary compliance also exist (32). Apparently there are few meaningful distinctions between leadership and other concepts of social influence. Thus, an understanding of the phenomena subsumed under the rubric of leadership may not require the construct of leadership (5).

While there is some agreement that leadership is related to social influence, more disagreement concerns the basic dimensions of leader behavior. Some have argued that there are two tasks to be accomplished in groups — maintenance of the group and performance of some task or activity — and thus leader behavior might be described along these two dimensions (1, 6, 8, 25). The dimensions emerging from the Ohio State leadership studies — consideration and initiating structure — may be seen as similar to the two components of group maintenance and task accomplishment (18).

Other dimensions of leadership behavior have also been proposed (4). Day and Hamblin (10) analyzed leadership in terms of the closeness and punitiveness of the supervision. Several authors have conceptualized leadership behavior in terms of the authority and discretion subordinates are permitted (23, 36, 51). Fiedler (14) analyzed leadership in terms of the

"The Ambiguity of Leadership" by Jeffrey Pfeffer. Reprinted with permission from *Academy of Management Review,* January 1977.

least-preferred-co-worker scale (LPC), but the meaning and behavioral attributes of this dimension of leadership behavior remain controversial.

The proliferation of dimensions is partly a function of research strategies frequently employed. Factor analysis on a large number of items describing behavior has frequently been used. This procedure tends to produce as many factors as the analyst decides to find and permits the development of a large number of possible factor structures. The resultant factors must be named and further imprecision is introduced. Deciding on a summative concept to represent a factor is inevitably a partly subjective process.

Literature assessing the effects of leadership tends to be equivocal. Sales (45) summarized leadership literature employing the authoritarian-democratic typology and concluded that effects on performance were small and inconsistent. Reviewing the literature on consideration and initiating structure dimensions, Korman (34) reported relatively small and inconsistent results, and Kerr and Schriesheim (30) reported more consistent effects of the two dimensions. Better results apparently emerge when moderating factors are taken into account, including subordinate personalities (50), and situational characteristics (23, 51). Kerr, et al. (31) list many moderating effects grouped under the headings of subordinate considerations, supervisor considerations, and task considerations. Even if each set of considerations consisted of only one factor (which it does not), an attempt to account for the effects of leader behavior would necessitate considering four-way interactions. While social reality is complex and contingent, it seems desirable to attempt to find more parsimonious explanations for the phenomena under study.

THE EFFECTS OF LEADERS

Hall asked a basic question about leadership: Is there any evidence on the magnitude of the effects of leadership (17, p. 248)? Surprisingly, he could find little evidence. Given the resources that have been spent studying, selecting, and training leaders, one might expect that the question of whether or not leaders matter would have been addressed earlier (12).

There are at least three reasons why it might be argued that the observed effects of leaders on organizational outcomes would be small. First, those obtaining leadership positions are selected, and perhaps only certain limited styles of behavior may be chosen. Second, once in the leadership position, the discretion and behavior of the leader are constrained. And third, leaders can typically affect only a few of the variables that may impact organizational performance.

Homogeneity of Leaders

Persons are selected to leadership positions. As a consequence of this selection process, the range of behaviors or characteristics exhibited by leaders is reduced, making it more problematic to discover empirically an effect of leadership. There are many types of constraints on the selection process. The attraction literature suggests that there is a tendency for persons to like those they perceive as similar (3). In critical decisions such as the selections of persons for leadership positions, compatible styles of behavior probably will be chosen.

Selection of persons is also constrained by the internal system of influence in the organization. As Zald (56) noted, succession is a critical decision, affected by political influence and by environmental contingencies faced by the organization. As Thompson (49) noted, leaders may be selected for their capacity to deal with various organizational contingencies. In a study of characteristics of hospital administrators, Pfeffer and Salancik (42) found a relationship between the hospital's context and the characteristics and tenure of the administrators. To the extent that the contingencies and power distribution within the organization remain stable, the abilities and behaviors of those selected into leadership positions will also remain stable.

Finally, the selection of persons to leadership positions is affected by a self-selection process. Organizations and roles have images, providing information about their character. Persons are likely to select themselves into organizations and roles based upon their preferences for the dimensions of the organizational and role characteristics as perceived through these images. The self-selection of persons would tend to work along with organizational selection to limit the range of abilities and behaviors in a given organizational role.

Such selection processes would tend to increase homogeneity more within a single organization than across organizations. Yet many studies of leadership effect at the work group level have compared groups within a single organization. If there comes to be a widely shared, socially constructed definition of leadership behaviors or characteristics which guides the selection process, then leadership activity may come to be defined similarly in various organizations, leading to the selection of only those who match the constructed image of a leader.

Constraints on Leader Behavior

Analyses of leadership have frequently presumed that leadership style or leader behavior was an independent variable that could be selected or trained at will to conform to what research would find to be optimal. Even theorists who took a more contingent view of appropriate leadership behavior generally assumed that with proper training appropriate behavior could be produced (51). Fiedler (13), noting how hard it was to change behavior, suggested changing the situational characteristics rather than the person, but this was an unusual suggestion in the context of prevailing literature which suggested that leadership style was something to be strategically selected according to the variables of the particular leadership theory.

But the leader is embedded in a social system, which constrains behavior. The leader has a role set (27), in which members have expectations for appropriate behavior and persons make efforts to modify the leader's behavior. Pressures to conform to the expectations of peers, subordinates, and superiors are all relevant in determining actual behavior.

Leaders, even in high-level positions, have unilateral control over fewer resources and fewer policies than might be expected. Investment decisions may require approval of others, while hiring and promotion decisions may be accomplished by committees. Leader behavior is constrained by both the demands of others in the role set and by organizationally prescribed limitations on the sphere of activity and influence.

External Factors

Many factors that may affect organizational performance are outside a leader's control, even if he or she were to have complete discretion over major areas of organizational decisions. For example, consider the executive in a construction firm. Costs are largely determined by operation of commodities and labor markets; and demand is largely affected by interest rates, availability of mortgage money, and economic conditions which are affected by governmental policies over which the executive has little control. School superintendents have little control over birth rates and community economic development, both of which

profoundly affect school system budgets. While the leader may react to contingencies as they arise, or may be a better or worse forecaster, in accounting for variation in organizational outcomes, he or she may account for relatively little compared to external factors.

Second, the leader's success or failure may be partly due to circumstances unique to the organization but still outside his or her control. Leader positions in organizations vary in terms of the strength and position of the organization. The choice of a new executive does not fundamentally alter a market and financial position that has developed over years and affects the leader's ability to make strategic changes and the likelihood that the organization will do well or poorly. Organizations have relatively enduring strengths and weaknesses. The choice of a particular leader for a particular position has limited impact on these capabilities.

Empirical Evidence

Two studies have assessed the effects of leadership changes in major positions in organizations. Lieberson and O'Connor (35) examined 167 business firms in 13 industries over a 20-year period, allocating variance in sales, profits, and profit margins to one of four sources: year (general economic conditions), industry, company effects, and effects of changes in the top executive position. They concluded that compared to other factors, administration had a limited effect on organizational outcomes.

Using a similar analytical procedure, Salancik and Pfeffer (44) examined the effects of mayors on city budgets for 30 U.S. cities. Data on expenditures by budget category were collected for 1951–1968. Variance in amount and proportion of expenditures was apportioned to the year, the city, or the mayor. The mayoral effect was relatively small, with the city accounting for most of the variance, although the mayor effect was larger for expenditure categories that were not as directly connected to important interest groups. Salancik and Pfeffer argued that the effects of the mayor were limited both by absence of power to control many of the expenditures and tax sources, and by construction of policies in response to demands from interests in the environment.

If leadership is defined as a strictly interpersonal phenomenon, the relevance of these two studies for the issue of leadership effects becomes problematic. But such a conceptualization seems unduly restrictive and is certainly inconsistent with Selznick's (47) conceptualization of leadership as strategic management and decision making. If one cannot observe differences when leaders change, then what does it matter who occupies the positions or how they behave?

Pfeffer and Salancik (41) investigated the extent to which behaviors selected by first-line supervisors were constrained by expectations of others in their role set. Variance in task and social behaviors could be accounted for by role-set expectations, with adherence to various demands made by role-set participants a function of similarity and relative power. Lowin and Craig (37) experimentally demonstrated that leader behavior was determined by the subordinate's own behavior. Both studies illustrate that leader behaviors are responses to the demands of the social context.

The effect of leadership may vary depending upon level in the organizational hierarchy, while the appropriate activities and behaviors may also vary with organizational level (26, 40). For the most part, empirical studies of leadership have dealt with first-line supervisors or leaders with relatively low organizational status (17). If leadership has any impact, it should be more evident at higher organizational levels or where there is more discretion in decisions and activities.

THE PROCESS OF SELECTING LEADERS

Along with the suggestion that leadership may not account for much variance in organizational outcomes, it can be argued that merit or ability may not account for much variation in hiring and advancement of organizational personnel. These two ideas are related. If competence is hard to judge, or if leadership competence does not greatly affect organizational outcomes, then other person-dependent criteria may be sufficient. Effective leadership styles may not predict career success when other variables such as social background are controlled.

Belief in the importance of leadership is frequently accompanied by belief that persons occupying leadership positions are selected and trained according to how well they can enhance the organization's performance. Belief in a leadership effect leads to development of a set of activities oriented toward enhancing leadership effectiveness. Simultaneously, persons managing their own careers are likely to place emphasis on activities and developing behaviors that will enhance their own leadership skills, assuming that such a strategy will facilitate advancement.

Research on the bases for hiring and promotion has been concentrated in examination of academic positions (e.g., 7, 19, 20). This is possibly the result of availability of relatively precise and unambiguous measures of performance, such as number of publications or citations. Evidence on criteria used in selecting and advancing personnel in industry is more indirect.

Studies have attempted to predict either the compensation or the attainment of general management positions of MBA students, using personality and other background information (21, 22, 54). There is some evidence that managerial success can be predicted by indicators of ability and motivation such as test scores and grades, but the amount of variance explained is typically quite small.

A second line of research has investigated characteristics and backgrounds of persons attaining leadership positions in major organizations in society. Domhoff (11), Mills (38), and Warner and Abbeglin (52) found a strong preponderance of persons with upper-class backgrounds occupying leadership positions. The implication of these findings is that studies of graduate success, including the success of MBA's, would explain more variance if the family background of the person were included.

A third line of inquiry uses a tracking model. The dynamic model developed is one in which access to elite universities is affected by social status (28) and, in turn, social status and attendance at elite universities affect later career outcomes (9, 43, 48, 55).

Unless one is willing to make the argument that attendance at elite universities or coming from an upper-class background is perfectly correlated with merit, the evidence suggests that succession to leadership positions is not strictly based on meritocratic criteria. Such a conclusion is consistent with the inability of studies attempting to predict the success of MBA graduates to account for much variance, even when a variety of personality and ability factors are used.

Beliefs about the bases for social mobility are important for social stability. As long as persons believe that positions are allocated on meritocratic grounds, they are more likely to be satisfied with the social order and with their position in it. This satisfaction derives from the belief that occupational position results from application of fair and reasonable criteria and that the opportunity exists for mobility if the person improves skills and performance.

If succession to leadership positions is determined by person-based criteria such as social origins or social connections (16), then efforts to enhance managerial effectiveness with the expectation that this will lead to career success divert attention from the processes of stratification actually operating within organizations. Leadership literature has been implicitly aimed at two audiences. Organizations were told how to become more effective, and persons were told what behaviors to acquire in order to become effective and, hence, advance in their careers. The possibility that neither organizational outcomes nor career success are related to leadership behaviors leaves leadership research facing issues of relevance and importance.

THE ATTRIBUTION OF LEADERSHIP

Kelley conceptualized the layman as:

an applied scientist, that is, as a person concerned about applying his knowledge of causal relationships in order to exercise control of his world (29, p. 2).

Reviewing a series of studies dealing with the attributional process, he concluded that persons were not only interested in understanding their world correctly, but also in controlling it.

The view here proposed is that attribution processes are to be understood not only as a means of providing the individual with a veridical view of his world, but as a means of encouraging and maintaining his effective exercise of control in that world (29, p. 22).

Controllable factors will have high salience as candidates for causal explanation, while a bias toward the more important causes may shift the attributional emphasis toward causes that are not controllable (29, p. 23). The study of attribution is a study of naive psychology — an examination of how persons make sense out of the events taking place around them.

If Kelley is correct that individuals will tend to develop attributions that give them a feeling of control, then emphasis on leadership may derive partially from a desire to believe in the effectiveness and importance of individual action, since individual action is more controllable than contextual variables. Lieberson and O'Connor (35) made essentially the same point in introducing their paper on the effects of top management changes on organizational performance. Given the desire for control and a feeling of personal effectiveness, organizational outcomes are more likely to be attributed to individual actions, regardless of their actual causes.

Leadership is attributed by observers. Social action has meaning only through a phenomenological process (46). The identification of certain organizational roles as leadership positions guides the construction of meaning in the direction of attributing effects to the actions of those positions. While Bavelas (2) argued that the functions of leadership, such as task accomplishment and group maintenance, are shared throughout the group, this fact provides no simple and potentially controllable focus for attributing causality. Rather, the identification of leadership positions provides a simpler and more readily changeable model of reality. When causality is lodged in one or a few persons rather than being a function of a complex set of interactions among all group members, changes can be made by replacing or influencing the occupant of the leadership position. Causes of organizational actions are readily identified in this simple causal structure.

Even if, empirically, leadership has little effect, and even if succession to leadership positions is not predicated on ability or performance, the belief in leadership effects and meritocratic succession provides a simple causal framework and a justification for the structure of the social collectivity. More importantly, the beliefs interpret social actions in terms that indicate potential for effective individual intervention or control. The personification of social causality serves too many uses to be easily overcome. Whether or not leader behavior actually influences performance or effectiveness, it is important because people believe it does.

One consequence of the attribution of causality to leaders and leadership is that leaders come to be symbols. Mintzberg (39), in his discussion of the roles of managers, wrote of the symbolic role, but more in terms of attendance at formal events and formally representing the organization. The symbolic role of leadership is more important than implied in such a description. The leader as a symbol provides a target for action when difficulties occur, serving as a scapegoat when things go wrong. Gamson and Scotch (15) noted that in baseball, the firing of the manager served a scapegoating purpose. One cannot fire the whole team; yet when performance is poor, something must be done. The firing of the manager conveys to the world and to the actors involved that success is the result of personal actions and that steps can and will be taken to enhance organizational performance.

The attribution of causality to leadership may be reinforced by organizational actions, such as the inauguration process, the choice process, and providing the leader with symbols and ceremony. If leaders are chosen by using a random number table, persons are less likely to believe in their effects than if there is an elaborate search or selection process followed by an elaborate ceremony signifying the changing of control, and if the leader then has a variety of perquisites and symbols that distinguish him or her from the rest of the organization. Construction of the importance of leadership in a given social context is the outcome of various social processes, which can be empirically examined.

Since belief in the leadership effect provides a feeling of personal control, one might argue that efforts to increase the attribution of causality to leaders would occur more when it is more necessary and more problematic to attribute causality to controllable factors. Such an argument would lead to the hypothesis that the more the *context* actually effects organizational outcomes, the more efforts will be made to ensure attribution to *leadership*. When leaders really do have effects, it is less necessary to engage in rituals indicating their effects. Such rituals are more likely when there is uncertainty and unpredictability associated with the organization's operations. This results both from the desire to feel control in uncertain situations and from the fact that in ambiguous contexts it is easier to attribute consequences to leadership without facing possible disconfirmation.

The leader is, in part, an actor. Through statements and actions, the leader attempts to reinforce the operation of an attribution process which tends to vest causality in that position in the social structure. Successful leaders, as perceived by members of the social system, are those who can separate themselves from organizational failures and associate themselves with organizational successes. Since the meaning of action is socially constructed, this involves manipulation of symbols to reinforce the desired process of attribution. For instance, if a manager knows that business in his or her division is about to improve because of the economic cycle, the leader may, nevertheless, write recommendations and undertake actions and changes that are highly visible and that will tend to identify his or her behavior closely with the division. A manager who perceives impending failure will attempt to associate the division and its policies and decisions with others, particularly persons in higher organizational positions, and to disassociate himself or herself from the division's performance, occasionally even transferring or moving to another organization.

CONCLUSION

The theme of this article has been that analysis of leadership and leadership processes must be contingent on the intent of the researcher. If the interest is in understanding the causality of social phenomena as reliably and accurately as possible, then the concept of leadership may be a poor place to begin. The issue of the effects of leadership is open to question. But examination of situational variables that accompany more or less leadership effect is a worthwhile task.

The more phenomenological analysis of leadership directs attention to the process by which social causality is attributed and focuses on the distinction between causality as perceived by group members and causality as assessed by an outside observer. Leadership is associated with a set of myths reinforcing a social construction of meaning which legitimates leadership role occupants, provides belief in potential mobility for those not in leadership roles, and attributes social causality to leadership roles, thereby providing a belief in the effectiveness of individual control. In analyzing leadership, this mythology and the process by which such mythology is created and supported should be separated from analysis of leadership as a social influence process, operating within constraints.

REFERENCE NOTES

1. Bales, R. F. *Interaction process analysis: A method for the study of small groups.* Reading, Mass.: Addison-Wesley, 1950.

2. Bavelas, Alex. Leadership: Man and function, *Administrative Science Quarterly,* 1960, 4:491–98.

3. Berscheid, Ellen, and Walster, Elaine. *Interpersonal attraction.* Reading, Mass.: Addison-Wesley, 1969.

4. Bowers, David G., and Seashore, Stanley E. Predicting organizational effectiveness with a four-factor theory of leadership, *Administrative Science Quarterly,* 1966, 11:238-63.

5. Calder, Bobby J. An attribution theory of leadership, in B. Staw and G. Salancik (eds.), *New directions in organizational behavior.* Chicago: St. Clair Press, 1976, in press.

6. Cartwright, Dorwin C., and Zander, Alvin. *Group dynamics: Research and theory,* 3d ed. Evanston, Ill.: Row, Peterson, 1960.

7. Cole, Jonathan R., and Cole, Stephen. *Social stratification in science.* Chicago: University of Chicago Press, 1973.

8. Collins, Barry E., and Guetzkow, Harold. *A social psychology of group processes for decision making.* New York: Wiley, 1964.

9. Collins, Randall. Functional and conflict theories of stratification, *American Sociological Review,* 1971, 36:1002-19.

10. Day, R. C., and Hamblin, R. L. Some effects of close and punitive styles of supervision. *American Journal of Sociology,* 1964, 69:499-510.

11. Domhoff, G. William. *Who rules America?* Englewood Cliffs, N.J.: Prentice-Hall, 1967.

12. Dubin, Robert. Supervision and productivity: Empirical findings and theoretical considerations, in R. Dubin, G. C. Homans, F. C. Mann, and D. C. Miller (eds.), *Leadership and productivity.* San Francisco: Chandler Publishing Co., 1965, pp. 1-50.

13. Fiedler, Fred E. Engineering the job to fit the manager, *Harvard Business Review,* 1965, 43:115-22.

14. Fiedler, Fred E. *A theory of leadership effectiveness.* New York: McGraw-Hill, 1967.

15. Gamson, William A., and Scotch, Norman A. Scapegoat in Baseball, *American Journal of Sociology,* 1964, 70:69-72.

16. Granovetter, Mark. *Getting a job.* Cambridge, Mass.: Harvard University Press, 1974.

17. Hall, Richard H. *Organizations: Structure and process.* Englewood Cliffs, N.J.: Prentice-Hall, 1972.

18. Halpin, A. W., and Winer, J. A factorial study of the leader behavior description questionnaire, in R. M. Stogdill and A. E. Coons (eds.), *Leader behavior: Its description and measurement.* Columbus, Ohio: Bureau of Business Research, Ohio State University, 1957, pp. 39-51.

19. Hargens, L. L. Patterns of mobility of new Ph.D.'s among American academic institutions, *Sociology of Education,* 1969, 42:18-37.

20. Hargens, L. L., and Hagstrom, W. O. Sponsored and contest mobility of American academic scientists, *Sociology of Education,* 1967, 40:24-38.

21. Harrell, Thomas W. High earning MBA's, *Personnel Psychology,* 1972, 25:523-30.

22. Harrell, Thomas W., and Harrell, Margaret S. Predictors of management success. *Stanford University Graduate School of Business, Technical Report no. 3 to the Office of Naval Research.*

23. Heller, Frank, and Yukl, Gary. Participation, managerial decision making, and situational variables, *Organizational Behavior and Human Performance,* 1969, 4:227-41.

24. Hollander, Edwin P., and Julian, James W. Contemporary trends in the analysis of leadership processes, *Psychological Bulletin,* 1969, 71:387-97.

25. House, Robert J. A path-goal theory of leader effectiveness, *Administrative Science Quarterly,* 1971, 16:321-38.

26. Hunt, J. G. Leadership-style effects at two managerial levels in a simulated organization, *Administrative Science Quarterly,* 1971, 16:476-85.

27. Kahn, R. L., Wolfe, D. M., Quinn, R. P., and Snock, J. D. *Organizational stress: Studies in role conflict and ambiguity.* New York: Wiley, 1964.

28. Karabel, J., and Astin, A. W. Social class, academic ability, and college "quality," *Social Forces,* 1951, 53:381-98.

29. Kelley, Harold H. *Attribution in social interaction.* Morristown, N.J.: General Learning Press, 1971.

30. Kerr, Steven, and Schriesheim, Chester. Consideration, initiating structure and organizational criteria — An update of Korman's 1966 review," *Personnel Psychology,* 1974, 27:555-68.

31. Kerr, S., Schriesheim, C., Murphy, C. J., and Stogdill, R. M. Toward a contingency theory of leadership based upon the consideration and initiating structure literature, *Organizational Behavior and Human Performance,* 1974, 12:62–82.

32. Kiesler, C., and Kiesler, S. *Conformity.* Reading, Mass.: Addison-Wesley, 1969.

33. Kochan, T. A., Schmidt, S. M., and DeCotiis, T. A. Superior-subordinate relations: Leadership and headship, *Human Relations,* 1975, 28:279–94.

34. Korman, A. K. Consideration, initiating structure, and organizational criteria — A review, *Personnel Psychology,* 1966, 19:349–62.

35. Lieberson, Stanley, and O'Connor, James F. Leadership and organizational performance: A study of large corporations, *American Sociological Review,* 1972, 37:117–30.

36. Lippitt, Ronald. An experimental study of the effect of democratic and authoritarian group atmospheres, *University of Iowa Studies in Child Welfare,* 1940, 16:43–195.

37. Lowin, A., and Craig, J. R. The influence of level of performance on managerial style: An experimental object-lesson in the ambiguity of correlational data, *Organizational Behavior and Human Performance,* 1968, 3:440–58.

38. Mills, C. Wright. The American business elite: A collective portrait, in C. W. Mills, *Power, politics and people.* New York: Oxford University Press, 1963, pp. 110–39.

39. Mintzberg, Henry. *The nature of managerial work.* New York: Harper and Row, 1973.

40. Nealey, Stanley M., and Blood, Milton R. Leadership performance of nursing supervisors at two organizational levels, *Journal of Applied Psychology,* 1968, 52:414–42.

41. Pfeffer, Jeffrey, and Salancik, Gerald R. Determinants of supervisory behavior: A role set analysis, *Human Relations,* 1975, 28:139–54.

42. Pfeffer, Jeffrey, and Salancik, Gerald R. Organizational context and the characteristics and tenure of hospital administrators, *Academy of Management Journal,* 1977, 20 in press.

43. Reed, R. H., and Miller, H. P. Some determinants of the variation in earnings for college men, *Journal of Human Resources,* 1970, 5:117–90.

44. Salancik, Gerald R., and Pfeffer, Jeffrey. Constraints on administrator discretion: The limited influence of mayors on city budgets, *Urban Affairs Quarterly,* in press.

45. Sales, Stephen M. Supervisory style and productivity: Review and theory, *Personnel Psychology,* 1966, 19:275–86.

46. Schultz, Alfred. *The phenomenology of the social world.* Evanston, Ill.: Northwestern University Press, 1967.

47. Selznick, P. *Leadership in administration.* Evanston, Ill.: Row, Peterson, 1957.

48. Spaeth, J. L., and Greeley, A. M. *Recent alumni and higher education.* New York: McGraw-Hill, 1970.

49. Thompson, James D. *Organizations in action.* New York: McGraw-Hill, 1967.

50. Vroom, Victor H. Some personality determinants of the effects of participation, *Journal of Abnormal and Social Psychology,* 1959, 59:322–27.

51. Vroom, Victor H., and Yetton, Phillip W. *Leadership and decision making.* Pittsburgh: University of Pittsburgh Press, 1973.

52. Warner, W. L., and Abbeglin, J. C. *Big business leaders in America.* New York: Harper and Brothers, 1955.

53. Weick, Karl E. *The social psychology of organizing.* Reading, Mass.: Addison-Wesley, 1969.

54. Weinstein, Alan G., and Srinivasan, V. Predicting managerial success of master of business administration (MBA) graduates, *Journal of Applied Psychology,* 1974, 59:207–12.

55. Wolfle, Dael. *The uses of talent.* Princeton: Princeton University Press, 1971.

56. Zald, Mayer N. Who shall rule? A political analysis of succession in a large welfare organization. *Pacific Sociological Review,* 1965, 8:52–60.

Part Four

Decision Making

Foundations of Decision Making

29. Judgmental Heuristics and Knowledge Structures

by Richard Nisbett and Lee Ross

The most characteristic thing about mental life, over and beyond the fact that one apprehends the events of the world around one, is that one constantly goes beyond the information given.

Jerome Bruner

The perceiver, as Bruner (1957) recognized, is not simply a dutiful clerk who passively registers items of information. Rather, the perceiver is an active interpreter, one who resolves ambiguities, makes educated guesses about events that cannot be observed directly, and forms inferences about associations and causal relations. In this chapter we explore the strategies that permit and encourage the perceiver to "go beyond the information given," that is, to venture beyond the most immediate implications of the data. We sketch some of the "knowledge structures" applied to understanding the world. These range from broad propositional theories about people in general to more schematic representations of objects, events, and actors. These structures house the person's generic knowledge and preconcep-

tions about the world and provide the basis for quick, coherent, but occasionally erroneous interpretations of new experience.

Before discussing these structures, we will introduce the reader to the "availability heuristic" and the "representativeness heuristic" — two simple judgmental strategies on which people seem to rely, and by which they sometimes are misled, in a variety of inferential tasks. In so doing, the chapter introduces the reader to a set of extraordinarily important contributions by Daniel Kahneman and Amos Tversky (1972, 1973, in press; Tversky & Kahneman, 1971, 1973, 1974). . . .

The heuristics to be explored are relatively primitive and simple judgmental strategies. They are not irrational and even nonrational. They probably produce vastly more correct or partially correct inferences than erroneous ones, and they do so with great speed and little effort. Indeed, we suspect that the use of such simple tools may be an inevitable feature of the cognitive apparatus of any organism that must make as

From Richard Nisbett and Lee Ross, *Human Inference: Strategies and Shortcomings of Social Judgment,* © 1980, pp. 43–62. Reprinted by permission of Prentice-Hall, Inc., Englewood Cliffs, N.J.

many judgments, inferences, and decisions as humans have to do. Each heuristic or, more properly, the misapplication of each heuristic, does lead people astray in some important inferential tasks. Since [we are] particularly concerned with inferential failings, it is the misuse of the heuristics — their application in preference to more normatively appropriate strategies — that we will emphasize.

Although we characterize the heuristics as "judgmental strategies," the term is misleading in that it implies a conscious and deliberate application of well-defined decision rules. The heuristics to be explored should be distinguished from straightforward computational or judgmental "algorithms" (such as the method for finding square roots or deciding whether one's bridge hand merits an opening bid), which generally are explicit and invariant both in the criteria for their use and the manner of their application. The intuitive psychologist probably would not assent to, much less spontaneously express, any general formulation of either heuristic. Instead, the utilization of the heuristics is generally automatic and nonreflective and notably free of any conscious consideration of appropriateness. As we shall see, the heuristics are not applied in a totally indiscriminate fashion. In many contexts in which a given heuristic would promote error, people refrain from using it and probably could articulate why its use would be foolish. On other logically equivalent and equally unpropitious occasions, people readily apply the same heuristic and may even attempt to justify its use.

THE AVAILABILITY HEURISTIC

When people are required to judge the relative frequency of particular objects or the likelihood of particular events, they often may be influenced by the relative *availability* of the objects or events, that is, their accessibility in the processes of perception, memory, or construction from imagination (cf. Tversky and Kahneman 1973). Such availability criteria often will prove accurate and useful. To the extent that availability is actually associated with objective frequency, the availability heuristic can be a useful tool of judgment. There are many factors uncorrelated with frequency, however, which can influence an event's immediate perceptual salience, the vividness or completeness with which it is recalled, or the ease with which it is imagined. As a result, the availability heuristic can be misleading.

Availability Biases in Frequency Estimation

Let us proceed first by introducing and then exploring in some detail three judgmental tasks for which application of the availability heuristic might lead one to biased estimates of the relative frequency of various objects or events. . . .

1. A pollster who asks a sample of American adults to estimate the "percentage of the work force who are currently unemployed" finds an "egocentric bias." That is, currently unemployed workers tend to overestimate the rate of unemployment, but currently employed workers tend to underestimate it.
2. An Indiana businessman confides to a friend, "Did you ever notice how many Hoosiers become famous or important? Look anywhere — politics, sports, Hollywood, big business, even notorious bank robbers — I couldn't guess the exact figures, but I bet we Hoosiers have far more than our fair share on just about any list in *Who's Who*."
3. A group of subjects consistently errs in judging the relative frequency of two kinds of English words. Specifically, they estimate the number of words beginning with particular letters (for example, *R* or *K*) to be greater than the number of words with those letters appearing third, although words of the latter type actually are far more numerous.

Examples 1 and 2 seem to present common and familiar errors, although one might not immediately recognize the role of availability factors in producing them. In fact, some readers might hasten to cite motivational or even "psychodynamic" factors that could induce unemployed workers to overestimate the commonness of their plight or that could prompt proud Indiana residents to exaggerate their share of the limelight. Example 3 seems less intuitively obvious and at first seems quite unconnected to the other two examples. Nevertheless, the chief source of error in all three cases seems to us to be the availability heuristic.

Consider Example 1, about estimates of unemployment. Here the bias in subjective availability can be traced to a bias in initial sampling. Unemployed people are more likely to know and meet other unemployed people than are job-holders, and vice versa. The reasons for such a sampling bias are hardly mysterious: The unemployed individual is likely to share the neighborhood, socioeconomic background, and occupation of other jobless individuals. He also is likely to encounter other unemployed people in such everyday endeavors as job-hunting, visiting employment agencies, collecting unemployment benefits, and shopping at stores offering cut-rate prices or easy credit. Indeed, he even may seek out such individuals for social comparison, information exchange, or general commiseration. Thus, to the extent that the unemployed person relies upon the sample generated by his personal experience, he will be misled about the commonness of unemployment. In the same manner, employed people, who are apt to live, work, and shop near one another, are apt to err in the opposite direction.

It is important to emphasize that the people in this hypothetical example would not be compelled to rely upon biased availability criteria in estimating the frequency of unemployment. They could try to recall media presentations of data, could apply some popular rule of thumb ("When there's an energy shortage, jobs disappear"), or could employ some more appropriate, "sampling procedure" ("How many people have I seen lining up outside my neighborhood unemployment office on the first of the month this year as compared with last year?"). They even could attempt to compensate for the biases distorting their samples of available data ("Hardly anyone I know is jobless, but of course, I don't get to meet many unemployed people, do I? I guess I'd better adjust my estimate upward!"). Indeed, it is quite likely that some people *would* avoid availability criteria or at least would attempt the necessary adjustments. ... However, we present experimental evidence showing that simple, tempting, availability criteria are used in contexts in which availability and frequency are poorly correlated and are used without appropriate adjustments for the factors that bias subjective experience.

Now let us consider Example 2, about the relative prominence of Indiana natives. The Hoosier's egocentric, estimate clearly contains some of the same features as in our initial example. That is, people from Indiana are disproportionately likely to know or hear about famous fellow Hoosiers. Beyond such biases in initial exposure, however, this example introduces the potential influence of additional biases in *storage*. When a national sportscaster says "Myra Swift of Grandville, Indiana and Mary Speed of Bigtown, Florida won gold medals in the Olympics yesterday," it is the accomplishment of his fellow Hoosier that the Indiana businessman is more likely to notice and to remember. Accordingly, the sample of famous people he subsequently can recall

from memory will reflect biases at the "storage" stage as well as at the sampling stage.

Biases in exposure, attention, and storage can arise, of course, from many factors besides the kinship between the perceiver and the object. As we shall see in later chapters, for instance, oddity or newsworthiness could accomplish the same end. Thus, people from all states might overestimate the number of very big, very small, very young, very pretty, or very hirsute Olympic gold medalists because such factors would bias the rater's likelihood of sampling, storing, and recalling the pertinent instances.

Example 3, about estimates of the frequency of the letter R in the first versus the third position, is subtler. In fact, readers who try the experiment themselves may find that they make the same incorrect assessments of relative frequency as did the original subjects. Once again, an inappropriate application of the availability criterion is the source of the difficulty. Like the subjects in Tversky's and Kahneman's (1973) demonstration, the reader probably finds that instances of words beginning with R are easier to generate spontaneously (at least in a casual first attempt) than are instances of words that have R as their third letter. The relative difficulty of generating words like "care," "street," and "derail," may give intereting hints of the storage and retrieval of one's vocabulary, but it says virtually nothing about objective work frequencies.

An analogy may be instructive here: In a quick search of the library, one would find it easier to find books by authors named Woolf than by authors named Virginia, or to find books about Australia than books by authors born in Australia. Such differences obviously would indicate little about the relative frequencies of such books in the library's collection. Instead, they would reflect the library's system for referencing books and granting access to them. By the same token, first letters apparently are more useful cues than third letter are for referencing and permitting access to the items in one's personal work collection. Once again, the use of criteria other than the subjective ease of generation (or, alternatively, recognition of relevant biases and adequate compensation) could lead people to a more accurate estimate.

Availability of Event Relationships and of Casual Explanations

Kahneman's and Tversky's work has been largely on the use of the availability heuristic in judgments involving the frequency or probability of individual events. Other research indicates that subjective availability may influence judgments of *relationships* between events, particularly *causal* relationships.

Jones's and Nisbett's (1972) account of the divergent causal interpretations of actors and observers — from which observers cite "dispositional" factors (traits, abilities, attitudes, ets.) to explain behaviors and outcomes that the actors themselves attribute to "situational" factors — is one case in point. For example, the actor who gives a dollar to a beggar is apt to attribute his behavior to the sad plight of the beggar, but the observer of the behavior is apt to attribute it to the actor's generosity. From the actor's perspective, it is the constantly changing features of the environment that are particularly salient or "available" as potential causes to which his behavior can be attributed. From the observer's perspective, the actor is the perceptual "figure," and the situation merely "ground," so that the actor himself provides the most available causal candidate. Indeed, by altering actors' and observers' perspectives through videotape replays, mirrors, or other methods, one can correspondingly alter the actor's and observers' causal assessments (cf. Arkin & Duval 1975; Duval & Wicklund 1972; Regan & Totten 1975; Storms 1973).

Subsequent research by a number of investigators, most notably Taylor and her associates (for example, Taylor & Fiske 1975, 1978), has demonstrated a more general point regarding availability and causal assessment. It appears that almost *any* manipulation that focuses the perceiver's attention on a potential cause, for example, on a particular participant in a social interaction, affects causal assessment. Whether the attentional manipulation is achieved by a blunt instruction about which participant to watch, subtle variations in seating arrangement, or by "solo" versus "nonsolo" status of, for example, female or black participants, the person made disproportionately "available" to onlookers is seen to be a disproportionately potent causal agent. (See also McArthur & Post 1977; McArthur & Solomon 1978.)

Availability effects also may account for other biases involving perceived causality. Consider Fischhoff's (1975; Fischhoff & Beyth 1975) reports on the subjective certainty of hindsight knowledge. These reports show that outcomes often seem in retrospect to have been inevitable. This may be because the antecedents and causal scenarios that "predicted" such outcomes have far greater "after-the-fact" availability than do antecedents or scenarios that predicted alternative outcomes that did not in fact occur. In a similar vein, Ross, Lepper, Strack, and Steinmetz (1977) demonstrated that *explaining* why some event is consistent with known preceding events (for example, explaining the suicide of a clinical patient whose case history one has examined) tends to increase the subjective likelihood that the event actually did occur. Again, the relevant mechanism appears to be the availability heuristic. The explanation creates a particular causal scenario, and its causal factors are disproportionately available to the perceiver when predictions are made later.

In both hindsight and explanation, the subjective ease of generation appears to be important. The subjects seem to respond not only to the mere presence of potential causal scenarios but also to the relative ease with which they were detected or invented. People probably implicitly assume this subjective ease of generation to be somehow symptomatic of the scenario's likelihood or of the explanation's aptness.

Appropriate and Inappropriate Applications of the Availability Heuristic

An indiscriminate use of the availability heuristic clearly can lead people into serious judgmental errors. It is important to reemphasize that in many contexts perceptual salience, memorability, and imaginability may be relatively unbiased and therefore will correlated with true frequency, probability, or even causal significance. In such cases, of course, the availability heuristic often can be a helpful and efficient tool of inference.

The same jobless individuals whose estimates of unemployment rates were distorted by the availability heuristic could make a reasonably accurate estimate of the preponderance of oak trees to maple trees in their neighborhood by using the same stategy. In estimating the frequencies of various types of trees, the individual's personal experiences and subsequent recollections would constitute generally unbiased samples. Similarly, the Indiana resident who was misled by the disproportionate availability of instances of famous fellow Hoosiers might have fared quite well if the same heuristic had been applied in estimating the success of German Olympians relative to Italian Olympians. Furthermore, the "east of generation" criterion would have helped rather than hindered Tversky's and Kahneman's subjects if the experimental task had been to estimate the relative frequencies either of (a) words beginning with *R* versus words beginning with *L*, or (b) words with *R* versus *L* in the third position. In either of these cases, differences in the relative ease of generation would have reflected differences in frequency quite accurately.

The normative status of using the availability heuristic, and the pragmatic utility of using it, thus depend on the judgmental domain and context. People are not, of course, totally unaware that simple availability criteria must sometimes be discounted. For example, few people who were asked to estimate the relative number of moles versus cats in their neighborhood would conclude "there must be more cats because I've seen several of them but I've never seen a mole." Nevertheless, . . people often fail to distinguish between legitimate and superficially similar, but illegitimate, uses of the availability heuristic.

THE REPRESENTATIVENESS HEURISTIC

The second judgmental heuristic to be introduced is one which Kahneman and Tversky (1972, 1973; Tversky & Kahneman 1974) termed the *representativeness* Heuristic. This heuristic involves the application of relatively simple resemblance or "goodness of fit" criteria to problems of categorization. In making a judgment, people assess the degree to which the salient features of the object are representative of, or similar to, the features presumed to be characteristic of the category.

In the following sections we try to provide a coherent grouping of examples. It should be emphasized, however, that our classification system is neither exhaustive nor theoretically derived. We also should note that we make no attempt to specify the precise criteria by which individuals calculate the representativeness of one object or event to another. (For the interested reader, a recent by already classic paper by Tversky, 1977, takes a first step in this direction by introducing a formal theory of similarity judgments.)

Judgments of the Degree to Which Outcomes Are Representative of Their Origins

People often are required to predict some outcome or judge the likelihood of some even on the basis of information about the "generating process" that produced it. On such occasions, the judgment is likely to reflect the degree to which the specified outcome represents its origin. Let us consider an example adapted from one used by Kahneman and Tversky (1972)

Subjects are asked to assess the relative likelihood of three particular sequences of birth of boys (B) and girls (G) for the next six babies born in the United States. These sequences are (i) BBBBBB, (ii) GGGBBB, (iii) GBBGGB.

According to the conventional probability calculation, the likelihood of each of these sequences is almost identical. (Actually, the first sequence is slightly more likely than either the second or third sequence, since male births are slightly more common than female births. The latter two sequences are simply different orderings of identical, independent events.) Subjects who rely upon their intuitions and upon the representativeness criteria which guide such intuitions, are apt to regard the GBBGGB sequence as far more likely than either of the other two. In doing so, they are responding to what they know about the population of babies and about the processes of "generation," that is, that each birth is a "random" event in which the probability of "boy" and "girl" are nearly equal. Only the GBBGGB sequence is "representative" of the generating process. The GGGBBB sequence seems too "orderly" to represent a random process. The BBBBBB sequence satisfies the criteria even less: It captures neither the randomness of the birth process nor the equal sex distribution of the population from which the six births were "samples."

The representativeness heuristic also accounts for the familiar "gamblers' fallacy." After observing a long run of "red" on a roulette wheel, people believe the that "black" is now due, because the occurrence of black would make the overall sequence of events more representative of the generating process than would the occurrence of another red. In a similar vein, any researcher who has ever consulted a random number table for an unbiased ordering of events has probably felt that the result was somehow insufficiently "representative" of a chance process, that it contained suspiciously orderly sequences, suspiciously long runs, suspicious overrepresentations or underrepresentations of particular numbers early or late in the sequence, and so forth (cf. Tversky & Kahneman 1971).

Judgments of the Degree to Which Instances Are Representative of Categories

Many everyday judgments require people to estimate the likelihood that some object or event with a given set of characteristics is an instance of some designated category or class. Typically, the judgments are made in relative terms, that is, is Event X more likely to be an instance of Class A or of Class B? Consider the following problem, which is similar in form to those in the empirical work by Kahneman and Tversky. . . .

The present authors have a friend who is a professor. He likes to write poetry, is rather shy, and is small in stature. Which of the following is his field: (a) Chinese studies or (b) psychology?

Those readers who quickly and confidently predicted "psychology" probably applies some version, whether sophisticated or crude, of conventional statistical canons. We congratulate these readers. We suspect, however, that many readers guessed "Chinese studies," or at least seriously considered that such a guess might be reasonable. If so, they probably were seduced by the representativeness heuristic. Specifically, they assessed the relative "goodness of fit" between the professor's personality profile and the predominant features of their stereotypes of Sinologists and psychologists. Finding the fit better for the former than for the latter, they guessed the professor's field to be Chinese studies.

In succumbing to the lure of the representativeness heuristic, what the reader likely has overlooked or not appreciated is some relevant category *base-rate* information. Let the reader who guessed "Chinese studies" now reconsider that guess in light of the relative numbers of psychologists and Sinologists in the population. Then consider the more restricted population of people likely to be friends of the authors, who themselves are psychologists. Surely *no* reader's implicit personality theory of the strength of association between academic discipline and the professor's various characteristics, that is, poetry-writing, shyness, and slightness of stature, warrants overriding such base-rate considerations.

Errors in problems of the Sinologist/psychologist variety may reflect that the judge has been led to answer the wrong question or, more specifically, to ponder the wrong conditional probability. The judge seems to be responding to the question "How likely is someone resembling the personality profile to be a psychologist (versus a Sinologist)?" The representativeness heuristic leads people to give a similar answer to the two questions, since it entails consideration only of the resemblance of the two occupational stereotypes to the given personality description. The error is the failure to consider the relevant base rates or marginal probabilities, a consideration which is irrelevant to the

first question but critical to the second. Although a much higher proportion of Sinologists than of psychologists may fit the profile, there would still be a much greater *absolute* number of psychologists than of Sinologists who fit it, because of the vastly greater number of psychologists than of Sinologists in the population. . . .

Judgments of the Degree to Which Antecedents Are Representative of Consequences

Earlier we contended that the availability of causal candidates, or of causal scenarios linking outcomes to potential antecedents, influences assessments of causality. We contend that representativeness criteria also may be important to such inferences. That is, a person who is required to account for some observed action or outcome may search the list of *available* antecedents for those that seem to be the most *representative* "causes" of the known "consequences."

Simple resemblance criteria appear to influence causal assessment just as they influence judgments of the representativeness of outcomes to origins or instances to classes. . . . Sometimes the resemblance criterion is used in a crude and unsophisticated way, as it is in primitive medical beliefs attributing a particular illness to an environmental agent with features resembling the illness. Sometimes its influence is less patent, as in the preference for motivational causes in explaining events with strong motivational or affective consequences or the preference for complicated, multifaceted causes for complicated, multifaceted outcomes.

Generally, the use of the representativeness heuristic in causal assessment is more than a simple comparison of the features of effects with those of their potential causes. Normally, people also use *theories* or general *knowledge* of the particular antecedents likely to cause or explain given outcomes and of the specific outcomes likely to follow given antecedents. A person's belief that the cause of Egypt's diplomatic initiative toward Israel was an heroic vision of Egypt's leaders rather than economic exigency does not reflect merely a crude assessment of the similarity between historic gestures and heroic visions. Instead, such assessments reflect judgments of the similarity of known effects and potential causes to tacit or explicit models of cause-and-effect relations in international conduct. Application of the representativeness heuristic to the assessment of causality thus ranges from the crude and questionable requirement that potential causes resemble effects, to normatively proper strategies based on a comparison of the similarity of observed effects and potential causes to generalized cause-and-effect models in the given domain.

Appropriate and Inappropriate Applications of the Representativeness Heuristic

Even more than the availability heuristic, the representativeness heuristic is a legitimate, indeed absolutely essential, cognitive tool. Countless inferential tasks, especially those requiring induction or generalization, depend on deciding what class or category of event one is observing; such judgments inevitably hinge upon assessments of resemblance or representativeness (cf. Tversky 1977). Even in our examples, the use of the representativeness heuristic produced errors only because it was overapplied or misapplies while normatively important criteria were overlooked. Let us briefly reconsider each of those examples.

In the case of the representativeness of the outcome to the oigin, the problem is clearly one of overapplication. The insight that the features of the sample ought to resemble those of the population or the generating process is generally valid. It leads people to recognize that an all-male or an all-white jury is more likely to reflect a biased selection procedure than will a jury with a more proportionate representation of the overall population. It also leads people to cry foul when a politician's cronies seem to enjoy a disproportionate share of good luck in their transaction with local or state agencies. Unfortunately, when people's understanding of the generating process and its implications is deficient — as when there are misconceptions about randomness — the representativeness heuristic will mislead.

In the second example, the Sinologist/psychologist problem, people are foiled mainly because important information is neglected, that is, the relevant base rates are ignored. In many circumstances, of course, such information is absent, and the representativeness heuristic has no serious contender. In other circumstances, base-rate information may have little practical significance. Sometimes the feature-matching process results in a category determination with a probability near 1.0, and when features are as powerfully diagnostic as that, there is little practical need to consider base rates. For example, in the Sinologist/psychologist problem, if the profile were extended to include the

information that the person speaks Chinese, knows no statistics, and has never heard of B. F. Skinner, the relevance of base-rate frequencies would dwindle to triviality. There are also occasions when representativeness criteria can be used directly without violating normative standards because the base rates or marginal probabilities are approximately equal. If the Sinologist/psychologist problem were altered to a decision between a sociologist and an historian, the representativeness heuristic would serve the judge quite well, providing that the relevant occupational stereotypes had at least some validity.

KNOWLEDGE STRUCTURES: THEORIES AND SCHEMAS

We have discussed some of the judgmental strategies that people use in a variety of social inference tasks. Often, however, people's understanding of the rapid flow of continuing social events may depend less on such judgmental procedures than on a rich store of general knowledge of objects, people, events, and their characteristic relationships. Some of this knowledge may be represented as beliefs or *theories*, that is, reasonably explicit "propositions" about the characteristics of objects or object classes. (For example: Joe is kind to small animals. Rotarians are public spirited. Adult neuroses have their "origin" in childhood trauma. Decision makers prefer minimax strategies.) People's generic knowledge also seems to be organized by a variety of less "propositional," more *schematic*, cognitive structures (for example, the knowledge underlying one's awareness of what happens in a restaurant, one's understanding of the Good Samaritan parable, or one's conception of what an introvert is like). To describe such knowledge structures, psychologists refer to a growing list of terms, including "frames" (Minsky 1975), "scripts" (Abelson 1976; Schank & Abelson 1977), "nuclear scenes" (Tomkins 1979), and "prototypes" (Cantor & Mischel 1977, in press), in addition to the earlier and more general term "schemas" (Bartlett 1932; Piaget 1936; also Rumelhart 1976). . . .

Theory-Based Judgments of Representativeness

As we noted earlier, assessments of representativeness often depend less on simple similarity criteria than on more sophisticated "theories" of the types of attributes and events that occur together, or that cause each other. For example, scandal in a parliamentary government is a "representative" cause of an impending election. When a scandal occurs we expect an election and when an election is called we are apt to cite any previous scandal as a contributing cause. The reason for such judgments clearly is not in the relative similarity of the outstanding features of political scandals and parliamentary elections. Rather, the judgment reflects one's adherence to a pair of "theoretical" propositions, first, that scandals weaken governments and second, that weakened governments in parliamentary democracies often must go to the electorate for a vote of confidence. Sometimes, as we shall see, the preconceptions governing causal inferences and likelihood assessments may best be regarded not as a set of propositions but as a schema or "script" (cf. Abelson 1976) in which a succession of "scenes" are linked in a single coherent structure — for example, accusations, denials, fresh accusations, limited acknowledgments of bad judgment and mendacity, resignations, and a final emotional appeal by the political leader for support at the polls.

People rely upon an enormous number of such theories, which are derived from personal experience and from the accumulated wisdom of one's culture, to decide on the representativeness of causes and effects, outcomes and outcome-generating processes, and objects and classes. The costs and benefits of relying upon such specific prior theories, rather than collecting and analyzing further data, for instance, depend both on the accuracy of the theories and on the feasibility of employing other, more empirical procedures. . . .

Schemas, Scripts, and Personae

To understand the social world, the layperson makes heavy use of a variety of knowledge structures normally not expressed in propositional terms and possibly not stored in a form even analogous to propositional statements. In describing these cognitive structures we shall use the generic designation "schema" and will comment in detail about only two types of schemas — event-schemas, or "scripts," and person-schemas, or "personae."

The most basic type of schema is probably that which underlies the use of common concepts or categories such as *dog, tree,* or *chair,* or concepts of far greater or lesser generality (*animals, flora,* and *furniture,* or *Airedales, Ponderosa pines,* and *Chippendales*). In recent years there has been an explosion of interest in

and research on people's use of categories, and we cannot digress to summarize this important and ever-expanding literature. Let us note merely that the "classic" view of a category, one that entails clearly specified boundaries and a set of defining characteristics necessary to and sufficient for category membership, has come under increasingly devastating attack (cf. Wittgenstein 1953; Rosch 1978; Tversky 1977). Gradually it has been supplanted by a more lenient and catholic view — one that allows ambiguous boundaries, recognizes a variety of differing bases for assessing category membership, and permits individual members to differ in their prototypicality. What both the traditional and newer views have in common is the notion that the category and the concept underlying it form an important basis for inference. That is, once the criteria for applying the concept have been met, the concept user readily assigns a number of additional characteristics to the entity. For example, upon deciding on the basis of a particular animal's appearance that it is a "dog," one makes the inferential leaps that it is trainable, capable of loyalty, able to bark, and likely to chase cats but is unlikely to climb trees, purr, or wash its coat.

In principle one could speak of a dog "schema," or even an Airedale schema or an animal schema. In practice, however, the term "schema" has come to be differentiated from the term "concept." Since its introduction in the 1930s by Bartlett (1923) and by Piaget (1936), the term "schema" has been used more and more to refer to those mental structures having a *dynamic* or *relational* aspect. For example, Piaget refers to a "thumb-sucking" schema and a "conservation" schema, both of which, despite the enormous difference in their level of abstractness, have dynamic relationships among the schema's components. In the former, the schema is a kind of mental summary of the sensory, cognitive, and motor experiences in a sequence of actions involving body parts. In the latter, the schema represents experiential knowledge of the relationship between mass and volume (or number and position) and the outcomes likely to result from various action sequences involving a fixed mass of material (or a fixed number of objects).

Kelley (1972b) introduced to the attribution literature the notion of a causal schema. Kelley used the term to refer primarily to a highly abstract, content-free notion of the formal relations among causes and effects. He proposed that people possess in very abstract and general form the notions of sufficiency and necessity in causal relations. This distinction underlies a number of specific causal schemas, such as the single necessary cause schema (in which the existence of the effect carries with it the certainty that a particular cause was present) and the multiple sufficient cause schema (in which the existence of the effect implies the possibility of each of several causes). There also are more complicated general schemas. For example, people may have a "discounting" schema: Given an effect capable of being produced by several causes and certain knowledge of the operation of a particular cause, people reduce their subjective probability that each of the other sufficient causes were operative. People also may possess an inhibitory cause schema: Given knowledge of the existence of a factor operating to block the occurrence of the effect, people infer that one or more facilitative causes were unusually powerful.

Though we are not confident that people actually possess such content-free causal schemas, we will use the term occasionally, to refer primarily to causal-analytic strategies that people do *not* seem to understand or to use in situations in which they would be helpful.

Scripts

The lexicons of cognitive social psychology and artificial intelligence recently were enriched by the introduction of the "script" concept (Abelson 1976, 1978; Shank & Abelson 1977). A script is a type of schema in which the related elements are social objects and events involving the individual as actor or observer. Unlike most schemas, scripts generally are event sequences extended over time, and the relationships have a distinctly causal flavor, that is, early events in the sequence produce or at least "enable" the occurrence of later events. A script can be compared to a cartoon strip with two or more captioned "scenes," each of which summarizes some basic actions that can be executed in a range of possible manners and contexts (for instance, the "restaurant script" with its "entering," "ordering," "eating," and "exiting" scenes). Alternatively, a script can be represented as a computer program with a set of tracks, variables, relationships, operations, subroutines, loops, and the like, which are "instantiated" with particular values for any particular application of the script. Thus, the restaurant script has a coffee shop track, a Chinese restaurant track, a cafeteria track, perhaps even a McDonald's track. The variable representing the decor may take on the value "fancy" or "crummy." The waiter values include "polite,"

"surly," and "bad enough to prompt a complaint." Exiting entails the operational options "pay waiter" or "pay cashier," and so forth.

Scripts can vary in many ways. They can be highly abstract, culturally pervasive, and may owe their existence only slightly to direct personal experience (for example, the script that links "temptation," "transgression," and "retribution"). Or they may be highly concrete, idiosyncratic, and directly tied to experience (for example, the scripted episode in which Daddy comes home from work, asks Mommy what's for dinner, she gets annoyed and sulks and, depending on what his day has been like, he either apologizes or gets angry too). The importance of scripts to the intuitive scientist lies in the speed and ease with which they make events (or secondhand accounts of events) readily comprehensible and predictable. Their potential cost, as always, is the possibility of erroneous interpretations, inaccurate expectations, and inflexible modes of response.

Personae

Central to any dramatic script is the *dramatis personae,* or cast of characters. Indeed, to specify the characters is often sufficient to convey much of the action of the script (for example, "the prostitute with the heart of gold and the scholarly but naive young man" or "the crusty but benign older physician and the hot-headed, idealistic young surgeon").

Social judgments and expectations often are mediated by a class of schemas which we shall term "personae," that is, cognitive structures representing the personal characteristics and typical behaviors of particular "stock characters." Some personae are the unique products of one's own personal experience (good old Aunt Mary, Coach Whiplasch). Others are shared within the culture or subculture (the sexpot, the earth-mother, the girl-next-door, the redneck, the schlemiel, the rebel-without-a-cause). Many of the shared personae are borrowed from fiction (Shakespeare's tortured Hamlet or television's bigoted Archie Bunker) or even from the popularized professional jargon of psychology and psychiatry (the authoritarian, the "Type A" personality, the anal-compulsive).

Our store of personae is augmented further by metaphors drawn from the animal kingdom and from the many occupational roles in our society. Animal or occupational personae are apt to be very simple and "concept-like," primarily highlighting a limited set of physical or behavioral characteristics. Hence, we readily understand, and are apt to be strongly influenced by, remarks like, "What do you see in that big *ox*," or "I wouldn't trust that *viper* if I were you," or "He wants you to be his Haldeman," or "Surgeon Blochit is a real butcher" (or, alternatively, "Butcher Phelps is a real surgeon").

In each instance the persona constitutes a knowledge structure which, when evoked, influences social judgments and behaviors. Once the principal features or beaviors of a given individual suggest a particular persona, subsequent expectations of and responses to that individual are apt to be dictated in part by the characteristics of the persona.

The concept of a persona is not essentially different from that of stereotype. We prefer the term persona, however, because it lacks the pejorative implications of the term "stereotype," which has been used to describe culturally shared, indeed hackneyed, notions of particular groups of people. The persona is also similar to the notion of a "person-prototype," proposed and investigated by Cantor and Mischel (1977).

Availability, Representativeness, and the Arousal of Knowledge Structures

The notion that the layperson's experience, understanding, and inferences are structured by a great and varied store of schemas is intuitively satisfying. Indeed, it has become increasingly clear to theorists working in almost all areas of psychology that the schema construct is a cornerstone of psychological theory (Neisser 1976). Workers in social interaction (Berne 1964; Goffman 1959), personality and psychopathology (G. Kelly 1955, 1958), visual perception (Minsky 1975), and especially in language comprehension and artificial intelligence (Abelson 1978; Bobrow & Collins 1976; Bower, Black & Turner in press; Rumelhart, 1976; Rumelhart & Ortony 1976; Schank 1975) all have made essentially the same point — that objects and events in the phenomenal world are almost never approached as if they were *sui generis* configurations but rather are assimilated into preexisting structures in the mind of the perceiver. . . .

It seems equally clear that the representativeness heuristic takes part in the selection of schemas. Indeed, the similarity of the data at hand to some stored representation of objects and events always has been presumed to be the chief determinant of schema arousal and application. But it also seems likely that purely incidental and irrelevant features of the stimulus may prompt the arousal of schemas tagged with similar incidental features. Thus, we have it on the testimony of Colonel House (May 1973) that, on the eve of World War I, President Woodrow Wilson was anguishing over the possibility of war with *Great Britain*. Why? Because, as on the eve of the War of 1812, the British were illegally searching American ships and, as Wilson agonized to House, "Madison and I are the only Princeton men to become President"(!) Apparently, the "search-ships/war with England" schema was a representative one for Wilson in part because of the irrelevant surface detail of the alma mater of the incumbent president.

Availability and representativeness determinants of schema arousal appear to be the probable focal guides of future research in this area. It will be fascinating to see whether these determinants operate in a normatively appropriate way, or whether, as in the Wilson anecdote, they operate so as to leave us at the mercy of arbitrary and incidental features of stimuli and structures.

Appropriate and Inappropriate Utilization of Knowledge Structures

It would be even more foolish to criticize people's general tendency to employ schemas and other knowledge structures than it would be to criticize their general tendency to rely on the availability and representativeness heuristics. Indeed, the primary reason for the widespread acceptance of the notion of schematic knowledge structures is that it is almost impossible to imagine how mental life could be managed without them. In a world characterized by recurrent stimuli presenting important functional equivalencies, any cognitive system that places a premium on minimizing computing time and effort must take advantage of such redundancy by storing generic concepts, events, event-sequences, and the like.

Despite the important efficiencies that accrue to the schema user, there seems little doubt there often are serious costs as well. Schemas are apt to be overused and misapplied, particularly to the social sphere, and they are apt to be used when other, less rapid and intuitive methods of judgment would fully merit the additional time and effort required.

In the physical world, stimuli categorized in a particular way, or events interpreted in terms of a given schema, may be similar to an extent rarely true in the social domain. In many important respects, it is only a slight overstatement to say that "if you've seen one oak tree, you've seen them all." The number of properties necessary to define uniquely many types of physical objects is highly limited. As a consequence, the number of properties of a particular object that must be perceived in order to place the object in its correct category also is limited. Moreover, once a physical object has been placed in some conceptual category, one can usually disregard much of the information that dictated the categorization (that is, information specifying exactly how, when, and under what observation conditions a particular tree satisfied the requirements for assignment to the "oak" category). Most important of all, classification of a physical object usually permits one to adduce or predict confidently additional properties of the object. Thus, once an object is correctly characterized as an oak tree, it is nearly certain that the tree will provide shade and acorns, that its wood will be hard and burn slowly, that all its leaves will drop in the fall, and so on.

It is quite different in the social domain, in which the observed properties are less diagnostic, in which the number of properties suggestive of a given category are not so sharply delineated, and in which the number of properties that can be inferred confidently, given correct categorization of the object, is very small. To appreciate these differences, let us note how the categorization of a person as a "bigot" differs from the categorization of an object as an oak tree. First, the number of properties that might indicate bigotry is, for all practical purposes, infinite, and information about the circumstances in which a particular person satisfied the "bigot" criterion can be ignored or forgotten only at one's peril. Similarly, the number of properties dictated by the categorization of someone as a bigot is large only in proportion to the naiveté of the perceiver. Few characteristics or behaviors can be confidently assumed about any particular "bigot." Schemas in the social domain rarely are more than rough outlines and tentative guides for perception and behavior. When they are relied on heavily, there are bound to be inferential errors and misguided actions.

E. R. May, in his fascinating book entitled *"Lessons" of the Past* (1973), presented some thought-provoking examples of erroneous political judgments and policies that seem to have originated in the overutilization or misapplication of particular schemas. For example, May describes how a schema, which might be termed the "Munich Conference" script, 'exerted an undue influence on the thinking of politicians (most notably

President Lyndon Johnson), who invoked the specter of the infamous "Munich Conference" to defend the aggressiveness of their military policy or the intransigence of their diplomacy. These politicians seem to have been influenced greatly by — or perhaps hoped to influence the public and their potential detractors through — a particularly vivid, historic script. The script has two scenes or vignettes, *"The Political Compromise,"* in which one yields to a power-hungry and unprincipled foe, and *"The Military Consequence,"* in which one's country or that of one's ally is subsequently overrun by the foe. To the extent that politicians rely on such historical scripts, they may be unduly dogmatic and constrained and may be unresponsive to features that ought to distinguish a current political decision from an historical one. They may even be unduly responsive to prominent but superficial considerations of script representativeness, that is, the Munich script may be particularly likely to be evoked if the foreign leader requests the conference in his own country rather than on neutral grounds or if he has a small moustache!

A "persona" can mislead as badly as a script can, as other examples from May's book show. President Harry Truman, a man not given to speaking kindly of all whom he met, demonstrated a peculiar willingness to trust his wartime ally, Joseph Stalin. His personal correspondences reveal a surprising source of this trust. To Truman, Stalin evoked the persona of Tom Pendergast, his former Missouri benefactor. Pendergast was a ruthless and corrupt political kingmaker, but he had always been completely trustworthy in his relations with Truman. Apparently because some of Stalin's characteristics were representative of the Pendergast persona, Truman seemed to feel that other Pendergast characteristics also could be assumed — specifically, trustworthiness in matters relating to Truman.

To May's examples, of schema-induced errors in the judgment of politicians, we add one related to us by Dorwin Cartwright. Cartwright told us that spokesmen for the pure sciences, lobbying for financial aid in the postwar period of the late forties and early fifties, effectively argued that the technological innovations of World War II had "depleted the stockpile of basic knowledge." Congressmen, accustomed to arguments about the depletion of stockpiles and the need for replenishing them, apparently accepted the idea that the "basic knowledge stockpile" was one of those depleted. The "stockpile" concept, as applied to basic scientific knowledge, is not entirely invalid, that is, the more knowledge the better, the more money and effort spent, the faster it will grow, and so on. But the "depletion" schema is invalid and highly misleading. For heavy use of basic scientific knowledge, far from exhausting the "stockpile," makes it grow. . . .

An example of inappropriate schema usage that may hit even closer to home is the behavior of the typical faculty committee charged to select students for a graduate program. A letter of recommendation for Elsa Doud may note that Ms. Doud was shy in Professor Smith's class at Ohio State. Doud's shyness and "midwesternness" may call to mind Priscilla Frimp, another shy midwestern woman who never made it through the program. The Frimp persona may then be used as a basis to reject Doud. Any reliance on personae in such a situation is utterly without foundation. The only currently valid grounds for predicting graduate performance seem to be the candidate's GRE (Graduate Record Examination) scores, grades, research experience, quality of undergraduate institution, and evaluations in letters of recommendation. Of course, if the Anti-Doud professor wishes to construct a shyness measure and can show that it is related to quality of the entire pool of applicants and reject those scoring high on it. If an interaction among shyness, sex, and region of the country is found, such that shyness is particularly crippling to the performance of midwestern females, then a lower cutoff point on the shyness scale may be set for midwestern females than for male or female students from other parts of the country. Unless the professor is willing to perform the requisite validation research, however, any persona ruminations should be kept out of the student procedure.

INFERENTIAL ADJUSTMENT AND ITS LIMITATIONS

In this chapter we described some inferential strategies on which the lay scientist seems to rely in forming judgments of the social world. There were two common themes in our observations. The first and more obvious — that people's errors and insights are intimately linked together and are typically a matter of appropriate versus inappropriate application of a given heuristic, theory, or schema — was reiterated often enough that we trust it needs no reemphasis. There was a second and less obvious theme that merits some elaboration. At several points we emphasized that it is not only people's eagerness to apply simple heuristics and immediately

available knowledge structures that leads to grief; it is also the failure to make necessary *adjustments* of initial judgments. That is, once a simple heuristic or or schema has been used, subsequent considerations fail to exert as much impact as common sense or normative considerations might dictate that it should.

Some simple, direct demonstrations of inadequate adjustment or "anchoring" effects were provided in work by Tversky and Kahneman (1974). In one study, for example, subjects were asked to adjust an arbitrary initial estimate of the percentage of African countries in the United Nations. Those starting with "anchors" of 10 percent and 65 percent produced "adjusted" estimates of 25 percent and 45 percent, respectively. The same anchoring effects were demonstrated with initial "estimates" dictated by the subject's own previous spin of a roulette wheel! Even though it would have been obvious to the subjects that these "starting points" were wholly arbitrary and unrelated to the judgment task, they nevertheless had an influence on final estimates.

Our present contention is essentially an extension of Tversky's and Kahneman's point about the effects of a cognitive "anchor." That is, once subjects have made a first pass at a problem, the initial judgment may prove remarkably resistant to further information, alternative modes of reasoning, and even logical or evidential challenges. Attempts to integrate new information may find the individual surprisingly "conservative," that is, willing to yield ground only grudgingly and primed to challenge the relevance, reliability, or authority of subsequent information or logical consideration. As a result, the method of first choice — and we believe heuristics and schemas to be such methods of first choice — may have disproportionate impact, while other methods (notably, methods considering pallid base lines, mitigating situational factors, possible sources of unreliability in the data, and the like) have relatively little impact.

SUMMARY

The chapter describes two of the general tools that people use to "go beyond the information given," judgmental heuristics and knowledge structures.

The availability heuristic is used to judge the frequency and likelihood of events and event-relations. Since the availability of remembered events is sometimes biased at the stage of sampling, sometimes at the stage of encoding and storage, and sometimes at the stage of retrieval, frequency and likelihood estimates often will be biased correspondingly.

The representativeness heuristic is used to estimate the likelihood of some state of affairs given knowledge of some other state of affairs, for example, the likelihood that an object is a member of some category because it has certain characteristics. Such judgments are based on the perceived similarity of the known characteristics of the object to the presumed essential characteristics of the category. The heuristic sometimes misleads because, in some circumstances, notably when diagnosticity is low or category base rates differ widely, mere similarity is an unreliable guide to likelihood.

In addition to heuristics, people use certain knowledge structures in approaching judgment tasks. These include relatively propositional structures such as theories and beliefs, and more schematic structures like scripts and personae. These knowledge structures are invaluable aids to understanding social events, but they may mislead to the extent that they are poor representations of external reality and to the extent that they preclude attention to the details of the actual object at hand.

The judgmental heuristics may prove to be the primary determinants of the arousal and application of the various knowledge structures. Availability of a given structure, including transient, arbitrary increments in its availability, may increase the likelihood of its application. The representativeness of a given structure, including the similarity of quite superficial and incidental features of the stimulus to features of the structure, may be a chief determinant of the arousal and application of a given structure.

It is emphasized that it is not the existence of heuristics and knowledge structures that can be criticized but rather, their overuse, misuse, and use in preference to more appropriate strategies. Even when more appropriate strategies are subsequently employed for a given judgmental task, the undue influence of the simpler, more intuitive strategies may persist.

REFERENCES

Abelson, R. P. Psychological implication. In R. P. Abelson, E. Aronson, W. J. McGuire, T. M. Newcomb, M. J. Rosenberg, & P. H. Tannenbaum (Eds.), *Theories of cognitive consistency: A sourcebook.* Chicago: Rand McNally, 1968.

Abelson, R. P. Script processing in attitude formation and decision making. In J.S. Carroll & J. W. Payne (Eds.), *Cognition and social behavior.* Hillsdale, N.J.: Lawrence Erlbaum, 1976.

Abelson, R. P. *Scripts.* Invited address to the Midwestern Psychological Association, Chicago, May 1978.

Arkin, R., & Duval, S. Focus of attention and causal attributions of actors and observers. *Journal of Experimental Social Psychology,* 1975, *11,* 427–438.

Bartlett, F. C. *Remembering.* Cambridge: Cambridge University Press, 1932.

Bem, D. J., & Allen, A. On predicting some of the people some of the time: The search for cross-situational consistencies in behavior. *Psychological Review,* 1974, *81,* 506–520.

Bem, D. J., & Funder, D. C. Predicting more of the people more of the time: Assessing the personality of situations. *Psychological Review,* 1978, *85,* 485–501.

Berne, E. *Games people play.* New York: Grove Press, 1964.

Borrow, D., & Collins, A. *Representation and understanding: Studies in cognitive science.* New York: Academic Press, 1976.

Bower, G., Black, J., & Turner, T. Scripts in text comprehension and memory. *Cognitive Psychology,* in press.

Bruner, J. S. Going beyond the information given. In H. Gulber and others (Eds.), *Contemporary approaches to cognition.* Cambridge, Mass.: Harvard University Press, 1957.

Cantor, N., & Mischel, W. Traits as prototypes: Effects on recognition memory. *Journal of Personality and Social Psychology,* 1977, *35,* 38–49.

Cantor, N., & Mischel, W. Prototypicality and personality: Effects on free recall and personality impressions. *Journal of Research in Personality,* in press.

Christie, R., & Geis, F. L. (Eds.), *Studies in Machiavellianism.* New York: Academic Press, 1970.

Collins, B. E. Four components of the Rotter internal-external scale: Belief in a difficult world, a just world, a predictable world, and a politically responsive world. *Journal of Personality and Social Psychology,* 1974, *29,* 381–391.

Crandall, V. C., Katkovsky, W., & Crandall, V. G. Children's beliefs in their own control of reinforcements in intellectual-academic achievement situations. *Child Development,* 1965, *36,* 91–109.

De Soto, C. B. The predilection for single orderings. *Journal of Abnormal and Social Psychology,* 1961, *62,* 16–23.

Duval, S., & Wicklund, R. A. *A theory of objective self-awareness.* New York: Academic Press, 1972.

Fischhoff, B. Hindsight ≠ foresight: The effect of outcome knowledge on judgment under uncertainty. *Journal of Experimental Psychology: Human Perception and Performance,* 1975, *1,* 288–299.

Fischhoff, B., & Beyth, R. "I knew it would happen" — remembered probabilities of once-future things. *Organizational Behavior and Human Performance,* 1975, *13,* 1–16.

Goffman, E. *The presentation of self in everyday life.* New York: Doubleday, 1959.

Hartshorne, H., & May, M. A. *Studies in the nature of character.* Vol. I. *Studies in deceit.* New York: Macmillan, 1928.

Heider, F. *The psychology of interpersonal relations.* New York: Wiley, 1958.

Higgins, E. T. & Rholes, W. S. Impression formation and role fulfillment: A "holistic reference" approach. *Journal of Experimental Social Psychology,* 1976, *12,* 422–435.

Higgins, E. T., Rholes, W. S., & Jones, C. R. Category accessibility and impression formation. *Journal of Experimental Social Psychology,* 1977, *13,* 141–154.

Hornstein, H. A., LaKind, E., Frankel, G., & Manne, S. Effects of knowledge about remote social events on prosocial behavior, social conception, and mood. *Journal of Personality and Social Psychology,* 1975, *32,* 1038–1046.

Jones, E. E., & Nisbett, R. E. The actor and the observer: Divergent perceptions of the causes of behavior. In E. E. Jones and others (Eds.), *Attribution: Perceiving the causes of behavior.* Morristown, N.J.: General Learning Press, 1972.

Kahneman, D., & Tversky, A. Subjective probability: A judgment of representativeness. *Cognitive Psychology,* 1972, *3,* 430–454.

Kahneman, D., & Tversky, A. On the psychology of prediction. *Psychological Review,* 1973, *80,* 237–251.

Kahneman, D., & Tversky, A. Intuitive prediction: Biases and corrective procedures. *Management Science,* in press.

Kelley, H. H. Causal schemata and the attribution process. In E. E. Jones and others (Eds.), *Attribution: Perceiving the causes of behavior.* Morristown: N.J.: General Learning Press, 1972. (b)

Kelly, G. *The psychology of personal constructs* (2 vols.). New York: Norton, 1955.

Kelly, G. Man's construction of his alternatives. In G. Lindzey (Ed.), *Assessment of human motives.* New York: Holt, Rinehart & Winston, 1958.

Kuhn, T. S. *The structure of scientific revolutions.* Chicago: University of Chicago Press, 1962.

Lefcourt, H. M. Internal vs. external control of reinforcement revisited: Recent developments. In B. A. Maher (Ed.), *Progress in Experimental Personality Research* (Vol. 6). New York: Academic Press, 1972.

Lewin, K. *A dynamic theory of personality.* New York: McGraw-Hill, 1935.

Markus, H. Self-schemata and processing information about the self. *Journal of Personality and Social Psychology,* 1977, *35,* 63–78.

May, E. R. *"Lessons" of the past.* New York: Oxford University Press, 1973.

McArthur, L. Z. & Post, D. Figural emphasis and person perception. *Journal of Experimental Social Psychology,* 1977, *13,* 520–535.

McArthur, L. Z., & Solomon, L. K. Perceptions of an aggressive encounter as a function of the victim's salience and the perceiver's arousal. *Journal of Personality and Social Psychology,* 1978, *36,* 1278-1290.

Minsky, M. A framework for representing knowledge. In P. H. Winston (Ed.), *The psychology of computer vision.* New York: McGraw-Hill, 1975.

Mischel, W. *Personality and assessment.* New York: Wiley, 1968.

Neisser, U. *Cognition and reality: Principles and implications of cognitive psychology.* San Francisco: Freeman, 1976.

Newcomb, T. M. *Consistency of certain extrovert-introvert behavior patterns in 51 problem boys.* New York: Columbia University, Teachers College, Bureau of Publications, 1929.

Piaget, J. *La naissance de l'intelligence chez l'enfant.* Neuchatel et Paris: Delachau et Niestle, 1936.

Regan, D. T., & Totten, J. Empathy and attribution: Turning observers into actors. *Journal of Personality and Social Psychology,* 1975, *32,* 850-856.

Rosch, E. Principles of categorization. In E. Rosch & B. Lloyd (Eds.), *Cognition and categorization.* Hillsdale, N.J.: Lawrence Erlbaum, 1978.

Ross, L. The intuitive psychologist and his shortcomings. In L. Berkowitz (Ed.) *Advances in Experimental Social Psychology* (Vol. 10). New York: Academic Press, 1977. (a)

Ross, L. Afterthoughts on the intuitive psychologist. In L. Berkowitz (Ed.), *Cognitive theories in social psychology.* New York: Academic Press, 1978.

Ross, L., & Anderson, C. Shortcomings in the attribution process: On the origins and maintenance of erroneous social assessments. In A. Tversky, D. Kahneman & P. Slovic (Eds.), *Judgment under uncertainty: Heuristics and biases.* New York: Cambridge University Press, 1980.

Ross, L., Lepper, M. R., Strack, F., & Steinmetz, J. L. Social explanation and social expectation: The effects of real and hypothetical explanations upon subjective likelihood. *Journal of Personality and Social Psychology,* 1977, *35,* 817-829.

Ross, L., Turiel, E., Josephson, J., & Lepper, M. R. *Developmental perspectives on the fundamental attribution error.* Unpublished manuscript, Stanford University, 1978.

Rotter, J. B. Generalized expectancies for internal versus external control of reinforcement. *Psychological Monographs,* 1966, *80* (609).

Rumelhart, D. E. Understanding and summarizing brief stories. In D. LaBerge & S. J. Samuels (Eds.), *Basic processes in reading: Perception and comprehension.* Hillsdale, N.J.: Lawrence Erlbaum, 1976.

Rumelhart, D. E., & Ortony, A. The presentation of knowledge in memory. In R. C. Anderson, R. J. Spiro, & W. E. Montague, (Eds.), *Schooling and the acquisition of knowledge.* Hillsdale, N.J.: Lawrence Earlbaum, 1976.

Schank, R. C. *Conceptual information processing.* Amsterdam: North Holland, 1975.

Schank, R., & Abelson, R. P. *Scripts, plans, goals and understanding: An inquiry into human knowledge structures.* Hillsdale, N.J.: Lawrence Erlbaum, 1977.

Seligman, M. E. P. *Helplessness: On depression, development and death.* San Francisco: W. H. Freeman, 1975.

Storms, M. D. Videotape and the attribution process: Reversing actors' and observers' point of view. *Journal of Personality and Social Psychology,* 1973, *27,* 165-175.

Taylor, S. E., & Crocker, J. C. Schematic bases of social information processing. In E. T. Higgins, P. Herman, & M. P. Zanna (Eds.), *The Ontario Symposium on Personality and Social Psychology* (Vol. 1). Hillsdale, N.J.: Lawrence Erlbaum, 1980.

Taylor, S. E., & Fiske, S. T. Point of view and perceptions of causality. *Journal of Personality and Social Psychology,* 1975, *32,* 439-445.

Taylor, S. E., & Fiske, S. T. Salience, attention and attribution: Top of the head phenomena. In L. Berkowitz (Ed.), *Advances in Experimental Social Psychology* (Vol. 11). New York: Academic Press, 1978.

Tomkins, A. Script theory: Differential magnification of affects. In H. E. Howes & R. A. Dienstbier (Eds.), *Nebraska Symposium on Motivation.* (Vol. 26). Lincoln, Neb.: University of Nebraska Press, 1979.

Tversky, A. Features of similarity. *Psychological Review,* 1977, *84,* 327-352.

Tversky, A., & Kahneman, D. Belief in the law of small numbers. *Psychological Bulletin,* 1971, *76,* 105–110.

Tversky, A., & Kahneman, D. Availability: A heuristic for judging frequency and probability. *Cognitive Psychology,* 1973, *5,* 207–232.

Tversky, A., & Kahneman, D. Judgment under uncertainty: Heuristics and biases. *Science,* 1974, *185,* 1124–1131.

Weber, M. *The protestant ethic and the spirit of capitalism.* (T. Parsons, trans.). New York: Scribner, 1930. (Originally published, 1904.)

Wittgenstein, L. *Philosophical investigations.* New York: MacMillan, 1953.

Two conflicting beliefs in a single
mind don't cohabit comfortably.
To defend his ego, man becomes

30. The Rationalizing Animal

Elliot Aronson

Man likes to think of himself as a rational animal. However, it is more true that man is a *rationalizing* animal, that he attempts to appear reasonable to himself and to others. Albert Camus even said that man is a creature who spends his entire life in an attempt to convince himself that he is not absurd.

Some years ago a woman reported that she was receiving messages from outer space. Word came to her from the planet Clarion that her city would be destroyed by a great flood on December 21. Soon a considerable number of believers shared her deep commitment to the prophecy. Some of them quit their jobs and spent their savings freely in anticipation of the end.

On the evening of December 20, the prophet and her followers met to prepare for the event. They believed that flying saucers would pick them up, thereby sparing them from disaster. Midnight arrived, but no flying saucers. December 21 dawned, but no flood.

What happens when prophecy fails? Social psychologists Leon Festinger, Henry Riecken, and Stanley Schacther infiltrated the little band of believers to see how they would react. They predicted that persons who had expected the disaster, but awaited it alone in their homes, would simply lose faith in the prophecy. But those who awaited the outcome in a group, who had thus admitted their belief publicly, would come to believe even more strongly in the prophecy and turn into active proselytizers.

This is exactly what happened. At first the faithful felt despair and shame because all their predictions had been for nought. Then, after waiting nearly five hours for the saucers, the prophet had a new vision. The city had been spared, she said, because of the trust and faith of her devoted group. This revelation was elegant in its simplicity, and the believers accepted it enthusiastically. They now sought the press that they had previously avoided. They turned from believers into zealots.

LIVING ON THE FAULT

In 1957 Leon Festinger proposed his theory of *cognitive dissonance,* which describes and predicts man's rationalizing behavior. Dissonance occurs whenever a person simultaneously holds two inconsistent cognitions (ideas, beliefs, opinions). For example, the belief that the world will end on a certain day is dissonant with the awareness, when the day breaks, that the world has not ended. Festinger manintained that this state of inconsistency is so uncomfortable that people strive to reduce the conflict in the easiest way possible. They will change one or both cognitions so that they will "fit together" better.

Consider what happens when a smoker is confronted with evidence that smoking causes cancer. He will become motivated to change either his attitudes about smoking or his behavior. And as anyone who has tried to quit knows, the former alternative is easier.

The smoker may decide that the studies are lousy. He may point to friends ("If Sam, Jack and Harry smoke, cigarettes can't be all that dangerous"). He may conclude that filters trap all the cancer-producing materials. Or he may argue that he would rather live a short and happy life with cigarettes than a long and miserable life without them.

The more a person is committed to a course of action, the more resistant he will be to information that threatens that course. Psychologists have reported that the couple who are least likely to believe the dangers of smoking are those who tried to quit — and failed. They have become more committed to smoking. Similarly, a person who builds a $100,000 house astride the San Andreas Fault will be less receptive to arguments about imminent earthquakes than would a person who is renting the house for a few months. The new homeowner is committed; he doesn't want to believe that he did an absurd thing.

When a person reduces his dissonance, he defends his ego, and keeps a positive self-image. But self-justification can reach startling extremes; people will ignore danger in order to avoid dissonance, even when that ignorance can cause their deaths. I mean that literally.

Suppose you are Jewish in a country occupied by Hitler's forces. What should you do? You could try to leave the country; you could try to pass as "Aryan"; you could do nothing and hope for the best. The first two choices are dangerous: if you are caught you will be executed. If you decide to sit tight, you will try to convince yourself that you made the best decision. You may reason that while Jews are indeed being treated unfairly, they are not being killed unless they break the law.

Now suppose that a respected man from your town announces that he has seen Jews being butchered mercilessly, including everyone who had recently been deported from your village. If you believe him, you might have a chance to escape. If you don't believe him, you and your family will be slaughtered.

Dissonance theory would predict that you will not listen to the witness, because to do so would be to admit that your judgment and decisions were wrong. You will dismiss his information as untrue, and decide that he was lying or hallucinating. Indeed, Eli Wiesel reported that this happened to the Jews in Sighet, a small town in Hungary, in 1944. Thus people are not passive receptacles for the deposit of information. The manner in which they view and distort the objective world in order to avoid and reduce dissonance is entirely predictable. But one cannot divide the world into rational people on one side and dissonance reducers on the other. While people vary in their ability to tolerate dissonance, we are all capable of rational or irrational behavior, depending on the circumstances — some of which follow.

DISSONANCE BECAUSE OF EFFORT

Judson Mills and I found that if people go through a lot of trouble to gain admission to a group, and the group turns out to be dull and dreary, they will experience dissonance. It is a rare person who will accept this situation with an "Oh, pshaw. I worked hard for nothing. Too bad." One way to resolve the dissonance is to decide that the group is worth the effort it took to get admitted.

We told a number of college women that they would have to undergo an initiation to join a group that would discuss the psychology of sex. One third of them had severe initiation: they had to recite a list of obscene words and read some lurid sexual passages from novels in the presence of a male experimenter (in 1959, this really was a "severe" and embarrassing task). One third went through a mild initiation in which they read words that were sexual but not obscene (such as "virgin" and "petting"); and the last third had no initiation at all. Then all of the women listened to an extremely boring taped discussion of the group they had presumably joined. The women in the severe initiation group rated the discussion and its drab participants much more favorably than those in the other groups.

I am not asserting that people enjoy painful experiences, or that they enjoy things that are associated with painful experiences. If you got hit on the head by a brick on the way to a fraternity initiation, you would not like that group any better. But if you volunteered to get hit with a brick *in order to join* the fraternity, you definitely would like the group more than if you had been admitted without fuss.

After a decision—especially a difficult one that involves much time, money, or effort—people almost always experience dissonance. Awareness of defects in the preferred object is dissonance with having chosen it; awareness of positive aspects of the unchosen object is dissonant with having rejected it.

Accordingly, researchers have found that *before* making a decision, people seek as much information as possible about the alternatives. Afterwards, however, they seek reassurance that they did the right thing, and do so by seeking information in support of their choice or by simply changing the information that is already in their heads. In one of the earliest experiments on dissonance theory, Jack Brehm gave a group of women their choice between two appliances, such as a toaster or a blender, that they had previously rated for desirability. When the subjects reevaluated the appliances after choosing one of them, they increased their liking for the one they had chosen and downgraded their evaluation of the rejected appliance. Similarly, Danuta Ehrlich and her associates found that a person about to buy a new car does so carefully, reading all ads and accepting facts openly on advertisements more selectively, and he will tend to avoid ads for Volkswagens, Chevrolets, and so on.

THE DECISION TO BEHAVE IMMORALLY

Your conscience, let us suppose, tells you that it is wrong to cheat, lie, steal seduce your neighbor's husband or wife, or whatever. Let us suppose further that you are in a situation in which you are sorely tempted to ignore your conscience. If you give in to temptation, the cognition "I am a decent moral person" will be dissonant with the cognition "I have committed an immoral act." If you resist, the cognition "I want to get a good grade (have that money, seduce that person)" is dissonant with the cognition "I could have acted so as to get that grade, but I chose not to."

The easiest way to reduce dissonance in either case is to minimize the negative aspects of the action one has chosen, and to change one's attitude about its immorality. If Mr. C. decides to cheat, he will probably decide that cheating isn't really so bad. It hurts no one; everyone does it; its part of human nature. If Mr. D. decides not to cheat, he will no doubt come to believe that cheating is a sin, and deserves severe punishment.

The point here is that the initial attitudes of these men is virtually the same. Moreover, their decisions could be a hair's breadth apart. But once the action is taken, their attitudes diverge sharply.

Judson Mills confirmed these speculations in an experiment with sixth-grade children. First he measured their attitudes toward cheating, and then put them in a competitive situation. He arranged the test so that is was impossible to win without cheating, and so it was easy for the children to cheat, thinking they would be unwatched. The next day, he asked the children again how they felt about cheating. Those who had cheated on the test had become more lenient in their attitudes; those who had resisted the temptation adopted harsher attitudes.

These data are provocative. They suggest that the most zealous crusaders are not those who are removed from the problem they oppose. I would hazard to say that the people who are most angry about "the sexual promiscruity of the young" are *not* those who have never dreamed of being promiscuous. On the contrary, they would be persons who had been seriously tempted by illicit sex, who came very close to giving in to their desires, but who finally resisted. People who almost live in glass houses are the ones who are most likely to throw stones.

INSUFFICIENT JUSTIFICATION

If I offer George $20 to do a boring task, and offer Richard $1 to do the same thing, which one will decide that the assignment was mildly interesting? If I threaten one child with harsh punishment if he does something forbidden, and threaten another child with mild punishment, which one will transgress?

Dissonance theory predicts that when people find themselves doing something and they have neither been rewarded adequately for doing it nor threatened with dire consequences for not doing it, they will find *internal* reasons for their behavior.

Suppose you dislike Woodrow Wilson, and I want you to make a speech in his favor. The most efficient thing I can do is to pay you a lot of money for making the speech, or threaten to kill you if you don't. In either case, you will probably comply with my wish, but you won't change your attitude toward Wilson. If that were my goal, I would have to give you a *minimal* reward or threat. Then, in order not to appear absurd, you would have to seek additional reasons for your speech—this could lead you to find good things about Wilson and hence, to conclude that you really do like Wilson after all. Lying produces great attitude change only when the liar is undercompensated.

Festinger and J. Merrill Carlsmith asked college students to work on boring and repetitive tasks. Then the experimenters persuaded the students to lie about the work, to tell a fellow student that the task would be interesting and enjoyable. They offered half of their subjects $20 for telling the lie, and they offered the others only $1. Later they asked all subjects how much they had really liked the tasks.

The students who earned $20 for their lies rated the work as deadly dull, which it was. They experienced no dissonance: they lied, but they were well paid for that behavior. By contrast, students who got $1 decided that the tasks were rather enjoyable. The dollar was apparently enough to get them to tell the lie, but not enough to keep them from feeling that lying for so paltry a sum was foolish. To reduce dissonance, they decided that they hadn't lied after all; the task was fun.

Similarly, Carlsmith and I found that mild threats are more effective than harsh threats in changing a child's attitude about a forbidden object, in this case a delightful toy. In the severe-threat condition, children refrained from playing with the toys and had a good reason for refraining—the very severity of the threat provided ample justification for not playing with the toy. In the mild-threat condition, however, the children refrained from playing with the toy but when they asked themselves, ''How come I'm not playing with the toy?'' they did not have a superabundant justification (because the threat was not terribly severe). Accordingly, they provided additional justification in the form of convincing themselves that the attractive toy was really not very attractive and that they didn't really want to play with it very much in the first place. Jonathan Freedman extended our findings and showed that severe threats do not have a lasting effect on a child's behavior. Mild threats, by contrast, can change behavior for many months.

Perhaps the most extraordinary example of insufficient justification occurred in India, where Jamuna Prasad analyzed the rumors that were circulated after a terrible earthquake in 1950. Prasad found that people in towns that were *not* in immediate danger were spreading rumors of impending doom from floods, cyclones, or unforeseeable calamities. Certainly the rumors could not help people feel more secure; why then perpetrate them? I believe that dissonance helps explain this phenomenon. The people were terribly frightened—after all, the neighboring villages had been destroyed—but they did not have ample excuse for their fear, since the earthquake had missed them. So they invented their own excuse; if a cyclone is on the way, it is reasonable to be afraid. Later, Durganand Sinha studied rumors in a town that had actually been destroyed. The people were scared, but they had good reason to be; they didn't need to seek additional justification for their terror. And their rumors showed no predictions of impending disaster and no serious exaggerations.

THE DECISION TO BE CRUEL

The need for people to believe that they are kind and decent can lead them to say and do unkind and indecent things. After the National Guard killed four students at Kent State, several rumors quickly spread: the slain girls were pregnant, so their deaths spared their families from shame; the students were filthy and had lice on them. These rumors were totally untrue, but the townspeople were eager to believe them. Why? The local people were conservative, and infuriated at the radical behavior of some of the students. Many had hoped that the students would get their comeuppance. But death is an awfully severe penalty. The severity of this penalty outweighs and is dissonant with the ''crimes'' of the students. In these circumstances, any information that put the victims in a bad light reduces dissonance by implying, in effect, that it was good that the young people died. One high-school teacher even avowed that anyone with ''long hair, dirty clothes, or [who goes] barefooted deserves to be shot.''

Keith Davis and Edward Jones demonstrated the need to justify cruelty. They persuaded students to help them with an experiment, in the course of which the volunteers had to tell another student that he was a shallow, untrustworthy, and dull person. Volunteers managed to convince themselves that they didn't like the victim of their cruel analysis. They found him less attractive than they did before they had to criticize him.

Similarly, David Glass persuaded a group of subjects to deliver electric shocks to others. The subjects, again, decided that the victim must deserve the cruelty; they rated him as stupid, mean, etc. Then Glass went a step further. He found that a subject with high self-esteem was most likely to derogate the victim. This led Glass to conclude, ironically, that it is precisely because a person thinks he is nice that he decides that the person he has hurt is a rat. "Since nice guys like me don't go around hurting innocent people," Glass's subjects seemed to say, "you must have deserved it." But individuals who have *low* self-esteem do not feel the need to justify their behavior and derogate their victims; it is *consonant* for such persons to believe they have behaved badly. "Worthless people like me do unkind things."

Ellen Berscheid and her colleagues found another factor that limits the need to derogate one's victim: the victim's capacity to retaliate. If the person doing harm feels that the situation is balanced, that his victim will pay him back in coin, he has no need to justify his behavior. In Berscheid's experiment, which involved electric shocks, college students did not derogate or dislike the persons they shocked if they believed the victims could retaliate. Students who were led to believe that the victims would not be able to retaliate *did* derogate them. Her work suggests that soldiers may have a greater need to disparage civilian victims (because they can't retaliate) than military victims. Lt. William L. Calley, who considered the "gooks" at My Lai to be something less than human, would be a case in point.

DISSONANCE AND THE SELF-CONCEPT

On the basis of recent experiments, I have reformulated Festinger's original theory in terms of the self concept. That is, dissonance is most powerful when self-esteem is threatened. Thus the important aspect of dissonance is not "I said one thing and I believe another," but "I have misled people — and I am a truthful, nice person." Conversely, the cognitions, "I believe the task is dull," and "I told someone the task was interesting," are not dissonant for a psychopathic liar.

David Mettee and I predicted in a recent experiment that persons who had low opinions of themselves would be more likely to cheat than persons with high self-esteem. We assumed that if an average person gets a temporary blow to his self-esteem (by being jilted, say, or not getting a promotion), he will temporarily feel stupid and worthless, and hence do any number of stupid and worthless things — cheat at cards, bungle an assignment, break a valuable vase.

Mettee and I temporarily changed 45 female students' self-esteem. We gave one third of them positive feedback about a personality test they had taken (we said that they were interesting, mature, deep, etc.); we gave one third negative feedback (we said that they were relatively immature, shallow, etc.); and one third of the students got no information at all. Then all the students went on to participate in what they thought was an unrelated experiment, in which they gambled in a competitive game of cards. We arranged the situation so that the students could cheat and thereby win a considerable sum of money, or not cheat, in which case they were sure to lose.

The results showed that the students who had received blows to their self-esteem cheated far more than those who had gotten positive feedback about themselves. It may well be that low self-esteem is a critical antecedent of criminal or cruel behavior.

The theory of cognitive dissonance has proved useful in generating research; it has uncovered a wide range of data. In formal terms, however, it is a very sloppy theory. Its very simplicity provides both its greatest strength and its most serious weakness. That is, while the theory has generated a great deal of data, it has not been easy to define the limits of the theoretical statements, to determine the specific predictions that can be made. All too often researchers have had to resort the very unscientific rule of thumb, "If you want to be sure, ask Leon."

LOGIC AND PSYCHOLOGIC

Part of the problem is that the theory does not deal with *logical* inconsistency, but *psychological* inconsistency. Festinger maintains that two cognitions are inconsistent if the opposite of one follows from the other. Strictly speaking, the information that smoking causes cancer does not make it illogical to smoke. But these cognitions produce dissonance because they do not make sense psychologically, assuming that the smoker does not want cancer.

One cannot always predict dissonance with accuracy. A man may admire Franklin Roosevelt enormously and discover that throughout his marriage FDR carried out a clandestine affair. If he places a high value on fidelity and he believes that great men are not exempt from this value, then he will experience dissonance. Then I can predict that he will either change his attitudes about Roosevelt or soften his attitudes about fidelity. But, he may believe that marital infidelity and political greatness are totally unrelated; if this were the case, he might simply shrug off these data without modifying his opinions either about Roosevelt or about fidelity.

Because of the sloppiness in the theory several commentators have criticized a great many of the findings first uncovered by dissonance theory. These criticisms have served a useful purpose. Often, they have goaded us to perform more precise research, which in turn has led to a clarification of some of the findings which, ironically enough, has eliminated the alternative explanations proposed by the critics themselves.

For example, Alphonse and Natalia Chapanis argued that the "severe initiation" experiment could have completely different causes. It might be that the young women were not embarrassed at having to read sexual words, but rather were aroused, and their arousal in turn led them to rate the dull discussion group as interesting. Or, to the contrary, the women in the severe-initiation condition could have felt much sexual anxiety, followed by relief that the discussion was so banal. They associated relief with the group, and so rated it favorably.

So Harold Gerard and Grover Mathewson replicated our experiment, using electric shocks in the initiation procedure. Our findings were supported — subjects who underwent severe shocks in order to join a discussion group rated that group more favorably than subjects who had undergone mild shocks. Moreover, Gerard and Mathewson went on to show that merely linking an electric shock with the group discussion (as in a simple conditioning experiment) did not produce greater liking for the group. The increase in liking for the group occurred only when subjects volunteered for the shock *in order to* gain membership in the group — just as dissonance theory would predict.

ROUTES TO CONSONANCE

In the real world there is usually more than one way to squirm out of inconsistency. Laboratory experiments carefully control a person's alternatives, and the conclusions drawn may be misleading if applied to everyday situations. For example, suppose a prestigious university rejects a young Ph.D. for its one available teaching position. If she feels that she is a good scholar, she will experience dissonance. She can then decide that members of that department are narrow-minded and senile, sexist, and wouldn't recognize talent if it sat on their laps. Or she could decide that if they could reject someone as fine and intelligent as she, they must be

extraordinarily brilliant. Both techniques will reduce dissonance, but not that they leave this woman with totally opposite opinions about professors at the university.

This is a serious conceptual problem. One solution is to specify the conditions under which a person will take one route to consonance over another. For example if a person struggles to reach a goal and fails, he may decide that the goal wasn't worth it (as Aesop's fox did) or that the effort was justified anyway (the fox got a lot of exercise in jumping for the grapes). My own research suggests that a person will take the first means when he has expended relatively little effort. But when he has put in a great deal of effort, dissonance will take the form of justifying the energy.

This line of work is encouraging. I do not think that it is very fruitful to demand to know what *the* mode of dissonance reduction is; it is more instructive to isolate the various modes that occur, and determine the optimum conditions for each.

IGNORANCE OF ABSURDITY

No dissonance theorist takes issue with the fact that people frequently work to get rewards. In our experiments, however, small rewards tend to be associated with greater attraction and greater attitude change. Is the reverse ever true?

Jonathan Freedman told college students to work on a dull task after first telling them *(a)* their results would be of no use to him, since his experiment was basically over, or *(b)* their results would be of great value to him. Subjects in the first condition were in a state of dissonance, for they had unknowingly agreed to work on a boring chore that apparently had no purpose. They reduced their dissonance by deciding that the task was enjoyable.

Then Freedman ran the same experiment with one change. He waited until the subjects finished the task to tell them whether their work would be important. In this study he found incentive effects: students told that the task was valuable enjoyed it more than those who were told that their work was useless. In short, dissonance theory does not apply when an individual performs an action in good faith without having any way of knowing it was absurd. When we agree to participate in an experiment we naturally assume that it is for a purpose. If we are informed afterward that it *had* no purpose, how were we to have known? In this instance we like the task better if it had an important purpose. But if we agreed to perform it *knowing* that it had no purpose, we try to convince ourselves that it is an attractive task in order to avoid looking absurd.

MAN CANNOT LIVE BY CONSONANCE ALONE

Dissonance reduction is only one of several motives, and other powerful drives can counteract it. If human beings had a pervasive, all-encompassing need to reduce all forms of dissonance, we would not grow, mature, or admit to our mistakes. We would sweep mistakes under the rug, or worse, turn the mistakes into virtues; in neither case would we profit from error.

But obviously people do learn from experience. They often do tolerate dissonance because the dissonant information has great utility. A person cannot ignore forever a leaky roof, even if that flaw is inconsistent with having spent a fortune in the house. As utility increases, individuals will come to prefer dissonance-arousing but useful information. But as dissonance increases, or when commitment is high, future utility and information tend to be ignored.

It is clear that people will go to extraordinary lengths to justify their actions. They will lie, cheat, live on the San Andreas Fault, accuse innocent bystanders of being vicious provocateurs, ignore information that might save their lives, and generally engage in all manner of absurd postures. Before we write off such behavior as bizarre, crazy, or evil, we would be wise to examine the situations that set up the need to reduce dissonance. Perhaps our awareness of the mechanism that makes us so often irrational will help turn Camus' observation on absurdity into a philosophic curiosity.

B.

Individual Decisions in Organizations

31. Decision-Making Strategies

Irving L. Janis and Leon Mann

When people are required to choose among alternative courses of action, what types of search, deliberation, and selection procedure do they typically use — that is, what decision-making strategy do they adopt?[1] Unfortunately, this question has so far received relatively little attention in behavioral science research. Most of the pertinent observations of decision-making strategies consist of case studies, impressionistic surveys, and anecdotes reported by scholars in administrative science and related fields that deal with organizational policy making. Administrative scientists have much more to say than social psychologists, both in their descriptions and in their theory, about when and why a decision maker uses one type of strategy rather than another. Although originally formulated in terms of organizational policy making by managers or bureaucrats, the concepts of specialists in organizational behavior embody relevant universal psychological assumptions about human

beings as imperfect decision makers. Accordingly, we shall examine the answers they give concerning how "administrative man" typically carries out the tasks of decision making. The answers provide essential background material that we shall draw upon in developing a conflict theory concerning the causes and consequences of defective information processing — a theory we believe to be equally applicable to personal decisions (pertaining to marriage, career, health, life style, and all sorts of personal matters) and to executive decisions in an organizational context.

OPTIMIZING AND THE PERILS OF SUBOPTIMIZING

Specialists in organizational decision making describe the optimizing strategy as having the goal of selecting the course of action with the highest payoff. Such a strategy requires estimating the comparative value of every viable alternative in terms of expected benefits and costs (see Young, 1966, pp. 138–47). But, as Herbert Simon (1976) has pointed out, human beings rarely adopt this decision-making approach: people simply do not have "the wits to maximize" (p. xxviii). Part of the problem is that determining all the potentially favorable and unfavorable consequences of all the feasible courses of action would require the decision maker to process so much information that impossible demands would be made on his resources and mental capabilities. In his attempts to obtain the degree of knowledge needed to anticipate alternative outcomes, the decision maker is likely to be overwhelmed by "information inundation, which can be quite as debilitating as information scarcity" (Miller and Starr, 1967, p. 62). Moreover, so many relevant variables may have to be taken into account that they cannot all be kept in mind at the same time. The number of crucially relevant categories usually far exceeds 7 ± 2, the limits of man's capacity for processing information in immediate memory (see Miller, 1956). Handicapped by the shortcomings of the human mind, the decision maker's attention, asserts Simon, "shifts from one value to another with consequent shifts in preference" (p. 83).

It is very costly in time, effort, and money to collect and examine the huge masses of information required when one uses an optimizing strategy to arrive at a decision. Furthermore, decision makers are often under severe pressure of time, which precludes careful search and appraisal. Managers in large companies, for example, seldom have time to engage in long-range planning because they are constantly occupied with current crises requiring emergency "fire fighting." The manager is likely to be "so busy solving immediate problems that he cannot effectively apply their solutions on a long-run recurrent basis; so busy manning the fire hose that he cannot devise a fire prevention program" (Young, p. 146).

As a result of personal limitations and various external constraints, a decision maker who does the best he can to use an optimizing strategy is still prone to such gross miscalculations that he ends up with an unsatisfactory *suboptimizing* solution, one that maximizes some of the utilities he expected to gain at the expense of losing other utilities. Miller and Starr (1967) cite the example of an executive who chooses a new job that is optimal in terms of his main professional objectives but requires so much overtime and travel that he has little time available

for family life. "This may have such adverse effects that the executive will find that his optimization in terms of one objective has produced an overall result which is much less than optimal in terms of all his objectives" (p. 48).

The perils of suboptimization abound in large organizations, where different units and different types of personnel have incompatible objectives. A hospital administrator may decide to hire a sizable number of paramedical aides to relieve overburdened nurses of nonprofessional chores and to provide additional services to the patients, such as writing letters for those who are incapacitated and separated from their families. But the additional personnel may unexpectedly overcrowd the hospital cafeteria, the rest rooms, the parking lot, and all the other employees' facilities to the point where the physicians, nurses, and orderlies become dissatisfied with the deterioration in their working conditions and demand that new facilities be built. The decisions made by policy makers in large organizations are, according to Young, "usually of a suboptimal nature, and only rarely can we assume that an ideal or unimprovable solution has been achieved" (p. 144). It needs to be emphasized, however, that a suboptimal policy is not necessarily unsatisfactory, even though it fails to attain all the policy makers' objectives; it may be a marked improvement over the former policy and constitute a step toward an optimizing solution.

Evidence from various social science disciplines indicates that, besides man's severe limitations as a processor of information, other recurrent conditions also militate against the use of an optimising approach, even though it might often seem to be the ideal strategy for making decisions (Brim et al., 1962; Etzioni, 1968; Johnson, 1974; Katona, 1953; Miller and Starr, 1967; Simmons et al., 1973; Steinbrunner, 1974; Taylor, 1965; Vroom and Yetton, 1973).

Contemporary developments in economics have emphasized the lack of realism of the assumption that individuals act so as to maximize their utility. There has not been an attack on the proposition that individuals should act so as to achieve a maximization of their utility. Rather, there has been sufficient evidence and supporting reasons to show that they do not act in this way. Among the reasons suggested have been the following: the inability of the individual to duplicate the rather recondite mathematics which economists have used to solve the problem of maximization of utility; the existence of other values (the higher values originally excluded by [Adam] Smith) which though not readily quantifiable, do cause divergences from the maximization of utility in the marketplace; the effect of habit; the influence of social emulation; the effect of social institutions.

. . . The work of psychologists would certainly tend to confirm the assertion that human beings have a variety of diverse motivations which do not lend themselves to maximization of utility—at least so long as utility is defined in terms of the satisfactions resulting from marketplace phenomena. . . . Similarly, sociologists have accumulated considerable evidence to demonstrate the enormous influence of social institutions, habit, and tradition on the choices and decisions made by individuals. The effect of these psychological and sociological factors leads individuals to make decisions and to take actions without recourse to maximization of utility in the classical economic sense. Alternatively phrased, it can be said that these factors cause people to act irrationally—but it should be noted that this is simply a matter of definition, rationality having been defined as maximization of economic utility [Miller and Starr, 1967, pp. 24–25].

Even in decisions made by business firms, where the overriding value would seem to be to make the greatest amount of profit, decision makers often do not orient themselves toward finding the course of action that will maximize profits and other tangible net gains. Without careful search and appraisal, corporation executives often make judgments about a multiplicity of conflicting objectives, including "good will," "growth potential," "acceptability within the organization," and other intangible gains that are difficult to measure in any way (see Johnson, 1974).

In a study of corporate decision making, Stagner (1969) found that many policy-making business executives, rather than focusing primarily on maximizing profit, were guided by numerous values pertaining to the future welfare of the organization. To examine high-level decision-making practices, Stagner mailed a questionnaire to 500 vice-presidential-level executives belonging to 125 of America's largest and most successful corporations, as selected by *Fortune* magazine. Returns were received from about 50 percent of the executives. The data revealed that in many firms cost and marginal-profit estimates are not carefully made. In fact, a substantial number of executives (28 percent) indicated that only "rough

estimates" were made of such variables; 65 percent of them reported that judgments about the company's public image often outweigh profit considerations; and 50 percent reported that considerable weight in making business decisions is attached to company tradition and past policies.[2]

Stagner points out that corporate decisions are not always made in terms of the long-range welfare of the organization, because some powerful executives are inclined to favor the objectives of their own division over those of the firm. Decisions by the manager of a unit are likely to be made with an eye toward local group loyalties and one-upmanship in the competitive struggle for power and influence among rival units, if not for personal advancement. According to numerous other observers, even when a policy maker is thinking in terms of the organization as a whole, he usually gives the devils of bureaucratic politics their due (Allison, 1971; Halperin, 1974; Lindblom, 1965; Johnson, 1974; Vroom and Yetton, 1973). Indeed, an executive risks failure if he overlooks the obligation to work out a policy that will be approved by higher executives or legal authorities within the organization and accepted by the managers who will be required to administer it. Then, too, he must try to avoid stirring up employee opposition, which could lead to disastrous slowdowns or a strike. Aside from the most obvious forms of employee resistance, there are other, subtle costs of implementing decisions that require the workers in a plant to change their work routines, to learn new operations, or to regroup into unaccustomed units: all such decisions result in some measure of lowered productivity.

Similarly, when an individual makes a vital decision bearing on his career, marriage, or health, or on any other aspect of his personal welfare, he does not think only about the major utilitarian goals to be attained. He also takes account of a multiplicity of intangible considerations bearing on the probably effects of the chosen and unchosen courses of action on relatives and friends. Anticipated feelings of high or low self-esteem with regard to living up to his own personal standards of conduct also affect his preferences for one alternative rather than another. . . .

Miller and Starr (1967) emphasize that there is no sound way to combine all the considerations involved in decision making into a single, objective utility measure, even though the decision maker might be capable of giving honest ratings of the subjective utility value of every consideration that enters into his choice.

The utility an individual gains from a commodity or a service can be measured to some degree by observable market phenomena (e.g., how much of the commodity he will buy at different prices). But there is no convenient measuring unit for the utility of an intangible such as dignity. Therefore, even if these other factors can be theoretically expressed in terms of [subjective] utility, the difficulties involved in measuring the utilities prevent the theory [of maximization of utilities] from satisfactorily explaining observed behavior and decisions [pp. 25–26].

Many behavioral scientists regard the optimizing strategy as an excellent *normative* (or *prescriptive*) model—that is, a set of standards the decision maker *should* strive to attain when making vital decisions (to avoid miscalculations, wishful thinking, and vulnerability to subsequent disillusionment). Some, however, like Miller and Starr, question whether optimizing would very often prove to be the optimal strategy in view of its high costs and the usual constraints on the decision maker's resources; they strongly oppose prescriptive recommendations that might inadvertently encourage decision makers to strive blindly for optimizing solutions, regardless of the circumstances. Even more objections have been raised against the assumption that the optimizing strategy provides an accurate *descriptive* model of how people actually *do* make decisions. The numerous critiques we have just summarized pose a major problem for the psychology of decision making: if optimizing is *not* the dominant strategy actually used by most decision makers most of the time, then what is?

SATISFICING

The most influential hypothesis concerning the way administrative man arrives at a new policy has been formulated by Herbert Simon (1976). The decision maker, according to Simon, *satisfices,* rather than maximizes; that is, he looks for a course of action that is "good enough," that meets a minimal set of requirements. Businessmen, for example, often decide to invest in a new enterprise if they expect it to return a "satisfactory profit," without bothering to compare it with all the alternative investments open to them. Sometimes more than one criterion is used, but always it is a question of whether the given choice will yield a "good enough" outcome. An executive looking for a

new job, for example, is likely to settle for the first one to come along that meets his minimal requirements— satisfactory pay, good chance for advancement, adequate working conditions, and location within commuting distance of his home. The satisficing strategy involves more superficial search for information and less cognitive work than maximizing. All that the person has to do is consider alternative courses of action sequentially until one that "will do" is found.

Simon argues convincingly that the satisficing approach fits the limited information-processing capabilities of human beings. The world is peopled by creatures of "bounded or limited rationality," he says, and these creatures constantly resort to gross simplifications when dealing with complex decision problems. Man's limited ability to foresee future consequences and to obtain information about the variety of available alternatives inclines him to settle for a barely "acceptable" course of action that is "better than the way things are now." He is not inclined to collect information about all the complicated factors that might affect the outcome of his choice, to estimate probabilities, or to work out preference orderings for many different alternatives. He is content to rely on "a drastically simplified model of the buzzing, blooming confusion that constitutes the real world" (Simon, 1976, p. xxix).

According to Johnson (1974), executives often feel so uncertain about the outcome of what seems to be the best choice that they forego it in order to play safe: they gravitate toward a more conventional, "second-best" choice that will cause little immediate disturbance or disapproval because it will be seen as "acceptable" by superiors and peers who will review the decision and by subordinates who will implement it. Cyert and March (1963) suggest that the more uncertainty there is about a long-term outcome, the greater the tendency to make a policy decision on the basis of its short-term acceptability within the organization.

Organizational theorists assume that individuals use a satisficing strategy in personal decisions as well as organizational decisions (Etzioni, 1968; Miller and Starr, 1967; Simon, 1976; Young, 1966). As Etzioni puts it, "Simon's important distinction between optimizing and 'satisficing' . . . is . . . independent of any socio-political system. It applies as much to a consumer in a supermarket as to the President of the United States" (p. 253). Whenever the consumer, the president, or anyone else is looking only for a choice that offers some degree of *improvement* over the present state of affairs, his survey, analysis, and evaluation are usually limited to just two alternatives — a new course of action that has been brought to his attention and the old one he has been pursuing. If neither meets his minimal requirements, he continues to look for other alternatives until he finds one that does. Consequently, the use of a satisficing strategy does not preclude contemplating a fairly large number of alternatives, but they are examined *sequentially*, with no attempt to work out a comparative balance sheet of pros and cons.

The simplest variant of the satisficing strategy takes the form of relying upon a single formula as the sole decision rule, which comes down to using only one criterion for a tolerable choice. Paradoxically, this crude approach often characterizes the decision-making behavior of people who are facing major personal decisions that will affect their future health or welfare. Men and women in serious trouble are likely to consult whichever physician or lawyer is recommended by a trusted friend and then to accept whatever course of action the adviser recommends, without spending the money and effort required to get a second opinion. The sole decision rule in such cases is often simply "Tell a qualified expert about your problem and do whatever he says — that will be good enough." Simple decision rules are also prevalent in consumer behavior. Studies of consumer purchases indicate that people in shops and supermarkets sometimes buy on impulse, without any advance planning or deliberation (Engel, Kollat, and Blackwell, 1968; Hansen, 1972). The person notices something attractive that he would like to have, and, if the price is within the range he regards as "reasonable," he immediately decides to buy it. A similar decision rule may come into play when a customer impulsively decides to appropriate an attractive piece of merchandise if he sees that no one in the store is looking.

Quasi-satisficing

Some people use a simple moral precept as the sole rule when making a decision to help someone in trouble. Schwartz (1970), in his account of the psychological basis of altruism, describes this approach as "moral decision making." Once the person realizes that someone requires aid and that there is some obvious way help can be given, he promptly takes action without deliberating about alternatives. This use of a simple decision rule is similar to a satisficing approach in all respects except one: the helper does not share the full-fledged satisficer's belief that his choice is *minimally* satisfactory. Instead of regarding his action as merely "good enough," the moral decision maker is convinced

that it is the *best,* that no other course would be morally justifiable. Later on we shall examine well-documented examples of moral decision making observed when a member of the family of a patient suffering from kidney disease is asked to donate his own kidney to save the relative's life.

When a decision maker does not accept responsibility for dealing with another person's problem, he is not likely to use a moral precept as his decision rule. The more responsibility he feels, the greater the likelihood that he will follow a simple normative prescription of offering help when someone needs it. To some extent, the findings from experiments on altruism by Bickman (1971, 1972), Latané and Darley (1970), Piliavin, Rodin, and Piliavin (1969, 1975), and others illustrate this relationship between perceived responsibility and a normative approach. The evidence indicates that a person is especially likely to help a stranger if he perceives that he is the only one available to give help. Not everyone, however, adheres to a simple normative rule when he perceives himself as responsible; some people weigh carefully the costs and benefits of giving aid to a needy person. The more frequently a person has told others he is committed to the moral norm that one should selflessly give aid to others when they need it, the greater the likelihood that he will subsequently use that norm as the basis for his decision to intervene.

When a person uses a simple normative precept as his sole decision rule, he usually feels it would be immoral for him to deliberate about any other options open to him. There is a moral-imperative quality to the norm that makes him resist violating it. When this normative decision rule is used, anticipated self-disapproval and social disapproval take precedence over any utilitarian considerations that might be implicated by the decision.

It is apparent from the examples just cited that personal choices based on a quasi-satisficing strategy that relies on a simple decision rule can result in either socially desirable or socially undesirable actions. The same can be said about domestic and foreign-policy decisions made by government leaders. Alexander George (1974) calls attention to the proclivity of national policy makers to rely on a simple formula rather than to attempt to master cognitively complex problems by means of careful search and analysis and weighing of alternatives. One type of decision rule frequently resorted to in a bureaucracy consists of using a simple criterion of "consensus," which requires only the single piece of information that could, in effect, be supplied by an opinion poll of the most powerful persons in the organization; thus, any policy is good enough to be adopted if the majority of influential people want it and will support it. Other simple decision rules sometimes used by policy makers consist of relying on, as a guide for action, a general ideological principle—e.g., "No appeasement of the enemy!"—or an operational code—e.g., the best tactic for dealing with an ultimatum from an enemy is to respond promptly with a more drastic ultimatum—(see George, 1974; Leites, 1953; Lindblom, 1965).

When making a major policy decision for which well-known historical precedents immediately come to mind, many national political leaders, according to historian Ernest May (1973) and political scientist Robert Jervis (1975), follow the simple decision rule "Do what we did last time if it worked and the opposite if it didn't."

Policy-makers ordinarily use history badly. When resorting to an analogy, they tend to seize upon the first that comes to mind. They do not search more widely. Nor do they pause to analyze the case, test its fitness, or even ask in what ways it might be misleading. Seeing a trend running toward the present, they tend to assume that it will continue into the future, not stopping to consider what produced it or why a linear projection might prove to be mistaken [May 1973, p. xi].

There is always a grave danger, as George (1974) points out, that relying on a simple decision rule will lead to a premature choice that overlooks nonobvious negative consequences. Some of those consequences might be averted if the decision were delayed until more thorough deliberation and evaluation were carried out after obtaining information from available intelligence resources.

What Are the Variables?

Although it is not explicitly stated in the descriptive accounts of satisficing and quasi-satisficing by Simon, Jervis, May, George, and others, these strategies differ from optimizing in more than one important dimension. We find that at least four different variables are involved.[3]

1. *Number of requirements to be met:* One characteristic feature of the satisficing strategy is that the testing rule used to determine whether or not to adopt a new course of action specifies a *small amount of requirements* that must be met, sometimes only one (e.g., that a personal choice should be acceptable to

one's spouse or that a policy choice should be acceptable to the majority of a policy-making group). The decision maker ignores many other values and spheres of interest that he realizes might also be implicated by his decision. In contrast, when the decision maker is using an optimizing strategy he takes account of a large number of requirements or objectives, with the intention of selecting the course of action that achieves the greatest possible satisfaction of the entire set of requirements. This is perhaps the most obvious characteristic that distinguishes satisficing from optimizing.

2. *Number of alternatives generated.* A decision maker using a satisficing strategy sequentially tests each alternative that comes to his attention; if the first one happens to be minimally satisfactory, he terminates his search. Since he makes little effort to canvass the full range of possible courses of action by searching his memory or by seeking suggestions from advisers, the decision maker is likely to generate *relatively few alternatives.* If he uses an optimizing strategy, on the other hand, the decision maker makes a thorough search and attempts to generate as *many* good alternatives as he can.

3. *Ordering and retesting of alternatives.* When using a satisficing strategy, the decision maker typically tests the alternatives only once and in a haphazard order, as one after another happens to come to his attention, until he finds one that meets his minimum requirements. When using an optimizing strategy, however, he selects the best alternatives and reexamines them repeatedly, ordering them in pairs or in some other way so as to make comparative judgments.

4. *Type of testing model used.* When testing to see if an alternative meets a given requirement, the satisficing decision maker typically limits his inquiry to seeing whether it falls above or below a *minimal cutoff point.* If there is more than one requirement, he treats each cutoff point in the same way, as equally important. In contrast to this simple, unweighted threshold model, the model used in the optimizing strategy is typically a weighted additive model, which requires the decision maker to arrive at an evaluation that takes account of the *magnitudes* of all the pros and cons with due regard for the relative importance of each objective. This gives him the opportunity to consider possible "tradeoffs" from gaining very high values in some important requirements in exchange for tolerating relatively low values on less important ones.

When a person's procedures fall at the low end of the continuum on all four variables, his decision-making strategy would be unambiguously classified as satisficing; when at the upper end of the continuum on all four variables, his strategy would be unambiguously classified as optimizing. But what if a person's pattern on the four variables is not consistent? Obviously, we can expect to find instances of quasi-satisficing or mixed strategies, where satisficing tendencies predominate on one or two variables but optimizing tendencies predominate on the others.

Even when someone warrants high ratings on all four variables, he might still fail to maximize all possible values, and hence fall far short of a genuinely optimizing strategy. Moreover, an unskilled or unwary decision maker with good intentions might obtain high ratings but nevertheless make gross miscalculations through ignorance, bias, overconcern about the foreseeable immediate consequences, or rigid belief in ''the too-ready assumption that actions which have in the past led to the desired outcome will continue to do so'' (Merton, 1936, p. 901). High ratings on the four variables might, therefore, be regarded as necessary, but not sufficient, conditions for optimizing.

Not unexpectedly, the four variables overlap to some extent with the seven criteria for vigilant information processing. . . . Anyone who uses a relatively pure satisficing strategy, as defined by the four variables, would obtain low scores on at least four of the seven variables that define vigilant information processing: he would fail to canvass a wide range of alternatives (criterion no. 1), to take account of the full range of short-term objectives and long-term values to be fulfilled by the choice (criterion no. 2), to weigh all he knows about the costs and risks of each alternative (criterion no. 3), and to reexamine the positive and negative consequences of all known alternatives (criterion no. 6). But the use of a satisficing strategy does not preclude meeting some of the criteria for vigilant information processing. Even within the confines of a pure satisficing strategy, a decision maker can still carry out an intensive search for relevant information, conscientiously assimilate information, and make provisions for implementation along with detailed contingency plans. Furthermore, it is possible for someone to meet all seven requirements for vigilant information processing and yet not obtain a high score on one or two of the variables that enter into the optimizing strategy, so that he would be classified as using a ''quasi-optimizing'' strategy. Taking account of the limitations of a ''pure'' optimizing strategy discussed

earlier, we expect that for purposes of predicting gross miscalculations in decision making and subsequent postdecisional regret, the seven variables specified as the criteria for vigilant information processing will prove to be more valuable than the set of four variables differentiating between satisficing and optimizing.

Elimination by Aspects

Instead of a single decision rule in a satisficing or quasi-satisficing strategy, a set of decision rules, involving perhaps up to half a dozen considerations, is sometimes used. Still, the decision maker does not engage in anything like the amount of cognitive work that would be required if he were to evaluate and weigh the alternatives using an optimizing strategy. One such multiple-rule variant, designated as the ''elimination-by-aspects'' approach, has been described by Tversky (1972). It consists essentially of a combination of simple decision rules, which can be applied to select rapidly from a number of salient alternatives one that meets a set of minimal requirements. Tversky illustrates this type of quasi-satisficing strategy by citing a television commercial screened in San Francisco. An announcer says:

There are more than two dozen companies in the San Francisco area which offer training in computer programing. [He puts some two dozen eggs and one walnut on the table to represent the alternatives.] Let us examine the facts. How many of these schools have on-line computer facilities for training? [*He removes several eggs.*] How many of these schools have placement services that would help you find a job? [*He removes some more eggs.*] How many of these schools are approved for veterans' benefits? [*This continues until the walnut alone remains. The announcer cracks the nutshell, revealing the name of the advertised company.*] This is all you need to know, in a nutshell.

When the elimination-by-aspects approach is used, decision making becomes essentially a sequential narrowing-down process, similar to the logic employed in the popular game Twenty Questions. Starting ordinarily with the most valued requirement, all salient alternatives that do not contain the selected aspect are eliminated, and the process continues for each requirement in turn until a single expedient remains. For example, in contemplating the purchase of a new car, the first aspect selected might be a $4,500 price limit; all cars more expensive than $4,500 are then excluded from further consideration. A second aspect might be high mileage per gallon; at this stage, all cars are eliminated that do not have this feature. Yet another aspect, say power steering, is examined for the remaining alternatives, and all cars not meeting this criterion are crossed off the "mental list." The process continues until all cars but one are eliminated.

Of course, the decision maker may run out of aspects before he arrives at a single remaining expedient; he will then have to introduce another decision rule in order to narrow his choice. Or he may run out of alternatives before he exhausts his list of minimal requirements. From a normative standpoint, however, a much more serious flaw of this complex form of satisficing lies in its failure to ensure that the alternatives retained are, in fact, superior to those eliminated. For example, in the alternative arrived at in the television commercial, the use of placement services as a criterion for elimination might lead to the rejection of programs whose overall quality far exceeds that of the advertised one despite the fact that they do not offer that particular service. Similarly, in the choice of a car, the use of power steering as a criterion for elimination could lead to rejection of vehicles otherwise far superior to the vehicle purchased. Part of the problem is that minor criteria may creep in early in the sequence or may survive to determine the final choice. Perhaps this drawback could be corrected in a way that would transform the elimination-by-aspects approach into a quasi-optimizing strategy by introducing procedures that reflect the decision maker's judgments about the differential weights to be assigned to various aspects. Even without any such refinement, however, this approach appears to be one of the most sophisticated and psychologically realistic of the quasi-satisficing strategies and might result in fewer miscalculations than the simpler variants that rely exclusively on a single decision rule (Abelson, 1976).

Some social science theorists would describe reliance on a single decision rule as less "rational" than the elimination-by-aspects approach, and all variants of satisficing as less "rational" than optimizing. But terms like *less rational, nonrational,* and *irrational* carry invidious connotations ("stupid," "crazy") that often do not correspond at all to the evaluations that would be made by objective observers. Indeed it could be argued that in certain circumstances it is not rational to waste time and effort in maximizing; even when the relevant information is available, a very simple form of satisficing sometimes may be the most sensible orientation, especially for many minor issues. For example, consumer research organizations have recommended that

when purchasing aspirin at a registered pharmacy, one should follow the simple rule of selecting whichever brand is cheapest (because all brands must meet rigorous U.S. government specifications and, despite advertising claims to the contrary, there are no significant differences among them). As Miller and Starr (1967, p. 51) point out, "It is always questionable whether the optimum procedure is to search for *the* optimum value." Accordingly, we avoid characterizing the satisficing strategy or any other decision-making strategy in terms of "rationality" or "irrationality." We do not intend to bypass the important issue of determining the conditions under which one or another decision-making procedure will have unfavorable consequences for the decision maker; but we shall attempt to relate specific types of conditions to specific types of unfavorable consequences without using overinclusive, misleading labels like *irrational.*

Incrementalism and Muddling Through

Organizational theorists recognize that despite its shortcomings, a satisficing strategy can result in slow progress toward an optimal course of action. Miller and Starr (1967), for example, speak about *incremental improvements* that sometimes come about as a result of a succession of satisficing policy choices, each small change presumably having been selected as "good enough" because it was seen as better than leaving the old policy unchanged. "Over time," Miller and Starr assert "both individuals and groups may be better off to move in incremental steps of reasonable size toward the perceived and bounded optimum than in giant strides based on long-range perceptions of where the ultimate optimal exists" (p. 51).

Charles E. Lindblom (1959, 1963, 1965) has given a detailed account of the incrementalist approach in an analysis of "the art of muddling through." When a problem arises requiring a change in policy, according to Lindblom, policy makers in government or large organizations generally consider a very narrow range of policy alternatives that differ to only a small degree from the existing policy. By sticking close to this familiar path of policymaking, the incrementalist shows his preference for the sin of "omission" over the sin of "confusion" (Lindblom, 1965, p. 146).

Incremental decision making is geared to alleviating concrete shortcomings in a present policy — putting out fires — rather than selecting the superior course of action. Since no effort is made to specify major goals and to find the best means for attaining them, "ends are chosen that are appropriate to available or nearly available means" (Hirschman and Lindblom, 1962, p. 215). The incremental approach allows executives to simplify the search and appraisal stages of decision making by carrying out successive comparisons with respect to policy alternatives that differ only slightly from the existing policy. Slovic (1971) postulates, on the basis of his experiments on the cognitive limitations displayed in gambling situations, that decision makers find the incremental approach attractive because it enables them to avoid difficult cognitive tasks: "Examination of business decision making and governmental policy making suggests that, whenever possible, decision makers avoid uncertainty and the necessity of weighting and combining information or trading-off conflicting values."

Often decision makers have no real awareness of trying to arrive at a new policy; rather, there is a never-ending series of attacks on each new problem as it arises. As policy makers take one small step after another to gradually change the existing policy, the satisficing criterion itself may change, depending on what is going wrong with the existing policy.[4] If there are strong objections to the policy on the part of other bureaucrats who have to implement it, the policy makers may find a satisficing solution that involves making a compromise in accord with the realities of bureaucratic politics. Incremental changes are often made primarily to keep other politically powerful groups in the hierarchy sufficiently satisfied so that they will stop complaining and will not obstruct the new trend (Halperin, 1974).

Braybrooke and Lindblom (1963) regard muddling-through incrementalism as the typical decision-making process of groups in pluralistic societies. Since the term *muddling through* evokes images of incompetence and aimlessness, it is tempting to conclude that it could be the preferred technique only of lazy or third-rate minds. But Braybrooke and Lindblom view it as the method by which societal decision-making bodies, acting as coalitions of interest groups, can effectively make cumulative decisions and arrive at workable compromises. Whenever power is distributed among a variety of influential executive leaders, political parties, legislative factions, and interest groups, one center of power can rarely impose its preferences on another and policies are likely to be the outcome of give and take among numerous partisans. The constraints of bureaucratic politics, with its shifting compromises and coalitions, constitute a major reason for the disjointed

and incremental nature of the policies that gradually evolve.

Lindblom and his associates argue that incremental decisions based largely on the criterion of consensus, rather than on the actual values implicated by the issue, may avoid some of the social evils of undemocratic, centralized decision making. But other social scientists point out that incrementalism based largely on keeping fellow power holders reasonably contented cannot be expected to do very much about the vital needs of underprivileged people and politically weak groups (see Etzioni, 1968, pp. 272–73; Dror, 1969, pp. 167–69.)[5] Moreover, there is no guarantee that in the atomic age our government leaders will always somehow muddle through successfully as they "stagger through history like a drunk putting one disjointed incremental foot after another" (Boulding, 1964, p. 931). On the one hand, incremental policy formation based on a succession of satisficing choices can have functional value for decision makers who want to avoid the risks of drastic societal changes that "may easily lead," as Popper (1963, p. 158) says, "to an intolerable increase in human suffering." But on the other hand, there is the danger that it can prove to be a zigzag passage to unanticipated disaster.

Relatively little is to be found in the social psychological literature about muddling through on personal decisions. Probably the same type of incremental change, based on a simple satisficing strategy, is adopted whenever a person is ignorant of the fundamental issues at stake or when he wishes to avoid investing a great deal of time and energy in wrestling with a problem that appears, at the time, insoluble. Important life decisions are sometimes incremental in nature, the end product of a series of small decisions that progressively commit the person to one particular course of action. A stepwise increase in commitment can end up locking the person into a career or marriage without his ever having made a definite decision about it. . . .

Many individuals do not make a deliberate occupational choice but in haphazard, trial-and-error fashion leave their job whenever something that seems somewhat better comes along. Ginzberg et al. (1951) suggest that incremental steps may determine the career choices made by a sizable number of people even in skilled occupations. A man or woman starts off getting a certain type of job training and then finds it more and more difficult to switch to another type of career. The person anticipates social disapproval for "wasting" his training, which tends to increase with each increment of training or advancement. And, of course, he is also deterred from changing by his own sense of prior investment of time, effort, and money in the direction he has already moved.

Matza (1964) indicates that the careers of lawbreakers are often arrived at in the same stepwise, drifting fashion, without any single stage at which the offenders decide they are going to pursue a life of crime. Rather, they start with minor offenses, get into more and more trouble with the police, and proceed slowly to enlarge their repertoire of criminal acts until they reach the point where they are regularly committing serious crimes. Each successive crime in the series appears to be not very much worse than the preceding one, and in this stepwise fashion the person proceeds to move from minor delinquency to major crime.

A similar stepwise process process has been reported for the decision to marry. Waller (1938, p. 259) noted that during the early decades of the twentieth century the process of mating unfolded gradually, in a series of steps whereby the person became increasingly committed in his own eyes and in those of others to the decision to marry. Each step involved the use of a few simple criteria, with no effort to weigh alternatives.

These observational reports about incremental decision making on such vital personal choices as marriage and career, although not sufficiently detailed to enable us to draw definitive conclusions about decision-making processes, suggest that the succession of small decisions may often be based on a satisficing or quasi-satisficing strategy, just as in the case of the incremental policy-making decisions described by administrative scientists.

MIXED SCANNING

Etzioni (1967) has outlined a conglomerate strategy called mixed scanning, which he sees as a synthesis of the stringent rationalism of optimizing and the "muddling," slipshod approach of extreme incrementalism, displayed by bureaucrats who use consensus as their only satisficing criterion. The mixed-scanning strategy has two main components: (1) some of the features of the optimizing strategy combined with essential features of the elimination-by-aspects approach are used for fundamental policy decisions that set basic directions; and (2) an incremental process (based on simple forms of satisficing) is followed for the minor or "bit" decisions that ensue after the basic policy direction is set, resulting in gradual revisions and sometimes preparing the way for a new fundamental decision. Etzioni argues that this mixture of substrategies fits the needs of democratic governments and organizations. In noncrisis periods, it is easier to obtain a consensus on "increments similar to the existing policies than to gain support for a new policy" (p. 294). But in times of serious trouble, a crisis stimulates intensive search for a better policy and serves "to build consensus for major changes of direction which are overdue (e.g., governmental guidance of economic stability, the welfare state, desegregation)" (p. 294).

Etzioni uses the term *scanning* to refer to the search, collection, processing, evaluation, and weighing of information in the process of making a choice — i.e., the main cognitive activities that enter into the orientation we call vigilant information processing. The intensiveness of scanning can vary over a wide range, from very superficial to extremely intensive, depending on how much "coverage" the decision maker strives for when he surveys the relevant fields of information, how much detail he "takes in," and how completely he "explores alternative steps." Each time he faces a dilemma that requires choosing a new course of action, he has to make a deliberate prior judgment about how much of his resources of time, energy, and money he is willing to allocate to search and appraisal activities.

Etzioni's description of the mixed-scanning strategy includes a set of rules for allocating resources to scanning whenever a policy maker faces the type of crisis that leads him to realize that earlier policy lines ought to be reviewed and perhaps changed.

Put into a program-like language, the [mixed-scanning] strategy roughly reads:

a. On strategic occasions . . . (i) list all relevant alternatives that come to mind, that the staff raises, and that advisers advocate (including alternatives not usually considered feasible).

(ii) Examine briefly the alternatives under (i). . . . and reject those that reveal a "crippling objection." These include: (a) utilitarian objections to alternatives which require means that are not available, (b) normative objections to alternatives which violate the basic values of the decision-makers, and (c) political objections to alternatives which violate the basic values or interests of other actors whose support seems essential for making the decision and/or implementing it.

(iii) For all alternatives not rejected under (ii), repeat (ii) in greater though not in full detail. . . .

(iv) For those alternatives remaining after (iii), repeat (ii) in still fuller detail. . . . Continue until only one alternative is left. . . .

b. *Before implementation* [in order to prepare for subsequent "incrementing"] (i) when possible, fragment the implementation into several sequential steps. . . .

(ii) When possible, divide the commitment to implement into several serial steps. . . .

(iii) When possible, divide the commitment of assets into several serial steps and maintain a strategic reserve. . . .

(iv) Arrange implementaion in such a way that, if possible, costly and less reversible decisions will appear later in the process than those which are more reversible and less costly.

(v) Provide a time schedule for the additional collection and processing of information. . . .

c. *Review while implementing.* (i) Scan on a semi-encompassing level after the first sub-set of increments is implemented. If they "work," continue to scan on a semi-encompassing level after longer intervals and in full, over-all review, still less frequently.

(ii) Scan more encompassingly whenever a series of increments, although each one seems a step in the right direction, results in deeper difficulties.

(iii) Be sure to scan at set intervals in full, over-all review even if everything seems all right. . . .

d. *Formulate a rule for the allocation of assets and time among the various levels of scanning.* . . . [pp. 286–88]

The only testing rule specified for fundamental decisions in the above program is one that would be rated as satisficing on one of the primary variables that defines the satisficing strategy — namely, rejecting every alternative that has a "crippling" objection, which is tantamount to using a minimal cutoff point. But instead of a quasi-satisficing approach, a quasi-optimizing approach could be used when dealing with those alternatives that survive the initial rejection test: each time the surviving alternatives are reexamined, the testing rule might be changed in the optimizing direction by raising the minimum standard (from "crippling" objections to more minor objections) or by introducing a comparative type of testing for selecting the least objectionable alternative. Etzioni no doubt assumes that the standards are raised each time the surviving alternatives are retested, since if the definition of *crippling* were to remain constant there would be little point in reexamining the alternatives, except to catch

and correct blatant errors made the first time. In any case, if we assume that the proposed upgrading of the testing rule is introduced into Etzioni's program for making fundamental decisions, the program would directly or indirectly embody the seven criteria we have specified for a vigilant information-processing orientation. Four of the criteria are explicitly mentioned (no. 1 — thorough canvassing of alternatives; no. 2 — taking account of the full range of objectives and values to be fulfilled; no. 4 — intensive search for new information; no. 7 — detailed provisions for implementation, with contingency plans). Moreover, in order to carry out all the quasi-optimizing steps conscientiously, the decision maker would be required by the program to meet the other three criteria as well (no. 3 — careful weighing of consequences of each alternative; no. 5 — thorough assimilation of new information; no. 6 — reexamination of consequences before making a final choice).

Although intended for policy makers, the same program, with minor modifications, could be applied to an individual's work-task decisions and to personal decisions involving career, marriage, health, or financial security. (Only a few slight changes in wording would be necessary — e.g., in step a (i), for personal decisions, *the staff* would be replaced by *family and friends*.)

The program for mixed scanning is presented by Etzioni primarily as a normative or prescriptive model, specifying what decision makers *should* do. The mixed-scanning strategy obviously has the virtue of adaptive flexibility at different stages of decision making, with a quasi-optimizing approach being used only while selecting the trunk of a new decision tree and a satisficing approach being used after the new fundamental policy has been chosen, as one moves out along the branches. Etzioni expects that decision makers will improve their effectiveness in attaining their actual goals if they follow his recommendations to differentiate "fundamental" from "bit" decisions and carry out the intensive scanning procedures he prescribes for the fundamental ones.

Etzioni suggests further that the mixed-scanning strategy may be an accurate descriptive model of what governmental policy makers *actually* do. He offers no systematic evidence, however, to support this hypothesis, although he mentions a few case studies that seem to fit the model. He challenges the overgeneralizations that have been drawn from the finding that the United States Congress generally makes only marginal (incremental) changes in the annual budget for federal agencies, raising or lowering the amounts allocated by just a slight percentage from the amounts allocated the preceding year (Fenno, 1966). He points out that congressmen occasionally make a fundamental decision to increase drastically the percentage of the gross national product to be devoted to the federal budget, as they did at the outbreak of the Korean War in 1950. The U.S. defense budget jumped from 5.0 percent of the GNP in 1950 to 10.3 percent in 1951; thereafter it fluctuated between 9.0 and 11.3 percent during the next decade, reflecting incremental decisions. Etzioni cites a similar jump in the budget for the national space agency in 1958, when Congress agreed to support a new program for space exploration, which was followed by incremental changes during the subsequent years. In these instances, what appears to be a series of incremental decisions turns out to be an extension of a fundamental, nonincremental policy decision. Whether the fundamental decision in each instance was made in the way described by Etzioni's program, however, requires further evidence — which Etzioni does not examine — concerning the procedures used by the decision makers in arriving at a new policy. It remains an open, empirical question whether any sizable population or subpopulation of decision makers does, in fact, proceed along the lines specified in Etzioni's description of the mixed-scanning strategy.

THE DECISION MAKER'S REPERTOIRE

Implicit in Etzioni's account is the assumption that every decision maker has in his repertoire all the component substrategies and orientations we have described in the preceding sections. Adopting a given strategy at one stage of the decision-making sequence does not preclude use of another strategy at a later stage, particularly if the earlier one proves ineffective in resolving the conflict. For some people, the work of making a decision involves switching from low-cost, low-energy substrategies to more costly, effortful ones as they realize they are unable to settle the decisional conflict.

We expect that when different strategies or substrategies are used, different information-processing orientations in the decision maker's repertoire come to the fore. When he is trying to optimize, as we have seen, the decision maker consistently behaves like an intelligent realist, pursuing maximum satisfaction or utility with single-minded attention. He uses his mental capacities to a remarkable degree while searching for all viable alternatives and trying to understand all their possible consequences.

When operating as a "mixed scanner," the decision maker solves the problem of his limited capacity to process information by classifying decisions as either fundamental or minor. He conserves his time and energy by scanning intensively only those choices that are the most important or most troublesome, treating all other choices much more superficially.

When satisficing, on the other hand, the decision maker deals with fundamental decisions in the same way as minor ones; he relies on one or a few rock-bottom principles that enable him to reduce a complex decisional problem into a matter of judging what will do and what won't do, which requires much less time and effort for search and appraisal. When in response to a profound challenge the decision maker functions as an incrementalist muddler, he resorts to the simplest form of satisficing, making only slight adjustments in an obsolete policy after doing little more than checking on the agreement of other interested parties. This crude form of satisficing is more likely than other strategies to lead to gross failures to meet the criteria for vigilant information processing. For vital decisions, the most damaging consequences are to be expected when the preliminary appraisal of the challenge is itself based on such a low level of vigilance that the the person fails to realize the importance of the objectives and values at stake. But a muddling strategy might be adaptive in a stable environment, where few fundamental challenges to existing policies are encountered.

According to a general assumption, . . . we expect that irrespective of the strategy adopted — i.e., whether the decision maker strives to optimize, settles for satisficing, or tries to follow a mixed strategy — the likelihood of miscalculation and postdecisional regret increases as a function of the degree to which he fails to engage in vigilant information processing (as defined by the seven criteria) during the period preceding commitment. Hence, according to this assumption, when attempting to predict the consequences of a satisficing strategy — or any other strategy — one needs to inquire into the degree to which the decision maker meets the seven criteria.

If we make the additional assumption that practically all the various strategies and substrategies we have discussed are in the repertoire of every decision maker, we find ourselves confronting a new set of research questions that need to be answered in order to develop an adequate descriptive theory of decision making. The old question, which has been addressed by many social scientists, was "Which strategy is the one most decision makers use most of the time?" The answer is still being debated, because no consistent evidence has as yet emerged. But the analysis presented in this chapter inclines us to be dubious about ever finding a general answer that will hold across all types of major and minor decisions, and in all circumstances. After all, being extremely careful to meet the criteria for vigilant information processing would be almost as inappropriate for a trivial or routine decision among substitutable alternatives as superficial satisficing would be for a major decision. In *Up the Organization*, Robert Townsend, the former chairman of the board of the Avis Corporation, gives some conventional wisdom, well known to business executives who have managed to survive at the top, about how to approach different kinds of decisions:

There are two kinds of decisions: those that are expensive to change and those that are not.

A decision to build the Edsel or Mustang (or locate your new factory in Orlando or Yakima) shouldn't be made hastily; nor without plenty of inputs from operating people and specialists.

But the common or garden-variety decision—like when to have the cafeteria open for lunch or what brand of pencil to buy—should be made fast. No point in taking three weeks to make a decision that can be made in three seconds—and corrected inexpensively later if wrong. The whole organization may be out of business while you oscillate between baby-blue or buffalo-brown coffee cups [Townsend, 1970, p. 45].

We suspect that in addition to using a simple satisficing approach to relatively unimportant decisions and an optimizing approach to the most important ones, many executives use some form of mixed strategy when dealing with decisions in the intermediate range that fall between the two extremes Townsend is talking about. The important point, however, is that people cannot be expected to use the same strategy for all types of decisions.

Instead of the old question, then, about which strategy is most prevalent, a new set of questions must be confronted: Under what conditions are people most likely to adopt a nonvigilant, satisficing strategy as opposed to a more vigilant one? Under what conditions are people most motivated to devote the resources of time, energy, and money necessary to seek an optimizing solution? What intervention procedures are available to remedy careless, superficial, or impulsive approaches to decision making when vital consequences are at stake?...

NOTES

1. In applying the term *strategy* for basic types of search and choice procedures—optimizing, satisficing, mixed scanning, etc.—we are following the terminology of George (1974), Etzioni (1968), and other social scientists who have made recent contributions to the analysis of decision-making processes. We do not use the term *strategy* in the technical meaning it has in game theory.

2. There are, of course, obvious weaknesses in questionnaire research on corporate decision making. Reliance on reports from a self-selected sample of vice-presidents can be a risky venture, since industrial executives are likely to be untrained observers with a strong inclination to bias their responses.

   To test the inter-observer reliability of his data, Stagner computed correlation coefficients for the responses provided by pairs of executives responding from the same firm. The level of correlation for pairs of executives describing the decision-making process for their firm was statistically significant ($r = +.46$, $N = 52$). While this level of agreement is encouraging, the amount of disagreement it implies susggests that, within firms, executives are not uniform in their observations of decision making. Moreover, no estimate can be made of the extent to which the correlation is inflated by the shared goals of so-called good public relations among the pairs of executives who decided to return the questionnaires. Nevertheless, some of the specific findings are not in accord with the usual myths and ideologies promoted by large corporations, which suggests that the executives in his sample were at least somewhat candid.

3. We are indebted to Robert Sternberg (private communication) for suggesting that the two main types of strategy described in the administrative sciences literature, optimizing and satisficing, are conglomerates of a number of different variables that should be specified.

4. Incrementalism, as described by Lindblom, is treated by most social scientists as a separate strategy, coordinate with the satisficing strategy. But it is apparent that it is a variant of the satisficing strategy once one recognizes that the content of the minimal requirements or the minimal cutoff points may change from one incremental decision to the next.

5. Dror's critique of the "science of muddling through" emphasizes that giving priority to the value of minimizing risks by continuing in the same direction may be appropriate in an unchanging social environment, but becomes inappropriate when conditions arise that require a fundamental change.

   Unless three closely interrelated conditions are concurrently met, incremental change by "successive limited comparison" is not an adequate method for policy making. *These three essential conditions are:* (1) *the results of present policies must be in the main satisfactory (to the policy makers and the social strata on which they depend), so that marginal changes are sufficient for achieving an acceptable rate of improvement in policy-results;* (2) *there must be a high degree of continuity in the nature of the problems;* (3) *there must be a high degree of continuity in the available means for dealing with problems.*

   When the results of past policies are undesirable, it is often preferable to take the risks involved in radical new departures. For instance, in newly developing states aspiring to accelerated socio-economic development, the policies followed by the former colonial policy makers clearly do not constitute an acceptable basis to be followed with only incremental change [Dror, 1969, pp. 167–168].

6. We expect that if we were to examine all the important decisions that any person makes in the course of his or her life, we would find considerable variation in the decision strategies that the person uses and corresponding variation in the degree to which the criteria for vigilant information processing are met. Some of that variation is undoubtedly attributable to cognitive limitations, some to bureaucratic politics (or its equivalent in the person's family and social network), and some to other familiar factors — objective features of the environment that facilitate or interfere with search and appraisal, the person's belief system about how to exercise good judgment, changes in the person's interests, willingness to take risks, level of aspiration, or other personality predispositions, etc. (see Barber, 1972; Elms, 1972, 1976). But if the influence of all of these variables could be assessed, a large amount of the variance would probably still remain unexplained. We believe that a big chunk of that remaining variance will be accounted for by the variables that emerge from our analysis . . . of the conditions under which one or another coping pattern is used to deal with the psychological stress generated by decisional conflict.

REFERENCES

Abelson, R. P. Script processing in attitude formation and decison making. In J. S. Carroll and J. W. Payne (Eds.), *Cognition and social behavior.* New York: Lawrence Erlbaum Associates, 1976.

Allison, G. T. *Essence of decision: Explaining the Cuban missile crisis.* Boston: Little, Brown, and Co., 1971.

Barber, J. D. *The presidential character: Predicting performance in the White House.* Englewood Cliffs, N.J.: Prentice-Hall, 1972.

Bickman, L. The effect of another bystander's ability to help on bystander intervention in an emergency. *Journal of Experimental Social Psychology,* 1971, *7,* 367–79.

Bickman, L. Social influence and diffusion of responsibility in an emergency. *Journal of Experimental Social Psychology,* 1972, *8,* 438–45.

Boulding, K. Review of *A strategy of decision. American Sociological Review,* 1964, *29,* 931.

Braybrooke, D., and C. E. Lindblom. *A strategy of decision.* New York: Free Press, 1963.

Brim, O. G., D. C. Glass, D. E. Lavin, and N. Goodman, *Personality and decision processes.* Stanford; Calif.: Stanford University Press, 1962.

Cyert, R. M., and J. G. March. *A behavioral theory of the firm.* Englewood Cliffs, N.J.: Prentice-Hall, 1963.

Dror, Y. Muddling through — science or inertia? In A. Etzioni (Ed.), *Readings on modern organization.* Englewood Cliffs, N.J.: Prentice-Hall, 1969.

Elms, A. C. *Social psychology and social relevance.* Boston: Little, Brown, 1972.

Elms, A. C. *Personality and politics.* New York: Harcourt Brace Jovanovich, 1976.

Engel, J. F., D. J. Kollat, and R. D. Blackwell. *Consumer behavior.* New York: Holt, Rinehart and Winston, 1968.

Etzioni, A. Mixed scanning: A third approach to decision making. *Public Administration Review,* 1967, *27,* 385-92.

Etzioni, A. *The active society.* New York: Free Press, 1968.

Fenno, R. F. *The power of the purse: Appropriations politics in Congress.* Boston: Little, Brown, 1966.

George, A. Adaptation to stress in political decision making. The individual, small group, and organizational contexts. In G. V. Coelho, D. A. Hamburg, and J. E. Adams (Eds.), *Coping and adaptation.* New York: Basic Books, 1974.

Ginzberg, E., S. W. Ginsburg, S. Axelrad, and J. L. Herma. *Occupational choice.* New York: Columbia University Press, 1951.

Halperin, M. H. *Bureaucratic politics and foreign policy.* Washington, D.C.: Brookings Institution, 1974.

Hansen, F. *Consumer choice behavior.* New York: Free Press, 1972.

Hirschman, A. O., and C. E. Lindblom. Economic development, research and development, policy making: Some converging views. *Behavioral Sciences,* 1962, *7,* 211-22.

Jervis, R. *Perception and misperception in international relations.* Princeton, N.J.: Princeton University Press, 1975.

Johnson, R. J. Conflict avoidance though acceptable decisions. *Human Relations,* 1974, *27,* 71-82.

Katona, G. Rational behavior and economic behavior. *Psychological Review,* 1953, *60,* 307-18.

Latane, B., and J. M. Darley. Social determinants of bystander intervention in emergencies. In J. Macauley and L. Berkowitz (Eds.), *Altruism and helping behavior.* New York: Academic Press, 1970.

Leites, N. *A study of Bolshevism.* New York: Free Press, 1953.

Lindblom, C. E. The science of muddling through. *Public Administration Review,* 1959, *19,* 79-99.

Lindblom, C. E. *The intelligence of democracy.* New York: Free Press, 1965.

Matza, D. *Delinquency and drift.* New York: Wiley, 1964.

May, E. R. *Lessons of the past.* New York: Oxford University Press, 1973.

Merton, R. K. The unanticipated consequences of purposive social action. *American Sociological Review,* 1936, *1,* 894-904.

Miller, D. W., and M. K. Starr. *The structure of human decisions.* Englewood Cliffs, N.J.: Prentice-Hall, 1967.

Miller, G. A. The magical number seven, plus or minus two. *Psychological Review,* 1956, *63,* 81-97.

Piliavin, I. M., J. A. Piliavin, and J. Rodin. Costs, diffusion, and the stigmatized victim. *Journal of Personality and Social Psychology,* 1975, *32,* 429-38.

Piliavin, I. M., J. Rodin, and J. A. Piliavin. Good Samaritanism: An underground phenomenon? *Journal of Personality and Social Psychology,* 1969, *12,* 289-99.

Popper, K. R. *The open society and its enemies.* Vol. 1. Princeton, N.J.: Princeton University Press, 1963.

Schwartz, S. Moral decision making and behavior. In J. Macauley and L. Berkowitz (Eds.), *Altruism and helping behavior.* New York: Academic Press, 1970.

Simmons, R. G., S. D. Klein, and K. Thornton. The family member's decision to be a kidney transplant donor. *Journal of Comparative Family Studies,* 1973, *4,* 88-115.

Simon, H. A. *Administrative behavior: A study of decision-making processes in administrative organization.* 2nd ed., New York: Macmillan, 1957; 3rd Ed., New York: Free Press, 1976.

Slovic, P. Limitations of the mind of man: Implications for decision making nuclear age. *Oregon Research Institute Bulletin,* 1971, *11,* 41-49.

Stagner, R. Corporate decision making: An empirical study. *Journal of Applied Psychology,* 1969, *53,* 1-13.

Steinbruner, J. D. *The cybernetic theory of decision.* Princeton, N.J.: Princeton University Press, 1974.

Taylor, D. W. Decision making and problem solving. In J. March (Ed.), *Handbook of organizations.* Chicago: Rand McNally, 1965.

Townsend, R. *Up the organization: How to stop the corporation from stifling people and strangling profits.* New York: Knopf, 1970.

Tversky, A. Elimination by aspects: A theory of choice. *Psychological Review,* 1972, *79,* 281–99.

Vroom, V. H., and P. W. Yetton. *Leadership and decision making.* Pittsburgh: University of Pittsburgh Press, 1973.

Waller, W. W. *The family: A dynamic interpretation.* New York: Cordon Co., 1938.

Young, S. *Management: A systems analysis.* Glenview, Ill.: Scott, Foresman, 1966.

32.   The Escalation of Commitment: A Review and Analysis

Barry M. Staw

Many of the most difficult decisions an individual must make are not choices about what to do in an isolated instance but are choices about the fate of an entire course of action. This is especially true when the decision is whether to cease a questionable line of behavior or to commit more effort and resources into making that course of action pay off. Do individuals in such cases cut their losses or escalate their commitment to the course of action? Consider the following examples:

1. An individual has spent three years working on an advanced degree in a field with minimal job prospects (e.g., the humanities or social science Ph.D.). The individual chooses to invest further time and effort to finish the degree rather than switching to an entirely new field of study. Having attained the degree, the individual is faced with the options of unemployment, working under dissatisfying conditions such as part-time or temporary status, or starting anew in a completely unrelated field.

2. An individual purchased a stock at $50 a share, but the price has gone down to $20. Because the individual is still convinced about the merit of the stock he buys more shares at this lower price. Soon the price declines further and the individual is again faced with the decision to buy more, hold what he already has, or sell out entirely (case taken from personal experience).

3. A city spends a large amount of money to improve the area's sewer and drainage system. The project is the largest public works project in the nation and involves digging 131 miles of tunnel shafts, reservoirs and pumping stations. The excavation is only 10% completed and is useless until it is totally finished. The project will take the next 20 years to complete and will cost $11 billion. Unfortunately, the deeper the tunnels go, the more money they cost, and the greater are the questions about the wisdom of the entire venture (*Time,* 1979, article on Chicago's "Deep Tunnel" project).

4. A company overestimates its capability to build an airplane brake that will meet certain technical specifications at a given cost. Because it wins the government contract, it is forced to invest greater and greater effort into meeting the contract terms.

From *Academy of Management Review* 1981, Vol. 6, No. 4, 577–587. Copyright © 1981 by the Academy of Management. Reprinted with permission.

As a result of increasing pressure to meet specifications and deadlines, records and tests of the brake are misrepresented to government officials. Corporate careers and credibility of the company are increasingly staked to the airbrake contract although many in the firm know the brake will not work effectively. At the conclusion of the construction period the government test pilot flies the plane; it skids off the runway and narrowly averts injuring the pilot (Vandiver, 1972).

5. At an early stage of the U.S. involvement in the Vietnam War, George Ball, then Undersecretary of State, wrote the following statement in a memo to Lyndon Johnson: "The decision you face now is crucial. Once large numbers of U.S. troops are committed to direct combat, they will begin to take heavy casualties in a war they are ill-equipped to fight in a noncooperative if not downright hostile countryside. Once we suffer large casualties, we will have started a well-nigh irreversible process. Our involvement will be so great that we cannot — without national humiliation — stop short of achieving our complete objectives. Of the two possibilities I think humiliation would be more likely than the achievement of our objectives — even after we have paid terrible costs." (Memo dated July 1, 1965, from *Pentagon Papers,* 1971.)

As evidenced in the above examples, many of the most injurious personal decisions and most glaring policy disasters can come in the shape of sequential and escalating commitments. From popular press accounts and the observation of everyday events it appears that individuals may have a tendency to become locked-in to a course of action, throwing good money after bad or committing new resources to a losing course of action. The critical question from an analytical point of view, however, is whether these everyday examples denote a syndrome of decisional errors or are just a post-hoc reconstruction of events. That is, do decisions about commitment to a course of action inherently lead individuals to errors of escalation or are we, as observers, simply labeling a subset of decisions whose outcomes turned out to be negative.

THE FALLIBLE DECISION MAKER

In the psychological literature there have been two primary ways of explaining decisional errors. One way is to point to individual limitations in information process-ing (e.g., Ross, 1977; Tversky & Kahneman, 1974; Slovic, Fishhoff, & Litchenstein, 1977). Individuals are limited in their ability and desire to search for alternatives and input information, recall information from memory, and to compare alternatives on multiple criteria. Because of the limitations to individual ability at each phase of cognitive information processing, the end-product of individual decisions may optimize neither personal utility nor collective welfare. A second way to explain decisional errors is to attribute a breakdown in rationality to interpersonal elements such as social power or group dynamics. Pfeffer (1977) has, for example, outlined how and when power considerations are likely to outweigh more rational aspects of organizational decision making, while Janis (1972) has noted many problems in the decision making of policy groups. Cohesive groups may, according to Janis, suppress dissent, censor information, create illusions of invulnerability, and stereotype enemies. Any of these by-products of social interaction may, of course, hinder rational decision making and lead individuals or collectivities to decisional errors.

Although the limitations to rationality posed by the group dynamics and information processing literatures can be relevant to commitment decisions, they do not seem to capture the central element of the commitment dilemma. When one reexamines the preceding case examples a salient feature is that a *series* of decisions are associated with a course of action rather than an isolated choice. The consequences of any single decision therefore can have implications about the utility of previous choices as well as determining future events or outcomes. This feature means that sunk costs may not be sunk psychologically but may enter into future decisions.

Under traditional models of economic rationality (e.g., Edwards, 1954; Vroom, 1964), resources should be allocated and decisions entered into when future benefits are greater than future costs. Losses or costs which may have been experienced in the past, but which are not expected to recur in the future, should not (at least from a normative perspective) enter into decision calculations. However, individuals may be motivated to rectify past losses as well as to seek future gain. One source of this motivation may be a desire on the part of individuals to appear rational in their decision making. A large literature on self-justification processes (Aronson, 1976; Festinger, 1957) supports this proposition and at least some of the tendency to escalate commitment may be explained by self-justification motives.

RESEARCH ON THE ESCALATION OF COMMITMENT

Self-Justification in Commitment Decisions

The largest and most systematic source of data on the justification of behavior is provided by the social psychological literature of forced compliance (see Wicklund & Brehm, 1976, for an excellent review). Typically, in forced compliance studies an individual is induced to perform an unpleasant or dissatisfying act when no compensating external rewards are present. It is generally predicted that individuals will bias their attitudes on the experimental task in a positive direction so as to justify their previous behavior (e.g., Festinger & Carlsmith, 1959; Pallak, Sogin, & Van Zante, 1974; Weick, 1964). Such biasing of attitudes is most likely to occur when individuals feel personally responsible for negative consequences (Cooper, 1971) and when these consequences are difficult to undo (Brehm & Cohen, 1961; Staw, 1974).

In a series of research studies, Staw and his associates (Staw, 1976; Staw & Fox, 1977; Staw & Ross, 1978) also utilized a self-justification framework in investigating whether decision makers can become overly committed to a course of action. However, the assumption underlying these studies was that individuals may go beyond the passive distortion of adverse consequences in an effort to rationalize a behavioral error. By committing new and additional resources, an individual who has suffered a setback could attempt to "turn the situation around" or to demonstrate the ultimate rationality of his or her original course of action.

In the first empirical test of an escalation effect, Staw (1976) used a simulated business case in which an administrator could recoup losses through the commitment of resources. While acting in the role of a corporate financial officer, business school students were asked to allocate research and development funds to one of two operating divisions of a company. Subjects were then given the results of their initial decisions and asked to make a second allocation of R&D funds. In this study, some participants also were assigned to a condition in which they did not make the initial allocation decision themselves, but were told that it was made earlier by another financial officer of the firm. The results of the experiment showed: (1) that subjects allocated more money to the declining rather than improving division, (2) that subjects allocated more money to the initially chosen division when they, rather than another financial officer, were responsible for the initial decision, and (3) there was a significant interaction such that subjects allocated more money under responsibility for negative consequences than would be expected by the two main effects acting alone. These findings supported the prediction that administrators may seek to justify an ineffective course of action by escalating their commitment of resources to it.

In a follow-up study, Staw and Fox (1977) again assigned subjects to both high and low responsibility conditions in the same type of experimental simulation. However, all subjects were run under a negative consequences condition which persisted over three time periods. Time was extended to see if the effects of high personal responsibility would persist or whether commitment could be built up over time even though a decision maker may not have been responsible for the original course of action (e.g., the Nixon administration became committed to the Vietnam War though it did not initiate it).

The results of this second study were more complex and difficult to interpret than the earlier Staw (1976) experiment. Although the effect of personal responsibility was replicated when simply considering time 1 data, there was a significant decline in commitment over time for high responsibility subjects, while low responsibility subjects maintained or slightly increased their commitment. In explaining these results, Staw and Fox noted that commitment did not diminish over time as one might expect when individuals are given negative feedback or "punishment" over repeated trials. For example, when high commitment was followed by further negative consequences, commitment was generally decreased, but when low commitment was followed by negative consequences, commitment was generally increased. Thus, it appeared from the data as though individuals were actively attempting to probe and learn from the system over time.

The results of the Staw (1976) and Staw and Fox (1977) studies, when considered together, did not provide evidence for a totally self-justifying administrator. The replicated effect of personal responsibility demonstrated that self-justification may motivate the commitment of resources to a course of action. However, when choosing to commit resources, subjects did not appear to persist unswervingly in the face of continued negative results or to ignore information about the possibility of future returns. These inconsistencies led Staw and Ross (1978) to a third study designed specifically to find out how individuals process information following negative versus positive feedback.

In the Staw and Ross (1978) study, both prior success/failure and causal information about a setback were experimentally varied. Results showed that subjects invested more resources in a course of action in which information pointed to an exogenous rather than endogenous cause of a setback, and this tendency was most pronounced when subjects had been given a prior failure rather than a success experience. The exogenous cause in this experiment was one which was both external to the program in which subjects invested and was unlikely to persist in the future, while the endogenous cause was a problem central to the program and likely to persist. These results can be interpreted as showing that individuals will reduce their commitment to a course of action where prospects for future gain are bleak, but that they will continue to invest large amounts of resources when provided an external cause of failure and some hope of recouping their losses. Unfortunately, individuals may selectively filter information so as to maintain their commitment to a policy or course of action (Lord, Ross, & Lepper, 1979; Caldwell & O'Reilly, 1980). One only has to recall the public statements of policy makers during the Vietnam War to appreciate the tendency to *find* exogenous and nonrecurring sources of setbacks (e.g., monsoon rains, equipment failures, and lead time for training allies).

External vs. Internal Justification

Although research on commitment has emphasized the role of justification, these studies have chiefly tapped what could be labeled an *internal justification* process. When justification is considered primarily as an intra-individual process, individuals are posited to attend to events and to act in ways to protect their own self-images (Aronson, 1968; 1976). But within most social settings, justification may also be directed externally. When faced with an external threat or evaluation, individuals may be motivated to prove to others that they were not wrong in an earlier decision and the force for such *external justification* could well be stronger than the protection of individual self esteem.

An empirical demonstration of the effect of external justification was recently conducted by Fox and Staw (1979). They hypothesized that administrators who are vulnerable to job loss or who implement a policy they know is unpopular would be especially motivated to protect themselves against failure. In such cases, where there is strong need for external justification, an administrator would most likely attempt to save a policy

failure by enlarging the commitment of resources. To test this idea, an experimental simulation was conducted in which business students were asked to play the role of administrators under various conditions of job insecurity and policy resistance. The effect of these manipulations upon resource allocation decisions confirmed the hypotheses. When a course of action led to negative results, the administrators who were both insecure in their jobs and who faced stiff policy resistance were most likely to escalate their commitment of resources and become locked-in to the losing course of action.

Norms for Consistency

In addition to the internal and external forms of justification, norms for consistency in action may be another major source of commitment. A lay theory may exist in our society, or at least within many organizational settings, that administrators who are consistent in their actions are better leaders than those who switch from one line of behavior to another. The possibility that there exists a shared norm for consistency in behavior is suggested by recent commentary in the popular press on the nature of leadership.

In a sense, Carter seems at last to have experienced ''his Bay of Pigs,'' the kind of crisis that historians tell us bares the true stuff of presidents, forcing them to search out the bedrock of their own convictions, to urge the nation toward the same conclusions, to make decisions that, if waffled later, could produce national trauma and personal political eclipse . . . leadership involves total belief and commitment.

(Hugh Sidey in Time, *December 11, 1978*)

. . . Carter has exacerbated many of the difficulties he has faced. His most damaging weakness in his first two years has been a frequent indecisiveness . . .

(Time, *February 5, 1979*)

A President must, plainly, show himself to be a man made confident by the courage of his own clear convictions. . . . The American people find it easy to forgive a leader's great mistakes, but not long meanderings.

(E. J. Hughes, in Fortune, *December 4, 1978*)

Reinforcing this notion of a preference or norm for consistency are the results of a national political survey. In the Gallup Poll on President Carter's popularity after his first year in office (Gallup, 1978), respondents who were dissatisfied with the President were asked why they felt this way. ''Indecisiveness'' was the second most frequent response given by the public and the only response that could be coded as a general pattern of behavior (others, e.g., related to specific issues of the economy, foreign policy or campaign promises).

These survey and anecdotal data point to the possibility of an implicit theory of leadership (Calder, 1977; Pfeffer, 1977b) in which effective administrators are seen as fully committed and steadfast to a course of action. In order to empirically test for the existence of such a lay theory, Staw and Ross (1980) conducted an experiment on the reactions of individuals to selected forms of administrative behavior. Subjects included practicing managers, undergraduates in business, and undergraduates in a psychology course. Each subject was asked to study a case description of an administrator's behavior and manipulated in these case descriptions was consistency vs. experimentation in the administrator's course of action as well as the ultimate success vs. failure of the administrator's efforts. In the consistency conditions, the administrator was portrayed as sticking to a single course of action through a series of negative results. In the experimenting conditions, the administrator was portrayed as trying one course of action and, when positive results did not appear, moving to a second and finally third alternative (as an administrator might behave within Campbell's [1969] ''experimenting society''). Ultimate success or failure of the administrator's actions was manipulated after two sets of negative results had been received by either the consistent or experimenting administrator.

Results showed that the administrator was rated highest when he followed a consistent course of action and was ultimately successful. There was also a significant interaction of consistency and success such that the consistent-successful administrator was rated more highly than would be predicted by the two main effects of these variables. This interaction supported a predicted ''hero effect'' for the administrator who remained committed through two apparent failures of a course of action, *only to succeed in the end*. Finally, the effect of consistency upon ratings of the administrator was shown to vary by subject group, being strongest among practicing administrators, next strong among business students, and weakest among psychology undergraduates. These results suggest not only that consistency in action is perceived to be part of effective leadership, but that this perception may be acquired through socialization in business and governmental roles.

TOWARD A THEORETICAL MODEL

In reviewing the research conducted to date it should be apparent that commitment is a complex process, subject to multiple and sometimes conflicting processes. Therefore, it may be helpful to consolidate in a single theoretical model the shape of the forces affecting commitment decisions, specifying their direction as well as possible impact. An attempt to reach such a model is presented in Figure 1.

The figure depicts four major determinants of commitment to a course of action: motivation to justify previous decisions, norms for consistency, probability of future outcomes, and value of future outcomes. Commitment research has concentrated upon the first two of these determinants, while the latter are obviously the two accepted determinants of economic and behavioral decision making. It should be apparent from our review that commitment research has focused upon the processes that may lead to departures from rational decision making, although such ''non-rational'' forces can often conflict and/or interact with traditional elements of rationality. After reviewing the major antecedents of commitment we will address some of these complexities and interactive features of the commitment process.

In examining Figure 1, motivation to justify decisions can be seen as a function of responsibility for negative consequences as well as both internal and external demands for competence. As depicted in the model, responsibility for negative consequences leads to a motivation to justify previous decisions, if there is a need to demonstrate competence to oneself or others. As already noted, the traditional literature on dissonance and self-justification considers only the internal desire of individuals to be correct or accurate in decision making, whereas the need to demonstrate competence to external parties may also be a potent force. Fox and Staw's (1979) operationalizations of job insecurity and policy resistance can be interpreted conceptually as manipulations of a need to externally demonstrate competence. However, while much research assumes a need for self-justification, few studies have actually manipulated internal competence needs. Certainly, Aronson (1968, 1976) speaks of self-esteem as a moderator of justification effects, but it is not yet clear whether a devaluation of self-esteem would lessen or intensify the need to demonstrate competence to oneself and there are no empirical results which clarify this issue. Therefore, at present, it must simply be

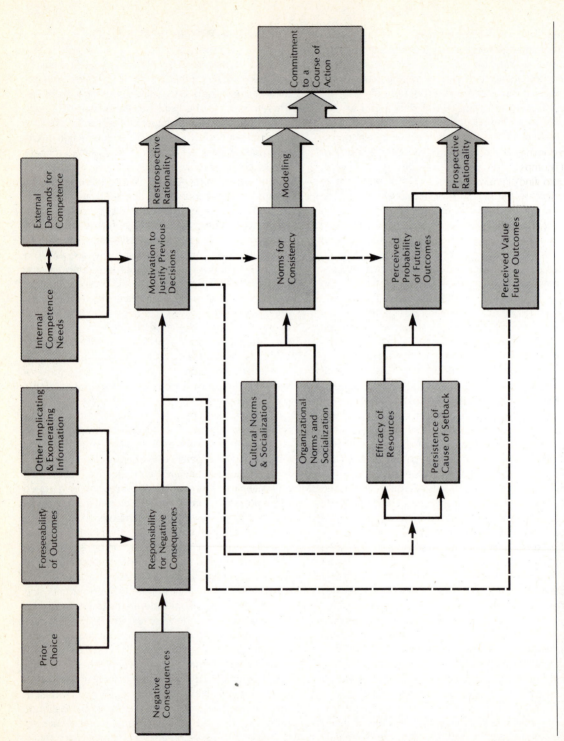

Figure 1. A Model of the Commitment Process.

posited that most individuals possess sufficient internal as well as external competence needs for negative consequences to evoke justification effects. Such predictions may be culture-bound, but emphases on individual rationality and competence are so strong in Western societies that they are likely to foster concomitant needs for rationalizing one's actions (Wicklund & Brehm, 1976). Likewise, because norms for rationality are so dominant in business and governmental organizations (Thompson, 1967), role occupants in these settings may also find it necessary to justify their actions to constituents within and outside the organization. In sum, it is somewhat ironic that both internal and external needs for competence can lead to justification, because justification is exactly what may detract from the rational or competent decision making that both individuals and organizations seek to achieve (Staw, 1980).

Returning to Figure 1, it can be noted that there are three determinants of responsibility for negative consequences. There is evidence from the forced compliance literature that prior choice (Collins & Hoyt, 1972; Linder, Cooper & Jones, 1967) and foreseeability of outcomes (Brehm & Jones, 1970; Cooper, 1971; Goethals, Cooper & Naficy, 1979) are antecedents of perceived responsibility. However, as is noted in the figure, there may be other implicating or exonerating information of relevance to the individual, since a person may be accused of error or may accept blame even when he or she may not have actively participated in a questionable decision (cf. Caldwell & O'Reilly, 1980). Although each of these antecedents of responsibility have not been tested in a commitment context, the overall effect of personal responsibility upon commitment has been replicated several times (Fox, 1980; Staw, 1976; Staw & Fox, 1977).

Prospective vs. Retrospective Rationality

As illustrated in Figure 1, forces for justification can lead to a form of retrospective rationality. The individual, when motivated by a need to justify, seeks to appear competent on *previous* as opposed to *future* actions (Staw, 1980). In contrast, SEU models of behavior posit that the individual is prospectively rational, seeking to maximize future utility. What adds to the complexity is the fact that *both* forces may be operative in commitment decisions.

As determinants of prospective rationality, some set of perceived probabilities and values should affect resource allocation decisions. Already within commitment situations we have validated the effects of the efficacy of resources (Staw & Fox, 1977) and the causal persistence of a setback (Staw & Ross, 1978). However, it is possible that individual perceptions of the likelihood and value of various outcomes are also influenced by justification motives. As shown in a recent experiment by Fox (1980), individuals make greater use of information that exonerates themselves of an earlier error than information that is implicating. Thus, it could be expected that motivation to justify decisions will affect the search for and storage of information by individuals. Likewise, having been responsible for negative consequences may make the achievement of future outcomes all the more important. The value of future returns may intensify as they may be needed to cover past losses. Hence, Figure 1 shows the interplay between some of the antecedents of justification with perceived probability and value of outcomes, the accepted elements of rational behavior. Because of these interactions (see dotted lines), it is not always clear whether behavior can be labeled as strictly prospectively or retrospectively oriented.

Modeling

In addition to the confluence of retrospective and prospective rationality, there is probably a third force of major importance to commitment decisions. As Staw and Ross (1980) have shown, individuals may become committed to a course of action simply because they believe consistency in action is an appropriate form of behavior. Individuals may model their own behavior on those they see as successful within organizations and/or society in general. These effects may be time-dependent (Gergen, 1976) since high level administrators may model their behavior on leadership stereotypes that exist in the culture at a given point in history. These effects may also be rather noncognitive since behavior may be modeled without a direct calculation of costs and benefits (cf., Bandura, 1971). Thus, the effect of norms for consistency is shown in Figure 1 as being determined by the cultural and organizational norms surrounding individuals and the effect of such norms is posited to lead directly to increases in commitment to a course of action. Obviously, norms could also be integrated into an SEU or expectancy model of decision making (e.g., Fishbein & Ajzen, 1975) and be viewed as one element of a prospectively rational decision to commit resources. Likewise, norms for consistency can themselves be viewed as an outgrowth of individual needs for cognitive consistency (Festinger, 1957) or socialization for consistency within the general society. The possible effect of justification upon norms for consistency is depicted by a dotted line in Figure 1, as is the possible effect of norms upon the perceived probability for future outcomes.

In summary, Figure 1 shows commitment to be a complex process dependent upon forces for retrospective rationality, prospective rationality, and behavioral modeling. I have emphasized that commitment decisions are different from simple isolated choices, and for that reason, I believe constructs other than SEU can explain much of the commitment process. The crucial feature of commitment decisions is that an entire series of outcomes are determined by a given choice, the consequences of any single decision having implications for past as well as future events. Thus, commitment decisions may be determined as much by a desire to rectify past outcomes as to attain future returns. In addition, because a series of decisions are associated together, norms for consistency in action may override SEU or economic considerations. Most of the antecedents we have explored must of course be viewed as very tentative determinants of commitment. At present, many of the proposed relationships are based as much on theoretical deduction as empirical evidence, and this is especially true for the interactive effects in Figure 1. While existing data have so far identified only simple antecedents of commitment, the model proposes that commitment is a complex product based on multiple and conflicting processes.

AN ASSESSMENT OF THE COMMITMENT PROCESS

We began this paper with a series of examples and an inquiry into whether commitment situations can inherently lead individuals into errors of escalation. The examples were tilted in the direction of an escalation of commitment and in each case the escalation seemed to lead to further problems or losses. Obviously, it is also possible that escalation of commitment can bring a turnaround of results and positive as well as negative consequences. But this is not the point. The crucial issue is whether there is a tendency to escalate commitment above and beyond what would be warranted by the "objective" facts of the situation. From our research, the answer to this question must be a qualified yes.

If a decision maker were to escalate commitment only when the facts warranted it, there should be no effects of justification or norms for consistency upon commitment. The only variables of relevance to "objective"

commitment decisions would be factors affecting the probability and value of future outcomes. However, knowledgeable observers of a commitment situation do not generally reach the same decisions as do actors who have experienced prior losses. In addition, there may be a simple preference on the part of individuals for consistency in behavior which may not be warranted by the facts of a commitment situation. Thus, motivation to justify and norms for consistency may each contribute to a general tendency to escalate. If future prospects are especially bleak, and this information is salient to the individual, escalation tendencies may be outweighed by these more pressing elements of the situation. Nonetheless, we believe we have identified some contributing elements to the commonly observed syndrome of escalating commitment.

Many researchers may object to the inclusion of "nonrational" elements into a decision framework and prefer to think of commitment strictly as a function of probabilities and valences in an expectancy theory sense (e.g., Edwards, 1954; Vroom, 1964). Of course it is even possible to collapse all the antecedents of commitment into factors affecting perceived probabilities and valences and finally into a SEU calculation. However, this would neither reduce the number of variables with which we must deal nor improve our understanding. It would simply constitute a semantic transformation of retrospective and normative factors into a purely prospective framework. As examples of this reasoning, factors such as personal responsibility for losses as well as political vulnerability could be reinterpreted as an increase in the value of future returns if a turnaround were to be reached, thus explaining additional commitment to a previously chosen course of action. We do not object to these interpretations and they may well be validated empirically. However, the usefulness of constructs such as justification and norms for consistency is that they make salient *to the researcher* variables which not only can explain escalation situations, but which would not be emphasized by research posed from other theoretical perspectives.

IMPLICATIONS

If we accept the conclusion that there is a tendency to escalate on the part of individuals, what are its implications? Perhaps the most likely victims of an escalation tendency will be behaviors that are perceptually associated as parts of a single course of action, because it is in these instances that both justification and consistency influences have been found to override more objective elements of the situation. Prime candidates for escalation therefore include resource allocation or investment decisions that are identified by an entering and exit value, life choices that are linked together by oneself or others with the label of a career, and policy decisions for which administrators are held accountable by others in an organization or by the general public. In these situations one must be especially wary of escalation tendencies and perhaps take counteractions to restore balance to decision making.

In counterbalancing an escalation tendency, the variables outlined in Figure 1 may again be of use. For example, individuals should seek and follow the advice of outsiders who can assess the relevant issues of a decision situation without being responsible for previous losses nor subject to internal or external needs to justify past actions. Likewise, organizations that have experienced losses from a given investment or course of action should rotate or change those in charge of allocating resources. One applied instance of such a counterbalancing strategy was recently uncovered by Lewicki (1980). In a comparative case study, procedures were examined in two banks for coping with the problem of delinquent loans. The more financially aggressive bank which had issued loans with greater risk utilized separate departments for lending and "workout," the latter department being in charge of efforts to recover the bank's investment from problem accounts. In contrast, the more conservative bank which had fewer delinquent loans had developed no formal procedure for separating responsibility for lending and workout, the original loan officer being charged with all phases of the loan relationship.

As a final note, this review should help us recognize how difficult it will be to achieve what Campbell (1969) has described as an "experimenting society." Our research has shown that administrators may become trapped in a course of action by external demands for success (Fox & Staw, 1979), and administrative experimentation may simply be viewed as an inappropriate form of leadership behavior (Staw & Ross, 1980). Thus, it may be important to revamp performance evaluation systems facing administrators so that the motivation for action will shift from the defense of past actions to attainment of future gain (e.g., from a retrospective to a prospective basis). It may also be necessary to retrain administrators and resocialize students entering governmental and business organizations about the merits of experimentation vs. consistency. In each of these ways the actions of decision makers can perhaps be tilted away from the tendency to escalate.

REFERENCES

Aronson, E. Dissonance theory: Progress and problems. In R. Abelson, E.; Aronson; W. McGuire; T. Newcomb; M. Rosenberg; & P. Tannenbaum (Eds.), *Theories of cognitive consistency*. Chicago: Rand McNally, 1968.

Aronson, E. *The social animal*. San Francisco: Freeman, 1976.

Bandura, A. *Psychological modeling: Conflicting theories*. Chicago: Aldine-Atherton, 1971.

Brehm, J. W.; & Cohen, A. E. *Explorations in cognitive dissonance*. New York: Wiley, 1962.

Brehm, J. W.; & Jones, R. A. The effect on dissonance of surprise consequences. *Journal of Personality and Social Psychology*, 1970, *6*, 420–431.

Calder, B. J. An attribution theory of leadership. In B. Staw & G. Salancik (Eds.), *New directions in organizational behavior*. Chicago: St. Clair Press, 1977.

Caldwell, D. F.; & O'Reilly, C. A. *Responses to failure: The effects of choice and responsibility on impression management*. Unpublished manuscript, 1980.

Campbell, D. T. Reforms as experiments. *American Psychologist*, 1979, *24*, 409–429.

Collins, B. E.; & Hoyt, M. F. Personal responsibility-for-consequences: An integration and extension of the "forced compliance" literature. *Journal of Experimental Social Psychology*, 1972, *8*, 558–593.

Cooper, J. Personal responsibility and dissonance: The role of foreseen consequences: An integration and extension of the "forced compliance" literature. *Journal of Experimental Social Psychology*, 1971, *8*, 558–594.

Edwards, W. The theory of decision making. *Psychological Bulletin,* 1954, *51,* 380–417.

Festinger, L. *A theory of cognitive dissonance.* Stanford: Stanford University Press, 1957.

Festinger, L.; & Carlsmith, J. M. Cognitive consequences of forced compliance. *Journal of Abnormal and Social Psychology,* 1959, *58,* 203–210.

Fishbein, M.; & Ajzen, I. *Belief, attitude, intention and behavior: An introduction to theory and research.* Reading, Mass.: Addison-Wesley, 1975.

Fox, F. V. Persistence: Effects of commitment and justification processes on efforts to succeed with a course of action, unpublished doctoral dissertation, University of Illinois, 1980.

Fox, F.; & Staw, B. M. The trapped administrator: The effects of job insecurity and policy resistance upon commitment to a course of action. *Administrative Science Quarterly,* 1979, *24,* 449–471.

Gallup, G. *The Gallup opinion index.* Princeton, N.J.: The American Institute of Public Opinion, March 1978.

Goethals, G.; Cooper, J.; & Naficy, A. Role of foreseen, foreseeable, and unforeseeable behavior consequences in the arousal of cognitive dissonance. *Journal of Personality and Social Psychology,* 1979, *37,* 1179–1185.

Hughes, E. J. The presidency versus Jimmy Carter. *Fortune,* December 4, 1978, p. 58.

Janis, I. *Victims of groupthink.* Boston: Houghton-Mifflin, 1972.

Lewicki, R. J. Bad loan psychology: Entrapment and commitment in financial lending, working paper 80-25, Graduate School of Business administration, Duke University, 1980.

Linder, E. D.; Cooper; J.; & Jones, E. E. Decision freedom as a determinant of the role of incentive magnitude in attitude change. *Journal of Personality and Social Psychology,* 1967, *6,* 245–254.

Lord, C.; Ross, L.; & Lepper, M. Biased assimilation and attitude polarization: The effects of prior theories on subsequently considered evidence. *Journal of Personality and Social Psychology,* 1979, *37,* 2098–2109.

Pallak, M. S.; Sogin, S. R.; & Van Zante, A. Bad decisions: Effects of volition, locus of causality, and negative consequences on attitude change. *Journal of Personality and Social Psychology,* 1972, *30,* 217–227.

Pentagon papers. *The New York Times* (based on investigative reporting of Neil Sheehan), New York: Bantam Books, 1971.

Pfeffer, J. The ambiguity of leadership. *Academy of Management Review,* 1977, *2,* 104–112 (a).

Pfeffer, J. Power and resource allocation in organizations. In B. Staw; & G. Salancik (Eds.), *New Directions in Organizational Behavior.* Chicago: St. Clair Press, 1977 (b).

Read, W. Upward communication in industrial hierarchies. *Human Relations,* 1962, *15,* 3-16.

Ross, L. The intuitive psychologist and his shortcomings: Distortions in the attribution process. In L. Berkowitz (Ed.), *Advances in experimental social psychology* (Vol. 10). New York: Academic Press, 1977.

Sidey, H. The crux of leadership. *Time,* December 11, 1978, p. 44.

Slovic, P.; Fischhoff, B.; & Lichtenstein, S. Behavioral decision theory. *Annual Review of Psychology,* 1977, *28,* 1-39.

Staw, B. M. Attitudinal and behavioral consequences of changing a major organizational reward: A natural field experiment. *Journal of Personality and Social Psychology,* 1974, *6,* 742–541.

Staw, B. M. Knee-deep in the big muddy: A study of escalating commitment to a chosen course of action. *Organizational Behavior and Human Performance,* 1976, *16,* 27–44.

Staw, B. M. Rationality and justification in organizational life. In B. Staw; & L. Cummings (Eds.) *Research in Organizational Behavior* (Volume 2). Greenwich, Conn.: JAI Press, 1980.

Staw, B. M.; & Fox, F. Escalation: Some determinants of commitment to a previously chosen course of action. *Human Relations,* 1977, *30,* 431–450.

Staw, B. M.; & Ross, J. Commitment to a policy decision: A multi-theoretical perspective. *Administrative Science Quarterly,* 1978, *23,* 40–64.

Staw, B. M.; & Ross, J. Commitment in an experimenting society: An experiment on the attribution of leadership from administrative scenarios. *Journal of Applied Psychology,* in press.

Time, The state of Jimmy Carter. February 5, 1979, p. 11.

Time, Money down the drain. June 25, 1979, p. 26.

Tversky, A., & Kahneman, D. Judgment under uncertainty: Heuristics and biases. *Science,* 1974, *185,* 1124–1131.

Vandiver, K. Why should my conscience bother me? In a. Heilbroner (Ed.), *In the name of profit.* Garden City, N.Y.: Doubleday, 1972.

Vroom, V. *Work and motivation.* New York: Wiley, 1964.

Weick, K. E. Reduction of cognitive dissonance through task enhancement and effort expenditure. *Journal of Abnormal and Social Psychology,* 1964, *68,* 533–539.

White, R. W. Motivation reconsidered: The concept of competence. *Psychological Review,* 1959, *66,* 297–334.

Wicklund, R.; & Brehm, J. *Perspectives on cognitive dissonance.* Hillsdale, N.J.: Lawrence Erlbaum Association, 1976.

33.   The Technology of Foolishness

James G. March

I

The concept of choice as a focus for interpreting human behavior has rarely had an easy time in the realm of ideas. It is beset by theological disputations over free will, by the dilemmas of absurdism, by the doubts of psychological behaviorism, by the claims of historical, economic, social, and demographic determinism. Nevertheless, the idea that humans make choices has proven robust enough to become a major matter of faith in important segments of contemporary Western civilization.

The major tenets of this faith run something like this: Human beings make choices. They do this by evaluating their alternatives in terms of their goals on the basis of information available to them. They choose the alternative that is most attractive in terms of the goals. The process of making choices can be improved by using the technology of choice. Through the paraphernalia of modern techniques, we can improve the quality of the search for alternatives, the quality of information, and the quality of the analysis used to evaluate alternatives. Although actual human choice may fall short of this ideal in various ways, it is an attractive model of how choices should be made by individuals and organizations.

Whatever the merits of such a faith within the academic worlds of philosophy, psychology, economics, history, and sociology, it is, I believe, a dominant view among businessmen, politicians, engineers, educators, scientists, and bureaucrats. It qualifies as a key part of the current conception of intelligence. It affirms the efficacy and possibility of intelligent human action.

These articles of faith have been built upon, and have stimulated, some scripture. It is the scripture of theories of individual and organizational decision making. The scripture is partly a codification of received doctrine and partly a source for that doctrine. As a result, our cultural ideas of intelligence and our theories of choice bear some substantial resemblance. In particular, they share three conspicuous interrelated ideas:

The first idea is the *preexistence of purpose.* We find it natural to base an interpretation of human choice

"The Technology of Foolishness" by James G. March from *Civiløkonomen* (Copenhagen) 18, no. 4, May 1971. Reprinted with permission of the author.

behavior on a presumption of human purpose. We have, in fact, invented one of the most elaborate terminologies in the professional literature: ''values,'' ''needs,'' ''wants,'' ''goods,'' ''preferences,'' ''utility,'' ''objectives,'' ''goals,'' ''aspirations,'' ''drives.'' All of these reflect a strong tendency to believe that a useful interpretation of human behavior involves defining a set of objectives that *(a)* are the prior attributes of the system, and *(b)* make the observed behavior in some sense intelligent vis-à-vis those objectives.

Whether we are talking about individuals or about organizations, purpose is an obvious presumption of the discussion. An organization is often defined in terms of its purpose. It is seen by some as the largest collectivity directed by a purpose. Action within an organization is justified (or criticized) in terms of the purpose. Individuals explain their own behavior, as well as the behavior of others, in terms of a set of value premises that are presumed to be antecedent to the behavior. Normative theories of choice begin with an assumption of a preexistent preference ordering defined over the possible outcomes of a choice.

The second idea is the *necessity of consistency*. We have come to recognize consistency both as an important property of human behavior and as a prerequisite for normative models of choice. Dissonance theory, balance theory, theories of congruency in attitudes, statuses, and performances have all served to remind us of the possibilities for interpreting human behavior in terms of the consistency requirements of a limited capacity information-processing system.

At the same time, consistency is a cultural and theoretical virtue. Action should be made consistent with belief. Beliefs should be consistent with each other, and stable over time. Actions taken by different parts of an organization should be consistent with each other. Individual and organizational activities are seen as connected with each other in terms of their consequences for some consistent set of purposes. In an organization, the structural manifestation of the dictum of consistency is the hierarchy with its obligations of coordination and control. In the individual, the structural manifestation is a set of values that generates a consistent preference ordering.

The third idea is the *primacy of rationality*. By rationality I mean a procedure for deciding what is correct behavior by relating consequences systematically to objectives. By placing primary emphasis on rational techniques, we implicitly have rejected—or seriously impaired—two other procedures for choice: *(a)* the

processes of intuition, by means of which people may do things without fully understanding why, and *(b)* the processes of tradition and faith, through which people do things because that is the way they are done.

Both within the theory and within the culture we insist on the ethic of rationality. We justify individual and organizational action in terms of an analysis of means and ends. Impulse, intuition, faith, and tradition are outside that system and viewed as antithetical to it. Faith may be seen as a possible source of values. Intuition may be seen as a possible source of ideas about alternatives. But the analysis and justification of action lies within the context of reason.

These ideas are obviously deeply embedded in the culture. Their roots extend into ideas that have conditioned much of modern Western history and interpretations of that history. Their general acceptance is probably highly correlated with the permeation of rationalism and individualism into the style of thinking within the culture. The ideas are even more obviously embedded in modern theories of choice. It is fundamental to those theories that thinking should precede action; that action should serve a purpose; that purpose should be defined in terms of a consistent set of preexistent goals; and that choice should be based on a consistent theory of the relation between action and its consequences.

Every tool of management decision that is currently a part of management science, operations research, or decision theory assumes the prior existence of a set of consistent goals. Almost the entire structure of microeconomic theory builds on the assumption that there exists a well-defined, stable, and consistent preference ordering. Most theories of individual or organizational choice behavior accept the idea that goals exist and that (in some sense) an individual or organization acts on those goals, choosing from among some alternatives on the basis of available information.

From the perspective of all of man's history, the ideas of purpose, consistency, and rationality are relatively new. Much of the technology currently available to implement them is extremely new. Over the past few centuries, and conspicuously over the past few decades, we have substantially improved man's capability for acting purposively, consistently, and rationally. We have substantially increased his propensity to think of himself as doing so. It is an impressive victory, won—where it has been won—by a happy combination of timing, performance, ideology, and persistence. It is a battle yet to be concluded, or even engaged, in many cultures of the world; but within most of the Western world, individuals and organizations see themselves as making choices.

II

The tools of intelligence as they are fashioned in modern theories of choice are necessary to any reasonable behavior in contemporary society. It is difficult to see how we could, and inconceivable that we would, fail to continue their development, refinement, and extension. As might be expected, however, a theory and ideology of choice built on the ideas outlined above is deficient in some obvious, elementary ways, most conspicuously in the treatment of human goals.

Goals are thrust upon the intelligent man. We ask that he act in the name of goals. We ask that he keep his goals consistent. We ask that his actions be oriented to his goals. But we do not concern ourselves with the origin of goals. Theories of individual and organizational choice assume actors with preexistent value systems.

Since it is obvious that goals change over time and that the character of those changes affects both the richness of personal and organizational development and the outcome of choice behavior, a theory of choice must somehow justify ignoring the phenomena. Although it is unreasonable to ask a theory of choice to solve all of the problems of man and his development, it is reasonable to ask how something as conspicuous as the fluidity of objective can plausibly be ignored in a theory that is offered as a guide to human choice behavior.

There are three classic justifications. The first is that goal development and choice are independent processes, conceptually and behaviorally. The second is that the model of choice is never satisfied in fact and that deviations from the model accommodate the problems of introducing change. The third is that the idea of changing goals is so intractable in a normative theory of choice that nothing can be said about it. Since I am unpersuaded of the first and second justifications, my optimism with respect to the third is somewhat greater than most of my fellows.

The argument that goal development and choice are independent behaviorally seems clearly false. It seems to me perfectly obvious that a description that assumes goals come first and action comes later is frequently radically wrong. Human choice behavior is at least as

much a process for discovering goals as for acting on them. Although it is true enough that goals and decisions are "conceptually" distinct, that is simply a statement of the theory. It is not a defense of it. They are conceptually distinct if we choose to make them so.

The argument that the model is incomplete is more persuasive. There do appear to be some critical "holes" in the system of intelligence as described by standard theories of choice. There is incomplete information, incomplete goal consistency, and a variety of external processes impinging on goal development — including intuition and tradition. What is somewhat disconcerting about the argument, however, is that it makes the efficacy of the concepts of intelligent choice dependent on their inadequacy. As we become more competent in the techniques of the model, and more committed to it, the "holes" become smaller. As the model becomes more accepted, our obligation to modify it increases.

The final argument seems to me sensible as a general principle, but misleading here. Why are we more reluctant to ask how human beings might find "good" goals than we are to ask how they might make "good" decisions? The second question appears to be a relatively technical problem. The first seems more pretentious. It claims to say something about alternative virtues. The appearance of pretense, however, stems directly from the theory and the ideology associated with it.

In fact, the conscious introduction of goal discovery as a consideration in theories of human choice is not unknown to modern man. We have two kinds of theories of choice behavior in human beings. One is a theory of children. The other is a theory of adults. In the theory of childhood, we emphasize choices as leading to experiences that develop the child's scope, his complexity, his awareness of the world. As parents, or psychologists, we try to lead the child to do things that are inconsistent with his present goals because we know (or believe) that he can only develop into an interesting person by coming to appreciate aspects of experience that he initially rejects.

In the theory of adulthood, we emphasize choices as a consequence of our intentions. As adults, or economists, we try to take actions that (within the limits of scarce resources) come as close as possible to achieving our goals. We try to find improved ways of making decisions consistent with our perceptions of what is valuable in the world.

The asymmetry in these models is conspicuous. Adults have constructed a model world in which adults know what is good for themselves, but children do not know what is good for themselves. It is hard to react positively to the conceit. Reaction to the asymmetry has, in fact, stimulated a rather large number of ideologies and reforms designed to allow children the same moral prerogative granted to adults — the right to imagine that they know what they want. The efforts have cut deeply into traditional child-rearing, traditional educational policies, traditional politics, and traditional consumer economics.

In my judgment, the asymmetry between models of choice for adults and models of choice for children is awkward; but the solution we have adopted is precisely wrong-headed. Instead of trying to adapt the model of adults to children, we might better adapt the model of children to adults. For many purposes, our model of children is better. Of course, children know what they want. Everyone does. The critical question is whether they are encouraged to develop more interesting "wants." Values change. People become more interesting as those values and the interconnections made among them change.

One of the most obvious things in the world turns out to be hard for us to accommodate in our theory of choice: A child of two will almost always have a less interesting set of values (yes, indeed, a *worse* set of values) than a child of twelve. The same is true of adults. Although one of the main natural arenas for the modification of human values is the arena of choice, our theories of adult and organizational decision making ignore the phenomenon entirely.

Introducing ambiguity and fluidity to the interpretation of individual and organizational goals obviously has implications for behavioral theories of decision making. The main point here, however, is not to consider how we might describe the behavior of individuals and organizations that are discovering goals as they act. Rather it is to examine how we might improve the quality of that behavior, how we might aid the development of interesting goals.

We know how to advise an organization or an individual if we are first given a consistent set of preferences. Under some conditions, we can suggest how to make decisions if the preferences are only consistent up to the point of specifying a series of independent constraints on the choice. But what about a normative theory of goal-finding behavior? What do we say when our client tells us that he is not sure his present set of values is the set of values in terms of which he wants to act?

It is a question familiar to many aspects of ordinary life. It is a question that friends, associates, students, college presidents, business managers, voters, and children ask at least as frequently as they ask how they should act within a set of consistent and stable values.

Within the context of the normative theory of choice as it exists, the answer we give is: First determine the values, then act. The advice is frequently useful. Moreover, we have developed ways in which we can use conventional techniques for decision analysis to help discover what our value premises are and to expose value inconsistencies for resolution. These techniques involve testing the decision implications of some successive approximations to a set of preferences. The object is to find a consistent set of preferences with implications that are acceptable to the person or organization making the decisions. Variations on such techniques are used routinely in operations research, as well as in personal counseling and analysis.

The utility of such techniques, however, apparently depends on the assumption that a primary problem is the excavation of preexistent values. The metaphors — "finding oneself," "goal clarification," "self-discovery" — are metaphors of search. If our value premises are to be "constructed" rather than "discovered," our standard procedures may be useful; but we have no a priori reason for assuming they will.

Perhaps we should explore a somewhat different approach to the normative question of how we ought to behave when our value premises are not yet (and never will be) fully determined. Suppose we treat actions as a way of creating interesting goals at the same time as we treat goals as a way of justifying action. It is an intuitively plausible and simple idea, but one that is not immediately within the domain of standard normative theories of intelligent choice.

Interesting people and interesting organizations construct complicated theories of themselves. In order to do this, they need to supplement the technology of reason with a technology of foolishness. Individuals and organizations need ways of doing things for which they have no good reason. Not always. Not usually. But sometimes. They need to act before they think.

III

In order to use the act of intelligent choice as a planned occasion for discovering new goals, we apparently require some idea of sensible foolishness. Which of the many foolish things that we might do now will lead to attractive value consequences? The question is almost inconceivable. Not only does it ask us to predict the value consequences of action, it asks us to evaluate them. In what terms can we talk about ''good'' changes in goals?

In effect, we are asked either to specify a set of supergoals in terms of which alternative goals are evaluated, or to choose among alternatives now in terms of the unknown set of values we will have at some future time (or the distribution over time of that unknown set of future values). The former alternative moves us back to the original situation of a fixed set of values—now called ''supergoals''—and hardly seems an important step in the direction of inventing procedures for discovering new goals. The latter alternative seems fundamental enough, but it violates severely our sense of temporal order. To say that we make decisions now in terms of goals that will only be knowable later is nonsensical—as long as we accept the basic framework of the theory of choice and its presumptions of preexistent goals.

I do not know in detail what is required, but I think it will be substantial. As we challenge the dogma of preexistent goals, we will be forced to reexamine some of our most precious prejudices: the strictures against imitation, coercion, and rationalization. Each of those honorable prohibitions depends on the view of man and human choice imposed on us by conventional theories of choice.

Imitation is not necessarily a sign of weak blood. It is a prediction. It is a prediction that if we duplicate the behavior or attitudes of someone else, the chances of our discovering attractive new goals for ourselves are relatively high. In order for imitation to be normatively attractive we need a better theory of who should be imitated. Such a theory seems to be eminently feasible. For example, what are the conditions for effectiveness of a rule that you should imitate another person whose values are in a close neighborhood of yours? How do the chances of discovering interesting goals through imitation change as the number of other people exhibiting the behavior to be imitated increases?

Coercion is not necessarily an assault on individual autonomy. It can be a device for stimulating individuality. We recognize this when we talk about parents and children (at least sometimes). What has always been difficult with coercion is the possibility for perversion that it involves, not its obvious capability for stimulating change. What we require is a theory of the circumstances under which entry into a coercive system

produces behavior that leads to the discovery of interesting goals. We are all familiar with the tactic. We use it in imposing deadlines, entering contracts, making commitments. What are the conditions for its effective use?

Rationalization is not necessarily a tricky way of evading morality. It can be a test for the feasibility of a goal change. When deciding among alternative actions for which we have no good reason, it may be sensible to develop some definition of how ''near'' to intelligence alternative ''unintelligent'' actions lie. Effective rationalization permits this kind of incremental approach to changes in values. To use it effectively, however, we require a better idea of the kinds of metrics that might be possible in measuring value distances. At the same time, rationalization is the major procedure for integrating newly discovered goals into an existing structure of values. It provides the organization of complexity itself becomes indistinguishable from randomness.

There are dangers in imitation, coercion, and rationalization. The risks are too familiar to elaborate. We should, indeed, be able to develop better techniques. Whatever those techniques may be, however, they will almost certainly stress the superstructure of biases erected on purpose, consistency, and rationality. They will involve some way of thinking about action now as occurring in terms of a set of unknown future values.

IV

A second requirement for a technology of foolishness is some strategy for suspending rational imperatives toward consistency. Even if we know which of several foolish things we want to do, we still need a mechanism for allowing us to do it. How do we escape the logic of our reason?

Here, I think, we are closer to understanding what we need. It is playfulness. Playfulness is the deliberate, temporary relaxation of rules in order to explore the possibilities of alternative rules. When we are playful, we challenge the necessity of consistency. In effect, we announce—in advance—our rejection of the usual objections to behavior that does not fit the standard model of intelligence.

Playfulness allows experimentation. At the same time, it acknowledges reason. It accepts an obligation that at some point either the playful behavior will be stopped or it will be integrated into the structure of intelligence in some way that makes sense. The suspension of the rules is temporary.

The idea of play may suggest three things that are, in my mind, quite erroneous in the present context. First, play may be seen as a kind of Mardi Gras for reason, a release of the emotional tensions of virtue. Although it is possible that play performs some such function, that is not the function with which I am concerned. Second, play may be seen as part of some mystical balance of spiritual principles: fire and water, hot and cold, weak and strong. The intention here is much narrower than a general mystique of balance. Third, play may be seen as an antithesis of intelligence, so that the emphasis on the importance of play becomes a support for simple self-indulgence. Without prejudicing the case for self-indulgent behavior, my present intent is to propose play as an instrument of intelligence, not a substitute.

Playfulness is a natural outgrowth of our standard view of reason. A strict insistence on purpose, consistency, and rationality limits our ability to find new purposes. Play relaxes that insistence to allow us to act ''unintelligently'' or ''irrationally,'' or ''foolishly'' to explore alternative ideas of possible purposes and alternative concepts of behavioral consistency. And it does this while maintaining our basic commitment to the necessity of intelligence.

Although play and reason are in this way functional complements, they are often behavioral competitors. They are alternative styles and alternative orientations to the same situation. There is no guarantee that the styles will be equally well developed. There is no guarantee that all individuals or all organizations will be equally adept in both styles. There is no guarantee that all cultures will be equally encouraging to both.

Our design problem is either to specify the best mix of styles or, failing that, to assume that most people and most organizations most of the time use an alternation of strategies rather than persevere in either one. It is a difficult problem. The optimization problem looks extremely difficult on the face of it, and the learning situations that will produce alternation in behavior appear to be somewhat less common than those that produce perseveration.

Consider, for example, the difficulty of sustaining playfulness as a style within contemporary American society. Individuals who are good at consistent rationality are rewarded early and heavily. We define it as intelligence, and the educational rewards of society are associated strongly with it. Much of the press from social

norms is in the same direction, particularly for men. Many of the demands of modern organizational life reinforce the same abilities and style preferences.

The result is that many of the most influential, best educated, and best placed citizens have experienced a powerful overlearning with respect to rationality. They are exceptionally good at maintaining consistent pictures of themselves, of relating action to purposes. They are exceptionally poor at a playful attitude toward their own beliefs, toward the logic of consistency, or toward the way they see things as being connected in the world. The dictates of manliness, forcefulness, independence, and intelligence are intolerant of playful urges if they arise. The playful urges that arise are weak ones.

The picture is probably overdrawn, but not, I believe, the implications. Both for organizations and for individuals reason and intelligence have had the unnecessary consequence of inhibiting the development of purpose into more complicated forms of consistency. In order to move away from that position, we need to find some ways of helping individuals and organizations to experiment with doing things for which they have no good reason, to be playful with their conception of themselves. It is a facility that requires more careful attention than I can give it, but I would suggest five things as a small beginning:

First, we can treat *goals as hypotheses*. Conventional decision theory allows us to entertain doubts about almost everything except the thing about which we frequently have the greatest doubt—our objectives. Suppose we define the decsion process as a time for the sequential testing of hypotheses about goals. If we can experiment with alternative goals, we stand some chance of discovering complicated and interesting combinations of good values that none of us previously imagined.

Second, we can treat *intuition as real*. I do not know what intuition is, or even if it is any one thing. Perhaps it is simply an excuse for doing something we cannot justify in terms of present values or for refusing to follow the logic of our own beliefs. Perhaps it is an inexplicable way of consulting that part of our intelligence that is not organized in a way anticipated by standard theories of choice. In either case, intuition permits us to see some possible actions that are outside our present scheme for justifying behavior.

Third, we can treat *hypocrisy as a transition*. Hypocrisy is an inconsistency between expressed values and behavior. Negative attitudes about hypocrisy stem from two major things. The first is a general onus against inconsistency. The second is a sentiment against combining the pleasures of vice with the appearance of virtue. Apparently, that is an unfair way of allowing evil to escape temporal punishment. Whatever the merits of such a position as ethics, it seems to me distinctly inhibiting toward change. A bad man with good intentions may be a man experimenting with the possibility of becoming good. Somehow it seems to me more sensible to encourage the experimentation than to insult it.

Fourth, we can treat *memory as an enemy*. The rules of consistency and rationality require a technology of memory. For most purposes, good memories make good choices. But the ability to forget, or overlook, is also useful. If I do not know what I did yesterday or what other people in the organization are doing today, I can act within the system of reason and still do things that are foolish.

Fifth, we can treat *experience as a theory*. Learning can be viewed as a series of conclusions based on concepts of action and consequences that we have invented. Experience can be changed retrospectively. By changing our interpretive concepts now, we modify what we learned earlier. Thus, we expose the possibility of experimenting with alternative childhoods. The usual strictures against ''self-deception'' in experience need occasionally to be tempered with an awareness of the extent to which all experience is an interpretation subject to conscious revision. Personal histories, like national histories, need to be rewritten rather continuously as a base for the retrospective learning of new self-conceptions.

C.

Group Process and Decision Making

34. Suppose We Took Groups Seriously . . .

Harold J. Leavitt

INTRODUCTION

This chapter is mostly a fantasy, but not a utopian fantasy. As the title suggests, it tries to spin out some of the things that might happen if we really took small groups seriously; if, that is, we really used groups, rather than individuals, as the basic building blocks for an organization.

This seems an appropriate forum for such a fantasy. It was fifty years ago, at Hawthorne, that the informal face-to-face work group was discovered. Since then groups have been studied inside and out; they have been experimented with, observed, built, and taken apart. Small groups have become the major tool of the applied behavioral scientist. Organizational Development methods are group methods. Almost all of what is called participative management is essentially based on group techniques.

So the idea of using groups as organizational mechanisms is by no means new or fantastic. The fantasy comes in proposing to start with groups, not add them in; to design organizations from scratch around small groups, rather than around individuals.

But right from the start, talk like that appears to violate a deep and important value, individualism. But this fantasy will not really turn out to be anti-individualistic in the end.

The rest of this chapter will briefly address the following questions: (1) Is it fair to say that groups have not been taken very seriously in organizational design? (2) Why are groups even worth thinking about as organizational building materials? What are the characteristics of groups that might make them interesting enough to be worth serious attention? (3) What would it mean "to take groups seriously?" Just what kinds of things would have to be done differently? (4) What compensatory changes would probably be needed in other aspects of the organization, to have groups as the basic unit? And finally, (5) is the idea of designing the organization around small face-to-face groups a very radical idea, or is it just an extension of a direction in which we are already going?

HAVEN'T GROUPS BEEN TAKEN SERIOUSLY ENOUGH ALREADY?

The argument that groups have not been taken "seriously" doesn't seem a hard one to make. The contemporary ideas about groups didn't really come along until the 30s and 40s. By that time a logical, rationalistic tradition for the construction of organizations already existed. That tradition was very heavily based on the notion that the individual was the construction unit. The logic moved from the projected task backward. Determine the task, the goal, then find an appropriate structure and technology, and last of all fit individual human beings into predefined man-sized pieces of the action. That was, for instance, what industrial psychology was all about during its development between the two world wars. It was concerned almost entirely with individual differences and worked in the service of structuralists, fitting square human pegs to predesigned square holes. The role of the psychologist was thus ancillary to the role of the designers of the whole organization. It was a backup, supportive role that followed more than it led design.

It was not just the logic of classical organizational theory that concentrated on the individual. The whole entrepreneurial tradition of American society supported it. Individuals, at least male individuals, were taught achievement motivation. They were taught to seek individual evaluation, to compete, to see the world, organizational or otherwise, as a place in which to strive for individual accomplishment and satisfaction.

In those respects the classical design of organizations was consonant with the then existent cultural landscape. Individualized organizational structures blended with the environment of individualism. All the accessories fell into place: individual incentive schemes for hourly workers, individual merit rating and assessment schemes, tests for selection of individuals.

The unique characteristic of the organization was that it was not simply a racetrack within which individuals could compete, but a system in which somehow the competitive behavior of individuals could be coordinated, harnessed and controlled in the interest of the common tasks. Of course one residual of all that was a continuing tension between individual and organization, with the organization seeking to control and coordinate the individual's activities at the same time that it tried to motivate him; while the competitive individual insisted on reaching well beyond the constraints imposed upon him by the organization. One product of this tension became the informal organization discovered here at Western; typically an informal coalition designed to fight the system.

Then it was discovered that groups could be exploited for what management saw as positive purposes, *toward* productivity instead of away from it. There followed the era of experimentation with small face-to-face groups. We learned to patch them on to existing organizations as bandaids to relieve tensions between individual and organization. We promoted coordination through group methods. We learned that groups were useful to discipline and control recalcitrant individuals.

Groups were fitted onto organizations. The group skills of individual members improved so that they could coordinate their efforts more effectively, control deviants more effectively and gain more commitment from subordinate individuals. But groups were seen primarily as tools to be tacked on and utilized in the preexisting individualized organizational system. With a few notable exceptions, like Rensis Likert (1961), most did not design organizations around groups. On the contrary, as some of the ideas about small groups began to be tacked onto existing organizational models, they generated new tensions and conflicts of their own. Managers complained not only that groups were slow, but that they diffused responsibility, vitiated the power of the hierarchy because they were too "democratic and created small in-group empires which were very hard for others to penetrate." There was the period, for example, of the great gap between T-group training (which had to be conducted on "cultural islands") and the organization back home. The T-groups therefore talked a lot about the "reentry problem," which meant in part the problem of movement from a new culture (the T-group culture) designed around groups back into the organizational culture designed around individuals.

But of course groups didn't die despite their difficulties. How could they die? They had always been there, though not always in the service of the organization.

They turned out to be useful, indeed necessary, though often unrecognized tools. For organizations were growing, and professionalizing, and the need for better coordination grew even as the humanistic expectations of individuals also grew. So "acknowledged" groups (as distinct from "natural," informal groups) became fairly firmly attached even to conservative organizations, but largely as compensating addenda very often reluctantly backed into by organizational managers.

Groups have never been given a chance. It is as though someone had insisted that automobiles be designed to fit the existing terrain rather than build roads to adapt to automobiles.

ARE GROUPS WORTH CONSIDERING AS FUNDAMENTAL BUILDING BLOCKS?

Why would groups be more interesting than individuals as basic design units around which to build organizations? What are the prominent characteristics of small groups? Why are they interesting? Here are several answers:

First, small groups seem to be good for people. They can satisfy important membership needs. They can provide a moderately wide range of activities for individual members. They can provide support in times of stress and crisis. They are settings in which people can learn not only cognitively but empirically to be reasonably trusting and helpful to one another. Second, groups seem to be good problem finding tools. They seem to be useful in promoting innovation and creativity. Third, in a wide variety of decision situations, they make better decisions than individuals do. Fourth, they are great tools for implementation. They gain commitment from their members so that group decisions are likely to be willingly carried out. Fifth, they can control and discipline individual members in ways that are often extremely difficult through more impersonal quasi-legal disciplinary systems. Sixth, as organizations grow large, small groups appear to be useful mechanisms for fending off many of the negative effects of large size. They help to prevent communication lines from growing too long, the hierarchy from growing too steep, and the individual from getting lost in the crowd.

There is a seventh, but altogether different kind of argument for taking groups seriously. Thus far the designer of organizations seemed to have a choice. He could build an individualized *or* a groupy organization. A groupy organization will, de facto, have to deal with individuals; but what was learned here so long ago is that individual organizations, must de facto, deal with groups. Groups are natural phenomena, and facts of organizational life. They can be created but their spontaneous development cannot be prevented. The problem is not shall groups exist or not, but shall groups be planned or not? If not, the individualized organizational garden will sprout groupy weeds all over the place. By defining them as weeds instead of flowers, they shall continue, as in earlier days, to be treated as pests, forever fouling up the beauty of rationally designed individualized organizations, forever forming informally (and irrationally) to harass and outgame the planners.

It is likely that the reverse could also be true, that if groups are defined as the flowers and individuals as the weeds, new problems will crop up. Surely they will, but that discussion can be delayed for at least a little while.

WHO USES GROUPS BEST?

So groups look like interesting organizational building blocks. But before going on to consider the implications of designing organizations around groups, one useful heuristic might be to look around the existing world at those places in which groups seem to have been treated somewhat more seriously.

One place groups have become big is in Japanese organizations (Johnson & Ouchi, 1974). The Japanese seem to be very groupy, and much less concerned than Americans about issues like individual accountability. Japanese organizations, of course, are thus consonant with Japanese culture, where notions of individual aggressiveness and competitiveness are deemphasized in favor of self-effacement and group loyalty. But Japanese organizations seem to get a lot done, despite the relative suppression of the individual in favor of the group. It also appears that the advantages of the groupy Japanese style have really come to the fore in large technologically complex organizations.

Another place to look is at American conglomerates. They go to the opposite extreme, dealing with very large units. They buy large organizational units and sell units. They evaluate units. In effect they promote units by offering them extra resources as rewards for good performance. In that sense conglomerates, one might argue, are designed around groups, but the groups in question are often themselves large organizational chunks.

GROUPS IN AN INDIVIDUALISTIC CULTURE

An architect can design a beautiful building which either blends smoothly with its environment or contrasts starkly with it. But organization designers may not have the same choice. If we design an organization which is structurally dissonant with its environment, it is conceivable that the environment will change to adjust to the organization. It seems much more likely, however, that the environment will reject the organization. If designing organizations around groups represents a sharp counterpoint to environmental trends, maybe we should abort the idea.

Our environment, one can argue, is certainly highly individualized. But one can also make a less solid argument in the other direction; an argument that American society is going groupy rather than individual this year. Or at least that it is going groupy as well as individual. The evidence is sloppy at best. One can reinterpret the student revolution and the growth of anti-establishment feelings at least in part as a reaction to the decline of those institutions that most satisfied social membership needs. One can argue that the decline of the Church, of the village and of the extended family is leaving behind a vacuum of unsatisfied membership and belongingness motives. Certainly popular critics of American society have laid a great deal of emphasis on the loneliness and anomie that seem to have resulted not only from materialism but from the emphasis on individualism. It seems possible to argue that, insofar as there has been any significant change in the work ethic in America, the change has been toward a desire for work which is socially as well as egoistically fulfilling, and which satisfies human needs for belongingness and affiliation as well as needs for achievement.

In effect, the usual interpretation of Abraham Maslow's need hierarchy may be wrong. Usually the esteem and self-actualization levels of motivation are emphasized. Perhaps the level that is becoming operant most rapidly is neither of those, but the social-love-membership level.

The rising role of women in American society also has implications for the groupiness of organizations. There is a moderate amount of evidence that American women have been socialized more strongly into affiliative and relational sorts of attitudes than men. They probably can, in general, more comfortably work in direct achievement roles in group settings, where there are strong relational bonds among members, than in competitive, individualistic settings. Moreover it is reasonable to assume that as women take a more important place in American society, some of their values and attitudes will spill over to the male side.

Although the notion of designing organizations around groups in America in 1974 may be a little premature, it is consonant with cultural trends that may make the idea much more appropriate ten years from now.

But groups are becoming more relevant for organizational as well as cultural reasons. Groups seem to be particularly useful as coordinating and integrating mechanisms for dealing with complex tasks that require the inputs of many kinds of specialized knowledge. In fact the development of matrix-type organizations in high technology industry is perhaps one effort to modify individually designed organizations toward a more groupy direction; not for humanistic reasons but as a consequence of tremendous increase in the informational complexity of the jobs that need to be done.

WHAT MIGHT A SERIOUSLY GROUPY ORGANIZATION LOOK LIKE?

Just what does it mean to design organizations around groups? Operationally how is that different from designing organizations around individuals? One approach to an answer is simply to take the things organizations do with individuals and try them out with groups. The idea is to raise the level from the atom to the molecule, and *select* groups rather than individuals; *train* groups rather than individuals, *pay* groups rather than individuals, *promote* groups rather than individuals, *design jobs* for groups rather than for individuals, *fire* groups rather than individuals, and so on down the list of activities which organizations have traditionally carried on in order to use human beings in their organizations.

Some of the items on that list seem easy to handle at the group level. For example, it doesn't seem terribly hard to design jobs for groups. In effect that is what top management already does for itself to a great extent. It gives specific jobs to committees, and often runs itself as a group. The problem seems to be a manageable one: designing job sets which are both big enough to require a small number of persons and also small enough to require only a small number of persons. Big enough in this context means not only jobs that would occupy the hands of group members but that would provide opportunities for learning and expansion.

Ideas like evaluating, promoting, and paying groups raise many more difficult but interesting problems. Maybe the best that can be said for such ideas is that they provide opportunities for thinking creatively about pay and evaluation. Suppose, for example, that as a reward for good work the group gets a larger salary budget than it got last year. Suppose the allocation for increases within the group is left to the group members. Certainly one can think up all sorts of difficulties that might arise. But are the potential problems necessarily any more difficult than those now generated by individual merit raises? Is there any company in America that is satisfied with its existing individual performance appraisal and salary allocation schemes? At least the issues of distributive justice within small groups would presumably be open to internal discussion and debate. One might even permit the group to allocate payments to individuals differentially at different times, in accordance with some criteria of current contribution that they might establish.

As far as performance evaluation is concerned, it is probably easier for people up the hierarchy to assess the performance of total groups than it is to assess the performance of individual members well down the hierarchy. Top managers of decentralized organizations do it all the time, except that they usually reward the formal leader of the decentralized unit rather than the whole unit.

The notion of promoting groups raises another variety of difficulties. One thinks of physically transferring a whole group, for example, and of the costs associated with training a whole group to do a new job, especially if there are no bridging individuals. But there may be large advantages too. If a group moves, its members already know how to work with one another. Families may be less disrupted by movement if several move at the same time.

There is the problem of selection. Does it make sense to select groups? Initially, why not? Can't means be found for selecting not only for appropriate knowledge and skill but also for potential ability to work together? There is plenty of groundwork in the literature already.

After the initial phase, there will of course be problems of adding or subtracting individuals from existing groups. We already know a good deal about how to help new members get integrated into old groups. Incidentally, I was told recently by a plant manager in the midwest about an oddity he had encountered; the phenomenon of groups applying for work. Groups of three or four people have been coming to his plant seeking employment together. They wanted to work together and stay together.

COSTS AND DANGER POINTS

To play this game of designing organizations around groups, what might be some important danger points? In general, a group-type organization is somewhat more like a free market than present organizations. More decisions would have to be worked out ad hoc, in a continually changing way. So one would need to schedule more negotiation time both within and between groups.

One would encounter more issues of justice, for the individual vis-a-vis the group and for groups vis-a-vis one another. More and better arbitration mechanisms would probably be needed along with highly flexible and rapidly adaptive record keeping. But modern record-keeping technology is, potentially, both highly flexible and rapidly adaptive.

Another specific issue is the provision of escape hatches for individuals. Groups have been known to be cruel and unjust to their deviant members. One existing escape route for the individual would of course continue to exist: departure from the organization. Another might be easy means of transfer to another group.

Another related danger of a strong group emphasis might be a tendency to drive away highly individualistic, nongroup people. But the tight organizational constraints now imposed do the same thing. Indeed might not groups protect their individualists better than the impersonal rules of present-day large organizations?

Another obvious problem: If groups are emphasized by rewarding them, paying them, promoting them, and so on, groups may begin to perceive themselves as power centers, in competitive conflict with other groups. Intergroup hostilities are likely to be exacerbated unless we can design some new coping mechanisms into the organization. Likert's proposal for solving that sort of problem (and others) is the linking pin concept. The notion is that individuals serve as members of more than one group, both up and down the hierarchy and horizontally. But Likert's scheme seems to me to assume fundamentally individualized organizations in the sense that it is still individuals who get paid, promoted and so on. In a more groupy organization, the linking pin concept has to be modified so that an individual might be a parttime member of more than one group, but still a real member. That is, for example, a portion of an individual's pay might come from each group in accordance with that group's perception of his contribution.

Certainly much more talk, both within and between groups, would be a necessary accompaniment of group emphasis; though we might argue about whether more talk should be classified as a cost or a benefit. In any case careful design of escape hatches for individuals and connections among groups would be as important in this kind of organization as would stairways between floors in the design of a private home.

There is also a danger of overdesigning groups. All groups in the organization need not look alike. Quite to the contrary. Task and technology should have significant effects on the shapes and sizes of different subgroups within the large organization. Just as individuals end up adjusting the edges of their jobs to themselves and themselves to their jobs, we should expect flexibility within groups, allowing them to adapt and modify themselves to whatever the task and technology demand.

Another initially scary problem associated with groups is the potential loss of clear formal individual leadership. Without formal leaders how will we motivate people? Without leaders how will we control and discipline people? Without leaders how will we pinpoint responsibility? Even as I write those questions I cannot help feel that they are archaic. They are questions which are themselves a product of the basic individual building block design of old organizations. The problem is not leaders so much as the performance of leadership functions. Surely groups will find leaders, but they will emerge from the bottom up. Given a fairly clear job description, some groups, in some settings, will set up more or less permanent leadership roles. Others may let leadership vary as the situation demands, or as a function of the power that individuals within any group may possess relative to the group's needs at that time. A reasonable amount of process time can be built in to enable groups to work on the leadership problem, but the problem will have to be resolved within each group. On the advantage side of the ledger, this may even get rid of a few hierarchical levels. There should be far less need for individuals who are chiefly supervisors of other individuals' work. Groups can serve as hierarchical leaders of other groups.

Two other potential costs: With an organization of groups, there may be a great deal of infighting, and power and conflict issues will come even more to the fore than they do now. Organizations of groups may become highly political, with coalitions lining up against one another on various issues. If so, the rest of the organizational system will have to take those political

problems into account, both by setting up sensible systems of intercommunications among groups, and by allocating larger amounts of time and expertise to problems of conflict resolution.

But this is not a new problem unique to groupy organizations. Conflict among groups is prevalent in large organizations which are political systems now. But because these issues have not often been foreseen and planned for, the mechanisms for dealing with them are largely ad hoc. As a result, conflict is often dealt with in extremely irrational ways.

But there is another kind of intergroup power problem that may become extremely important and difficult in groupy organizations. There is a real danger that relatively autonomous and cohesive groups may be closed, not only to other groups but more importantly to staff advice or to new technological inputs.

These problems exist at present, of course, but they may be exacerbated by group structure. I cannot see any perfect way to handle those problems. One possibility may be to make individual members of staff groups part-time members of line groups. Another is to work harder to educate line groups to potential staff contributions. Of course the reward system, the old market system, will probably be the strongest force for keeping groups from staying old-fashioned in a world of new technologies and ideas.

But the nature and degree of many of the second order spinoff effects are not fully knowable at the design stage. We need to build more complete working models and pilot plants. In any case it does not seem obvious that slowdowns, either at the work place or in decision-making processes, would necessarily accompany group based organizational designs.

SOME POSSIBLE ADVANTAGES TO THE ORGANIZATION

Finally, from an organizational perspective, what are the potential advantages to be gained from a group-based organization? The first might be a sharp reduction in the number of units that need to be controlled. Control would not have to be carried all the way down to the individual level. If the average group size is five, the number of blocks that management has to worry about is cut to 20 percent of what it was. Such a design would also probably cut the number of operational levels in the organization. In effect, levels which are now primarily supervisory would be incorporated into the groups that they supervise.

By this means many of the advantages of the small individualized organization could be brought back. These advantages would occur within groups simply because there would be a small number of blocks, albeit larger blocks, with which to build and rebuild the organization.

But most of all, and this is still uncertain, despite the extent to which we behavioral scientists have been enamoured of groups, there would be increased human advantages of cohesiveness, motivation, and commitment, and via that route, both increased productivity, stronger social glue within the organization, and a wider interaction between organization and environment.

SUMMARY

Far and away the most powerful and beloved tool of applied behavioral scientists is the small face-to-face group. Since the Western Electric researches, behavioral scientists have been learning to understand, exploit and love groups. Groups attracted interest initially as devices for improving the implementation of decisions and to increase human commitment and motivation. They are not loved because they are also creative and innovative, they often make better quality decisions than individuals, and because they make organizational life more livable for people. One can't hire an applied behavioral scientist into an organization who within ten minutes will not want to call a group meeting and talk things over. The group meeting is his primary technology, his primary tool.

But groups in organizations are not an invention of behavioral types. They are a natural phenomenon of organizations. Organizations develop informal groups, like it or not. It is both possible and sensible to describe most large organizations as collections of groups in interaction with one another; bargaining with one another, forming coalitions with one another, cooperating and competing with one another. It is possible and sensible, too, to treat the decisions that emerge from large organizations as a resultant of the interplay of forces among groups within the organization, and not just the resultant of rational analysis.

On the down side, small face-to-face groups are great tools for disciplining and controlling their members. Contemporary China, for example, has just a fraction of the number of lawyers in the United States. Partially this is a result of the lesser complexity of Chinese society and lower levels of education. But a large part of it, surprisingly enough, seems to derive from the fact that modern China is designed around small groups. Since small groups take responsibility for the discipline and control of their members, many deviant acts which would be considered illegal in the United States never enter the formal legal system in China. The law controls individual deviation less, the group controls it more (Li, 1971).

Control of individual behavior is also a major problem of large complex western organizations. This problem has driven many organizations into elaborate bureaucratic quasi-legal sets of rules, ranging from job evaluation schemes to performance evaluations to incentive systems; all individually based, all terribly complex, all creating problems of distributive justice. Any organizational design that might eliminate much of that legalistic superstructure therefore begins to look highly desirable.

Management should consider building organizations using a material now understood very well and with properties that look very promising, the small group. Until recently, at least, the human group has primarily been used for patching and mending organizations that were originally built of other materials.

The major unanswered questions in my mind are not in the understanding of groups, nor in the potential utility of the group as a building block. The more difficult answered question is whether or not the approaching era is one in which Americans would willingly work in such apparently contra-individualistic units. I think we are.

REFERENCES

Johnson, Richard T., and Ouchi, William G. ``Made in America (under Japanese Management).'' *Harvard Business Review*, September-October 1974.

Li, Victor. ``The Development of the Chinese Legal System.'' *China: The Management of a Revolutionary Society*, edited by John Lindbeck. Seattle: University of Washington Press, 1971.

Likert, Rensis. *New Patterns of Management*. New York: McGraw-Hill, 1961.

The U.S. road to disaster — in Vietnam,
the Bay of Pigs, Korea, and Pearl Harbor —
is paved with

35.   Groupthink

— the desperate drive for consensus at any
cost that suppresses dissent among the
mighty in the corridors of power.

Irving L. Janis

''How could we have been so stupid?'' President John F. Kennedy asked after he and a close group of advisers had blundered into the Bay of Pigs invasion. For the last two years I have been studying that question, as it applies not only to the Bay of Pigs decision makers but also to those who led the United States into such other major fiascos as the failure to be prepared for the attack on Pearl Harbor, the Korean War stalemate, and the escalation of the Vietnam War.

Stupidity certainly is not the explanation. The men who participated in making the Bay of Pigs decision, for instance, comprised one of the greatest arrays of intellectual talent in the history of American Government — Dean Rusk, Robert McNamara, Douglas Dillon, Robert Kennedy, McGeorge Bundy, Arthur Schlesinger Jr., Allen Dulles, and others.

It also seemed to me that explanations were incomplete if they concentrated only on disturbances in the behavior of each individual within a decision-making body: temporary emotional states of elation, fear, or anger that reduce a man's mental efficiency, for example, or chronic blind spots arising from a man's social prejudices or idiosyncratic biases.

I preferred to broaden the picture by looking at the fiascos from the standpoint of group dynamics as it has been explored over the past three decades, first by the great social psychologist Kurt Lewin and later in many experimental situations by myself and other behavioral scientists. My conclusion after poring over hundreds of relevant documents — historical reports about formal group meetings and informal conversations among the members — is that the groups that committed the fiascos were victims of what I call ''groupthink.''

''GROUPY''

In each case study, I was surprised to discover the extent to which each group displayed the typical phenomena of social conformity that are regularly encountered in studies of group dynamics among ordinary citizens. For example, some of the phenomena appear to be completely in line with findings from social-psychological experiments showing that powerful social pressures are brought to bear by the members of a cohesive group whenever a dissident begins to voice his objections to a group consensus. Other phenomena are reminiscent of the shared illusions observed in encounter groups and friendship cliques when the members simultaneously reach a peak of ''groupy'' feelings.

Above all, there are numerous indications pointing to the development of group norms that bolster morale at the expense of critical thinking. One of the most common norms appears to be that of remaining loyal to the group by sticking with the policies to which the group has already committed itself, even when those policies are obviously working out badly and have unintended consequences that disturb the conscience of each member. This is one of the key characteristics of groupthink.

1984

I use the term *groupthink* as a quick and easy way to refer to the mode of thinking that persons engage in when *concurrence seeking* becomes so dominant in a cohesive ingroup that it tends to override realistic appraisal of alternative courses of action. Groupthink is a term of the same order as the words in the newspeak vocabulary George Orwell used in his dismaying world of *1984*. In that context, groupthink takes on an invidious connotation. Exactly such a connotation is intended, since the term refers to a deterioration in mental efficiency, reality testing, and moral judgments as a result of group pressures.

The symptoms of groupthink arise when the members of decision-making groups become motivated to avoid being too harsh in their judgments of their leaders' or their colleagues' ideas. They adopt a soft line of criticism, even in their own thinking. At their meetings, all the members are amiable and seek complete concurrence on every important issue, with no bickering or conflict to spoil the cozy, "we-feeling" atmosphere.

KILL

Paradoxically, soft-headed groups are often hard-hearted when it comes to dealing with outgroups or enemies. They find it relatively easy to resort to dehumanizing solutions—they will readily authorize bombing attacks that kill large numbers of civilians in the name of the noble cause of persuading an unfriendly government to negotiate at the peace table. They are unlikely to pursue the more difficult and controversial issues that arise when alternatives to a harsh military solution come up for discussion. Nor are they inclined to raise ethical issues that carry the implication that *this fine group of ours, with its humanitarianism and its high-minded principles, might be capable of adopting a course of action that is inhumane and immoral.*

NORMS

There is evidence from a number of social-psychological studies that as the members of a group feel more accepted by the others, which is a central feature of increased group cohesiveness, they display less overt conformity to group norms. Thus we would expect that the more cohesive a group becomes, the less the members will feel constrained to censor what they say

out of fear of being socially punished for antagonizing the leader or any of their fellow members.

In contrast, the groupthink type of conformity tends to increase as group cohesiveness increases. Groupthink involves nondeliberate suppression of critical thoughts as a result of internalization of the group's norms, which is quite different from deliberate suppression on the basis of external threats of social punishment. The more cohesive the group, the greater the inner compulsion on the part of each member to avoid creating disunity, which inclines him to believe in the soundness of whatever proposals are promoted by the leader or by a majority of the group's members.

In a cohesive group, the danger is not so much that each individual will fail to reveal his objections to what the others propose but that he will think the proposal is a good one, without attempting to carry out a careful, critical scrutiny of the pros and cons of the alternatives. When groupthink becomes dominant, there also is considerable suppression of deviant thoughts, but it takes the form of each person's deciding that his misgivings are not relevant and should be set aside, that the benefit of the doubt regarding any lingering uncertainties should be given to the group consensus.

STRESS

I do not mean to imply that all cohesive groups necessarily suffer from groupthink. All ingroups may have a mild tendency toward groupthink, displaying one or another of the symptoms from time to time, but it need not be so dominant as to influence the quality of the group's final decision. Neither do I mean to imply that there is anything necessarily inefficient or harmful about group decisions in general. On the contrary, a group whose members have properly defined roles, with traditions concerning the procedures to follow in pursuing a critical inquiry, probably is capable of making better decisions than any individual group member working alone.

The problem is that the advantages of having decisions made by groups are often lost because of powerful psychological pressures that arise when the members work closely together, share the same set of values, and, above all, face a crisis situation that puts everyone under intense stress.

The main principle of groupthink, which I offer in the spirit of Parkinson's Law, is this: *The more amiability and esprit de corps there is among the members of a policy-making ingroup, the greater the danger that independent critical thinking will be replaced by groupthink, which is likely to result in irrational and dehumanizing actions directed against outgroups.*

SYMPTOMS

In my studies of high-level governmental decision makers, both civilian and military, I have found eight main symptoms of groupthink.

1. Invulnerability

Most or all of the members of the ingroup share an *illusion* of invulnerability that provides for them some degree of reassurance about obvious dangers and leads them to become overoptimistic and willing to take extraordinary risks. It also causes them to fail to respond to clear warnings of danger.

The Kennedy ingroup, which uncritically accepted the Central Intelligence Agency's disastrous Bay of Pigs plan, operated on the false assumption that they could keep secret the fact that the United States was responsible for the invasion of Cuba. Even after news of the plan began to leak out, their belief remained unshaken. They failed even to consider the danger that awaited them: a worldwide revulsion against the U.S.

A similar attitude appeared among the members of President Lyndon B. Johnson's ingroup, the "Tuesday Cabinet," which kept escalating the Vietnam War despite repeated setbacks and failures. "There was a belief," Bill Moyers commented after he resigned, "that if we indicated a willingness to use our power, they [the North Vietnamese] would get the message and back away from an all-out confrontation. . . . There was a confidence — it was never bragged about, it was just there — that when the chips were really down, the other people would fold."

A most poignant example of an illusion of invulnerability involves the ingroup around Admiral H. E. Kimmel, which failed to prepare for the possibility of a Japanese attack on Pearl Harbor despite repeated warnings. Informed by his intelligence chief that radio contact with Japanese aircraft carriers had been lost, Kimmel joked about it: "What, you don't know where the carriers are? Do you mean to say that they could be rounding Diamond Head (at Honolulu) and you wouldn't know it?" The carriers were in fact moving full-steam toward Kimmel's command post at the time. Laughing together about a danger signal, which labels it as a purely laughing matter, is a characteristic manifestation of groupthink.

2. Rationale

As we see, victims of groupthink ignore warnings; they also collectively construct rationalizations in order to discount warnings and other forms of negative feedback that, taken seriously, might lead the group members to reconsider their assumptions each time they recommit themselves to past decisions. Why did the Johnson ingroup avoid reconsidering its escalation policy when time and again the expectations on which they based their decisions turned out to be wrong? James C. Thompson Jr., a Harvard historian who spent five years as an observing participant in both the State Department and the White House, tells us that the policymakers avoided critical discussion of their prior decisions and continually invented new rationalizations so that they could sincerely recommit themselves to defeating the North Vietnamese.

In the fall of 1964, before the bombing of North Vietnam began, some of the policymakers predicted that six weeks of air strikes would induce the North Vietnamese to seek peace talks. When someone asked, "What if they don't?" the answer was that another four weeks certainly would do the trick.

Later, after each setback, the ingroup agreed that by investing just a bit more effort (by stepping up the bomb tonnage a bit, for instance), their course of action would prove to be right. *The Pentagon Papers* bear out these observations.

In *The Limits of Intervention,* Townsend Hoopes, who was acting Secretary of the Air Force under Johnson, says that Walt W. Rostow in particular showed a remarkable capacity for what has been called "instant rationalization." According to Hoopes, Rostow buttressed the group's optimism about being on the road to victory by culling selected scraps of evidence from news reports or, if necessary, by inventing "plausible" forecasts that had no basis in evidence at all.

Admiral Kimmel's group rationalized away their warnings, too. Right up to December 7, 1941, they convinced themselves that the Japanese would never dare attempt a full-scale surprise assault against Hawaii because Japan's leaders would realize that it would precipitate an all-out war which the United States would surely win. They made no attempt to look at the situation through the eyes of the Japanese leaders — another manifestation of groupthink.

3. Morality

Victims of groupthink believe unquestioningly in the inherent morality of their ingroup; this belief inclines the members to ignore the ethical or moral consequences of their decisions.

Evidence that this symptom is at work usually is of a negative kind—the things that are left unsaid in group meetings. At least two influential persons had doubts about the morality of the Bay of Pigs adventure. One of them, Arthur Schlesinger, Jr., presented his strong objections in a memorandum to President Kennedy and Secretary of State Rusk but suppressed them when he attended meetings of the Kennedy team. The other, Senator J. William Fulbright, was not a member of the group, but the President invited him to express his misgivings in a speech to the policymakers. However, when Fulbright finished speaking the President moved on to other agenda items without asking for reactions of the group.

David Kraslow and Stuart H. Loory, in *The Secret Search for Peace in Vietnam,* report that during 1966 President Johnson's ingroup was concerned primarily with selecting bomb targets in North Vietnam. They based their selections on four factors—the military advantage, the risk to American aircraft and pilots, the danger of forcing other countries into the fighting, and the danger of heavy civilian casualties. At their regular Tuesday luncheons, they weighed these factors the way school teachers grade examination papers, averaging them out. Though evidence on this point is scant, I suspect that the group's ritualistic adherence to a standardized procedure induced the members to feel morally justified in their destructive way of dealing with the Vietnamese people—after all, the danger of heavy civilian casualties from U.S. air strikes was taken into account on their checklists.

4. Stereotypes

Victims of groupthink hold stereotyped views of the leaders of enemy groups: they are so evil that genuine attempts at negotiating differences with them are unwarranted, or they are too weak or too stupid to deal effectively with whatever attempts the ingroup makes to defeat their purposes, no matter how risky the attempts are.

Kennedy's groupthinkers believed that Premier Fidel Castro's air force was so ineffectual that obsolete B-26s could knock it out completely in a surprise attack before the invasion began. They also believed that Castro's army was so weak that a small Cuban-exile brigade could establish a well-protected beachhead at the Bay of Pigs. In addition, they believed that Castro was not smart enough to put down any possible internal

uprisings in support of the exiles. They were wrong on all three assumptions. Though much of the blame was attributable to faulty intelligence, the point is that none of Kennedy's advisers even questioned the CIA planners about these assumptions.

The Johnson advisers' sloganistic thinking about "the Communist apparatus" that was "working all around the world" (as Dean Rusk put it) led them to overlook the powerful nationalistic strivings of the North Vietnamese government and its efforts to ward off Chinese domination. The crudest of all stereotypes used by Johnson's inner circle to justify their policies was the domino theory ("If we don't stop the Reds in South Vietnam, tomorrow they will be in Hawaii and next week they will be in San Francisco," Johnson once said). The group so firmly accepted this stereotype that it became almost impossible for any adviser to introduce a more sophisticated viewpoint.

In the documents on Pearl Harbor, it is clear to see that the Navy commanders stationed in Hawaii had a naive image of Japan as a midget that would not dare to strike a blow against a powerful giant.

5. Pressure

Victims of groupthink apply direct pressure to any individual who momentarily expresses doubts about any of the group's shared illusions or who questions the validity of the arguments supporting a policy alternative favored by the majority. This gambit reinforces the concurrence-seeking norm that loyal members are expected to maintain.

President Kennedy probably was more active than anyone else in raising skeptical questions during the Bay of Pigs meetings, and yet he seems to have encouraged the group's docile, uncritical acceptance of defective arguments in favor of the CIA's plan. At every meeting, he allowed the CIA representatives to dominate the discussion. He permitted them to give their immediate refutations in response to each tentative doubt that one of the others expressed, instead of asking whether anyone shared the doubt or wanted to pursue the implications of the new worrisome issue that had just been raised. And at the most crucial meeting, when he was calling on each member to give his vote for or against the plan, he did not call on Arthur Schlesinger, the one man there who was known by the President to have serious misgivings.

Historian Thompson informs us that whenever a member of Johnson's ingroup began to express doubts, the group used subtle social pressures to "domesticate" him. To start with, the dissenter was made to feel at home, provided that he lived up to two restrictions: (1) that he did not voice his doubts to outsiders, which would play into the hands of the opposition; and (2) that he kept his criticisms within the bounds of acceptable deviation, which meant not challenging any of the fundamental assumptions that went into the group's prior commitments. One such "domesticated dissenter" was Bill Moyers. When Moyers arrived at a meeting, Thompson tells us, the President greeted him with, "Well, here comes Mr. Stop-the-Bombing."

6. Self-Censorship

Victims of groupthink avoid deviating from what appears to be group consensus; they keep silent about their misgivings and even minimize to themselves the importance of their doubts.

As we have seen, Schlesinger was not at all hesitant about presenting his strong objections to the Bay of Pigs plan in a memorandum to the President and the Secretary of State. But he became keenly aware of his tendency to suppress objections at the White House meetings. "In the months after the Bag of Pigs I bitterly reproached myself for having kept so silent during those crucial discussions in the cabinet room," Schlesinger writes in *A Thousand Days*. "I can only explain my failure to do more than raise a few timid questions by reporting that one's impulse to blow the whistle on this nonsense was simply undone by the circumstances of the discussion."

7. Unanimity

Victims of groupthink share an *illusion* of unanimity within the group concerning almost all judgments expressed by members who speak in favor of the majority view. This symptom results partly from the preceding one, whose effects are augmented by the false assumption that any individual who remains silent during any part of the discussion is in full accord with what the others are saying.

When a group of persons who respect each other's opinions arrives at a unanimous view, each member is likely to feel that the belief must be true. This reliance on consensual validation within the group tends to replace individual critical thinking and reality testing, unless there are clear-cut disagreements among the members. In contemplating a course of action such as the invasion of Cuba, it is painful for the members to confront disagreements within their group, particularly if it

becomes apparent that there are widely divergent views about whether the preferred course of action is too risky to undertake at all. Such disagreements are likely to arouse anxieties about making a serious error. Once the sense of unanimity is shattered, the members no longer can feel complacently confident about the decision they are inclined to make. Each man must then face the annoying realization that there are troublesome uncertainties and he must diligently seek out the best information he can get in order to decide for himself exactly how serious the risks might be. This is one of the unpleasant consequences of being in a group of hardheaded, critical thinkers.

To avoid such an unpleasant state, the members often become inclined, without quite realizing it, to prevent latent disagreements from surfacing when they are about to initiate a risky course of action. The group leader and the members support each other in playing up the areas of convergence in their thinking, at the expense of fully exploring divergencies that might reveal unsettled issues.

"Our meetings took place in a curious atmosphere of assumed consensus," Schlesinger writes. His additional comments clearly show that, curiously, the consensus was an illusion — an illusion that could be maintained only because the major participants did not reveal their own reasoning or discuss their idiosyncratic assumptions and vague reservations. Evidence from several sources makes it clear that even the three principals — President Kennedy, Rusk and McNamara — had widely differing assumptions about the invasion plan.

8. Mindguards

Victims of groupthink sometimes appoint themselves as mindguards to protect the leader and fellow members from adverse information that might break the complacency they shared about the effectiveness and morality of past decisions. At a large birthday party for his wife, Attorney General Robert F. Kennedy, who had been constantly informed about the Cuban invasion plan, took Schlesinger aside and asked him why he was opposed. Kennedy listened coldly and said, "You may be right or you may be wrong, but the President has made his mind up. Don't push it any further. Now is the time for everyone to help him all they can."

Rusk also functioned as a highly effective mindguard by failing to transmit to the group the strong objections of three "outsiders" who had learned of the invasion plan — Undersecretary of State Chester Bowles, USIA Director Edward R. Murrow, and Rusk's intelligence chief, Roger Hilsman. Had Rusk done so, their warnings might have reinforced Schlesinger's memorandum and jolted some of Kennedy's ingroup, if not the President himself, into reconsidering the decision.

PRODUCTS

When a group of executives frequently displays most or all of these interrelated symptoms, a detailed study of their deliberations is likely to reveal a number of immediate consequences. These consequences are, in effect, products of poor decision-making practices because they lead to inadequate solutions to the problems under discussion.

First, the group limits its discussions to a few alternative courses of action (often only two) without an initial survey of all the alternatives that might be worthy of consideration.

Second, the group fails to reexamine the course of action initially preferred by the majority after they learn of risks and drawbacks they had not considered originally.

Third, the members spend little or no time discussing whether there are nonobvious gains they may have overlooked or ways of reducing the seemingly prohibitive costs that made rejected alternatives appear undesirable to them.

Fourth, members make little or no attempt to obtain information from experts within their own organizations who might be able to supply more precise estimates of potential losses and gains.

Fifth, members show positive interest in facts and opinions that support their preferred policy; they tend to ignore facts and opinions that do not.

Sixth, members spend little time deliberating about how the chosen policy might be hindered by bureaucratic inertia, sabotaged by political opponents, or temporarily derailed by common accidents. Consequently, they fail to work out contingency plans to cope with foreseeable setbacks that could endanger the overall success of their chosen course.

SUPPORT

The search for an explanation of why groupthink occurs had led me through a quagmire of complicated theoretical issues in the murky area of human motivation. My belief, based on recent social psychological research, is that we can best understand the various symptoms of groupthink as a mutual effort among the group members to maintain self-esteem and emotional equanimity by providing social support to each other, especially at times when they share responsibility for making vital decisions.

Even when no important decision is pending, the typical administrator will begin to doubt the wisdom and morality of his past decisions each time he receives information about setbacks, particularly if the information is accompanied by negative feedback from prominent men who originally had been his supporters. It should not be surprising, therefore, to find that individual members strive to develop unanimity and esprit de corps that will help bolster each other's morale, to create an optimistic outlook about the success of pending decisions, and to reaffirm the positive value of past policies to which all of them are committed.

PRIDE

Shared illusions of invulnerability, for example, can reduce anxiety about taking risks. Rationalizations help members believe that the risks are really not so bad after all. The assumption of inherent morality helps the members to avoid feelings of shame or guilt. Negative stereotypes function as stress-reducing devices to enhance a sense of moral righteousness as well as pride in a lofty mission.

The mutual enhancement of self-esteem and morale may have functional value in enabling the members to maintain their capacity to take action, but it has maladaptive consequences insofar as concurrence-seeking tendencies interfere with critical, rational capacities and lead to serious errors of judgment.

While I have limited my study to decision-making bodies in Government, groupthink symptoms appear in business, industry and any other field where small, cohesive groups make the decisions. It is vital, then, for all sorts of people — and especially group leaders — to know what steps they can take to prevent groupthink.

REMEDIES

To counterpoint my case studies of the major fiascos, I have also investigated two highly successful group enterprises, the formulation of the Marshall Plan in the Truman Administration and the handling of the Cuban missile crisis by President Kennedy and his advisers. I have found it instructive to examine the steps Kennedy took to change his group's decision-making processes. These changes ensured that the mistakes made by his Bay of Pigs ingroup were not repeated by the missile-crisis ingroup, even though the membership of both groups was essentially the same.

The following recommendations for preventing groupthink incorporate many of the good practices I discovered to be characteristic of the Marshall Plan and missile-crisis groups:

1. The leader of a policy-forming group should assign the role of critical evaluation to each member, encouraging the group to give high priority to open airing of objections and doubts. This practice needs to be reinforced by the leader's acceptance of criticism of his own judgments in order to discourage members from soft-pedaling their disagreements and from allowing their striving for concurrence to inhibit critical thinking.

2. When the key members of a hierarchy assign a policy-planning mission to any group within their organization, they should adopt an impartial stance instead of stating preferences and expectations at the beginning. This will encourage open inquiry and impartial probing of a wide range of policy alternatives.

3. The organization routinely should set up several outside policy-planning and evaluation groups to work on the same policy question, each deliberating under a different leader. This can prevent the insulation of an ingroup.

4. At intervals before the group reaches a final consensus, the leader should require each member to discuss the group's deliberations with associates in his own unit of the organization — assuming that those associates can be trusted to adhere to the same security regulations that govern the policy-makers — and then to report back their reactions to the group.

5. The group should invite one or more outside experts to each meeting on a staggered basis and encourage the experts to challenge the views of the core members.

6. At every general meeting of the group, whenever the agenda calls for an evaluation of policy alternatives, at least one member should play devil's advocate, functioning as a good lawyer in challeng-ing the testimony of those who advocate the majority position.

7. Whenever the policy issue involves relations with a rival nation or organization, the group should devote a sizable block of time, perhaps an entire session, to a survey of all warning signals from the rivals and should write alternative scenarios on the rivals' intentions.

8. When the group is surveying policy alternatives for feasibility and effectiveness, it should from time to time divide into two or more subgroups to meet separately, under different chairmen, and then come back together to hammer out differences.

9. After reaching a preliminary consensus about what seems to be the best policy, the group should hold a "second-chance" meeting at which every member expresses as vividly as he can all his residual doubts, and rethinks the entire issue before making a definitive choice.

HOW

These recommendations have their disadvantages. To encourage the open airing of objections, for instance, might lead to prolonged and costly debates when a rapidly growing crisis requires immediate solution. It also could cause rejection, depression and anger. A leader's failure to set a norm might create cleavage between leader and members that could develop into a disruptive power struggle if the leader looks on the emerging consensus as anathema. Setting up outside evaluation groups might increase the risk of security leakage. Still, inventive executives who know their way around the organizational maze probably can figure out how to apply one or another of the prescriptions successfully, without harmful side effects.

They also could benefit from the advice of outside experts in the administrative and behavioral sciences. Though these experts have much to offer, they have had few chances to work on policy-making machinery within large organizations. As matters now stand, executives innovate only when they need new procedures to avoid repeating serious errors that have deflated their self-images.

In this era of atomic warheads, urban disorganization and ecocatastrophes, it seems to me that policymakers should collaborate with behavioral scientists and give top priority to preventing groupthink and its attendant fiascos.

36.   Improving Group Performance Effectiveness

J. Richard Hackman and Charles G. Morris

When decision makers in public and private institutions in this society are faced with genuinely important tasks, it is likely that they will assign those tasks to groups for solution. Sometimes the reason is simply that one individual could not be expected to handle the task by himself (e.g., formulating a new welfare policy, which requires a diversity of knowledge and skills). Other times it is because decision makers assume that the added human resources available in a group will lead to a product higher in *quality* — or at least lessen the chances that the product will be grossly defective.

Given current knowledge about group effectiveness, the state of affairs described above is not an occasion for optimism. Although literally thousands of studies of group performance have been conducted over the last several decades, we still know very little about why some groups are more effective than others. We know even less about what to do to improve the performance of a given group working on a specific task.

GROUP PROCESS AS A POSSIBLE KEY

We suggest that one key to understanding the effectiveness of small groups is to be found in the ongoing *interaction process* that takes place among members as they work on a task. At one extreme, for example, group members may work together so badly that members do not share with one another uniquely held information that is critical to the problem at hand; in this case, the quality of the group outcome surely will suffer. On the other hand, group members may operate in great harmony, with the comments of one member prompting quick and sometimes innovative responses in another, which then leads a third to see a synthesis between the ideas of the first two, and so on; in this case, a genuinely creative outcome may result.

In general, social psychologists have tended toward a rather pessimistic view of group process, describing it as something that, for the most part, impairs task effectiveness. One well-known theory of group performance, for example, deals with interaction process almost exclusively in terms of "process losses" that prevent a group from approaching its optimal or potential productivity (Steiner, 1972). And it turns out that predictions of group productivity based on this view of group process are, for many tasks, reasonably accurate.

Other social psychologists suggest that the interaction among group members helps to catch and remedy errors which might slip by if individuals were doing the task by themselves. Thus, the argument goes, although groups may be slow and inefficient because of process problems, their use is more than justified when the *quality* of a solution (i.e., freedom from errors) is of paramount importance (cf. Taylor & Faust, 1952). Recent work by Janis (1972), however, calls into question the efficacy of group interaction for finding and correcting errors, at least under some circumstances. Janis shows that as members become excessively close-knit and generate a clubby feeling of "we-ness," there may be a marked decrease in the exchange of discrepant or unsettling information, and a simultaneous unwillingness to deal seriously with such information even when it is forced to their attention. Janis suggests that the principles of "groupthink" help to explain a number of highly significant and unfortunate decisions made by top-level government officials, such as the Bay of Pigs invasion, and Britain's "appeasement" policy toward Hitler before World War II. Apparently even for some very important decisions, patterns of group interaction can develop which allow large and significant errors of fact and judgment to "slip through" and seriously impair group effectiveness.

A more optimistic view of the role of group process is offered by Collins and Guetzkow (1964), who propose that, in some circumstances, interaction can result in "assembly-effect bonuses." That is, patterns of interaction may develop in which the individual inputs of group members combine to yield an outcome better than that of any single person — or even than the sum of individual products. The literature reviewed by Collins and Guetzkow, however, offers little help in understanding how to create such bonuses. The "brainstorming" fad of the late 1950s seemed to offer one clear instance in which the assembly-effect bonus led to group outcomes of higher creativity than those obtained by pooling the products of individuals; yet subsequent research failed to reveal any creative bonuses which were attributable to the group interaction process per se.

Organizational psychologists involved with experiential "training groups" or with "teambuilding" activities also tend to be optimistic about the possibility of enhancing the effectiveness of groups by alternating group processes. In general, they assume that members of many task groups are inhibited from exchanging ideas and information and from working together in a concerted fashion to complete the task. Interpersonal training activities are intended, at the least, to remove some of the emotional and interpersonal obstacles to effective group functioning and thereby to permit group members to devote a greater proportion of their energies toward actual work on tasks. Unfortunately, while there is substantial evidence to show that such interpersonal training activities do alter what goes on among group members (and how members feel about that), it remains unclear whether or not such training improves the effectiveness of the group.

In sum, there is substantial agreement among researchers and observers of task-oriented groups that something important happens in group interaction that can affect performance outcomes. There is little agreement about just what that "something" is, when it will enhance (or when it will impair) group effectiveness, and how it can be monitored, analyzed, and altered. It is to these questions that we now turn.

HOW GROUP INTERACTION PROCESS AFFECTS GROUP PERFORMANCE

We suggest that the impact of group interaction on group effectiveness is *not* direct, but instead operates by affecting three "summary variables" that do directly determine how well a group does on its tasks. These variables can be used to summarize the causes of task effectiveness. The influence of group interaction process on performance effectiveness, then, can be understood by examining how process affects:

1. The level of *effort* the group applies to carrying out its task;
2. The adequacy of the *task performance strategies* used by the group in carrying out the task;
3. The level and appropriateness of the *knowledge and skills* brought to bear on the task by group members.

To the extent that interaction processes control or influence these three summary variables, we believe, then the performance of a group working on almost any task will be substantially affected. The remainder of this section extends and elaborates this proposition.

Summary Variable 1: Members' Efforts

For most group tasks, effort counts heavily in determining how well the group performs. Group interaction can affect the level of effort actually brought to bear on the task in two ways: (1) by influencing how well the efforts of individual members are *coordinated,* and (2) by influencing the *level* of effort members choose to expend working on the task (i.e., their task motivation).

Coordination of Members' Efforts. When task effectiveness is affected by the amount of effort group members apply to their work, then it is important that members coordinate their activities in a way that minimizes the amount of effort that is "wasted." In a tug-of-war, for example, a group will do quite poorly unless some means is devised to ensure that its members all pull at the same time.

Whenever the efforts of individual group members must be coordinated to accomplish some task, there always is some "slippage" that keeps the group from achieving its potential productivity (i.e., that which would be obtained if the efforts of each member were fully useable by the group). Moreover, the larger the group, the greater the process loss, simply because the job of getting all members functioning together in a coordinated fashion becomes increasingly difficult as the number of members increases (Steiner, 1972).

Raising or Lowering the Level of Members' Efforts. While individual members usually approach a given group task with some notion about how hard they expect to work on it, what happens in the group can radically alter that expectation in either direction.

Presumably, an individual will increase his level of effort to the extent that working hard with the other group members leads to the satisfaction of his personal needs or the achievement of his personal goals. If his task-oriented efforts are reinforced, he should work harder on the task; but if his efforts are ignored or punished, his effort should decrease. Thus, social interaction can importantly affect how much effort an individual chooses to expend in work on the group task.

The depression of members' efforts has been explored by Steiner (1972) in terms of a "motivation decrement" that becomes more of a problem as the size of the group increases. Members presumably feel that their own efforts are less critically needed in larger groups, because there are many other people available to do the work. Moreover, individuals may find it increasingly difficult to obtain satisfaction of their own needs because of the limited amount of "air time" available to individual members of large groups.

Little research has been conducted on how motivation *increments* might be created—i.e., patterns of interaction in the group that would prompt members to work especially hard on the group task. The feasibility of creating such increments in task-oriented groups is explored later in this paper.

Summary Variable 2: Task Performance Strategies

As used here, "strategy" refers to the choices made by group members about how the group will go about performing the task. For example, a group might decide to opt for a very high quality product at the expense of quantity of production (a strategy choice about outcomes); or members might decide to free-associate about ideas for proceeding with the task before actually starting work on it (a strategy choice about procedure).

Strategy choices can be very important in determining how well a group does its task (cf. Hackman & Morris, 1975), and group interaction can affect the strategies actually used by a group in two ways: (1) by influencing how preexisting notions about "appropriate" strategy are actually *implemented* in doing the task, and (2) by affecting the *development* of strategies for proceeding with the task that are new to the group and uniquely suited to its task.

Implementing Existing, Shared Strategies.   As people gain experience with various tasks in the course of their everyday lives, strategies for working on these tasks become well-learned. When the task is a familiar one, group interaction may serve mainly as a vehicle for implementing an already well-learned strategy for proceeding with the task, and no evidence of "working on performance strategy" may be visible in the overt interaction among members. It is true, nonetheless, that members inevitably will encounter interpersonal obstacles that impair their efficiency in implementing even a very well-learned strategy—in other words, a process loss that makes the group less effective than it could be.

Developing or Reformulating Strategic Plans.   Few tasks constrain a group from overtly discussing and reformulating its performance strategies (or from developing new strategies from scratch). Yet, there appears to be a pervasive norm in groups *not* to address such matters explicitly, even when group members are aware that it is to their advantage to plan strategies before starting actual work on the task (Shure, Rogers, Larsen, & Tassone, 1962; Weick, 1969, pp. 11-12).

To the extent that norms against strategy planning exist, the chances are lessened that the preexisting strategies members bring to the group will be altered and improved upon, or that new (and possibly more effective) strategies will be generated by group members. This obviously can limit the effectiveness of the group on many types of tasks.

On the other hand, there is evidence that in some circumstances overt consideration and discussion of task performance strategies can "unfreeze" group members from their traditional and well-learned approaches to task performance, and thereby open the possibility that a new and more effective way of proceeding will be invented. In one study, for example, discussion about strategy tended to occur only when a group member made a suggestion that was deviant from preexisting and shared notions about what would be an "appropriate" strategy for the task at hand (e.g., suggesting a bizarre solution to a routine problem-solving task). Yet, even as group members explained to the deviant why his ideas were faulty, they fell into a discussion of alternative ways of proceeding with the task, some of which subsequently were adopted and led to significant increases in measured group creativity (Hackman & Morris, 1975). Such findings suggest that it may be possible to help groups improve their effectiveness on some tasks by encouraging members to examine and alter existing norms that discourage open discussion of strategies.

Summary Variable 3: Members' Knowledge and Skill

The knowledge and the skills of group members — and the way these are brought to bear on the group task — is the final summary variable to be considered. In this case, the functions of group interaction are as follows: (1) group process is the means by which the contributions of different members (who presumably differ in the amount of task-relevant talent they bring to the group) are *assessed and weighted;* and (2) the patterns of interaction that develop in the group can lead to *changes in the level of talent* held by members and applicable to the task.

Assessing and Weighting Knowledge and Skill of Members.   For tasks on which knowledge or skills are important in determining performance, it often is possible to predict how well the group will do solely on the basis of the talents of its members (Davis, 1969; Kelley & Thibaut, 1969; Steiner, 1972). The specific predictive model required, of course, depends on the task. For some tasks, the group will operate at the level of its *most* competent member, as in Steiner's "disjunctive" model of group performance (e.g., a track team). For others, performance will be determined by the *least* competent group member, as in Steiner's "conjunctive" model (e.g., a roped-together mountain climbing team). For still others, the group would be expected to perform approximately at the level of its "average" member.

In general, tests of such predictive models have been reasonably successful. Of special interest, however, is the recurrent finding that when actual group productivity is at variance with predictions, it is usually because the model has overpredicted group performance. That is, given the level of members' talent, the group "should" have performed better than it actually did. The implication is that the interaction process of the group, through which the talents of members are assessed, weighted, and brought to bear on the task, must have been inadequate in some way.

For some tasks, such process losses should not be substantial. For example, when the specific knowledge or skill required is obvious, and when obtaining the solution does not involve complex teamwork among members, sophisticated or subtle social processes are not required to identify the necessary talents and to apply them to the task. Instead, group interaction may serve merely as a vehicle for exchanging data, and for informing other members that one "knows the answer." There is little opportunity in such circum-

stances for process foul-ups (cf. Laughlin, Branch, & Johnson, 1969).

On other tasks, however, the role of group process may be more substantial and the risk of process losses substantially greater. A novel case in point is the prediction of the performance of professional athletic teams from data about the skills of individual team members (Jones, 1974). As would be expected, substantial relationships were found between measures of individual skill and team performance: teams with better athletes did better. However, the *level* of prediction attained was higher for some sports than for others. For example, nearly 90 percent of the variation in baseball team effectiveness was predictable from measures of team member skill, as compared with only about 35 percent for basketball teams. As the author notes, success in basketball is especially dependent upon personal relations and teamwork among players. Thus, process losses might be more likely to impair basketball team effectiveness than would be the case for other team sports.

We have suggested above that when the primary functions of group interaction are to assess, weight, and apply members' talent, process losses are inevitable, and that for some types of tasks the potential losses are greater than for others. In every case, however, considerations of group process determine how *near* a group comes to its potential performance, given the capabilities of its members.

Affecting the Level of Talent Available to the Group. Group interaction process can, at least potentially, serve as a means for actually increasing the total amount of members' talent available to the group for work on the task. The issue here is *not* the simple exchange or coordination of existing knowledge and skill, as discussed above; that function of group interaction does not result in a net increase in the total supply of talent available to the group. Instead, the present focus is on how group members can do more than merely share among themselves what they already know — and instead work as a group to gain knowledge or generate skills which previously did not exist within the group.

Virtually no controlled research has been carried out on this latter function of group interaction. The "training group" approach to the development of interpersonal skills (Argyris, 1962; Bradford, Gibb, & Benne, 1964; Schein & Bennis, 1965) postulates that group members can effectively use one another as resources to increase members' individual competence and thereby increase the level of competence in the group as a whole. But the social processes through which such learning takes place are only beginning to be illuminated (cf. Argyris & Schon, 1974), and additional research on the talent-enhancing functions of group interaction is much needed.

We have examined above the impact of group interaction process on each of three summary variables: (1) the level of effort brought to bear on the task; (2) the task performance strategies implemented by group members in carrying out the task; and (3) the level of knowledge and skill at the disposal of the group for task work. The impact of group interaction on each of these three summary variables is shown in Table 1. This table shows that the functions served by interaction process are quite different for each of the three summary variables. The implication is that a researcher who is attempting to understand the process determinants of group performance will have to examine different aspects of the group process, *depending on which of the summary variables are operative in the particular task situation being considered.* By the same token, the approach an interventionist would take in attempting to help group members create more task-appropriate patterns of interaction would vary depending on the variables operative for the task being performed.[1]

As noted in column A of Table 1, there are inevitable process losses associated with each of the three summary variables. A group can never handle the process issues in column A perfectly; the group's performance therefore will depend, in part, on how successful members are in finding ways to minimize these process losses. At the same time (column B) there are potentially important (but often unrecognized) process *gains* associated with each of the summary variables. That is, at least the possibility exists for group members to find and implement new, task-effective ways of interacting which will make it possible for them to achieve a level of effectiveness which could not have been anticipated from knowledge about the talents and intentions of group members before the start of work on the task. In the section to follow, we explore possibilities for achieving such performance-enhancing process gains.

INTERVENTIONS FOR IMPROVING GROUP EFFECTIVENESS

In this section, we attempt to show how group effectiveness can be improved above the level expected in column A of Table 1 by planned alteration of three aspects of the overall performance situation—three "input variables." In particular, as shown in Figure 1: (1) performance strategies can be made more appropriate

Table 1. Summary of the Proposed Functions of Group Interaction

Summary Variables Postulated as Important in Affecting Performance Outcomes	Impact of Interaction Process on the Summary Variables	
	A Inevitable process losses	B Potential for process gains
Members' efforts brought to bear on the task	Interaction serves as the less-than-perfect means by which members' efforts are coordinated and applied to the task.	Interaction can serve to enhance the level of effort members choose to expend on task work.
Performance strategies used in carrying out the task	Interaction serves as a less-than-perfect "vehicle" for implementing preexisting strategies brought to the group by members and (often) shared by them.	Interaction can serve as the site for developing or reformulating strategic plans to increase their task-appropriateness.
Members' knowledge and skills used by the group for task work	Interaction serves as a less-than-perfect means for assessing, weighting, and applying members' talents to the task.	Interaction can serve as a means of increasing the total pool of knowledge or skills available to the group (i.e., when the group is the site for generating new knowledge or skills by members).

Factors which are manipulable
to change group process and performance

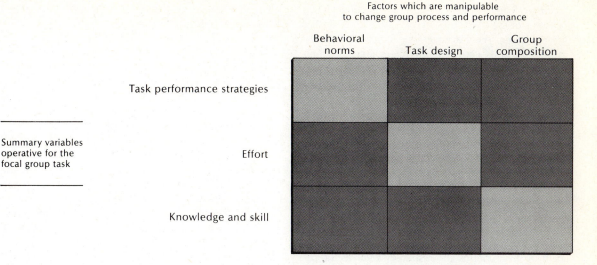

| | Behavioral norms | Task design | Group composition |

Task performance strategies

Summary variables
operative for the
focal group task

Effort

Knowledge and skill

Figure 1.   The Three Summary Variables and Input Factors Which May Be Altered to Influence Them. (*Note:* Shaded cells represent sites that are particularly promising for changes aimed at improving group performance effectiveness.)

for each task by the modification of group *norms:* (2) members' efforts can be increased by the redesign of the group *task;* and (3) the level and utilization of members' knowledge and skills can be improved by altering the *composition* of the group. All three factors affect (and are affected by) the interaction process of the group, and all can be adjusted or "set" before the start of task performance activities to minimize the chances of significant process losses — and to increase the likelihood that process gains will materialize.

Task Performance Strategies

The strategies used by members of a group to perform tasks often are well codified as behavioral norms of the group. Group members typically share a set of expectations about proper approaches to each task, and enforce adherence to those expectations. Such norms often make it unnecessary to manage and coordinate members' behavior explicitly; everyone knows how things should be done, and everyone does them that way.

Ideally, the presence of such norms should contribute to the effectiveness of the group — simply because little time would have to be spent on moment-by-moment

behavior-management activities, leaving more time for actual task work. However, this advantage will accrue only if the norms which guide the selection and use of performance strategies are fully appropriate to the task. If existing norms about strategy are dysfunctional for effectiveness, then performance is likely to suffer unless the norms are changed — despite their time-saving advantages.

As discussed earlier, the problem is that reconsideration of strategic norms in task-oriented groups rarely occurs spontaneously, and may be actively resisted by the group.[2] The challenge, then, is to create conditions that encourage group members to engage in serious explorations of their norms about strategy when there is reason to believe that existing norms are not optimal for the task at hand. Three general approaches for creating such conditions are presented and evaluated below.

Diagnosis-Feedback.   The Return Potential Model proposed by Jackson (1965) can help group members gain increased understanding of group norms and can serve as a basis for planning changes in norms. This model addresses the distribution of potential approval (and disapproval) group members feel for various specific behaviors that might be exhibited in a given situation. Its usefulness as a diagnostic device derives, in large part, from its potential for generating quantitative measures of the characteristics of specific group norms (for examples, see Hackman, 1976; Jackson, 1965). These measures can help members increase their understanding of existing group norms and serve as a basis for deciding whether (and how) they wish to change them.

Diagnostic data about group norms also could be generated using other devices, including observation of behavior in the group by a consultant. The idea is simply to provide systematic and verifiable data about group norms, so that members have a concrete basis for planning how those norms might be altered to make them more appropriate to the demands of the task and the personal needs of the members themselves.

Process Consultation.   A second general approach to changing group norms about strategy involves the use of an outside consultant to help group members discover and implement new, more task-effective ways of working together. In its most flexible and general form, process consultation involves joint work by the consultant and the group to diagnose the state of the group, and to plan what to do on the basis of that diagnosis (Schein, 1969).

In most applications of process consultation, the consultant spends considerable time with group members, helping them to examine existing norms and to experiment with new ways of behaving. Therefore, broad-gauge process consultation is most effective over the long term — and then only if group members develop their own diagnostic and action skills which reduce their dependency on the consultant and, in effect, allow group members to consult with themselves about the most effective task and interpersonal processes to use in various situations.

An alternative consultative approach, which would appear more useful in the short term, is to educate group members in specific strategic alternatives or techniques for carrying out the task. A number of such techniques have been proposed, such as setting time limits for discussion, temporally separating the generation of ideas from their evaluation, focusing on analysis of the task before beginning to perform it, setting aside time to locate facts and potential obstacles to implementation of the solution, devising specific structures for exchanging ideas and information among group members, and so on (cf. Kepner & Tregoe, 1965; Maier, 1963; Osborn, 1957; Varela, 1971). Some of the techniques proposed are based on research findings; others derive more from intuitive considerations. All are intended to provide procedural strategies which will be immediate aids to group effectiveness.

There are at least two problems with short-term, technique-based approaches to changing preexisting group norms about strategy. First, the value of any given technique depends on the task; yet there is very little information available which would help group members to select those strategic approaches likely to be particularly useful for a given task. Second, some of the techniques involve the use of group relations skills which may not be valued or well-practiced by group members. Moreover, the strategy cannot help the group unless members are both motivated and sufficiently skilled to use it appropriately. At present, little is known about how to introduce such techniques and to train members in their effective utilization.

Probably the most straightforward process consultative technique — for helping members explicitly consider their norms about strategy — is simply to provide the group with a "preliminary task" before they begin work on the primary task. This preliminary task would require members to discuss the task performance strategies they plan to use on the main task — and to consider revising or replacing them if warranted by the discussion. Since in most circumstances, the immediate demands of the primary task drive out any tendencies toward strategy planning, introduction of a preliminary group task could help "hold off" such immediate task demands until strategy planning had been completed. Moreover, the intervention capitalizes on the tendency of group members to follow rather slavishly the demands of tasks they see as legitimate (March & Simon, 1958, p. 185; Shure et al., 1962).

In one recent study, groups (whose main task was assembly of a number of types of electrical components) were given a preliminary task that explicitly required members to discuss their performance strategy before beginning work on the main task (Hackman, Brousseau & Weiss, 1976). Members of experimental groups did follow the requirements of the preliminary task and discussed their strategic options extensively. Control groups, however, engaged in virtually no spontaneous discussion of strategy, and proceeded immediately to work on the main task in ways that were consistent with their private, a priori notions about how such a task should be done.

Use of a preliminary task does not, of course, guarantee that any new performance strategies that are generated will be more task-effective than members' private, prior hypotheses about how the task should be done. For example, in the study described above, it was found that discussion of strategy increased group effectiveness *when the task required cooperation and coordination among members.* In another task condition, however, where the task did *not* require high interdependence among members, there were no differences in effectiveness between those groups that discussed their performance strategy and those that did not. This finding reemphasizes the importance of the group task in determining what aspects of group process are critical to group effectiveness in a given instance.

Task Design.   Both the diagnosis-feedback and the process consultation approaches require group members to address directly group norms about performance strategy, and both require some intervention by an outside consultant or researcher. A third general approach to the change of group norms about strategy — task design — deals with norms less directly, and minimizes the role of "outsiders" in the group itself.

Specifically, the group task can be arranged so that it requires, suggests, or provides cues which prompt specific ways of going about performing the task. For example, if a task which requires the assembly of small mechanical devices is physically laid out in a linear fashion, with chairs and equipment for group members placed along the side of a long narrow table, members almost certainly will assume that they should form an assembly line and will proceed to operate as if that is the optimal way of doing the task. But if materials are arranged around a circular table, with a full complement of equipment provided for each member, a strategy of individual assembly probably will be adopted instead, with just as little overt discussion.

At the extreme, of course, a task can be designed so that *no* discretion about strategy is left to the group: members are informed exactly how to proceed to achieve the goal. This is the approach often taken by consultants who attempt to increase the creativity of groups. In the synectics approach, for example, group members are provided with tasks and exercises which specify exactly what strategies group members are to use in working on the task — strategies which are designed explicitly to facilitate the production of original solutions (Prince, 1970). The ultimate success of the group, of course, depends partly on the adequacy of those task-specified strategies.

While, from an "engineering" perspective, task design offers considerable appeal as a device for helping group members utilize more task-effective performance

strategies in their work, responsibility for the strategies remains outside the group itself. The task serves simply to get potentially task-effective patterns of behavior under way; whether such behaviors will "stick" and become incorporated into the normative structure of the group depends, in large part, on whether members find the behaviors instrumental for achieving their goals. Diagnosis-feedback and process consultation, on the other hand, probably are less efficient in any given instance, but have the advantage that the group itself "owns" the new procedures it has devised. Moreover, as group members use these techniques, they may learn some group-relations skills or develop some norms that can be usefully applied to other tasks, or in other groups.

Members' Efforts

There is considerable evidence that the effort members expend on a group task, like the performance strategies they use, is powerfully affected by the norms of the group, especially when members value their membership in that group. Much less is known about what determines the *direction* of group norms — that is, whether the norms will encourage high or low effort on the task (Hackman, 1976).

We suggest that whether a group develops a norm of high or low effort depends substantially on the quality of the experiences members have as they work on the task — and that these experiences, in turn, are largely determined by the task itself. For example, if members find the task activities frustrating and unpleasant, they are likely, after some time, to notice the adverse attitudes of others in the group — and perhaps to share these reactions verbally. Gradually, through such interaction, group members may come to an implicit or explicit agreement that the best way to minimize the unpleasantness they experience is to minimize the energy invested in doing the task. If, on the other hand, members find their work on the task exciting, fulfilling, or otherwise rewarding, these experiences also are likely to be shared with one another, and a norm of high effort may be the result.

To the extent that the quality of members' experiences does depend partly on the task itself, then it may be useful to consider task redesign as a strategy for increasing members' efforts, rather than to attempt to address directly norms about effort. To do the latter, in many cases, would be attacking the outcropping of the problem rather than the problem itself.

What task characteristics are likely to lead to high commitment by group members to work hard on the task? Research data suggest that an individual's task motivation often is enhanced when jobs are high on the following five dimensions: (1) skill variety — the degree to which the individual does a number of different things on the job involving use of his or her valued skills; (2) task identity — the degree to which he or she does a whole and visible piece of work; (3) task significance — how much the results of work on the job will affect the psychological or physical well-being of other people; (4) autonomy — the personal initiative and discretion the individual has on the job; and (5) feedback — the degree to which the person learns while working how well he or she is doing (Hackman & Oldham, 1976).

If a group task were designed with these or similar characteristics in mind, one might expect to observe an increase in the motivation of individual group members to work energetically on the task. The result should be a considerable increase in the overall level of effort the group expends on the task (a "process gain"), and over time this increase should be reinforced by the emergent normative structure in the group. Again, as with most of the possibilities for enhancing group effectiveness introduced in this section, research tests remain to be done.

Knowledge and Skill of Members

Consider now tasks for which the utilization of members' knowledge and skills strongly determine group effectiveness. As suggested earlier, the single most powerful point of leverage on group effectiveness for such tasks is simply group composition; a group made up of competent people will do better than a group composed of less competent members (cf. Varela, 1971, pp. 153-157). But if it is assumed that the group originally has been composed to maximize the level of task-relevant talent present, what can be done to increase the utilization and development of that talent in the service of the group task? How, for example, can the group operate to minimize the inevitable process losses which occur when information is combined and members' contributions are evaluated, or to increase the level of knowledge and skills of individual members so that the total pool of talent available to the group also increases?

Achieving such states of affairs in a group is neither a straightforward nor a short-term proposition. Groups usually have difficulty dealing effectively with individual differences in competence: when weighting of in-dividual contributions is done in the group, difficult issues of interpersonal competitiveness, evaluation, and differential status come very quickly to the fore. Dealing with such issues openly is, for most members of most groups, highly threatening and anxiety-arousing. Group members are likely to erect protective shells around themselves in such circumstances, and, as a result, the group as a whole loses access to much of the talent already present within its boundaries. And the chances of members' using one another to learn genuinely innovative patterns of behavior — or to seek out and internalize knowledge that initially is foreign to them — are very slim indeed.

How might a group break out of such a self-defeating pattern of behavior? Possibly the group task could be structured to require explicit and overt treatment of individual differences in knowledge and skill; or perhaps intervention could be made to help members become aware of (and possibly change) existing group norms specifying how such matters are handled in the group. Such interventions can ensure that issues of individual differences in knowledge and skill are brought to the attention of group members — and can prompt explicit discussion of them. But successful resolution of such matters once they have surfaced may be extraordinarily difficult.

What are needed, it seems, are interventions which will help group members learn *how* to deal effectively with issues of individual differences within the group and how to create a climate which supports and facilitates learning and sharing of learning. This suggests the need for a rather long-term program of process consultation (or "team building"), in which members gradually build a climate of interpersonal trust within the group, leading to a reduction in the level of personal threat they experience in the group setting. As such a climate develops, members may become better able to experiment with new forms of behavior and become increasingly ready to engage in the usually-risky and always-anxiety-arousing activities required to extend one's knowledge and skills in a public setting. Even in the long term, however, there is no guarantee that the group will develop into a site for individual learning and heightened sharing among group members: the process is a fragile one, and fragile things break.

What *is* relatively certain is that if such a long-term team-building program is successful, the members themselves will almost invariably be changed as a consequence — that is, they will perhaps take more risks, experiment more, and be more willing to tolerate stress and anxiety in the interest of increasing and sharing their personal knowledge and skill (cf. Argyris & Schon, 1974). When such a point is reached, if it is reached, the group will have become ''recomposed,'' not by the removal of incompetent members and substitution of more competent ones, but by changes in the attitudes, skills, and behavioral styles of the existing members.

So we come full circle for tasks on which group effectiveness is strongly determined by the level and utilization of members' knowledge and skills. At the first level, we have noted that the most efficient and straightforward means for improving group effectiveness on such task is through group composition: put good people in the group. To move beyond that level, we believe, also requires attention to the composition of the group — but through changes within the group itself, changes in the personal attitudes and interpersonal skills of individual members.

CONCLUSIONS AND IMPLICATIONS

Elusiveness of General Theory

While there have been numerous attempts to integrate findings about group effectiveness and to draw general conclusions about behavior in groups, so far no general theory of small-group effectiveness has appeared.

We suggest here the possibility that no single theory can ever encompass and deal simultaneously with the complexity of factors which can affect a group's task effectiveness. Instead, it may be necessary to settle for a number of smaller theories, each of which is relevant

to a specific aspect or phase of the performance process, or to performance effectiveness under certain specified circumstances. One intent of the present paper has been to help structure the domain within which such smaller theories might be developed. In particular, we have attempted to examine in some depth (1) the role of the group interaction process as a major determinant of group productivity; (2) three summary variables (effort, performance strategies, knowledge and skill) which are proposed as devices for summarizing the most powerful proximal causes of group effectiveness; and (3) some selected ''input'' variables that we see as having powerful influence on group performance, and thus as being useful points of leverage for changing performance — whether directly, or through the interaction process of the group.

A general framework suggesting how these three classes of variables interact in the task-performance sequence is shown in Figure 2. Further research on this input-process-output sequence for different types of tasks may lead to additional understanding that will aid both in predicting and in changing group effectiveness in a large number of performance settings. But a general and unified theory of group effectiveness, we believe, is currently out of reach — and is likely to remain so.

Elusiveness of General Interventions

There is no dearth of small-group intervention techniques available to the practitioner interested in trying to change group behavior and task effectiveness. Yet, just as we have argued that there is not likely to be a general

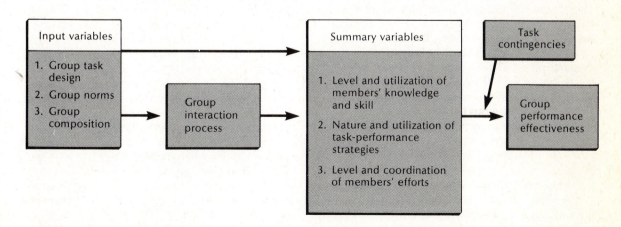

Figure 2.   Framework Showing the Relations Among Certain Input Variables, Group Interaction Process, and the Three Summary Variables in Influencing Group Performance Effectiveness.

theory of group effectiveness, we also eschew the notion that there can be any single intervention package which will be universally helpful in improving group effectiveness.

Consider, for example, small-group "team building," a popular intervention technique which focuses on the interpersonal relationships and social climate present in the group. Team-building may be of great use in helping group members develop the capability to utilize their knowledge and skills effectively on a task. For this reason, the technique may aid performance effectiveness on tasks for which knowledge and skill are critical. But team-building may be actively dysfunctional (at least in the short term) for tasks where effort is the most important factor, because the energies of group members are siphoned away from the task itself and applied instead to the exciting and involving interpersonal processes which take place during the team-building process. Similarly, redesign of the group task may aid effectiveness on tasks where effort is an important determinant of productivity, but be much less useful as an intervention if the problem is one of faulty performance strategies.

In general, intervention techniques which have been offered as devices for improving group effectiveness fall into two classes: (1) interpersonal techniques, often utilizing experiential learning devices intended to improve the quality of the relationships among group members; and (2) procedure-oriented techniques, which provide group members (often via the group leader) with specific strategies for going about their work on the task in a more effective manner.

Relatively little research has been done to assess the value of such techniques for improving the task effectiveness of groups. In general, however, research suggests that interpersonal interventions are powerful in changing patterns of behavior in the group — but that task effectiveness is rarely enhanced (and often suffers) as a consequence. Procedure-oriented interventions, on the other hand, often may be helpful in improving effectiveness for the task immediately at hand, but rarely can they be incorporated readily into the ongoing process of the group (cf. Hackman & Morris, 1975).

What seems needed, then, are the following:

1. Development of interventions which enhance effectiveness in the short term, *and* which simultaneously lead to alterations in group processes so that greater overall competence of the group as a performing unit is achieved.

2. Development of a taxonomy of groups, tasks, and situations which specifies the potential utility of various interventions for different types of performance situations. Recent work by Herold (in press) offers some promising leads toward such a taxonomy. In the meantime, however, we believe that interventionists will have to rely on especially careful *diagnoses* of the task, the group, and the situation — and tailor their change-oriented activities to what those diagnoses reveal.

Toward Increased Self-Management by Task Groups

As techniques for modifying situations and intervening in group processes become known and tested, it is tempting for a consultant to a group (whether outsider or group leader) to use this knowledge, perhaps covertly, to move the group toward greater effectiveness. And, indeed, this "engineering" approach has been advocated and used with apparent success in some situations (Varela, 1971, chap. 6).

We believe, however, that, in the long term, it is better if the group members themselves develop the skills and the understanding to manage their *own* development as a productive unit. This will lessen the reliance of the group on the continued expertise of the consultant, and often may increase the commitment of group members to the group and its goals — because they come increasingly to "own," and therefore care about, its processes and its products. Moreover, the problems of a group often are highly idiosyncratic, hinging on rather unique coincidences of people, tasks, and situations. Relying on specific advice and assistance from an outside professional on an ongoing basis would, it appears, be a grossly inefficient way to improve the long-term effectiveness of the group.

There are two major — and quite different — hurdles to be overcome if a group is to gain increased self-control over its own task-performance processes and increased competence in managing its performance activities. The first is the development of a heightened awareness of the determinants of group processes and group performance. The second is the development of the competence (both technical and interpersonal) to respond adaptively to the newly understood problems and opportunities.

Outside assistance would seem to be critical in helping a group overcome both of these hurdles. Members must break out of the reactive stance most people assume in task-performance situations, and take a more active, seeking, and structuring orientation toward their task and interpersonal environment. This is unlikely to occur spontaneously, for reasons discussed at several points throughout this paper. It is, however, likely to become self-perpetuating, once group members become more aware of the determinants of their behavior (assuming that they decide that they do, in fact, wish to take a more active stance toward the task and social environment). With the aid of a competent leader or consultant, the traditional implicit norm of reactivity can be replaced by a new norm of proaction on the part of both individual group members and the group as an interacting unit.

Group members themselves, for example, probably should be as involved as possible in diagnostic activities aimed at determining the demands of the task and the resources the group has at hand to work on the task. By participating in such diagnoses, members should achieve the fullest possible awareness and understanding of the factors which affect their own performance activities and their effectiveness as a group. They should, therefore, become increasingly well-prepared to engage in new activities intended to reduce their process losses — and to chart avenues for realizing previously unrecognized possibilities for process gains.

An especially critical point is reached when group members have become aware of the need for change and have developed the motivation to initiate and carry through specific changes. At this point, they may be in rather desperate need of assistance to learn how, competently, to do what they already want to do — and they may not be aware of many of the problems that they will face in implementing their plans. This is especially important for changes involving the internal process of the group: merely wanting to be "less punitive in dealing with ideas" for example, while often an admirable goal and one that may be task-effective on many tasks, is extraordinarily difficult for most members of most groups to carry off successfully. Similarly, changing the task of the group — something most members of most groups take as an unalterable — requires the use of personal and interpersonal skills which are not well-practiced. Again, members will require assistance in finding ways to carry out their intentions.

The challenge to the consultant is to help the group members to raise their collective consciousness about what "might be" and to learn how to achieve their newly-found aspirations. The challenge to the small-group researcher is to provide, for the consultant and the group members alike, the knowledge and the tools that will help them get there from here.

NOTES

1. In many complex organizational tasks, all three summary variables will be operative, and a researcher or interventionist would need to examine all of the entries in Table 1 to ascertain the process determinants of performance problems, and opportunities for the development of potential process "gains."

2. The problem may not be as great when the group is dealing with a strange or unfamiliar task. In such cases, few cues will be present in the task materials to engage members' learned views about how they "should" proceed on the task — and they may be forced to discuss strategic options in order to arrive at a shared and coordinated plan for dealing with the task.

REFERENCES

Argyris, C. *Interpersonal competence and organizational effectiveness.* Homewood, Ill.: Irwin-Dorsey, 1962.

Argyris, C., & Schon, D. *Theory in practice.* San Francisco: Jossey-Bass, 1974.

Bradford, L. P., Gibb, J., & Benne, K. (Eds.), *T-Group theory and laboratory method.* New York: Wiley, 1964.

Collins, B. E., & Guetzkow, H. *A social psychology of group processes for decision-making.* New York: Wiley, 1964.

Davis, J. H. *Group performance.* Reading, Mass.: Addison-Wesley, 1969.

Hackman, J. R. Group influences on individuals. In M. D. Dunnette (Ed.), *Handbook of industrial and organizational psychology.* Chicago: Rand-McNally, 1976.

Hackman, J. R., & Morris, C. G. Group tasks, group interaction process, and group performance effectiveness: A review and proposed integration. In L. Berkowitz (Ed.), *Advances in experimental social psychology* (Vol. 8). New York: Academic Press, 1975.

Hackman, J. R., & Oldham, G. R. Motivation through the design of work: Test of a theory. *Organizational Behavior and Human Performance,* 1976, 16, 250–279.

Hackman, J. R., Brousseau, K., & Weiss, J. A. The interaction of task design and group performance strategies in determining group effectiveness. *Organizational Behavior and Human Performance,* 1976, 16, 350–365.

Herold, D. M. Group effectiveness as a function of task-appropriate interaction processes. In J. L. Livingstone (Ed.), *Managerial accounting: The behavioral foundations.* Columbus, Ohio: Grid Publishers, in press.

Jackson, J. Structural characteristics of norms. In I. D. Steiner & M. Fishbein (Eds.), *Current studies in social psychology.* New York: Holt, 1965.

Janis, I. L. *Victims of groupthink: A psychological study of foreign-policy decisions and fiascos.* New York: Houghton-Mifflin, 1972.

Jones, M. B. Regressing group on individual effectiveness. *Organizational Behavior and Human Performance,* 1974, 11, 426–451.

Kelley, H. H., & Thibaut, J. W. Group problem solving. In G. Lindzey & E. Aronson (Eds.), *The handbook of social psychology* (2nd ed.). Reading, Mass.: Addison-Wesley, 1969.

Kepner, C. H. & Tregoe, B. B. *The rational manager: A systematic approach to problem solving and decision making.* New York: McGraw-Hill, 1965.

Laughlin, P. R., Branch, L. G., & Johnson, H. H. Individual versus triadic performance on a unidimensional complementary task, as a function of initial ability level. *Journal of Personality and Social Psychology,* 1969, 12, 144–150.

Maier, N. R. F. *Problem solving discussions and conferences: Leadership and skills.* New York: McGraw-Hill, 1963.

March, J. G., & Simon, H. A. *Organizations.* New York: Wiley, 1958.

Osborn, A. F. *Applied imagination* (Rev. ed.). New York: Scribner, 1957.

Prince, G. M. *The practice of creativity.* New York: Harper & Row, 1970.

Schein, E. H. *Process consultation.* Reading, Mass.: Addison-Wesley, 1969.

Schein, E. H., & Bennis, W. *Personal and organizational change through group methods.* New York: Wiley, 1965.

Shure, G. H., Rogers, M. S., Larsen, I. M., & Tassone, J. Group planning and task effectiveness. *Sociometry,* 1962, 25, 263–282.

Steiner, I. D. *Group process and productivity.* New York: Academic Press, 1972.

Taylor, D. W., & Faust, W. L. Twenty questions: Efficiency in problem solving as a function of size of group. *Journal of Experimental Psychology,* 1952, 44, 360–368.

Varela, J. A. *Psychological solutions to social problems.* New York: Academic Press, 1971.

Weick, K. E. *The social psychology of organizing.* Reading, Mass.: Addison-Wesley, 1969.

Part Five

Organizational Effectiveness and Change

A.

Foundations of Organizational Rationality

37. Goals and Effectiveness

Richard H. Hall

The plan of this reading is to examine the nature of organizational goals, as abstractions and as practical and research issues, and then to consider varying approaches to effectiveness. Since effectiveness can be approached from more perspectives than just that of the organization itself, the discussion here will examine the other parties concerned with respect to how an organization accomplishes what it sets out to do and how it affects them.

ORGANIZATIONAL GOALS

"An organizational goal is a desired state of affairs which the organization attempts to realize."[1] This desired state of affairs is by definition many things to many people. In a large organization, top executives may see the organization seeking one kind of state while those in the middle and lower echelons may have drastically different goals for the organization and for themselves personally. Even in an organization in which there is high participation in decision making and strong membership commitment, it is unlikely that there will be totally unanimous consensus on what the organization should attempt to do, let alone on the means of achieving these ends.

The goal idea at first glance seems most simple in the case of profit-making organizations. Indeed, much of the research on effectiveness has used this type of organization because of goal clarity. The readily quantifiable profit goal is not such a simple matter, however. It is confounded by such issues as the time perspective (long-run or short-run profits); the rate of profit (in terms of return to investors); the important issue of survival and growth in a turbulent and unpredictable environment that might in the short run preclude profit making; the intrusion of other values, such as providing quality products or services, or benefiting mankind; and the firm's comparative position vis-à-vis others in the same industry. Leaving aside for the moment the question of *whose* goals these alternative values might represent, the difficulties apparent in the straightforward profit-making firm are indicative of the difficulties inherent in determining what the goals of an organization really are. When the situation is shifted to a consideration of the goals of a government agency, university, or church, the determination of the organization's goals becomes almost impossible.

Take, for example, the case of a governmental regulative agency charged with administering the public utilities laws and regulations of a state. A casual view suggests that this is a unitary goal, assuming that the laws and regulations are clearly stated. However, this assumption is seldom met, given the large number of lawyers and other technical experts employed by the agency for the purpose of developing and defending interpretations of the existing laws. Administration in such a case is not a simple matter either, since the choice between active and passive administration is a political and organizational football. The well-known distinction between the letter and the intent of the law becomes an issue for such agencies as they develop their operating procedures. What is the goal for the agency? If it is staffed by personnel who have values above and beyond simply administering the existing laws (every organization contains personnel with differing values), their own values toward social action or inaction can clearly modify the stated goals of the organization. In the case of the public utilities agency, beliefs in such diverse areas as air and water pollution, the nature of the publics served by the agency (the public, segments of the public, or the organizations involved), the desirability of maintaining certain public services despite their unprofitability (as in the case of railroad passenger service), and competition versus monopoly in public services — these merely exemplify the range of alternatives available as goals for this organization aside from those found in its formal charter.

The three commonly stated goals of colleges and universities — teaching, research, and public service —

are almost by definition too vague to serve as much of a guide for organizational analysis or practice. In the light of contemporary reality, it can also be seen that they have become essentially incompatible in practice. Universities and colleges tend to concentrate on one of the three goals to the exclusion of the others. While emphases change, the basic issue of deciding among these goals remains. And also, since each contains vast uncertainties — exactly what is meant by good teaching, research, or service? — the use of the goal concept in this setting becomes excruciatingly difficult.

With an understanding of some of the difficulties in the utilization of the goal concept, let us examine the concept more systematically.

The Meaning of Organizational Goals

Organizational goals can be approached from a variety of perspectives. Parsons has cogently pointed out that organizational goals are intimately intertwined with important and basic societal functions, such as integration, pattern maintenance, and so on.[2] From this point of view, organizational goals are really an extension of what the society needs for its own survival. At the other extreme is the position that organizational goals are nothing more than the goals of the individual members of the organization. Both positions disguise more than they illuminate. If the level of analysis is kept in the broad societal-function framework, the variations in goals and activities among organizations performing the same basic functions are ignored. If the level of analysis focuses on just the variety of individual goals, the whole point of organizations is missed — if there were only individual goals, there would be no point in organizing. Clearly, many individuals may have the same goal, such as making a profit, furthering a cause, or destroying an enemy. Clearly also, however, when these people come together in the form of an organization, the profit, cause, or destruction becomes an abstraction toward which they work together.

Organizational goals by definition are creations of individuals, singly or collectively. At the same time, the determination of a goal for collective action becomes a standard by which the collective action is judged. As we will see, the collectively determined, commonly based goal seldom remains constant over time. New considerations imposed from without or within deflect the organization from its original goal, not only changing the activities of the organization, but also becoming part of the overall goal structure. The important point is that the goal of any organization is an abstraction distilled from the desires of members and pressures from the environment and internal system. While there is never 100 percent agreement among members as to what organizational goals are or should be, members can articulate a goal that is a desired state for the organization at some future point in time.

This approach is in some ways similar to that of Herbert Simon. Simon's major focus is on decision making within the organization. He notes that:

When we are interested in the internal structure of an organization, however, the problem cannot be avoided. . . . Either we must explain organizational behavior in terms of the goals of the individual members of the organization, or we must postulate the existence of one or more organizational goals, over and above the goals of the individuals. [3]

Simon then goes on to differentiate between the goals or value premises that serve as inputs to decisions and motives, and the causes that lead individuals to select some goals over others as the basis for their decision making. He keeps the goal idea at the individual level, but offers the important notion that the goals of an organization at any point in time are the result of the interaction among the members of the organization.

To this we would add that external conditions also affect the nature of an organization's goals. An example is the case of many current military organizations. The official goal is typically to protect the state and its people from external threats. The leaders of the military organization may come to believe, for any number of reasons, that the goal is to be victorious over a wide variety of enemies (this is not necessarily the same as protecting the state). This then becomes the goal until it is modified by interactions or conflicts with lower-level personnel, or with external forces in the form of some type of civilian control, with the goal again becoming altered to engagement in limited wars without winning or protecting the state. In this hypothetical and oversimplified example, the goals of individual organization members, particularly those in high positions, are crucial in goal setting. These goals are modified in the course of internal and external interactions.

In Simon's approach, goals become constraints on the decision-making process. The constraints are based on abstract values around which the organization operates. Decisions are made within the framework of a set of constraints (goals), and organizations attempt to make decisions that are optimal in terms of the sets of constraints they face. While the approach taken here is not based solely on the decision-making framework, the perspective is the same. Organizational actions are constrained not only by goals, but also by the external and internal factors that have been discussed. In probably the great majority of cases, goals are one, if not the only, relevant constraint.

Operative Goals

Treating goals as abstract values has the merit of showing that organizational actions are guided by more than the day-to-day whims of individual members. At the same time, abstract values are just that — abstract. They must be converted to specific guides for the actual operations of an organization. Perrow takes this position when he distinguishes between "official" and "operative" organizational goals. [4] Official goals are "the general purposes of the organization as put forth in the charter, annual reports, public statements by key executives and other authoritative pronouncements." Operative goals, on the other hand, "designate the ends sought through the actual operating policies of the organization; they tell us what the organization actually is trying to do, regardless of what the official goals say are the aims."

This distinction is grounded in reality. Two organizations, both with the official goal of profit making, may differ drastically in the amount of emphasis they place on making profits. Blau's examination of two employment agencies with the same goals shows wide variations between the agencies in what they were actually trying to accomplish. [5] In his discussion of this point, Perrow states:

Where operative goals provide the specific content of official goals, they reflect choices among competing values. They may be justified on the basis of an official goal, even though they may subvert another official goal. In one sense they are means to official goals, but since the latter are vague or of high abstraction, the "means" become ends in themselves when the organization is the object of analysis. For example, where profit making is the announced goal, operative goals will specify whether quality or quantity is to be emphasized, whether profits are to be short run and risky or long run and stable, and will indicate the relative priority of diverse and somewhat conflicting ends of customer service, employee morale, competitive pricing, diversification, or liquidity. Decisions on all these factors influence the nature of the organization, and distinguish it from another with an identical official goal.[6]

From this perspective, operative goals become the standards by which the organization's actions are judged and around which decisions are made. In many cases these operative goals reflect the official goals, in that they are abstractions made more concrete. However, operative goals can evolve that are basically unrelated to the official goals. In this regard, Perrow notes:

Unofficial operative goals, on the other hand, are tied more directly to group interests, and while they may support, be irrelevant to, or subvert official goals, they bear no necessary connection with them. An interest in a major supplier may dictate the policies of a corporation executive. The prestige that attaches to utilizing elaborate high-speed computers may dictate the reorganization of inventory and accounting departments. Racial prejudice may influence the selection procedures of an employment agency. The personal ambitions of a hospital administrator may lead to community alliances and activities which bind the organization without enhancing its goal achievement. On the other hand, while the use of interns and residents as "cheap labor" may subvert the official goal of medical education, it may substantially further the official goal of providing a high quality of patient care.[7]

Operative goals thus reflect the derivation and distillation of a set of goals from both official and unofficial sources. These operative goals are developed through interaction patterns within the organization, but persist after the interactions are completed. They reflect the "desired state of affairs," or abstract official goals, the modifications and subversions of these by personnel in decision-making positions, and the force of pressures from the external environment. It is the combination of official goals with internal and external factors that leads to an existing set of operative goals.

If the use of unofficial goals is carried too far, of course, every organization could be viewed as having a huge, perhaps infinite, number of such goals. The distinction must be made, therefore, between goals and operating policies and procedures. The latter are the exact specifications, formally or informally stated, of what individual actors at all levels are to do in their daily activities. Goals, on the other hand, remain at the abstract level, serving as constraining or guiding principles from which policies and procedures can be derived. Operative goals are abstractions in the same way as official goals. They are a set of ideas about where the organization should be going, which are operationalized into specific plans and procedures.

The Determination of Organizational Goals

How does one find out exactly what the goals of an organization are? From the research point of view, this is a vital step if there is to be any concern with issues such as effectiveness, personnel and resource allocation, or optimal structuring. In a very real sense, organizational research must be concerned with goals if it is to be anything more than simply descriptive. For the member of the organization at any level, goal determination is similarly vital. If he misses what the goals really are, his own actions may not only not contribute to the organization, they may contribute to his own organizational demise. Members of organizations must know the "system" if they are to operate within it or to change it. From the discussion above, it should be clear that the "system" is much more than official statements.

The vital importance of understanding operative goals can perhaps best be exemplified by an actual case.[8] The case in point is the familiar one of the goals of a university. The University of Minnesota *Faculty Information* booklet contains the following statements:

TEACHING
The University emphasizes excellence in teaching. The first duty of every faculty member engaged in instruction is the communication of knowledge and values to students, and the stimulation of their intellectual ability, curiosity, and imagination.

RESEARCH
Research is the second strong arm of the University. The faculty member is aided in obtaining funds and facilities for research, and is encouraged to contribute to the ever-expanding realms of human knowledge.

PUBLIC SERVICE AND PROFESSIONAL COMMITMENTS

. . . .

UNIVERSITY SERVICE

. . . .

COMMUNITY SERVICE

. . . . [9]

As everyone must know, these goals are not equally stressed, even though the official pronouncement would lead one to believe otherwise. If a new (or old) faculty member actually believed what he read, he would probably soon find himself at a distinct disadvantage. One of the questions asked of the faculty, in at least one department, when salary increases for the coming year were being considered was the number of offers from other universities that each had received. The larger the number of offers, apparently, the greater the likelihood of receiving a substantial raise, and vice versa. But the vast majority of such offers are forthcoming to those who are active in the research side of the goal equation, since the other factors cannot be readily visible to other institutions. This is not an unusual case, nor is the meaning of it limited to colleges and universities. Knowledge of operative goals is imperative for effective functioning and for the effective implementation of one's own ideas. At the extreme, such knowledge is necessary for individual survival in organizations.

Operative-goal determination for the individual is obviously important. It is plainly part of the ongoing organizational system, also, and thus central to organizational functioning. It is equally important for the organizational analyst. The significance of operative goals forces the analyst to go beyond the more easily determined official goals. The key to finding out what the operative goals are lies in the actual decisions of the top decision makers in the organization. The kinds of decisions they make about allocation of resources (money, personnel, equipment, etc.) are a major indicator. In a study of juvenile correctional organizations, Mayer Zald found that resources were consistently allocated to the custodial and traditional aspects of the institutions rather than to professional treatment personnel, despite official pronouncements that rehabilitation was the goal.[10] Although lower-level personnel influence the decisions made in the organization, it is the people near or at the top who have the major and sometimes final say in organizational matters.

The determination of these operative goals is more easily said than done. Organizations may be reluctant to allow the researcher or member access to the kinds of records that show the nature of resource allocation. In interviews they may tend to repeat the official goal as a form of rhetoric. However, the analyst or member can determine operative goals through the use of multiple methods of data collection from a variety of goal indicators, such as the deployment of personnel, growth patterns among departments, examination of available records and so on.

Since operative goals reflect what the major decision makers believe to be the critical areas and issues for the organization, it follows that the operative goals will shift as internal and external conditions impinge upon the organization. . . . these conditions can deflect the organization from a pursuit of its goals. In a real sense, the operative goals are deflected by these threats or conditions during periods of severe stress. At the same time, *the operative goals will usually reflect some variation on the theme of the official goal.* That is, operative goals are generally based on the official goals, even though there is not perfect correspondence. Profit-making organizations vary in their emphases: colleges and universities pay more or less attention to teaching, research, and so on; and hospitals are concerned to varying degrees with teaching, patient care, and research. If the official goals remain the same when pressures, conditions, and priorities change, the shift in operative goals will be mainly in emphasis.

Changes in Organizational Goals

Organizational goals change for three major reasons. The first is direct pressure from external forces, which leads to a deflection from the original goals. Second is pressure from internal sources. This may lead the organization to emphasize quite different activities than those originally intended. The third factor is changed environmental and technological demands that lead the organization to redefine its goal. While this is similar to the first reason, the factors here occur in *indirect* interaction with the organization, whereas in the first case the organization is in *direct* interaction with the relevant environmental factors.

The impact of external relationships on goals is best seen in Thompson and McEwen's analysis of organization-environmental interactions.[11] They note that organizational goal setting is affected by competitive, bargaining, cooptative, and coalitional relationships with the environment. In the competitive situation — "that form of rivalry between two or more organizations which is mediated by a third party" — organizations must devote their efforts toward gaining support for their continued existence. Competition is most easily seen among business firms that compete for the customer's dollar, but it is also very evident among government agencies as they compete for a share of the tax dollar or among religious organizations as they compete for members and their support. (Religious and other voluntary organizations must also compete with alternative organizations for members and money.) Competition partially controls the organization's "choice of goals" that its energies must be turned to the competitive activity. Continuous support is vital for continued survival as an organization.

Bargaining also involves resources, but in this case the organization is in direct interaction with supplier, consumer, and other organizations. In the bargaining situation, the organization must "give" a little to get what it desires. Bargaining takes place in standard relationships between two organizations, as in the case where a routine supplier is asked to alter its goods for the organization. This "custom" order will cost the supplier more money and hence he bargains for a better price, with the organization bargaining to get its custom equipment at the old price. Thompson and McEwen note that universities will often bargain away the name of a building for a substantial gift. Government agencies may bargain by not enforcing certain regulations in order to maintain support for the seeking of other goals. The impact of bargaining is more subtle than that of competition, but it has a similar impact on goal setting.

Cooptation is "the process of absorbing new elements into the leadership or policy-determining structure of an organization as a means of averting threats to its stability or existence."[12] The classic study of cooptation is Selznick's *TVA and the Grass Roots,* in which he documents the impact of bringing new societal elements into the governing structure of the TVA.[13] The organization shifted its emphases partially as a result of new pressures brought to bear in the decision-making system. It is no accident that boards of directors or trustees contain members from pressure groups important to the organizations involved. If a member of a group that is antipathetic to the organization can be brought into the organization, the antipathy can be minimized. At the same time, the presence of that person on a controlling board has an influence on decisions made, even though the hostility rate may be down. The recent movement toward "student power" among high school and college students is interesting to observe in this regard. It is predicted that student members of college and university governing bodies and boards of trustees will be coopted — that is, the students will become part of the power structure and

take its view — but also that the organizations involved will find their goal setting at least minimally influenced by the presence of the students. Cooptation is thus a two-way street. Both those coopted and those doing the coopting are influenced.

The final type of external relationship is coalition, or the "combination of two or more organizations for a common purpose. Coalition appears to be the ultimate or extreme form of environmental conditioning of organizational goals."[14] While seeking common purposes, coalitions place strong constraints on the organizations involved, since they cannot set goals in a unilateral fashion.

Although it is clear that other environmental factors also affect the nature of organizational goals, Thompson and McEwen's analysis centers around transactions with other organizations. They suggest a very important consideration in the determination of the operative goals of an organization: Organizations operate in a "field" of other organizations,[15] and these affect what the focal organization does. While this has been amply demonstrated in economic analysis of market competition, the impact goes beyond this type of relationship. The interactions we have described are direct evidence that the use of official-goal statements would be misleading, since the transactions with other organizations by definition would deflect an organization from its official goal.

Operative goals are also affected by what goes on inside an organization. A given set of goals may be altered drastically by changes in the power system of the organization; new types of personnel, as in the case of a sudden influx of professionals; and the development of new standards that supersede those of the past. Etzioni has called this phenomenon "goal displacement."[16]

Goal displacement is clearly evident in Robert Michels' analysis of Socialist parties and labor unions in Europe in the early twentieth century.[17] In this study he developed the idea of the "iron law of oligarchy." Michels pointed out that these revolutionary groups began as democratic organizations. The need for organization to accomplish the revolutionary purposes (operative goals) led to the establishment of leaders of the organizations. The leaders, tasting power, did not want to relinquish it, and therefore devoted much of their energies to maintain their positions. Since members of most voluntary organizations, even revolutionary parties, are politically indifferent, and since the skills necessary for leading the parties are not universally distributed, the leaders could rather easily perpetuate themselves in power — in part by coopting or purging the young potential leaders. The emphasis in the parties shifted to organizational maintenance, at the expense of militancy and revolutionary zeal. Close parallels to this situation exist in contemporary revolutionary and militant movements of every political and social persuasion.

A different form of goal displacement can be seen in Robert Scott's analysis of the "sheltered workshop for the blind."[18] When these workshops were formed in the early twentieth century, the overall goal was to integrate the blind into the industrial community. However, it was recognized that many blind people could not work in regular factories, and so the sheltered workshops were developed to provide the blind with work (making brooms and mops, weaving, chair caning, etc.) as a social service. Owing to a series of events, the workshops began to define themselves as factories in competition with nonblind producers of goods. The emphasis shifted from helping the blind to employing competent workers (not necessarily mutually exclusive categories), and the social-service function largely fell by the wayside. Part of the reason for the shift in emphasis lay in changed environmental conditions, with an increased demand for the workshops' products. But it appears that these demands could have been resisted and the original intent of the workshops maintained intact. The internal decision-making process led to the development of clearly different goals from those professed at the outset.

Still another type of displacement can be seen in what Etzioni calls "overmeasurement" and Bertram Gross labels "number magic."[19] Both refer to the tendency for organizations of all types to organize their energies (goals) around activities that are easily quantified. Easy quantification leads to counting publications of university faculty rather than evaluating classroom performance, looking at output per worker rather than "diligence, cooperation, punctuality, loyalty, and responsibility,"[20] and counting parishioners in a church rather than assessing the spiritual guidance of the parishioners.[21] These examples could be multiplied many times for many organizations. The obvious solution to this problem is to use multiple indicators for determining the extent to which organizations are achieving their goals. When this is not done and the easily quantifiable measure is stressed, organizational goals become deflected toward the achievement of the easily measured aspect.[22] This may in turn actually defeat the purpose for which the organization was designed.

These internal sources of goal change can be found in any organization and are a basic part of the determination of the operative goals. In the extreme cases discussed here, the changes are rather clearly dysfunctional in terms of the official and original operative goals; but the processes inherent in these changes are a normal part of the goal-setting process.

The final source of goal change is a more generalized environmental pressure — generalized, that is, in terms of falling within abstract categories such as technological development, cultural changes, and economic conditions; however, the impact on the organization is direct. Several studies are available that provide direct evidence for this basis of goal change. Perhaps the most dramatic evidence comes from David L. Sills' analysis of the national Foundation for Infantile Paralysis.[23] Although the study was completed before the transition to be discussed was accomplished, the change in operative goals is very evident. The foundation was formed to assist in the prevention and treatment of polio through research, coordinating, and fund-raising activities. At the time the foundation was organized, polio was a major health problem, highlighted by Franklin D. Roosevelt's crippled condition as a result of the disease. Roosevelt himself founded the organization in 1938 at the height of his own popularity and the seriousness of the polio problem. The organization grew rapidly, and its March of Dimes became a very successful volunteer fund-raising effort.

In less than two decades, the organization accomplished its primary goal. Through the development of the Salk and Sabine vaccines, polio has largely been eliminated as a serious health hazard. Rehabilitation facilities have been consistently improved to assist those who suffer from the effects of polio contracted in the past (the number of new cases at present is insignificant). For the organization, these events presented a clear dilemma. The choice was between going out of business and developing a new goal. The latter alternative was chosen, as the organization decided to concentrate on "other crippling diseases," with particular emphasis on birth defects. Sills suggests that the presence of a strong national headquarters together with committed volunteers should maintain the organization over time. The historical evidence seems to confirm this, although the organization does not appear to be as strong as it was during the polio epidemics.

The volunteer and nonvolunteer members of this organization had a vested interest in its maintenance. At the same time, technological developments outside the organization made its continuation questionable because of its operative goals at that time. The focus of the organization shifted to adapt to the changed technology. While some of the operative goals remained the same, others shifted to meet the new concerns.

The impact of technological shifts can also be seen in Lawrence and Lorsch's analysis of firms in the plastics industry. In this case, technological change, in the form of a rapidly changing "state of the art," is an ever-present and pressing factor of the environment. In discussing the performance of organizations in this industry, Lawrence and Lorsch comment:

The low-performing organizations were both character-ized by their top administrators as having serious difficulty in dealing with this environment. They had not been successful in introducing and marketing new products. In fact, their attempts to do so had met with repeated failures. This record, plus other measures of performance available to top management, left them with a feeling of disquiet and a sense of urgency to find ways of improving their performance.[24]

This sense of urgency would be translated into altered operative goals for the organization as it seeks to cope more effectively with the rapidly changing technological system.

Technology is not the only environmental factor impinging upon the organization, despite its apparent centrality. The general values in the environment surrounding an organization also affect its operation. Burton Clark's analysis of the adult education system in California indicates clearly that an organization is vitally affected by the values of those whom it serves and whose support it seeks.[25]

The adult education system's official goals are concerned with relatively lofty matters, such as awareness of civic responsibilities, economic uplift, personal adjustment in the family, health and physical fitness, cultural development, broadened educational background, and the development of avocational interests. This educational system suffers from a number of handicaps. It is part of the public educational system but not part of the normal sequence. It is a "peripheral, nonmandatory" part; and this marginality is heightened by the fact that the system operates on an "enrollment economy." That is, school income is determined largely by attendance (paid) in classes. If attendance declines, support for the program from tax revenues is likely also

to decline. Course enrollments become "*the* criterion by which courses are initiated and continued."[26]

Courses are offered only if they are popular. It is not surprising, therefore, to find classes in cake decorating, rug making, and square dancing. While these are legitimate avocational activities, the pressure for courses such as these precludes much attention being paid to the other official goals and increases the criticisms of the adult education program from other segments of the educational enterprise. The adult education administrators are thus caught in the bind of trying to maintain attendance in the face of competing demands for the potential student's time and trying to satisfy the pertinent criticism of other educators and members of the legislature. The values of the clientele are inconsistent with those of the system itself. The organization adapts to their demands, but then finds itself out of phase with another part of its relevant environment.

Organizations in the service area are constantly confronted with changed values that make their services in greater or lesser demands. Colleges and universities were unprepared for the rise in enrollments caused by the increased valuation placed on education during most of the 1960s. While demographic conditions would have led to a prediction of some increase, more than the expected proportions of high school graduates opted for college as opposed to other endeavors (for whatever reason). These changed values have obviously affected the goals of the organizations as they are forced to "process" students at the expense of some of the traditional goals.[27]

Shifts in cultural values and their impact on the goals of organizations are obvious in the profit-making sector also. While the goals of profit may remain, the operative goals shift as more energies are put into market research and as organizations redefine themselves as "young" organizations for the "now" generation. These are often more than advertising slogans, in that internal transformations have occurred to refocus the organizations' activities.

Shifts in the economic and political systems surrounding an organization would have similar influences on the goals of the organization involved. While much more than goals are affected by these interactions with the environment, it should be clear that organizational goals, like the organizations for which they serve as constraints and guides for action, are not static. Internal and external factors affect them. The relative strength of the various factors affecting goals, which would include the decision-making and power processes within the organization, have not been determined. We do know that these factors are operative, but we cannot specify the conditions under which the importance of these factors varies.

The Utility of the Goal Concept

The factors that affect goals, and the fact that the meaningful goals for an organization are not those officially pronounced, might lead us to reject the goal concept altogether. But there is still the simple but basic fact that the organization would not exist if it were not for some common purpose. Except in the case of conscription, as in the military system or the public schools, members come to the organization willingly, if not enthusiastically. In all cases, the organization engages in some activity. This activity is not simply random behavior; it is based on some notion of what the purpose of the action is.

This purpose or goal is the basis for organizational activities. It is true that means can come to be emphasized more heavily than the goal itself, that members of the organization may have no idea of why they are doing what they are doing, and that ritualistic adherence to outmoded norms may become the norm; but these behaviors would be impossible without the presence of a goal. Even when forgotten or ignored, the goal is still the basis for the organization, since the means would not have developed without it in the first place.

From the discussion above, it is clear that most organizations have more than one goal. These multiple goals may be in conflict with one another; even then, they are still a basis for action. The action itself may or may not conflict with conflicting goals. The relative importance of the goals can be determined by the way the organization allocates its resources to them. Since both external and internal pressures affect goals, along with the more rational process of goal setting, goals cannot be viewed as static. They change, sometimes dramatically, over time. These changes, it should be stressed, can occur because of decision making within the organization. This decision making is almost by definition a consequence of internal or external forces. Goal alterations decided within the organization are a consequence of the interactions of members who participate in the goal-setting process. This can be done by an oligarchic elite or through democratic processes (in very few organizations would a total democracy prevail).

Shifts in goals can also occur without a conscious decision on the part of organization members — that is, as a reaction to the external or internal pressures without a conscious reference to an abstract model of where the organization is going. While this is not goal-related behavior, the persistence of such activities leads to their becoming operative goals for the organization, as where the organization focuses its efforts on achieving easily measured objectives at the expense of more central but less easily measured goals.

It is at this point, of course, that the goal concept is most fuzzy. If an organization is oriented toward some easily quantifiable objective for the sake of measuring its achievements, the analyst can stand back and say, "Aha, this organization isn't doing what it is supposed to do!" At the same time, the easily quantified goal is an abstraction despite its easy quantification, just as is the possibly more lofty objective that serves as the analyst's point of departure. The analyst can also point out the deflections that occur as a result of the external and internal pressures discussed. Concentration upon deflections from official goals, whether they are due to quantification or external and internal pressures, can lead to the decision that goals are really not relevant for organizational analysis. It is at this point that the work of Perrow and Simon is most pertinent. Perrow's emphasis on the operative goals, however they are developed, and Simon's notion that goals place constraints on decision making both suggest that goals are relevant, even central, for organizational analysis. It does not matter what the source of operative goals might be; what does matter is that they come into the decision-making and action processes of the organization. They are still abstractions around which the organization and its members behave.

The goal concept, with the modifications we have discussed, is vital in organizational analysis. The dynamics of goal setting and goal change do not alter the fact that goals still serve as guides for what happens in an organization. If the concept of goals is not used, organizational behavior becomes a random occurrence, subject to whatever pressures and forces exist at any point in time. Since organizations have continuity and do accomplish things, the notion of goals as abstractions around which behavior is organized remains viable.

The analysis of goals is a rather empty exercise until the second part of the equation is added. Since a goal is something that is sought, the seeking leads to the issue of goal accomplishment, or effectiveness. Since goals are seldom accomplished, except in rare cases such as that of the National Foundation for Infantile Paralysis, *effectiveness* is a more usable term than *accomplishment*. The discussion of effectiveness that follows is based on the goal notion that has been developed . . . that organizations attempt to be rational and goal-seeking, but are deflected by the kinds of pressures and forces that have been described.

EFFECTIVENESS

Effectiveness has been defined as the "degree to which [an organization] realizes its goals."[28] From the discussion of goals, it should be clear that effectiveness is not a simple issue. The basic difficulty in analyzing it is the fact of multiple and often conflicting goals in many organizations. Effectiveness in one set of endeavors may lead to noneffectiveness in another, particularly in the case of multipurpose organizations.

Effectiveness is a difficult issue from another standpoint. *Efficiency* is often confused with effectiveness. Etzioni defines efficiency as the "amount of resources used to produce a unit of output."[29] Clearly, an organization can be efficient without being effective, and vice versa. Recent controversies regarding certain poverty programs illustrate this point. The costs (efficiency) of producing a well-trained and well-adjusted person who came from a disadvantaged background were higher than those of producing a college graduate at some elite universities. The programs may have been effective — although this was never directly confirmed — but they were not efficient, at least from the point of view of many legislators. Efficiency and effectiveness are often closely related, but it is dangerous to assume without careful investigation that they are identical.

Despite the difficulties with the concept of effectiveness, it is one that captures the attention of almost everyone concerned with organizations. For the organization member, the effectiveness issue really boils down to the question, "Is it worth it?" While not every member is concerned with the issue, certainly those in decision-making positions are. For the organizational analyst, the same question applies, since he also wants to know whether the relationships he is examining mean anything.

The Goal Approach

The interest in effectiveness has not led to a definitive set of studies or conceptual approaches to the issue. A good part of the difficulty in assessing effectiveness lies in the problems surrounding goals. Most analyses of effectiveness are built around some version of a goal model of organization. In a relatively early study of effectiveness, Basil Georgopoulos and Arnold Tannenbaum argued that measures of effectiveness must be based on organizational means and ends, rather than relying on externally derived criteria.[30] They found that productivity, flexibility, and absence of strain and conflict were both interrelated and associated with independent assessments of effectiveness. These indicators of effectiveness were closely related to the goals of the organizations studied.

In a major effort to make some sense of the effectiveness issue, James Price has recently compiled a set of propositions dealing with effectiveness.[31] The propositions are drawn from some fifty research monographs (not all concerned specifically with effectiveness) and deal with a variety of qualities assumed by Price to be indicators of effectiveness — including productivity, morale, conformity, adaptiveness, and institutionalization. Productivity is taken as the indicator most closely related to effectiveness. Unfortunately, as Price notes, the indicators themselves do not vary together in actual practice, and what might be related to morale might be unrelated to productivity. This problem illustrates a major issue in the analysis of organizational effectiveness: Since organizations generally pursue more than one goal, the degree of effectiveness in the attainment of one goal may be inversely related to the degree in the attainment of other goals. This sort of thing does occur quite often, apparently, and so organizations must choose between the goals they seek to attain, thus reinforcing the idea that the operative goals of the organization are the result of internal choice processes and external pressures. This point also raises the strong possibility that *organizations cannot be effective,* if the idea is accepted that almost every organization has multiple goals.

Despite these problems, which Price acknowledges in part, he then links organizational characteristics to effectiveness. He suggests, for example, that organizations are likely to be more effective when they have a high degree of division of labor, specialized departmentalization, and continuous systems of assembling output. . . . Also related to effectiveness are such things as the acceptance of the legitimacy of the decision-making system, a high degree of organizational autonomy, and high rates of communication within the organization.[32] Although the propositions may be oversimplified, as William Starbuck has suggested,[33] they provide a starting point from which systematic examinations of effectiveness may begin. Rather than proposi-tions, Price's work actually presents a series of hypotheses about effectiveness that are subject to empirical verification.

An additional problem with the Price inventory, and one that characterizes most effectiveness studies, is the use of productivity as the major indicator. This is misleading and/or inapplicable in service organizations and less than perfect in many production organizations. The positive role of conflict in certain circumstances is also typically ignored.

The Price analysis is based on the assumption that organizations are goal-seeking entities. It also recognizes that the attainment of one goal may operate against (be dysfunctional for) the attainment of another. The more complex the organization in terms of the operative goals on which it is based, the more difficult the effectiveness issue becomes. The problem becomes further com-pounded, of course, when an organization stresses the easily quantifiable measures of effectiveness when these are not true indicators of its total purposes.

The System-Resources Approach

Stanley Seashore and Ephraim Yuchtman[34] have at-tempted to avoid some of the pitfalls of the goal approach by essentially ignoring organizational goals in their analyses of effectiveness. They criticize those who use the goal approach on the ground that the determi-nation of goals is extremely difficult, if not impossible. Their criticism is largely of those who advocate the use of the official, rather than operative goals. Where they do consider the operative goals, they note that there are often conflicting goals for the same organization. Instead of the goal model, Seashore and Yuchtman suggest the use of a "system-resources" model for the analysis of organizational effectiveness.

The system-resources approach is based on the idea of the organization as an open system. As such, it engages in exchange and competitive relationships with the environment. Effectiveness becomes the "ability of the organization, in either relative or absolute terms, to exploit its environment in the acquisition of scarce and valued resources."[35] These resources are acquired in the competitive and exchange relationships. An organiza-tion is most effective when it "maximizes its bargaining position and optimizes its resource procurement." This approach links the organization back into the society by noting that it is in interaction with the environment and thus must gain resources from that source.

In an empirical examination of this approach, Seashore and Yuchtman used data from 75 insurance sales agencies located in different communities through-out the United States. Data from these agencies were factor-analyzed. The analysis yielded ten factors that were stable over time. These were:

1. Business volume
2. Production cost
3. New member productivity
4. Youthfulness of members
5. Business mix
6. Manpower growth
7. Management emphasis
8. Maintenance cost
9. Member productivity
10. Market penetration[36]

These factors are not taken as indicators for all organizations. The factors of youthfulness of members, for example, while related to performance in this case, may be part of a phase or cycle in the life of these organizations. In interpreting the results of this analysis, Seashore and Yuchtman note that factors such as business volume and penetration of the market could be considered goals, but member productivity and youthfulness certainly cannot. They conclude that while not all the factors associated with performance can be considered as goals, they can be regarded as important resources gleaned from the environment.

This approach would essentially do away with goals as a component of the analysis of effectiveness. It also suggests that there is no universal standard by which effectiveness can be judged, making the effectiveness issue one that would have to be handled organization by organization, or at least type of organization by type of organization.

Viewed from another perspective, the Seashore-Yuchtman approach does not differ markedly from the one that has already been discussed. The acquisition of resources from the environment is based upon the official goal of the organization (Seashore and Yuchtman use the term *ultimate criterion*[37]). Movement toward this goal or ultimate criterion is difficult if not impossible to measure. The next step is to specify the operative goals (*penultimate criteria* in the Seashore-Yuchtman ap-proach) and other activities in which the organization engages. Performance or effectiveness according to these criteria is more easily assessed. Growth in business volume is an operative goal in this sense, while youthfulness in members is merely a cyclical factor associated with performance on the other factors. The issue of goals versus resource allocation is therefore in many ways an argument over semantics. The acquisition of resources does not just happen.[38] It is based on what the organization is trying to achieve — its goal — but is accomplished through the operative goals. The Seashore-Yuchtman perspective is very useful in its attention to environmental transactions and its use of organizationally based data. Although they argue against the goal model, their own work is not that much different from the perspective taken here. Their approach is an empirical verification of the importance of the operative-goal concept.

This discussion of organizational effectiveness leads to the conclusion that there is no single indicator of effectiveness, even a group of common indicators, that can be used across organizations. Instead, the approach must be that operative goals serve as the bases for assessments of effectiveness. These operative goals are built around acquiring and maintaining environmental support. To these external considerations must be added the internal factors that Price suggests — morale, adaptiveness, and so on.

The Multiple Criteria of Effectiveness

The relevance of the multiple-criteria approach to effectiveness is seen in practice when data from business managers is considered. Thomas Mahoney and William Weitzel examined the criteria that managers used in assessing the performance of subunits under their direction.[39]

General business managers tend to use productivity and efficient performance. These high-order criteria refer to measures of output, whereas lower-order criteria tend to refer to characteristics of the organization climate, supervisory style, and organizational capacity for performance. The research and development managers, on the other hand, use cooperative behavior, staff development, and reliable performance as high-order criteria; and efficiency, productivity, and output behavior as lower-order criteria.[40]

These differences can be found within the same organization.

This research demonstrates the fact that effectiveness criteria as developed by the organization itself do not vary together. In a very real sense, the complex organization thus cannot be effective, if effectiveness is

taken in a global or ultimate sense. It can be effective on one or several criteria, but must be less effective or ineffective on others. In fact, efforts to increase effectiveness on one criterion can provide an oppositional force to achieving effectiveness on another. The fact that choices among criteria must be made reinforces the utility of the goal concept, since these choices will be based at least partially on the operative goals of the moment.

Implicit in the discussions of effectiveness, regardless of perspective, is the assumption that the organization operates in a relatively free market and the customer or client is free to select an alternative organization if his needs are not being met. When he shifts to another organization, resources are not allocated to the original organization and effectiveness diminishes. In the goals perspective, profits or community support would decrease as this occurs. The free-market assumption is an important one and makes sense for many organizations. There are, however, many organizations that have an essentially captive market. This can be most easily seen in the case of some service organizations, such as schools or public welfare agencies, but it is also the case for the military and for many business organizations that enjoy a near monopoly in an area. In these cases, an important consideration in the effectiveness equation is typically ignored — the response of the customer or client to the organization.

If the client is not receiving the services he feels are important to him, the organization cannot be judged as being totally effective, regardless of what the organization members themselves think. For example, if a particular form of public welfare makes the recipients feel degraded and does not help them move into a more meaningful life style, the welfare system in question is not as effective as it might be. In fact, it could be posited that the conditions under which the organization might judge itself to be effective, such as the number of cases handled or the amount of money disbursed, might be counter to the client perception of what the organization should be doing.

This consideration raises again the point that it is difficult for organizations to be effective. In this case the organization might be achieving its multiple goals as it sees it, but be ineffective in accomplishing what its clients see as being of primary importance. In issues like this, of course, it is difficult, if not impossible, to determine the extent to which the "experts" in the organization should be listened to as opposed to a concern with lay opinion. The potential for conflict must be recognized, however, and the organization should be aware of the values of its constituents.

Recent client and consumer movements should bring this issue into the open more clearly. At the present time, it is difficult to determine how the organizations involved will react, other than with resistance.

SUMMARY AND CONCLUSIONS

This reading has been concerned with two central but controversial issues in organizational analysis. Perspectives on goals have ranged from seeing them as the key to understanding organizations to considering them of no use whatsoever. The approach taken here has been to acknowledge the fact that official goals do not tell us very much about the organization, and to adopt instead the operative-goal concept, as a means of focusing on what organizations actually do. The operative goals serve as abstract ideas around which behavior is organized. These ideas take the form of constraints on decision making in determining where the organization's

resources will be placed. The operative goals can and usually do change as a result of internal and external factors. These changes can deflect the organization quite dramatically from its original (official) purposes, reflecting a response to reality in most cases. Changes in goals can also lead to the disintegration of an organization, if the new operative goals do not allow the organization to have sufficient resources brought in to ensure survival. Operative goals are translated into policies that guide the day-to-day activities of the organization. Changes in policy reflect alterations in the pattern of the organization's goals.

Effectiveness was treated within the operative-goals framework. Since the very concept of operative goals suggests a complex goals structure, effectiveness cannot be viewed from an all-or-none perspective. Effectiveness is a relative phenomenon, with an absence of covariation among many of the criteria and possibly inverse relationships among others. The complexity of organizations, almost by definition, precludes effectiveness on all criteria. The specific type of effectiveness sought reflects the operative goals as they have evolved over time.

NOTES

1. Amitai Etzioni, *Modern Organizations* (Englewood Cliffs, N.J.: Prentice-Hall, Inc., 1964), p. 6.

2. Talcott Parsons, *Structure and Process in Modern Societies* (New York: The Free Press, 1960), pp. 17–22 and 44–47.

3. Herbert A. Simon, "On the Concept of Organizational Goal," *Administrative Science Quarterly* 9, no. 1 (June 1964): 2.

4. Charles Perrow, "The Analysis of Goals in Complex Organizations," *American Sociological Review* 26, no. 6 (December 1961): 855.

5. Peter M. Blau, *The Dynamics of Bureaucracy* (Chicago: University of Chicago Press, 1955).

6. Perrow, "Analysis of Goals," pp. 855–56.

7. Ibid., p. 856.

8. Cases and case studies are useful as examples, but they cannot be used as bases for generalizations concerning other organizations, even of a very similar type.

9. *Faculty Information* (Minneapolis: University of Minnesota, 1966), pp. 7–8.

10. Mayer N. Zald, "Comparative Analysis and Measurement of Organizational Goals: The Case of Correctional Institutions for Delinquents," *The Sociological Quarterly* 4, no. 2 (Spring 1963): 206–30.

11. James D. Thompson and William J. McEwen, "Organizational Goals and Environment: Goal Setting as an Interaction Process," *Administrative Science Quarterly* 23, no. 1 (February 1958).

12. Ibid., p. 27.

13. Philip Selznick, *TVA and the Grass Roots* (New York: Harper Torchbook Edition, 1966).

14. Thompson and McEwen, "Organizational Goals and Environment," p. 28.

15. For a further discussion of this point, see Roland L. Warren, ''The Interorganizational Field as a Focus for Investigation,'' *Administrative Science Quarterly* 12, no. 3 (December 1967): 396–419.

16. Etzioni, *Modern Organizations,* p. 10.

17. Robert Michels, *Political Parties* (New York: The Free Press, 1949).

18. Robert A. Scott, ''The Factory as a Social Service Organization: Goal Displacement in Workshops for the Blind,'' *Social Problems* 15, no. 2 (Fall 1967): 160–75.

19. Etzioni, *Modern Organizations,* pp. 8–10; and Bertram M. Gross, *Organizations and Their Managing* (New York: The Free Press, 1968), p. 293.

20. Gross, *Organizations and Their Managing,* p. 295.

21. Etzioni, *Modern Organizations,* p. 10.

22. For an extended discussion of this point, see W. Keith Warner and A. Eugene Havens, ''Goal Displacement and the Intangibility of Organizational Goals,'' *Administrative Science Quarterly* 12, no. 4 (March 1968): 539–55.

23. David L. Sills, *The Volunteers* (New York: The Free Press, 1957).

24. Paul R. Lawrence and Jay W. Lorsch, *Organization and Environment: Managing Differentiation and Integration* (Cambridge: Harvard Graduate School of Business Administration, 1967), p. 42.

25. Burton R. Clark, ''Organizational Adaptation and Precarious Values,'' *American Sociological Review* 21, no. 3 (June 1956): 327–36.

26. Ibid., p. 333.

27. The case of the WCTU, discussed earlier, illustrates what happens when an organization *does not* adapt to changed values. The current shifts in college enrollment illustrate still another shift of values.

28. Etzioni, *Modern Organization,* p. 8.

29. Ibid.

30. Basil S. Georgopoulos and Arnold S. Tannenbaum, ''A Study of Organizational Effectiveness,'' *American Sociological Review* 22, no. 5 (October 1957): 534–40.

31. James L. Price, *Organizational Effectiveness: An Inventory of Propositions* (Homewood, Ill.: Richard D. Irwin, Inc., 1968).

32. Ibid., pp. 203–4.

33. William H. Starbuck, ''Some Comments, Observations and Objections Stimulated by 'Design of Proof in Organizational Research,' '' *Administrative Science Quarterly* 13, no. 1 (June 1968): 135–61.

34. Stanley E. Seashore and Ephraim Yuchtman, ''Factorial Analysis of Organizational Performance,'' *Administrative Science Quarterly* 12, no. 3 (December 1967): 377–95; and Yuchtman and Seashore, ''A System Resource Approach to Organizational Effectiveness,'' *American Sociological Review* 32, no. 6 (December 1967): 891–903.

35. Yuchtman and Seashore, ''A System Resource Approach,'' p. 898.

36. Seashore and Yuchtman, ''Factorial Analysis,'' p. 383.

37. Ibid., p. 378.

38. Mayer N. Zald, in ''Urban Differentiation, Characteristics of Boards of Directors, and Organizational Effectiveness,'' *American Journal of Sociology* 73, no. 3 (November 1967), uses the acquisition of resources as the criterion for effectiveness. In this case, the presence of high-status members on the boards of directors of YMCA branches is related to effectiveness because of their success in bringing in resources.

39. Thomas A. Mahoney and William Weitzel, ''Managerial Models of Organizational Effectiveness,'' *Administrative Science Quarterly* 14, no. 3 (September 1969): 357–65.

40. Ibid., p. 362.

Strategies for Increasing Effectiveness

38. Learning from the Japanese: Prospects and Pitfalls

Robert E. Cole

It has become extraordinarily fashionable in recent years for leading management experts to trumpet the potential for learning from the Japanese. Particular attention has been called to the advantages of Japanese management style and techniques, especially as they relate to the organization and training of the labor force.

What accounts for this surge of interest? The enormity of Japan's economic success as it moved to the second largest economy outside of the communist bloc and its successful penetration of Western markets are clearly the major factors. When you are getting hurt at the marketplace, you are inclined to sit up and listen.

Yet, there are still many American managers who would dismiss the Japanese experience as one that grew out of Japan's unique cultural heritage and therefore could not have much applicability for U.S. firms. The ranks of this core group, while still strong, have been thinned by the recent invasion of Japanese-operated subsidiaries in the United States. The bulk of the reports on this "invasion" have reported the activities of Japanese companies quite favorably. They emphasize their ability to import Japanese management techniques and philosophy and apply them successfully to their management of American workers.

This turn of events has made it more difficult for the doubters to claim these approaches will work only in the rarified atmosphere of Japanese cultural conditions. Above all, the Japanese are now seen as having a winning package that has catapulted them to success. That American managers are beginning to study carefully and apply Japanese practices in this environment is not surprising. Yet, they often make such decisions in the absence of very hard data showing the applicability of these practices. For example, the literature on the practices of Japanese subsidiaries in the

United States is very impressionistic and lacks systematic comparisons, not to speak of control groups. Yet, as Herbert Simon (Carnegie Mellon University's Nobel laureate in economics) has shown us in his observations on the adoption of computers in the 1960's, management decisions are often based on the fads of the moment rather than some carefully calculated economic rationality.

In one sense, then, these developments must be reckoned as quite positive. In the area of worker-manager relationships, American managers have historically kept themselves unusually insulated from the experiences of other industrial nations; one need only contrast U.S. practices with those in Western Europe where large amounts of information and learning experiences are exchanged. No doubt this is a function of the unique relationship worked out in the course of our history between human and national resources in a relatively isolated geographical setting.

What, then, are the prospects of learning from the Japanese in the area of worker-manager relationships? To answer this question, two approaches are useful:

1. Consider the obverse case — that is, what has been the experience with the Japanese in borrowing from the Americans in this area.
2. Consider the concrete example of Japanese quality control circles (QC Circles).

THE PATTERN OF JAPANESE BORROWING

When the United States was unquestionably the most advanced industrial nation in the early postwar period, in addition to being the conqueror and occupying power of Japan, it was not surprising that the Japanese were willing and eager to learn from American management techniques. Generally, the Japanese were willing to make the assumption that American management techniques must be the most advanced, independent of any objective confirmation. These developments were part of a "management boom," as it was called in Japan, during which American management formulas and techniques were introduced into all spheres of business administration from the 1950s, particularly personnel administration.

The attention the Japanese pay to Western developments in management theory and practice is still astonishing. A significant component of the large literature on management and work in the Japanese language consists of translations and analyses of the work of Western scholars. One estimate puts translations alone at 9 percent of the some 1,000 books published a year. The research and proposals of American organizational specialists such as Rensis Likert, Peter Drucker, Chris Argyris, Douglas McGregor, and Frederick Herzberg are widely known, and the use of their ideas is commonplace in large Japanese firms. Indeed, Japanese managers are often surprised when they visit the United States to find such hostility to their ideas on the part of many American managers.

We can get a sense of the Japanese capacity to borrow and adapt Western organizational technology to their own needs through a brief tracing of the introduction of QC circles. QC circles may represent the most innovative process of borrowing and adaption in the personnel policies of large Japanese companies in the postwar period.

Before 1945, Japan had only moderate experience with modern methods of statistical quality control. An early postwar effort was organized by U.S. occupation officials to have American statisticians go to Japan and teach American wartime industrial standards to Japanese engineers and statisticians. Prominent in this early effort was a series of postwar lectures beginning in 1950 undertaken by Dr. William Deming to teach statistical quality control practices. Indeed, the Deming Prize was established to commemorate Dr. Deming's contribution to the diffusion of quality control ideas in Japan; an annual competition by major firms for the award serves further to promote the spread of these ideas. These various efforts were a major factor contributing to the formal adoption of Japanese Engineering Standards (JES) provided for by legislation in 1949. The Korean War had a further impact on the acceptance of these standards. In order to win military procurement orders from the American military between 1954 and 1961, the quality standards defined by the U.S. Defense Department had to be met.

In 1954 Dr. J. Juran, the noted quality control expert, arrived in Japan for a series of lectures. He emphasized a newer orientation to quality control, stating that it must be an integral part of the management function and practiced throughout the firm. In practice, this meant teaching quality control to middle management.

From 1955 through 1960 these ideas spread rapidly in major firms. But there was a critical innovation on the part of the Japanese. In the Japanese reinterpretation, each and every person in the organizational hierarchy from top management to rank-and-file employees received exposure to statistical quality control knowledge and techniques. Workers began to participate in study groups to upgrade quality control practices. This practice gave both a simple and most profound twist to the original ideas propagated by the Western experts. Quality control shifted from being the prerogative of a minority of engineers with limited shop experience ("outsiders") to being the responsibility of each employee. Instead of adding additional layers of inspectors, reliability assurance and rework personnel when quality problems arise, as is customary in many U.S. firms, each worker, in concert with his or her workmates, is expected to take responsibility for solving quality problems.

This pattern of taking ideas developed in America for management employees and applying them to hourly personnel is not unique to QC circles. Rather, it is a distinctive approach adopted by the Japanese manager. For example, the American ideas on career development that have so much currency today in the personnel administration field were developed and are being applied to management personnel in the United States. The Japanese, however, have taken these same ideas and applied them to their hourly-rated personnel.

To fully understand the process of borrowing and adaptation, it is important to understand why these transformations of American ideas take place. What is it about the Japanese environment of the firm in Japan that makes their response so different from American firms in this regard? We can offer three levels of explanation: cultural, sociological, and economic.

In the cultural area, the Confucianist doctrine of perfectability of man harmonizes nicely with a belief in the educability and the potential of even blue collar workers to contribute to the firm. The Japanese

manager tends to view his employees as having sociopsychological needs, which, if nurtured, will yield economic returns to the firm. They see all regular male employees as resources with substantial potentialities for human growth. This contrasts sharply with the doctrine of original sin that characterizes our Judeo-Christian heritage. Here the emphasis is on the fundamental weaknesses and limitations of man.

While it is appealing to lay the difference in willingness to invest in training and responsibility at the feet of Confucianism versus Christianity, this explanation is much too simplistic. In constructing a value-added explanation, we can add first a set of sociological factors. A matter of particular relevance here is the impact of racial, ethnic, and religious differences between the managerial and worker classes. Japan is a remarkably homogenous country in race, ethnicity, religion, and culture. To be sure, there is a significant Korean and Eta minority, but they are by-and-large excluded from the large-scale manufacturing sector and relegated to various retail and wholesale trades. For all practical purposes this means that the Japanese manager can accept the proposition that the average worker is really not so very different from them and that "there for the grace of God go I." I maintain that this is a profound point critical to understanding the willingness of Japanese employers to invest in the training of and provide responsibility for blue collar employees.

There is a fundamental egalitarianism in Japanese industry that is quite impressive and is apparent to most careful observers: *Japanese managers believe in their labor force.* They believe that given the opportunity, their labor force can and wants to contribute to organizational goals.

Compare this approach to the situation in American industry. We have a management that is largely white Anglo-Saxon Protestant and a labor force that often

---

How QC Circles Work

A QC circle is a relatively autonomous unit composed of a small group of workers (ideally about ten), usually led by a foreman or senior worker and organized in each work unit. Participants are taught elementary techniques of problem solving including statistical methods. It is in principle a voluntary study group that concentrates on solving job-related quality problems. These problems are broadly conceived as improving methods of production as part of company-wide efforts. Some typical efforts include reducing defects, scrap, rework, and down-time. These activities in turn are expected to lead to cost-reduction and increased productivity. At the same time, the circles focus on improving working conditions and the self-development of workers. The latter includes: development of leadership abilities of foreman and workers, skill development among workers, improvement of worker morale and motivation, the stimulation of teamwork within work groups, and recognition of worker achievements. Above all, the circles involve recognition that hourly workers have an important contribution to make to the organization.

comprises diverse racial, religious, and ethnic groups. Cultural gaps reflecting the failures of our public school education system are also wider in the United States. These differences make it much more difficult for management to put itself in the role of the ordinary production worker. Rather, this bifurcation of functions by race, religion, and ethnicity makes it much easier for American managers to see themselves as an elite whose superior education entitles them to make all the important decisions. It makes it easier to dismiss the idea that investment in education and training of ordinary blue collar workers or the sharing of decision making with them would make a significant contribution to the firm.

The final factor in this value-added explanation is an economic one. You can believe all you want in Confucianism and egalitarianism, but if your firm is not growing, you are not likely to make major investments in employee training and education, particularly if you have high rates of employee turnover.

The difference between the U.S. and Japanese economies is obvious in this respect. For the better part of the postwar period, Japanese managers have operated in the context of a high growth-rate economy and, until the early 1970s, a labor surplus economy. Investments in education and training that would enable workers to better participate in organizational decisions could be recouped. Promotion opportunities for talented and even not-so-talented workers were quite large. Moreover, the system of lifetime employment, especially in large Japanese firms, meant that the probability of employees staying on at the same firm was much higher in Japanese than in U.S. firms. Under these conditions, it was not unreasonable for Japanese employers to make large investments in employee training and education. It was easier for them to treat all employees as important resources. In the United States, high turnover and sluggish growth rates in many industries made such investment less likely. Employers were more likely to see hourly rate employees as interchangeable parts, particularly in the context of a large army of reserved unemployed.

EFFECTS OF QC CIRCLE PRACTICES

The QC circle movement in Japan has grown explosively. The number of QC circles registered with the Union of Japanese Scientists and Engineers (JUSE) increased from 1,000 in 1964 to some 87,000 by 1978. With an average of almost ten members a circle, the membership totalled 840,000. Unregistered QC circles are estimated conservatively to total an additional five times the number of registered circles, with a membership of some four million. With a total Japanese labor force of some 37 million in 1978, this means that approximately one out of every eight Japanese employees was involved in QC circle activity. The movement has drawn most of its members from hourly employees in the manufacturing sector. These summary figures are inflated because the data do not strictly discriminate between QC circles and some other forms of small group activity such as zero-defect programs, industrial engineering teams, improvement groups, and so on. Nonetheless, we are dealing with a movement that has had a significant impact on managerial practices and the degree of employee participation in the workplace.

Three characteristics of the QC circles as they have evolved in Japan are particularly significant.

- The QC circle is not a response to specific problems. Rather, it is a continuous study process operative in the workshop. That is, it functions as monitoring behavior that scans the environment for opportunities, does not wait to be activated by a problem, and does not stop its activities when a problem has been found and solved. This is a rare quality and constitutes an enormous asset where operative.

- Most U.S. motivational schemes assume that workers know how to raise productivity and improve quality but that they are holding back for no justifiable reason. Operator indifference or even sabotage are assumed to be the normal problems which management must combat. Under these assumptions, close supervision and/or financial incentives is the common response. The QC circle, to the contrary, starts with the assumption that the causes of poor quality performance are not known by either management or workers and that analysis is needed to discover and remedy these causes. A corollary of this assumption is that you must provide participants with the tools and the training necessary to discover causes and remedy them.

- Even if the solutions arrived at by workers are no better than those arrived at by technical personnel, we can anticipate that workers will more enthusiastically carry out solutions to problems that they have solved. You tend to carry out with enthusiasm policies where you have been part of the problem-solving process. This is one of the most fundamental of motivational principles.

It should be noted that the QC circles do not always perform in Japanese companies as they do on paper.

Because of Japan's remarkable economic success, we have a tendency to see the Japanese as miracle men who never make mistakes. Some of their common problems are:

— For all the emphasis on voluntarism in QC circle activity, there is a great deal of top-down control in many companies. A significant minority of workers see the circles as a burden imposed on them by management rather than their own program. Thus, the circles often take on somewhat of a coercive aspect that is not the best incentive for motivating workers to produce innovative behavior.

— While in theory there is equal emphasis on the development of worker potential and productivity, in practice the emphasis on productivity has played a more prominent role. This leads workers to often question the benefits that the circles have for them.

— As the QC circle movement has developed, there is a tendency toward the routinization of that original spontaneity. This leads to workers going through the motions and turns their participation into ritualistic behavior.

THE PATTERN OF U.S. BORROWING

We are now in the remarkable situation in which the transmission of information on quality control practices is coming, full circle, back to the United States. Over 100 American firms have now adopted or are in the process of adopting some version of the QC circles. They include firms of different sizes, industries and technologies. Some of the early innovators are: American Airlines, Babcock & Wilcox, Champion Spark Plugs, Honeywell Corporation, Cordis-Dow, Federal Products, Ford Motor Company, General Motors Corporation, Hughes Aircraft, J. B. Lansing, Lockheed Missile and Space Company, Mercury Marine, Pentel of America, Rockwell International, Solar Turbines, Verbatim Corporation, Waters Associates, and Westinghouse Defense and Electronics Center. In truly American fashion, a variety of consultants have sprung up to implement the QC circles, and the circles are now a regular feature in seminars offered by leading management organizations. The American Society for Quality Control is also providing more publicity and information on the subject. Two former employees of Lockheed Missile and Space Company who were involved with the QC circle program have not only set up their own consultant firm but have also established the International Association of Quality Circles (IAQC). In short, a broadly based publicity campaign designed to diffuse the QC circle practice is beginning to develop and accumulate momentum.

Conversations with officials in various companies suggest a variety of incentives, often multiple, responsible for their decision to introduce QC circles. Some of these more commonly mentioned include: need to maintain or improve quality, search for new ways to raise productivity, fear of a plant closing or shutting down of a product line unless more productive methods are found, worry about a direct Japanese threat to one's market position, desire to reduce the likelihood of unionization, desire to improve relations with existing unions, and a concern with reducing the adversary relation between management and workers. In a very real sense, we have a case of solutions chasing problems. The packaged solution, wrapped in the winning colors of Japan, is being exhibited and marketed for all potential buyers. Management, the consumer, is carefully examining the wares and asking if this solution might not speak to some of its problems. Despite the variety of explanations company officials give for their interest, the desire to raise productivity and improve quality seems paramount, often in the face of increasing competition from the Japanese. With these concerns goes the recognition that perhaps they have underutilized the worker as an organizational resource.

If one examines the industry composition of the early innovators, one finds further confirmation of this position. They tend to be characterized by firms in which quality has long been an unusually important consideration such as aerospace, pharmaceuticals, and high technology companies, as well as those firms in which a stronger concern for quality has recently come to the fore (often through the vehicle of increasing numbers of product liability suits) as in the case of the automobile. The auto industry receptivity involves a case in which producers are being increasingly criticized for the quality of their product at the same time that the Japanese are making sharp inroads on their markets backed by substantial evidence for the claim that the Japanese are both more responsive to the consumer as well as producing a high-quality product.

The reaction of Japanese firms operating in the United States is interesting. Pentel of America is one Japanese subsidiary that has a QC circle program here. Its parent firm in Japan is a leading maker of pens and won the 1978 Deming Prize for the most successful QC circle program. Pental has nonetheless had some difficult start-up problems with its circle program in the United

States, as has another major Japanese firm in California, whose efforts to establish a circle program have been resisted by its American managers.

What is perhaps most curious is that a number of Japanese firms with established and successful QC circle programs in Japan have not pushed for their adoption in their U.S. subsidiaries. Matsushita Electric, a pioneer in the Japanese QC circle effort, does not have QC circles in its Chicago Quasar plant. One of the American managers explained to me that they were proceeding very cautiously. (See Cole, ``Will QC Circles Work in the U.S.?'' *Quality Progress,* July 1980.) By this he seemed to mean that he doubted whether American employees had sufficient organizational commitment to make the QC concept work in America. Many Japanese subsidiaries in the United States seem to be adopting a wait-and-see attitude. For all the ballyhoo about their success in the U.S., Japanese managers in this country feel quite unsure of their ability to understand and master the intricacies of American labor-management relations.

Most of the experiences with QC circles have been quite shallow; few companies have had the circles in operation more than two years. Thus, it would be premature to make assessments as to their suitability to the American environment.

There are those who would argue that workers are the same everywhere and that few adaptations will have to be made to fit the circle concept to the needs of American managers and workers. Experience thus far suggests this is a fallacious view and that unless the circles are adapted to U.S. conditions, they will fail here. Just as the Japanese adapted Western ideas on quality control to develop the QC circle, so will the Americans have to adapt QC circles to fit the needs of American management and labor. This has been most vividly demonstrated in the very use of the term *quality control circles.* Many companies have found that this name itself does not sit well with workers and unions; in particular the word ``control'' has coercive tones that many firms would prefer to avoid. Consequently, they have chosen other names such as *Employee Participation Circles* and *Quality Circles.* Some companies, however, have stuck with the name Quality Control Circles.

A second area in which adaptation is taking place concerns the role of the union. In Japan, the unions have usually been consulted by management at the time of the introduction of circles but have had relatively little to do with circle operations once they were established other than to monitor excessive demands on workers. In heavily unionized industries in America, this does not

seem to be a suitable strategy. It was a strategy that was tried in Lockheed Missile and Space Company, which seemingly had the most successful program in the U.S. But when a strike occurred and the workers and union did not receive what they felt was their due at the end of the strike, they responded by reducing their participation in the circles. To be sure, there were other important factors involved. But loss of key personnel and failure to institutionalize QC circles were extremely significant in contributing to the decline of circle activity at Lockheed.

In a number of other firms, management has simply installed the circles with only minimum consultation with the unions. The consequences were predictable; the unions saw the circles as just one more attempt to extract increased productivity from the workers without sharing the rewards and/or as an attempt to win the loyalty of workers away from the union. Union leaders put pressure on workers not to cooperate, and the circles either never got off the ground or collapsed soon after they were started.

In one company, a poor choice of circle leader in the trial program nearly wrecked the initiative with circles. A worker hostile to the local union committeeman was appointed as QC circle leader. The union committeeman did everything in his power to sabotage the program and reduce worker participation in the circles. Failure was narrowly avoided by bringing in a national headquarters union official, who was sympathetic to the program. He smoothed the ruffled feathers of the local committeeman and explained the rationale for the program from a union perspective.

If the circles are to be introduced in a union situation, they need to be part of the program. The union needs to have a ``piece of the action'' so that success rubs off on them as well. Otherwise they will see QC activity as an attempt to weaken the union, as indeed it is in some companies. If management tries to go it alone, the union will find a thousand ways to sabotage the program. In a number of firms, I asked managers responsible for initiating the QC circle program how they would do it if they could start all over. Again and again, the answer came back that ``I would design it together with the union so that they felt they had a stake in its success.'' One strategy for involving the union is to create a steering committee for the circles with local union leaders as members.

A third area in which adaptation is occurring concerns the voluntary character of participation. We have seen how the Japanese approach often takes on coercive tones through pressures from either management or peer groups. In the United States the voluntaristic principle will have to be maintained more firmly to fit with the expectations of American workers and unions. Should this not be the case, workers will in all likelihood reject the QC circles; the experiences with the zero defect movement are suggestive in this regard. Adherence to the voluntaristic principle may make getting the circles started more difficult in the beginning. On the other hand, there are far greater rewards associated with the operation of the circles if you stick to a voluntary approach for workers. Genuine enthusiasm for developing innovative suggestions is more likely to emerge.

A related problem of adapting the circles to the United States environment concerns the nature of peer pressure. In large-scale Japanese organizations, for a variety of reasons management has been able to mobilize a good deal of peer pressure on behalf of organizational goals. This was not always the case, but it has been true to a large extent since the early 1960s. Thus, they have been able to use peer pressure on the shop floor to encourage workers to join and participate in circle activities. In the United States, given the adversary relationships that predominate between management and labor, it is difficult to mobilize such pressures. The circles are often seen as just one more in a series of management gimmicks designed to hustle the workers. When I asked one worker why he was suspicious of the circles, he replied, "I'm a union man." He reported that although 40 percent of the hourly personnel in the plant were participating in the circles, there was still a lot of resistance, especially from the older workers who didn't see any virtue in circle activity and didn't think they were likely to change the way things had always been done. In expressing their hostility, the noncircle participants referred to those in the circles as "circle jerks," and those in the circles were clearly quite defensive on the subject.

Given this often hostile atmosphere reported in both union and nonunion firms, two strategies seem relevant.

- The volunteers must struggle to develop ways to make their circle activity provide benefits for all workers as a way of providing its worth and making their participation legitimate in the eyes of their co-workers.
- The introduction of the circles must be done carefully and gradually with attention to reaching opinion leaders among the hourly-rate personnel and local union officials. Ultimately, the opponents of the circles among the shop personnel will change their

minds only when they see changes on the shop floor which they believe are serving worker interests.

Still another area in which adaptation of Japanese practices is taking place is that of wage payments for circle activity. In those situations in which circle activity is conducted on overtime, which is often the case in high volume production operations, American managers will have to pay normal overtime rates. This is not always the case in Japan where sometimes nominal payments are made. Given the practice of permanent employment in Japan, circle activity can be seen as just one of a long stream of contributions that the worker makes to the organization and that will be recognized over the long haul in promotion or wage increases.

In the United States the absence of this long-term commitment means that workers expect their rewards to be more immediate. Instead of monetary incentives for circle suggestions, Japanese employers rely heavily on providing recognition to circle participation through a variety of activities. Again, this makes sense in the context of long-term employee commitment. In the absence of such commitment, U.S. managers will have to provide greater financial rewards for circle suggestions. Not all U.S. companies using circles have accepted this position, but one strategy that does seem to be emerging is that the circle suggestions are channeled into existing suggestion systems with any payments being split among circle members.

One additional point deserves mention here. The provision of recognition to circle members can be complementary to the use of financial incentives. Firms with QC circles have generally found that there is an enormous craving for recognition on the part of participating workers that can be met in a relatively cost-free fashion. Management presentations, meeting in management reserved rooms, T-shirts imprinted with the name of the company circle program have all been found to be useful approaches. The point is not that you can buy off the workers cheap through figuring out some gimmick for recognition. Rather, there is a demand on the part of workers for recognizing their dignity as individuals and their ability to make meaningful contributions to their organization. They want to be recognized both financially and otherwise.

POTENTIAL FOR EXPANSION

Potentially one of the most exciting areas for adaptation of Japanese practices lies in the scope of QC circle activity. The Japanese have concentrated almost exclusively on applying the circles to hourly-rated personnel. U.S. companies have recently made a few breakthroughs to salaried personnel, but even here success is far from assured.

This is a case in which U.S. ignorance of Japanese practices may have been an asset. Most U.S. companies adopting circles have not known that the Japanese have not applied the circles very extensively to white collar workers. Consequently, the American companies have not been subject to any restraint in this area that might otherwise have been the case. As a result, a number of U.S. firms are experimenting with QC circles for technical and staff personnel, office personnel, and even union-management circles. It is too early to evaluate such efforts, but there may be something in the U.S. environment that makes circle activity among salaried personnel more feasible than is the case in Japan. It will be an interesting area to watch.

A final area in which adaptation will have to take place and is taking place is in the treatment and behavior of middle management. While strong top-level management support is critical to the success of the QC circle program, it is the lack of middle management support in many adopting American companies that has proved to be the major obstacle to their success. This has not been a major problem in Japanese companies where traditionally a strong consensus has usually been forged between top management and middle management before innovations are introduced. Top management usually works through middle management in implementing the circles; it may be characterized as a top-to-middle-down model. In U.S. companies that have adopted the circles, more often than not, middle management has been bypassed in introducing the circles with predictable results. They came to see the circles as a threat to their own positions and not necessarily incorrectly so. Thus, insuring the cooperation of middle management in the United States requires the initiation of formal guidelines.

Middle management resistance can take many forms. At one plant, the staff person in charge of QC circles (facilitator) was astonished to find suddenly that his best circle leader was transferred into a section where there was no opportunity to lead QC circles because of a hostile supervisor in his new department. The facilitator had lost his best leader and gained nothing. When he asked the supervisor who ordered the change his reason for making the transfer, the supervisor replied that it was a normal operating decision. He said he didn't take the circles into consideration in making his decision. It was not that the supervisor was hostile to the circles

as much as that he did not see any connections between his responsibilities and circle activity. Consequently the circles had a low priority vis á vis other demands being made upon him. While this was not a conscious attempt at sabotage, it had the same effect.

In another company the circles and the facilitator were instructed to make reports to the manufacturing manager. Middle management felt that the information contained in these reports was a way of checking up on them. They responded by refusing to cooperate with the facilitator. The facilitator, recognizing her problem, asked top management to call off the reports so that she could win the confidence of middle management.

In general, two strategies for involving middle management in QC circles seem advisable. First, a concerted training program involving all middle management supervisors should be established so that even those who do not volunteer to participate will at least understand the program's needs and operation. The emphasis should not be to pressure middle managers into involvement but to win them over gradually through an educational process. It must be made absolutely clear, however, that they will not be allowed to block the program's installation. One way of involving middle managers more fully in circle activity is to create a steering committee in which both union leaders and middle management are well represented.

A second strategy for harnessing middle management cooperation involves performance appraisal. In some companies the degree of success in circle activities is a factor in their performance ratings. When middle managers understand that top management gives the circles high priority, they will have a stronger incentive to pursue circle activity. This kind of restructuring of middle management priorities can take place only when top management is committed to circle activity. The ideal, however, is to get middle managers to see circle activity as a tool for better accomplishing their everyday objectives.

SUMMING UP THE BASICS

Six basic principles of QC circle activity seem operative. They are:

1. *Trust your employees.* Accept that they will work to implement organizational goals if given a chance.
2. *Build employee loyalty to the company.* It will pay off in the long run.
3. *Invest in training and treat employees as resources which, if cultivated, will yield economic returns to the firm.* This involves the development of worker skills.

Implicit in this perspective is that you aim for long-term employee commitment to the firm.

4. *Recognize employee accomplishments.* Symbolic rewards are more important than you think. Show workers that you care about them as individuals.
5. *Decentralize decision making.* Put the decisions where the information is.
6. *Work should be seen as a cooperative effort with workers and managers doing the job together.* This implies some degree of consensual decision-making.

A simple examination of these principles should lead most readers to respond, "What's the big deal? — there is nothing new here." We can make two responses to that. First, as noted earlier, while the ideas may not be new with regard to managerial personnel, they are new with regard to blue collar applications. Secondly, all these six principles can be found in any good survey of behavioral science literature in the United States. What is particularly fascinating is that the Japanese have taken many of the basic ideas developed in the American behavioral sciences and acted to institutionalize them in daily practice in their firms.

In thinking about this matter further, consider the following analogy to technological hardware. The transistor was invented in the United States but was initially commercialized most successfully in Japan. Now many Americans like to emphasize that the invention is the really important thing and that took place in America. So they conclude with a sigh of relief that we still maintain our position of leadership. This interpretation totally misses the point! Much of the history of America's successful industrialization can be attributed to our ability to take inventions developed in Europe and commercialize them successfully in the United States. The jet engine, for example, was invented in England but commercialized in the United States. It is just this that the Japanese are increasingly doing to us now, and it is a terrible mistake to downplay the creativity needed to take an invention and adapt it to commercial possibilities. This applies just as much to organizational software (including techniques for organizing the labor force) as it does to technological hardware. Although the management principles operative in the QC circle may not strike an American manager as terribly original, it is the ability of the Japanese to synthesize these principles in a system and institutionalize them in daily practice that is extraordinarily original.

Simon Kuznets, in his pathbreaking study of industrialization (*Modern Economic Growth,* Yale University Press, 1966), maintains that the increase in the stock of useful knowledge and the application of this knowledge are the essence of modern economic growth. This increase, in turn, rests on some combination of the growing application of science to problems of economic production and changes in individual attitudes and institutional arrangements which allow for the release of these technological innovations. As industrialization spread through the world, technological and social innovations cropped up in various centers of development. These innovations were the outcome of a cumulative testing process by which some forms emerged superior to others; each historical period gave rise to new methods and solutions. The economic growth of a given nation came to depend upon adoption of these innovations, Kuznets concludes, by stressing the importance of the "worldwide validity and transmissibility of modern additions to knowledge, the transnational character of this stock of knowledge, and the dependence on it of any single nation in the course of its modern economic growth."

We are dealing here with the borrowing and adaptation of social innovations. Although Kuznets speaks of both technological and social knowledge, his reasoning applies most forcefully to the realm of technological choice. It is here that the selection of the most progressive technique will be made most unambiguously in terms of cost-benefit analysis. For example, the blast furnace using a hot blast and a mineral fuel adopted in nineteenth-century America was clearly superior, in terms of reducing costs and increasing productivity, to its predecessor based on charcoal technology. One can make a similar point with regard to adaptation of technology to specific environmental conditions. Thus, to pursue the steel-making example, the basic oxygen furnace developed in Austria depended, in part, for its success on the availability of special heat-resistant brick used to line the converters that were not available outside of Austria. It was not until comparable heat resistant bricks were developed outside of Europe that the basic oxygen furnace became economically feasible in North America and Japan.

With social knowledge and institutional arrangements, the situation is more complex. To be sure, certain institutional arrangements are fairly rapidly grasped under the right conditions as being essential to economic progress. Consider the spread of the joint stock company, double-entry bookkeeping and the diffusion of multidivisional decentralized management structure. Many other institutional innovations, however, are not easily compared and evaluated vis á vis existing arrangements. This is because social innovations often interact with a variety of other processes in a way that obscures their respective contributions to economic growth. Furthermore, the output of social innovations is often not as easily quantified as is usually the case with hard technology.

It is the lack of clarity in these relationships and the abundance of unwarranted inferences that lead to an element of fad in the adoption of social innovations and give free rein to arguments grounded more in ideology and power relationships than in tested generalizations. A rapid rate of diffusion of a particular social innovation may reflect these considerations more than the proven superiority of the innovation in question. Ironically, the claims to superiority of one social arrangement over another often are cloaked in the language of objective social science.

Thus, the task of evaluating the applicability of Japanese management practices in the United States and judging what are to be the needed adaptations is a herculean task. Many claims are being made and often by those with vested interests in the outcome. How is one to separate the wheat from the chaff? How are we to insure diffusion of best practice? There are no simple answers to these questions. The problem is made more difficult by our dependency on consultants for diffusing information on such innovations. Naturally, they treat such information as proprietary. Yet, consultants possess and diffuse both good and bad information in varying proportions. It is extremely difficult for the manager to separate the good consultants from the bad consultants. By the nature of their business, consultants don't like to talk about failure. Moreover, each consultant is devoted to creating a differentiated product that they can market over a broad client base. For all these as well as other reasons, the manager seeking to identify a program in work restructuring that fits his or her needs has great difficulty.

Yet, even here the Japanese case may be instructive. In the case of QC circles, a nonprofit professional association (Union of Japanese Scientists and Engineers) set up a structure that provides for a standardized collection of information (including a central repository) and a "public testing" of strategies and programs. This information is then fed back to individual firms in a variety of packages carefully tailored for different levels of personnel. The Union of Japanese Scientists and Engineers helps develop a consensus on what constitutes best practice and encourages the dissemination of these ideas. It may be time for organizations such as the American Society for Quality Control and the American Society for Training and Development to assume such functions. There is already some movement in this direction, and it is my hope that it will crystallize in a concrete form.

To be sure, even if successfully applied to American firms, QC circles will continue to evolve into new forms of worker participation in decision making. If one could say that their major contribution was to convince American management that hourly-rated workers do have an important contribution to make to the organization and are prepared to do so when given the opportunity, then the innovation will have had a lasting impact in America.

39. Beyond Management and the Worker: The Institutional Function of Management

Jeffrey Pfeffer

Theory, research, and education in the field of organizational behavior and management have been dominated by a concern for the management of people *within* organizations. The question of how to make workers more productive has stood as the foundation for management theory and practice since the time of Frederick Taylor. Such an emphasis neglects the institutional function of management. While managing people within organizations is critical, managing the organization's relationships with other organizations such as competitors, creditors, suppliers, and governmental agencies is frequently as critical to the firm's success.

Parsons (1960) noted that there were three levels in organizations: (1) the technical level, where the technology of the organization was used to produce some product or service; (b) the administrative level, which coordinated and supervised the technical level; and (c) the institutional level, which was concerned with the organization's legitimacy and with organization-environment relations. Organization and management theory has primarily concentrated on administrative level problems, frequently at very low hierarchical levels in organizations.

Practicing managers and some researchers do recognize the importance of the institutional context in which the firm operates. There is increasing use of institutional advertising, and executives from the oil industry, among others, have been active in projecting their organizations' views in a variety of contexts. Mintzberg (1973) has identified the liaison role as one of ten roles managers fill. Other authors explicitly have noted the importance of relating the organization to other organizations (Pfeffer & Nowak, unpub. ms.; Whyte, 1955).

Saying that the institutional function is important is different from developing a theory of the organization's relationships with other organizations, a theory which can potentially guide the manager's strategic actions in performing the function of institutional management. Such a theory is needed, and data are accumulating to construct such a theory.

The purposes of this article are: (a) to present evidence of the importance of the institutional function of management; and (b) to review data consistent with a model of institutional management. This model argues that managers behave as if they were seeking to manage and reduce uncertainty and interdependence arising from the firm's relationships with other organizations. Several strategic responses to interorganizational exchange, including their advantages and disadvantages, are considered.

INSTITUTIONAL PROBLEMS OF ORGANIZATIONS

Organizations are open social systems, engaged in constant and important transactions with other organizations in their environments. Business firms transact with customer and supplier organizations, and with sources of credit; they interact on the federal and local level with regulatory and legal authorities which are concerned with pollution, taxes, antitrust, equal employment, and myriad other issues. Because firms do interact with these other organizations, two consequences follow. First, organizations face uncertainty. If an organization were a closed system so that it could completely control and predict all the variables that affected its operation, the organization could make technically rational, maximizing decisions and anticipate the consequences of its actions. As an open system, transacting with important external organizations, the firm does not have control over many of the important factors that affect its operations. Because organizations are open, they are affected by events outside their boundaries.

Second, organizations are interdependent with other organizations with which they exchange resources, information or personnel, and thus open to influence by them. The extent of this influence is likely to be a function of the importance of the resource obtained, and inversely related to the ease with which the resource can be procured from alternative sources

From *Academy of Management Review* 1, 1976, pp. 36–46. Reprinted by permission.

(Jacobs, 1974; Thompson, 1967). Interdependence is problematic and troublesome. Managers do not like to be dependent on factors outside their control. Interdependence is especially troublesome if there are few alternative sources, so the external organization is particularly important to the firm.

Interdependence and uncertainty interact in their effects on organizations. One of the principal functions of the institutional level of the firm is the management of this interdependence and uncertainty.

THE IMPORTANCE OF INSTITUTIONAL MANAGEMENT

Katz and Kahn (1966) noted that organizations may pursue two complementary paths to effectiveness. The first is to be as efficient as possible, and thereby obtain a competitive advantage with respect to other firms. Under this strategy, the firm succeeds because it operates so efficiently that it achieves a competitive advantage in the market. The second strategy, termed "political," involves the establishment of favorable exchange relationships based on considerations that do not relate strictly to price, quality, service, or efficiency. Winning an order because of the firm's product and cost characteristics would be an example of the strategy of efficiency; winning the order because of interlocks in the directorates of the organizations involved, or because of family connections between executives in the two organizations, would illustrate political strategies.

The uses and consequences of political strategies for achieving organizational success have infrequently been empirically examined. Hirsch (1975) has recently compared the ethical drug and record industries, noting great similarities between them. Both sell their products through gatekeepers or intermediaries — in the case of pharmaceuticals, through doctors who must write the prescriptions, and in the case of records, through disc jockeys who determine air time and, consequently, exposure. Both sell products with relatively short life cycles, and both industries place great emphasis on new products and product innovation. Both depend on the legal environment of patents, copyrights, and trademarks for market protection.

Hirsch noted that the rate of return for the average pharmaceutical firm during the period 1956–66 was more than double the rate of return for the average firm in the record industry. Finding no evidence that would enable him to attribute the striking differences in profitability to factors associated with internal structural arrangements, Hirsch concluded that at least one factor affecting the relative profitability of the two industries is the ability to manage their institutional environments, and more specifically, the control over distribution, patent and copyright protection, and the prediction of adoption by the independent gatekeepers.

In a review of the history of both industries, Hirsch indicated that in pharmaceuticals, control over entry was achieved by (a) amending the patent laws to permit the patenting of naturally occurring substances, antibiotics; and (b) instituting a long and expensive licensing procedure required before drugs could be manufactured and marketed, administered by the Food and Drug Administration (FDA). In contrast, record firms have much less protection under the copyright laws; as a consequence, entry is less controlled, leading to more competition and lower profits. While there are other differences between the industries, including size and expenditures on research and development, Hirsch argued that at least some of the success of drug firms derives from their ability to control entry and their ability to control information channels relating to their product through the use of detail personnel and advertising in the American Medical Association Journals. Retail price maintenance, tariff protection, and licensing to restrict entry are other examples of practices that are part of the organization's institutional environment and may profoundly affect its success.

MANAGING UNCERTAINTY AND INTERDEPENDENCE

The organization, requiring transactions with other organizations and uncertain about their future performance, has available a variety of strategies that can be used to manage uncertainty and interdependence. Firms face two problems in their institutional relationships: (a) managing the uncertainty caused by the unpredictable actions of competitors; and (b) managing the uncertainty resulting from noncompetitive interdependence with suppliers, creditors, government agencies, and customers. In both instances, the same set of strategic responses is available: merger, to completely absorb the interdependence and resulting uncertainty; joint ventures; interlocking directorates, to partially absorb the interdependence; the movement and selective recruiting of executives and other personnel, to develop interorganizational linkages; regulation, to provide government enforced stability; and other political activity to reduce competition, protect markets and sources of supply, and otherwise manage the organization's environment.

Because organizations are open systems, each strategy is limited in its effect. While merger or some other interorganizational linkage may manage one source of organizational dependence, it probably at the same time makes the organizations dependent on yet other organizations. For example, while regulation may eliminate effective price competition and restrict entry into the industry (Jordan, 1972; Pfeffer, 1974a; Posner, 1974), the regulated organizations then face the uncertainties involved in dealing with the regulatory agency. Moreover, in reducing uncertainty for itself, the organization must bargain away some of its own discretion (Thompson, 1967). One can view institutional management as an exchange process — the organization assures itself of needed resources, but at the same time, must promise certain predictable behaviors in return. Keeping these qualifications in mind, evidence on use of the various strategies of institutional management is reviewed.

Merger

There are three reasons an organization may seek to merge — first, to reduce competition by absorbing an important competitor organization; second, to manage interdependence with either sources of input or purchasers of output by absorbing them; and third, to diversify operations and thereby lessen dependence on the present organizations with which it exchanges (Pfeffer, 1972a). While merger among competing organizations is presumably proscribed by the antitrust laws, enforcement resources are limited, and major consolidations do take place.

In analyzing patterns of interorganizational behavior, one can either ask executives in the organizations involved the reasons for the action, or alternatively, one can develop a hypothetical model of behavior which is then tested with the available data. Talking with organizational executives may not provide the real reasons behind interorganizational activity since (a) different persons may see and interpret the same action in different ways; (b) persons may infer after the fact the motives for the action or decision; and (c) persons may not be motivated to tell the complete truth about the reasons for the behavior. Much of the existing literature on interorganizational linkage activity, therefore, uses the method of empirically testing the deductions from a hypothetical model of interorganizational behavior.

The classic expressed rationale for merger has been to increase the profits or the value of the shares of the firm. In a series of studies beginning as early as 1921, researchers have been unable to demonstrate that merger active firms are more profitable or have higher stock prices following the merger activity. This literature has been summarized by Reid (1968), who asserts that mergers are made for growth and that growth is sought because of the relationship between firm size and managerial salaries.

Growth, however, does not provide information concerning the desired characteristics of the acquired firm. Under a growth objective, any merger is equivalent to any other of the same size. Pfeffer (1972a) has argued that mergers are undertaken to manage organizational interdependence. Examining the proportion of merger activity occurring within the same two-digit SIC industry category, he found that the highest proportion of within-industry mergers occurred in industries of intermediate concentration. The theoretical argument was that in industries with many competitors, the absorption of a single one did little to reduce competitive uncertainty. At the other extreme, with only a few competitors, merger would more likely be scrutinized by the antitrust authorities and coordination could instead be achieved through more informal arrangements, such as price leadership.

The same study investigated the second reason to merge: to absorb the uncertainty among organizations vertically related to each other, as in a buyer-seller relationship. He found that it was possible to explain 40 percent of the variation in the distribution of merger activity over industries on the basis of resource interdependence, measured by estimates of the transactions flows between sectors of the economy. On an individual industry basis, in two-thirds of the cases a measure of transactions interdependence accounted for 65 percent or more of the variation in the pattern of merger activity. The study indicated that it was possible to account for the industry of the likely merger partner firm by considering the extent to which firms in the two industries exchanged resources.

While absorption of suppliers or customers will reduce the firm's uncertainty by bringing critical contingencies within the boundaries of the organization, this strategy has some distinct costs. One danger is that the process of vertical integration creates a larger organization which is increasingly tied to a single industry.

The third reason for merger is diversification. Occasionally, the organization is confronted by interdependence it cannot absorb, either because of resource or legal limitations. Through diversifying its activities, the organization does not reduce the uncertainty, but makes the particular contingency less critical for its success and well-being. Diversification provides the organization with a way of avoiding, rather than absorbing, problematic interdependence.

Merger represents the most complete solution to situations of organizational interdependence, as it involves the total absorption of either a competitor or a vertically related organization, or the acquisition of an organization operating in another area. Because it does involve total absorption, merger requires more resources and is a more visible and substantial form of interorganizational linkage.

Joint Ventures

Closely related to merger is the joint venture: the creation of a jointly owned, but independent organization by two or more separate parent firms. Merger involves the total pooling of assets by two or more organizations. In a joint venture, some assets of each of several parent organizations are used, and thus only a partial pooling of resources is involved (Bernstein, 1965). For a variety of reasons, joint ventures have been prosecuted less frequently and less successfully than mergers, making joint ventures particularly appropriate as a way of coping with competitive interdependence.

The joint subsidiary can have several effects on competitive interdependence and uncertainty. First, it can reduce the extent of new competition. Instead of both firms entering a market, they can combine some of their assets and create a joint subsidiary to enter the market. Second, since joint subsidiaries are typically staffed, particularly at the higher executive levels, with personnel drawn from the parent firms, the joint subsidiary becomes another location for the management of competing firms to meet. Most importantly, the joint subsidiary must set price and output levels, make new product development and marketing decisions and decisions about its advertising policies. Consequently, the parent organizations are brought into association in a setting in which exactly those aspects of the competitive relationship must be jointly determined.

In a study of joint ventures among manufacturing and oil and gas companies during the period 1960–71, Pfeffer and Nowak (in press, a, b) found that 56 percent involved parent firms operating in the same two-digit

industry. Further, in 36 percent of the 166 joint ventures studied, the joint subsidiary operated in the same industry as *both* parent organizations. As in the case of mergers, the proportion of joing venture activities undertaken with other firms in the same industry was related to the concentration of the firm's industry being intermediate. The relationship between concentration and the proportion of joint ventures undertaken within the same industry accounted for some 25 percent of the variation in the pattern of joint venture activities.

In addition to considering the use of joint ventures in coping with competitive interdependence, the Pfeffer and Nowak study of joint ventures examined the extent to which the creation of joint subsidiaries was related to patterns of transaction interdependence across industries. While the correlations between the proportion of transactions and the proportion of joint ventures undertaken between industry pairs were lower than in the case of mergers, statistically significant relationships between this form of interorganizational linkage activity and patterns of resource exchange were observed. The difference between mergers and joint ventures appears to be that mergers are used relatively more to cope with buyer-seller interdependence, and joint ventures are more highly related to considerations of coping with competitive uncertainty.

Cooptation and Interlocking Directorates

Cooptation is a venerable strategy for managing interdependence between organizations. Cooptation involves the partial absorption of another organization through the placing of a representative of that organization on the board of the focal organization. Corporations frequently place bankers on their boards; hospitals and universities offer trustee positions to prominent business leaders; and community action agencies develop advisory boards populated with active and strong community political figures.

As a strategy for coping with interdependence, cooptation involves some particular problems and considerations. For example, a representative of the external organization is brought into the focal organization, while still retaining his or her original organizational membership. Cooptation is based on creating a conflict of interest within the coopted person. To what extent should one pursue the goals and interests of one's organization of principal affiliation, and to what extent should one favor the interests of the coopting organization? From the point of view of the coopting organization, the individual should favor its interests, but not to the point where he or she loses credibility in the parent organization, because at that point, the individual ceases to be useful in ensuring that organization's support. Thus, cooptation requires striking a balance between the pressures to identify with either the parent or coopting institution.

Furthermore, since cooptation involves less than total absorption of the other organization, there is the risk that the coopted representative will not have enough influence or control in the principal organization to ensure the desired decisions. Of course, it is possible to coopt more than a single representative. This is frequently done when relationships with the coopted organization are particularly uncertain and critical. Cooptation may be the most feasible strategy when total absorption is impossible due to financial or legal constraints.

Interlocks in the boards of directors of competing organizations provide a possible strategy for coping with competitive interdependence and the resulting uncertainty. The underlying argument is that in order to manage interorganizational relationships, information must be exchanged, usually through a joint subsidiary or interlocking directorate. While interlocks among competitors are ostensibly illegal, until very recently there was practically no prosecution of this practice. In a 1965 study, a subcommittee of the House Judiciary Committee found more than 300 cases in which direct competitors had interlocking boards of directors. In a study of the extent of interlocking among competing organizations in a sample of 109 manufacturing organizations, Pfeffer and Nowak (unpub. ms.) found that the proportion of directors on the board from direct competitors was higher for firms operating in industries in which concentration was intermediate. This result is consistent with the result found for joint ventures and mergers as well. In all three instances, linkages among competing organizations occurred more frequently when concentration was in an intermediate range.

Analyses of cooptation through the use of boards of directors have not been confined to business firms. Price (1963) argued that the principal function of the boards of the Oregon Fish and Game Commissions was to link the organizations to their environments. Zald (1967) found that the composition of YMCA boards in Chicago matched the demography of their operating areas, and affected the organizations' effectiveness, particularly in raising money. Pfeffer (1973) examined the size, composition, and function of hospital boards of directors, finding that variables of organizational context, such as ownership, source of funds, and location, were important explanatory factors. He also found a relationship between cooptation and organizational effectiveness. In 1972, (1972b) he found that regulated firms, firms with a higher proportion of debt in their capital structures, and larger firms tended to have more outside directors. Allen (1974) also found that size of the board and the use of cooptation was predicted by the size of the firm, but did not replicate Pfeffer's earlier finding of a relationship between the organization's capital structure and the proportion of directors from financial institutions. In a study of utility boards, Pfeffer (1974b) noted that the composition of the board tended to correlate with the demographics of the area in which the utility was regulated.

The evidence is consistent with the strategy of organizations using their boards of directors to coopt external organizations and manage problematic interdependence. The role of the board of directors is seen not as the provision of management expertise or control, but more generally as a means of managing problematic aspects of an organization's institutional environment.

Executive Recruitment

Information also is transferred among organizations through the movement of personnel. The difference between movement of executives between organizations and cooptation is that in the latter case, the person linking the two organizations retains membership in both organizations. In the case of personnel movement, dual organizational membership is not maintained. When people change jobs, they take with themselves information about the operations, policies, and values of their previous employers, as well as contacts in the organization. In a study of the movement of faculty among schools of business, Baty et al. (1971) found that similar orientations and curricula developed among schools exchanging personnel. The movement of personnel is one method by which new techniques of management and new marketing and product ideas are diffused through a set of organizations.

Occasionally, the movement of executives between organizations has been viewed as intensifying, rather than reducing, competition. Companies have been distressed by the raiding of trade secrets and managerial expertise by other organizations. While this perspective must be recognized, the exchange of personnel among organizations is a revered method of conflict *reduction* between organizations (Stern et al., 1973). Personnel motivation inevitably involves sharing information among a set of organizations.

If executive movement is a form of interfirm linkage designed to manage competitive relationships, the proportion of executives recruited from within the same industry should be highest at intermediate levels of industrial concentration. Examining the three top executive positions in twenty different manufacturing industries, the evidence on executive backgrounds was found to be consistent with this argument (Pfeffer & Leblebici, 1973). The proportion of high level executives with previous jobs in the same industry but in a different company was found to be negatively related to the number of firms in the industry. The larger the number of firms, the less likely that a single link among competitors will substantially reduce uncertainty, but the larger the available supply of external executive talent. The data indicated no support for a supply argument, but supported the premise that interorganizational linkages are used to manage interdependence and uncertainty.

The use of executive movement to manage noncompetitive interorganizational relationships is quite prevalent. The often-cited movement of personnel between the Defense Department and major defense contractors is only one example, because there is extensive movement of personnel between many government departments and industries interested in the agencies' decisions. The explanation is frequently proposed that organizations are acquiring these personnel because of their expertise. The expertise explanation is frequently difficult to separate from the alternative that personnel are being exchanged to enhance interorganizational relationships. Regardless of the motivation, exchanging personnel inevitably involves the transfer of information and access to the other organization. It is conceptually possible to control for the effect of expertise — in other words, taking expertise into account, is there evidence that recruiting patterns reflect the influence of factors related to institutional management?

Regulation

Occasionally, institutional relationships are managed through recourse to political intervention. The reduction of competition and its associated uncertainty may be accomplished through regulation. Regulation, however, is a risky strategy for organizations to pursue. While regulation most frequently benefits the regulated industry (Jordan, 1972; Pfeffer, 1974a), the industry and firms have no assurance that regulatory authority will not be used against their interest. Regulation is very hard to repeal. Successful use of regulation requires that the firm and industry face little or no powerful political opposition, and that the political future can be accurately forecast.

The benefits of regulation to those being regulated have been extensively reviewed (Posner, 1974; Stigler, 1971). Regulation frequently has been sought by the regulated industry. Currently, trucking firms are among the biggest supporters of continued regulation of trucking. Since the Civil Aeronautics Board was created in 1938, no new trunk carriers have been started. Jordan (1970) found that air rates on intrastate (hence not regulated by the CAB) airlines within California are frequently 25 percent or more lower than fares on comparable routes of regulated carriers. Estimates of the effects of regulation on prices in electric utilities, airlines, trucking, and natural gas have indicated that regulation either increases price or has no effect.

The theory behind these outcomes is still unclear. One approach suggests that regulation is created for the public benefit, but after the initial legislative attention, the regulatory process is captured by the firms subject to regulation. Another approach proposes that regulation, like other goods, is acquired subject to supply and demand considerations (Posner, 1974). Political scientists, focusing on the operation of interest groups, argue that regulatory agencies are "captured" by organized and well-financed interests. Government intervention in the market can solve many of the interdependence problems faced by firms. Regulation is most often accompanied by restriction of entry and the fixing of prices, which tend to reduce market uncertainties. Markets may be actually allocated to firms, and with the reduction of risk, regulation may make access to capital easier. Regulation may alter the organization's relationships with suppliers and customers. One theory of why the railroads were interested in the creation of the Interstate Commerce Commission (ICC) in 1887 was that large users were continually demanding and winning discriminatory rate reductions, disturbing the price stability of railroad price fixing cartels. By forbidding price discrimination and enforcing this regulation, the ICC strengthened the railroads' position with respect to large customers (MacAvoy, 1965).

Political Activity

Regulation is only one specific form of organizational activity in governmental processes. Business attempts to affect competition through the operation of the tariff laws date back to the 1700s (Bauer et al., 1968). Epstein (1969) provided one of the more complete summaries of the history of corporate involvement in politics and the inevitability of such action. The government has the power of coercion, possessed legally by no other social institution. Furthermore, legislation and regulation affect most of our economic institutions and markets, either indirectly through taxation, or more directly through purchasing, market protection or market creation. For example, taxes on margarine only recently came to an end. Federal taxes, imposed in 1886 as a protectionist measure for dairy interests, were removed in 1950, but a law outlawing the sale of oleo in its colored form lasted until 1967 in Wisconsin.

As with regulation, political activities carry both benefits and risks. The risk arises because once government intervention in an issue on behalf of a firm or industry is sought, then political intervention becomes legitimated, regardless of whose interests are helped or hurt. The firm that seeks favorable tax legislation runs the risk of creating a setting in which it is equally legitimate to be exposed to very unfavorable legislation. After an issue is opened to government intervention, neither side will find it easy to claim that further government action is illegitimate.

In learning to cope with a particular institutional environment, the firm may be unprepared for new uncertainties caused by the change of fundamental institutional relationships, including the opening of price competition, new entry and the lack of protection from overseas competition.

CONCLUSION

The institutional function of management involves managing the organization's relationships with other organizations. Table 1 presents strategies of institutional management with their principal advantages and disadvantages. From observation of organizational activities, the most common response to interdependence with external organizations seems to be the attempt to develop some form of interorganizational linkage to ensure the continuation of favorable relationships with important organizations in the environment.

All such interfirm linkages have costs, with the most fundamental being the loss of the organization's autonomy. In return for the certainty that one's competitors will not engage in predatory price cutting, one must provide assurances about one's own behavior. For example, cooptation involves the possibility of acquiring the support of an external organization, but at the same time the firm gives up some degree of privacy over its internal information and some control over its operations and decisions.

Variables affecting responses to the organization's environment can be specified. Actions taken to manage interdependencies are related to the extent of the interdependence and its importance to the organization. The response to competitive interdependence is related to measures of industry structure, and particularly to the necessity and feasibility of developing informal, interorganizational structures. Two important issues remain. First, is effective institutional management associated with favorable outcomes to the organization? Second, given the importance of institutional management, why are some organizations more successful than others at this task?

The effect of institutional management on firm performance is difficult to measure, and seldom has been examined. To examine the effect of successful institutional management, an outcome measure is needed. Profit is only one possibility, because there is evidence that the reduction of uncertainty may be sought regardless of its effect on profit (Caves, 1970). Whatever criterion is chosen is affected by many factors. To attribute a result to institutional management, other causes must be controlled. Nevertheless, institutional management receives a great deal of management attention in some firms and a firm's interorganizational relationships may be important to its success and survival.

Of even more fundamental interest is the question of why some firms are able to develop more effective strategic responses to their institutional environments. It is possible that effective institutional management requires fundamentally different structures of top management, of the development of excess managerial capacity, or the development of particular types of information systems. It is easier to find successful institutional management than to identify critical variables enabling it to develop in the first place. For example, some universities have better relationships with their state legislatures than do others. It is possible to retrospectively infer explanations as to why this is so.

Table 1. Advantages and Disadvantages of Strategies of Institutional Management

Strategy	Advantages	Disadvantages
Merger	Completely absorbs interdependence	Requires resources sufficient to acquire another organization
		May be proscribed by antitrust laws, or infeasible for other reasons (e.g., a governmental unit cannot be absorbed by a firm)
Joint ventures	Can be used for sharing risks and costs associated with large, or technologically advanced activities	Is available only for certain types of organizations, though less restricted than merger (COMSAT, for instance, brings together government and business)
	Can be used to partially pool resources and coordinate activities	
Cooptation	Relatively inexpensive	May not provide enough coordination or linkage between organizations to ensure performance
		Coopted person may lose credibility in original organization
Personnel movement	Relatively inexpensive Almost universally possible	Person loses identification with original organization, lessening influence there
		Linkage is based on knowledge and familiarity, and on a few persons at most, not on basic structural relationships
Regulation	Enables organization to benefit from the coercive power of the government	Regulation may be used to harm the organization's interests
Political activity	Enables organization to use government to modify and enhance environment	Government intervention, once legitimated, may be used against the organization as well as for its benefit

What remains to be done is to explain those factors that could be designed into an organization initially to ensure effective institutional management in the future.

Considering its probable importance to the firm, the institutional function of management has received much less concern than it warrants. It is time that this aspect of management receives the systematic attention long reserved for motivational and productivity problems associated with relationships between management and workers.

REFERENCES

Allen, Michael Patrick. "The Structure of Interorganizational Elite Cooptation: Interlocking Corporate Directorates." *American Sociological Review* 39 (1974): 393–406.

Baty, Gordon B.; Evan, William M.; and Rothermel, Terry W. "Personnel Flows as Interorganizational Relations." *Administrative Science Quarterly* 16 (1971): 430–43.

Bauer, Raymond A.; de Sola Pool, Ithiel; and Dexter, Lewis Anthony. *American Business and Public Policy.* New York: Atherton Press, 1968.

Bernstein, Lewis. "Joint Ventures in the Light of Recent Antitrust Developments." *The Antitrust Bulletin* 10 (1965): 25–29.

Caves, Richard E. "Uncertainty, Market Structure, and Performance: Galbraith as Conventional Wisdom." In *Industrial Organization and Economic Development*, edited by J. W. Markham and G. F. Papanek, pp. 283–302. Boston: Houghton Mifflin, 1970.

Epstein, Edwin M. *The Corporation in American Politics*. Englewood Cliffs, New Jersey: Prentice-Hall, 1969.

Hirsch, Paul M. "Organizational Effectiveness and the Institutional Environment." *Administrative Science Quarterly* 20 (1975): 327–44.

House of Representatives, Staff Report to the Antitrust Subcommittee of the Committee on the Judiciary. *Interlocks in Corporate Management*. Washington, D.C.: U.S. Government Printing Office, 1965.

Jacobs, David. "Dependency and Vulnerability: An Exchange Approach to the Control of Organizations." *Administrative Science Quarterly* 19 (1974): 45–59.

Jordan, William A. *Airline Regulation in America: Effects and Imperfections*. Baltimore: Johns Hopkins University Press, 1970.

_____. "Producer Protection, Prior Market Structure and the Effects of Government Regulation." *Journal of Law and Economics* 15 (1972): 151–76.

Katz, Daniel, and Kahn, Robert L. *The Social Psychology of Organizations*. New York: John Wiley, 1966.

MacAvoy, Paul W. *The Economic Effects of Regulation*. Cambridge, Mass.: MIT Press, 1965.

Mintzberg, Henry. *The Nature of Managerial Work*. New York: Harper and Row, 1973.

Parsons, Talcott. *Structure and Process in Modern Societies*. Glencoe, Illinois: Free Press, 1960.

Pfeffer, Jeffrey. "Merger as a Response to Organizational Interdependence." *Administrative Science Quarterly* 17 (1972): 382–94. (a)

_____. "Size and Composition of Corporate Boards of Directors: The Organization and its Environment." *Administrative Science Quarterly* 17 (1972): 218–28. (b)

_____. "Size, Composition and Function of Hospital Boards of Directors: A Study of Organization-Environment Linkage." *Administrative Science Quarterly* 18 (1973): 349–64.

_____. "Administrative Regulation and Licensing: Social Problem or Solution?" *Social Problems* 21 (1974): 468–79. (a)

_____. "Cooptation and the Composition of Electric Utility Boards of Directors." *Pacific Sociological Review* 17 (1974): 333–63. (b)

_____, and Leblebici, Huseyin. "Executive Recruitment and the Development of Interfirm Organizations." *Administrative Science Quarterly* 18 (1973): 449–61.

_____, and Nowak, Phillip. "Joint Ventures and Interorganizational Interdependence." *Administrative Science Quarterly,* in press. (a)

_____. "Organizational Context and Interorganizational Linkages Among Corporations." Unpublished manuscript, Berkeley: University of California.

_____. "Patterns of Joint Venture Activity: Implications for Antitrust Policy." *The Antitrust Bulletin,* in press. (b)

Posner, Richard A. "Theories of Economic Regulation." *Bell Journal of Economics and Management Science* 5 (1974): 335–58.

Price, James L. "The Impact of Governing Boards on Organizational Effectiveness and Morale." *Administrative Science Quarterly* 8 (1963): 361–78.

Reid, Samuel R. *Mergers, Managers, and the Economy*. New York: McGraw-Hill, 1968.

Sayles, Leonard R. *Managerial Behavior: Administration in Complex Organization*. New York: McGraw-Hill, 1964.

Stern, Louis W.; Sternthal, Brian; and Craig, C. Samuel. "Managing Conflict in Distribution Channels: A Laboratory Study." *Journal of Marketing Research* 10 (1973): 169–79.

Stigler, George J. "The Theory of Economic Regulation." *Bell Journal of Economics and Management Science* 2 (1971): 3–21.

Thompson, James D. *Organizations in Action*. New York: McGraw-Hill, 1967.

Whyte, William F. *Street Corner Society*. Chicago: University of Chicago Press, 1955.

Zald, Mayer N. "Urban Differentiation, Characteristics of Boards of Directors and Organizational Effectiveness." *American Journal of Sociology* 73 (1967): 261–72.

40. Change

Theodore Caplow

Suppose that a football reformer observed the obvious fact that the object of the game is to make touchdowns. This would lead immediately to the important discovery that if the two teams would only cooperate, hundreds of touchdowns could be made in a game, while only one or two of them are made when each opposes the other.

Thurman Arnold

CHANGE AND INNOVATION

No organization exists in a vacuum. Every organization must submit to the demands of its environment, and these demands vary as the environment changes. There have even been more or less serious attempts to apply Darwin's model of natural selection and the survival of the fittest to organizations.[1] Even the most passive organization is compelled to modify itself from time to time in response to irresistible changes in its environment. A well-known study of a civic association was published under the title, "The Reluctant Organization and the Aggressive Environment," and the title tells the whole story. The organization in question sought to do as little as possible, but other civic associations pushed and pulled it into one new activity after another.

Impulses toward change may also appear in an organization without any outside stimulus. Organizations, like individuals, engage in campaigns of self-improvement. Many large organizations have planning departments to provide a steady flow of innovations.

Planning does not protect an organization from unforeseen changes: in the first place, it cannot control the external environment, and in the second place, carefully planned changes in one part of an organization usually cause unexpected stresses in other parts.

The most elementary forms of organizational change are growth and decline. Few human organizations come to rest at the exact equilibrium point between growth and expansion.[2] Most organizations, at any given time, are either expanding or contracting. Within limits, both processes are cumulative. Growth facilitates further

1. See Howard E. Aldrich, *Organization and Environments* (Englewood Cliffs, N.J.: Prentice-Hall, 1979), pp. 26–55.

2. For an interesting discussion of organizational stability and instability, see John W. Meyer and Brian Rowan, "Institutionalized Organizations: Formal Structure as Myth and Ceremony," in O. Grusky and G. A. Miller, *The Sociology of Organizations: Basic Studies,* second edition (New York: Free Press, 1981), pp. 530–54.

growth; decline paves the way for further decline. Turning points are relatively infrequent. An organization may grow continuously from the time it is founded until it reaches a turning point and then decline continuously until it disappears.

Growth and decline call for numerous adjustments in an organization, and that is where we begin our discussion of the manager's responsibility for adapting to change. Then, we will consider the types of adaptation required by market pressures, social change, technological change, and creative innovation.

GROWING, STABLE, AND DECLINING ORGANIZATIONS

In some fields of activity, like banking and politics, an organization's growth rate is a direct measure of its success. In any field, the growing organization has certain natural advantages. Its expanding resources pay for past mistakes and offer protection against current risks. The expansion of its program creates new opportunities for people already in the organization and attracts desirable recruits. Decision-making is easy, or seems easy, because good decisions are confirmed, and poor decisions are masked, by continuing growth. The decision-maker has a wider range of choices than he would have in a stable or declining organization.

For the very same reasons, mistakes are likely to be made in the management of a growing organization, even if the mistakes do not show. It is probably harder to run a growing organization really well than to run the same type of organization in a stable phase, and the more rapid the growth, the more difficult the task.

Managerial Problems in Growing Organizations

It is obvious that a manager of given ability can control a small organization more firmly than a large one, supervise more of its activity directly, observe more of what goes on, and understand a larger proportion of the relationships his subordinates have with each other and with outsiders. As the organization grows, control becomes more complex by the mere accretion of numbers. There are ways of reducing the complexity by delegating responsibility and installing better data systems, but there is no way of avoiding it altogether.

The diminution of consensus about organizational goals is a normal consequence of growth, attributable in part to the inherent difficulty of getting a larger number

of people who know each other less well to agree about anything, in part to the importation of new people and ideas, but mostly to the brute fact that as an organization grows, its relationships to its members and to the environment necessarily change, so that its original goals become less congruent with its current program. These problems are magnified by discontinuities of scale. No organization can grow indefinitely in small increments. Sooner or later it makes a quantum leap that transforms its whole character: the company acquires a second factory in another state; summer camp adds a winter program; the family has its first child. Often the people involved may not realize that anything significant has occurred until they discover by experience that their familiar procedures no longer work and that their familiar routines have been bizarrely transformed.

One sign of discontinuity is the breakdown of organizational norms. There is a point in the growth of nearly every organization when internal theft becomes a problem and new security measures must be devised. In growing organizations that are badly run, a criminal underground may develop.

The growth of an organization makes some of its people obsolete. Some of its original members — perhaps those who deserve most of the credit for growth — will be unwilling or unable to adjust to the new order, and will be left by the wayside.

While the growing organization discards some of its insiders, its dependence on outsiders increases, because the expanded program requires transactions with an expanded environment or because growth has been achieved by mortgaging resources or assuming long-term commitments. Most successful private enterprises in the United States have gone this route, sacrificing independence for growth and eventually falling under the control of outside investors.

The problems of managing a growing organization are not insurmountable, but they do become more severe as the rate of growth accelerates, and organizations that grow very rapidly are often managed so badly that they ultimately collapse.

The standard methods for coping with rapid expansion in an organization (of any size) are:

1. team management,
2. decentralization of operating responsibilities,
3. standardization of procedures,
4. centralization of financial control,
5. expansion of communication facilities.

This formula, although derived from case studies of organizations of varying size, bears a close resemblance to the Sloan plan for General Motors. . . . The resemblance is not coincidental, since the Sloan plan was, in fact, designed for a rapidly expanding organization and worked well for upward of forty years until General Motors reached a level of relative stability and began to encounter a different set of problems. The same organization that had coped so well with the problems of expansion became remarkably maladroit when asked to cope with consumer activists, federal regulation of engine emissions, and the design constraints introduced by high-priced gasoline.

Although the formula set forth above calls to mind a giant organization, I have seen it applied with notable success to middle-sized and even tiny organizations — a piano company expanding in the manufacture of electric organs, a civic orchestra becoming a full-time professional orchestra, a research institute outgrowing the converted barn in which it started.

Under team management, the single, ultimately responsible head of the organization to whom this book is addressed sometimes becomes two or three people who divide the job up or do it jointly.[3] More commonly under team management, the manager of the organization can still be identified but has one or two close associates whose authority is nearly equal to his own. The reason for team management in rapidly expanding organizations is that there are at least three separate managerial jobs to be done: running the existing operation, supervising the expansion, and coping with the unpredictable problems that expansion creates.

But since there are built-in limits to the size of a managerial team (no executive committee is likely to function well with more than five members), the continued expansion of an organization continuously threatens to overload the management team unless the responsibility for routine and subsidiary operations is spun off as soon as possible to subordinate managers. Hence the need for decentralization. Decentralization is only feasible, however, if procedures are standardized and financial controls are tightened; otherwise it amounts to anarchy. When decentralization has been accomplished, there remains the danger that the organization's ability to react to events as a unit will suffer because its decentralized parts lack a common viewpoint. Hence the need for expanded communications.

Managerial Problems in Stable Organizations

By a stable organization, I mean one that is not growing or declining significantly. It need not be stable in all other respects.

Some organizations are inherently stable because they are designed to operate with a membership of fixed size — a troupe of aerialists, for example, or a string quartet, or a state legislature. Some, such as the Central Mental Hospital described by Erving Goffman in his notable book on asylums,[4] must confine their activities to fixed facilities, and therefore have approximately stable populations.

Some other organizations are stable by deliberate choice, steering a careful course between the temptation to grow and the danger of declining. A considerable number of small communities and small associations are run this way, and even a few sizable businesses. One Great Lakes shipping line, for example, operated the same fleet of eleven bulk carriers out of the same port for a period of thirty-two years, spanning the entire career of one fleet manager, without adding or losing a single ship and without ever replacing a captain for any reason but retirement. The Comédie Française, the French National Theater, has maintained an approximately constant membership for more than 300 years. It is a cooperative headed by the actor of longest service. A new recruit becomes an associate member after a year's probation and a formal debut in a role of his or her choice but cannot become a sociétaire until a vacancy is created by the resignation or death of a member.[5]

As a general rule, morale is higher in stable organizations than in either growing or declining ones, but that is not to say that the stable organization is free of problems. There is the constant problem of assuring that the measures taken to prevent growth do not overcarry and lead into a spiral of decline. Stable organizations tend to be inflexible and set in their ways, and since they generally have low turnover they are apt to become

---

3. A full description of team management may be found in Peter H. Drucker, *Management: Tasks, Responsibilities, Practices* (New York: Harper and Row, 1974).

4. Erving Goffman, *Asylums* (New York: Anchor Books, 1961).

5. *International Herald Tribune,* October 22, 1980.

more inflexible as their members age. The ragged, long-bearded crew of the Flying Dutchman's ship, as described in the old sea legend, were not unlike the personnel of some other organizations that have been stable for a long time. A middle-aged colleague of mine who joined the staff of a famous and extremely stable scientific institute in Paris said that he felt conspicuous at staff meetings because he was the only person present without a hearing aid.

Because of their built-in resistance to change, stable organizations are vulnerable to certain types of crisis. Crises of succession, when they occur in stable organizations, are especially severe, since career frustration in a stable organization is a more serious matter than in a dynamic organization. I knew a man who served for seventeen years as the associate director of a stable industrial laboratory, secure in the knowledge that when the director reached the mandatory retirement age, the place would be his, and that he would then have fourteen more years to run the laboratory before his own retirement. In due course, the director retired and, to everybody's surprise, a younger man from outside was selected for the post. My friend's reactions were violent, running from initial shock into a nearly suicidal depression that required him to take a long leave of absence. When he recovered, he returned to work in his old job, with the fixed intention of taking revenge at the first opportunity. As it turned out, the new director was sufficiently incompetent to fail at his job even without my friend's assistance. Between them, they wrecked the organization beyond repair within two years.

Such disasters are avoidable provided that the stable organization refrains from actions — such as disrupting an orderly succession — that are incompatible with long-term stability. Some Oxford and Cambridge colleges have remained stable for centuries. The best account of how such an organization handles a crisis of succession may be found, lightly disguised as fiction, in C. P. Snow's novel *The Masters,* in which the fellows of a Cambridge college, selecting their new head in a bitterly contested election, take elaborate account of the motives and expectations of all concerned in order to arrive at the least disruptive choice.

The principal elements of the formula for managing a stable organization are these:

1. adherence to traditional procedures,
2. slow-moving, intensive problem-solving efforts,
3. democratic participation in decision-making,
4. meticulous and accessible records and accounts,
5. a system for the designation of successors designed to prevent surprises.

A stable organization cannot be maintained for long unless it has the wholehearted support of its members and they keep a vigilant lookout for incipient signs of growth or decline. In order for the organization to obtain that much support from its members, it must assure that their expectations are rarely disappointed, and in order to do that, it must follow a slow participatory mode of problem-solving. The manager of a stable organization is less of an initiator and more of a representative than the managers of growing and declining organizations, and his success is measured by how well he expresses the wishes of his constituents.

Managerial Problems in Declining Organizations

Organizations decline for a variety of reasons, not all of which signify failure. A few types of organization have a built-in, normal rate of decline. An organized alumnae group, like the Old Ivy class of 1985, begins its existence with a maximum roster and declines over the years as members die or are lost from sight, until the roster is emptied seventy or eighty years later. Veterans' organizations follow a similar course. Some very important types of organizations anticipate cyclical decline as a matter of course. Standing armies and navies grow rapidly in wartime and decline even faster when the war comes to an end. Some organizations are plunged into a decline by achieving their original goals. The associations formed to combat tuberculosis and poliomyelitis are classic, much-studied examples.

Tax-supported agencies decline when their appropriations are reduced. Schools, hospitals, and other service institutions decline when shifts of population reduce the demand for their services. A commercial enterprise may decline because of shrinking markets. The producers of washtubs, laundry soap, blueing, and other materials for doing laundry by hand have sold their products in a shrinking market for decades since the invention of washing machines.

As a general rule, it is much more difficult to manage a declining organization than a stable or growing one. The growing organization is rarely confronted by a truly insoluble problem — there is usually some way around it. The stable organization has learned to keep insoluble problems at bay, or it would not be stable. But the declining organization has problems that cannot be solved.

Morale is usually low in declining organizations. Because of the organization's diminishing ability to meet its commitments, it must often disappoint the legitimate expectations of its members. In addition, they experience an automatic status deflation as the organization's importance diminishes and the importance of their own activities is correspondingly reduced. When the decline of an organization is unscheduled, there is certain to be some loss of confidence in its program; this is likely to occur even when the decline is scheduled. Few professional groups are less certain of their own purposes than the officers of a peacetime army. This loss of confidence breeds cynicism and encourages corruption. Declining organizations are susceptible to exploitation by outsiders, and looting by their own members.

The productivity of declining organizations is typically low because of inadequate resources to keep up with technological progress and the difficulty of recruiting competent replacements when positions fall vacant.

A specific malady that afflicts declining organizations may be called "Parkinsonitis," after the brilliant satirist who invented Parkinson's Law.[6] Its leading symptom is the expansion of administrative overhead as the operations contract. In a case of Parkinsonitis, the number of administrators and the costs of administration actually increase with each decrease in the number of people and activities to be administered. Parkinson presented figures for the Royal Navy between 1914 and 1928. During that period, the number of capital ships in commission decreased by 68 percent and the number of naval personnel by 32 percent, while the number of Admiralty officials increased by 78 percent, from 2,000 to 3,569. Another set of figures presented in the same essay showed a nearly fourfold increase in the staff of the British Colonial Office between 1935 and 1954, during which period the colonial empire administered by that office was liquidated. More recently, John Freeman and Michael T. Hannon have demonstrated the existence of Parkinsonitis in California school districts with an elaborate mathematical model.[7]

The new manager of a declining organization starts with two strikes against him. First, he is sure to find numerous deficiencies. Second, his chance of ultimate success is poor. Nevertheless, even declining organizations need to be managed, and there is the consoling thought that failure in the management of a declining organization is not much of a disgrace, while success is a notable achievement.

The formula for managing a declining organization may be summarized as follows:

1. reduce administrative overhead at a faster rate than the shrinkage of other activities,
2. drop the nonessential parts of the organizational program,
3. identify the inefficient and corrupt units and eliminate them,
4. when the organization has been stripped of its nonessential functions and purged of its worst abuses, look for new activities and goals.

ADJUSTING TO MARKET PRESSURES

Aside from the permanent decline that leads to extinction, every healthy organization is susceptible to temporary phases of decline due to competition, scarcities, rising costs, or declining revenues.

Competition

Every organization in the world competes with other organizations for resources, influence, manpower, and clients. Most organizations are simultaneously pitted against several distinct sets of competitors. A manufacturer of table linen competes, of course, with other linen manufacturers but also with linen importers, with manufacturers of paper napkins, plastic tablecloths, place mats, and disposable fabrics, and with commercial linen services and discount houses that buy linen from captive suppliers.

A noncommercial institution also has separate sets of competitors. A private liberal arts college, for example, competes intensely and consciously with other colleges in its league — those of about the same size and type in the same region, but it is also willy-nilly in competition with publicly supported institutions from state universi-

6. C. Northcote Parkinson, *Parkinson's Law and Other Studies in Administration* (Boston: Houghton-Mifflin, 1957).

7. John Freeman and Michael T. Hannan, "Growth and Decline Processes in Organizations," in D. Katz, R. Kahn and S. Adams, *The Study of Organizations* (San Francisco: Jossey-Bass, 1980), pp. 43–58.

ties down to community colleges, and with alternative institutions such as vocational schools and service academies.

When market conditions are highly favorable, competitive efforts are directed almost exclusively against nearby competitors — against the other middle-size manufacturers of fine table linen, or against the other second-rank New England women's colleges. When market conditions turn unfavorable, the competitive focus shifts to more remote but more threatening competitors: the paper goods industry, the community colleges. The most successful competitors are generally those who are able to see a coming change of competitive focus earlier than their peers.

Scarcities

The most dangerous kind of market pressure is an absolute scarcity of something the organization requires for its program. A relative scarcity of material or manpower will be reflected, of course, in rising costs, and a relative scarcity of clients and customers will take the form of declining revenues. An absolute scarcity is a different sort of problem, and not particularly uncommon.

An absolute scarcity occurs when, for example: the balsa wood used for model planes is no longer available because of a trade embargo; the county hospital cannot be staffed because physicians' services have been priced out of reach; the Sunday school must be abandoned because the congregation has few young children; the municipal auditorium is condemned after a fire and there is no other hall large enough for the civic orchestra's concerts; the abandonment of air service to an island resort keeps all the tourists away; the exhaustion of the silver lode closes down the mine and the mining town.

An absolute scarcity cannot be argued with or fiddled with. It calls for imaginative and *quick* innovation, before the organization founders.

Rising Costs

Rising costs may reflect the appearances of relative scarcities, as when a poor flax crop raises the price of linen or a shortage of psychological counselors increases the salaries that must be offered to hire one. But there are many other reasons why costs rise, some of them internal to the organization, such as ineffective administration, worn-out equipment, or embezzlement; some of them external, such as new taxes, increased postal rates, or inflation. Some of these factors raise costs gradually, but others work abruptly so that, for example, every rise in fourth-class postage rates spells the end for some magazines, and every extension of minimum-wage coverage puts a stop to various small enterprises. The effect of rising costs is most dramatic when the organization is not free to pass on increases to its customers or clients. But even when it is, there comes a point where further increases reduce revenues. That is the problem that faces private liberal arts colleges. Their tuition fees are already very high in relation to the ability of students' families to pay, and further increases to meet rising costs drive so many students away to publicly-supported institutions that total revenues decline. Urban mass-transit systems have been caught in a similar spiral for many years. Increasing costs of labor, fuel, and equipment force them to increase their fares periodically, but every increase reduces the number of passengers, which soon calls for a further increase of fares, which reduces the number of passengers still more, and so on down the spiral of insolvency. The fundamental remedy for rising costs due to inflation is technological improvement, and the usual remedy for rising costs due to government intervention is lobbying, but these measures are not necessarily effective. The liberal arts college cannot introduce much technological improvement without changing its institutional character and losing much of its remaining clientele, and the operators of urban bus lines can bring only a limited influence to bear on government policy.

Declining Revenues

Declining revenues have much the same effect as rising costs, but in the typical case they are a little more under the organization's control, since the decline can sometimes be arrested by vigorous cultivation of an existing clientele or by reaching out for new clients. Advertising and promotion offer the commercial enterprise innumerable opportunities to turn declining sales trends around. Intelligent programs of attracting students enable some liberal arts colleges to flourish when most are declining. Hospitals, churches, schools, clubs, civic associations, and innumerable other organizations that depend on voluntary support are often able to reverse a declining revenue trend by intensive cultivation of their existing constituencies, or by reaching out for new supporters.

Responding to Market Pressures

The formula for responding to market pressure may be briefly summarized as follows:

1. *Remember that no trend lasts forever.* The time of peace is the time to prepare for war, and the time of increasing revenue is the time to plan and prepare for a phase of declining revenue.
2. *Every technological improvement should be justified by cost reduction.* Technological improvements are possible in nearly every organized human activity, but since it is also possible to burden nearly any activity with new devices that are not really needed, a technological improvement should not be adopted unless it offers a significant reduction of cost.
3. *Make multiple responses to market pressure whenever possible, and determine by trial and error which responses are most effective.* An organization's response to market pressure is affected not only by unpredictable fluctuations of the market but also by the reactions of competitors. This field of action resembles a storm at sea more than it resembles a field to be plowed and planted. To get through it safely, you need to stand by your instruments, take continuous readings, and be prepared to change course frequently.

ADJUSTING TO SOCIAL CHANGE

No organization can be completely insulated from the currents of social change in the surrounding society. And all societies change continually — not only advanced, industrial societies but *all* societies. The changes that occur in our own society can be classified in many different ways, but those that have the most impact on organizations fall conveniently into four categories: demographic shifts, changes of public policy, changes in social values, and changes in organizational styles.

Demographic Shifts

Demographic shifts occur because of the growth or decline of population in a given territory, or changing rates of growth or decline; because of migration from country to city, from central city to suburb, and from region to region; because of fluctuations in birth rates, death rates, and other vital statistics; and because of the changes in the age, sex, ethnicity, and other characteristics of given populations that are induced by all of the foregoing processes.

Every demographic shift has some effect on organizations, and some of these effects ripple on for decades. For example, the rise in the United States birth rate that occurred in the late 1940s necessitated a great expansion of elementary schools in the 1950s, of high schools a little later, and of colleges and universities in the 1960s. The sharp decline of the same birthrate that occurred in the 1970s calls for a shrinkage of educational institutions in the 1980s that will continue at least until the end of the century.

To take another familiar example, the migration of urban dwellers to the suburbs has profound effects upon the city churches they formerly attended, which respond to the problem of declining attendance and interest in a variety of ways. Some urban churches follow their congregations to the suburbs. Some continue to operate on a much reduced scale for a remnant of elderly parishioners, some go out of existence, and some reorganize to serve a new clientele.

No national population in the modern world has a fixed size, distribution, or composition; all of them are continuously changing. Hence, all modern organizations are subject to continuous demographic shifts that change the number and type of people available for participation in their programs.

Changes of Public Policy

Changes in public policy have frequent and unpredictable effects upon organizations of every kind in every modern society. In the People's Democracies, no aspect of organizational life falls outside the sphere of official control. Under a freer form of government, the jurisdiction of the state is more limited, but the expenditures of all levels of government in the United States account for more than a third of the gross national product, and governmental control over nongovernmental organizations is expressed by an unending stream of statutes, regulations, and rulings emitted by legislatures, courts, and administrative agencies. Even the most private association, like a fishing club, must file a tax statement, apply for licenses, conform to health, safety, and zoning regulations, pay minimum wages, refrain from illegal discrimination, operate equipment in a prescribed manner, and so on and so forth. An establishment of a more public character, like a hospital, operates within an intricate maze of government controls.

There are hundreds of separate government bodies with the power to alter some of the public policies that control the operation of a hospital, and many of them are hyperactive in developing new policies and procedures. For example, in the reimbursement of hospitals from public funds for patient charges, about the only thing that can be taken for granted concerning the policies and procedures in effect at a given time is that they will not be the same twelve months later.

A statute or court ruling intended to accomplish some unrelated purpose may transform an organization's environment beyond recognition, as has repeatedly happened in recent years to organizations as diverse as nursery schools, nursing homes, and tree nurseries, within my own observation. In the case of the nursery schools, a careless phrase in a state law on the licensing of school teachers had the effect of requiring nursery schoolteachers to have bachelor's degrees in education, thereby eliminating a good proportion of the nursery schools in that state and tripling the average charges of those that remained. In the case of nursing homes, a small change in the regulations concerning Medicare eligibility forced large nursing homes to dismantle their facilities for intensive medical care. In the case of the tree nurseries, a minor revision in the tax regulations concerning depletion allowances made Christmas tree nurseries highly attractive to investors at one time, while another minor revision some years later made them instantly unprofitable.

In the great expansion of federal jurisdiction that began around 1964 and continued until 1980, many activities that were already regulated by state and local agencies were brought under federal jurisdiction as well. While, at the same time, federal agencies with somewhat contradictory mandates, like the Department of Energy and the EPA, devised innumerable regulations that took little account of the regulations of competing agencies. Lending institutions, elementary schools, trucklines, hospitals, pharmaceutical manufacturers, automobile manufacturers, racetracks, food distributors, express services now have to cope with 10 to 20 regulatory agencies whose requirements are sometimes redundant, incoherent, or flatly contradictory and always impose a considerable burden of recordkeeping and other paperwork.[8] The organization that tries to

cope with government regulation in an imaginative way and the manager who devotes much time to regulatory matters are both asking for trouble. Conforming to burdensome regulations — or for that matter, evading them — is a matter for experts, for accountants, lawyers, and other professionals who specialize in such matters. Enterprises that deal with regulatory agencies through an intermediary body like a trade association, have a much easier time of it than those that attempt to deal directly with government agencies and improvise their responses to regulatory pressure.

The realm of public policy constitutes a Pandora's box of unexpected surprises, sometimes pleasant but more often unpleasant for the modern organization. Nearly every sizable organization is continually engaged in lobbying and litigation, either directly or through representative associations. Nevertheless, since changes in public policy come from so many different quarters, an organization will often be unaware that some significant modification is about to be required in its program until the change is upon it. The Buckley amendment requiring educational institutions to give students access to confidential records about themselves, which transformed the record-keeping procedures of educational institutions, was enacted and took effect before the affected institutions or their official lobbyists were aware that such a measure was pending.

Changes in Social Values

Changes in social values are even more unpredictable in the long run than changes in public policy, but since they are much less abrupt, they permit more planning and adaptation. Changes in social values involve such matters as the relationship between the sexes, the attitudes of young people toward their elders, the limits of legitimate authority, the recognition or denial of property rights, the importance attached to education and to leisure, the role of religion in daily life, the tolerance accorded to people of different color or descent, and the definition of what constitutes acceptable appearance, speech, and behavior in various settings. No organization is impermeable to changes in social values, but most organizations do not absorb such changes passively; they either encourage or resist them. With respect to such a matter as the equalization of sex

8. See *Gains and Shortcomings in Resolving Regulatory Conflicts and Overlaps* (Washington, D.C.: U.S. General Accounting Office, PAD-81-76, June 23, 1981).

roles, a strong organization is likely to be either far ahead of, or far behind, the general social trend. Few organizations, however, remain unaffected.

Changes in Organizational Styles

Organizational styles change as frequently as styles in clothing or entertainment. Fashions and fads in organizational matters are partly derived from the external environment and partly self-generated. Modern organizations of the same type stay in close touch through conventions and periodicals, so that any significant innovation in an organization is noticed almost immediately by other organizations in the same set, and any innovation that has been adopted by a number of organizations in a set becomes almost irresistible to the others. A bank without a computer, or a church without a revised liturgy, would be a rarity today, although the advantage of either innovation is open to question.

When an organization is confronted with an external social change that invites or compels action, the manager ought to be mindful of the following rules:

1. *Do not be taken unaware.* It is the manager's personal responsibility to be aware of changes in the external environment that affect the organization's program, and this responsibility can never really be delegated.
2. *Do not allow the organization to react hastily.* The problems of adjusting an organization to external change are inherently complex, and the probability of finding the right solution is necessarily low.
3. *Specify the end condition to be achieved and then work backward step-by-step to find the appropriate means.* This is known as the sequential method of solving social problems; I have described it in detail in another book.[9]
4. *Make sure that you have a substantial consensus within the organization before responding to external changes.* The existence of a consensus is ascertained by consultation with the people directly or indirectly affected by the proposed course of action. If there is no consensus, it must be developed by having the same people study the problem until they arrive at agreement (or, in extreme circumstances, by a drastic reorganization). How much consensus is enough is always a good question, but it is easy to underestimate the resistance to change

that can be mustered by a disgruntled minority, or by the one wicked witch not invited to the christening.
5. *When following organizational fashions, do not be the last with the old nor the first with the new.* This is an old doctor's adage concerning the application of new remedies. It rests on the commonsense observation that the first users of a new remedy are the ones most likely to suffer from its unknown side effects, while the last users have the least advantage of its benefits.

ADJUSTING TO TECHNOLOGICAL PROGRESS

In an advanced technological society, all organizations, including those that have nothing to do with industrial production, are offered a continuous stream of technologically improved devices. The museum of antique furniture is offered a computerized catalog system. The rowing club can pace its practice sessions with an electronically activated timer and can substitute fiberglass for wooden oars.

From the technological standpoint, an improvement is an improvement; even the casual observer can usually determine which of two related devices is more advanced along the vector of technological progress. But the problem of whether an organization needs, wants, or can make use of a given bit of new technology is not so easily resolved. It is possible to automate a dairy farm so that the cows are fed and milked without any human intervention, but it is not economically practical to do so except with a very large herd.

From the organizational standpoint, technological improvement usually involves both advantages and disadvantages. The advantages are along the lines of greater speed, scope, capacity, and precision and (sometimes) lower unit costs. The disadvantages are along the lines of the loss of autonomy, waste of skills, reduction in cooperative effort, decreased control, and (sometimes) increased unit costs.

Hence, the adjustment of an organization to technological progress in its field involves two separate tasks: first, choosing or rejecting new technological improvements as they are offered; second, incorporating whatever improvements are chosen into the organizational program with minimum damage. In many

---

9. Theodore Caplow, *Towards Social Hope* (New York: Basic Books, 1975).

technically oriented organizations, there is the third task of contributing to the development of new technology by research and experimentation.

Choosing or Rejecting New Technology

This task is more of a pitfall for small organizations than for large ones. Large organizations, with their specialized technical facilities, participate directly in the current of ongoing research and usually have rational procedures for appraising the advantages and disadvantages of a proposed bit of new technology. There are some notable exceptions, however. The U.S. Postal Service, for example, has so powerful a tradition of technological ineptness that private message and parcel service are able to compete with it effectively, despite the enormous subsidy it enjoys.

In any case, the rules of thumb for choosing or rejecting a new bit of technology are the same for organizations of every size. They may be summarized as follows:

1. Adopt a technological improvement when it offers a large reduction of cost, or an unmistakable gain of efficacy, without any increased cost.
2. Reject a technological improvement when its effects on cost or efficacy are uncertain.
3. Adopt a technological improvement if it can be introduced on an experimental basis without serious jeopardy to the organizational program in case of failure.
4. Reject a technological improvement that exposes the organization to disaster in case of failure.

Incorporating New Technology into an Organization

The decision to adopt a new bit of technology is frequently made at the top level of an organization (or by outsiders, in the case of organizations that are components of larger ones) without any serious attention to the problem of fitting the innovation into the organization. That is where the sociological fun begins.

The installation of a new bit of technology in an organization bears some resemblance to the modernization of a primitive village by well-meaning outside

experts. The things that can go wrong because the experts fail to take full account of the customs and beliefs of the natives were admirably cataloged by Conrad Arensberg and Arthur Niehoff in the manual they prepared for American experts working overseas.

They had many anecdotes to tell about misdirected technological improvements; for example, in Laotian villages, Leghorn and Rhode Island Red roosters were put into village flocks to raise a more productive mixed breed:

Some American chickens survived but even these got no chance to prove their usefulness. They rarely were able to mate with the local hens because they were no match for the gamecocks that served as roosters in the local flocks. The chicken expert tried to get around this difficulty by demanding that a villager get rid of all of his local roosters before he would put some American ones in the flock. This worked for one generation. Then the sons of the American roosters and the Lao hens took over. Being half village chicken, they were tougher fighters than their fathers, and kept the latter from mating. In this manner, each generation became inferior in size and egg-producing ability, but superior in fighting. [10]

The reason that the American expert could not overcome these difficulties was that he never fully visualized the difference between the American system of raising chickens in a tightly controlled hen house environment and the Laotian system of letting the chickens forage for themselves, nor did he perceive the bad connection between cock-fighting and poultry raising.

Exactly the same sort of incomprehension often attends the introduction of a technological innovation in a sophisticated enterprise. A textbook publisher who installed an automated shipping system in a computerized warehouse discovered that his salesmen were ordering out huge numbers of examination copies under fictitious names and hoarding them. The new system, it turned out, had an average delivery time of around fifteen days, much less than that of the previous system; but, unlike the previous system, it was incapable of delivering a book overnight on a salesman's rush order. Since the salesman depended on such rush orders

---

10. Conrad N. Arensberg and Arthur H. Niehoff, *Introducing Social Change: A Manual for Americans Overseas* (Chicago: Aldine, 1964), p. 77.

whenever a buyer showed interest, they bypassed the new warehouse and improvised a makeshift system of their own in order to get their work done.

What appears to be an irrational resistance to technology often turns out, in closer analysis, to be rational enough from the standpoint of the resisters. The Lancaster weavers who smashed the power looms at the very beginning of the Industrial Revolution feared that their wages would be lowered by the new invention and they were perfectly right.

Even when the resistance to an invention is irrational, it may be quite reasonable in terms of the information available to the resisters. The fault in such cases lies with the innovators for not having sufficiently studied the environment in which they proposed to operate.

To take another example from the modernization of developing countries, the team of agronomists from the University of Iowa who attempted to introduce an improved variety of seed corn in highland Guatemala discovered that although the local farmers took the corn gratefully enough, they fed it to their animals instead of planting it. After two or three seasons of this charade, the agronomists, on the advice of an astute Indian, put a high fence studded with No Trespassing signs around their compound and stopped giving their seed corn away. But they left the fence unguarded at night and enough corn was stolen and planted to establish the new variety. In that part of the world, nearly every family has its own subvariety of corn, and it is much too valuable to give away. But if it appears really superior, the neighbors will pilfer some to try out.

The first series of experiments at the Western Electric plant in Hawthorne more than half a century ago, which had such a profound effect on the development of industrial sociology, attempted to demonstrate the effect of improved lighting on the productivity of factory work groups. In one of these experiments, a test group was chosen to work under progressively improving illumination. It was carefully matched with a control group, working under constant illumination. The results were startling. The increase of productivity in the control group was nearly the same as the increase in the experimental group. In a follow-up experiment, both the test group and the control group were placed in artificial light, and this time the level of illumination in the test group enclosure was gradually decreased. Again, the efficiencies of the test group and the control group increased at about the same rate. Not until the test group's illumination was reduced to the approximate brightness of moonlight, so that they could barely see their materials, did output begin to decrease.

The implication of this experiment was that the level of illumination had only a minor influence on productivity in that particular setting, but that the amount of supervisory attention received by a work group had a major influence. Both the test group and the control group were closely watched, fussed over, and consulted by supervisors during the course of the experiment; the favorable effects of this increased attention overcame the minor effects of varying illumination.

In general, the successful introduction of a technological innovation depends upon predicting with reasonable accuracy (1) what functions the innovation will perform and how these will affect the organization's structure, and (2) obtaining—preferably in advance—the consent and cooperation of the people who are expected to make the innovation work.

The usual procedures for accomplishing these purposes may be summarized as follows:

1. Before committing the organization to a technological innovation, it is essential to obtain empirical evidence that the innovation is workable, by means of a pilot installation or by close observation of a comparable organization in which it is already operational.
2. The more people involved in preliminary discussion of, and planning for, the innovation, the more successful it is likely to be.
3. When resistance to an innovation begins to develop, stop the clock and resolve the problem before proceeding further. Resistance of this kind should not be approached as an obstacle to be surmounted. It may be solidly grounded on technical or social facts that need to be taken into account.
4. Try to determine in advance, primarily by consultation outside and inside the organization, the probable defects of a proposed innovation so as to be prepared to cope with them as they appear.
5. A technological innovation should be monitored for a considerable period of time after its installation in order to detect those malfunctions that take some time to develop and in order to measure the results of the innovation when it settles into a steady state of operation.

CREATIVE INNOVATION

March and Simon, in their classic treatise on the theory of organization, hypothesize that "most innovations in an organization are a result of borrowing rather than invention."[11] The borrowing is accomplished either by direct imitation of other organizations or by importing people who have experience elsewhere. The practice of borrowing makes eminent good sense, particularly for small organizations, since the borrower is spared the cost of invention and testing and is protected from the errors in trial-and-error testing.

Nevertheless, any organization may occasionally invent a new technical or social device, and some organizations and branches of organizations specialize in creative innovation. This activity is undertaken with varying degrees of seriousness in scientific laboratories, research and development teams, advertising agencies, law firms, and a few high-level planning agencies.

Under primitive conditions, creative innovation is the exclusive prerogative of a few individuals who have the rare talent of perceiving possibilities to which their fellows are blind. While filming the lives of monkeys (red-faced macaques) on the island of Kochima, a team of Japanese zoologists actually saw a young female, whom they nicknamed Imo, hit on the idea of washing a sweet potato in the lake before eating it. After about a month, she was imitated by another monkey, and ten years later, the practice had spread throughout the band. Later, Imo made a second fundamental discovery when she found a way of separating grain from sand by tossing a pawful of grain on the surface of the water and letting the sand sink. "She was something of a monkey Prometheus," wrote one observer.[12]

The characteristics of inventive geniuses do not change very much as we ascend the evolutionary scale. They are rare, conscious of their special gifts, and capable of making multiple discoveries under the right conditions. Creative innovators seem to have distinctive mental and personality traits. They rate high on conceptual fluency and flexibility, respond to stimuli in original and atypical ways, and enjoy complex problems. They are likely to be stubborn about their opinions, somewhat lonely, impulsive, and resistant to authority. In other words, they are not good executive material.[13]

The question of how to design an organization to encourage and facilitate creative innovation cannot, in the present state of knowledge, be answered by a formula. There is considerable disagreement among successful research administrators about how much autonomy the creative innovator needs to have. The question is complicated by the fact that in contemporary science, technology, and social management, the problems to be solved by creative innovation sometimes call for massive team efforts. The individual capable of original discoveries does not lose his importance, but his work must now be coordinated with the less original efforts of numerous hardworking collaborators.

The available research evidence suggests that administrative style, tables of organization, and operating procedures are less important in creative organizations than in those with more routine programs. The most productive research organization I have ever observed was Millard Hansen's Social Science Research Center at the University of Puerto Rico — although it was enmeshed in the toils of an old-fashioned, slow moving, bilingual bureaucracy. The secret of the center's success seems to have been that project directors were very carefully selected and then given unlimited responsibility for their projects and as much support as the center could provide with no questions asked and few reports required. The classic prototype of the American industrial laboratory, the research division of General Electric under Irving Langmuir, operated in a similar fashion.

On the other hand, the two greatest achievements of American technology, the Manhattan project and the NASA moon program, were carried out by tightly administered organizations, each of which had a rather narrow and rigid division of labor. In contrast to the absence of deadlines in Hansen's center and Langmuir's laboratory (other than those self-imposed by individuals), some effective research organizations not only impose deadlines but use the trick of a suddenly advanced deadline to achieve breakthroughs on stubborn problems.

---

11. James G. March and Herman A. Simon, *Organizations* (New York: John Wiley and Sons, 1958), p. 188.

12. The original observations are somewhat inaccessible, but the film has been widely shown, and a good summary may be found in Vitus B. Droscher, *The Friendly Beast* (New York: Harper and Row, 1971), pp. 191–92.

13. Gary A. Steiner, *The Creative Organization* (Chicago: University of Chicago Press, 1965).

While the optimum design for a creative organization cannot be completely specified, there are a few well-established principles for managing a creative organization, which may be stated as follows:

1. Identify the creative individuals on whom the success of the organization depends, on the basis of their demonstrated performance.
2. Make sure that you and they share a common view of the organization's goals, whether broadly or narrowly defined.
3. Provide them with all the support the organization can muster.
4. Protect them from bureaucratic interference.
5. Reward them as lavishly as possible.

It is obvious from the foregoing that the noncreative people in a creative organization will suffer from relative deprivation, and that the creative people will sometimes get in each other's way. Successful research organizations are seldom characterized by high morale, but that matters little if they are able to make new discoveries.

SYSTEMATIC PLANNING

The reader, if he or she has any organizational experience at all, will not have needed this book to learn that management is more an art than a science, although the findings of social science may assist us in practicing the art. He or she would not have needed a book, either, to learn that both pleasures and pains are associated with the headship of anything. "Is it not passing brave to be a King and ride in triumph through Persepolis?" asked Christopher Marlowe in *Tamburlaine*. "Uneasy lies the head that wears a crown," his greater contemporary wrote in *Henry IV*.

The principles of conduct proposed in the foregoing pages can be read backward as signposts pointing toward the pitfalls into which a manager may fall, and sometimes *must* fall. The balance between success and failure in running an organization is so delicate that common sense tells us to count no manager successful until he has retired and gone away.

Is there some sure method of tipping this uncertain balance in our favor? The answer is *no* if we want to be guaranteed against unknown dangers, unprovoked hostility, and the consequences of our own mistakes. The answer is *yes* if we want to maintain authority, encourage communication, achieve high levels of productivity and morale, and adapt successfully to change. A nearly magical enhancement of the manager's personal capability can be achieved nine times out of ten by an intelligent emphasis on planning.

In nearly every kind of organization, the manager has a primary responsibility for planning that is not likely to be questioned or disputed.[14] Even a manager with very limited authority, like the principal of a public school or the president of a civic association, is usually free to launch as much planning activity as he wants and can enlist others in a planning program without meeting much resistance.

Not all of what passes for organizational planning deserves the name. Some so-called plans are really sales prospectuses. Others are science fiction. In a few interesting cases, the sole function of planning is to direct attention away from the real problems. Serious planning, by contrast, is marked by an emphasis on contingency and by a meticulous interest in small details.

Planning may, of course, be short-term, middle-term, or long-term; routine or episodic; problem-oriented or goal-oriented, participant or nonparticipant. But the essential features of a well-conceived planning program are not very much affected by these distinctions. They are as follows:

1. A detailed description of the current state of the organization and of the relevant features of the environment.
2. An analysis of past trends in the organization and in the environment to provide a basis for extrapolating the same trends into the future.
3. A division of the future into a sequence of successive stages and a description of the conditions to be achieved at each stage.
4. Estimates of the organizational inputs required to move from each stage to the next of the planned sequence.
5. Specification of the external conditions required to carry the plan through its successive stages.

---

14. For discussion of the president's role in corporate planning, see Myles L. Mace, "The President and Corporate Planning," in Harvard Business Review, *On Management* (New York: Harper and Row, 1976), pp. 119–42.

6. A method for measuring plan fulfillment at each stage.
7. Provisions for revising the plan in case of over-fulfillment, underfulfillment, or unforeseen contingencies.

The direct advantages of planning are obvious. The indirect benefits are not quite so obvious but they are equally real and just as important.

Self-appraisal

In organizations that practice continuous short-term planning, for example in companies that set production or sales quotas for six months or a year ahead, the pressures for achievement on the one hand, and the politics of quota-setting on the other hand, force every unit of the organization—down to the individual worker—to practice continuous self-appraisal. In middle- and long-term planning, a major planning episode usually begins with a self-survey in which units assess their past progress, present performance, and potential capability in relation to the organization's stated goals. This experience, repeated at reasonable intervals and in a reasonably democratic spirit, has all sorts of wonderful side effects. It is by far the most effective way of clarifying the organization's purposes and bringing the activities of component units into alignment with them. It leads units to uncover and resolve many structural and operating problems that would otherwise go untreated. It elicits information and suggestions from parts of the organization that do not normally play much part in formulating policy, while the need to combine the reports of lower units at each level provokes intense communication—upward, downward, and sideways—about organizational problems.[15]

Clarification of Goals

No matter how clearly the initial goals of an organization are stated or understood, some ambiguities, differences of opinion, and misunderstandings are sure to develop in the course of normal operations, with the result that one part of the program pulls against another, or some units spend their energies undoing the work of other units. Planning brings these contradictions to light and provides incentives to resolve them, at least within the confines of the plan.[16]

New Possibilities

Part of the magic of planning is the inevitable discovery of possible courses of action not previously imagined or noticed. The simple procedure of arranging alternatives and contingencies in an orderly way often leads to useful new strategies that would not otherwise have been suggested.

Improved Information

Nearly the first thing that happens in the preparation of an organizational plan is that people find they need information that is not readily available, either because the reporting system is not set up to deliver it, or because it has not been collected, or because it needs to be obtained from outside the organization. When the reporting system has been modified to produce the needed information, or channels to outside sources of information have been established, there is likely to be a permanent improvement in the flow of routine information.

How Not to Plan

Planning, like any other magic, can turn against its user. The failures of planning loom so large in the current world that they deserve separate consideration. Defective planning is one of the hallmarks of modern bureaucracy; it takes several familiar forms:

1. *Setting organizational objectives without participation and consent.* This is the characteristic form of planning in the Soviet economy and, to a lesser extent, in the other centralized economies of eastern Europe. It is one of the principal reasons why their productivity lags so far behind that of the partially planned economies of western Europe, despite the advantage of more tightly disciplined labor forces in the eastern countries.
2. *Planning with unlimited resources.* The whole point of planning is that it enables an organization to adjust

---

15. Such a situation is described in detail by Neal Gross, Joseph B. Giacquinto, and Marty Bernstein, in *Implementing Organizational Innovations* (New York: Basic Books, 1971).

16. Needless to say, some of the contradictions will persist in reality whether or not they are resolved within a plan. For a despairing view of planning under those conditions, see W. Richard Scott, *Organizations: Rational, Natural and Open Systems* (Englewood Cliffs, N.J.: Prentice-Hall, 1981), pp. 270–75.

its program to existing constraints in a realistic way. Limited resources constitute the fundamental constraint in most cases. If, for some reason, the resources potentially available to an organization are limited only by its demands, there will be a tendency to plan for maximum growth rather than maximum effectiveness. This is a common occurrence in government agencies when they draw on resources that, at least in the short and middle term, are virtually unlimited. It occurs also in some private organizations whose budgets are so small in relation to the sources from which they draw support as to be practically unlimited. For example, the private security forces of larger private institutions seem to develop in a less effective way when planned than when unplanned, since the planning of security services is conventionally oriented toward expansion rather than efficiency.

3. *Master planning.* Master planning is an aberration of the planning process to which American communities are particularly susceptible. The preparation of a master plan is a gigantic effort, altogether out of scale with routine planning activities. The typical master plan is not a statement of intentions but a mixture of practical possibilities and pious hopes that refer to some future time too remote to be controlled from the present. In many cases, the master plan takes so long to prepare that it is outdated before it is published. Master plans seldom specify intermediate stages in detail and, because of their gigantic scale, are not easily amended to take account of intervening events. But the overhanging presence of a master plan has a tendency to inhibit or interfere with realistic planning on a smaller scale.

4. *Planning by outsiders.* It is a common practice for large-scale organizations of every kind to bring in outside experts to do their long-term planning. In some instances where the plan involves very little besides the installation of a new technology, as in the construction of a water purification plant, this procedure makes sense. In the more usual situation, in which modifications in the structure or functions of a living organization are contemplated, it is nearly impossible for outsiders to plan effectively, however knowledgeable and experienced they may be. Consultants are useful to get the planning process going, to suggest new methods and new systems, and to carry styles of self-improvement from one organization to another; but they cannot successfully plan the future of an organization to which they do not belong. That is the inherent responsibility of the organization's active members. Without their consent and participation, planning is a hollow show.

41. The Experimenting Organization: Problems and Prospects

Barry M. Staw

The last decade has seen a burgeoning of interest in the evaluation of social programs. Social scientists have increasingly focused their attention upon conceptual definitions of evaluation (e.g., Bennett & Lumsdaine, 1975; Campbell, 1969; Scriven, 1967; Wortman, 1975), the development of evaluation research methodologies (e.g., Campbell & Stanley, 1966; Cook & Campbell, 1976; Riecken & Boruch, 1975), and the political dynamics of evaluating various action programs (e.g., Banner, 1974; Berk & Rossi, 1976; Weiss, 1973, 1975). In short, there appears to be good progress toward what Campbell (1974) has labeled as "the experimenting society."

Although evaluation research has heightened in popularity during recent years, it is important to recognize that most of this activity has been centered on

Portions of this paper were presented at *The Experimenting Organization Symposium* during the 1976 national convention of the American Institute for Decision Sciences.

the evaluation of externally visible health, education, and welfare programs introduced by public sector organizations. Few evaluation research studies are conducted *within* public or private organizations to test whether internal innovations are effective or not. Rarely are persons trained in social research assigned to internal evaluation tasks. Instead, research-oriented staff are generally confined to established organizational functions, such as personnel selection, testing, and market research. Even the academic discipline of organizational behavior, whose function it is to study the internal workings of organizations, has largely ignored evaluation research as an important input to administrative decision making or the assessment of various programs *within* organizations. The purpose of the present paper is therefore to explore some of the implications of evaluation research for organizational decision processes and to discuss the problems as well as the prospects for the "experimenting organization."

THE CURRENT STATE OF ADMINISTRATIVE DECISION MAKING

Most organizational decisions are, by necessity, formulated within a context of uncertainty. For example, when deciding to start a new employee compensation scheme, a new program for task redesign, or a new training procedure, an administrator is often quite uncertain whether it will prove effective or not. In facing these kinds of decisions, the administrator usually comes armed only with a "lay psychology of organizational effectiveness." That is, through personal trial and error experiences in organizational settings, and both direct and indirect observations of the previous experiences of others, the administrator may have constructed his own theory to explain the internal workings of organizations (Staw, 1975). The administrator may have constructed his own personality theory to explain the relative productivity of different individuals (Bruner & Taguiri, 1954), his own interpersonal theory to explain what makes some groups more effective than others (Staw, 1975), and his own organizational theory to explain the chief determinants of an efficient administrative unit (Likert, 1967). The problem that remains, however, is that these lay theories may or may not be correct.

The major shortcoming of lay theories of organizational effectiveness is the methodological weakness of their supporting data. The administrator, for example, may construct a theory merely from the static observa-

tion of two groups differing in both performance and some other property A. If the differences between the two groups on both performance and property A are substantial, the individual is likely to conclude that A is a cause of performance. Moreover, if several groups are observed with the same pattern of data, the individual's confidence in this causal inference is likely to increase. Unfortunately, neither of these sources of cross-sectional data provides a highly valid basis for causal inference. In the case of the two-group comparison, statistical instability may have accounted for the result; in the comparison of many such groups, the threat of statistical instability is lessened, but the accuracy of causal inference is not greatly increased. The problem with drawing causal inference from a static-group comparison is that any other factor may have caused both property A and performance to vary together, and the direction of causation may merely be reversed.

The individual, in constructing his own theory or organizational effectiveness, may also utilize longitudinal data. Rather than relying solely upon static differences between individuals or groups, a person may look for covariation over time. A number of laboratory studies (e.g., Bavelas et al., 1965; Heider & Simmel, 1944; Michotte, 1963) have shown, for example, that causal inferences are most likely to be drawn when two variables covary over time and a change in one variable closely follows a change in another. Unfortunately, however, one's casual experience in observing covariation over time generally consists of only the weakest of longitudinal designs. For example, using Campbell and Stanley's (1966) notation in which X represents a change in an independent variable or treatment (e.g., a new job procedure) and O represents an observation of a dependent variable (e.g., work performance), the typical administrator has probably experienced some of the following "pre-experimental" designs:

1. $O \, X_1 \, O$
2. $O \, X_1 \, X_2 \, O$
3. $X_1 \, X_2 \, X_3 \, O$

As shown in the first example, the administrator may have changed X and then observed a change in the observation O from time 1 to time 2. In the second example, the administrator may have made multiple changes and observed a complex effect. Finally, in the third case, the administrator may have made multiple changes with only one post-treatment observation. Unfortunately, in none of these data-gathering instances can one be very confident of valid causal inference, regardless of the level or apparent change in the dependent variable(s).

THE ATTRIBUTION OF A CAUSAL RELATIONSHIP

The study of how individuals draw causal inferences from the data around them is the chief focus of attribution theory (Kelley, 1967). In general, empirical data has shown individuals to follow a relatively rational procedure of induction. Individuals look for salient differences or covariation from which to draw inferences and they employ a "discounting principle" in which confidence in causal inference is decreased when there exist salient alternative causes of the same phenomena (e.g., Bem, 1976; Calder & Staw, 1975; Deci, 1971; Jones et al., 1961; Jones & Harris, 1967; Kruglanski et al., 1971; Lepper et al., 1973; Staw, 1976a; Strickland, 1958; Thibaut & Riecken, 1955). More recently, Kelley (1973) has expanded this "discounting principle" in causal reference to encompass both inhibitory and facilitative causes. For example, if a new work training program accomplishes a goal in the face of an inhibitory cause (e.g., a strike or raw materials shortage) the new program would likely be given more credit as a causal factor than if such inhibitory forces were not present. Likewise, if the same new training program accomplishes a goal when other facilitative forces are present (e.g., an influx of more educated workers or improved physical surroundings), the impact of the new program would likely be discounted.

Methodologists in the evaluation area have also been concerned with facilitative and inhibitory causes that are external to a new program or experimental treatment. Campbell (1971), for instance, has systematically outlined a number of threats to the internal validity of experimental results. Because threats to internal validity are factors that can either hide a true effect of a treatment or make it appear overly robust, they are actually quite similar to Kelley's facilitative and inhibitory causes of a phenomenon. In Table 1, for example, are listed nine possible threats to the internal validity of experimental results. When any of them are judged to be present, one's confidence that a given treatment has caused a change in a dependent variable *ought* to be lessened. Also in Table 1 is a list of threats to external validity. These rival hypotheses limit the confidence one has in generalizing the results found in one situation to

that of a new setting. The closer situation *A* resembles situation *B,* the more confidence one *should* have in an *A*-to-*B* generalization. Obviously, it would be useful to know if uninitiated observers of social phenomena also take these threats to internal and external validity into consideration and whether they are judged to be equally or differentially weighted in importance.

Given the present trend of research findings in the attribution area (c.f. Kelley, 1973), it is not unlikely for researchers to find individuals drawing causal inferences and making generalizations in much the same fashion as do social researchers. Although their terminology would no doubt be different, individuals are probably aware of threats to both internal and external validity. Thus, the principle shortcoming of lay theories of effectiveness is not likely to be the administrator's *innate* capacity for drawing causal inferences and generalizing from them, but the difficulty of being accurate given the incomplete and confounded data with which he must work. Because most administrative experiences conform to neither sound experimental or quasi-experimental designs, the administrator is forced to draw inferences from only the weakest of data sets.

DATA GENERATED BY 'EXPERTS'

In facing a decision to start a particular innovation, an administrator may sometimes attempt to go beyond his lay psychology of effectiveness and turn to behavioral scientists for help. Behavioral scientists have laid claim to a relatively objective view of persons and things (e.g., technology, structure) within organizational settings, and have amassed a very large body of research findings. Moreover, researchers in organizational behavior frequently view their role as one of providing practicing administrators with theories that are an improvement over the commonly held lay theories of practitioners (e.g., Behling & Schiesheim, 1976; Filley et al., 1976). It must be noted, however, that many of the "expert" theories are based upon research designs that are not far in advance of those used by the lay observer of behavior.

One problem with data generated in the field of organizational behavior is that it merely feeds back to administrators their own lay theories of effectiveness. This problem stems from the fact that most data are based on cross-sectional surveys that relate various self-report measures to measures of performance. Research data, for example, show that questionnaire

Table 1.

Threats to Internal Validity	Threats to External Validity
1. *History:* events, other than the experimental treatment, occurring between pretest and posttest and thus providing alternate explanations of effects.	1. *Interaction effects of testing:* the effect of a pretest in increasing or decreasing the respondent's sensitivity or responsiveness to the experimental variable, thus making the results obtained for a pretested population unrepresentative of the effects of the experimental variable for the unpretested universe from which the experimental respondents were selected.
2. *Maturation:* processes within the respondents or observed social units producing changes as a function of the passage of time per se, such as growth, fatigue, secular trends, etc.	
3. *Instability:* unreliability of measures, fluctuations in sampling persons or components, autonomous instability of repeated or "equivalent" measures. (This is the only threat to which statistical tests of significance are relevant.)	2. *Interaction of selection and experimental treatment:* unrepresentative responsiveness of the treated population.
	3. *Reactive effects of experimental arrangements:* "artificially"; conditions making the experimental setting atypical of conditions of regular application of the treatment: "Hawthorne effects."
4. *Testing:* the effect of taking a test upon the scores of a second testing. The effect of publication of a social indicator upon subsequent readings of that indicator.	
5. *Instrumentation:* in which changes in the calibration of a measuring instrument or changes in the observers or scores used may produce changes in the obtained measurements.	4. *Multiple-treatment interference:* where multiple treatments are jointly applied, effects atypical of the separate application of the treatments.
6. *Regression artifacts:* pseudo-shifts occurring when persons or treatment units have been selected upon the basis of their extreme scores.	5. *Irrelevant responsiveness of measures:* all measures are complex, and all include irrelevant components that may produce apparent effects.
7. *Selection:* biases resulting from differential recruitment of comparison groups, producing different mean levels on the measure of effects.	6. *Irrelevant replicability of treatments:* treatments are complex, and replications of them may fail to include those components actually responsible for the effects.
8. *Experimental mortality:* the differential loss of respondents from comparison groups.	
9. *Selection-maturation interaction:* selection biases resulting in differential rates of "maturation" or autonomous change.	

Note: *Internal validity* refers to the level of confidence one has in whether a change in variable X actually causes a change in variable Y.

External validity refers to the level of confidence one has in whether such a causal relationship can be generalized.

From D. T. Campbell, "Reforms as Experiments," *American Psychologist* 24 (1969): 409–29. Copyright 1969 by the American Psychological Association. Reprinted by permission of the author.

responses to items on influence, openness to change, cohesiveness, and so on correlate significantly with organizational performance. However, research has shown (see Staw, 1975) that beliefs about performance *also* influence one's beliefs about other processes that occur in social situations. Once one knows that an individual, group, or organization is a high or low performer, one is likely to make consistent attributions along many other dimensions. For example, regardless of the actual processes that may have occurred in a group, it has been shown that knowledge that the group was effective will lead to the attribution that it was also cohesive, high in communication, and high in mutual

influence. Thus, when the organizational researcher attempts to show that various self-report measures are the causes of performance, he may merely be tapping a preexisting, lay theory of effectiveness.

In addition to the attributional problem in interpreting cross-sectional data, there are also recognized difficulties of reversed or reciprocal causation. As an example of some high quality cross-sectional research which may still be subject to these difficulties, let us examine the work of Hackman and Oldham (1976). These researchers measured job characteristics using both observer and self-rating forms and correlated these data with measures of work performance. Several characteristics of job enrichment (e.g., task variety, significance, identity) correlate significantly with performance and would seem to be determinants of task behavior in organizations. However, caution must be exercised in drawing such causal inferences since the best performers in an organization are likely to be given the most enriched and responsible jobs. And, although the Hackman and Oldham data show that the relationship between task characteristics and performance is strongest for persons with potent high-order needs, this moderated relationship could also be causally reversed. That is, high performance may not only generally lead supervisors to assign enriched jobs to subordinates, but this effect may be especially strong for those with high needs for autonomy and self-actualization. These persons may not merely wait for challenging jobs to be assigned; they may *actively lobby* for them.

Because of the difficulties of interpreting cross-sectional survey data, many researchers have resorted to laboratory experimentation. Laboratory experimentation provides much greater confidence in causal inference (i.e., internal validity) because changes in one variable are introduced and effects observed in a second variable, while extraneous factors are controlled. However, with each addition of experimental control, the laboratory situation becomes more and more divorced from everyday behavior. Hence, laboratory experiments often rank low in external validity, and one cannot often generalize their results to the organization with confidence. The greater the difference in research participants, experimental treatments, and setting from that of the real world, the lower is the external validity.

The organizational researcher often faces a dilemma in attempting to increase both internal and external validity. Those techniques that aid the interpretability of cause-effect relationships often decrease external validity, while efforts to make effects more generalizable often reduce internal validity. What is needed, therefore, are coordinated efforts tying together both laboratory and field research, and also field studies that utilize methods with greater internal validity. To date, there are few findings that have been tested in both the laboratory and field settings, or through a series of controlled field experiments.

Aside from the traditional concerns for internal and external validity of research data, there are several additional factors that may limit the applicability of research findings. First, within the behavioral sciences as a whole, there is a serious under-reporting of negative results (Notz et al., 1976). Data that are statistically significant and easily interpreted with a preexisting hypothesis are much more likely to be published than negative or inconsistent data. While this practice substantially reduces the volume of material for members of the field to process, it also limits the representativeness of published research results.

A second limitation is the frequent use of reconstructed logic in the presentation of research studies. As Notz et al. (1976) have noted, theories are often either fitted to data *post facto* or are amplified in those aspects that are consistent with the reported findings. Hypotheses and research designs are seldom as explicitly a priori as they are presented in published form. In large part, this bias is due to the fact that the author is judged professionally in the role of *advocate* — that is, on the basis of the consistency of his argument as well as the strength of his data. Because of the use of reconstructed logic, undue faith is often awarded to a particular theory, especially if its author is an articulate advocate.

A third, and perhaps most serious, problem in applying organizational research findings stems from a common misunderstanding of normative versus descriptive research. Most descriptive studies endeavor to report on cause-effect relationships found in the behavior of groups, individuals or organizations. The documentation of such findings can comprise a science of behavior and lead to a more accurate description of the social world. However, from a normative perspective, some authors have used these descriptive data to posit what *should* be done in a given situation. For example, Vroom and Yetton (1973) posit conditions when leaders should be participative or authoritarian in order to achieve maximum results. Their theoretical model is based upon a large amount of descriptive research in small group behavior and is likely to be accurate. But, as Argyris (1976) has cogently noted, Vroom and Yetton have implicitly accepted and made the status quo a desirable state by building it into their normative model. Argyris would argue that knowledge of individuals' reactions to participative or authoritarian management does not mean these reactions cannot be changed in the future. Thus, in deriving prescriptive statements from descriptive data, the researcher should be aware of his tacit role of either defender of tradition or change agent. As Gergen (1973) has noted, knowledge of cause-effect relationships is basically historical knowledge. Not only can one never be really confident of effects in future situations (Campbell, 1975), but, even when there is high external validity, specific actions can often be taken to change future states.

THE CONTRIBUTION OF BEHAVIORAL SCIENCES TO ADMINISTRATION

It may seem that we have painted a dark outlook for the contribution of behavioral science to practicing administrators. We have noted that research findings may be questionable in terms of either internal or external validity and are seldom high on both dimensions. We have noted that there is bias in the selection of published research to favor both statistically significant results and reconstructed logic. Finally, we have noted that what should exist need not be the same as what currently exists, and prescriptive statements need not be totally consistent with previous descriptive research. What is the purpose of these caveats and where do they lead the practicing administrator?

At present, the behavioral sciences utilize what Schon (1971) has labeled a center-periphery model of dissemination. As shown in Figure 1, the model rests on the assumption that internally and externally valid findings are held by behavioral researchers (who are presumably at the center of knowledge), and that the primary job is to disseminate the expertise to users at the periphery. Obviously, as we have seen, this is an erroneous view of the applicability of behavioral research. Because there are few behavioral principles that can be readily applied in a formula-like fashion, potential users might well be cautious of the zealous purveyor of such research findings.

A more realistic view is to acknowledge the uncertainty present in the social sciences and to accept the source of innovation at a more local level. From the administrator's point of view, behavioral findings should be appraised in terms of *best guesses;* what is most likely, second most likely, and least likely to work. Once the existing research literature is assessed in terms of its

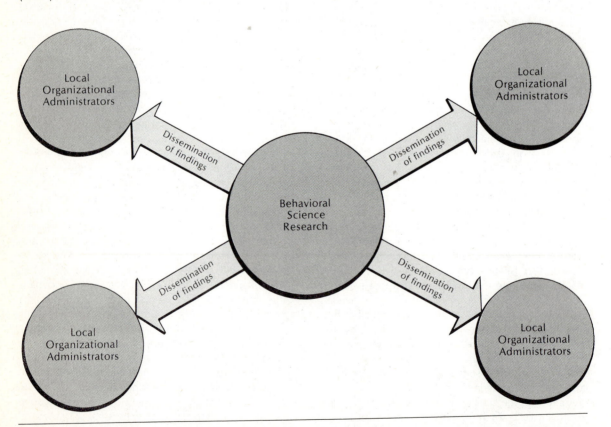

Figure 1.   The Center-Periphery Model of the Dissemination of Knowledge.

From W. W. Notz, P. E. Salipante and J. A. Waters, ''Innovation in Situ: A Contingency Approach to Human Resource Development,'' Working Paper. Dept. of Administrative Sciences, University of Manitoba, Winnepeg, Canada, 1976.)

internal and external validity, the administrator should *experimentally* undertake the seemingly best course of action. As shown in Figure 2, the administrator can be the focus of innovation utilizing the social science community as peripheral resources. The practitioner can be the one who ultimately tests the usefulness of any given theory or set of research findings (Notz et al., 1976).

When the role of behavioral science shifts from center to periphery, its educational task also shifts. Instead of persuading practitioners to adopt one particular theory and reject another, it may expend more energy to training practitioners in evaluation skills—skills needed to ascertain whether a particular program is working or not. These evaluation skills can be viewed as tools that improve upon those normally available to the lay administrator in assessing cause-effect relationships. Because there are already entire

volumes devoted to the development of appropriate evaluation techniques, we will mention only a few methods that are especially applicable to organizational administrators.

Methods of Evaluating Change in Large Organizations

When an organization is large, it is often possible to introduce a change (e.g., job redesign, participation system, incentive scheme) on a truly experimental basis. That is, individuals or intact work groups may be assigned randomly to experimental and control conditions and measures taken both before and after the experimental treatment or change. Such an experimental design is shown below:

$$R\ O\ X\ O$$
$$R\ O\ \ \ O$$

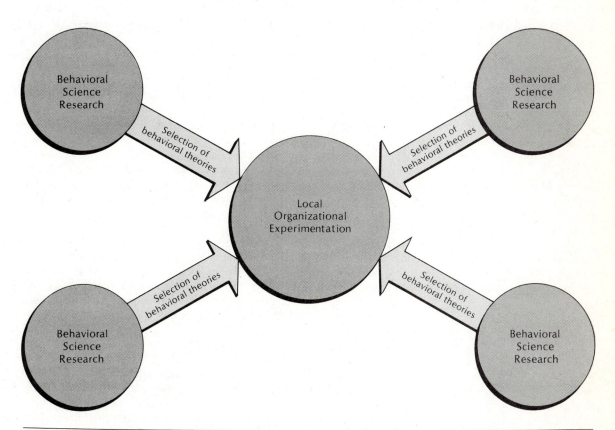

Figure 2.   The Organizational Experimentation Model.

(From W. W. Notz, P. E. Salipante and J. A. Waters, "Innovation in Situ: A Contingency Approach to Human Resource Development." Working Paper. Dept. of Administrative Sciences, University of Manitoba, Winnipeg, Canada, 1976.)

In the [preceding] design, the existence of a cause-effect relationship can be assessed with relative confidence. If job enlargement is introduced by random assignment, for example, then any increase in job satisfaction over the control group (those for whom jobs were left unchanged) can be attributed to the enlargement. Randomization controls for history, maturation, selection, selection-maturation, and regression by equalizing experimental and control groups on all dimensions except the treatment. Instrumentation and testing can also be readily controlled by administering the same measures to both experimental and control groups. Mortality can present a problem for interpretation if it is treatment-induced (e.g., job enlargement causes greater or lesser turnover in the experimental than in the control group), but this threat can be easily measured and assessed. Finally, statistical instability may confound results if the sample size of the experimental and control groups are small or variability extremely large, but this is readily assessed through standard statistical tests of significance.

As Cook and Campbell (1976) have noted, there are several conditions that are especially conducive to true experimentation in organizations. The most common are when demand outstrips supply or when an innovation cannot be delivered to all individuals or units at once. In such situations, the most equitable way of distributing an improvement (e.g., job change) is through random assignment. Moreover, even when a bias can be firmly established for need priority, experimentation is frequently still possible. If the population is large enough, individuals (or groups) can be ranked in terms of their need priority. Those who clearly need the treatment can be given it immediately, and those who definitely do not need it can be denied the opportunity. However, within a range of "need ambiguity" individuals or groups can be randomly assigned to experimental and control groups. If this subgroup is large enough, a true experiment may result.

Perhaps the most important factor that is conducive to true experimentation is uncertainty over the results of an innovation. If it is not clear whether a change is helpful, the most reasonable procedure from a managerial point of view is to administer the treatment through random assignment. And, when a change is thought almost certainly to be costly to individuals or groups, random assignment removes the onus from the administrator. When lotteries are expected in a field setting, they provide data especially high in internal as well as external validity (see, e.g., the draft lottery studies conducted by Notz et al., 1971; Staw, 1974; and Staw et al., 1974).

Though true experimentation ranks highest in valid causal inference, it is not always the most practical course of action in the administrative settings. Individuals cannot always be randomly assigned to experimental and control groups because such a procedure might disrupt normal production systems (e.g., in the case of job enlargement) or produce inequities between experimental and control groups (e.g., in the case of incentive or reward changes). In addition, there may be too few intact work groups for randomization to work effectively in equating the experimental and control groups. In such cases, the best procedure is to employ a time-series design. A time-series design basically utilizes a large number of observations before and after an experimental change and may or may not involve a comparison group. Shown below is a time-series design using two intact groups, one of which has received an experimental treatment.

$$O\ O\ O\ X\ O\ O\ O$$
$$O\ O\ O\quad O\ O\ O$$

The groups shown above are not randomly assigned and may not be perfectly comparable. However, by taking numerous measures of a dependent variable before and after a change, one can rule out such common threats to internal validity as testing, maturation, regression, and instrumentation. History remains the most problematic aspect of the time-series design. One must ask whether any other external event (other than the experimental change) could have caused a substantial shift in the dependent variable. For example, has production changed due to a new job standards, plant modernization, leadership changes or any other factor in addition to the introduction of job enlargement? A control group that is measured before and after the change will aid in this inference process, if these two groups are believed to be subject to similar exogenous forces.

Time-series designs are the most easily implemented within organizational settings, because they involve little or no disruption of ongoing operations. What they demand, however, is extensive use of archival data. It is rarely possible to gather enough questionnaire data to construct a time-series of before and after observations of attitudes toward various aspects of organizational life. However, it is possible to utilize routinely collected behavioral observations such as absenteeism, turnover and production. In addition, an administrator can creatively collect data on many surrogates of attitudinal variables (Webb et al., 1966). For example, how early in the day a worker starts his cleanup may be indicative of his attitude toward the job; the number of cigarette butts found in the ashtrays during departmental meetings may be representative of intradepartmental conflict or tension; the number of employees using company's product (e.g., in an automobile plant) may relate to organizational loyalty or identification.

Although the time-series design explicitly demands nothing more than careful documentation and observation, its power can also be improved by an administrative attitude of tentativeness. That is, if an innovation is first implemented on an experimental basis to a small sample within an organization, it may be subsequently administered on an increasingly inclusive basis. Such a replicated time-series design offers both a powerful basis from which to infer cause-effect relations and a great deal of generalizability. A replicated time-series design is shown below:

$$O\ O\ O\ X\ O\ O\ O\ O\ O\ O\ O\ O\ O$$
$$O\ O\ O\ O\ O\ O\ X\ O\ O\ O\ O\ O\ O$$
$$O\ O\ O\ O\ O\ O\ O\ O\ O\ X\ O\ O\ O$$

By staging the introduction of a change at several different points in time, one can readily rule out history as an alternative explanation of the change in a dependent variable. In addition, one can be relatively more certain that the observed change was not due to mere statistical instability, and can be more confident that the change will be applicable to multiple units in the organization.

The major requirement of a replicated time-series design is separation of the various treatment groups. If the groups can communicate and/or observe each other, the change in one group may spill over or diffuse to the others. This could result in either interunit jealously resulting in deterioration in attitudes or the expression of rivalry, which could improve morale. Obviously under these conditions, the introduction of an innovation to an observing group differs from the initial innovation and does not constitute a true replication. A second and more serious problem for interpreting time-series designs, however, is the requirement of a relatively quick, high-impact treatment. If a change is slow and incremental (as in many O.D. interventions) it is often difficult to separate treatment-induced change from statistical error and other internal influences. Still, irrespective of these limitations,

time-series techniques are a powerful tool in the evaluation of large-scale administrative changes. (For discussion of the data analysis techniques available for time-series studies, see Glass et al., 1975; McCain & McCleary, 1976; and Nelson, 1973).

Methods of Evaluating Change in Small Administrative Units

We have seen that it is often possible for the administrator to make large-scale changes and to use these changes to infer cause-effect relationships. Does the administrator of a small unit (e.g., imagine one is supervising four people on a face-to-face basis) also have the capacity to make such valid causal inferences?

An immediate response to the above query is, "no, the small unit administrator is armed merely with theory rather than method." The administrator of a small, face-to-face unit cannot readily assign two people to a job-enlargement condition while leaving two others' jobs alone. Moreover, a random assignment with such small samples (coupled with the high degree of interaction among all the individuals involved) would provide little improvement in internal validity. A time-series analysis is possible with few subjects (see Chassan, 1967), although obviously changes will be more difficult to infer due to the statistical instability of such a small sample.

Must we then conclude that our only real leverage in improving decision-making skills of the small-unit administrator is in theory transmission? Certainly, in its role of training future administrators, the field of organizational behavior is chiefly involved in transmitting "expert" theories of leadership, motivation and group process and dispelling "lay" theories. Yet, there is room for methodological skills at this level, also. When sample size is small and statistical power weakened, one should turn to more qualitative research techniques. Training for the evaluation of small-unit changes should concentrate upon interviewing and observational techniques. Administrators can be trained to recognize facial expressions, physical distance and other nonverbal cues in evaluating the attitudes and beliefs of others. In addition, administrators can be trained to conduct clinically oriented interviews to discover the source and possible remedies of problems. Related techniques of interaction analysis and sensitivity training are already available and are used in professional school programs. What is necessary is to recognize these tools as data-gathering devices and couple them with other less obtrusive forms of measurement (Webb et al., 1966). For example, if the administrator changes the jobs of several of his employees, he should look for behavioral indicators of changes in attitude and performance in addition to those that result from direct questioning and interviewing. Unfortunately advocates of qualitative and quantitative research techniques have not recognized the special role and utility of each other's methodology. Proponents of qualitative techniques are often more interested in promoting new forms of human interaction than using their techniques in objective data gathering. Meanwhile, proponents of quantitative analysis have tended to restrict their attention to the testing of theory rather than to how practitioners can measure and evaluate their own changes. Needless to say, there is a great deal to be gained by a practitioner's synthesis of both forms of analysis.

Formative versus Summative Evaluation

To this point our discussion has centered on how behavioral science might improve causal inference in administrative settings. However, the evaluation techniques elaborated so far attack only part of the problem. Although tools such as experimental and quasi-experimental design help one to gather internally valid data, they presume a clearly formulated or at least explicitly chosen program of action. It is assumed, for example, that in evaluating the results of job enlargement, administrators know what job enlargement is and have chosen a particular aspect of it (e.g., increased task variety) to implement. The process of inferring whether a treatment "worked" or has had a positive effect is referred to as *summative evaluation*. The process of selecting program goals and building a treatment is referred to as *formative evaluation*. Formative evaluation resembles the pilot study stage of a research project in which the researcher gathers information about how he should proceed with a full-scale test of his hypothesis. As Wortman (1975) notes, the procedures involved in formative evaluation remain more of an art than a science. There is no convenient list of threats to validity, techniques, and methods for conducting a formative evaluation. Presumably, however, the successful "builder" of treatments must search for the correct blend of expert and lay theories of organizational effectiveness, be able to evaluate their prospects of success in his own situation, and conduct some inquiry (e.g., through interviews with other administrators, subordinates,

search of prior records) into the likely consequences of his actions.

Wortman (1975) has described how formative and summative evaluation can be effectively combined in program evaluation. His basic point is that the qualitative and quantitative techniques used in formative and summative evaluations can be complementary rather than competing forms of evaluation. Thus, one might imagine an administrator first making small-scale changes (as in a pilot study) and using primarily qualitative analysis techniques. Then, once the administrator has a greater source of knowledge and has built what he thinks is a good treatment, he may implement this change on a larger-scale basis. The large-scale change can be evaluated using experimental and/or time-series research designs.

Problems in Moving from Formative to Summative Evaluation

Though the sequential use of formative and summative evaluation makes intuitive sense, is it realistic in most administrative settings? The principal problem seems to be when, and if, one can move from formative to summative evaluation. At what stage is the administrator willing to regard his change as "in place" and ready for testing? As Lindblom (1959) has noted, the answer may be *never!*

The administrative process, as Lindblom notes, may be a perpetual sequence of making incremental changes or "tinkering with the treatment." Lindblom describes the public administrator, for example, as one who makes a number of successive limited comparisons rather than attempting to comprehensively analyze problems, set specific goals, and implement solutions. In Lindblom's view, incrementalism is the most rational way to address any complex social problem, and he labels this process as "the science of muddling through."

The incrementalism explicit in Lindblom's "science of muddling through" is not inconsistent with the concept of the experimenting organization. In fact, an administrator's willingness to change policy or course of action on the basis of data is the *essence* of social experimentation. However, there may be important differences between the administrator's and the organization's *preferred* form of incrementalism. From the organization's point of view, it would seem generally preferable to build a treatment through formative evaluation and then subject it to a rigorous test through summative evaluation. This procedure would be quite consistent with an evolutionary model of organizations in which evaluation research functions as a device to aid selection and retention processes (Pondy, 1977; Weick, 1969). But, from the individual administrator's point of view, it may seem preferable to forge an acceptable treatment through a succession of limited comparisons without ever being subjected to a summative evaluation. By remaining at the formative evaluation stage, administrators may continuously revise a program (or even its goals) to meet the demands of clients and other administrators. Lindblom would argue that this process of revision never ends for administrators, especially in the public sector. Of necessity, the administrator may have to continuously shape and reshape a program to retain the support of shifting coalitions of power within organizations and their environments. Obviously, such political considerations will often determine the nature and scope of any evaluation effort, and must be seriously examined in the initial design of a program evaluation.

The Trapped Administrator

Although administrators are often willing to make incremental changes in a treatment, they are frequently hesitant to ''backtrack'' or make changes that can be construed as an admission of previous error. In fact, there are some visible cases, such as the U.S. intervention in the Indochina War, that seem to indicate that decision makers will even escalate their commitment following negative results rather than undertake any major shifts in policy. The Indochina War effort was similar to an investment decision context in which it was possible to recoup an initial loss by increasing one's subsequent investment. Similar situations might also exist in organizations, such as when one must decide how much advertising is needed to successfully launch a new product or how much R&D expenditure is needed to build a new or improved product. Each of these situations poses a dilemma when negative results occur. Does one accept one's losses and scuttle the program or escalate one's investment in an effort to turn the situation around?

Using a simulated business decision case, Staw (1976b) experimentally tested for the tendency to escalate following the receipt of negative consequences. In his study, business school students were asked to allocate research and development funds to one of two operating divisions of a company. They were then given the results of their initial decisions and asked to make a second allocation of R&D funds. In this

study, some subjects also were assigned to a condition in which they did not make the initial allocation decision *themselves,* but were told that it was made earlier by another financial officer of the firm. The results of the experiment were as follows: (1) there was a main effect of responsibility such that subjects allocated more money when *they,* rather than another financial officer, had made the initial decision; (2) there was a main effect of consequences such that subjects allocated more money to the declining rather than improving division; and (3) there was a significant interaction of responsibility and consequences. That is, subjects allocated even more money when they were responsible for negative consequences that would be expected by the two main effects acting alone. Personal responsibility for negative consequence, therefore, may lead to the greatest likelihood of escalation behavior.

From the experimental results described above and observational evidence of real-world escalations (see, e.g., *The Pentagon Papers*), it seems possible that administrators can become trapped by their own previous mistakes. It seems that a key problem the administrator faces is knowing when it is appropriate to accept one's losses or enlarge the stakes. Hindsight yields examples of leaders who are perceived as strong and courageous following *either* of these two strategies. For example, Lyndon Johnson's leadership ability was assailed for following the escalation route. However, if Johnson had succeeded in ''winning the war'' in Indochina, he no doubt would have been hailed widely as a wise and bold leader. Unfortunately, from the administrator's perspective, there are no available statistical techniques that will substitute for qualitative judgment on this classic investment problem.

Staw and Fox (in press) found that many decision makers attempt to ''test the system'' by allocating a substantial amount of resources to the problem and then, if no effect results, reduce their commitment substantially. This strategy would seem appropriate for treatments that require a large, immediate expenditure of resources to create an impact (e.g., advertising a new product), but quite inappropriate for treatments that require a slow, building commitment (e.g., many O.D. interventions). As mentioned earlier, the latter treatments not only pose difficulties in judgment, but are especially troublesome for detecting changes using statistical techniques such as time-series analysis (Glass et al., 1975).

In addition to the problem of knowing how much investment is enough to create a change, there is likely to be a second and even more important cause of the trapped administrator. From the administrator's point of view, a program must sometimes be *made to work at almost any cost.* A program that fails is frequently treated as an administrative failure and can be cause for demotion or dismissal. Few organizations have assimilated an experimental philosophy in which ineffective programs are merely replaced by other more promising programs. Instead, programs are advocated and implemented by ambitious administrators who, in case of failure, are replaced by other more promising candidates. Thus, evaluation apprehension (Rosenberg, 1969) is a likely cause of administrative defense and advocacy of programs that appear to others as obvious failures. Moreover, because evaluation in organizations is frequently *ad hominem,* there may also be pressure throughout the system to bias the data forming the basis of program evaluation. Close associates of administrative heads may be hesitant to relay negative information (Janis, 1972; Tesser & Rosen, 1975), and lower level officials may be selective in the information they pass upward (Cohen, 1958; Read, 1962). As Thompson (1967) has noted, there may be enormous pressure at the individual, group and organizational levels to report successes and deemphasize any information that can be construed as a failure. Clearly, a great deal of work needs to be done to design an organizational system that can effectively monitor, feed back, and utilize negative as well as positive data.

Some Organizational Solutions to Evaluation Apprehension

The most obvious solution to the apprehension that often accompanies evaluation research is to take specific measures to insure that one is evaluating *programs* and not *people.* As Campbell has noted (personal communication, 1976), decisions about the salary, grade, or promotions of program administrators should be divorced from program evaluation and reporting procedures. Campbell also goes so far as to state that program funding decisions should be removed from evaluation research activities. Taken literally, this solution is quite similar to that frequently advocated (e.g., Porter et al., 1975) for other kinds of performance evaluation systems within organizations. For example, in the personnel evaluation context, it is not in the employee's best interest to present any negative information to his superior. However, it is precisely such weaknesses that need to be communicated in order for the supervisor to properly counsel and

guide the employee for improvement. Hence, it is sometimes recommended that performance evaluation be temporally (and even functionally) separated for salary review and employee development sessions. The only hitch is that, even when there is temporal spacing or some other form of separation, any perceived relationship between communicated negative information and salary decisions is likely to lead to future defensiveness and data filtering.

In the contexts of both program evaluation and personnel evaluation, there is a very real conflict between the organizational functions of feedback and resource allocation. The desire to know what programs are working well and to allocate money to the most effective is similar to the need to know who are the best performing workers in order to allocate rewards as a consequence of performance. From the organization's point of view, rewards that are not contingent upon behavior will lead to a decrease in task motivation (Hamner, 1973; Nord, 1971); likewise, resources that are not allocated to the most effective programs (or perhaps program administrators) may be misspent or wasted. However, from the individual employee or program administrator's point of view, efforts will be taken to insure that reports are positive, show improvement, or closely follow *whatever criteria* is utilized in resource allocation decisions.

Given the inherent conflict between resource allocation and feedback processes, program evaluation will no doubt always retain some aspects of a "police function." Teams of evaluators may be viewed warily, and data may continue to be made available only selectively. At the same time, evaluators will attempt to find unobtrusive and seemingly uncorrupted measures of program effectiveness. If organizations opt to recognize such conflict as intractable, they may concentrate on developing structures to manage the conflict. One possibility is that of building a quasi-legal system within organizations in which advocacy (both pro and con) is voiced, evidence is presented, and then resource allocation decisions are made by a single authority or unbiased panel. Although Wolf (1974) has discussed such a possibility within educational organizations, there have as yet been no known attempts to implement such a system.

A second and apparently more popular way of dealing with the conflict between resource allocation and feedback is to attempt to reduce it by decoupling these organizational processes. Summative or outcome evaluation can be deemphasized, and instead efforts can be made to concentrate on formative evaluation in which the program is changed. Formative evaluation is less likely to be threatening than summative evaluation because it is focused upon improving the program rather than evaluating its impact vis-à-vis other uses for resources. Unfortunately, deemphasis of summative evaluation may also drastically reduce organizational efficiency or cost effectiveness. A better strategy for decoupling feedback and allocation processes is for the organization to guarantee continued funding of a particular organizational unit, but to encourage that unit to experiment among various programs. Carried to its extreme, the organization could reward organizational units and administrators, not on their overall results, but on the quality of their experimentation and program evaluation techniques.

A third solution to evaluation apprehension is to design organizational reward systems so that resources are highly contingent upon performance. However, at the same time, one might also institute an evaluation research group as an in-house consulting unit. The idea here is to actually *increase* pressure upon individuals and work units to perform, but also to offer free evaluation consulting as an aid to improve local performance. Obviously, for this solution to work, the in-house consulting group must be perceived to be politically neutral and the data offered to program evaluators held confidential. If such a system functioned successfully, organizational units might be encouraged to experiment in order to increase their own monitored effectiveness. Organizational units might simultaneously utilize two methods and then choose the best, or sequentially explore new program tools and procedures.

Operationalism versus Goal Accomplishment

In addition to the problem of data biasing, one other key difficulty with program evaluation merits attention in this paper. Within organizations, program evaluation may often be troubled by a confusion between measured improvement and goal accomplishment. That is, there may tend to be undue emphasis upon a particular indicator or operationalization of effectiveness at the expense of the construct of effectiveness itself. The problem is best illustrated in the context of performance contracting for education. When private contractors are paid on the basis of improvement in students' reading or math scores, they tend to "teach for the test," giving repeated examples of old test materials and spending most of the class time on tested skills (Stake, 1971).

Although tested scores may improve, educational effectiveness of the program may thus be low. Similarly, organizational units may spend an undue amount of effort on those behaviors that are measured and weighted heavily within a program evaluation (Ridgeway, 1956; Thompson, 1967). Patients may not be referred to hospitals in order to keep a mental health program's hospital recidivism rate low; poor workers may be encouraged to stay on the job to keep employee turnover down, and work quantity may be emphasized at the expense of quality.

One solution to this problem is to use multiple indicators or operationalizations of the construct of effectiveness (Campbell, 1974). For example, in addition to measuring the number of absences before and after a program of applied reinforcement for work attendance (e.g., Lawler & Hackman, 1969), one should also measure work quality, quantity, and satisfaction. As shown by Staw & Oldham (1976), it is possible that there are some positive consequences of absenteeism, and that strong inducements for attendance could actually lead to decrements in work performance. The crucial point is that program evaluators should try to avoid concentrating upon single indicators of success.

Of course, even with multiple operationalizations of the effectiveness criterion, there may still be some focusing of local effort upon a presumed hierarchy of results. Regardless of the number of indicators of success, program administrators may attempt to discern which are *the* most important indicators in a final judgment affecting resource allocation decisions (Pfeffer, 1977). The weighting of effectiveness indicators should thus be made an *explicit and public aspect* of the evaluation process so that local organizational units can legitimately focus their attention on the most important criteria. No doubt, it will frequently be necessary for an evaluation team to get higher level management to specify clearly what their criteria for effectiveness are. This process, not unlike the setting of organizational objectives (Drucker, 1954; Odiorne, 1965), may even prove to be one of the most valuable aspects of program evaluation. For example, when administrators and participants of a program disagree on what criteria a program should be evaluated, such disagreement can often be translated into a positive program of participative goal setting. And, participation of program administrators, participants, and higher level management in criteria selection may turn out to be one of the most important necessary conditions of successful program evaluation within organizations.

CONCLUSION

In this paper, we have discussed several of the difficulties facing evaluation research within organizations. We have offered some suggestions to minimize problems such as evaluation apprehension, biasing of data, and over-focusing upon operationalized measures of effectiveness. Still, we do not wish to promote the naive impression that program evaluation is easy, foolproof, or necessarily accurate. Some problems such as those discussed here may be endemic to any attempt to assess the effectiveness of an organizational program.

Our main purpose has been to promote a cautious optimism about evaluation activities within organizations. Administrators have been viewed here as having the innate capacity to make relatively rational causal inferences and to be able to evaluate both large and small unit changes. In fact, the chief difficulty confronting organizational administrators in our view is the lack of appropriate data and research design capability *within* organizations. Instead of merely proffering new or revised theories for administrators to use in an "across the board" fashion, behavioral scientists should therefore concentrate more on transferring methodological skills to practicing administrators so that they can experimentally test the usefulness of various theories, including their own. In this way, organizational researchers may provide the greatest contribution to the organizations they study.

REFERENCES

Argyris, C. "Problems and New Directions for Industrial Psychology." In *Handbook of Industrial Organizational Psychology,* edited by M. D. Dunnette. Chicago: Rand McNally, 1976.

Banner, D. K. "The Politics of Evaluation Research." *Omega* 2 (1974): 736–74.

Bavelas, A.; Hastorf, A. H.; Gross, A. E.; and Kite, W. R. "Experiments in Alteration of Group Structure." *Journal of Experimental Social Psychology* 1 (1965): 199–218.

Behling, O., and Schreisheim, C. *Organizational Behavior: Theory, Research, and Application.* Boston: Allyn and Bacon, 1976.

Bem, D. J. "Self-perception: The Dependent Variable of Human Performance." *Organizational Behavior and Human Performance* 2(1976): 105–21.

Bennett, C. A., and Lumsdaine, A. A. "Social Program Evaluation: Definitions and Issues." In *Evaluation and Experiment: Some Critical Issues in Assessing Social Programs,* edited by C. A. Bennett and A. A. Lumsdaine. New York: Academic Press, 1975.

Berk, R. A., and Rossi, P. H. "Doing Good or Worse: Evaluation Research Politically Reexamined." *Social Problems* 23 (1976): 337–49.

Bruner, J. S., and Taguiri, A. "The Perception of People." In *Handbook of Social Psychology,* edited by G. Lindzey. Reading, Massachusetts: Addison-Wesley, 1954.

Calder, B. J., and Staw, B. M. "Self-perception of Intrinsic and Extrinsic Motivation." *Journal of Personality and Social Psychology* 31 (1975): 599–605.

Campbell, D. T. "Reforms at Experiments." *American Psychologist* 24 (1969): 409–429.

_____. "Methods for the Experimenting Society." *Evaluation Research Program Paper Series, No. 5.* Evanston, Illinois: Northwestern University, 1974.

_____. "Assessing the Impact of Planned Social Change." In *Social Research and Public Policies,* edited by G. M. Lyons. Hanover, New Hampshire: University Press of New England, 1975.

_____, and Stanley, J. C. *Experimental and Quasi-Experimental Designs for Research.* Chicago: Rand McNally, 1966.

Chassan, J. B. *Research Designs in Clinical Psychology and Psychiatry.* New York: Appleton-Century-Crofts, 1967.

Cohen, A. R. "Upward Communication in Experimentally Created Hierarchies." *Human Relations* 11 (1958): 41-53.

Cook, T. D., and Campbell, D. T. "The Design and Conduct of Quasi-Experiments and True Experiments in Field Settings." In *Handbook of Industrial and Organizational Psychology,* edited by M. D. Dunnette. Chicago: Rand McNally, 1976.

Deci, E. L. "The Effects of Externally Mediated Rewards on Intrinsic Motivation." *Journal of Personality and Social Psychology* 18 (1971): 105-15.

Drucker, P. *The Practice of Management.* New York: Harper & Row, 1954.

Filley, A. C.; House, R. J.; and Kerr, S. *Managerial Process and Organizational Behavior.* Glenview, Illinois: Scott, Foresman, & Co., 1976.

Gergen, K. V. "Social Psychology as History." *Journal of Personality and Social Psychology* 26 (1973): 309-20.

Glass, G. V.; Willson, V. L.; and Gottman, J. M. *Design and Analysis of Time-Series Experiments.* Boulder, Colorado: Colorado Associated University Press, 1975.

Hackman, J. R., and Oldham, G. R. "Motivation Through the Design of Work." *Organizational Behavior and Human Performance,* 1976.

Heider, F., and Simmel, M. "An Experimental Study of Apparent Behavior." *American Journal of Psychology* 57 (1944): 243-59.

Janis, I. L. *Victims of Groupthink: A Psychological Study of Foreign Policy Decisions and Fiascoes.* Boston: Houghton Mifflin Co., 1972.

Jones, E. E.; Davis, K. E.; and Gergen, K. E. "Role Playing Variations and Their Informational Value for Person Perception." *Journal of Abnormal and Social Psychology.* 63 (1961): 302-10.

_____, and Harris, V. A. "The Attribution of Attitudes." *Journal of Experimental Social Psychology* 3 (1967): 1-24.

Kelley, H. H. "Attribution Theory in Social Psychology." In *Nebraska Symposium on Motivation,* edited by D. Levine. Lincoln: University of Nebraska Press, 1967.

_____. "The Processes of Causal Attribution." *American Psychologist* 28 (1973): 107-28.

Kruglanski, A. W.; Freedman, I.; and Zeevi, G. "The Effects of Extrinsic Incentives on Some Qualitative Aspects of Task Performance." *Journal of Personality* 39 (1971): 606-17.

Hamner, W. C. "Reinforcement Theory and Contingency Management in Organizational Settings." In *Organizational Behavior and Management: A Contingency Approach,* edited by H. L. Tosi and W. C. Hamner. Chicago: St. Clair Press, 1974.

Lawler, E. E., and Hackman, J. R. "Impact of Employee Participation in the Development of Pay Incentive Plans: A Field Experiment." *Journal of Applied Psychology* 53 (1969): 467-71.

Lepper, M. R.; Greene, D.; and Nisbett, R. E. "Undermining Children's Intrinsic Interest with Extrinsic Rewards: A Test of the Over-justification Hypothesis." *Journal of Personality and Social Psychology* 28 (1973): 129-37.

Likert, R. *Human Organization: Its Management and Value.* New York: McGraw-Hill, 1967.

Lindblom, C. E. "The Science of Muddling Through." *Public Administration Review* 19 (1959): 79-88.

McCain, L. J., and McCleary, R. "The Statistical Analysis of Interrupted Time Series Quasi-Experiments." In *The Design and Analysis of Quasi-Experiments in Field Settings,* edited by T. D. Cook and D. T. Campbell. Chicago: Rand McNally, 1976.

Michotte, A. *The Perception of Causality.* New York: Basic Books, 1963.

Nelson, C. R. *Applied Time Series Analysis for Managerial Forecasting.* San Francisco: Holden Day, 1973.

Nord, W. R. "Beyond the Teaching Machine: The Neglected Area of Operant Conditioning in the Theory and Practice of Management." *Organizational Behavior and Human Performance* 4 (1969): 375-401.

Notz, W. W.; Salipante, P. E.; and Waters, J. A. "Innovation in Situ: A Contingency Approach to Human Resource Development." Working paper, Department of Administrative Sciences, University of Manitoba, Winnipeg, Canada, 1976.

_____; Staw, B. M.; and Cook, T. D. "Attitude Toward Troop Withdrawal from Indochina as a Function of Draft Number: Dissonance or Self-Interest?" *Journal of Personality and Social Psychology* 20 (1971): 118–26.

Odiorne, G. S. *Management by Objectives.* New York: Pitman Publishing Co., 1965.

Pentagon Papers, The New York Times (based on investigative reporting of Neil Sheehan). New York: Bantam Books, 1971.

Pfeffer, J. "Power and Resource Allocation in Organizations." In *New Directions in Organizational Behavior,* edited by B. M. Staw and G. R. Salancik. Chicago: St. Clair Press, 1977.

Pondy, L. R. "Two Faces of Evaluation." In *Accounting for Social Goals and Social Organization,* edited by H. W. Metton and D. Watson. Columbus, Ohio: Grid Publishing Co., 1977.

Porter, L. W.; Lawler, E. E.; and Hackman, J. R. *Behavior in Organizations.* New York: McGraw-Hill, 1975.

Read, W. "Upward Communication in Industrial Hierarchies." *Human Relations* 15 (1962): 3–16.

Ridgeway, V. "Dysfunctional Consequences of Performance Measures." *Administrative Science Quarterly* 1 (1956): 240–47.

Riecken, H. W., and Boruch, R. F., eds. *Social Experimentation: A Method for Planning and Evaluating Social Intervention.* New York: Academic Press, 1974.

Rosenberg, M. J. "The Conditions and Consequences of Evaluation Apprehension." In *Artifact in Behavioral Research,* edited by R. Rosenthal and R. L. Rosnow. New York: Academic Press, 1969.

Schon, D. A. *Beyond the Stable State.* New York: Random House, 1971.

Scriven, M. "The Methodology of Evaluation." In *Perspectives of Curriculum Evaluation,* edited by R. W. Tyler, R. M. Gagné, and M. Scriven. Chicago: Rand McNally, 1967.

Stake, R. E. "Testing Hazards in Performance Contracting." *Phi Delta Kappan* 52 (1971): 583–88.

Staw, B. M. "Attitudinal and Behavioral Consequences of Changing a Major Organizational Reward: A Natural Field Experiment." *Journal of Personality and Social Psychology* 29 (1974): 742–51.

_____. "Attribution of the 'Causes' of Performance: A General Alternative Interpretation of Cross-Sectional Research on Organizations." *Organizational Behavior and Human Performance* 13 (1975): 414–32.

_____. *Intrinsic and Extrinsic Motivation.* Morristown, N.J.: General Learning Press, 1976. (a)

_____. "Knee-Deep in the Big Muddy: A Study of Escalating Commitment to a Chosen Course of Action." *Organizational Behavior and Human Performance* 16 (1976): 27–44. (b)

_____, and Fox, F. W. "Escalation: Some Determinants of Commitment to a Previously Chosen Course of Action. *Human Relations,* in press.

_____; Notz, W. W.; and Cook, T. D. "Vulnerability to the Draft and Attitudes Toward Troop Withdrawal from Indochina: Replication and Refinement." *Psychological Reports* 34 (1974): 407–17.

_____, and Oldham, G. R. "Some Functional Consequences of Absenteeism." Working paper, Northwestern University, 1976.

Strickland, L. H. "Surveillance and Trust." *Journal of Personality* 26 (1958): 200–15.

Tesser, A., and Rosen, S. "The Reluctance to Transmit Bad News." In *Advances in Experimental Social Psychology,* edited by C. Berkowitz. New York: Academic Press, 1975.

Thibaut, J. W., and Riecken, H. W. "Some Determinants and Consequences of the Perception of Social Causality." *Journal of Personality* 24 (1955): 113–33.

Thompson, J. D. *Organizations in Action.* New York: McGraw-Hill, 1967.

Vroom, V. H. and Yetton, P. W. *Leadership and Decision Making.* Pittsburgh: University of Pittsburgh Press, 1973.

Webb, E. J.; Campbell, D. T.; Schwartz, R. D.; and Sechrest, L. *Unobtrusive Measures: Non-Reactive Research in the Social Sciences.* Chicago: Rand McNally, 1966.

Weick, K. E. *The Social Psychology of Organizing.* Reading, Mass.: Addison-Wesley, 1969.

Weiss, C. H. "Where Politics and Evaluation Research." *Evaluation* 1 (1973): 37–45.

_____. ''Evaluation Research in the Political Context.'' In *Handbook of Evaluation Research,* edited by E. L. Struening and M. Guttentag. Beverly Hills, California: Sage Publications, 1975.

Wolf, R. L. *The Application of Select Legal Concepts to Educational Evaluation.* Ph.D. dissertation, University of Illinois at Urbana-Champaign, School of Education, 1974.

Wortman, P. M. ''Evaluation Research: A Psychological Perspective.'' *American Psychologist* 30 (1975): 562–75.